Greek Tragedy

Greek Tragedy

MODERN ESSAYS IN CRITICISM

Edited by Erich Segal
Yale University

1817

HARPER & ROW, PUBLISHERS, New York
Cambridge, Philadelphia, San Francisco,
London, Mexico City, São Paulo, Sydney

A hardcover edition of this book is published by Oxford University Press, Oxford,
England under the title OXFORD READINGS IN GREEK TRAGEDY. It is here
reprinted by arrangement.

GREEK TRAGEDY. Copyright © 1983 by Erich Segal. All rights reserved. Printed in
the United States of America. No part of this book may be used or reproduced in any
manner whatsoever without written permission except in the case of brief quotations
embodied in critical articles and reviews. For information address Harper & Row,
Publishers, Inc., 10 East 53rd Street, New York, N.Y. 10022.

FIRST U.S. EDITION

Library of Congress Cataloging in Publication Data
Main entry under title:

Greek tragedy.

Includes bibliographical references.
1. Greek drama (Tragedy)—History and criticism—Addresses, essays, lectures.
I. Segal, Erich, 1937-   .
PA3133.G68 1984   882′.01′09   83-47542
ISBN 0-06-015203-6   84 85 86 87 88 10 9 8 7 6 5 4 3 2 1
ISBN 0-06-091080-1 (pbk.)   84 85 86 87 88 10 9 8 7 6 5 4 3 2 1

PREFACE

This anthology is intended for the general reader as well as the classicist. All Greek quotations have therefore been translated, and footnotes segregated to the end of the book. Readers need not consult these to follow the arguments of the essays. For those unfamiliar with some of the terms commonly employed in discussions of Greek Tragedy, there is a glossary on p. 452.

This collection makes no claim to be either definitive or comprehensive. Indeed, no single volume could possibly treat all thirty-three extant Greek tragedies. Moreover, it seemed wise to devote more than one essay to some of the plays most often read (e.g., *Oedipus*, *Medea*). Several excellent articles had to be omitted, either because they were too specialized (metrical analyses, textual criticism) or incomprehensible without a thorough knowledge of Greek. Space limitations also precluded publication of excerpts from 'general' works like John Jones's *On Aristotle and Greek Tragedy*, Walter Burkert's studies of tragedy and ritual, or Brian Vickers's *Towards Greek Tragedy*.[1]

Still, there is a reasonably broad spectrum of critical approaches, including structuralist (Vernant, C. Segal), Marxist (Thomson), and even such 'contemporary' issues as the role of women in society (Winnington-Ingram, Knox). They were, however, chosen for their inherent merit, not with an eye on critical fashion.

Those seeking further reading on Greek Tragedy may consult the excellent bibliographies in *L'année philologique*, the *Classical World Surveys*[2], *Lustrum* (often in German), and the New Surveys in the Classics, published at intervals by *Greece & Rome*.

---

[1]Cf. John Jones, *On Aristotle and Greek Tragedy*, (London, 1962); Walter Burkert's work includes 'Greek Tragedy and Sacrificial Ritual', *Gk. Rom. Byz. Stud.* 7 (1966), 87–129, and, of related interest, *Structure and History in Greek Mythology and Ritual*, Sather Classical Lectures, Vol. 47 (Berkeley and Los Angeles, 1979); Brian Vickers, *Towards Greek Tragedy: Drama, Myth and Society* (London, 1973).

[2]*Aeschylus*: A. G. McKay, 'A Survey of recent (1947–54) work on Aeschylus', *CW* 48 (1954–5), 145–50; 153–9; and 'Aeschylean Studies', Vol. 59 (1965–6), 40–8, 65–75. *Sophocles*: G. M. Kirkwood, 'A review of recent Sophoclean Studies' (1945–56), *CW* 50 (1956–7), 157–72. *Euripides*: H. W. Miller, 'A Survey of recent Euripidean scholarship, 1940–54', *CW* 49 (1955–6), 81–92; and 'Euripidean Drama 1955–65', *CW* 60 (1966–7), 177–87; 218–20.

The three surveys are contained in the *Classical World Bibliographies: Greek*

I am extremely grateful for the generous good counsel of several scholars. My gratitude to W. G. Arnott, Hellmut Flashar, C. J. Herington, Bernard Knox, Hugh Lloyd–Jones, A. G. McKay, Carroll Moulton, Charles Segal, and Oliver Taplin. Professors Segal and Winnington-Ingram kindly revised their essays for this collection. Valuable criticisms were offered by the readers and editors at the Oxford University Press. It is always a pleasure to acknowledge the untiring assistance of the librarians at the Institute of Classical Studies in London.

I hope this volume will be of use to many, and perpetuate enthusiasm for the masterpieces that constitute the first great drama of the western world.

London,   ERICH SEGAL
16 June 1982

Drama and Poetry (ed. Walter Donlan), Garland Publishing, New York–London, 1978. The Surveys editor, Professor McKay, is hopeful of publishing updated bibliographies in the near future.

CONTENTS

EMOTION AND MEANING IN
GREEK TRAGEDY

OLIVER TAPLIN

I shall attempt to characterize what kind of effect Greek tragedy has — used to have, may have — on a member of the audience. This attempt calls for a basic consideration of the nature of the art-form, and some of the most familiar doctrines about it will have to be cleared from the air. The life-breath of Greek tragedy often seems stifled by antiquarian patronizing and by text-book clichés, clichés which I find trotted out in the programme-notes to almost every modern production.

My working assumption is that the tragedians were free in their use of theatrical techniques, that they chose to convey their meaning by certain actions and sequences of action rather than others, and that this artistic choice directs us to their purpose. But most critics have written not of freedom but of constraints, limitations, rules. In some ways Aristotle's *Poetics* sets the example for this approach, though at least Aristotle was being prescriptive, not descriptive. But in his wake more petty and more authoritarian critics have so extended and rigidly codified the 'rules' of Greek tragedy as to obscure and even deny its lively freedom. Overgeneralizations and simplifications have become common textbook doctrine; and instead of illuminating tragedy these clichés have mortified and alienated it. Some will have to be cleared out of the way in order to approach the experience of the audience of a Greek tragedy. This negative progress will, I hope, constantly be bringing our positive goal nearer.

To react against the imposition of rules by critics is not for a moment to deny that the Athenian theatre was in many respects highly conventional. Innumerable conventions governing diction, tone and propriety

From *Greek Tragedy in Action* (London: Methuen and Co., 1978). Reprinted with minor revisions by permission of the author and the publisher. © 1978 Oliver Taplin.

defined the genre and sustained its elevation. Others regulated, and at the same time made familiar, the technical medium.[1] Some may strike us as awkwardly restrictive (e.g., those governing the handling of the chorus or stichomythia); others are still dramatic common sense and seem too obvious to notice (e.g., only one character speaks at a time, characters normally speak on entry). Very few of these 'laws' are unbreakable. Two conventions, for instance — both with sound practical justification — are that the chorus should not go off in the middle of the play, and that wounds and death should not be presented on stage. Yet there are counter-examples to both: the former in *Eum.* and *Ajax*, the latter in *Ajax*, *OT* and *Hipp*. These unwritten laws are not really restrictions or limitations, they are rather the familiar framework which supports any great cultural florescence. When the artist has accepted forms and his audience shares a complex of expectations, then, since the audience is more sensitive and receptive, the art form can be accordingly more highly developed. So the circumscriptions are liberating (most, if not all, worthwhile human activities need rules). It is only after the flowering is over that the rules become a bondage and the art tends either towards lifeless imitation (like the tragedy of later antiquity) or towards an indiscriminate formlessness (like today?). These flexible defining rules of the game are not like the stiffly distorting overgeneralizations I am complaining of.

Take this, for instance: 'all the important *action* in Greek tragedy takes place off stage: on stage it is merely spoken and sung about.' My claim is, on the contrary, that it is the action which takes place *on* stage which *is* important, and is part of what the play is about: the action off-stage is only of interest in so far as it is given attention on stage. The error comes about from a simple-minded preconception of what constitutes action; it only counts the huge violent events of narrative history — battles, riots, miracles, natural disasters and so forth. This is to miss the point that the stuff of tragedy is the individual response to such events; not the blood, but the tears. It is the life-sized actions of this personal dimension which are the dramatist's concern, and which he puts on stage. (It is above all the film which, for better or for worse, has obscured this distinction.)

I move on to a more evidently attractive fallacy, and one which has, in fact, influenced our contemporary theatre: that Greek tragedy is in one way or another a *ritual* event. This is, I think, true only in so far as all human activities are 'rituals', a use of the word which renders it virtually meaningless. On any useful definition of ritual, Greek tragedy is simply and demonstrably not a ritual. The whole point about ritual is that it should always be the *same*: it is the aim of its performers to repeat the rigmarole as perfectly, as identically as possible.[2] Whatever its origins Greek tragedy as we know it retains no such repeated elements, neither in part nor in whole. Of course there are all the conventions just discussed above, but they promote diversity, not repetition. Many attempts have been made to find invariable ritual elements in Greek tragedy, but all have failed and all (so far as I can see) are bound to fail. Probably the best known is the struggle, death, lament and rebirth of the 'year spirit', a pattern of fertility ritual which Gilbert Murray extended to Greek tragedy. But not one single tragedy we have can be claimed without distortion actually to follow this pattern; in particular Greek tragedy does not go in for resurrection or rejuvenation.

Now there certainly are some ritual procedures during the course of the events of the plays, for example supplication, or ghost-raising, or the hunting *kōmos*. But these are used *within* the plays, they are not imposed on them from without. Greek tragedy reflects and exploits the rituals of the real world, of course: but it is not itself a ritual. When the playwright set about composition, in other words, he did not have to follow any imposed ritual formula or sequence.

I would go further and suggest that it was a necessary precondition of the great age of Greek tragedy that the drama should *not* have been a ritual. It had to be human and various, beyond the control of repeated superstition, ancestral taboo, actions stylized and codified beyond anything mimetic — it had to exploit ritual, not just conserve and subserve it. This break with the repetitiousness of ritual may well have been one of the great achievements of tragedy's creators. The impulse among modern critics to impose ritual patterns was largely inspired by the rise of comparative anthropological studies.[3] For when it was seen how rituals, including some semi-dramatic rituals, are so extremely important in primitive societies, it was an obvious step to expect ritual patterns in Greek tragedy. What this approach, which is still active, underestimates is the extent to which classical Greek culture had gone beyond the 'primitive', and moved on in the direction, whether or not one regards it as a beneficial progress, taken since by Western civilization.

But a further argument is advanced by those who claim that tragedy was a ritual, the fact that the tragedies were performed as part of the programme of the city festival of Dionysus, an annual event of several days which included many traditional ritual events — processions, sacrifices, etc.[4] The plays were performed within the sacred area of Dionysus, in the presence of his priest, and were preceded and followed by fixed rituals. All true. But the fact is that these circumstances have left no trace whatsoever on the tragedies themselves, no trace of the Dionysiac occasion, the time of year, the priests, the surrounding rituals, nothing.

We could not tell one single thing about the Festival from the *internal* evidence of the plays; it is all supplied by external evidence.

Unimaginable? We may go to a secular play or concert which is part of a church festival, is given in a church and is even preceded by some prayers from the priest; but does that make the performance a ritual or attendance a religious experience? You have only to contrast it with the lessons, litany and liturgy of a church service. But surely, it may still be claimed, tragedy was, none the less, a religious experience for the audience, seeing that they were participating in a sacred festival. Is going to the *Nutcracker* a religious experience since it is part of the annual festival commemorating Christ's birth (or making the winter solstice, if you prefer)? For the Athenians the great Dionysia was an occasion to stop work, drink a lot of wine, eat some meat, and witness or participate in the various ceremonials, processions and priestly doings which are part of such holidays the world over. It was also the occasion for tragedy and comedy; but I do not see any way in which the Dionysiac occasion invades or affects the entertainment. Some Athenians complained that the tragedy was 'nothing to do with Dionysus' (cf. our Christmas): but whatever everyone else went for it was evidently not another ritual, nor in any obvious or overt sense for a religious experience. To put it another way, there is nothing intrinsically Dionysiac about Greek tragedy.

Next a dogma which is, if anything, even more widespread and more misleading: that 'they all knew the story already'. This promotes several misconceived inferences: that Greek tragedy was a repository of traditional tales, that the dramatist's composition is 'dictated by the myth', that there is no element of suspense or surprise, that the tragedy is the working out of fate or destiny, that the characters are puppets of the gods. All these clichés I regard as more or less wrong.

Greek tragedy almost invariably drew on stories about the distant heroic age of Greece, the period which in historical terms we now call the Late Bronze Age or 'The Mycenaean Age', those few generations of mightly exploits, turmoil and splendour, which were the setting of most traditional Greek heroic song, both in epic and lyric. But these stories were not history, nor were they canonized in any definitive collection of 'Greek myths'. Their oral transmission 'at mother's knee' was no doubt subject to the huge variations which characterize nearly all such oral traditions, variations of emphasis and the mood no less than of narrative content (whatever 'deep structures' the reductionist sage may claim to detect). It is likely, in any case, that the tragedians drew predominantly on literary sources. Here, too, there was almost limitless variation, the product of centuries of re-arrangement and invention, a process which the tragedians themselves continued. Not even the myths of the *Iliad* and *Odyssey* are definitive. The only full coincidence with Homer in surviving tragedy, *Rhesus* and *Iliad* 10, reveals many important divergencies. Or take the myth of Orestes. In the story alluded to several times in the *Odyssey* (and also, it seems, in early lyric) Aegisthus is the chief agent of Agamemnon's murder and chief object of Orestes' vengeance: but the whole shape of the *Oresteia* is moulded by Aeschylus' decision, possibly innovatory, to make Clytemnestra the sole murderer and chief victim of vengeance. Then we all know from Sophocles that when Oedipus discovered the truth he blinded himself and went into exile, while Jocaste hanged herself. In the version in *Odyssey* 11 Epicaste (as she is called) hangs herself, but there is nothing about Oedipus' blinding: he rules on in Thebes. And a line in the *Iliad* (23.679) implies that he fell in battle there. Then in Euripides' *Phoenician Women* Oedipus is blind but still in Thebes many years after the discovery of the truth – and Jocaste? She is still alive. Then, again, in Aeschylus' original version of the *Seven against Thebes* Oedipus had no daughters; the death of his sons was the end of his line. Examples like this may be multiplied, and even more so if vase-paintings are brought into play. Very little was immutably fixed.

But even if the myths were much more rigidly laid down than my argument claims, this would still be of minimal consequence for the literary criticism of tragedy, since the mere *story*, such as may be excerpted in a collection of 'Greek Myths', has no significant bearing on the quality of the play. The mere story is shared by good and bad dramatists alike – it may be indistinguishable in Sophocles and in a fifth-rate hack. What matters, for the dramatist and his audience, is the way he has *shaped* the story, the way he has turned it into drama. The constraint is minimal: the scope for artistry enormous.[5] The area of artistic initiative may be conveyed by a crude catalogue of some of the decisions in question: which brief section is to be taken from the continuum of the myth, which events are to be emphasized or played down, which characters, which aspects, which motifs and images? The identity and role of the chorus, the sequence of events, the exposition, the shape of the acts and of the ending, the use of the lyric, whether choral, monody or lyric dialogue; and last but not least, all the aspects of theatrical and visual technique (the subject of *Greek Tragedy in Action*): all have to be decided on. The list could be extended and elaborated to fill volumes: for these factors are, in effect, the playwright's medium and, thus, our means to literary criticism and interpretation. What we ask is *how* the dramatist has wrought his play, and why he has done it in his particular way, for he had deliberated on this process and made his decisions. The constraint of his myth, in so far as it is fixed, is only of marginal influence. The standard comparison of Aeschylus' *Choephoroi* with the *Electras* of Euripides and Sophocles shows this process of artistic shaping in practice. The range of variation is even better brought out by looking at Aeschylus' *Seven against Thebes*, Sophocles' *Antigone*, and Euripides' *Phoenician Women*.[6]

Now let us look at this issue from the side of the audience. They did not know the 'plot' in advance, for they did not know what version, what variations and innovations the playwright would use — no doubt they were eager to find out. Still less did they know how he would shape his plot, how he would dramatize it: that is precisely what they went to see. In this respect the audience approached the drama, I would maintain, virtually free of preconceptions. It was then the dramatist's task to enthrall their minds, to fill them with the knowledge, thoughts and feelings which he wished to conjure up, and to the exclusion of all others. That is why each tragedy is more or less self-contained in narra- tive, and includes even the most elementary facts in its exposition — which is quite uncalled for if they 'knew it already'. The dramatist would, naturally, prepare for and foreshadow the course of his plot (hence 'tragic irony'), though even here there is plenty of scope for surprise and suspense. He might even call to mind previous versions of his story, earlier dramatizations or, above all, Homer; he will then arouse complex associations and expectations which he can confirm or vary or contradict. But such allusions should only receive as much attention as the spellbinder allows; and what is not alluded to does not, within the play, exist. Far from knowing it all already, the audience knows what it is told, thinks and feels what it is aroused to think and feel.

A brief paragraph on the related misconception that Greek tragedy basically shows the working of Fate, of men fastened to the puppetry of higher powers — a notion with an enduring fascination, for Thomas Hardy for example.[7] Most cultures have their expressions of fatalism; they are one of our chief sources of solace in the face of the pointless waste of ill fortune: 'che sarà, sarà', 'God's will be done', 'his number was up', 'it is written' . . . The ancient Greeks were as prone as any to resort to such notions, though, naturally enough, after rather than before the event, and after disaster rather than good fortune. And like most cultures, for a pattern or purpose behind catastrophe they looked to superhuman forces, personal or impersonal. But this tendency does not, within the whole compass of a drama, preclude the free will of the characters or their responsibility, nor does it render their whole life puppetry. Most of the time they are presented as free agents working out their own destinies — as a rule disastrously, since this is tragedy.

But sometimes they are seen in fatalistic terms; and sometimes the two motivations, human and superhuman, are seen conspiring together, both logically sufficient conditions of the outcome, yet both at work. But never, except perhaps in mad scenes, are the characters of Greek tragedy portrayed as automata or marionettes. Even when they are viewed as victims of the gods, they remain human and independent.

Compared with the 'myth fallacy' and the 'ritual fallacy' relatively few critics are the prisoners of my last trap, what might be called the 'propaganda fallacy'. This is the supposition that a Greek tragedy was primarily or significantly shaped by the desire to promote a certain line on a specific contemporary issue (in politics or philosophy or whatever). The advocates of such a view will have for a start to allow that such propaganda is *cryptic*, if it is true that there is not one single specific allusion to a contemporary person or event in all of Greek tragedy.[8] So far as I can see this is in fact the case. There is not one anachronism to be noted as such, no overt rupture of the dramatic illuson of the remote heroic world. To avert misunderstanding, I hasten to grant that in a sense — in the most important sense — Greek tragedy is entirely topical and the mirror of its own times. It was composed for the audience of fifth-century Athenians, not for a Bronze Age audience; and its general preoccupations, moral, social and emotional, are those of its age. Thus, it is a tissue of technical anachronisms in the strictest historical sense: my point is that they are not to be noticed as such, they are admitted only as long as they are congruous with the heroic world of the far past in which the play is set.

As a warning consider these three facts (all in my view beyond dispute, though not, in fact, undisputed). Nowhere in Greek tragedy is there any direct address to the audience or any other reference to it; nowhere in Greek tragedy does the dramatist use the first person of himself or refer to himself in any way; and nowhere in Greek tragedy is there any reference of any kind to the theatre, to drama, actors, etc. No 'gentle spectators', no 'humble author', no 'all the world's a stage'. All three absences are in direct contrast to the Old Comedy of Aristophanes and to most later drama, which likes to exploit the tension between the world of audience and the world of the play, between these two competing types of reality.[9] This invariable refusal to admit the existence of audience and actors and playwright, or to admit that the play is not the real world, confirms the claim that the dramatic illusion is inviolable. The world of the play never acknowledges the world of the audience: the distancing remains always intact. This is by no means to deny the relevance of the tragedy to the world of the audience; but the relevance is not that of propaganda.

What then *is* the relevance of Greek tragedy to its audience? Now that some more modern dogmas have been cleared aside, we might turn to the ancient Greek sources to see what they thought their tragedies were about.[10] They give us, I think, some views which are interestingly wrong, and some which tally so well with my own experience that I am unable to improve on them.

By far the most substantial fifth-century discussion of tragedy is the second half of Aristophanes' *Frogs*. One theme is particularly persistent: that tragedy *teaches* its audience. 'We poets make men better citizens' (1009 f.). 'Boys have a schoolteacher to instruct them, grown-ups have poets' (1054 f.). In Plato too this is generally regarded as the dramatist's chief claim. This may seem fair enough — most of us decide that art is didactic in one sense or another — but both Aristophanes and Plato apply the notion in disappointing ways. Thus, they both speak of poets, including tragedians, as though it was claimed for them that they actually taught various practical skills — strategy, sailing, economics, cobbling, or whatever it may be. Plato's Socrates has a good time at the expense of this absurdity: obviously for such expertise you go, not to poetry, but to a technical manual or to a living authority.

Another questionable assumption is that the poet's teaching is contained in the words of certain of his lines, and so can be extracted from the work (like a tooth). Aristophanes scarcely seems to doubt that the 'message' of a play by Aeschylus or Euripides — and the man's personal moral views also — is purveyed by certain sententious lines from his work. The same assumption has been shared by the generations of critics down to the present day who have put together a picture of the dramatist from a patchwork of quotations. Obviously this is a hazardous, if not downright foolish, method, since each quotation has a context within the drama as a whole, a context from which (in any good playwright) it is indivisible. The dramatizer of conflict has to be able to put both sides of a case: which side is his message? Furthermore, admirable sentiments may be put in the mouth of a villain, and objectionable ones in the mouth of a virtuous character who does not act upon them (like Hippolytus' notorious line 'my tongue swore, but my heart did not confirm it'). Sometimes, it is true, a final message is drawn from the tragedy as a whole — messages like 'life is full of unexpected turns', 'call no man happy until he is dead', 'think on a mortal level'. But these are the traditional maxims of the Greeks, the property of every grandfather: one need not go to tragedy to learn these. As always, as soon as the message of a work of art is reduced to a sentence it becomes banal.

But the idea that tragedy teaches is not to be abandoned just because it has been applied sophistically. We might well agree in general terms that, in so far as tragedy teaches, it does so through the work *as a whole*, through the way that human life is portrayed and not merely by individual spoken lines. So the audience learns, in so far as it learns, by way of the whole experience. That is to say, the intellectual burden of the tragedy and its value as teaching has to do with the quality of the audience's experience.

We do have a scrap of fifth-century criticism which seems to be developing this very train of thought. It is a single sentence, a fragment torn from its surrounding discourse, but we know it was written apropos of tragedy: 'The man who deceives shows more justice than he who does not; and the man who is deceived has more wisdom than he who is not' (*ho te apatēsas dikaioteros tou mē apatēsantos, kai ho apatētheis sophōteros tou mē apatēthentos*). These are the words of Gorgias, the Sicilian theorist and teacher of rhetoric, who worked in Athens in the last quarter of the fifth century, and who is best known for his discomfiture in Plato's *Gorgias*.[11] Inevitably any interpretation of this sentence is speculative, but there is one which seems to me to make very good sense, whether or not it is what Gorgias meant. The tragedian who succeeds in enthralling his audience does more justice by the effect this has on his audience than the playwright who fails to captivate them: likewise the member of the audience who succumbs to the spell of the play will through that experience be a better, wiser man than the member who resists and remains unmoved. On any interpretation the key word is, of course, *apatān*, to deceive, trick, beguile (perhaps conveyed by the English word-play that tragedy 'takes in' its audience). It is a balanced paradox, typical of Gorgias' manner, that deceit should be the means of justice and wisdom. It is also a shrewd reply to all those moralists, above all Plato himself, who have complained that fiction is all lies. The deceit, Gorgias implies, is temporary and it is beneficial. Truth and falsity are not the category relevant to the case: the worth of the work of art depends rather on whether it is convincing, on whether it interests, enthralls, moves its audience.

How, then, does this 'deceit' take effect? Gorgias' own views are, I suggest, worth pursuing; and the following passage, which comes from his virtuoso apologia for Helen, surely has tragedy in mind. 'All poetry I consider and define as discourse in metre. There comes over the audience of poetry a fearful horror and tearful pity and doleful yearning. By means of the discourse their spirit feels a personal emotion on account of the good and bad fortune of others.'[12] This passage alone should be enough to rescue Gorgias from the common slander that he was merely a word-juggler. Above all he sees that *emotions* are at the heart of tragic poetry. And what is more he has put his finger on one of the most vital and remarkable features of this experience: that the emotions are generous — altruistic almost — that we feel disturbed personally for *other* people, for people who have no direct connection with us and indeed belong to another world from ours. (What's Hecuba to us?) This outgoing emotion, as opposed to introverted self-absorption, is characteristic of Greek tragedy, and of most (perhaps all) great tragedy. This point is well brought home by the anecdote in Herodotus (6.21) about Phyrnichus, a contemporary of Aeschylus, who produced a tragedy about the sack of Miletus, a recent outrage on a city closely connected with Athens. Phyrnichus was prosecuted and fined for reminding the Athenians of their *own* troubles; this is not the playwright's function.

Can we characterize these tragic emotions? Gorgias' list is, I think, extraordinarily apt, and far more evocative than Aristotle's terse and derivative 'pity and fear' (*eleos kai phobos*). Literally Gorgias writes 'ultra-fearful shuddering and much-weeping pity and grief-loving longing'. The greatest of these is surely pity, however much Plato and Nietzsche may protest (how deluded Nietzsche was in claiming the Greeks as his authority for denouncing pity). We feel an overwhelming *compassion* for these other people who undergo the tribulations, pain and waste which are the stuff of tragedy. Yet this compassion is seldom if ever separable from other emotions. We pity Agamemnon, Oedipus, Agaue; yet at the same time we feel horror, alarm (*phrīkē*); and at the same time we *want* Agamemnon to be murdered, Oedipus to find out the truth, Agaue to recognize her son's head. We have a longing (*pothos*) which wants grief (*philopenthēs*): it is such sweet sorrow. I shall return to the paradoxical pleasure of these doleful feelings; the important new point for now is that the emotions of the tragic experience are *complex*, and they are of course ever-shifting. Perhaps, indeed, the better the tragedy, the more complex and labile the emotions it arouses. This may be why there are certain strong emotions which Greek tragedy does not as a rule subject us to, notably hatred and lust. These are domineering and single-minded obsessions which do not permit mental companions.

It seems to me, then, that Gorgias is right that tragedy is essentially the *emotional experience of its audience*. Whatever it tells us about the world is conveyed by means of these emotions. Plato agreed with Gorgias in this, but he disapproved of the process and regarded it as harmful. Aristotle agreed with him too, but, contrary to Plato, regarded it as beneficial and salutary. Plato's objection was that such emotions are not the province of the highest part of the soul, the intellectual part. This is the forefather of the error made by so many later critics who have not acknowledged the centrality of emotion in the communication of tragedy. They think that if tragedy is essentially an emotional experience, it must be *solely* that; and they think this because they assume that strong emotion is necessarily in opposition to thought, that the psychic activities are mutually exclusive. But is this right? Understanding, reason, learning, moral discrimination; these things are not, in my experience, incompatible with emotion (nor presumably in the experience of Gorgias and Aristotle): what is incompatible is cold insensibility. Whether or not emotion is inimical to such intellectual processes depends on the *circumstances in which it is aroused*.

The characteristic tragic emotions – pity, horror, fascination, indignation, and so forth – are felt in many other situations besides in the theatre. Above all we suffer them in the face of the misfortunes of real life, of course. What distinguishes the experience of a great tragedy? For one thing, as already remarked, we feel for the fortunes of people who have no direct personal relation to us: while this does not decrease the intensity of the emotion, it affords us some distance and perspective. We can feel and at the same time observe from outside. But does this distinguish tragedy from other 'contrived' emotional experiences (most of them tending to the anti-intellectual), for example an animal hunt, a football match, an encounter group, reading a thriller, or watching a horror movie? Well, the experience of tragedy is by no means a random series of sensations. Our emotional involvement has perspective and context at the same time, and not just in retrospect. Thus the events of the tragedy are in an ordered *sequence*, a sequence which gives shape and comprehensibility to what we feel. And, most important of all, the affairs of the characters which move us are given a moral setting which is argued and explored in the play. They act and suffer within situations of moral conflict, or social, intellectual and theological conflict. The quality of the tragedy depends *both* on its power to arouse our emotions *and* on the setting of those emotions in a sequence of moral and intellectual complications which is set out and examined. Tragedy evokes our feelings for others, like much else; but it is distinguished by the order and significance it imparts to suffering. So if the audience is not moved, then the tragedy, however intellectual, is a total failure: if its passions are aroused, but in a thoughtless, amorphous way, then it is merely a bad tragedy, sensational, melodramatic.

Thus it is that our emotions in the theatre, far from driving out thought and meaning, are indivisible from them: they are simultaneous and mutually dependent. The experience of tragedy can achieve this coherence in a way that the emotional experiences of real life generally cannot because they are too close, too cluttered with detail and partiality, to be seen in perspective. Tragedy makes us feel that we understand life in its tragic aspects. We have the sense that we can better sympathize with and cope with suffering, misfortune and waste. It is this sense of understanding (not isolated pearls of wisdom) that is the 'message' of a tragedy, that the great playwright imparts. This is well put in T. S. Eliot's essay 'Shakespeare and the Stoicism of Seneca', where he argues that it is the quality of the emotional expression rather than the quality of the philosophy which makes literature great, which makes it 'strong, true and informative . . . useful and beneficial in the sense in which poetry is useful and beneficial'. 'All great poetry' Eliot writes 'gives the illusion of a view of life . . . for every precise emotion tends towards intellectual formulation'.

'*Illusion*'? Maybe; but emphatically not because the play is a fiction and the audiences' experiences the product of temporary artifice. (And all for nothing! For Hecuba?) Their experiences, both emotional and intellectual, are none the less real, and become part of the real person. The experience is not erased when we leave the theatre. Tragedy is only an illusion in so far as any claim to make sense of all the evils of our life is an illusion (and perhaps tragedy does not claim this). The 'tragedies' of real life, unlike those of the stage, are often shapeless, sordid, capricious, meaningless. But supposing this to be true (as I do), what then? It is not *human* to be content with this useless, even if ultimate, truth. We *must* try to understand, to cope, to respond. It is in this attempt that tragedy — that most great art — has its place. For it gives the hurtful twists of life a shape and meaning which are *persuasive*, which can be lived with. And that endurance and perspective are none the less real. As Gorgias so neatly put it 'the man who is deceived has more wisdom than he who is not.' And so in the end the 'deceit' is true to life and part of life and makes life the better for it.

By enthralling its audience tragedy unites emotion and meaning so as to give us an experience which, by creating a perspective on the misfortunes of human life, helps us to understand and cope with those misfortunes. There is nothing new or startling in this conclusion; but if it is along the right lines there is no harm in its being repeated and rephrased. *We* are now the audience of Greek tragedy. Are the actions and emotions and ideas I have been considering irremediably inaccessible? They still have the power, surely, to amaze indeed the very faculties of eyes and ears.

2

DECISION AND RESPONSIBILITY IN THE
TRAGEDY OF AESCHYLUS

ALBIN LESKY

What I want to present here is an interpretation of four passages from
the extant dramas of Aeschylus. Our point of departure will be the text
and not any general consideration. I also want to avoid committing myself right at the outset on the question whether we have to exclude the
idea of personal will from the tragedies merely because we do not find
in them a corresponding term for it. I do want, however, to confess to
one belief. It seems to me just as wrong to interpret the great poetry of
the Greeks out of the ideas of our times, out of that *'Impertinente Nähe'*
('audacious Proximity') that Nietzsche spoke of, as it is wrong to regard
the Greeks as completely different people, severed from our world by
an unbridgeable gulf. The Aristotelian golden mean will here too be the
best guide.

Let us begin with a passage from the *Suppliants*, a passage to which
Professor Snell has also attributed particular significance.[1] I would like
to emphasise, however, that, if I begin with a scene from the *Suppliants*,
this does not mean that I have returned to the old view that dated
the play in an early period. On the ground of the well-known papyrus-
fragment of a Didascalia [production record] it seems to me on the
contrary quite inevitable to date the performance of the play in the
middle or in the second half of the 460s.

The situation in the first part of the drama needs no special introduction. The chorus is formed by the daughters of Danaos, who have
fled to Argos from the impetuous and repulsive wooing of the sons of
Aigyptos. (Incidentally, I shall take it for granted that the twelve
members of the chorus represented all fifty daughters of Danaos.) Near
the town of Argos, they have taken refuge at a large altar, where the
images or symbols of a number of gods are combined. The king of the

From *Journal of Hellenic Studies* 86 (1966), 78–86. Reprinted with minor revisions
by permission of the Society for the Promotion of Hellenic Studies.

country comes to inquire about the business of the strange crowd. He learns of their desire to be received in the city and given protection against their Egyptian pursuers. The daughters of Danaos point out their relationship with Io, the woman of Argos. The king finds himself facing a momentous decision. The suppliants have sought the protection of Zeus *hikesios*, (god of suppliants), and regard for suppliants *is* a religious commandment, which ranks high in the canon of ethical norms. On the other hand, to receive the Danaides means that he will have to fight against the sons of Aigyptos, who will come in arms to force their uncle's daughters to marry them. The king now has to choose one way out of this dilemma. The manner in which he does this and the part that free choice and force respectively play in his decision are important not only for the course of the action in the *Suppliants*; a study of this passage will help our understanding of other, more difficult passages. In a lengthy epirrhematic scene, the chorus in its stanzas entreats the king to grant the requested protection. The king tries to escape by pointing out that the decision rests not with him but with the people of Argos. He inquires about the reason for the flight of the Danaides without, however, receiving a satisfactory answer to his question. It already becomes obvious in this passage that the king has recognised the difficulty of his decision. He expresses this clearly in his first speech which follows the quick movement of the preceding scene. Here we find the magnificent image of the diver, who has to fathom great depths with a clear eye. The city should not suffer damage from a fight, nor should a curse be brought down on Argos by abandoning the fugitives who are seeking protection at the altar of the gods (417). To the request of the chorus to consider the righteous command of the god (437) the king at the beginning of his second great speech, which surpasses the first in length and intensity, answers with the assurance that he indeed has (438). The hopelessness of the situation becomes evident; there is no solution without great pain (442). And when the king finally says he had rather be ignorant of the peril than aware of it, this is an attempt — however futile it may be — to evade the decision. And so it is interpreted by the chorus. For now the leader of the chorus announces that their words of awe and reserve have come to an end. New and different things are foreshadowed. The king is horrified to hear in answer to his questions that the girls would hang themselves on the images of the gods if their request were refused. This, however, would bring an inexpiable defilement and great disaster upon the city. The king knows this (473). Once more he weighs disaster against disaster, bloodshed against abandoning the fugitive. The girls' threat, however, has tipped the scale and what follows are simply the measures the king takes to protect the girls. It may be said right away that the theme of a final decision by the people of Argos has lost much of its weight. Later it will cause suspense, above all it will lead up to the song of blessing for Argos, in which the poet was interested mainly for political reasons. The fact, however, is that the decision was reached with the words of the king and that he made it in full consciousness of his responsibility.

But was the choice between two possibilities made in full freedom of will? This is the central question. First it has to be remarked that the poet presents in a very elaborate scene what is going on in the minds of the persons involved. It cannot be shown in detail here, but at least it should be mentioned briefly that Aeschylus elaborates the psychological development of the characters more fully than his successors. One may compare how in Sophocles' *Philoctetes* the change in Neoptolemos is shown as something completed whereas its development is hardly indicated at all. We may compare Euripides who contrasts Iphigeneia begging for her life and her later readiness to sacrifice herself without developing this change of attitude step by step. And let us compare with that the fully developed scene at the end of *Agamemnon*, when Klytaimnestra in spiritual combat with the chorus step by step changes from her ecstatic admission of her deed to a recognition of the fatal chain of events.

But let us return to the *Suppliants*. We may clearly distinguish two stages, which I should like to call recognition or, as it were, diagnosis and decision. It seems important that the decision does not immediately spring from the recognition. In the interchange between the chorus and the king, as well as in his speeches, the situation is thoroughly analysed. The conclusion is that disaster stands against disaster, that each decision must entail a catastrophe. There is no way out of the deadlock between equally strong forces. But a new element is introduced; the threat of girls to hang themselves on the images of the gods, the threat of unspeakable desecration. Now the decision is made, but the king adds two expressions we must not neglect; *anankē* and the wrath of Zeus. Of course, the decision remains a personal one, and he bears the responsibility for it. It has often been surmised, and in fact it seems very likely, that the full tragic consequence of this decision is the king's death, in the second part of the trilogy, in the fight that arose over the fate of the Danaides. But on the other hand we cannot fail to see that the king's decision was made under heavy pressure. We can anticipate a phrase that will concern us presently. 'He has taken upon him the yoke of *Anankē*.' Freedom and compulsion are united in a genuinely tragic way.

Yet another thing that is extremely characteristic of Aeschylus can be seen from this interpretation. It was Aeschylus who discovered the problem of the uncertainty inherent in every human action. Man through his actions exposes himself to uncertainty. Many human actions have a double aspect — this holds true if not for all human actions, at least for all those which presuppose a decision. To protect the suppliants means disregarding the interests of the city; by giving preference to these, the king would prove his sense of responsibility towards the Polis, and yet he would gravely sin against Zeus, who protects the fugitives.

After these considerations let us now turn to a passage in *Agamemnon*, which has in recent years been the subject of lively discussion. It is the report given by the old men of Argos in the initial choral passage about the events before the departure of the fleet from Aulis. The external course of events can be outlined in just a few words. A strange omen appears to the Greeks. Two eagles differing in their plumage rend a pregnant hare. Without difficulty Calchas interprets the omen to signify the capture of Troy by the two Atreidai and the destruction of its possessions. But he adds that Artemis is angry because the two eagles did not even spare the young in the hare's womb. It must be feared that by an unfavourable wind she will prevent the fleet from sailing and demand another sacrifice that could bring about never-ending hatred. And so it happens. The fleet is held fast and the prophet announces that only the sacrifice of Iphigeneia can calm the winds and make departure possible. Agamemnon, after a heavy inner conflict, determines to sacrifice Iphigeneia, and she dies on the altar of the goddess. There is no word of her being saved. We may assume that the poet in the words of the chorus (247) passes over a tale current at that time which told how Iphigeneia was saved by Artemis. This would have been unsuitable, if Agamemnon's deed was to have its full weight.

The question now is this: Does Agamemnon's decision to sacrifice his own daughter spring from his own will? Is it the result of a free choice? Such eminent interpreters of Greek tragedy as Dodds[2] and Kitto[3] answer the question in the affirmative, whereas such outstanding scholars as Page[4] and Rivier[5] deny that there was a choice between two possibilities. Agamemnon could not act differently, he had no choice; for it would be unthinkable that he should stop his campaign and refrain from his punishment of Troy. It is important to point out that Agamemnon himself describes such an action as that of a *liponaus* (ship deserter) with which Professor Fraenkel rightly compares *lipotaxis* as a current term for (military) deserter.

But would it have been absolutely impossible for Agamemnon to dismiss the fleet and to discontinue the campaign so that there was no question of a free choice? Must we not remember that Agamemnon's situation is developed in an entirely different way in another drama? I am thinking of *Iphigeneia in Aulis* by Euripides, where in the rapid shift of scenes at the beginning Agamemnon and Menelaus one after the other seriously consider discontinuing the campaign and are willing to dismiss the fleet. Of course, we at once have to raise the objection that the dramas by Euripides and by Aeschylus are not the same, just as Euripides' *Herakles* cannot be compared to Sophocles' *Ajax* in spite of an externally similar situation. What we have to do, therefore, is to turn back to the text, and we shall there find support for the two contrary opinions. For the text of our choral passage shows a psychological development similar to the one we saw in the king of Argos in the *Suppliants*. As a matter of fact, the two passages have a good deal in common, which manifests itself in verbal parallels, and this can help us in our understanding of the far more difficult lines in *Agamemnon*.

The first reaction of the Atreidai to the prophet's revelation is utter horror. They beat their sceptres on the ground, tears spring from their eyes. After line 205 we hear about Agamenmon only. We see him, like the king of Argos, facing two alternatives which both lead to disaster. Agamemnon's conclusion 'which of these courses is free from evil'? (211) corresponds exactly to the words with which the king of Argos summarises the situation (*Supp.* 471). The scale at this point is not yet tipped, although the necessity of a choice between two equally disastrous possibilities has become evident. In both plays, however, there is at this point a change which quickly brings about the decision. In the *Suppliants* it comes from outside; the girls' threat to commit suicide at the altar forces the king to give in. In *Agamemnon*, however, the change takes place in the soul of the hesitant hero. 'How am I to become the deserter of my ships (*liponaus*) losing my allies?' (212) Agamemnon asks, and as soon as he utters this phrase, by which he envisages the disgrace and shame he would incur by deserting his post, the scales are no longer even. His decision no longer springs from a free choice between equal possibilities; one has to be avoided at any cost. Iphigeneia *has* to be sacrificed. It is still the king's personal decision springing from his will but the freedom of will is overshadowed by the overwhelming force of the situation which clearly influences the decision. Thus, it is correct to speak of a free choice up to a point. As for the final decision, however, I agree with Rivier that *acte volontaire, nécessité*, and *perturbation* are united in it. Two more parallels in the text indicate that we have correctly compared the ways in which a decision is reached in the *Suppliants* and in *Agamemnon*. Agamemnon's decision to sacrifice Iphigeneia because it was *themis* (ordained) to do so is followed by the sceptical and resigned words (217) which echo *Suppliants* (454), in which the king expresses his sombre premonition of things to come. However, it is far more important still that in both cases the decision is connected with the word *ananke*. It is *ananke* to the king of Argos to avoid the anger of the Zeus of the suppliants. And Agamemnon, it is said, after making his decision took the yoke of *ananke* upon him (218).

Thus far we may confidently draw the parallel but here it ends and our task is to examine what is different in *Agamemnon* and what new motives significant for Aeschylus are introduced.

The king of Argos was drawn from outside into a fatal situation. Agamemnon, however, right from the beginning is involved in the fatal series of events that concern the house of the Atreidai; he is a key-figure in a drama 'whose central problem consists in the connexion between guilt and atonement', as Professor Fraenkel put it. The sacrifice of Iphigeneia is not only a horrible necessity imposed upon him, it is at the same time, his personal and his passionately desired deed, for which he is responsible and for which he has to atone. If one makes a clear logical distinction, of course, one will say: 'A man who acts under necessity is not acting voluntarily.' But to insist upon logical consistency would mean that we should have to reject considerable parts of Aeschylus' tragedies, for many of the tragic situations he presents do, in fact, spring from the rationally indissoluble fusion of necessity and personal will. The words of the passage we are concerned with, express this in a way that leaves no doubt about fusion. First of all, the way Agamemnon expresses his decision in the monologue reported by the chorus: there is no longer any question of shrinking back in despair from the necessity; *themis* must cover not only the deed as such, but also the impetuous desire for it (214). In the following strophe the chorus sings of the 'evil-counselling, merciless infatuation, first cause of ill [*prōtopēmōn*]' (222) which has befallen Agamemnon. This distraction, bordering on insanity, encourages people to horrible deeds.

I must object to the attempt to disparage these words of the chorus as a personal opinion or even a misunderstanding on its part. It is also impossible to interpret the words of the chorus as relating to the irrational sphere only, which has nothing to do with the will that springs from rational consideration. The words in our passage do not permit of this interpretation. The metaphor taken from wind and seafaring (219) expresses the change that has taken place in Agamemnon, the change by which horror at the dreadful alternatives is replaced by the readiness to sacrifice Iphigeneia. The image of 'the turn', incidentally, is also used by the king in the *Suppliants*, though during this state of indecision (442). It is highly characteristic of Aeschylus that in one and the same sentence he speaks of the *anankas lepadnon* ('yoke of necessity') that Agamemnon had to take upon himself and simultaneously calls his change of will, the *phrenos tropaia*, vile and abominable. Thus, what Agamemnon is forced to do under the yoke of *anankē* is at the same time what he wants to do, the crime that entails guilt and atonement, that he will have to atone for with his own fall. The words of the chorus also clearly indicate that the king is not just carried away by irrational forces but rationally accepts his fatal deed (221). Thus we are shown from a new angle the double aspect of human action. The sacrifice of Iphigeneia is necessary because of a fatal situation, and at the same time is not only accepted, but passionately desired by Agamemnon, and therefore he is responsible for it. It might seem a rationally acceptable solution to assume that once Agamemnon has surrendered to the necessity, forces are released in him that makes him passionately seek to fulfil his aim. But I seriously wonder whether we should not be reading too much of modern psychology into Aeschylus. It seems to me more correct simply to state this union of external coercion and personal readiness; the meaning of this genuinely Aeschylean union is that in this way man, acting out of necessity, has to take upon himself guilt and the need for atonement under the divine order.

Logically, this union cannot be analysed; in fact, the stumbling-block in the way of an attempt at logical analysis goes much farther. This was shown by Professor Page in the introduction to his edition. Is not the campaign against Troy a just punishment inflicted on behalf of the highest god, Zeus, who protects the rights of hospitality? Thus Agamemnon acts on behalf of the god who wills this punishment. And yet the price for this punishment is a terrible guilt, for which the king has to atone with his death. Here there is no rational consistency. But the campaign against Troy is obviously another example of the twofold judgement to which human action is so often subject in Aeschylus. The anapaests before the first Stasimon and its first strophe stress that it was Zeus' punishment that came upon Troy (367). But in the course of the Stasimon we are brought to see the other aspect of this victory. Instead of the many warriors an urn returns and the victims of the war are mourned (447). And when it is said later on in the Stasimon that the gods do not overlook mass-murderers (460) – and that the Erinyes destroy unjust felicity, we no longer think of Troy, but of the returning conquerors and their king. He will be struck by the lightning from the eyes of Zeus, the same Zeus who as the protector of the rights of hospitality wanted Troy to be destroyed. Agamemnon himself, on his return, speaks with a shudder of the catastrophe which came on a flourishing city 'for the sake of a woman' (823). The two contrary conceptions of Zeus we have developed are juxtaposed with epigrammatic brevity in the passage with which we are immediately concerned. In the introductory lines it is said about the Atreidai that 'Zeus guardian of host and guest sent them against Alexander because of a promiscuous woman' (61). However, when the chorus tells of Agamemnon's fatal decision and at once marks it as a horrible crime, the deed is described as 'to aid a war to avenge a woman' (225). Let us go back to the *Suppliants* again for a moment, where the king regards it as particularly grave that men should die for the sake of women (477). Thus, Agamemnon's double fate of victory and atonement corresponds to the double meaning the poet clearly and explicitly gives to the campaign against Troy. . . .

We have seen the king of Argos and Agamemnon in situations in which necessity and man's personal decision to act are indissolubly united. The situation is basically the same in two other dramas by Aeschylus. The figure of Eteokles in the last part of the Theban trilogy has in recent years become the subject of a lively discussion. For our present purposes we must focus our attention on a certain scene in the final part. Almost all interpreters regard the speech of Eteokles that begins at line 653 as a turning-point in the course of the action. Eteokles has learned from a messenger that the attacker at the city's seventh gate will be his own brother Polyneikes, and he bursts out in a desperate lament, whose tragic content was impressively expounded by Professor Fraenkel in his analysis of the seven pairs of speeches. I cannot enter here in detail upon the way in which the poet has left in the dark the time when the defenders were allocated to the seven gates. In any case it was his intention to make us realise that it is Eteokles' fate to face his own brother at the seventh gate and that this is brought about by the curse that the house of the Labdakadai is under, and which took new effect in Oedipus' curse upon his sons. Thus, Eteokles in the words just mentioned recognizes the fatal fulfilment of his father's curse. After his first outburst of despair he tries to compose himself and we find him ready to take up the fratricidal fight and thus to fulfil his fate.

But that is not yet all. In the subsequent dialogue with the chorus which presently takes lyrical form, there emerges surprisingly a new theme, which, however, will not be unfamiliar to us after what has been said already. The chorus reminds Eteokles of the inexpiable crime of fratricide, and when the king points out that this is a question of honour the chorus retorts that he is not only accepting the fatal conflict but that he is desiring it out of his own will. In the very first lines of the chorus the word *orgē* [passion, anger] (678) is used, which at once reminds us of the *orga periorgōs epithumein* ('insanely, mad lusting after') spoken in a closely similar situation in *Agamemnon*; in its first stanza, however, the chorus speaks of 'mad lust for battle', of the 'evil passion' of Eteokles. And in the following stanza it accuses the king of being driven too much by the desire to commit a murder which will bear bitter fruit, to shed blood he must not touch. Do we not find here again what our analysis of the passage in Agamemnon so clearly showed: man being led by fate to a terrible deed, which, however, he not only accepts but desires and passionately undertakes?

My view, however, is in contrast with an interpretation which by now has become something of a *fable convenue*. According to this interpretation the words of the chorus I have cited simply spring from a misunderstanding. It is women who are speaking here, and the heroism of Eteokles, who saves his city, is incomprehensible to them, and thus they misinterpret his attitude. In my view this way of understanding the scene is mistaken because it totally fails to recognize the characteristically Aeschylean union of fatal necessity and personal will. It not only has no support in the text, but contradicts it in a number of essential points. If it had been the poet's intention to confront Eteokles with a female chorus that misunderstood him, he would have indicated this misunderstanding. At least he would have made Eteokles contradict the women, which, however, Eteokles never does. . . . Furthermore, the words the chorus speaks about the two brothers after the catastrophe, 'they perished for their impious intent' (831), aptly express the degree of free will the poet recognizes in Eteokles. Thus, the deed of Eteokles, too, reveals the twofold aspect of human action; the king's defense of Thebes, which proves his heroism, becomes at the same time the terrible crime of fratricide. This aspect reveals Aeschylus' conception of the old idea of a curse lying on a family, to which he gave a new and profound meaning; the effect of the curse consists in a crime renewed from generation to generation.

The most significant traits that our analysis has shown are to be seen very clearly in another Aeschylean figure, in Orestes. I shall try to be brief here because I have dwelt upon the problems concerning the figure elsewhere.[6] Suffice it to say here as much as necessary to place the figure of Orestes in *Choephoroi* in the context of our analysis. The necessity imposed upon man from without is particularly emphasized in this case by Apollo's command that he should exact vengeance on his own mother. In his speech before the great Kommos he goes to great lengths in describing the horrors with which the god threatened him in case he should refuse to obey. Opinions differ on this great Kommos between Orestes, Elektra, and the chorus. By some it is interpreted as a mere description of the situation with no intention on the part of the poet to reveal what is going on in Orestes' soul. In contrast to that, I have given a dynamic interpretation of the Kommos, not, however, in the sense that Orestes only here makes the decision to murder his mother; that decision is made before he enters the stage. I believe I have shown, however, that what goes on in Orestes is the same thing that we have been able to observe with Agamemnon and Eteokles; once they are determined to commit the dreadful deeds under the coercion of necessity, one to kill his own daughter and the other to take up the fatal fight against his brother, they at once begin to desire the disastrous deed. In this respect I basically agree with Professor Rivier who says in his study of Aeschylus 'At no moment does the act he must perform lose its necessary character but once again, the hero must accept, he must give in to necessity.'[7] May I remind you, without repeating my own line of argumentation, that during the whole Kommos neither Apollo's command nor even the god's name is ever mentioned? May I also remind you how the chorus and Elektra urge on Orestes with their reports of Klytaimnestra's vile deed. When he bursts out in the words 'She will pay for dishonouring my father by the action of the gods and by the action of my hands' (435) he is no longer acting only on behalf of Apollo, but he wants to do the deed that he must do just as in Agamemnon and in Eteokles compulsion and volition are one.

Once again we can see here the twofold judgement of the deed. Orestes is the obedient servant of the god of Delphi, he is the faithful son of his father as the chorus calls him (1051), he is the deliverer of Argos, and yet his deed is a terrible crime. Already in *Agamemnon* Cassandra says prophetically that Orestes will be the one to complete the desecration of the family (1283), (and she calls him 'the son that slays his mother, an atoner for his father') (1281), giving in a nutshell the two aspects of his deed. It is also characteristic how the chorus immediately after trying along with Elektra to strengthen Orestes' will speaks of 'sorrow inbred in the race', 'bloody stroke of ruin', and 'pain impossible to ease'. It is the same chorus that at the end of the drama places Orestes' deed among the crimes in the house of the Atreidai and once more emphasizes the duality of its judgement: 'and now thirdly, has there come from somewhere a deliverer . . . or shall I say a doom? ' (1073).

To conclude our observations we may take it as proved that two elements of high significance in Aeschylus can be clearly shown: the close union of necessity imposed by the gods and the personal decision to act. This union leaves a certain space for the will of the individual but at the same time limits it. Secondly, we have seen what an important part in Aeschylus' dramas the ambiguity of human action plays. It can be the fulfilment of a duty, obedience to a divine order; and yet at the same time be a dreadful crime.

What I have tried to show here, of course, touches upon a problem which has recently been discussed and which is contained in the title to a well-known book by Karl Reinhardt, *Aischylos the Theologian*. Now, Aeschylus certainly was not a theologian in the sense that he wanted to work out a logically well-founded system. But with all the powers of his mind, he wrestled with the problems arising from the conflict between human existence and divine rule. He does not present a solution in the manner of a well-solved mathematical problem, and for this he may be criticised by those who have such a solution to offer. The tragic power of his dramas, however, springs from those antitheses I have tried to show here. We may apply to our subject what Virginia Woolf said about the language of Aeschylus: 'There is an ambiguity which is the mark of the highest poetry.'[8]

3

THE SHIELD OF ETEOCLES

HELEN H. BACON

The climax of *Seven Against Thebes* is Eteocles' decision at the end of the central messenger scene to meet his brother Polyneices in single combat at the seventh gate. The meaning of this decision, for the city and for Eteocles, is the focus of most of the critical discussion about the play.[1] Both Patzer[2] and Lesky[3] have suggested that in the course of the play Eteocles progresses from uncertainty, or blindness, to knowledge about the workings of the family curse, and that in this progress the central messenger scene plays a crucial role. Neither scholar has discussed the way the language and imagery of the play substantiate this view — nor the way these suggest that the knowledge involved is that fundamental kind of knowledge which we associate with all the stories connected with the family of Oedipus — knowledge of our real relation to those who are most close (*philoi*) to us.[4]

In the central scene in which Eteocles makes his decision, the purpose of the impious shouts, the noisy trappings, and above all of the shield devices, of the first five attackers is to terrify the Theban defenders. Eteocles is not terrified. He recognizes the shields as masks of terror, mere appearances, without real power to harm. The shield device of Polyneices is a mask of a more insidious kind. It represents the bearer, not as omnipotent in his defiance of the gods, but as reverently carrying out the behests of Dike. But the seer, Amphiaraus, has made it clear that there is no Dike that will justify an assault on the mother city by one of her own sons (lines 580-6). Amphiaraus, who does not wish to *seem* but to *be aristos* [best, most noble], has no device on his shield. He alone has no mask. Because he can distinguish illusion from reality he is master of himself, though not of his circumstances. He has accepted death in a doomed expedition in which he is participating against his will. He does not need either the mask of terror which would disguise his helplessness, or the mask of virtue which would disguise his desires.

From *Arion* 3.3 (Autumn 1964) 27-38. Reprinted by permission of the author and *Arion*.

In this central and crucial scene one of the things the shields do is to focus our attention on the problem of knowing what is *really* to be feared.

To Eteocles what is really to be feared is Polyneices and his mask of virtue. Against the masks of terror of the first five attackers he takes calm and effective measures of defense. Towards Amphiaraus he expresses grief for a just man forced against his will to be part of an impious venture. But when the messenger describes Polyneices and his shield, bearing a figure of Dike leading home a man in armour, Eteocles responds with a cry which reflects his horror both in words and in its broken rhythm (lines 653-5).

O my sorrowful race, the race of Oedipus, made mad by the gods, and terribly hated by the gods, alas now in truth my father's curses are being fulfilled.

Eteocles' decision to face his brother in single combat, which comes at the end of this speech, is a decision to *know*, at whatever price, the ultimate meaning of Polyneices' so modest appearing shield device (lines 659-61):

We will soon *know* in what direction the device will fulfill itself, whether the gold inscribed letters, babbling with a wandering of the mind, *will* lead him home.

Near the end of the *kommos* both brothers are described as having achieved knowledge — knowledge of the power of the fury (lines 986-990):

Cho. O grievous Fate, giver of heavy gifts, and lady shade of Oedipus, black Erinys, truly you are *overwhelming*.
Ant. Indeed you *know* her [or *nun*, now] by experiencing [her].
Ism. And *you* have *learned* no later [than he]

The absolutely just division of the wealth of Oedipus, which they have achieved in death, is a kind of knowledge. They are equal in this as in everything else.

In Sophocles' three plays about the house of Laius the central theme of knowing is carried by images of seeing and hearing. In *Seven Against Thebes* too seeing and hearing are crucial. The experiences in which what *seems* must be distinguished from what *is* are transmitted to the mind by the eyes and the ears.

War is presented as visible and audible horror. Perhaps because the chorus can hear more than they can see of the approaching army, sound predominates in their first two songs and in the exchanges with Eteocles which come between them – the clash of harness, chariots, arms, the thud of hooves, the screams of pain and grief, the shouts of rage and greed, and the wonderful variety of noises in the words themselves. And there are the chorus's own cries of terror.

In the central messenger scene the emphasis shifts from the audible to the visible – to the terror-inducing shield devices and to speech made visible in impious slogans inscribed on the shields. But here too the other aspect of the terror of war is noise – the noises that come from the shields themselves, the noises of the horses and their gear, the insolent screams of the warriors, and the same lavish vocabulary of noise that we heard in the first two choral songs. Amphiaraus shows his aloofness from the war and his difference from the other champions, by having no shield device. And equally important, he speaks in the tones of ordinary conversation (*badzō, legō, audaō* ['speak'] as compared with *bremō* (call out), *boaō* (roar), *autō* [shout], *epalaladzō* [battle cry]), and has no noise-making accoutrements.

The messenger who is the means by which the sights and sounds of the war outside the gates are transmitted is called a *katoptēs* (one who sees, lines 41, 369). His function – accurately to convey what comes to him through his eyes and ears – is several times referred to (lines 36-8, 40-1, 66-9, 375, 651-2). In this, as in every other story that has to do with the family of Oedipus, the eyes and ears as vehicles of knowledge have special prominence.

The problem of *knowing* where the danger really is – who is really the stranger, the enemy, the outsider, haunts the play in many forms. Ares, whose statue stands on the stage as one of the seven gods of the city, who is twice the ancestor of all the Thebans – both through his daughter Harmonia and through the Spartoi – is also the *xenos* . . . *Chalybos Skythōn apoikos* (the stranger, the Chalybian settler from Scythia, lines 727-8), the *pontios xeinos* (the stranger from beyond the sea, lines 941-2), a stranger from a distant land who, as an outsider, can make a just and equal division of the inheritance of the sons of Oedipus. Dike is one of blood (line 415) with the Thebans, but has nothing to do with the birth or nurture of Polyneices (lines 662-671). Although Aeschylus refers to the attackers collectively as Achaeans (lines 28 and 324) and Argives (line 120) his emphasis on the violence and strangeness of their speech and behavior has led some scholars to believe that he wished to present them as non-Greeks. They are *both* strangers and fellow Greeks.[5]

The images of a loud and overwhelming storm at sea, and of an uncontrolled beast, which are repeatedly used to describe the stranger army (lines 62-4, 84-5, 114-15, 213, 229, 362), are used by Eteocles of the Theban chorus's cries of fear (lines 192, 181, 186, 280). The chorus fears the noise of war *outside* the gates. Eteocles fears the noise of the chorus *inside* the city, as a kind of magic practiced by woman, which can unman the citizens (lines 191-2, 237, 254), and help those *outside* by causing the citizens 'to be sacked by themselves *from within*' (lines 192-4). The 'real' danger is inside the city. It has the overwhelming force and strangeness of a storm at sea or a savage beast. In this scene all Eteocles' strength is organized to keep this force locked up — to keep the women 'inside' where they belong, away from the statues of the gods and the affairs of men (which are 'outside'), and to substitute for their wild outpouring of feeling the impersonal formulae of a victory chant (lines 265-70). By reducing them to silence after repeated attempts (lines 232, 250, 252, 262) he does, perhaps, for the moment, succeed. But the harshness of his language and the intensity of his horror of women (lines 18, 187-90, 194-5, 256) leave one with the feeling that the success is somehow against nature, and therefore unstable.

The attackers themselves, as almost all critics recognize, are destroyed more by the violence within them, which provokes the wrath of the gods, than by the action of the Thebans (lines 444-6 and 508-20).

There is a danger 'outside' which must not be let in, and a danger 'inside' which must not be let out. The same images of an alien and overwhelming force and noise are used of both. The problem is to know who really *is* the stranger, the outsider, the enemy.

This ambiguity about who is really an enemy and an outsider, and about where he is, is the ambiguity of the house of Laius itself. The homeless stranger who slew Laius, solved the riddle of the sphinx, and so won the kingdom of Thebes with the hand of the queen, was in reality the son of the king he slew and the queen he married, and the legitimate heir to the throne, *philos* — a blood relative, and an insider in every sense. At some point in the trilogy, *Laius, Oedipus, Seven Against Thebes*, his sons, who were also his brothers, became his rivals over the land and the city which was the mother of all three. 'They are all too close in blood' (line 940). But they are also, for three generations, enemies and strangers to each other.

The engulfing force which destroys Eteocles and Polyneices is, like the attacking army and the terror-stricken chorus, described in images of storm (lines 689-91, 707-8, 758-61, 769-71, 848-60) and of violent animality. The words with which Eteocles rejects the chorus's entreaty that he propitiate the fury echo those of Tydeus rejecting the advice of Amphiaraus. Both refuse to 'fawn on fate' (lines 383 and 704). Eteocles' echoing of Tydeus at this crisis of the play indicates that his defiance, like that of Tydeus, is insane and self-destructive. The defiance of Eteocles

and Polyneices is also compared by verbal echoes to the defiance of
Laius, whose 'defiant, disobedient counsels' (line 842) led him, against
the command of the Delphic oracle, to beget a child. Over the bodies of
the two brothers the chorus sing 'you did this defiant, disobedient [also
incredible?] thing' (line 846), and (lines 876–8) 'Not listening to those
who are near to you [*apistoi philōn*], not worn out by misfortune
[evil?], having taken by force the house of your father.'

Apistoi philōn can imply defying the ties of blood as well as disregarding the advice of friends. In taking by force the house of their
father, they put themselves in the same relation to Oedipus that Oedipus
was in to Laius. When the sons are laid beside their father-brother in
Theban earth they share their mother with him, as he shared her with
his father, Laius. *pēma patri pareunon* (line 1004), disastrous sharing of
a father's bed, are the last words of the *kommos*.

The strangers outside the gates of Thebes do not *break in*. But the
passion and fury of those who are *philoi* (the word is particularly important in the *kommos*, line 971:

Ant.: You perished at the hands of a *philos*.

Ismene: And you slew a *philos*. (cf. line 940 *homaimoi*, and lines
932-3)) *break out* and sweep the whole race of Laius to destruction
(lines 689-92). The Ares inside the house of Laius is more terrible,
more insatiable, and more sterile than the Ares that storms outside the
gates. Eteocles and Polyneices learn its full power and meaning only at
the moment of their mutually inflicted deaths.

The engulfing passion, the danger which breaks out from inside, is
incestuous rivalry – of Oedipus with Laius, of Eteocles and Polyneices
with Oedipus and with each other – over the city, the land, the woman
who is the source of their life ('the mother spring' as Amphiaraus calls
Thebes, line 584). For the house of Laius the female is destruction. It
was where three ways meet, in the sphere of Hecate, the goddess of the
moon, of magic, and of all dark incomprehensible female functions,
that Oedipus committed the act of violence against his father that led
to his incestuous marriage. The only sizable fragment from the earlier
part of the tetralogy *Laius, Oedipus, Seven Against Thebes, Sphinx*, is a
description of the place where the three ways meet (Mette, frag. 172 =
Nauck, frag. 173). The sphinx also is a female and a destroyer of men,
as is the fury, who appears in this play only in her destructive aspect.

Let us now return to the crucial scene, the scene in which Eteocles
makes his decision to face his brother in single combat, and consider
how this central theme – coming to know what is the real danger for
the house of Laius – figures there.

Tydeus sets the tone of violence, defiance, and animality, which threatens the city. This is elaborated in the next five attackers and negated in the defenders, and above all in Amphiaraus. In Capaneus, Eteoclus, Hippomedon, Parthenopaeus, these qualities are conveyed not only by words, appearance, behavior, but by the shield devices which grow progressively more threatening — a naked man carrying a torch and shouting 'I shall burn the city,' a hoplite carrying a ladder with which to scale the walls, Typhon wreathed in snakes and breathing smoke, the man-eating sphinx with a dead Theban in her claws. The shield of Tydeus, which leads the list, bears a starry night with a full moon. Should not it too threaten the city?

To all the shield devices, including that of Tydeus, and to all the ill-omened words of the attackers, Eteocles responds with the traditional defense against magic. He turns both the words and the visible symbols back on their originators so that they work to the destruction of the bearer.[6] Against the shield of Hippomedon, and perhaps, as Verrall in his edition of the play suggested, against the shields of the others too, he produces an actual shield device, Zeus to overcome Typhon.[7] There is plenty of evidence that shield devices like the ones in this passage were actually used to cause fear in the enemy.[8] I have found no explanation of the nature of the threat on the shield of Tydeus, although the fact that it is the first in a list of threatening shield devices, and the fact that Eteocles takes measures to turn its menace back onto Tydeus, make it clear that Aeschylus meant it to seem threatening.

If I have rightly interpreted the play the tranquil starry night with its effulgent full moon is the most comprehensive threat of all for the house of Laius. Night and the moon, as well as magic and all things female, are the sphere of Hecate, who presides over the place where three ways meet, who shares with the fury, the daughter of the night, the attributes of torches, dogs, snakes, and whips. The moon on the shield is *nyktos ophthalmos*, eye of night, and it is as an eye that can cast a spell on whatever it falls on that it sheds its radiant but baneful light over the scene.[9]

The eye is the instrument of knowledge, and the fury knows all. Her unsleeping eye will find the violator of Dike at last, and when he is found he will not escape knowledge of the nature of her power. Tydeus, with the eye of night on his shield, is literally what Amphiaraus calls him, 'summoner of the fury' (line 574).

The shield of Tydeus with its brazen bells which 'shriek fear' (line 386) and its terrible eye which glares fear (cf. lines 53 and 498) sums up the sight and sound imagery of the play. The four shields that follow cannot but be seen as a continuation of this imagery, shouting and glaring the inescapable knowledge which the sons of Oedipus will achieve by mutual slaughter.

The shields, like the shield of Tydeus, all have voices. The slogan on Capaneus' shield *phonei* (shouts) (line 434), the slogan on Eteoclus' shield *boa* (roars) (line 468), and the many references to the metal of which they are made, particularly in this context of metallic noises, accentuate their noisiness. They are also, all of them, like the shield of Tydeus, eyes.

The very large number of references to the circularity of the shields (lines 489, 496, 540, 590, 591, 643) should be understood as indications of their affinity with eyes. The tendency among editors from the earliest times to reduce this number by emendation (lines 590 and 642) overlooks this function.

The roundness of the shields is emphasized in two other ways. The Argive shield, whose distinctive character was that it was round and white, is mentioned in the first choral song (line 89), and suggested again in the double reference to the gate of Proetus (lines 377 and 395) at which Tydeus is stationed. The Argive Proetus with his brother Acrisius, was known to tradition as the 'discoverer' of the Argive shield (Apollodorus, *Bibl.* 2.2). The Argive inventor of the shield is stressed just at the moment when the Argive shield becomes the focus of the action.

The Argive shield appears in *Aeneid* 3 (lines 635-7) in the description of the blinding of the Cyclops:

> et telo lumen terebramus acuto
> ingens quod torva solum sub fronte latebat,
> Argolici clipei aut Phoebeae lampadis instar.

> and with a sharp weapon we bore his eye out,
> his lone huge eye lying deep in his savage forehead
> like an Argive shield or the lamp of Phoebus.

Here too the round white Argive shield is associated with a baleful single eye, and the shining disk in the sky — the sun apparently. I wish it were the moon.[10]

The barely human Tydeus has a shield device which, on the surface at least, is not horrible at all. As the champions grow more human and less terrifying the shield devices grow more monstrous. The maiden-faced Parthenopaeus, who ends the sequence, carries the sphinx with a dead Theban in her claws. But also, as we have discovered, the tranquil beauty of Tydeus' shield masks the deadliest threat to the house of Laius. Similarly out of the girlish face of Parthenopaeus stare the eyes of the gorgon (line 537). This is still another expression of the ambiguity about what is really terrible, the confusion between what seems and what is, that haunts the house of Laius in this play.

The descriptions of the warriors with their shields express not only the Ares outside the gates which fails to break in, but also the Ares inside the house of Laius which is about to break out, and make itself known to Eteocles and Polyneices.

Polyneices, appealing to Dike and the ancestral gods of Thebes, is as much a contrast to the other attackers in appearance and behavior as Eteocles himself. But he proclaims his willingness to kill his brother, and Amphiaraus makes it plain that his assault on the city is nothing less than an assault on the mother who gave him life (line 584). The gap between being and seeming is not hard to see in Polyneices.

The hatred and violence masked by Eteocles' reverent and controlled manner breaks out only at the end of his response to the messenger's description of Polyneices and his shield (lines 672-5).

> I shall go and face him in battle *myself*. Who has *more right*? ruler to
> ruler, brother to brother, *hater* to *hater* I shall stand.

He then immediately demands his greaves. Schadewaldt has suggested that this is the signal for bringing his battle equipment, which he then assumes in the traditional order — greaves, breastplate, sword, helmet, shield, and spear.[11] This arming on stage is a visual enactment of the hardening of Eteocles' deadly purpose. With the assumption of each item in the traditional list his opposition to the chorus grows more frenzied, until at last he stands before them fully armed and ready to kill. As Schadewaldt points out, there are numerous precedents in other plays of Aeschylus for such concretizations and externalizations of inner experience. To Schadewaldt's already compelling list of arguments for this proposal I would like to add the following, which help to round out the interpretation of the play which I have been presenting here.

When Eteocles proclaims his hatred and calls for his greaves the chorus beg him not to become 'like in passion (*orgē*) to him who is most evilly spoken of (or evilly named?, lines 677-8),' that is, Polyneices. In the exchange with the chorus which follows he reveals for the first time the animal passions which make him in fact *orgēn homoios*, equal in passion, to his brother who is preparing to assault the mother city. I share Lesky's belief that this is the only way to understand Eteocles' assent to the chorus's description of him as mad (line 686), carried away by *atē* (line 687), full of *kakos erōs* evil love (line 688) and 'fierce biting desire' (line 692).[12]

If, as this indicates, Eteocles becomes in this scene Polyneices' equal in passion, is it not appropriate, almost necessary, that he should at the same time assume arms which will be the counterpart of the arms of Polyneices? At the end of the scene the contrast of the first part of the play should be eliminated. He should be the mirror image of his brother — transformed from what he *seems* to what he *is*, from a man in control of himself and his people to a man possessed by the fury. If he is not, the absolute equality of rights and wrongs so often proclaimed in the last two songs of the chorus has little real connection with the action.

As Schadewaldt points out, the six well defined sections of the exchange between Eteocles and the chorus correspond in number to the six items of equipment that are called for in a traditional arming scene. I believe that the moments when Eteocles receives the two last, and most significant, items are also indicated verbally in the text.

The chorus urge Eteocles not to provoke the fury while she still seethes (*eti zei* line 708). It is the metaphor of the storm. Eteocles replies (lines 709-11), 'The curses of Oedipus have boiled up' (*exezesen*. I cannot find one English root to cover the implications of *zeō* and *ekzeō*). 'All too true were the visions of appearances in sleep, which apportioned the wealth of my father.' He sees this as the moment when the fury fulfills the curse. At this point the traditional order of arming demands that he be handed his shield. And if he is handed a shield, can the shield device be hidden or absent? I think not. So what will it be? What, if not the fury whom he is saluting as he takes the shield in hand? It is under her sign that he launches the war when he hears the first report of the oath taking and lot drawing in the prologue (lines 69-72). To the defense of Thebes he summons not only Zeus, Earth, and the gods of the city, but also (line 70) 'the *overwhelming* Curse and Fury of my father.'

The fury is properly invoked here. As the enforcer of the Dike of kindred she should protect the city against the assault of the impious son, Polyneices. But in calling her up to defend the city Eteocles calls her up to destroy himself. It is equally her obligation to punish Eteocles' crime against the source of life (whatever it was that makes him, equally with Polyneices, one who 'has taken by force his father's house,' lines 877-8, must have been presented in the preceding play). It is as *megasthenēs*, overwhelming, that Eteocles and Polyneices come to know her in the *kommos* (line 988). Eteocles, who summons her as protector, must also come to know her as destroyer. She has here the same terrible duality which characterizes everything female throughout the play.

The fury is certainly the proper counterpart to Dike on the shield of Polyneices. To appeal to Dike is to appeal to the fury that will enforce Dike — his own Dike, but also his brother's Dike, for they are equal in this as in everything else. Each brother is subject to the law he invokes against the other. This is the inescapable knowledge which the shields express.

It is with the receiving of the spear that the transformation of Eteocles from seeming to being is complete. I would put this action not where Schadewaldt puts it at the last line of the scene, but five lines earlier when Eteocles, rejecting the chorus's plea that he not go to the seventh gate says (line 715), 'Now that I am *whetted* you will not blunt me with speech'. The moment in which he imagines himself as a spear is the right moment for him to take the spear in hand. In the *kommos* 'god's sayings (the Delphic prophecy to Laius) are not blunted' (line 844) and Ares, 'the equal apportioner of wealth, the fulfiller of the father's curse' (lines 944–6), 'the stranger from over the sea' (lines 941–2) is called 'whetted steel' (line 944). With the assuming of the spear Eteocles too becomes 'whetted steel,' in fact the *xenos Chalybos Skythōn apoikos*, Ares, the bitter but just resolver of strife, the visible expression of the sharp point of Apollo's word to Laius. There is one more step in his transformation. Rejecting the last appeal of the chorus he says (line 717), 'A man in *full armor* must not assent to this word'. He is now the exact counterpart of the *anēr teuchēstēs* on the shield of Polyneices (line 644), no longer a man, but from head to foot the noisy, glaring, rending metal that will make the absolutely just division of the wealth of Oedipus.

4

SALAMIS SYMPHONY:
THE *PERSAE* OF AESCHYLUS

S. M. ADAMS

This drama has received much less than justice. Fine qualities within it have been recognized and fully, sometimes brilliantly, appreciated: it is distinguished by splendid descriptions of battle; it offers opportunities for effective pageantry; it is notable for some interesting moves in the direction of what the word drama afterwards came to mean. But there has been, I think, no recognition and appreciation of its real structure. Yet it is a highly finished example of the art that Aeschylus knew and practised. It is a composition in three movements marked off from each other by concluding choral lyrics and followed by a kind of scherzo, the whole being knit together by recurrent themes and by a simple governing design. This design has not been recognized, and the work has therefore not been seen for what it is. That is because it has been interpreted on the basis of a wrong assumption.

Critics have assumed that the dramatist's purpose was to show his audience that the Persian defeat at Salamis was the punishment of Xerxes' *hybris*. But it is surely most unlikely that an Athenian audience needed to be shown the application to Xerxes of a doctrine with which the city had been more than familiar since the time of Solon. The case of Xerxes was a most obvious and striking instance of the operation of the law. Master of all the wealth and power of Asia, he had *koros* on a breath-taking scale. His attempt to add free Hellas to the Persian Empire was clearly *hybris*, on a scale hardly less enormous. His defeat at the hands of a force numerically so inferior could be explained only on the assumption of punitive intervention by some god or gods; and the point at which he incurred divine wrath was quite manifest in his most striking act, the bridging of the Hellespont.[1] Even if this explanation of Salamis was not universally seen in 480, it must by 472 have become public

From *Studies in Honour of Gilbert Norwood*, edited by Mary White, pp. 46–54. Copyright, Canada, 1952 by University of Toronto Press. Reprinted by permission of University of Toronto Press.

property. Assuredly it did not take Aeschylus eight years to see it. Nor was he the craftsman to be content with teaching in slow evolvement a lesson everyone in Athens had long since learned — however many *parerga* he might be able to produce along the way. This cannot have been the dramatist's purpose.

It is a very different matter if he is exhibiting to his audience the way in which a truth already known to them was made known to the persons in the drama. That is the form Greek tragedy normally takes. It is the form in which Aeschylus has cast his *Persae*. He is delighting his audience with an imaginative conception of how the lesson of Salamis came home to the Persians, represented here by the Chorus who, incidentally, represent not only the surviving manhood of Persia but also the Persian women, for whom they are at pains to speak. The central figure is thus the Chorus. The drama is appropriately named for them. It is with them the dramatist is primarily concerned. The individual *dramatis personae* are introduced for their effect upon the Chorus and for their function in the simple mechanism of the piece;[2] such effects as they otherwise produce, however dramatic in the later sense of the word or magnificent in themselves, are incidental. All these incidental effects must have been received with lively satisfaction; but unquestionably interest was centred on what we must see as the action of the drama: the process in which the Chorus's first vague misgivings are developed into final comprehension. The audience know in advance the truth that is to come out; they see it stirring in the minds of the Chorus; it draws nearer; it arrives — and then Aeschylus, artist that he is, gives more than was expected.

I have called the *Persae* a symphony. For that neither explanation nor apology seems necessary; since Walter Headlam first drew attention to the similarity between that musical technique and the technique of Aeschylus the point has been well pressed with regard both to whole trilogies and to individual dramas. Certainly, if ever the three-movement form — the trilogy form — is to be found reproduced within a single drama, we should find it here; for the *Persae* belonged to a trilogy of unconnected pieces and we might therefore expect it to prove a kind of trilogy in miniature. That is what I think it is, the fourth movement representing to some extent the satyr-play while forming part of an artistic whole.

The following analysis is offered in support of this view. It contains a good deal that has been said before but must be repeated here for the argument's sake; on the other hand, the use of recurrent themes to link the movements can be little more than hinted at.

The first movement (1–289) might be called Realization of Foreboding. Its technique is that which Aeschylus brought to perfection in the *Agamemnon*: foreboding, vague at first, gathers intensity despite attempts to down it and is at last shown justified in the event.

Against a background theme of Persia's wealth the Chorus sound the note at once (8-15). They are disturbed by the fact that Asia's might has 'gone,' by the army's growling at a young man's rashness, and by the absence of news; the striking brevity, vagueness and harshness of the words in vs. 13 suggest that it is Xerxes' 'youthful rashness' that disturbs them most. They seek to suppress the foreboding, turning to the theme of Persian power in a sweeping survey, resonant with barbaric names, of the army's far-flung sources. But something brings foreboding back; they are chanting again (59-64) of the might that has 'gone,' of Asia sighing for her sons, of parents and wives fearful as they count the days.

In vs. 50 they have defined the army's purpose as 'to cast upon Greece their enslaving yoke [*zugon*].' Perhaps it was these words that brought foreboding back. If so, Aeschylus has traced for us the source of the old men's foreboding from Xerxes' rashness to the project of enslaving Greece. In any case, the expression has another function. A metaphor so trite to us as hardly to be noticed has to the Athenian audience its full value. It establishes for the rest of the drama the equation *zugon* = slavery. The first effect of this is soon apparent. In the opening strophe of the following stasimon the old men sing that the army has 'cast a yoke upon the neck of the Sea.' In the light of the equation that means 'enslaved the Sea.' They do not see in this 'yoking,' as the audience does, a damning act of supreme *hybris*, but it is plain enough that it is preying on their minds: there is something very wrong about it. Aeschylus has brought forward the third and most vital source of their misgivings.

The first strophe thus contains two themes that fight for mastery in the ode: the King's 'city-sacking' army, inspiring confidence; and the yoking of the Sea, occasioning foreboding. The old men turn for confidence to the thought of the army's power; this time it is that power as wielded by the King. It is a majestic statement, but it fails; the other theme breaks through. 'Of no man is it told that he stands against a mighty flood of men and though his barriers are strong holds back the irresistible wave of the Sea' (87-90). The suppressed foreboding has dictated the metaphor and so forced itself into consciousness and speech. That is why they swerve to the thought of vss. 93-100;[3] what they are saying here is, in effect, 'But suppose Xerxes is the victim of *apatē* (deception)? What if this whole expedition, and this yoking of the Sea, are the product of divinely-sent Illusion?' 'With seeming kindliness she lures a man into the snares of Ate; and thence he cannot escape.'

What follows may be a mere extension of these thoughts or it may be (as I prefer to believe) an attempt to fight down the renewed foreboding by justifying Xerxes' actions as consistent with Persia's divinely-ordered destiny. It is a short-lived effort. In pursuance of that destiny, they sing, the Persians 'learned to look upon the sacred province of the waters.' They meant merely to describe ships 'that with slender rigging give passage to men'; but the insuppressible thought of the yoked Sea so affects their language that the words mean also the bridge of boats, 'a device giving passage to the army by means of slender cables' (112–114). Foreboding triumphs completely; the rest of the ode is given over to it.[4]

In this state of mind the old men propose to contemplate the possibilities; but Atossa appears. She too has forebodings, which she makes no attempt to hide, and her greater frankness increases the emotional tension. When the Chorus have assured her of their loyal support she describes a dream and an omen that have caused her fears: the dream was of a disastrous attempt by her son to *yoke* two maidens of the same race; the omen, an eagle fleeing from and ravaged by a hawk. That both of these portend evil is only too clear, and we have an appropriate return to trochaic rhythm. But the old men play their part: after they have urged the Queen to make to the gods and to Darius such prayers as the circumstances plainly demand, they firmly assert that the outcome will be good in every way: with due observance of the right course of action they seek to make dream and omen better by calling them good.

Again an attempt to build confidence fails. Whatever virtue the Chorus's pronouncement may contain is counteracted by Atossa's curiosity concerning Athens. The old men are compelled to tell her facts as alarming to themselves in the telling as they are to her, and culminating in a mention of Marathon not less shattering because veiled. Foreboding has reached its peak, and at this moment a Messenger is seen approaching in haste. In one short speech that gathers up the themes of wealth and power, completes the growing implication of the verb *oixomai* (to be ruined), and returns to us the very words of the Chorus,[5] he announces disaster:

O cities of the whole extent of Asia's land,
O Persian land and harbor that enfolds great wealth,
A single stroke has brought about the ruin of great
Prosperity, the flower of Persia fallen and gone (*oixetai*).   (249–252)

Foreboding has been brought to realization in fact; and the movement ends with the music of a *kommos*.

Compared with the first movement, the second (290–597) is very simple in design. In it we have Realization of Divine Visitation. The Chorus, who now know that they were right in feeling that there was something very wrong in Xerxes' actions, are made to feel that his defeat was brought about by some *daimon* or spirit of vengeance.

The movement opens with Atossa's anxiety concerning her son's own fate — a little passage handled with exquisite restraint and showing the shape of things to come in the dramatic art — and is linked to the first movement by the Messenger's recital of Persian names: a return in different key of the names-theme in the parodos. But in her first words Atossa forecasts the dominant thought: 'Necessity dictates that men should bear / The ills the gods bestow' (293-294). The thought itself soon comes. Telling of the overwhelming numerical superiority of Xerxes' ships, the Messenger says (345-346):

> No, not by numbers, but some Spirit crushed the host,
> Threw in an evil fate against us on the scales.

His narratives follow, introduced (353-354) by:

> The one that started the whole disaster, lady, was
> Some Curse or Evil Spirit that appeared from somewhere.

There are three narratives; the trilogy-form holds in this still smaller compass. First is the magnificent account of Salamis. To this Atossa responds (433-434) with a 'reminiscence' of the Chorus's unfortunate metaphor (87-90), forecast by the Messenger's 'the streaming Persian force withstood the shocks' (412-413):

> Aee! A huge sea of ills has broken out
> And overwhelmed the Persians and all the barbarian race.
>
> (433-34)

This is another link with the preceding movement. But the dominant theme returns when the story of the slaughter on Psyttalea has been told: Atossa exclaims (472-473):

> O hateful Spirit, Deceitfully it seems you've worked
> upon the Persians' minds.

And when the Messenger has recounted the disasters on the overland retreat, the Coryphaeus says (515-516):

> O Spirit of Suffering, with what a heavy leap —
> Too heavy! you jumped upon the entire Persian race.

The thought is thus voiced by Messenger, Atossa, and Coryphaeus in turn. This order is significant; certainty of divine causation comes last, and therefore with most telling force, to the Chorus, the object of chief concern.

The explanation of Salamis has thus advanced from vague misgivings to consciousness of intervention by some avenging power. Atossa, fulfilling her function as part of the dramatic machinery to bring on the Ghost of Darius, departs to arrange for the prayers and offerings recommended in the first movement by the Coryphaeus, the dramatist allowing her a further display of maternal anxiety; and the movement ends with an ode which brings the women of Persia once more into the picture, states the personal responsibility of Xerxes, stresses the part played by the ships and the Sea,[6] laments the breakdown of Persian overlordship and the consequent recrudescence of freedom, and brings in again (594) the theme of the yoke.

The third movement (598-908) sets forth Realization of *Hybris*. Atossa enters with offerings.[7] To our surprise the Ghost of Darius is to be conjured up. Unless the changed situation is enough to account for it, this seems to lack motivation; but it may be argued that every play is entitled to one unmotivated turn; even that masterpiece of construction, the *Oedipus Tyrannus*, has its Corinthian Messenger. An incantation to raise the dead, dramatized, is performed; the Ghost rises, and the long-awaited explanation is at hand.

With his unfailing dramatic skill Aeschylus postpones the great moment and doubles the interest by showing the truth dawning first upon Darius himself. In conversation with the Coryphaeus the Ghost learns what has happened, and it is all brought back to us, thus linking this movement to the first and second: the attempt to conquer Athens, the bridging of the Hellespont, the *daimon*. He understands; and the validity of the explanation he is about to give is attested by oracles once given to him, oracles which he was sure had reference to a much more remote future.

His explanation (744-751) is explicit save in one respect: Xerxes brought about this disaster through youthful rashness; he hoped to hold the sacred Hellespont in bonds, like a slave; he sought to change the natural order of the strait; he thought to master all the gods, Poseidon in particular – and was not this infatuation on his part? Here are *Thrasos* [Rashness], *Apatē* [Deceit], *Elpis* [Hope]; and Atossa immediately supplies the note of *Peitho*, telling of the evil counsellors who won Xerxes to the attempt on Greece. But though the idea of *Hybris* underlies it all the word itself has yet to be spoken.

The big moment, then, has arrived, but there is more to come. After a solemn passage in which the contrast between Xerxes and his godly predecessors is set forth and a stern warning issued against any further attack on the Greeks, the dramatist by a skilful transition passes to the subject of the forthcoming Persian defeat at Plataea; and now at last (808) the missing word comes out in fitting context and with fitting emphasis:

> The crown of wretched suffering awaits them there,
> Requital for their *hybris* and their godless thoughts.

There is no anticlimax here. On Salamis is piled Plataea. On the *hybris* of Xerxes is piled the *hybris* shown by the Persians in plundering the images of the gods of Greece and utterly destroying their temples. The treatment rises to the measure of the theme. Few passages in Aeschylus match 800–828 in straightforward poetic power;[8] never, in iambics at any rate, has the doctrine of *hybris* received more effective exposition.

The truth is home. The yoking of the Sea has been shown to the Chorus as the damning act of *hybris*; the *daimon* has been identified for them as Poseidon. They understand now that the Sea rejected the yoke and has taken vengeance through Ionian ships and hands on the man who tried to enslave it — and on all the Persian race as well; that was inevitable.[9]

The rest of the episode is concerned with the thought of Xerxes' torn robes; this theme, a variant, so to speak, of the theme of wealth, has been recurrent throughout the drama and has yet to reach its culmination.[10] The movement concludes with an ode which surveys the Empire that has been, and on reaching the name of the Cyprian Salamis brings the thought full circle; it ends with the perfect touch: 'The Sea struck its blows.' (908).

The trilogy is complete. What, then, of the rest of the drama?

In the first place, it is a scene significant in the history of drama. In the *Supplices* the story told is the story of the Chorus themselves. Of what lies between nothing can be said with any certainty. Here, for the first time in extant drama, we have a work built on the story of an individual. But the Chorus remain the central figure in the presentation of his story; the action of the piece concludes without the audience so much as seeing him. Sound instinct prompts this final spectacle of the man himself in the full realization of his offence and its punishment. The audience have heard his story; it will give them satisfaction to see him and hear what he has to say and what the Chorus have to say to him. Dramatic genius has taken a forward step; here is the suggestion of a new technique: the telling of one man's story for the dramatic values to be derived from the man himself, as well as those arising from the story and from the reactions of the Chorus. Aeschylus may have been quite aware of what he was doing, or it may have been a matter in which, as Sophocles is reputed to have said of him, he did the right thing without knowing it. At all events, he did it. It may be thought tentative, or crude; but the way lay open to the *Seven*.

The manner in which the scene could be added would suggest itself: the miniature trilogy could be rounded off with a miniature satyr-play. It could not be other than an appendage, and that was what the satyr-play was. Yet in so small a compass as a single drama it could hardly be entirely detached from what preceded. It must form part of an artistic whole, yet differ from the trilogy movements sufficiently to leave them artistically intact, their action being finished.

No one can fail to notice a difference. The scene is certainly not 'funny,'[11] as some editors appear to have thought it, at least in parts. But even after allowance is made for the fact that it is cast in a barbaric mould to portray Oriental abandonment to grief, it seems definitely lighter in mood and thinner in content; and the cries, lamentations, and gesticulations of King and Chorus surely pertain rather to the satyr-play than to serious drama.

Yet it hovers between these two types, for it is bound to the trilogy in what is clearly conceived as an artistic whole. Old themes recur. We have, for instance, in the opening anapaests the *daimon* and the verb *oixomai*; and when Xerxes displays his tattered robes and empty quiver the themes of wealth and power end in excellent symbolism. More effective perhaps than anything else is the recital of Persian names. We heard this theme in the first movement when the great army was described as rushing forth to conquest; we heard it in the second movement, creating dismay; we hear it again now, sung in abandonment to woe. It is no doubt a mechanical device, but it certifies the unity of the work.

Such is the structure of the *Persae* as I see it. Those with whom the interpretation finds favour will at least be freed from any feeling of surprise that not a single Greek is mentioned in the drama; Aeschylus was too good an artist for that.

5

THE *SUPPLIANTS* OF AESCHYLUS

HUGH LLOYD-JONES

No papyrus discovery of modern times has given a ruder shock to ortho-doxy than the fragment of a didascalic notice published in 1952 in Part XX of the Oxyrhynchus series.[1] Most living scholars had been brought up to take it for granted that the *Suppliant Women* was the earliest play of Aeschylus, produced perhaps as early as the beginning of the fifth century. This fragment indicates that the Danaid trilogy, of which the *Suppliant Women* is the first play, won first prize in a year in which the runner-up was Sophocles; and Sophocles competed first in 470, 469 or 468. The indication of date in the notice is mutilated; we read only the letters EPIAR[. AR might possibly be the beginning of the word *archontos*, but it was more probably the beginning of the name of Archedemides, archon in 464/3; in either case, the name of Sophocles supplies a *terminus post quem*. Desperate attempts were made to save the orthodox belief. The production of the late sixties might, it was argued, have been a revival; or the play might have been written forty years earlier and produced only in the sixties; the three leading advocates of these suggestions averaged about eighty years of age. But Albin Lesky (*Hermes* 82, 1954, 1 f.) pointed out that in the present state of the evidence it would be perverse to deny that a first production in the sixties is virtually certain, and this view is now gener-ally accepted. Without wishing to abuse the advantage given us by the new evidence in order to patronise our predecessors, we may find it useful to investigate the causes of such a persistent and such an important error. Such an inquiry may help us to avoid similar mistakes in future; it may also throw light upon the *Suppliant Women* in particular and upon the art of Aeschylus in general.

Most of the scholars who had assigned the Danaid trilogy to a late date had argued from supposed allusions to contemporary political events; most of those who put it early had argued from an analysis of its style,

From *Antiquité Classique* 33 (1964), 355–74. Reprinted with minor revisions by permission of the author and *Antiquité Classique*.

diction, metre and dramatic technique. The former method was employed first at the beginning of the nineteenth century, when the school of Boeckh, Otfried Mueller and Welcker began to apply the data of history and archaeology to the interpretation of Greek literature. Otfried Mueller,[2] following Boeckh, felt little doubt that the trilogy must have been produced while the Athenian alliance with Argos made in 461 was in effect. In the Oresteia, produced in 458, Agamemnon rules not in Mycenae, as in Homer, nor in Sparta or Amyclae, as in the lyric poets, but in Argos; and Orestes promises that Argos will requite his acquittal by an Athenian court by helping Athens in time of war. That is generally held to allude to the alliance. Now in the *Suppliant Women*, after Danaus has announced the ratification by the Argive demos of the king's decision to protect his daughters against their pursuing cousins, the Aegyptiads, the Chorus expresses its gratitude by a solemn prayer to all the gods that Argos may enjoy prosperity and be free from war and pestilence (625 f.). This ode conforms to a standard pattern for invoking blessings on a city that has its origins in early epic:[3] in this it resembles the ode of benediction upon Athens sung by the chorus of the *Eumenides* (916 f.). Mueller connected this ode with the friendship between Athens and Argos. He believed that at this time Argos must have had a democratic constitution; and he saw allusions to this fact in several passages in the play which insist upon the Argive king's incompetence to make a decision that may involve war without the consent of the popular assembly.

Other scholars protested that the alleged political allusions gave no clear evidence for the play's date.[4] The ode of blessing upon Argos, they objected, is wholly suited to its context in the play; it is natural for the Danaids to return thanks, and to do so in terms of a known pattern of benediction. The force of this objection must be acknowledged; without denying that the ode may be intended to allude to the alliance, we can hardly accept it as a certain indication of the play's date. But what if it is taken together with the alleged allusion to democracy at Argos? During the great scene in which the Danaids supplicate the Argive king Pelasgus, the king warns them that he cannot promise them support without the consent of the whole citizen body (368-9). The Danaids insist that he, the king, is the sole ruler, dwelling on the notion of monarchical supremacy with an intensity characteristic of their oriental origin (370 f.). Later in that scene the king fears that if he acts without the consent of the demos the people may say of him, in case of a disaster, 'In doing honour to strangers you have ruined the city' (397 f.). Finally he summons Danaus before the assembly, complaining as he does so of the people's readiness to make complaint against their

ruler (480-8). After the king has persuaded the multitude Danaus returns,
and vividly describes how the sky was thick with right hands raised in
favour of the decision (607-8). Later, in the hymn of blessing, there is
mention of 'the people, that rules the city' (699).

'The praise of democratic Argos in these lines', it was claimed as
recently as 1960,[5] 'is totally irrelevant in any mythological situation'.
That statement is a little sweeping. Even an epic kingdom had its popular assembly, as we know from several places in the Iliad. 'The Greeks at
Troy', writes Andrewes,[6] 'will feel and will be safer if they have a king
to tell them what to do, but — and that is the point of the meetings and
the speeches — they must also feel sure about their king, confident that
he can cope with their situation and with them, and that he will continue
to fulfil their own obscurely felt purposes.' Aeschylus' allusions to the
powers of the assembly are perfectly consonant with this state of affairs.
Even the king's fear of being found fault with by his subjects could well
be found in Homer; at the crisis of his fate Hector is prevented from
taking refuge in Troy by the thought that people will reproach him for
not having taken the advice of Polydamas to order a retreat earlier.[7] It
may well be that the poet has been led by the added importance of
assemblies in his own times to lay special emphasis on the powers of the
epic demos, as Euripides does in his *Orestes*; but in doing this he is not
guilty of an anachronism. The possibility that he had a contemporary
Argive democracy in mind must certainly be reckoned with; but we
cannot feel certain that it was not the importance of the assembly in his
own city that was in his mind.

The need for caution at this point becomes even greater when we
consider how little we know about the Argive constitution during the
fifth century. Herodotus[8] says that after the disastrous defeat by Sparta
in 494 Argos was ruled for a time by slaves. This statement is usually
interpreted in the light of the testimony of Aristotle and Plutarch that
after this event certain of the perioikoi — 'the best' of them, in Plutarch's
words — were admitted to the citizenship.[9] Did their admission make
the constitution more democratic? And if so, how much more? We can
hardly hope to know. The slaves, according to Herodotus, were eventually expelled from Argos and seized Tiryns, from which they were ejected
about the middle of the sixties. After that the Argolid was again controlled by the descendants of its former rulers. Did the constitution
become less democratic? Again, we do not really know. Themistocles,
who took refuge in Argos about 470-69, was eventually forced to leave
in obedience to Spartan pressure. Was that because an aristocratic, and
therefore pro-Spartan government was in power? or was it simply due
to Argive weakness? The fact that Argos made offerings at Delphi at

about this time has been thought to strengthen the former supposition; but Delphi was a panhellenic shrine, and the argument is not a safe one. Again, it has often been inferred that when Argos made the alliance with Athens in 461 a democratic government must have been in power. But this inference is not valid; the ancient rivalry of Argos and Sparta must have been strong before democracy was thought of in either place. To sum up, our evidence for the nature of the Argive constitution during this period is almost negligible, though such indications as there are make somewhat against the likelihood that it was democratic. After all, where in mainland Greece outside Athens was there a real democracy before the Athenian Empire had advertised this form of government?

We must conclude that it is possible, but far from certain, that the play contained 'praise of Argive democracy'. If it did, then it is likely that as Otfried Mueller supposed Argos was democratic at time of its production. That runs counter to the views of other historians,[10] who believed that a democratic Argos, containing enfranchised perioikoi, had taken in Themistocles about 470, but that an aristocratic Argos ruled by the descendants of those defeated at Sepeia in 494 had expelled him a few years later. They suppose that the supplication of the Danaids at Argos was meant to remind the Athenian audience of 463 of the supplication of Themistocles in about 470, and that the praise of Argive democracy was meant not for the present prospective allies of Athens but for an Argive democracy suppressed by them some years earlier. Both these suppositions are unlikely. If the play praises the Argive democracy, it probably praises a contemporary democracy, as Mueller thought. But we have seen that independent evidence for the existence of democracy at Argos in 463 is not strong. Its weakness does not favour the possibility — and it is no more — that the play does not praise Argive democracy at all. We must conclude that even if Boeckh and Mueller were right in thinking the play referred to the political situation of the late sixties, the grounds adduced by them for dating at that time were far from sufficient to prove their case.

Those who have argued from the play's style, diction, metre and technique have argued with few exceptions, for an early date. Let me first deal briefly with the linguistic and stylistic arguments. It has commonly been maintained that these strongly favour an early date; and yet the upholders of this view, like those who deny the authenticity of the end of the *Seven Against Thebes*[11] or the whole of the *Rhesus*, have not so far offered a close and detailed examination of the relevant material. That would need considerable space; at present it will be enough to point out that the assertions made by believers in an early date have not so far been adequately grounded. For the least incomplete statement that any of them has offered we must go to such a gravely inadequate production as the late F. R. Earp's study of the style of Aeschylus.[12] The *Suppliant Women* has not more compounds than other plays, nor more hapax legomena, nor more similes or metaphors; the number of epic words is higher, but not significantly higher, than in the other plays. There are thirty words which Earp considers to be rare, nine more than in the *Persae*, which comes next in this respect; but of these thirty ten occur in two brief passages, amounting together to less than sixty lines, in which the poet is clearly making a special effort to convey the effect of outlandish speech and which are, moreover, deeply corrupt.

So much for the evidence from diction. Earp finds the style markedly different from that of Aeschylus' other works. 'In parts of it', he writes, (p. 63) 'the various forms of ongkos (majestic style) are not laid with the brush but spread with a trowel, and very little of the surface escapes. We find here all the qualities parodied by Aristophanes . . . ' In fact we find these qualities everywhere in Aeschylus. Do we find in the *Suppliant Women* anything too extreme for the poet who called fishes 'children of the undefiled' (*Pers.* 578), or dust 'mud's thirsty sister' (*Agam.* 494 -5) or who wrote the first stasimon of the *Seven* (287. f.) with its astonishing description of the horrors that accompany the sack of cities?

Metrical arguments advanced in favour of the early date are not substantial. Advocates of the late dating were able to point to one archaic feature of the *Persae* which is wanting in the *Suppliant Women*. Aristotle says that in early times the regular dialogue metre of tragedy was the tetrameter, and in the *Persae* it is used for two whole scenes. The other party retorted that the *Agamemnon* also contains two tetrameter scenes. But there the scenes are shorter, and the tetrameters seem to be used just as they are in later tragedy, to convey the notion of speed and excitement. The use of tetrameters in the *Persae* is different, and the difference may well be significant.

The most noteworthy metrical argument deployed on either side of the controversy rests on the observation of E. C. Yorke in 1936[13] that the incidence of resolutions would indicate for the *Suppliants*, with one resolution in 11 trimeters, a date between the *Persae*, with one in nine, and the *Seven*, with one in 12; in all the other plays, resolution is considerably more frequent. As Yorke recognised, this test is not one that can be applied rigidly or by itself. But Zielinski[14] had shown that in the case of Euripides, where our material is ampler than it is for Aeschylus, the order indicated by the incidence of resolution closely corresponds with the order so far as it is known from external evidence. That warrants us in treating this indication with special respect, especially now that it is confirmed by the evidence of the papyrus.

We now come to arguments which have been far more influential in creating belief in an early date, those based on dramatic technique. Aristotle (*Poet.*, 1449 A 17) says that the choral element in early tragedy was very great, and that Aeschylus reduced it. The choral element in the *Suppliants* is greater in proportion to the whole than in any other surviving play of Aeschylus, and hence it is inferred that it must be earlier than the others.[15] This argument has had great influence, and yet its weaknesses are obvious. First, it is not safe to assume that the choral part was reduced at a uniform rate, so that each successive play had less chorus than the one before. Next, the subject-matter of the *Suppliants* clearly required that the choral element should be very great; can we be sure that a poet writing after the choral element in most plays had been considerably reduced would not have made an exception for a play dealing with this subject? In this play the chorus is protagonist, but that does not help to prove that the play is early. Even in the *Eumenides* it is at least deuteragonist, and that play was produced in 458; even as late as Euripides' *Bacchae*, we find a chorus deeply implicated in a play's action.

Closely connected with the argument from the large amount of choral utterance is the argument from the poet's restricted use of the second actor.[16] Like the *Persae* and the *Seven*, the *Suppliants* is a play for two actors, but there are only two passages, neither of them very long, where two actors take part in a dialogue together. Throughout the great supplication scene which is the kernel of the play, the chorus sings lyrics and the coryphaeus speaks iambics in the effort to persuade the king while Danaus stands silent on the stage. Only when the supplication is over and the king has consented does Danaus give tongue,[17] and then it is only to ask the king for an escort for himself and his daughters as they enter the city. Later in the play there is another dialogue between actors, between the king and the Egyptian herald (911 f.). Aeschylus, it is argued, was not used to the luxury of a second actor, and therefore failed to put it to the effective use he might have done.

It must be acknowledged that in one scene, at least, the scene between Pelasgus and the Egyptian herald, Aeschylus does put the second actor to an effective use. Compare the scene with other tragic episodes of the same nature — one thinks of the dialogues of Prometheus with Hermes (*P.V.* 944 f.) and of Demophon with the herald of Eurystheus in Euripides' *Heraclidae* (120 f.) — and the scene in the *Suppliants* emerges well from the comparison. Was the writer of that scene really incapable of using a second actor skilfully in other places? To answer the question we must ask in what other places he might have used one. We can only answer, in the supplication scene; the other scenes are only brief interludes that give little occasion for a dialogue. Would the supplication scene be more effective if Danaus shared with the chorus and the coryphaeus the task of supplication? From the standpoint of modern dramatic naturalism the scene would have greater verisimilitude; but whether the emotional effect at which the poet aims would have been more successfully conveyed is a different question. The assignation of the main part to the chorus is not inconsistent with the technique used by Aeschylus in his other works. When in the *Persae* the Messenger first announces the defeat at Salamis (249 f.) an epirrhematic scene of 35 lines between messenger and chorus takes place before the Queen of Persia says a word. When she does speak (290 f.), the Queen explains her silence as being due to the shock she has received; this is not the only case in which a silence imposed on Aeschylus by a technical reason is motivated by a dramatic one. After that epirrhematic scene comes a dialogue between Queen and Messenger in which both speak long rheseis; out of 242 lines (290–531), only two are spoken by the chorus. The next scene in this play to contain an epirrhematic element is that of the invocation of Darius' ghost. After the initial stasimon, Darius opens with a speech of thirteen trimeters (681 f.). The chorus in a brief stanza in ionics protest that they are too terrified to speak with him; the king in three tetrameters urges them to speak; and the chorus in an antistrophe at all points symmetrical to the strophe repeat their refusal. At this point the King instructs the Queen to replace the chorus as his interlocutor, which she continues to be throughout the tetrameter scene that follows; it contains a stichomythia, but also several long rheseis. In the *Seven* there are two epirrhematic scenes between Eteocles and the chorus; in the first (181 f.), the king pleads with the Theban women not to spread despondency by excessive prayer and lamentation, in the second (677 f.), the women plead with the king not to take the field against his brother. Both scenes are unlike that in the *Persae* and like that in the *Suppliants* in the sense that each comprises an agon, an attempt by one party to win over the other to his point of view. Each of these scenes consists of a succession of brief dochmiac stanzas by the chorus punctuated by trimeters, never more than three together, spoken by the actor; each continues with a one-one stichomythia; after the first comes a long rhesis by the actor; after the second, a stasimon. Had he wished the poet could have introduced an actor, Antigone, perhaps, or Iocaste, to plead with Eteocles; yet all trimeters are spoken by the coryphaeus.

Aeschylus' practice seems to be that when an epirrhematic episode verges into one containing long speeches, an actor takes over from the chorus; but so long as not more than three trimeters at a time are being spoken on the side the chorus represents, these are given to the coryphaeus. The reason for this arrangement seems clear enough; in a scene of this kind the trimeter utterances on the side of the chorus are so closely bound up with the lyrics that they cannot be given to an actor. If the chorus takes the main part throughout the supplication scene, that does not mean that they and not Danaus take the lead in the family's counsels; we are explicitly told more than once that this is not so. The predominance of the chorus in this scene is due to a technical reason, inconsistent with the principles of modern naturalism but fully comprehensible in the context of an Aeschylean tragedy.

The belief that in the *Suppliants* the chorus numbered not twelve, as in the rest of Aeschylus, but fifty originated in consequence of the belief that the *Suppliants* was a very early play. But once in being it helped to maintain the belief in an early date, and its credentials must certainly be re-examined now. Otfried Mueller in 1833 first combined the statement of Pollux that the tragic chorus originally numbered fifty with the assumption that the fifty Danaids must be represented by fifty choreutae; despite the sound sense of Pickard-Cambridge,[18] the belief still flourishes. The number of the Danaids is never actually mentioned in the text; but the Danaids say that Aegyptus has fifty sons, and the number appears in most known versions of the story. Wilamowitz was a strong believer in the theory,[19] and indeed enlarged on it with a remarkable extension. He suggested (first in 1923)[20] that in the scene in which the Danaids are threatened by the Egyptian herald, the lyrics assigned in the manuscript to the herald should really be given to a secondary chorus of the herald's fifty Egyptian henchmen. There are good reasons for thinking that the play had one such subsidiary chorus. The lyrical dialogue in the exodos is generally thought to take place between the main chorus of Danaids and a subsidiary chorus of their handmaidens. If the handmaidens have no special function, there is no reason why they should be explicitly introduced at l. 975 f.; and it is hardly possible, after the passionate unanimity of the Danaids against marriage that has been maintained throughout the play, for half of them suddenly and temporarily to defend Aphrodite's functions. A satisfactory parallel is supplied by the subsidiary chorus of Propompoi in the exodos of the *Eumenides*. No such evidence for the chorus of Egyptians is furnished by the test. Yet Wilamowitz' theory[21] was believed by Paul Maas and Walter Kranz. Five years after the publication of the new evidence for the date of the trilogy, Denys Page[22] wrote of the *Suppliants*: 'It is a play of movements and multitudes. The scene is filled, and vacated, by very large throngs of persons, for the most part, of dusky complexion and unfamiliar costume. There is a moment when we stop and ask, how many persons are in sight? On a mound or platform are Danaus and his

fifty daughters, each (unless the poet misleads us) with an attendant girl;
in the scene below are a herald and his Egyptian escort, presumably
equal in number to the screaming women whom they would carry away;
to them enters the king of Argos with a bodyguard presumably equal in
number to the Egyptians whom they repulse. Can the total be less than
203? The multitude, outlandish costumes, the black faces, the threats
of the one party and the screams of the other, compose a scene without
parallel in the remains of Greek tragedy'. Again, W. S. Barrett, in his
great edition of the *Hippolytus* published this year writes (p. 368) that
in this passage a secondary chorus of Egyptians, 'announced at 825 f.,
sings in alternation with the main chorus'. But look at 825 f. and at
every other part of the text, and you find no plurals but singulars; the
text contains not one scrap of support for Wilamowitz' theory. It is
true that the members of a chorus might be referred to in the singular;
but the onus of proof is on those who believe in a plurality.

   Let us examine the reasons for Wilamowitz' belief. 'So long as it is
uttering its threats', he writes,[23] 'the secondary chorus can be singing,
but when its members rush to the attack and try to lay hands on individual girls, this is no longer possible, so the herald speaks . . . '. In fact
there is nothing whatever in the text to suggest that the herald or any
one person 'rushes to the attack' or 'tries to lay hands on individual
girls'. Behind this naturalistic argument lies the assumption that a single
herald could not throw fifty Danaids into the state of panic that is
apparent from their utterances. Since we are dealing with a medium so
utterly remote from modern stage naturalism as Aeschylean tragedy, it
is hardly safe to assume that one herald could not have terrified fifty
Danaids. But if it turns out that there is no need to imagine that there
were any more than twelve choreutae, the main support for Wilamowitz' conjecture will collapse. Maas (*vid. l.c.*) advocated the theory on
the ground that it harmonises with his rule that characters of low social
standing do not sing in tragedy.[24] Whether a herald is of low social
standing is debatable; and though Maas in defence of his rule deprived
the Nurse in Sophocles' *Trachiniae* of her lyrics, he still had to admit
one somewhat considerable exception, the Phrygian slave's aria in the
Orestes of Euripides. This is not the kind of rarity that can be ruled out
simply because it is rare. A further objection against Wilamowitz' theory
has been impressed upon me by Richmond Lattimore. He points out
that it is hardly consonant with Greek practice for a herald to arrive at
a foreign city with a demarche accompanied by a military force. What
we should expect is what happens in the analogous scene in Euripides'
Heraclidae; the Herald arrives alone, presents his demand and when it is
refused goes off to tell his master, who will now bring up his army

(214 f.). If we follow the natural indications of the text, that is what happens here.

We must now return to the arguments for thinking there were fifty members of the chorus. It rests on a combination of the statement of Pollux (4, 110) that the early tragic chorus numbered fifty with the naturalistic assumption that fifty Danaids could be represented only by fifty choreutae. I wonder how many of the subscribers to this theory have been aware that in the passage to which they assign such weight Pollux says that the number continued to be fifty until the production of the *Eumenides*, when the fifty Erinyes so much scared the Athenians that they reduced the numbers. Anyone who has more than a superficial acquaintance with the *Onomasticon* is aware that this statement is only too characteristic of its author, whose authority in this matter we should be wise not to take too seriously. Wilamowitz' statement that it would be 'absurd' for twelve choreutae to represent fifty Danaids (*Aischylos*: *Interpretationen*, p. 4) is the mere assertion of a naturalistic prejudice. In a play about this subject, the Danaids would have to be the chorus. It would hardly be putting too great a strain on the imagination of the audience to ask them to take twelve to represent fifty; the poet made it a little easier for them by making only one reference, and that oblique, to the number of the sisters. The decisive parallel is supplied by the *Suppliants* of Euripides; there the chorus numbers fifteen, but we are told four times in the text that it consists of the mothers of the seven chiefs who have perished before Thebes (12, 100-2, 598, 963-5). 'The number seven', writes Wilamowitz in the introduction to his translation of that play,[25] 'only signifies a conventional number which is practically equivalent to a proper name'. Exactly; so, in the *Suppliants* of Aeschylus, does the number fifty.

The question of the number of the sisters affords a convenient transition from arguments based on technique to arguments based on content. It has been argued that the legend, with its strong element of the folktale, could have been used only in a very early tragedy. Such an argument need not detain us; one has only to remember, say, the legend of Oedipus. The feature that has struck some people as particularly primitive is of course the number of Danaids and Aegyptiads. Naturalistic prejudices die hard when the number of children people have is in question, yet this number is a matter of fashion, and fashion varies. According to the manuscripts of the Agamemnon (1605) twelve children of Thyestes were served up to him by Atreus; Page follows Emperius in altering that number to two, remarking that twelve is 'a ludicrous multitude in this context'. Ludicrous, maybe, to most of us; but not, I think, to the author of the Prometheus plays, the *Sphinx*, the *Phorcides*, the *Psychostasia*. The theme clearly lends itself to the composition of an Aeschylean trilogy, similar in many respects to the Oresteia. The issue between Danaids and Aegyptiads supplies a conflict, not unlike that between the two branches of the house of Pleisthenes; and by means of the device of treating the antipathy of the Danaids towards their cousins as though it were an antipathy towards marriage in general, Aeschylus contrived to make the clash of individuals symbolise a clash of cosmic principles.

The persons offered by the legend are suited to Aeschylus' purpose; but the poet's characterisation of them has seemed to many to prove the trilogy to be an early work. Danaus in particular has been severely criticised. He has been found dull, prosy, irrelevant; he has been called a mere appendage of the daughters who call him the leader of their company. The question of Danaus' character is clearly bound up with that of the handling of the second actor. If in the supplication scene the Chorus does the talking, that does not mean that Danaus simply obeys his daughters' will. They tell us he is their leader, and there is no reason why we should not believe them. Throughout the play identity of purpose between father and daughters is complete, and when they speak together, Danaus is always in command. That is the point of his warnings to his daughters to behave discreetly; if we consider them without first clearing our minds of naturalistic prejudices, it is easy to mistake their purpose. A recent writer on the style of Aeschylus[26] has said that Danaus 'is portrayed as given to proverbs and maxims and admonitions', and takes this as an instance of the weakness in characterisation of the early Aeschylus. If the word 'portrayed' means 'characterised as an individual', Danaus is not 'portrayed' at all. He is simply the father and counsellor who must show wisdom and resource in defending the interests of his family. For him to warn his daughters against the desires their beauty may excite is highly relevant to the theme of the nature of marriage and the power of Aphrodite which must have been central to the trilogy, as we can see from the last scene of the *Suppliants*, the speech of Aphrodite from the *Danaides* and the subject of the accompanying satyr-play, the *Amymone*. The didactic manner of Danaus' utterance, far from being meant to characterise him as a somewhat fussy and sententious old gentleman, simply expresses his function after the austere and formal fashion of Aeschylean tragedy. In Danaus as a person Aeschylus takes no interest whatsoever, any more than he takes an interest in the Queen of Persia, or in Orestes — whose lack of colour is such a grievous disappointment to such members of the individualising school as have remarked it — or in Oceanus, whose static dignity has been so grotesquely misrepresented as the false civility of a disloyal friend.

Neither is Aeschylus interested in the personality of Pelasgus, which some modern critics have analysed with great care. Some have pronounced him a weak character because, like Agamemnon or the Homeric Hector, he shows respect for public opinion; others have praised the psychological skill shown by the poet in depicting the mental turmoil into which he is thrown by the need to make his agonising decision. The dramatic possibilities of that decision are indeed exploited with great power; but the poet is not concerned to show the effect upon Pelasgus as a person having a particular character of the situation in which he finds himself. Pelasgus is simply a good and conscientious king, confronted with a grim dilemma; either he must receive the suppliants, thus risking war with all its horrors, or he must bring down on himself and his people the wrath of Zeus, protector of suppliants. The moment the Danaids play their trump card, the threat of suicide, the king throws in his hand; in the Aeschylean world the hazards of war, grievous as they may be, are nothing compared with the pollution to which the suicide at the altars of rejected suppliants will expose the polis. Like Eteocles, like Agamemnon at Aulis, Pelasgus can make only one choice.

What the ancients called *ethos* required that the characters in a work of literary art should be depicted as being the kind of people likely to perform the actions that the story gives them. The persons of Aeschylus have enough character to satisfy that requirement and no more. One factor in making it hard for us to see this has been the existence of three of them who strike us as having, in a sense, marked individuality. Clytemnestra is a peculiar case; the actions given her by the story are of such a special kind that in order to seem capable of them she must seem abnormal, and to explain them the poet suggests that she, like her sister Helen, is a peculiar kind of being sent into the world by Zeus in order to accomplish a destructive purpose. Eteocles and Agamemnon have acquired peculiarity in a different way, from the duality of the function assigned them by the plot of the trilogy. Each is the good king, the shepherd of his people, and yet each has laboured from birth under a curse; their actions must reflect this double destiny, and hence their character acquires a double aspect. It is by an accident that these three characters acquire individuality, an accident that may be called the beginning of character-study in European drama.[27]

We may now look back and survey the arguments used to try to date the trilogy before the publication of the papyrus. Before that time, the materials for determining the date did not exist. Walter Nestle's writings during the thirties[28] certainly ought to have warned scholars that their confidence in the early date was much exaggerated, and he will always be remembered with admiration for his stand against dogmatic orthodoxy.

But even if Nestle had been spared to offer the exhaustive treatment of
the subject that he promised, the severe limitations of our knowledge of
Aeschylus would hardly have allowed him to put the case for a late date
beyond reasonable doubt. Seven complete plays, with fragments, is
simply not enough; after a hundred and fifty years of doctoral disserta-
tions, people who confidently claim to *know* the date of Sophocles'
Electra or *Trachiniae* are living in a private world. But now that we have
external evidence for the date of the Danaid trilogy, we can see that the
internal evidence in no way makes against its reliability; and it may be
instructive to examine the reasons for the old dogmatism.

At the root of it lies a prejudice, in essence metaphysical, which
originated in antiquity; the belief that an art form develops in the same
way as an animal or a plant, and that its development can be studied by
the same kind of method. That prejudice can be seen at work in the
earliest and in many ways the best study of Greek tragedy known to us.
Aristotle had taken over from his master, Plato, the belief that each
individual and each abstract entity is what it is by virtue of its conformity
to a fixed type, its participation in a given form. He adapted Plato's
theory of forms in the light of his own favourite scientific discipline, that
of biology; each species had its proper nature, to whose full realisation
its whole development must tend. Tragedy 'attained its nature' (*Poet.*,
1449a15) apparently when Sophocles wrote the pattern drama, the
Oedipus Tyrannus; earlier efforts were seen by Aristotle as marking
stages in a movement, irregular, perhaps, but none the less continuous,
that culminated at that point in time. Aristotle must have thought of
Aeschylus, when he thought of him at all, as an imperfect struggler towards the ideal, the Sophoclean pattern. That way of looking at the
growth of tragedy as a kind of linear progression has been taken for
granted as the only way by the great majority of modern scholars.
Wilamowitz did not question it; how much less most of his immediate
successors, obsessed with the notion of development to such a point
that in a series of ponderous tomes they remorselessly exhibit the growth
of early Greek literature as a process culminating in Plato, smearing the
sublime simplicity of the early Greeks with a thick, clogging treacle of
Hegelian metaphysics! Yet common sense reminds us that the analogy
between a plant or animal on the one hand and an art form on the
other is not necessarily a close one; even in the case of a plant or an
animal, the question as to what exactly is its proper nature and when it
has attained it is one that different people may answer in different ways.
The dangers involved in the attempt to confine within the strait-jacket
of Platonic or Aristotelian idealism the untidy, wasteful, infinite pullu-
lation of the forms of life is particularly well illustrated by the result of

treating Aeschylean tragedy as a mere imperfect stage on the way to Sophoclean perfection, or to the ideal tragedy as it is conceived by a modern taste nurtured on Shakespearian individualism and Ibsenian naturalism.

Suppose we try the experiment of treating Aeschylean tragedy, at least for a moment, as though it had a form and principles of its own, ceasing for the time being to regard it as an imperfect groping towards the perfections realised by later dramatists. Our material is so scanty that we shall run the risk of making some mistakes; but we know enough about it for the attempt to be worth making, and by making it we become alive to features of tragic technique that would otherwise escape us.

In an Aeschylean tragedy the chorus is as a rule deeply involved, at least emotionally, in the action; it may be deuteragonist or even protagonist. The choral part is greater in proportion to the whole than in later tragedy, especially when the chorus is most deeply implicated in the action. The actors are there in order to enact the plot, not in order to display their individual characters; in so far as they have character, they have such character as their acts require. Stichomythia is frequent, and is of a stiffer and more formal kind than that of Sophocles; free dialogue is rare, and in the *Suppliants* and the *Seven* scarcely occurs at all. An agon may take the form of stichomythia or, when a special effect of intensity is aimed at, of an epirrhematic scene. Long rheseis by actors may follow one another, with or without the interposition of brief choral comments, but no agon consisting of long rheseis is found in what we have of Aeschylus. The chorica do not neatly divide the dialogue portion into scenes of approximately equal length; the space between two chorica may be occupied by a single rhesis. Actors as well as choruses speak in a manner that is grand, formal, ceremonious. Neither the language nor the style has any close relation to that of ordinary life; humble figures, the herald in the *Agamemnon* and the nurse in the *Choephori*, are the licensed exceptions that prove the rule. The style and diction, with all their richness and with all their beauty, preserve an element of archaic roughness, distasteful to certain persons and to certain ages, yet giving to the verse a special simplicity and a special strength.

Bernard Ashmole in a memorable paper (*Proc. Brit. Acad.* 1962, p. 217) has reminded us of what he calls 'the pained surprise with which our grandfathers first beheld the sculptures of Olympia'. Those sculptures and the tragedies of Aeschylus have many qualities in common. Even in periods, like the present, when it is not fashionable to dislike these qualities, many people, some of them by no means without taste, view them with aversion. No wonder, when we consider the low esteem enjoyed by Aeschylus between his own time and the nineteenth century; in the violence with which the very people who most insist on the excellence of all genuine Greek tragedy declaim against any passage which they have persuaded themselves is an interpolation, we can recognise a reaction that is only human. It has been easier to patronise the *Suppliants* as a monument of primitive drama rather than to understand it; yet the qualities which it exhibits, whether they deserve praise or not, are those that are typical of Aeschylean tragedy. The force and passion of the opening anapaests make them almost the finest beginning to any play of Aeschylus; the lyrics, though damaged by corruption, are of superb quality; the scene with the herald, though the most corrupt of all, is dramatic to a high degree; and above all the supplication scene is hardly much inferior to the great kommos of the *Choephori*. What has told most against the play in modern estimation is the stilted character of much of the trimeter part. That is a feature of any play of Aeschylus, but most of all of this one. Those who dislike it have a perfect right to; but some will find it less displeasing once they have got used to the undoubted fact that Aeschylus wrote in a convention even more remote from modern naturalism than either of the other great tragedians, and in character for its own sake he took no interest whatsoever.

6

THE GUILT OF AGAMEMNON[1]

HUGH LLOYD-JONES

In recent years the general view of the theology and morality of Aeschylus which we still find expressed in the most popular handbooks of Greek tragedy has come under fire;[2] fire which its defenders have so far been unwilling or unable to return. That Aeschylus was a bold religious innovator propounding advanced doctrines can no longer be assumed without argument; neither can one take for granted that his outlook on morality in general and on justice in particular was as advanced as it was once usual to maintain. Aeschylean justice, it is now beginning to be realized, had more in common with the ancient Hebrew justice that demanded eye for eye and tooth for tooth than with the exalted conceptions attributed to the poet by modern theorists. But whatever view we take of Aeschylus' notion of justice, we are not likely to dispute the paramount importance of justice in his work, and especially in the *Oresteia*. If I begin, then, with the assumption that the *Oresteia* is concerned with justice, human and divine, I shall be on safe ground.

The first and greatest of its three plays shows how the leader of the Greek expedition against Troy, the chosen instrument of Zeus' chastisement of the Trojans, comes to a miserable end. The train of events that leads to this conclusion has been set in motion long before the play begins, when the Greek fleet is assembled at Aulis on its way to Troy. The goddess Artemis becomes incensed with Agamemnon, and sends unfavourable winds that prevent the fleet from sailing. Either the great expedition, ordered by Zeus, must be abandoned, or the king must sacrifice his own daughter to appease the goddess. He consents to the sacrifice. This action earns him the bitter enmity of his wife, who at home in Argos plans his murder. She has at hand an instrument ready to her purpose. Agamemnon's father, Atreus, has long ago massacred the children of his brother, and has served him at a banquet with their flesh. One survivor has escaped, and he is now a grown man waiting for his revenge.

From *Classical Quarterly* 12 (1962), 187–99. Reprinted with minor revisions by permission of the author and Oxford University Press.

The constant preoccupation of the poet with guilt and retribution creates a strong impression in the hearer's mind that the exact assessment of Agamemnon's guilt must be important for the understanding of the play. And yet there is no agreement among scholars as to the nature of that guilt. Agamemnon has been sent against Troy by Zeus himself; and yet Zeus allows him to perish miserably. Why? Is it for having consented to his daughter's sacrifice? If so, how far is his punishment the work of Zeus, and how far is it the consequence of the wrath of Artemis? The motive for that wrath is itself a subject of acute controversy. Or is Agamemnon punished for his remorseless extirpation of the Trojans, and the destruction of their city together with its temples and its altars? What part is played in his destruction by the curse brought down upon his family by the monstrous action of his father, Atreus? Or is he punished for his own pride and arrogance? Most modern scholars, with the notable exception of Eduard Fraenkel, have seen him, if not as an arrogant and cruel despot, at least as something not far removed from one. Or can it be that several, or all of, these factors contribute somehow to his ruin? If so, how far can we hope to assign to each its proper degree of importance in working to this end?

All these questions are controversial. The most learned of Aeschylean scholars, to whom every serious student of the play must acknowledge a large debt, has even warned us that 'it would be absurd to attempt an exact calculation as to the degree of efficacy in each of the different elements that work together towards Agamemnon's fatal end'.[3] It is indeed important to guard against attacking the complicated task of unravelling these twisted strands with any excessive confidence that we shall reach a clear-cut answer. Yet it is agreed that the trilogy is concerned with justice, guilt, and retribution; and that seems to me to justify a fresh attempt to discover how the poet meant us to suppose these notions are exemplified in his work. Whether the results which are arrived at are absurd will be for the reader to judge.

The Chorus in its opening anapaests (60 f.) strongly asserts that the cause of the Atreidae against the Trojans is a just cause. They have been sent against Troy by Zeus, the guardian of the law of host and guest: Zeus, who has been outraged by Paris' crime against the sacred laws of hospitality. At the beginning of the first stasimon (367 f.), the point is further reinforced. The Chorus has just been told that Troy has fallen. 'They can speak of a stroke from Zeus', they begin; 'this, at least, one can make out.' Later in the play the same truth is strongly insisted on both by the Herald and by the King himself. And yet it is by the will of Zeus, as the loyal elders themselves finally acknowledge, that Agamemnon comes to his miserable end.

The reasons begin to emerge in the parodos, in that great choral ode which describes what has happened ten years earlier, when the Greek fleet lay encamped at Aulis on its way to Troy. The portent of the eagles that tore and devoured a pregnant hare has taught Calchas, the prophet of the Greek army, that Troy is destined to fall to the expedition; it has taught him also that Artemis is incensed against its leaders, the Atreidae. In the whole play nothing is more controversial than the reasons for Artemis' anger, but in an investigation of the guilt of Agamemnon the problem of her motive is not one that we can avoid.

'In time', says Calchas (126 ff.), 'this expedition captures Priam's city; and all the plentiful herds of the people before the walls shall Fate violently ravage. Only may no envious grudge from the gods strike beforehand and cast into darkness the great bit for Troy's mouth that is the host encamped. For in pity Artemis bears a grudge against the winged hounds of her father that slaughter the poor trembling hare with all her young before the birth; and she loathes the feast of the eagles. . . . The Fair One, kindly as she is towards the helpless offspring of ravening lions and pleasant to the suckling young of all creatures that roam the wild, demands fulfilment of what these things portend; favourable is the portent, yet fraught with blame. And I invoke the blessèd Healer, that she prepare not against the Danaoi lengthy delays in port caused by adverse winds that hold fast the ships, striving to bring about another sacrifice, one without song or banquet, a worker of quarrels born in the house and fearless of the husband. For there abides a terrible, ever re-arising, treacherous keeper of the house, unforgetting Wrath, child-avenging.'

The ancient epic called the *Cypria* accounted for the wrath of Artemis by means of a story not mentioned by Aeschylus. According to Proclus' summary of the plot of this lost work (O.C.T. of Homer, v. 104), Agamemnon had shot a stag, and in his triumph boasted that as an archer he surpassed even Artemis. A similar story is told by Sophocles in his *Electra* (563 f.). That story is not mentioned here; but can we rule out the possibility that it was, none the less, the reason for the wrath of Artemis that Aeschylus had in mind? If that is so, it follows that he has set down Artemis' anger to an obscure and arbitrary grievance, a grievance so trivial that it is not worth mentioning in the play at all. It would certainly be unsafe to deny *a priori* that this could be the case; but the conclusion is such a strange one that it seems hardly reasonable to adopt it without further examination of the evidence. Does the portent give us any clue to the reason for the goddess's anger?

Calchas says that she is angry because she loathes the feast of the eagles; and the eagles, he says, stand for the Atreidae. Here, say some

scholars, we have the explanation of her anger: she hates the eagles, and
the eagles stand for the Atreidae; therefore she conceives a hatred for
the Atreidae. This interpretation seems to me to rest on an intolerable
confusion between the world of the portent and the world of the reality
it happens in order to symbolize. The eagles and the hare belong to the
world of the portent; that portent symbolizes an event which is to
happen in the real world. The eagles stand for the Atreidae; so it is
natural to infer that the hare must stand for some other figure or figures
belonging to the real world. We can hardly avoid supposing that it stands
for the Trojans and their city. So when Calchas says (137) Artemis
abhors the eagles' feast, he must mean that Artemis abhors the coming
destruction of Troy, which the Atreidae are destined to accomplish.

I believe that this conclusion is confirmed by the words of Calchas'
explanation of the portent. But the point is not to be grasped immediately, for like most Greek prophets Calchas casts his interpretation in
riddling language. 'In time', he begins (126 f.), 'this expedition captures
Priam's city; and all the plentiful herds of the people before the walls
shall fate violently ravage.' This is strange language. We should have expected that the tearing of the pregnant hare would stand for the annihilation of the Trojans, not only men, women and children, but even
the unborn; we can scarcely help remembering the speech of Agamemnon
to Menelaus in the sixth book of the *Iliad* (57 f.), in which he declares
that not even the unborn children of the Trojans shall escape his vengeance. Yet when it comes to the explanation of the portent, we are
told that the Achaeans will destroy the Trojan . . . cattle!

That seems incredible; and I have suggested that the explanation lies
in the habit Greek prophets had of referring to people by the names of
animals.[4] If so, 'the abundant herds of the people' will mean 'the abundant herds *that are* the people'. This is confirmed by the presence of
the words 'before the walls'; for the Trojan cattle did not perish before
the walls, but the Trojan men did perish 'in front of the city'.

If it is correct, the close correspondence of the portent with the future
reality must be taken as established. The eagles stand for the Atreidae;
the hare and its young stand for Troy and its inhabitants. What reason
does Calchas give for the pity felt by Artemis for the hare? He says that
Artemis is the patroness of the young of all wild animals; and according
to many modern interpreters this fact in itself is enough to explain her
anger against the Atreidae. But this is out of the question. Just as both
eagles and hare correspond to figures of the real world, so must the
motive assigned to the goddess for championing the hare represent a
motive for championing what the hare represents in the world of reality.
We have seen that in the real world the hare represents the Trojans. Has

Artemis a special motive for championing the Trojans that may correspond in the world of reality to the motive assigned her in the world of
the portent for championing the hare?

She has, in fact, an excellent motive; for in the *Iliad* and in the whole
poetical tradition Artemis together with her brother Apollo appears
as a loyal partisan of Troy against the invaders. This supplies a motive
for her hostility to the Atreidae that is fully sufficient to explain her
action. The last scholar to put forward a view at all similar to this
weakened his case by regarding the sacrifice of Iphigeneia as 'an atonement payable in advance for the destruction of Troy'.[5] This language is
too legalistic: it is a mistake to talk of 'sin' and 'atonement' in this
connexion. In Aeschylus, as in Homer, the lesser gods have a position in
no way comparable with that of Zeus; they may range themselves on
either side in the Trojan conflict, but Zeus for the first time holds the
balance and will in the end decide the issue. Artemis' blow against
Agamemnon is one move in the struggle; it is the attempt of a pro-Trojan
goddess to strike at the invaders before the invasion: Artemis must be
seen not as a judge punishing a sin, but as a powerful enemy striking at
an enemy. Zeus will not prevent Artemis from bringing about the sacrifice; and Calchas hints that this may have consequences beyond itself.
Why may it have these consequences? 'There abides', he says (152 ff.),
'a terrible, ever re-arising, treacherous keeper of the house, unforgetting
wrath, child-avenging.' That is usually taken as an allusion to Clytemnestra; indeed, some scholars have thought that it identifies the Wrath
with her. But if I am right in translating *palinortos* by 'ever re-arising', the
reference cannot be limited to her. There is a possibility (see Denniston-
Page, ad loc.) that the word may mean 'arising in the future'; and in
view of that I do not press the point. But it is worth noticing that if
palinortos here could bear its natural meaning, the reference would be
to a child-avenging wrath that is 'ever again arising'. And that could
only be the ancient wrath of the House of Atreus.

After the narrative of Calchas' prophecy, the Chorus enters upon the
famous invocation that is often called the 'hymn to Zeus' (160 ff.). Why
does the Chorus choose this moment for the invocation? The question
is not one which every editor of the play has tried to answer; but the
choral lyrics of Aeschylus are not normally irrelevant to the dramatic
situation, and there is no reason why this one should form an exception
to the rule. What is the situation at this point? Zeus has sent the Atreidae
against Troy; but Artemis has confronted them with the intolerable
choice between abandoning the expedition Zeus has ordered or con-
senting to Iphigeneia's killing. Where might Agamemnon have looked
for help? And where might the elders of Argos appeal in the face of the

anxiety that even now, ten years later, still torments them in consequence of what happened at Aulis? Only Zeus could have helped him, and them, to cast from their minds 'the burden of futile worry' (165). Zeus' power is over all, and he teaches men, by means of bitter experience, to obey his stern law of reciprocal justice. Artemis has faced Agamemnon with a terrible alternative. Zeus has sent him against Troy; surely he can hope for aid from Zeus.

Yet the Chorus does not appear at all confident that such aid will be forthcoming. 'Why not?', the audience may wonder. The Chorus gives no indication of the reason for its fears; at this point, the audience can only ponder on the riddling final words of the prophecy of Calchas. But, in the light of a full knowledge of the play, the reader may well wonder, 'Will aid from Zeus be forthcoming for the son of Atreus?'

From the invocation the Chrous returns abruptly to the scene at Aulis, and Agamemnon's grim dilemma. Should he have given up his expedition and gone home? Many scholars have been of this opinion. But in his brilliant introduction to the play D. L. Page has argued that Agamemnon has no choice. Zeus, he has pointed out, has ordered the expedition; it is his will that Troy shall fall. Hear the words attributed to Agamemnon (214 f.): 'That they should desire with passion exceeding passion a sacrifice to still the winds, a sacrifice of maiden's blood, is right in the sight of heaven'. It is no use trying to water down the final word *themis*, whose emphatic position no less than its solemn association lends it great weight in this place. Yet we must notice that Agamemnon's action is described by the Chorus in words that leave no doubt that it is considered a crime (218 f.): 'And when he had taken upon him the bridle of compulsion, and the wind of his purpose had veered and blew impious, impure, unholy, from that moment he reversed his mind to a course of utter recklessness. For men are made bold by evil-counselling shameless infatuation, the beginning of woe. So he brought himself to sacrifice his daughter, in aid of a war to avenge a woman's loss and as advance payment for his ships.'

We are faced with an apparently glaring contradiction. We must agree with Page that Agamemnon has no choice but to sacrifice his daughter; the expedition had to sail. Yet E. R. Dodds[6] is equally right in insisting that his action was, and is meant to be regarded as, a crime. The text is explicit on this point. Can it be that both are right? Can Zeus have forced Agamemnon to choose between two crimes, either of which was certain to result in his destruction? My answer to this question would be, Yes.

The words just now quoted which describe how Agamemnon made his decision imply that he is mentally deranged (222). These words recall the famous passage in the nineteenth book of the *Iliad* in which Agamemnon tries to account for his reckless behaviour in provoking Achilles. 'I was not responsible', he exclaims, 'but Zeus and my portion and the Erinys that walks in darkness, who while I speak put cruel Ate in my mind' (86-88). Infatuation, *parakopē*, in the *Agamemnon* is hardly distinct from Ate in the *Iliad*; and Ate is commonly an instrument of Zeus.

Zeus is indeed determined that the fleet must sail; Agamemnon has indeed no choice. But how has Zeus chosen to enforce his will? Not by charging Calchas or some other accredited mouthpice to inform the king of his decision; but by sending Ate to take away his judgement so that he cannot do otherwise. Does it follow that Agamemnon is not held responsible for his action? Certainly not. In Homer Agamemnon excuses his behaviour by pointing to the action of Ate on his mind; but it does not occur to him to deny his responsibility, or to shuffle out of paying the enormous compensation which he has promised to Achilles. It is the same in Aeschylus. Zeus has taken away Agamemnon's judgement; but that does not absolve Agamemnon from the guilt his error will incur. Nothing could better illustrate the saying of Aeschylus' Niobe that Zeus makes a fault in men, when he is determined utterly to destroy a house (fr. 277, Loeb edition, pp. 15-16).

But what leads Zeus to determine to destroy a house? A famous chorus of the *Agamemnon* (750 f.) gives a definite answer to this question; and it stands in such a context that we can hardly doubt that the belief which it expresses is meant to be regarded as a true one. Prosperity in itself, the Chorus insists, is not sufficient to arouse the anger of the gods; only crime brings down punishment on a man or on his descendants after him. Despite the Chorus's claim of originality, this doctrine is not, of course, peculiar to Aeschylus; Page (loc. cit., p. 136) has reminded us that it is found in two places in the fragments of Solon, a writer not unfamiliar to Aeschylus' audience. It is likely to represent Aeschylus' own belief. If so, it is unlikely that Zeus' decision to destroy Agamemnon is without a motive.

Zeus has faced Agamemnon with an impossible alternative. Also, he has taken away his judgement, so that he takes a fatal course; not that the other choice would not have been equally fatal. Why has he done this? Why, in using Agamemnon to punish Troy, has he chosen a course which must lead inevitably to the ruin of Agamemnon? Do we know of any guilt previously attaching to the King himself? No. But do we know of any guilt attaching to his ancestors? More than half the play has elapsed before we hear anything of such guilt. But let me continue with the commentary on the play's successive scenes that I have begun, resuming from the scene that follows the parodos.

Running right through the play we find a deliberate parallel between the fate of the house of Priam and the fate of the house of Atreus; equally pervasive, only less important, is the parallel between the fate of Helen and the fate of Clytemnestra. Again and again we find this sequence repeated; first, pious moralizings as the working of Zeus' law is traced in the just punishment of Troy; next, gradually increasing realization, both by the audience and by the Chorus, that what is true of Troy may prove true also of Troy's conquerors; lastly, agonized apprehension. This is the pattern of scene after scene and chorus after chorus. It was the pattern of the Chorus's initial anapaests together with the parodos; it is the pattern of the scene between Clytemnestra and the Chorus that follows.

In the first of her two great speeches in that scene (281 ff.), Clytemnestra describes the rapid journey from Troy to Argos of 'the light lineally descended from the fire of Ida' (311). Some people see nothing in the Beacon Speech but an irrelevant, if magnificent, geographical excursus. No one could be more reluctant than I to attribute to ancient authors anything like what is generally meant by the modern term 'symbolism'. But I cannot doubt that in Clytemnestra's mind the fire from Ida stands for the avenging fire of Zeus; nor that the Beacon Speech is highly relevant to the parallel between the fates of the Priamidae and that of the Atreidae which I have just mentioned. In the second of her speeches in this scene (320 f.) Clytemnestra paints for the Chorus a vivid picture of what she imagines to be happening in the captured city. If the conquerors show piety, she says, towards the gods of the conquered land and towards their shrines, then they may escape being conquered in their turn. But if they commit sacrilege, they may provoke revenge; and even if they avoid sacrilege, they may arouse the vengeance of the spirits of the dead. Clytemnestra's pretended fears are obviously her secret hopes. This speech looks forward to the later scene in which the Chorus gradually extracts from the innocently optimistic Herald the news of the storm that has scattered the returning ships. This disaster was directly provoked by the sacrilege Clytemnestra had anticipated, and its occurrence greatly facilitated the accomplishment of her plan; for it was owing to the storm that Agamemnon returned in a single ship and without his brother. The adventures of Menelaus after the storm formed the subject of the satyr-play that accompanied the trilogy, the *Proteus*; this, too, may help to explain the importance assigned by the poet to the brothers' separation.

The first stasimon begins on a note of triumph and ends on one of disaster. From the theme of the just punishment of Troy, the Chorus passes to that of Helen and the lives sacrificed for her sake, and ends on a note of anxious foreboding (459 f.) 'My anxious thought waits to hear something yet shrouded in darkness. For the gods are not unwatchful of the killers of many; and in time the black Erinyes consign to darkness him who is fortunate without justice, reversing his fortune and ruining his life; and he has no protection once he is among the vanished. To be praised exceedingly is dangerous. . . . My choice is the prosperity that comes without envy. May I not be a sacker of cities, nor yet be made captive by others and see my life waste away.' It is remarkable that Agamemnon's own loyal councillors can seem to imply that he is 'fortunate without justice'. If he has killed many, is it not because he is the minister of Zeus' vengeance? If he has made war and sacrificed his daughter for the sake of Helen, has it not been at Zeus' order?

The scene of the Herald repeats the now familiar sequence of hope and triumph followed by the slow realization that all is not well; it ends with the Chorus forcing the Herald, much against his will, to describe the disaster of the storm. Then the second stasimon takes up once more the theme of Helen, and illustrates her nature by the fable of the lion cub. It shows Helen to be in a sense a daemonic being, one sent into the world for the express purpose of causing havoc and destruction. We are meant to remember that Clytemnestra is her sister; later in the play, the Chorus itself will observe the similarity of their careers (1468 f.). From the theme of Helen, the Chorus goes on to speak of guilt and divine justice (750 f.). Prosperity does not of itself provoke the anger of the gods; evil deeds alone bring down divine justice either on their doer or on his descendants after him.

Immediately after this famous passage the King enters the stage; we can hardly doubt that the words the Chorus has lately uttered somehow apply to his case. The elders welcome him. In the past they have criticized his conduct in making war to recover Helen; but now that his plan has been successfully accomplished, they are glad to greet him with enthusiasm and to warn him against secret enemies. Perhaps the presentation of the King himself may furnish some clue to the problem of his guilt. But the character assigned him by the poet has been, and is, the subject of acute controversy. 'It is a common view', wrote Fraenkel in 1942,[7] '. . . that king Agamemnon is either the villain of the piece or, at any rate, a reckless, overbearing and impious tyrant.' His own view is very different. For him Agamemnon is 'in everything . . . a great gentleman, possessed of moderation and self-control';[8] he is 'every inch a king'; 'his every word and gesture is expressive of a powerful sincerity'.[9] Page takes a view of Agamemnon's character not widely removed from that against which Fraenkel has so energetically protested. 'His first address does not endear him,' he writes, 'he is ready with pious phrases, he greets success with gratitude, but without surprise. . . . He neither mentions his wife nor expresses pleasure in his home-coming . . .' (loc. cit., pp. xxxiii f.). When he gives in to Clytemnestra and fatally consents to make a triumphal entry into the palace, treading underfoot the purple tapestries normally reserved as offerings to the gods, that happens, according to Page, 'simply because he is at the mercy of his own vanity and arrogance, instantly ready to do this scandalous act the moment his personal fears of divine retribution and human censure are, by whatever sophistry, allayed' (loc. cit., p. 151),

Let us investigate the reasons for this singular disagreement. Fraenkel seems to me to have established that his calling the gods 'jointly responsible' for his victory does not immediately convict the King of hybris; such language was for a Greek perfectly consistent with a properly respectful attitude.[10] But it cannot be denied that in his opening speech Agamemnon looks back upon his ruthless extirpation of his enemies with a fierce satisfaction. 'The blasts of destruction still have life; and the embers as they die with the dead city waft upwards the rich incense of its wealth' (819-20). 'There is no sentimental lamentation in this fine sentence,' writes Fraenkel (p. 378), 'but a true note of profound sympathy.' A few lines later Agamemnon says, 'The ravening lion leaped over the wall, and lapped his fill of the blood of kings' (827-8). I find no sympathy, profound or otherwise, in that sentence or in anything that Agamemnon says about the Trojans; and I find it difficult to deny that the complaisance with which he views the extermination of his enemies must bode ill for him. Clytemnestra has, we know, been hoping that the Greeks will commit some act of sacrilege and provoke the anger of the gods; and the Herald has told us, in a line most unconvincingly obelized by Fraenkel (527), that the altars and shrines of the gods are to be seen no more. Agamemnon now boasts of the city's total destruction; are we to suppose that he has somehow managed it in such a way as to leave the shrines intact?[11] It is true that in his vengeance Agamemnon has acted as the minister of Zeus. But is it no less true that it is dangerous to be a sacker of cities, and that the destruction of the Trojan temples must provoke divine resentment.

We must agree with Page that the grimness and harshness of Agamemnon make an unfavourable impression; but we cannot deny that there is much in the situation that makes this understandable. It is hardly reasonable to reproach him with his coldness to his wife; it seems clear that rumours of what is going on at home have found their way to him. Nor is his behaviour at any point undignified; here we must contrast him with Aegisthus, whom the poet has portrayed in a most unsympathetic fashion. Both recent editors have remarked on the meanness of his conduct and the vulgarity of his language: what purpose had the poet in depicting him in such a way if not that of showing his enemy in a comparatively sympathetic light? Further, we must note the trust and affection of the humble Watchman who speaks the prologue; he looks forward to clasping in his own his master's well-loved hands. Notice, too, the attitude of the Chorus. They acknowledge to the King himself that they have criticized his conduct in the past. But they are glad to welcome him back from Troy with a friendly greeting; and their sincerity is proved by their lamentations at the miserable end of him whom they call their 'kindly guardian' (1452). Fraenkel and Page are both right; we have here a character of light and shade. This conclusion is confirmed by a comparison of Aeschylus' Agamemnon with that of Homer; the two are remarkably alike. Homer's Agamemnon is not, on the whole, an agreeable character. He is proud and irascible, to such an extent that he becomes involved in quarrels with his allies that have disastrous consequences. He is utterly determined to exterminate the enemy, declaring to Menelaus that even the unborn children in the womb shall perish (6. 57 f.). He is ready to proclaim in open council that he prefers the captive concubine Chryseis to his wife Clytemnestra (1.113 ff.). But these defects cannot blind the reader to his magnificent heroic qualities. He is a good fighter, at his best in a difficult situation; his management of affairs is, as Apollo says in the *Eumenides* (631-2), on the whole successful. Like many hot-tempered men he is capable of behaving with dignity and nobility, as his reconciliation with Achilles plainly shows.

Let us now examine the crucial scene in which Clytemnestra induces her husband to tread upon the purple tapestries (932 ff.). Why does Agamemnon end by succumbing to his wife's persuasion? Fraenkel (loc. cit., p. 441) argues that he yields partly out of chivalry towards a lady, partly because after long years of struggle he is weary and his nerve finally gives way. This is not convincing. Chivalry of such a kind seems to be a medieval and a modern rather than an ancient concept; and the psychological explanation that the King sees through his wife but is too weary to oppose her has a decidedly modern ring. It is a far cry from Aeschylus' Agamemnon to Mann's Aschenbach; nor is such a notion firmly grounded in the text. Must we then believe with Page that Agamemnon secretly longs to make a triumphal entry, and eagerly grasps at the sophistical excuses offered by the Queen? Or should we rather accept a third explanation lately offered us by Hermann Gundert,[12] who has argued that Agamemnon surrenders because he has been outwitted, and that he has been outwitted because Zeus has taken away his wits?

With these three theories in mind let us turn to the text. 'In a moment of fear', says Clytemnestra, 'might you not have vowed to the gods that you would do this?' This is no argument; an offering made to discharge a vow would have been in honour of the gods, but what Clytemnestra is proposing would be in honour of the King himself. Agamemnon knows this, and might have said it; what he does say is that, on the advice of an accredited exegete, he would have done so. 'What do you think Priam would have done?', the Queen asks. This again is a sophism; Priam was not only a barbarian, but a man under a curse. This too Agamemnon knows and might have said; instead he is content with the dry answer, 'Yes, *he* certainly would have done it.' 'Have no scruple, then,' says Clytemnestra, 'for the reproach of men.' Agamemnon could have answered that the reproach of men did not worry him, but that what he dreaded was the anger of the gods. Instead, he lamely replies, 'Yes, but public opinion is a great power.' Considered in terms of what we know of Aeschylean morality, this answer surely indicates a moral blindness. 'But the man who arouses no jealousy is not enviable', says the Queen. Agamemnon knows that to incur *phthonos* ('envy') is dangerous; yet he can counter only with the feeble complaint that a woman ought not to desire contention. 'But for the fortunate', his wife answers, 'it is becoming to yield the victory.' 'Do you think victory in this contest so important?' 'Be persuaded; if you give in to me, you are the winner.' The King has no answer to this; and after removing his boots in a futile gesture of appeasement, he enters the palace.

Agamamnon's answers to the last two questions give a definite indication that he has provoked divine *phthonos*: the more closely we consider them, the harder it becomes to accept Fraenkel's explanation of Agamemnon's conduct. Must we agree with Page that he gives in 'simply because he is at the mercy of his own vanity and arrogance'? Here we are troubled by the empirical fact that during a performance of the play we find ourselves at this point regarding Agamemnon not with contempt, but with compassion. Note in particular the lines that immediately precede the stichomythia (926 f.). The king has replied to his wife's long and effusive speech of welcome with a curt and almost brutal refusal to accept her praise. But the conclusion of his speech, summing up his attitude, makes him, almost for the first time, sympathetic. 'Apart from foot-wipers and embroideries sounds the voice of fame; and good sense is the god's greatest gift. Men should call him happy who has ended his life in the prosperity that we desire. And if in all things I can act thus, I lack not confidence.' These do not seem the accents of hypocrisy. Yet in the scene that follows, Clytemnestra twists her husband round her little finger; he is as helpless as Thrasymachus before Socrates against her devastating dialectic.

How can we account for Agamemnon's rapid collapse? Page's view that under temptation he reveals his secret moral weakness is not a wholly convincing explanation of the change in him. Here we must carefully consider the explanation offered by Gundert, that Zeus and his portion and the Erinys have put Ate into his mind, to use the words put into Agamemnon's mouth in the nineteenth book of the *Iliad* (quoted on p. 63). A parallel which seems to me to lend strong support to Gundert's view is furnished by that scene in the *Seven Against Thebes* in which the Messenger describes to Eteocles the seven champions who are arrayed against the seven gates. Against the first six Eteocles dispatches champions from his own command. At the seventh gate stands Eteocles' own brother Polyneices. Like Agamemnon Eteocles is a harsh and grim character who is yet not unsympathetically portrayed. He knows that if he fights his brother he will not survive; he knows that pollution of the most hideous sort is caused by the shedding of a brother's blood; and yet he cannot bring himself to do as the Chorus wishes and send another in his place. The reason for this is clearly indicated in the text, as Friedrich Solmsen has shown in an important article;[13] Eteocles is in the power of the Erinys. In Agamemnon's case the evidence of the text is less positive; but I have little doubt that Gundert is right in thinking that the reason for his behaviour is the same.

Not that Gundert's explanation seems to me entirely sufficient; in a curious way I believe that he and Page are both partly right. Gundert goes too far in arguing that Agamemnon reveals no *hybris*, but mere stupidity; for when Zeus takes away a man's wits, he sends upon him a moral blindness. Zeus' action in sending Ate upon Agamemnon causes Agamemnon to commit a crime; so far Page is right; but in so far as the crime is the result of Zeus' action, Gundert has supplied an element of the truth which Page's explanation has ignored. It is clear that we have come upon an anomaly similar to that which so much perplexed us in the matter of Agamemnon's fatal decision at Aulis. There Page argued that Agamemnon could not be held responsible; Dodds argued that his action was a crime, and was called a crime by the Chorus; both views, I have argued, contain an element of truth. Here too it is the same. In one sense Agamemnon is guilty; Page has shown that he utters words that are bound to bring down on him divine envy, and we know that he will presently pay the penalty. Yet in a certain sense Agamemnon is innocent; he acts as he does because Zeus has taken away his wits. But why has Zeus done so? For the same reason as at Aulis; because of the curse. As Agamemnon succumbs, vanquished by the irresistible persuasion of Helen's sister, the destined instrument of his destruction, we look upon him not with scorn, but with compassion. Guilty as he is, he is not, like Aegisthus, mean and contemptible; destined as he is to ruin, at once guilty and innocent, he is a truly tragic figure.

The King disappears into the palace; the Chorus sings the third stasimon, full of ominous foreboding; and we are already waiting for Agamemnon's death-cry. But we are kept waiting till the end of the Cassandra scene. That scene occupies nearly 300 lines, not much less than one-fifth of the entire play. The power and beauty of that scene are so overwhelming that it is easy to forget to inquire what is its function in the unfolding of the plot. What is that function? Cassandra makes a desperate effort to get across to the uncomprehending Chorus a warning of Agamemnon's mortal danger which it is inevitably bound not to grasp. This provides a wonderful opportunity for the working up of an uncanny atmosphere and for the gradual building up of suspense. But this is not all. Since the narrative of the prophecy of Calchas, the audience has felt that there is some dark factor in the situation which has only been hinted at; something which if known would do more to explain the sinister forebodings of the Chorus than any vague talk of murmurs in the city against the princes. What that something is is instantly known to the foreigner Cassandra, whom Clytemnestra has supposed may be ignorant of Greek. No sooner does she begin to move in the direction of the door than she sees in a vision (1096) the murdered children of Thyestes. Soon after she exclaims that even now a mighty evil is being plotted in the house (1102); and she describes in confused and agitated utterance a vision of the approaching murder. During the first part of the scene Cassandra speaks in lyrics; that part concludes with her calling to mind the fate of her own family and nation, and recalling once more to the audience the parallel, so often suggested during the first four great odes, between the fate of the Priamidae and the fate of the Atreidae. Then by a last great effort she collects herself, and in trimeters instead of lyrics, in speech instead of song, she openly declares to the Chorus (1178 f.) that the house of Atreus is beset by the Erinyes; that it is haunted by the spirits of the murdered children; that she and Agamemnon are presently to die an awful death; and that they will not go unavenged. And just before her final exit, she returns once more (1287 f.) to the fate of Troy and the not dissimilar fate of its conquerors.

We cannot regard the Cassandra scene as a mere episode, one whose presence may be amply justified by its effect but which is not essential to the development of the plot. Cassandra supplies us, first obscurely and later at the climax explicitly, with the vital piece of information that gives the missing clue for which we have so long been seeking. One main contribution of the scene to the unfolding of the plot is Cassandra's futile warning; but a more important one is her bringing into the open, for the first time in the play, the origin and nature of the curse.

There follows the scene in which Clytemnestra, standing over the dead bodies of the murdered pair, boldly confronts the Chorus and exults in her revenge. Returning to the theme so often played on in the early lyrics of the play, the Chorus cries out against Helen; now her deadly work has achieved its final triumph. 'O mad Helen,' they exclaim (1455 f.), 'you who alone destroyed those many, all those many lives beneath Troy, now have you crowned yourself with the last, the perfect garland, not to be forgotten, by means of the blood not washed away.' Clytemnestra forbids the Chorus to blame Helen. Next the old men address the daemon of the house (1468 f.): 'Daemon, you who fall upon the house and the two Tantalids, and exercise through women an evil sway. . . .' 'Now you have set right your utterance', the queen replies, 'by calling on the daemon of this race, thrice glutted.' 'Great is the daemon of whom you speak,' says the Chorus, 'evil is his wrath, insatiate of baneful fortune. Woe, woe, through the will of Zeus, the cause of all, the doer of all. For what is fulfilled for men without Zeus? Which of these things is not god-ordained?'

These words of the Chorus are not spoken idly. We can now trace, from the primal *Atē* of Thyestes, the grand design of Zeus. The action of the Theban trilogy, almost the only other of which we have a reasonable knowledge, is determined from the start by the curse upon Laius; so, I feel certain, is the action of the *Oresteia* by the curse upon Atreus. From his birth Agamemnon's fate, like that of Oedipus or Eteocles, has been determined; he is the son of the accursed Atreus. Zeus uses him as the instrument of his vengeance upon Troy; but he uses him in such a fashion that his own destruction must inevitably follow. At the outset of the expedition, Artemis, a partisan of Agamemnon's enemies, demands of him blood for blood. Agamemnon cannot refuse, for it is Zeus' will that the fleet sail; and Zeus sends Ate to take away his judgement and force him to consent. The King bows to the goddess's demand: and his consent brings down upon him the vengeance of his wife, who shares her sister's uncanny and daemonic nature serving like her as an instrument of Zeus' destructive purpose. Even his righteous revenge upon the Trojans involves Agamemnon in yet further guilt. In one sense, it is a triumph of divine justice; in another, an atrocious crime; the instrument of Zeus' punishment of Troy must himself be punished. But such guilt as the King contracts from the sacrifice of his daughter and from the annihilation of Troy with its people and its temples is only a consequence of the original guilt inherited from Atreus; the curse comes first, and determines everything that follows. Zeus brings about the ruin of Priam; Zeus brings about the ruin of Agamemnon. The Chorus of the *Agamemnon*, like Sophocles' women of Trachis,[14] can justly echo Homer's words at the beginning of the *Iliad* and say that all that has happened has been in accordance with the will of Zeus.

7

IMAGERY AND ACTION IN THE *ORESTEIA*

ANN LEBECK

Several major systems of imagery in the *Oresteia* have a specific purpose: they turn the events of the drama into a concrete illustration of the principle *pathein ton erxanta* ('the doer suffers'). The gnome itself is not stated until the end of *Agamemnon*: yet the idea of like for like is communicated on the level of imagery from the beginning of the play. Further, a variety of expressions which suggest the proverb prepare for the statement of the gnome itself. The majority of these involve repetition of *paschō* (suffer), *draō* (act), and *prattō* (do) or verbal parallelism of some kind. They recur with increasing frequency in the final half of *Agamemnon*.[1]

Introduced at the close of the first drama, the gnome and its equivalent 'blood for blood' are central to the action of *Choephori*. However, as the trilogy progresses the proverb takes on other overtones. A divine decree in *Agamemnon* (1563-64), in *Choephori* it is shown to be untenable, a vicious unending circle of injustice.[2] Orestes' last words to Clytemnestra sum up the situation with an irony born of understanding: 'You slew whom you ought not have slain, now in requital suffer what you ought not suffer' (930).

In *Eumenides*, along with Erinyes, the gnome undergoes a final metamorphosis: from doing ill and suffering harm to doing good and faring well. From the lament of the Furies in the parodos to the words of Athena at the close:

> *Chor.* Ho, ho! Out upon it! We have suffered, dear ones —
> much have I suffered, and all in vain! —
> we have suffered a grievous blow, alas, a hurt unbearable.
>
> (143-145)
>
> Such are the actions of the younger gods. . . .   (163)

Excerpted from *The Oresteia: A Study in Language and Structure*, (Cambridge, Mass.: Harvard University Press, 1971), pp. 59-73. Abridged, with some Greek, French and German passages replaced by English translation.

> *Ath.*   to do good and receive good, and in goodly honor
>   to have a portion in this land most dear to the gods.   (868–869)

In *Agamemnon* this gnomic statement is illustrated by three systems
of imagery: that of sacrifice, that of the hunt, and that of the marriage
ritual.

Sacrifice

Each complex of imagery has its origin in an idea or a concrete act. His
subject matter offers Aeschylus two traditions: the sacrificial feast served
Thyestes and the sacrifice of Iphigenia.[3] These two events are the point
of departure for the image of murder as a ritual act which appears
throughout the *Oresteia*. Agamemnon dies in requital for the crime of
Atreus and the crime at Aulis. The image of his own death as sacrifice
makes that death parallel to the two crimes of which he is guilty. It is
just requital, like for like. The connection between these three decisive
events, gradually established by recurrent imagery, is made explicit at
the end of *Agamemnon*. The recurrence of the sacrifice motif in *Choephori* and *Eumenides* links the action of these two plays to its initial
cause, the murder of Agamemnon. In *Choephori* the 'sacrifice' of
Clytemnestra is performed by Orestes to avenge Agamemnon, and in
Eumenides the Furies demand the 'sacrifice' of Orestes in payment for
the matricide.[4]

As was stated, this motif has particular significance with regard to
the ritual murder of Iphigenia and Thyestes' children. However, it also
connects Agamemnon's death with the other wrong for which he is held
responsible, the destruction of Ilium and death of men in battle. The
ololygmos[5] (victory cry) and sacrifice of thanksgiving with which
Clytemnestra greets the news of victory over Troy (26–29, 587, 595)
are echoed by the *ololygmos* raised in her victory over Troy's conqueror:

> *Cassandra*:   a raging hell-mother, breathing truceless war
>   against her own! And how she cried out in joy,
>   she who dares all things, as though at the turning-point of battle!
>   (1235–37)

The motif appears more and more often as the moment of Agamemnon's
death approaches. The first intimations that his death approximates a
sacrificial rite[6] appear in the form of irony rather than imagery. Clytemnestra invites Cassandra to come and stand at the altar and partake of
the ceremony which will soon take place within:

> Since without anger Zeus has made you with our house
> a sharer in lustral water, with many slaves
> taking your stand near the altar of Zeus, god of possessions. . . .
> (1036-38)

When her efforts at persuasion fail she refuses to waste further time: inside the house the sheep stand ready at the hearth for slaughter (1055-59).[7] As Clytemnestra knows, the sacrifice to which she alludes is the murder of Agamemnon. In Cassandra's vision this motif is raised to the level of metaphor: Agamemnon's death becomes a sacrifice offered by his wife (1235-37).[8] Later she perceives that her own death is the sacrificial rite to which Clytemnestra had invited her:

> Instead of my father's altar (*bōmou*), a chopping-block (*epixēnon*) awaits me,
> soon to be red with my hot blood when I am struck before the sacrifice. (1277-78)

She is to be a victim, not a celebrant as she once was at her father's altar.[9] The chorus echo her image twenty lines further on, asking how she can approach the house with the acquiescence of a beast whom the god himself drives to the altar. She hesitates before entering and complains that the house reeks with the smell of blood (1309). The chorus answer that it is the smell of sacrifice, unaware that the sacrificial victim is their king.

When Clytemnestra describes the murder to the chorus, she draws another image from the sphere of ritual: the blood which spurts from the third blow is a drink-offering poured to Hades *nekrōn sōtēr* (lord of the dead 1385-87), a parody of the third libation offered to Zeus *sōtēr* ('Zeus the savior').[10] This image suggests another. The libation of blood falls upon Clytemnestra like a shower of spring rain and she, in turn, pours back over the corpse a funeral libation of curses, letting him drink from the cup which he himself has filled.

The libation image which she uses here for blood develops an idea introduced by her earlier irony. She invited Cassandra to enter and join the rite of *chernibes* within (1036-38). The ceremony mentioned is one of purification: wetting the hands and sprinkling lustral water.[11] Just as in 1385-87 the shedding of blood becomes a libation offered to the gods, so here the sprinkling of holy water suggests the bloodshed uppermost in Clytemnestra's mind.[12]

There is as well another connotation in the irony of Clytemnestra's *chernibes*: the sprinkling of water precedes the actual ceremony of sacrifice. Just as *chernibes* precede the slaughter of a sacrificial animal,

so the bath of Agamemnon ends with his death. One of the words
which Cassandra uses for the bath is *lebēs* (1129), a word frequent in
the *Odyssey*[13] for the basin that holds the purifying water.

In the final lyric, following Clytemnestra's description of the murder,
the chorus pick up her image of a blood libation and drink-offering of
curses, the cup drained by Agamemnon (1397-98). They ask what evil
drink inspired her to bring about this sacrifice and the people's curse
which will follow hard upon it.

> Woman, what evil
> food nurtured by the earth or what drink
> sprung from the flowing sea have you tasted,
> that you have put on yourself this murder, and incurred the
>   people's curses?   (1407-10)[14]

Clytemnestra then joins their metaphor of sacrifice to the actual sacrifice
of Iphigenia. They have no right to accuse her since they brought no
charge against the man who sacrificed his own child (1417). When the
chorus threaten that she must pay for her deed in kind (1429-30), she
swears an oath that she is without fear:

> I swear by the Justice accomplished for my child,
> and by Ruin and the Erinys, to whom I sacrificed this man. . . .
>   (1432-33)

This metaphor ['I sacrificed'] reflects a specific ritual: *sphazō*, as a
sacrificial term, refers to the act of cutting a victim's throat. Whenever
an important oath is sworn it is accompanied by a sacrificial offering;
the sacrifice itself is the *horkōmosion*, the victims are *horkia*.[15] Thus in
1432-33 Agamemnon is the victim sacrificed to seal that oath which
Clytemnestra swore in the name of Dike.

The Hunting Net

Just as the image of sacrifice links the murder of Agamemnon to the
sacrifice of Iphigenia, so that of the net and the hunt shows the causal
connection between his death and the capture of Troy.[16] These two
images originate in a concrete object and the manner of its use: the
robe thrown over Agamemnon by Clytemnestra before he is slain. This
imagery develops slowly in the course of the drama; its significance
does not become apparent until the audience are shown the real 'net'.[17]
Although there can be no certainty, it seems probable that the robe is a
traditional 'given' rather than an invention of Aeschylus. It is closely
connected with the active part played by Clytemnestra, a role assigned

her in Pindar's 11th *Pythian* as well as in the *Oresteia*. Thus it would seem that the two poets are following the same version of the myth.[18]

The image of the net appears for the first time in the anapestic introduction to the first stasimon (355-361).[19] These anapests are addressed to Night and Zeus, who worked together in accomplishing Troy's fall. The imagery here operates on two different levels. Within the immediate context the description of Night casting her netlike cover over the towers of Troy is an image for the onset of dark. Troy was captured during the night just past (264-265, 279) which enveloped it in darkness. This is the concrete circumstance to which the image is directly related. Within the context of the drama, the net belongs to a system of imagery by which Aeschylus unites the capture of Troy and the murder of Agamemnon so that they illustrate the gnome *pathein ton erxanta*. The address to Night and Zeus can be seen from two similar standpoints. Within the immediate context *nyx philia* (the dear night) is specifically the preceding night which brought to birth the dawn of capture (264-267). But within the context of the trilogy this partnership of Zeus and Night introduces a major theme. *Nyx philia* is more than the particular night on which Troy fell; she is also Night, mother of the Erinyes, as the close of the ode suggests.[20] The phrase *megalōn kosmōn kteateira* ('[Night] possessor of great glories' 356) yields two corresponding levels of meaning. The 'adornments' or 'honors' of Night suggest, primarily, the stars. But as the chorus go on to tell of her role in the capture of Troy, the *kosmōn* which she possesses (or acquires) imply both the honor of victory won with her aid and the great power of Night as a primal force, a force with which even Zeus must reckon. Zeus and Night work equally to bring about Troy's fall. Night casts a net (357); Zeus shoots an arrow (363). Thus there is implicit here that harmonious union established at the end of the trilogy when Zeus and Night's daughters, the Erinyes, are once more reconciled.[21]

The net image of the first stasimon raises another point concerning imagery in the *Oresteia*. It is sometimes an error to regularize these images so that they are exactly congruent with the specific act or object which provided a point of departure. Dumortier, for example, maintains, 'A true and precise description of the realities to which the poet alludes in his images is thrust upon us from the very beginning.'[22] Actually, one need know next to nothing about hunting techniques in fifth century Greece in order to analyze the net images of *Agamemnon*. It is, however, important to realize (and can be grasped from a quick look at *LSJ* as well as by reading the *Cynegetica* [Xenophon's treatise on hunting]) that these images are imprecise, their employment 'catachrestic'. They paint a picture drawn from fantasy, a blend of fishing and hunting which corresponds to no hunt in this world.

In 357-358 Night casts down over Troy an enveloping net, *steganon diktyon*. The chorus continue:

> so that none full grown
> nor any of the young could overleap
> slavery's mighty
> dragnet, of all-capturing destruction.   (358-361)

The image of the net reappears full-blown when Clytemnestra describes the murder (1372-83).[23] There is the same 'inconsistency' here as in the introduction to the first stasimon. In 1374-76 she surrounds Agamemnon with a hunting net too high for leaping over (cf. 358-359). In 1382-83 she says of the robe:

> A covering inextricable, like a net for fish,
> I threw around him, an evil wealth of raiment. . . .

A subsidiary motif accompanies the hunting image: that of the dog tracking down its prey. Again there is a parallel between Troy and the house of Atreus. For Agamemnon the net is a robe, Clytemnestra the dog who drives her game into the net. (She calls herself a faithful watchdog in 607 and Cassandra describes her as hateful bitch in 1228.) For Troy the net is night, the Greek huntsmen with a pack of hounds (*kynagoi*, 694); and in the omen which portends Troy's fall a hare is torn apart by winged hounds (136). The watchman awaits the fire signalling that fall *kynos dikēn* (dog-like; 3); as parallel to this Cassandra tracks the scent of bloodshed in the house of Atreus (1093) and knowledge flashes upon her like fire (1256).

In *Choephori* the robe-net is spread out on stage like the carpet in *Agamemnon* (*Cho.* 980-1000). Before the crime Electra tells how she was shut off by Clytemnestra like a savage dog (446); afterward Orestes sees the avengers of his mother as angry hounds (924 and 1054).

In *Eumenides* the Furies find that Orestes has leapt like a fawn through their net (111-112). Moreover, the previous canine metaphors were an anticipation fulfilled here when image becomes action: the Furies enter as a pack of hounds tracking their quarry by his bloody spoor.

The Robe, the Net, the Bond of Fate

At the end of *Choephori* a new metaphor is used to describe the robe with which Clytemnestra entrapped Agamemnon. Orestes calls it a bond (*desmon*, 981).[24] Then in *Eumenides*, immediately before the first stasimon, Orestes prays that Athena may come as deliverer to loose him:

> may she come — for she hears me even from afar, goddess that
>   she is —
> that she may grant me release from this my plight!   (297-298)

The Erinyes answer that neither Apollo nor Athena's strength can give protection. They nullify his prayer for a *lytērios* (releaser) with the *desmios hymnos*, their binding spell (306).

All earlier images of destiny and destruction as something that entangles man, an object hindering movement, curbing freedom, culminate in this spell with which the Furies bind Orestes. Behind the image is an idea, a concept of destiny found among many Indo-European peoples. Man's fate is a fabric spun of individual threads and allotted him at birth, his death a bond the gods bind round him.[25]

The hunting net, the yoke, the shackle, and the fetter comprise a major system of kindred imagery. Study of these images reveals a complex interrelation between the object or act for which the image stands, the image itself, and a universal symbol of mythopoeic value, that is, a symbol which gives insight into the nature of the world and man's place in it. The perfection of imagery in the *Oresteia* results in part from this: the particular act or object passes into image and image passes into universal symbol with a fluidity which blurs the moment of transition. The image itself stands halfway between the two, representing both, yet identical with neither, possessing an independent life with which its own concreteness has endowed it. Because of this tangibility, because of the insistence with which repetition thrusts it on the mind, the image becomes more real than that which suggested it.

First, the images of binding and entangling are based upon the physical mechanics by which Agamemnon's death is brought about. A whole complex of imagery is explored before the hearer becomes aware of the act and object which engendered it. The moment when he perceives the connection between the two, between the net imagery and Agamemnon's murder, is a high point in the drama. Proceeding from there one may realize that the carpet, the entangling robe, and all related images are themselves symbols of the interwoven strands of fate by which Agamemnon is held fast. The destiny which waits to net him in the bath was called up by the choice at Aulis when he fastened on necessity's yoke (218); it was confirmed when the night of capture fell on Troy and darkness took the city in a net of ruin which none escapes (360-361). And Agamemnon's own ruin becomes inevitable when he sets foot on rich woven garments (948-949) and finally falls with feet entangled in a garment's evil wealth (1382-83). Yet the image of the net, of things which trap and bind, the dramatization of this image in the carpet scene, are more than metaphors for the means used to murder Agamemnon. They are an image for the course of his whole life, his tragedy. Then, passing beyond that single life and death, they reach the realm of myth, turning his story into a symbol of the trap which is man's destiny.

The Telos *of Marriage and the* Telos *of Death*

Another system of imagery links the destiny of Troy with that of Agamemnon and, at the same time, establishes an implicit connection between the city's fall and the sacrifice of Iphigenia. Images drawn from the rite of marriage as well as that of sacrifice surround Agamemnon's death. The two overlap, insofar as sacrifice is a part of the wedding ceremony; however, the former is more closely linked with Iphigenia, the latter with Troy. Both Troy's fall and the murder of Agamemnon appear on the level of imagery as the consummation (*telos*) of a marriage ritual.

The ominous use of auspicious words which appears in all the tragedies of Aeschylus has special significance in the *Oresteia*. It reflects the movement of the trilogy from anxious rejoicing to despair, and from despair to joy freed of anxiety.[26] In *Agamemnon* those forces which should be beautiful, benevolent, and life-giving are converted into their opposites. Words of good omen and the images to which they give rise have an ominous undertone in the first play. Artemis the kindly and the fair (140) becomes hostile; Helen, flower of love which pricks the heart (743), becomes an Erinys causing brides to weep (749); the wife becomes the instrument of death (1116). In *Eumenides* the proper balance is restored: words of good omen regain their natural significance and all that was malevolent and destructive shows once more its gracious aspect. The Erinyes are first accused by Apollo of scorning the claims of love and covenant of wedlock:

> *Apollo*:   Indeed you dishonour and reduce to nothing
> the pledges of Hera the Fulfiller (*teleias*) and of Zeus,
> and the Cyprian is cast aside in dishonour by your plea,
> she from whom comes to mortals what they hold most dear.
>
> (213–216)

At the end they are persuaded by Athena to receive sacrifices which celebrate the marriage rite:

> As first fruits of this great land
> you shall have forever sacrifice in thanks for children
> and the accomplishment (*telous*) of marriage, and you shall
>   approve my words.   (834–836)

The motif of a disastrous wedding and the mode of its development in *Agamemnon* merit study in detail.

In the parodos *proteleia* appears twice: first in connection with the Trojan War (65–66), then with the sacrifice of Iphigenia (227). In each case a dissonance is involved. The customary significance of the word, its association with the marriage ceremony, clashes with the inauspicious meaning forced upon it by the context.[27] *Proteleia* are, in general, any preliminary sacrifice, specifically that which precedes the marriage rite. The latter signification is underlined by the phrase *proteleia naōn* (initiating sacrifice for ships) which, by similarity in sound, evokes the full title of the wedding ritual: *proteleia gamōn* (initiating sacrifice for marriage). And Artemis, to whom Iphigenia is offered up, is one of the divinities to whom such wedding sacrifices were made.[28] Each time the word occurs in *Agamemnon*, a reference to Helen is close beside it, strengthening the suggestion of a fatal wedding. She is mentioned in 62 and in 225–226. The third occurrence is in the lion parable (720), framed by a description of Helen.[29]

In the first stasimon Helen departs quickly, bringing a dowry of destruction to Ilium (406). Similarly, in the second stasimon, with a spear for her bridegroom, she vanishes with uncanny ease. The Wrath which sent Helen as Troy's bride and sorrow (*kēdos*) turns the wedding song to threnody (699–711). The city cries that Paris takes destruction to his bed (712–713). The image appears again in 720 and 745. As Troy's fall was the consummation of Helen's marriage, so there awaits Agamemnon at the hands of his own wife a *telos* for which the deaths at Troy and the slaying of Iphigenia and Thyestes' children were *proteleia*:

> Ah, ah, mad Helen,
> you who alone destroyed the many, the very many
> lives beneath Troy,
> now you have put on yourself the *last* (*telean*) the perfect garland,
> (1455–58)

> the ancient savage avenger
> of Atreus, the cruel banqueter,
> slew him in requital,
> sacrificing a grown man (*teleon*) after children.   (1501–04)

The 'net' in whose embrace he falls is the partner to his bed and to his murder (1116–17). Like Paris (713), he too might be called *ton ainolektron* (ill-bedded). Once again the fates of Troy and Agamemnon run parallel: for both ruin is the outcome of a disastrous marriage.

The association of death with marriage is facilitated by the various meanings associated with *telos* and its cognates. The word covers an area of meaning so vast as to be untranslatable. The philologist, faced with a term whose many meanings he cannot correlate, usually assumes derivation from several different words originally distinct. It is more cogent to assume the essential unity of such a word even if the philologist can find no logical connection between its meanings.[30] The concept of fulfillment, consummation, or completion might be the single primary significance which embraces all the rest.

Aeschylus uses *telos* in many ways, playing upon its various meanings.[31] Such word play is effected when meaning in the immediate context clashes with the thematic and more profound significance which the word acquires through constant repetition. Thus the meaning of major importance in the context of the trilogy is momentarily replaced by another sense in which the word can be understood. The one does not completely replace the other; rather the two are evoked simultaneously. The effect of this technique can be more easily appreciated in the case of *dikē*. Each time *dikē* appears in the accusative as a quasi-preposition, in the narrower sense 'plea', 'sentence', 'trial', or is suggested by phonetic similarity, it calls up the broader, more frequently repeated meaning which is a major theme of the trilogy.

In the case of *telos* the number of possible meanings is multiplied several times, making it more difficult to determine the thematic importance of the word.[32] This much is certain: the meaning of *telos* which is significant for the trilogy as a whole, that against which every secondary meaning plays, is a religious one.[33] It is difficult to be more precise. *Telos* denotes the fulfillment or consummation of one's destiny, the end of a process of becoming, the completion of a cycle.[34] Marriage is a *telos*, initiation into the mysteries is a *telos*, death is a *telos*.[35] All these associations are evoked each time the word occurs.

The second stasimon provides a good example of significant repetition over a small area. The entire lyric, which immediately precedes Agamemnon's entrance, is dominated by the idea of *telos* (700, 720, 745, 751-752), as is the prayer of Clytemnestra which follows his exit. In the second stasimon consummation of the marriage ritual shades into fulfillment and completion of Troy's destined end. The former is a metaphorical statement of the latter.

What awaits Agamemnon inside the palace is also conceived as a *telos* in every sense. It is the *telos* of a sacrifical ceremony, of marriage, of initiation into some mystery. And all these are images for the actual *telos*, that of death. The word occurs again and again in the scene between Agamemnon and Clytemnestra, climaxed by her final prayer to Zeus *teleios* (accomplisher; 973).[36] She calls the spreading of the carpet a *telos* (908); he agrees that to walk upon it is a *telos* (934). As he disappears within she prays:

While the root lives, it brings its foliage to the house,
giving protection from Sirius with shade; so your
coming is the arrival of summer warmth in winter
cold. So too when Zeus makes the unripe grape give wine,
within the house cool chases summer heat, provided
that the master fulfills his function (*teleiou*) in the
house. Zeus, giver of fulfillment (*teleie*), now
fulfill (*telei*) my prayers. Attend to that for which
you do intend fulfillment (*telein*).   (966-974)

The first comparison (968-969) is based on opposition to the original statement (966-967): from cooling shade as a protection against heat (967) to summer warmth as protection from winter cold (969). The second member of the comparison (970-71) reverses that which immediately preceded, returning to the original idea: pleasant cool in the midst of summer's heat. Lines 969-971, which range these two elements of comparison side by side, are framed by repetition of the same thought and construction: 968 matches 972. As leaves are the *telos* of the root, as wine is the *telos* of the grape, Agamemnon's death is the *telos* for which Clytemnestra prays.[37]

8

CLYTEMNESTRA
AND THE VOTE OF ATHENA

R. P. WINNINGTON-INGRAM

It will not be disputed that the relationship between the sexes was a subject of great interest to Aeschylus. The *Suppliants* turns on the question of marriage, willing or unwilling; and this is true, whether the Danaids were actuated by a passionate celibacy or by a horror of what they considered incest. The loss of the succeeding play renders the interpretation of the Danaid trilogy speculative. But in the *Oresteia*, Aeschylus returns to similar themes: marriage, wife and husband, the relative status of men and women. The last issue becomes explicit during the trial of Orestes, when Apollo proclaims the superiority of the male, and Athena endorses his judgement with her vote. This scene, if variously interpreted, has been recognised to be important. Equally it has been recognised that Clytemnestra, for whose murder Orestes was on trial, is herself depicted as an anomaly: a woman with the mind and counsel of a man.[1] The connexion between these two aspects of the trilogy deserves perhaps a further examination.

It is first necessary to consider the characterisation of Clytemnestra. Quite apart from the issues raised in the *Eumenides*, it is doubtful whether the accepted 'masculinity' of Clytemnestra has received attention commensurate with the stress which the poet has laid upon it, nor has it been fully considered in relation to the motives of her conduct. Some, indeed, will deprecate the psychological approach to an Aeschylean character.[2] But there are no *a priori* grounds on which we can decide up to what point the poet's interest in character developed, as develop it admittedly did. Clytemnestra is the test-case, and we must judge by what we find.

In any play — certainly a Greek play — the first references to a character are likely to be revealing. The Watchman in his opening soliloquy does not at first refer to Clytemnestra directly: he speaks (11) of 'a woman's heart of manly counsel' which has set him at his post. He is a

From *Journal of Hellenic Studies* 68 (1948), 130–47. Reprinted with revisions by permission of the author and the Society for the Promotion of Hellenic Studies.

servant in fear, and after this paradoxical phrase we know whom he fears. He is a servant in sorrow for his master's house, and hints at the adultery of his mistress (18 f.). When the beacon shines out, he calls to Clytemnestra, but we do not yet hear her name. It is Agamemnon's wife (26) whom he bids leap from her bed (which should be Agamemnon's bed) and raise the woman's cry of joy. But Agamemnon's wife has another consort; the woman has the mind of a man.

Clytemnestra is not addressed by name till 84, during the anapaests of the Chorus, when she makes a silent appearance to supervise the sacrifices.[3] She is addressed as daughter of Tyndareus, which immediately associates her with her sister Helen (62) for whom the Greeks and Trojans have fought a terrible war. As Helen was the bane first of Menelaus and then of Paris, so will Clytemnestra be of Agamemnon and later of Aegisthus. Disdaining to reply to the Chorus, she re-enters the palace, not to appear for 150 lines. The song of the Chorus is meantime concerned with the sacrifice of Iphigeneia, and we wonder what effect that sacrifice has had upon this woman of manly counsel. Iphigeneia, Aegisthus (hinted at only), the masculinity of Agamemnon's wife: the elements of the situation are now before us. It remains to see how they are combined.

The Chorus round off their ode with words intended for the ear of the approaching queen, when they call her 'the sole bulwark of the Apian land'. The chorus-leader speaks to her: 'I have come to pay homage, Clytemnestra, to your rule (258).' The word is *kratos* and (with *kratein*) is commonly used in the trilogy to denote authority, domestic or political. Indeed, to revert to the Watchman's speech, it is, in fact, from the verb *kratei* (10) that the audience derives its first impression of the queen.[4] 'I watch,' said the Watchman, 'for so rules a woman's hoping heart of manly counsel.' The words will be met again at salient points in the trilogy. Now Clytemnestra stands before us as a ruler, as sole ruler, but only in the absence of her husband. 'It is right,' says the chorus-leader, 'to honour the wife of a reigning prince, when the male throne is left empty' (259 f.).

The closing words of the chorus-leader, the opening words of the queen, have intricate associations. For instance, when the queen speaks of the night as of a mother that has given birth to the day (265, 279), it is to remind us of her own motherhood, of Iphigeneia, and of the theme of heredity which runs through the trilogy. The reference back to her masculinity is equally unmistakable. The leader suggests (262) that Clytemnestra's messengers of good may be merely hopes. This suggestion she rejects (266), and announces the capture of Troy. What then *is* the evidence (272)? A god. Is it a dream then (274)? Is it a rumour (276)? 'You make light indeed of my understanding, as though I were a young

girl.' Clytemnestra does not forget these accusations which impute to
her the psychology, not only of a child, but of a woman, given to
irrational hopes and, where her emotions are involved, easily convinced.
When, in two brilliant speeches, her imagination has ranged over land
and sea and over the scenes of siege and capture, 'Here,' she says, 'you
have my woman's words (348).' No wonder the chorus-leader makes
amends: 'Lady, you speak like a wise man' (351). It is a compliment
which she has virtually demanded. On this note the scene ends, as it
began.

The Chorus sing their first *stasimon*. What begins as 'an exultant
hymn for triumph over Troy' ends in 'apprehension for the conqueror.'[5]
It is almost with relief that they remember the news may not be true
and return to their former allegations.[6] Good tidings have been brought
by fire (475). But are they true? To trust such a message is childish (*cf.*
277), witless (contr. 351). To believe too readily is just like a woman
(483, 485, 487). Better evidence, however, than the beacons is now at
hand in Agamemnon's herald. Him they cannot disbelieve. But Clytemnestra herself has no need of a herald, except to carry a message to her
husband; and in this message are reiterated the words — man, woman,
husband, wife.[7] With irony and with a brazenness that deceives none of
her listeners, she maintains the role of the conventional wife, the home-
keeper, the watch-dog. When she speaks of the faithful wife who has
never tampered with any seal, we think of Aegisthus. She is as innocent of joys from another man as . . . of the tempering of bronze: and
we are reminded that this is no ordinary woman, subject to feminine
weakness.

From this message we may pass rapidly to her greeting of Agamemnon.[8] The Chorus try to warn him on his entrance (808 f.), but he does
not understand. He is proud, self-conscious, and sententious. His mind
is on war and politics (matters outside a woman's sphere), concerning
which he will 'take counsel'. He turns to enter his palace with the prayer
that Victory, which has attended him, may remain still constant. On
the word *nikē* Clytemnestra enters. The speech she now makes, her
longest in the play, is of outstanding importance. In it all the elements
of her character and situation are combined.

To Iphigeneia she does not refer openly, but when she speaks of a
child who should have been present (877 ff.), Iphigeneia, as well as
Orestes, is in her mind.[9] The references to Aegisthus are clear and ex-
tensive, as Headlam has shown.[10] But when Clytemnestra speaks of 'the
fearful hardship for a woman without man to sit solitary at home' (861
f.), issues are raised which transcend adultery and go back to the man-
woman of the Prologue. To the sister of Helen physical celibacy may

not have been congenial: but this is unimportant. That Clytemnestra had been literally, 'without man' is an ironical lie; but that is not all. Where this woman had sat solitary during her husband's absence was upon his throne, as the Chorus pointed out on her first speaking entrance;[11] and this to her was not 'hardship'. Now the royal man returns, and the glories of his state are described by Clytemnestra herself with fulsome rhetoric (896 ff.). The whole passage is dominated, like Clytemnestra's address to the Herald, by the theme of the relationship between man and woman.

The thesis of this article — and it is supported by the continual emphasis which the dramatist places upon the sexual antithesis and upon the anomalous personality of Clytemnestra — is that she hated Agamemnon, not simply because he had killed her child, not because she loved Aegisthus, but out of a jealousy that was not jealousy of Chryseis or Cassandra, but of Agamemnon himself and his status as a man. For she herself is of manly temper, and the dominance of a man is abhorrent to her. Thus, when she kills her husband, it is not only an act of vengeance, but also a blow struck for her personal liberty.[12] The same motive explains her choice of Aegisthus. Agamemnon, for all his weakness at Aulis and in the scene which follows, was a lion of the Pelopid house, a great warrior and conqueror. Aegisthus is seen in the vision of Cassandra as a lion indeed (a Pelopid), but a cowardly lion, and later as a wolf mating with this human lioness in the absence of the noble lion (1224, 1259). He was 'keeping the home' (1626) while the Greeks were at Troy. This was the woman's part. Aegisthus is addressed as a woman by the Chorus at the end of the play (1625),[13] and Orestes in the *Choephori* implies the same charge (304). This woman-man was chosen by the man-woman to be her mate. The return of her husband is a threat. Yet so great is she that she does not fear his return, but rather longs passionately for it, because it will give her the opportunity of avenging herself and of demonstrating her superiority. It is in the light of this situation that the next scene must be considered — the scene in which Clytemnestra induces Agamemnon to enter the palace treading on scarlet draperies.

Why is she at such pains that he should make his entrance so? Is it merely that the act is *epiphthonon* (envy-provoking), and that by putting him in the wrong before the gods she will facilitate her triumph? The symbolism of the act is unmistakable:[14] but was this her only motive? Again, why does Agamemnon give way so easily? Because he is a doomed sinner blinded by Ate? Some critics[15] have objected to the psychological interpretation of this scene, and yet both Clytemnestra's desire and Agamemnon's compliance have a psychological explanation.

It is suggested above that, in the last analysis, Clytemnestra killed her husband because he was a man and in order to avenge herself upon his male supremacy. But to kill him was only half of her victory. First she must prove herself the stronger. Her physical victory is won, necessarily, by craft; the spiritual contest is on equal terms, and in it Agamemnon will be compelled, as his own words reveal,[16] to play the woman's part.

'Pamper me not so,' he says, 'as though I were a woman; nor adore me as though I were a barbarian, with loud open-mouthed prostrations' (918 ff.). The protests are complementary and significant. Just as the conqueror of Priam is to be reduced to barbarism, so the cuckold of Aegisthus is to be reduced to effeminacy. If, then, he was so closely aware of the implications of his act, is it not unnatural that he should comply so readily? It is not unnatural, because his desire to tread those scarlet draperies is stronger than he knows, because he feels in his heart of hearts that such honour is no more than due to the conqueror of Troy.[17] Out come the copy-book maxims.[18] But they are too many; he protests too much; and, though he ends his speech with a refusal, the signs of weakness are evident. For the keynotes of his character are vanity and ambition. Ambition led him to sacrifice Iphigeneia at Aulis in order that he might become a sacker of cities. Now vanity tells him what is the fitting reward for the conqueror.

Clytemnestra turns from rhetoric to argument.[19] The brief dialogue which follows is the crisis of the play. It is a contest between two wills, in which the woman plays upon the weakness of the man, putting forward argument after argument which he ought to reject in terms but does not. The closing lines are particularly revealing (940 ff.). 'It is not for a woman to thirst for battle,' underlines the reversal of the normal roles. Clytemnestra's reply is itself based upon a conventional conception of the relation of man to woman, and so is irresistible to Agamemnon, who condescends to her: 'Do you too desire a victory in strife?' 'Be persuaded (*pithou*),' she replies, 'you are still the master (*krateis*) if you make a voluntary concession to me.' Every word is significant. *pithou*: and to be easily persuaded is the mark of the woman. *krateis*: yet the mastery at this very moment passes from him. *hekon* (willingly): for unless this is so, half the sweetness of her victory is lost. At 944 the victory is won.

After the victory of *peithō* (persuasion), the victory of *bia* (force). But this is delayed by the master-stroke of the Cassandra scene, which serves manifold purposes, most of them irrelevant to the present investigation. One aspect, however, is relevant, for Cassandra also has her place in what may be termed the sexual pattern of the play. The last words of Agamemnon proclaim his own subjection (956). A few lines earlier, commending his concubine to the queeen, he had said: 'No one submits willingly to the yoke of slavery (953).' Yet this is a precise description of his own behaviour and condition. Thus at the outset a point of comparison is established between Cassandra and Agamemnon in respect of bonds and freedom. The scene in which Clytemnestra bids her come down from the chariot and enter the palace is parallel to the scene between husband and wife which has just been examined. As an ingredient of her triumph, Clytemnestra means to kill Cassandra, as she means to kill Agamemnon; but in this instance also she wills to win a victory of persuasion, even where she could command (1052). But Cassandra makes no move and the queen admits defeat (1055, 1068). This slave has not yet learnt, like Agamemnon, to bear the yoke (1066). Her enslavement is of the body only.[20] When she has finished her prophesying, she faces her fate, recoils from it, but goes to meet it bravely, entering the palace a free soul.[21] Thus the slave proves herself superior to the conqueror, the barbarian to the Greek, the woman to the man.

After the murder of Agamemnon, the play falls into three parts: the speeches in which Clytemnestra justifies herself to the Chorus, the Kommos in which her anapaests alternate with their lyrical laments, and the Aegisthus scene. It is during the first two of these only, out of the whole play, that she can discard ironical pretence and stand revealed in her true colours. She exults, to the amazement of the Chorus. She claims that the deed of her hand was just; and then in two speeches she advances her justification.

The theme of the first speech is Iphigeneia. The Chorus wish to proceed against Clytemnestra for the murder of her husband. But what opposition did they make when Agamemnon sacrificed his own daughter — her daughter — at Aulis 'to charm the winds from Thrace'? The point is unanswerable, and is not answered by the Chorus. 'Great are your designs' is their comment, for at the end of her speech the queen had spoken not as mother, but as competitor for power who has gained one victory of force and is prepared to gain another.

Her second speech is more complex. From Iphigeneia it moves to Aegisthus; from Aegisthus to the infidelities of Agamemnon, to Chryseis and Cassandra. The sequence of thought is subtle and will, it is to be hoped, continue to defy the transpositions of editors. Clytemnestra swears 'by Justice fully taken for my child, by Ate and Erinys', that she has no fear — 'so long as Aegisthus lights fire upon my hearth.' Thus the ground of her confidence is not only Justice, not only Iphigeneia, but Aegisthus. Now, as we have seen, the significance of Aegisthus lies in his function as a substitute for Agamemnon. As a person he is effeminate and she can dominate him; but as a male he can command force and so is a necessary tool for her masculine will. The mention of Aegisthus leads Clytemnestra to accuse Agamemnon of sexual infidelity.

Is this simply a parry to the similar charge which has been brought, and will continue to be brought against her? If so, the charges cancel out,[22] and the amours of Agamemnon are not valid to justify Clytemnestra. Yet she reverts to this theme again in the *Choephori* (918). Was sexual jealousy then among her motives? But if Clytemnestra was jealous, she was jealous primarily of Agamemnon himself, who went to Troy and came back a conqueror, while she, knowing herself to be the stronger personality, was left to keep the home. If she was jealous of the Chryseids and Cassandra, perhaps it was not simply that they had shared his bed, but that Chryseis had shared his hut beneath the walls of Troy (1439), and Cassandra his life on board the ship (1442 f.).[23] But the significance of the charge is still not exhausted, for there is a link of primary importance between the first speech dealing with Iphigeneia and the second speech dealing with sexual infidelity.

Agamemnon died justly, because he had killed Iphigeneia; Agamemnon's death was 'not undeserved' (1443), because he had insulted Clytemnestra in her status as a wife (1438). To the latter charge, when it is repeated in the *Choephori*, Orestes replies by quoting, in effect, a 'double standard' of morality (*Cho.* 919), which is a symbol of that inferiority against which Clytemnestra chafed. No less, however, did the act of Agamemnon in sacrificing his daughter strike at the relationship of husband and wife and emphasise the inferior status of the wife. In considering the dramatic function of Iphigeneia, we need not over-simplify or suppose that, if Clytemnestra's deed was an act of self-liberation, vengeance for her daughter was a mere pretext. Doubtless she had loved her daughter; doubtless that love had turned into a hatred of her husband.[24] It is not merely, however, that two separate motives had combined to make her kill her husband. For the motives are inextricably connected. Clytemnestra describes her daughter as 'the dearest fruit of my labor-pains' (1417); later as a shoot or branch (1525). The terms insist upon the intimate physical connexion between mother and child.[25] In each case the phrase is completed by words expressive of the father's share in the child. 'His own child, my dearest birth-pang' (1417 f.). 'My branch raised up by him' (1525). It has already been noted that when, in her first speech to Agamemnon, Clytemnestra referred to the absent Orestes, she did so in terms which could apply to Iphigeneia. 'Wherefore there stands not by our side, as should have stood, the child, the ratification of my faith and yours. . . . ' Such was the value that Agamemnon placed upon the pledge of their mutual love, claiming full rights of disposal in a child that was hers no less than his. Thus both the offences of which

Clytemnestra accuses her husband are sins against marriage and strike at the status of the woman in marriage.[26]

On neither score can a defence be made by the Chorus for all their loyalty to the dead. They pray for death themselves. This is not the place for a full analysis of the ensuing Kommos, in which the traditional form of lamentation is complicated by a divergence of sympathy between the participants, by argument and counter-argument, and by reference to the deepest philosophical issues of the trilogy. The Chorus apostrophise the *daimon* 'that falls upon the house'; and, with the mention of the *daimon*, Clytemnestra, who had exultantly claimed full responsibility (1406), now changes her ground.

She sees herself, or would have the Chorus see her, not as the wife of Agamemnon, but as the embodiment of an ancestral curse (1497 ff.). The instrument of the curse indeed she is, but personal responsibility Aeschylus will not allow her to disclaim (1505 ff.); the less so perhaps that she is actuated by motives extraneous to the bloody history of the house of Atreus.[27] It is at this point that she returns (1521 ff.) to the theme of Iphigeneia, with that phrase which links her and Agamemnon as parents of the murdered child, and thus relates her vengeance as a mother to her status as a wife. Yet again she returns (1555 ff.) to Iphigeneia, and it is the climax of bitterness when she tells how the daughter will meet her father at the rapid Ford of Sorrows, will fling her arms about his neck and kiss him. Yet when she has played this her strongest card, she reverts to the Daimon. For she knows, without the Chorus's ominous suggestions of further bloodshed, that the matter is not ended by appeal to the memory of Iphigeneia; that she cannot claim to be the embodiment of the Daimon and deny its implications. It is a change of mood indeed when she tries to strike a bargain with the ancestral curse and so rid the palace of 'the madness of mutual slaughter' (1567 ff.). But such compromise is futile; and Aegisthus is a symbol of its futility.

The entry of Aegisthus is an effective piece of bathos. The stage, which has held only Clytemnestra and her victims, now fills with soldiers. The queen stands silent while Aegisthus, who has had no share in the emotional tension of the preceding scene, makes a forensic speech.[28] A crude character, he prides himself on his cunning, his worldly wisdom, his clear-sightedness (1623).[29] He advances the male interpretation of the death of Agamemnon, in terms of fathers, sons and brothers, and of the competition for power. For this death he takes full credit to himself, claiming the male prerogative of planning and decision; he claims full authority in the state (1638 ff.). But which is the ruler? Which is the man? The Chorus-leader calls him the woman and taunts him with his home-keeping (1625 ff.);[30] and the audience will draw the correct conclusion. Yet this is the person that Clytemnestra has hailed as her shield of confidence (1437). For it is part of her predicament that she cannot dispense with the formal protection of a man and of the armed force which a man alone can command. Between the death of Agamemnon and the entry of Aegisthus Clytemnestra spoke without pose or dissimulation. Now she enters upon her new role, the consort of Aegisthus as formerly of Agamemnon. She listens with contempt to the altercations of the men; and when these threaten to lead to bloodshed, she intervenes with good counsel, but closes with her old irony: 'Such is a woman's word, if it is worth hearing' (1661). The quarrel continues to reverberate until she ends it and the play with two significant lines. 'Pay no regard to these idle yelpings; I and thou, as masters of this house, will make good order' (1672 f.). Mastery in the dual number (*kratounte*); but the first person singular (*egō*), from word-order and rhythm, receives great emphasis. It is Clytemnestra who will, in fact, be master, and it was for this mastery that she killed her husband.

kratei (10) was the first indication of the character of Clytemnestra; *kratos* (258) greeted her first speaking appearance; the ironical *krateis* (943) marked the climax of her struggle with Agamemnon; and with *kratounte* (1673) the first play ended. The *Choephori* opens with *kratē* — with Orestes appealing to Hermes Chthonius: 'who watchest over my father's sovereignty.' For the son has now returned to claim his birthright and to retrieve the defeat, the loss of mastery, which his father had suffered. Here, as elsewhere in this play, the reference is primarily political; but, since Orestes is to renew with Clytemnestra the duel between man and woman, it is personal also. It is both personal and political, for she is now the real master of house and state, whose harsh government is revealed by the Chorus of female slaves who enter with Electra — servants in fear, as the Watchman of the *Agamemnon* was a servant in fear. If Clytemnestra does not dominate the second play as she dominated the first, her near presence is always felt; and, though her part is short, the scenes where she confronts her son are the peaks of dramatic interest in the play.

The immediate preparation for entry is a striking theatrical effect. For Orestes, in his role of Phocian messenger, bids the servant summon one in authority, a woman — or better a man . . . 'man speaks to man with confidence and makes plain his evidence' (663 ff.). It is Clytemnestra who enters. What does she say? She behaves with formal propriety as the lady of a house. She offers the hospitable services for which a woman is responsible — the bath and the bed; 'but if anything needs be done requiring counsel, that is the work of men,' to whom she will communicate it. But 'counsel' and 'men' in juxtaposition must recall the *androboulon kear* ('man-counselling heart') of Clytemnestra; and there is significance even in the hospitality she offers. For, using the functions of a woman to carry out her manly counsel, she had killed her husband in a bath.[31] She dissimulates, as in the *Agamemnon*; but when, after the false news, which she receives with coldness and reserve,[32] she rounds off the scene by saying that she will communicate these things to the masters of the house and will take counsel, we know who is the master and who the counsellor.

The expected catastrophe is postponed, as in the *Agamemnon* by the Cassandra scene, so here by the entry of Orestes' Nurse. This simple soul takes us back to the past, and in so doing illuminates the immediate future. Soon mother and son will face one another, and she will plead with him by her motherhood. So the poet reminds us of the infancy of Clytemnestra's child. At the same time, he makes the Nurse, and not Clytemnestra, display a mother's affection and a mother's grief.[33] He achieves two purposes which may conflict upon the level of prosaic logic, but combine poetically to enhance the scene between unnatural mother and unnatural child; and it is to this scene that the Chorus now look forward (827 ff.), when Clytemnestra will cry *teknon* ('child') and Orestes will harden his heart.

The reference to Clytemnestra prepares the entry of Aegisthus, as hers was prepared by expectation of him. He cannot enter the trilogy without bathos, and his very inferiority is a commentary upon her predicament. Hypocritical, pompous, and with a good conceit that he cannot be imposed upon, he is now to be the vehicle of subtle irony. For, like the Elders in the *Agamemnon*, he doubts that the news is true; and he uses the same metaphor of fire to express his doubt (845 f.). Thus for the last time Clytemnestra is accused – and by one who should have known better – of a woman's weak credulity. Yet this time the accusation is justified. For Clytemnestra no longer controls the situation. She is numbered among the deaf and the sleepers (881); she asks, not answers, questions (885). Nevertheless, it is the circumstances that have changed, not the fibre of the woman. This is clear in the contest which follows.

The death-cry of Aegisthus is heard, and the Chorus-leader says that the issue of the battle is now decided (874). But this is not true: the real battle has not yet begun – the contest between mother and son which resumes the contest between husband and wife and which, like that earlier battle, is fought with the twin weapons of *peithō* and of *bia*. 'The dead the living slay,' cries the Servant to Clytemnestra (886); and she reads the silly riddle with characteristic speed. 'By craft we shall perish as we slew.' She demands a 'man-slaying axe',[34] to decide the issue of victory or defeat. It is her instinct to do battle as a man. She does not realise that Aegisthus is dead; the words of the Servant did not imply it. But the sight of Orestes and Pylades with drawn swords reveals to her the true situation and her own ignominious weakness. The 'might' of Aegisthus (her 'shield' of the *Agamemnon*) has perished;[35] for a woman force, unprepared by cunning, was futile, and on this occasion the cunning had been used against her. The weapon of persuasion remains. With a swift efficiency she turns to wheedle her son as she had wheedled her husband; and the scene which follows is parallel to the scene in which she persuaded Agamemnon to tread the scarlet draperies. At the word *teknon*, at the sight of the breast, Orestes hesitates. Will Clytemnestra win yet another victory? But Apollo speaks, with the voice of Pylades. 'I count thee victor (903),' replies Orestes; for the victory in the contest belongs neither to the son nor to the mother, but to the god of Delphi.

Clytemnestra, however, does not easily accept defeat; and in the following thrust and parry we are taken back to the fundamental issues. For Orestes now threatens her life, as Agamemnon had threatened her liberty. To Orestes, indeed (as to the Choruses in both plays), the explanation of her conduct lies in her passion for Aegisthus (894 f.), whom she had preferred to Agamemnon in life, with whom she must sleep in death (904 ff.). Clytemnestra replies with an appeal which misses the reality by an equal margin: 'I nursed you and would grow old beside you' (908). Not only is this appeal already somewhat prejudiced by the Nurse's speech: it is inherently absurd, for Clytemnestra no more needs a son in her old age than she needed a husband in her prime; and the reply of Orestes means more than he knows: 'Could you who killed my father live with me?' The dialogue as it proceeds is packed with meanings that do not relate to our present theme. But, when Orestes charges his mother with selling him into slavery, the climax is approaching. 'Where, she asks, 'is the price which I received in exchange (916)?' It is a price which Orestes is ashamed to put into words. To such a simple charge, she makes a simple reply; she advances, as she had advanced in the *Agamemnon*, the infidelities of her husband. The lines which follow are the very core and centre of the dialogue.[36]

'Do not criticise him who works, you who sit within.' 'It is grief for women to be parted from their man, my child.' 'Yes, but the man's work supports them while they sit within' (919–21). The two lines spoken by Orestes are straightforward statements of male superiority. The husband supports the wife with his labour, with his valour, and in return demands that he be free from her criticism. 'Sitting within' (919) is reiterated and re-emphasised by 921. For this was Clytemnestra's situation, while Agamemnon was at Troy; and her own intervening comment carries us back to the entry of Agamemnon and her speech of greeting (*Agam.* 861 ff.). Then, when she deprecated solitude, it was an ironical lie, which yet hinted at the crude assumptions of Orestes. Yet, in reducing her to the level of her paramour, it is such an over-simplification of the relationship between man and woman as the rest of the trilogy repudiates. It is corrected by that twofold reference to the woman who sits at home, which implies the collision of the powers and gifts of Clytemnestra with the conditions of her life as a woman.[37] The price which she received for the murder of her husband and for the banishment of her son was indeed Aegisthus, whose outward protection it was part of her humiliation to need, but whose weak character allowed her to continue the male role. Her predicament and its sorry solution lead as directly to the matricide (922) as the husbandhood of Agamemnon led to his murder (*Agam.* 1405).

Clytemnestra has a speaking part in the *Eumenides* also, but the short scene in which her ghost upbraids the sleeping Furies tells us little about Clytemnestra living. The woman who in the *Agamemnon* despised the 'plausible visions of a dream' (*Agam.* 274 f.), but in the *Choephori* allowed her action to be governed by a dream (*Cho.* 32 ff.), is now herself a dream in the minds of her avengers (116). This is in itself a symbol of that decline in psychological interest which the broad design of the trilogy imposed upon the dramatist. In the *Eumenides*, the divine powers and the general issues hold the stage; and it is through the utterances of gods that the special case of Clytemnestra is set against a wider background. But amid the debates of the gods we shall do well to remember the woman of the earlier plays.

These debates turn largely upon the relative status of man and woman. The Furies are the champions of Clytemnestra — of Clytemnestra as mother. But Apollo, in defending Orestes, speaks for Agamemnon, not only as a husband, but as man (625 ff.); he disparages the motherhood of Clytemnestra, denying the right of the female to be regarded, in the full sense, as parent of the child (658 ff.). Athena casts her vote for Orestes frankly on grounds of preference for the male (737). But these pronouncements come at the end of a long process of argument, which must now be examined.

The scene between Apollo and the Furies at Delphi (179–234) is a kind of preliminary, in the absence of the defendant, to the later trial before the Areopagus. It serves to present in a vivid form the direct clash, in interest and point of view, between the two parties. 'Your oracle bade that he should kill his mother.' 'My oracle bade that he should bring vengeance for his father' (202 f.). To the Furies it seems

inconsistent — and perhaps it is — that the god who accepts the polluted
man should hurl abuse at his 'escort' (206). There may, in fact, be more
in common between the two parties than either could willingly admit.
'We drive matricides from their homes.' 'When a woman kills her husband,
what then?' (210 f.). The answer, as Apollo knows, is that, according to
his own code, the son must avenge the father or suffer persecution by
Furies. But it is a good point to make against his opponents. When they
reply that in such a case no kindred blood is shed (212), the narrowness
of their interests is revealed; and Apollo retorts effectively that they
dishonour the institution of marriage, pledged by Zeus and Hera — they
dishonour Cypris and the love of man and woman (213 ff.). This solemn
reference to marriage is clearly of the first importance, and, whether
Apollo is fully entitled to his argument or not, he gets on the whole the
better of the first exchange, despite the arrogant violence of his partisanship. But this is only a preliminary contest. We must now pass to the
trial itself.

The entry of Apollo to witness and to plead, is dramatic,[38] but his
wrangle with the Furies is not immediately resumed. Instead, the Furies
address to Orestes questions which are intended to elicit facts, but which
soon lead to controversy. The rival claims of the dead are starkly juxtaposed (598 f.). Orestes bases his case upon the crimes of his mother,
who had killed a man, a husband and a father. He asks, as Apollo had in
effect asked (211), why the Furies did not pursue Clytemnestra when
she was alive (604), and he receives the same answer: 'She was no kin of
the man she slew.' We are back to the issue of the earlier scene. But,
where Apollo's rejoinder had referred to the institution of marriage,
Orestes asks, bitterly, whether he was, in fact, of his mother's blood
(606). 'A false step,' observes Professor Thomson; and so it is, for Orestes
bases his reply on the weakness, not (like Apollo) on the strength of his
case. Yet it is in this kinship of blood that the horror of matricide
resides. 'How then,' say the Furies, 'did she nurture thee beneath her
girdle? Dost thou abjure thy mother's blood?'[39] They appeal to the
apparent fact and to the universal sentiment of mankind; and at this
point the reaction of the audience is bound to be sympathetic. The
position is beyond Orestes, who invokes the aid of Apollo. The god will
return to the question of kinship between mother and son, but his
earlier arguments also must be carefully examined.

Apollo makes four speeches, in the first of which he seeks to dispose
of the matter on the basis of authority. He is the prophet who never lies
(615);[40] he is the mouthpiece of Zeus. But not only are 'appeals to
authority useless when there is a conflict of authority':[41] this appeal is
subtly prejudiced for an Athenian audience: 'Never yet,' says Apollo,

'have I spoken on my throne of prophecy, concerning man, woman, or city, what was not ordered by Zeus, father of the Olympians' (616 ff.). 'Concerning the city': from the god who medised [i.e. went over to the Medes — ed.].[42] And if he could be wrong about politics, he is not necessarily right about man and woman. The appeal was to Zeus, but for Aeschylus the will of Zeus is something to be anxiously explored, not accepted upon the authority of an Apollo. Did Zeus say: 'Avenge a father's death and pay no honour to a mother?' This is the reply of the Furies (622-4), and Apollo must now argue the point.

His argument is a simple one. The death of a man is different (625) — different, that is, from the death of a woman. This particular man is qualified as noble and as a king, by divine right. His death is rendered the more shocking by the fact that a woman killed him, not in open fight, but by treachery: the method is described in detail. The speech must be read in the light of earlier plays. Craft (which it is perhaps not for Apollo to disparage)[43] was imposed upon Clytemnestra, since in the circumstances of her life it was impossible for her to fight as an Amazon (or as a goddess). Yet with the weapons at her command she fought, and reversed the roles, so that Agamemnon became the woman, she the man. We cannot judge Apollo's argument out of all relation to the portraits of man and woman in the *Agamemnon*, and Aeschylus has ensured that we shall not do so in two ways: by reference to the general-ship of Agamemnon (631 f.), and by reference to the manner of his death. Agamemnon was killed on his return 'from warfare, where he had, for the most part, won success'. There had, as Headlam says, been 'unfortunate incidents'.[44] Then why refer to them? In order to remind the audience of Iphigeneia, of Clytemnestra's justification (such as it was), of Agamemnon's weakness at Aulis — and at Argos. For when Apollo speaks of the robe, the embroidered garment with which Clytem-nestra fettered her husband (635), we are meant to think not only of the material, but of the spiritual entanglement; not only of the robe, but of the carpet (*Agam.* 923), by means of which she had subjected his will to hers and forced him to accept the feminine role.[45] There is thus a certain irony in justifying the matricide on the grounds that Clytem-nestra the woman had killed Agamemnon the man.

Apollo's argument does not impress the Furies. They return to Zeus. Does Zeus, who bound his father Cronus, give greater honour to a father's fate (640 ff.)? A debating-point which causes Apollo to lose his temper.[46] By making the obvious retort that bonds are not to be compared with death, which is irrevocable,[47] he plays into the hands of his opponents. For, as they are quick to remark, this is the very charge against Orestes — that he had shed a 'mother's kindred blood'. Thus Apollo is forced

back to the very point at which Orestes had handed over his defence
(606). Unless he can dispose of it, the matricide stands condemned.

Apollo puts forward (658 ff.) the famous physiological argument,
which has been so much discussed. The mother, while she has the function
of nourishing the child in the womb, is not the true parent or progenitor,
but a stranger who gives safe keeping to another's plant. The purpose of
this argument is to defend matricide from the charge that it violates the
relation of kinship, and the god has been driven to the position at which
it is the only argument which can do so. Such a doctrine, perhaps already
known in Athens,[48] might be welcomed in a masculine society as a
counterpoise to the manifest uncertainty of fatherhood. For, if one
thing is sure, it is that the mother carries and bears the child, and the
intimacy of this relationship is confirmed by instinct and emotion. When
Orestes first questioned the tie of blood between himself and Clytemnestra, the audience was bound to share in the indignation of the Furies.
Did Aeschylus intend that they should now accept, upon the authority
of Apollo (already damaged), a physiological theory which deprived the
mother of real kinship with her child?

Aeschylus was a poet, not a physiologist. On the physiological theory,
as such, the poet passes no judgement, but the inference which depreciates
the relationship of mother and child he cannot accept without undermining one of the bases of tragic emotion in his trilogy. Not only does
the dramatic tension of the *Choephori* derive from this relationship,[49]
but in the *Agamemnon* also interest is focused upon the relationship of
Clytemnestra to her daughter Iphigeneia and upon the violation of a
mother's rights. Yet, if she is not fully the parent of Orestes, she is not
fully the parent of Iphigeneia either. This is the kind of point on which
we should expect Aeschylus to give verbal guidance to his audience; and
he does so. The word *ernos* (plant, shoot), which occurs twice in this
speech (661, 666), had been used by Clytemnestra of Iphigeneia in a
striking passage.[50] But that is not all. The mother, says Apollo, 'like a
stranger keeps safe the plant (*ernos*) — provided a god blast it not (661).'
Why make this qualification?[51] To remind us of the pregnant hare of
the *Agamemnon* and her offspring (*Agam.* 120), of the offence against
motherhood which called down the wrath of Artemis and led to the
sacrifice of Iphigeneia. For the hare was both the symbol and the cause
of Iphigeneia's death.[52]

With this argument, so deadly to the tragedy and yet the only argument which can represent the matricide as a blameless act, Apollo's
bolts are all shot (676).[53] The Furies are equally ready for the verdict to
be pronounced. If the audience at this stage makes its own summing-up,
it may feel that the balance has been held steady between Apollo and

the Furies. Both parties have been shown to disparage an intimate human relationship. If the weakness of the Furies in disregarding the marriage-tie is obvious, the attempt of Apollo to brush aside the tie of blood between mother and child in the superior interest of the male has been subtly criticised, his consistency and his authority impugned. When the votes of the human jurors are counted, they are found to be equal; and this verdict not only corresponds to the balance of argument, but is a sign that Orestes was confronted with an intolerable dilemma, being subjected to contradictory claims *both* based upon the blood-tie and backed by the law of the vendetta. It has been well said that 'Aeschylus was not interested in the solution of an insoluble conundrum'.[54] What Orestes did was terrible: what else, in the social circumstances, Orestes could have done, it is not the purpose of the dramatist to show; his eyes are on the future. But the matricide is acquitted, and the acquittal is brought about by the 'vote' of Athena, given for a specific reason. Apollo is so treated in the trilogy that we can to a considerable extent discount his *ex cathedra* pronouncements. Athena, with her dignity and courtesy, is far more impressive; as the protectress of the men of Athens and foundress of the Areopagus she carries more weight.

The reason which she gives for her support of Orestes is already hinted at in the closing speech of Apollo, who quotes her as evidence in favour of his theory of parentage (662 ff.). For Athena, daughter of Olympian Zeus, was not nurtured in the darkness of the womb (665). As evidence, the analogy has little weight, for all human beings are so nurtured, nor can Apollo's physiology abolish this physical fact (659). But if his case is not strengthened thereby, the audience is prepared for the partisanship of the goddess. When the time comes, Athena could not give her reason more explicitly. She votes,[55] not out of pity, not out of respect for the suppliant, not in order to gain advantage for her city, but on these grounds. 'No mother bore me. The male I commend in all things — except for marriage — with all my heart, and am strongly on the father's side. Thus I will not pay more regard to the death of a woman who killed a man, the master of a house.' This is the climax of the man-woman theme. 'Zeus,' said the Furies to Apollo (640) 'pays more regard to a father's fate, by your account'; and Apollo's view is now ratified by Athena. How is this to be explained? We may fall into error if we attempt to answer this question without reference to Clytemnestra.

For there is a sense in which Athena is the counterpart of Clytemnestra and serves as the poet's final comment upon her character and motives. When Orestes reached Athens, he prayed to Athena, wherever she might be, whether in Libya or 'whether, like a bold captain (296), she surveys the plain of Phlegra'. For Athena fights like a man. In fact, she was neither in Libya nor at Phlegra, but in the Troad, as she tells in her first words (397 ff.), taking possession of the land which the leaders and princes of the Achaeans had given her as the prize of war. For she had fought at Troy; and Orestes (454 ff.) can refer to her comradeship-in-arms with Agamemnon. Athena fought at Troy; Clytemnestra, left to keep the home, hated the very Chryseis who had shared Agamemnon's hut and the Cassandra who had sailed with him on his homeward voyage. When he returned, she could not kill him in fair fight ('like an Amazon, with far-shot arrows'), but with craft and traps. Everything, then, that Clytemnestra's nature demanded and her sex forbade or hampered, Athena is free to do, by virtue of her godhead. She is god-goddess to Clytemnestra's man-woman; and her masculinity wins her praise and worship, while that of Clytemnestra leads to disaster for herself and others. There is thus a bitter irony, when the goddess, who in all things commends the male and is free to exercise her preference in action, condemns the woman of manly counsel for seeking the domination which her nature demanded.

Yet it is altogether unnatural that Athena should vote as she does. Herself in authority, she respects the status of the master. Daughter of Zeus, she can sympathise with the relationship of child to father, and so votes for Orestes. But the issue of the trial had come to turn upon two other relationships, in which she had no part. The argument was between Apollo, who stood (at least at 213 ff.) for the marriage-tie, and the Furies, who stood for the bond between child and mother. Upon this issue Athena, who was born of no mother, the virgin-goddess who eschewed wedlock, gives her vote; and since there can be no question upon which side it will be cast, we should at least ask how much validity and what precise significance attaches to this vote. The matter must be considered in two ways: in terms of theology and in terms of society.[56]

Theologically, Athena has importance, for Aeschylus, only as a potential spokesman of the will of Zeus. Apollo, with considerable pomp, had claimed to speak for his father, but this claim was prejudiced in various ways. Athena also is a child of Zeus, and, as her bearing is more dignified, so her solutions are clearly better than Apollo's. At the voting, she speaks for herself and makes no claim to higher authority, but later, when she brings her divine persuasion to bear upon the Furies, she makes reference to her father's will.[57] 'Bright testimony,' she tells them, 'came from Zeus; and he who gave evidence was he himself who prophesied that Orestes for this deed should not come to harm' (797 ff.). This must, of course, be read in the light of her preceding remarks: that the Furies were not defeated, that the outcome of the trial was an equally divided vote, which was an honest one (796). It is noteworthy that the key-word *dikē* (justice)[58] is associated with the equal votes of the human jurors and that the wording of the oracle is negative. Orestes — and this is the will of Zeus — was to suffer no harm for what he did (799). For the main responsibility rested upon Apollo, who gave the oracle — that is to say, upon the social code under which Orestes acted. This code was imperfect and embodied 'justice' to a limited degree. We see it in the process of supersession. This is the significance of the reference to Zeus in the next speech of Athena. Tactfully, yet firmly, she reminds the Furies of the thunderbolt of Zeus — which had already been employed against recalcitrant divinities of an older generation.[59] The will of Zeus for the evolution of human society is not to be frustrated. But there is no need of the thunderbolt in this case (829), for the Furies recognise Zeus as all-powerful (918) and accept their place in the new order which his daughter has established in Athens.[60]

It is generally recognised that a great part of the interest in the trilogy, and particularly in the *Eumenides*, is sociological, in the sense that Aeschylus has dramatised a signal advance in the organisation of human society — from the vendetta to the court of law. The point need not be laboured. Athena succeeds where Apollo failed, because his code was still tied to the obsolete blood-feud.[61] The dilemma which faced Orestes could only be escaped by the establishment of a court of law to try cases of homicide. The divided vote seems to recognise this fact; and the jurors who returned this verdict were, in fact, those Athenians who are represented as at once the pioneers and beneficiaries of the new order. But their goddess did not give the vote which acquitted Orestes on the ground that he had been placed in an impossible position: she gave it out of preference for the male. Has this fact, too, a sociological significance?

So Professor Thomson argues. 'If we ask why the dramatist has made the outcome of the trial turn on the social relations of the sexes, the answer is that he regarded the subordination of women, quite correctly, as an indispensable condition of democracy . . . a necessary consequence of the development of private property.'[62] That Aeschylus has, in fact, made the outcome of the trial depend upon the relationship between the sexes cannot be denied; and it is the less possible to disregard the emphatic pronouncement of Athena because it is not only the trial but, if the foregoing analysis has been correct, the whole trilogy which turns upon this relationship. One may doubt, however, whether the simple statement (made by Professor Thomson in a different context)[63] that to Aeschylus 'the subjection of women was not only just but preferable to the liberty which they had formerly enjoyed' is an adequate description of the dramatist's views.

It might, for instance, be considered that Aeschylus adopted a strange method of proclaiming the natural superiority and rightful dominance of the male, when he opened his trilogy with a play in which the man — husband, king, and general — is routed upon every plane by the woman. And not by one woman only, if the superiority of Cassandra to her conqueror is admitted. It is, indeed, striking how interest and sympathy are concentrated upon the women in the *Agamemnon*, where, to set against Iphigeneia, Clytemnestra, and Cassandra, we have the humiliated Agamemnon and the ignominious Aegisthus.[64]

But Clytemnestra, it will be said, is an abnormal woman, in that she has the mental characteristics of a man. This is true, and it is the cause of a personal tragedy which is almost Sophoclean. This tragedy, given its final touch of irony by the words of Athena, is absolute, since it was impossible in Clytemnestra's own society, and equally impossible in democratic Athens, for a woman of dominating will and intelligence to exploit her gifts to her own satisfaction and for the advantage of the community. The underlying social problem is one which has only been solved partially and intermittently in human history. If Aeschylus, who had fought against Artemisia at Salamis, realised the normal predicament of such a woman in a predominantly male society, this does not mean that he saw how it could be avoided, or that, when he made Athena proclaim the primacy of the male, he did not recognise that this was a historical necessity Her words, at that solemn moment, were not vain; nor could they be. Yet, even so, we have not perhaps exhausted the significance of the theme.

The trilogy treats of the relationship between man and woman and of the institution of marriage. Against this institution, Clytemnestra rebels, partly because it is ill adapted to such as her, partly because, in the matter of Iphigeneia, her husband had violated the basis of mutual respect upon which marriage should stand. Clytemnestra is not only the tragic exception, over whom the general rule rides roughshod: she is a symbol of all wives and mothers who suffer from the inferior status of the woman in marriage. It is for this reason, if for no other, that the dramatist has taken pains that Iphigeneia shall not be forgotten in the *Eumenides*. The foundation of the Areopagus solved, triumphantly, the social problem of homicide. Did Athena's proclamation of male superiority solve the social problem of the relationship of the sexes in marriage? Did democratic Athens in the fifth century solve this problem, or did Aeschylus think that it had done so?

Athens did not. We need not indeed suppose that the most extreme statements of feminine subjection tell the whole truth, or that no respectable woman in Athens had any scope for the development of her personality, or that there was no equality, no mutual respect, in any Athenian marriage. There is evidence to the contrary.[65] But the impression remains that in this field of social life the Athenians had, on the whole, failed to achieve a harmonious balance and, in degrading the status of women, had committed an injustice which damaged their society.[66] Euripides was very conscious of this, and his Medea speaks for her sex. But did not Clytemnestra do the like? It is hard to believe that Aeschylus, whose women have such powers and courage, regarded with complacency a state of affairs which can have changed but little in the generation which separates the *Oresteia* from the *Medea*.

At this point we badly miss the end of the Danaid trilogy, which Aeschylus may have been able to take for granted, when in the closing scene of the *Eumenides* he passes to other themes. For the earlier trilogy also dealt with the institution of marriage; and, if it led to the conclusion that the married lot must be accepted by women, there is some reason to suppose that it was also concerned with their dignity in marriage.[67] The *Oresteia* makes by implication the same claim on behalf of women – a claim which was, broadly, not met by Athenian society. Aeschylus, who regarded, and rightly regarded, the Athenian democracy as a new peak in social achievement, to which the closing scenes of the *Eumenides* are, in one respect, a triumphant hymn, was not necessarily its blind propagandist.[68] Athena, who inaugurates the new order with dignity and patience, does not necessarily speak the final word of the wisdom of Zeus, when she gives her vote to Orestes with such an explicit absence of sympathy for the opposite cause. To achieve her ends she employs the sovereign democratic virtue of Persuasion; yet *Peithō* had work still to do, in creating a just social order, which was beyond the imagination of this masculine goddess, but not perhaps beyond the poet's.[69]

9

PROMETHEIA

GEORGE THOMSON

Prometheus, it was once said, is the patron saint of the proletariat.

It was Prometheus who bestowed on man the gift of fire, which he had brought down from the sun stored in a fennel stalk. That is the primitive nucleus of the myth, which can be traced in this or similar forms all over the world. It is a genuine folk-memory of the earliest and one of the most revolutionary steps in the advancement of material technique.

In the myth of Prometheus, the first of these technical advances became a symbol for the rest. Fire stands for the material basis of civilisation. That is the one constant element in the myth. The others vary, because the myth has a history of its own, being continuously reinterpreted and adapted to new developments in the process of which it is a symbol. The higher stages of that process were conditional, as we have seen, on the division of society into economically unequal classes — into those that performed the actual labour of production and those that enjoyed the wealth and leisure thus produced. This division created, among the rulers, the need to justify their privileged position, and, among the ruled, a sense of frustration springing from the perception that their own wealth and leisure had not kept pace with the increasing productivity of their work. The primitive form of the myth, which simply registered the pride of the community in the success of its collective struggle against its material environment, was no longer adequate, because out of the struggle between man and Nature had now emerged the struggle between man and man. Accordingly, it was complicated and elaborated.

The peasants of Hesiod were hungry and oppressed. Why were they condemned to toil so hard and enjoy so little? Because man had sinned against his masters. Once the human race had lived in happiness without sickness or labour or the need to win their bread in the sweat of their brows. That was the Reign of Kronos, when the untilled earth had

From *Aeschylus and Athens*, 4th ed., pp. 297–324. Copyright 1941 by Lawrence & Wishart Ltd. Reprinted with revisions by permission of Lawrence & Wishart Ltd.

brought forth of itself abundance of good things, which all men enjoyed in common; and in those days, of course, they had possessed the gift of fire. This happy state of things was brought to an end through the culpability of Prometheus, who, at a banquet of the gods, tried to cheat Zeus of the special portion which was his due. In punishment for this offence, Zeus deprived man of fire. Prometheus replied by stealing it from heaven and restoring it to man. Zeus then impaled him on a rock, where he was tormented by an eagle, which visited him daily to devour his liver, until he was released by Herakles. Meanwhile, the human race remained in possession of the gift of fire, but to it was added another gift — Pandora and her box, which, when the lid was removed, let loose over the world labour, sorrow, sickness and a multitude of plagues. And so, Hesiod tells his listeners, had it not been for Prometheus, who provoked the gods into withholding from men their means of living, 'you would have been able to do easily in a day enough work to keep you for a year, to hang up your rudder in the chimney corner, and let your fields run to waste.'

Thus, for the peasants of Hesiod, Prometheus, the pioneer in man's conquest of nature, has been degraded to the level of a common malefactor. Material progress has been complicated by the class struggle in such a way that for them, instead of enlarging, it has diminished the sum of human happiness. Such was the form which the myth had assumed under the aristocracy. But that form was not final any more than the aristocracy itself.

The story of Prometheus is not mentioned in the Homeric poems, nor, so far as we know, was it treated in choral lyric. It was not the sort of story to appeal to members of the aristocracy. In our records, its next exponent after Hesiod is Aeschylus himself; but, while his version was doubtless to a large extent his own creation, it contains certain structural features which clearly have their roots in the mystical teaching of the Orphics. At the beginning of the trilogy, Prometheus describes himself as banished from the company of the gods and as about to endure an agony that will last thousands of years; throughout the first play his torments are described with reference to the idea of Ananke or Necessity; at the end of it he is hurled down into Hades, whence, at the opening of the second, he has been brought up again to earth; and, finally, after his penance has lasted for a total period of 30,000 years, he is readmitted to Olympus. This is the Orphic Wheel of Necessity — the cycle that leads the soul from divinity to birth and death and thence back to divinity. In the words of Empedokles:

There is an oracle of Necessity, an ordinance of the gods, ancient, eternal and sealed by broad oaths, that whenever one of the *daímones*, whose portion is length of days, has sinfully stained his hands with blood or followed strife or forsworn himself, he shall be banished from the abodes of the blessed for thrice ten thousand seasons, being born throughout the time in all manner of mortal shapes, exchanging one toilsome path for another. . . . One of these am I now, an exile and a wanderer from the gods, because I put my trust in insensate strife.

Alas, unhappy race of men, bitterly unblest, such are the groans and struggles from which ye have been born!

But at the last they appear among mankind as prophets, poets, physicians and princes; and thence they arise as gods, exalted in honour, sharing with the other gods a common hearth and table, free from the miseries of mortality, without part therein, untroubled.

Set against this background, the sufferings of the Aeschylean Prometheus appear as the sufferings of man himself, cast down from heaven into misery and death but destined to rise again.

The cults of Prometheus were few and insignificant. At Athens, he was worshipped in the Academy together with Athena and Hephaistos, who were also closely associated with the handicrafts that man had learned from his control of fire. All three were honoured with torch races, run by the *épheboi* from some point outside the city to one of the altars within it with the object of renewing the sacred fire. In origin, these races were probably ordeals of initiation, like the foot-races at Olympia.

Prometheus was delivered by Herakles, a figure far more prominent both in myth and cult, and far too complex to be discussed in detail here. He was a son of Zeus by Alkmene, a descendant of Io, and he was sent into the world to clear it of primeval monsters for the benefit of man. The last of his labours was a descent into Hades, for which he prepared himself by initiation at Eleusis, and after it he ascended into heaven and received in marriage Hera's daughter, Hebe. Here, too, we can discern traces of the mystical sequence of strife, death, and deification.

Turning to the *Prometheus Bound*, the first question that we ask ourselves is, where does the poet intend our sympathies to lie as between the two antagonists? It is a vital question, because the answer to it necessarily reveals so much in both the poet and his critics. If modern readers of the play have given sharply divergent answers to this question, it is not, as we shall see, because there is any ambiguity in the play itself, but because, on an issue so crucial as that of rebellion against the established order, they have been forced to disclose their own attitude to contemporary society.

Zeus is a tyrant and his rule is a tyranny. We learn this from his own ministers, who are proud of it (10); from Prometheus, who denounces it (222, 305, 357, 736, 756, 909, 942, 956-9, 996); from the Ocean

Nymphs, who deplore it (184); and from the God of Ocean, who is resigned to it (310). The fact is incontestable, and the only question is how the dramatist intended his audience to interpret it.

The history of the tyranny at Athens has been reviewed in an earlier chapter, where we saw how the progressive character of its opening phase became obscured in retrospect by the reactionary tendencies which it had subsequently developed. We also saw that, when the Athenians had to face a Persian landing at Marathon, the exiled Hippias was on the Persian side; and, even after the Persian menace had been removed, Athenian democrats found it necessary to remain constantly on their guard against the danger that some influential aristocrat, a Militades or an Alkibiades, might make a bid for the position which Hippias had lost. The result was that, in the fifth century at Athens, there grew up a traditional conception of the tyrant, endowed with all the qualities which the people had experienced in Hippias; and eventually, owing partly to similar experiences elsewhere and partly to the dominant influence exercised by Attic writers in the development of thought, this tradition became fixed. Thus, Herodotus describes the tyrant as irresponsible, with a dangerous tendency towards pride, suspicions of his best citizens, and, above all, violent, a ravisher of women. Similar arguments are repeated by Theseus in his dispute with the herald from Argos in the *Suppliants* of Euripides. The tyrant is a law to himself; he cuts off his leading citizens as he might the tallest ears of corn (in accordance with the advice which, so Herodotus tells us, was actually given by one tyrant to another); and, lastly, parents cannot safeguard their daughters from his violence.

The tragedians were naturally quick to turn this tradition to dramatic advantage. In the *Antigone*, for example, the heroine bitterly declares that one of the privileges of the tyranny is to do and say what it likes; and in the *Persians* Atossa raises her defeated son above the reach of popular reproach with the significant reminder that he is not responsible to his people. In the *Œdipus Tyrannus*, as Sheppard has shown, the character of the king is thrown into ominous relief by a number of such allusions, which, though for the most part implicit, were readily appreciated by an audience made familiar with such technique by Aeschylus.

The ministers whom Zeus has appointed to escort Prometheus to his place of confinement are Might and Violence, the one signifying his power, the other the method by which he exercises it. He is described as harsh (186, 324), as irresponsible (324), as unconstitutional, acknowledging no laws but his own, a law to himself (150, 402, 187); he is suspicious of his friends — a feature described expressly as characteristic of the tyrant (224-5); implacable and impervious to persuasion (34, 184-5,

333); and, above all, in his treatment of Io, he reveals his violence (735-8). The brutality of this episode is not, as in the *Suppliants*, veiled in lyric poetry; on the contrary, the poet seems to be at pains to fill his audience, like his own Oceanids, with abhorrence. Zeus tried first persuasion and then threats to bend the unhappy girl to his will. This is the method Prometheus expected of him, and it is typical of the tyrant. Hence there can be no question where the sympathies of an Athenian audience must have lain — or, indeed, of any popular audience — when Prometheus breaks off his prediction of Io's future agonies with the impassioned cry (736):

> You see how he behaves
> To all the same, inhuman, brutal tyrant.

In view of this evidence, it is fairly clear that those critics who can pass judgment against the hero who has dared to rebel against this heartless despotism have been influenced by factors independent of the dramatist's intention.

The characterisation of Prometheus is more complex. In the opening scene, the sinister figure of Violence eyes the prisoner in silence. Might assails him with insults as he spurs Hephaistos to the task of binding him, but does not address him directly till he flings at him his parting taunt (82-7). Hephaistos alone is filled with compassion. He recognises his crime, by which indeed, as god of fire, he has been particularly affected; yet he forgets his own loss in sympathy for the sufferer. Prometheus is silent.

The compassion of Hephaistos is that of kin for kin (14, 39). The same feeling prompts the visit of the Ocean Nymphs (129-30) and is professed by their father Ocean (289-90), who counsels moderation, but with an underlying subservience to authority that marks him as a type of the trimmer or conformer; and Prometheus dismisses him with politely veiled contempt. The Ocean Nymphs have said nothing in the presence of their father, but after his departure they are forced to confess that with them, too, sympathy is tempered with disapproval. So far the indignation of Prometheus has been controlled; but during his discourse with Io we feel the anger rising in him, and, when his enemy's victim is carried away in a sudden agony of pain, the reaction is immediate. The Nymphs, horrified and terrified, bow down in helpless submission. Prometheus, on the other hand, hurls at his antagonist a speech of reckless denunciation and defiance. Yet he does not forfeit our sympathy, because this change of attitude corresponds to our own reaction to the brutality of Zeus manifested in the spectacle of Io. The Nymphs remonstrate, but he is deaf to their appeals. Hermes arrives with a peremptory demand that he shall reveal the secret with which he threatens his master's supremacy; yet even Hermes, when he perceives the prisoner's state of mind, joins with the Nymphs in a sincere attempt to reason with him. But Prometheus, who received the insults of Might in silence, himself assails Hermes with insults; and in dramatic fulfilment of his own prayer (152-7, 1050-1) he is cast into the pit of Tartarus. The ambivalent effect of the last scene on the audience is faithfully reflected in the attitude of the Chorus, who, while disapproving as strongly as Hermes of the prisoner's lack of restraint, nevertheless refuse to desert him.

Thus, the play ends in a deadlock. The ruler of the gods is a tyrant, the champion of mankind has been reproved by his own friends for exceeding the bounds of moderation. The wrath of Zeus is a disease, and the unrestraint of Prometheus is a disease. This metaphor, which is of course intended to suggest the hope of a cure to come, recurs again and again throughout the play. The world is out of joint, and only a change in both antagonists can set it right.

While insisting on the tyrannical nature of the rule of Zeus, Aeschylus is careful to impress on us at the outset, and to remind us repeatedly, that his power is new. He is displaying the world not as it is now but as it was in the beginning. In the course of 30,000 years, taught by experience, the adversaries will be reconciled. So we are told, early in the play, by Prometheus himself, whose vision is as yet unclouded by passion (190-2). Later, forgetting his own prophecy, he can foresee nothing in store for his enemy but destruction (907-27); but the truth re-emerges in his final altercation with Hermes (980-83). Reminded of his lost bliss, Prometheus inadvertently utters a cry of grief — 'Ah me!' — of which Hermes is quick to take advantage:

'Ah me!' — that is a cry unknown to Zeus.

At the mention of his enemy, Prometheus recovers himself:

Time, as he grows old, will teach everything.

But again Hermes is ready with his retort:

Yes, *you* have yet to learn where wisdom lies.

With this allusion to the doctrine of wisdom through suffering, the scattered hints of an impending change in both antagonists are significantly brought together at the end of the play.

It is clear, therefore, that in the sequel both antagonists will learn by experience; but of course that is very far from saying that Prometheus ought not to have done what he has done. It is true that, when they hear

of his theft of fire, the Oceanids exclaim, shocked by his audacity, that
he has sinned; but, if so, it is a sin which has saved humanity from annihilation, and, if any further doubt remain as to the dramatist's attitude
on this point, it is dispelled by the hero's narration of the consequences
of his sin for the destiny of man (442–471):

> Now listen to the sufferings of mankind,
> In whom, once speechless, senseless, like an infant,
> I have implanted the faculty of reason . . .
> At first, with eyes to see, they saw in vain,
> With ears to hear, heard nothing, groping through
> Their lives in a dreamlike stupor, with no skill
> In carpentry or brickmaking, like ants
> Burrowing in holes, unpractised in the signs
> Of blossom, fruit and frost, from hand to mouth
> Struggling improvidently, until I
> Chartered the intricate orbits of the stars;
> Invented number, that most exquisite
> Instrument, and the alphabet, the tool
> Of history and chronicle of their progress;
> Tamed the wild beasts to toil in pack and harness
> And yoked the prancing mounts of opulence,
> Obedient to the rein, in chariots;
> Constructed wheelless vehicles with linen
> Wings to carry them over the trackless ocean . . .
> And yet more matter is there to admire
> In the resource of my imagination,
> And this above all. When sickness struck them down,
> Having no herbal therapy to dispense
> In salves and potions, their strength neglected ran
> To waste in moping ignorance, till I
> Compounded for them gentle medicines
> To arm them in the war against disease . . .
> At last, who else can boast to have unlocked
> The earth's rich subterranean treasure-houses
> Of iron, copper, bronze, silver and gold?
> That is my record. You have it in a word:
> Prometheus founded all the arts of man.

All this, as the details of the passage show, belongs to the tradition
of the Pythagoreans — the same tradition which we have illustrated from
Hippokrates' account of the origin of medicine; and the striking
thing about it is its bold materialism. This combination of materialism
with mysticism, which we have already noticed in the work of Aeschylus,
was evidently characteristic of the early Pythagoreans. We find it again
in Empedokles, whose preoccupation with the revival of magical practices

and beliefs did not prevent him from making solid contributions to science. How the Pythagoreans reconciled these two sides to their teaching, we do not know; but it seems clear that, while the first was derived from the Orphic movement, of which their own was an offshoot, they owed the second to their political activity in the initial stage of the democratic revolution; and from them it was transmitted through Hippokrates and the sophists to Demokritos and Epicurus.

The mystical form in which Aeschylus has clothed this tradition does not disguise its essential significance — on the contrary, the myth itself has been reinterpreted so as to throw into relief the underlying doctrine that progress is the outcome of conflict. If Prometheus has erred, it is because *es ist der Mensch solang' er strebt*. The champions of a new order offend inevitably against the old. If Prometheus has to suffer, it is because man himself has suffered in the course of his advancement. Without suffering he would have lacked the stimulus to invention. The truth which both Aeschylus and Hippokrates, in different ways, were seeking to express was one that had been grasped in practice by primitive man from the earliest stages of his history and was eventually formulated by Epicurus in the words:

Human nature was taught much by the sheer force of circumstances, and these lessons were taken over by human reason, refined and supplemented.

The view of human progress expressed by Aeschylus is therefore not far removed from the position of modern dialectical materialism:

Until we acquire knowledge of the laws of nature, which exist and act independently of our mind, we are slaves of 'blind necessity.' When we acquire knowledge of them, we acquire mastery of nature.

Intelligence, the gift of Prometheus, had made man free, because it had enabled him to comprehend, and so to control, the laws of nature. Freedom consists in the understanding of necessity.

The *Prometheus* contains very little action; yet it is intensely dramatic. Technically, it is the most accomplished of the extant plays, and shows that by the end of his life Aeschylus had become an absolute master of his craft. It is therefore worth examining in some detail from this point of view.

The play contains three marked pauses. The first is at the end of the *párodos* (192) after Prometheus' first prediction of the future, which carries us, without revealing the intermediate steps, to the ultimate reconciliation, and at the same time lets fall the first allusion to his secret. The second comes at the end of the second episode (525), where he declines to reveal this secret, which, we are now told, is to be the means of his deliverance. And the third comes at the end of the next episode (876), after he has predicted the actual coming of his deliverer. These pauses divide the play into four movements. In the first, Prometheus is nailed to the rock; in the second he relates the past history of gods and men, in the third he predicts the future; in the fourth, he is cast into Tartarus.

Each of these movements has an internal structure of its own. Each falls into three parts, except the third, which falls into two such sets of three. Further, in each set of three, there is an organic relation between the first and third parts, the second being in the nature of a digression or development. Thus, in the first movement, Prometheus is punished by his enemies; he delivers his soliloquy; and he is visited by his friends, the Ocean Nymphs. In the second, he relates the story of the war among the gods and his own services to Zeus; he is interrupted by the visit of the God of Ocean; and he proceeds to relate his services to man. In the first part of the third movement, Io appears and entreats him to reveal her future; at the request of the Oceanids she tells the story of her past; and then, after predicting her wanderings as far as the borders of Asia, Prometheus hints at the fall of Zeus and his own deliverance. In the second part, he continues his prophecy as far as her destination in Egypt; then, in proof of his veracity, he reverts to her past (thus completing her own account); and, finally, he predicts her ultimate fate and the coming of his deliverer. In the fourth movement, he alludes once again, more openly, to his secret, which, he now declares, will effect his enemy's downfall; the emissary of Zeus seeks in vain to extort his secret from him; and Prometheus is cast into Tartarus.

Now turn to the choral odes, which are integral links in this development. In the *párodos*, the Oceanids offer the sympathy of the gods (160-61); Prometheus goes on to relate his services to the gods. In the first *stásimon* (397-435) they sing of the compassion of mankind: Prometheus relates his services to humanity. In the second *stásimon* (526-60) they sing of the helplessness of man and contrast his present state with the happiness of his wedding day: Io appears, helpless mortal persecuted by a brutal suitor (739-40). The theme of the third *stásimon* (887-907) is wisdom; and this prepares us for the final scene, in which they join with Hermes in an appeal to the sufferer to follow the course of wisdom.

Thus, the subject of the first movement is the binding of Prometheus — the present; of the second, the history of the past; of the third, the destiny of Io and the birth of Herakles — the future; and the fourth movement, with its increase of the penalty, balances the first. Yet, throughout the play, these threads of present, past and future are interwoven with such skill that at each turning-point our attention is thrown with increasing emphasis on the future. The opening speech of Might ends with a declaration that Prometheus must be taught by suffering to accept the tyranny of Zeus (10-11) while the speech of Hephaistos which follows ends with a suggestion that the tyrant himself, in course of time, will change his ways (35); and both these themes will be developed in the *párodos* (168-85). In the middle of his task Hephaistos utters the impassioned cry, 'Alas, Prometheus! it is for you I weep' (66). The retort of Might comes at the close of the scene, where our attention is redirected to the future (85-7):

> We called you God of Foresight. It's a lie.
> Now you need all your foresight for yourself
> To shuffle off *this* masterly work of art.

And again this parting insult will be answered at the end of the first movement, where we are permitted a glimpse of the final reconciliation, welcomed by both antagonists (186-92).

We are brought back abruptly to the past (193). At the request of the Nymphs, who entreat him to 'reveal all things', Prometheus reluctantly begins his exposition. Later, shocked by his audacity, the Nymphs are anxious to change the subject (261-2); but now it is Prometheus who insists on continuing, urging them to listen to his revelation of the future (272-3). Then comes the interlude — the visit of the God of Ocean. After his departure the exposition is resumed, leading to the end of the second movement, where, eagerly questioned about the secret to which he alluded at the end of the first, Prometheus draws back, refusing to disclose it (522-5):

> No, think of other things. The time to speak
> Of that is still far distant. It must be hidden.
> That is my secret, which if closely kept
> Contains my sure hope of deliverance.

To resume, we have seen that the opening speeches of the play ended by directing our attention to the future, thus anticipating the close of the binding scene and the climax at the end of the first movement, the last speech of the *párodos*. The second movement began by taking us back into the past; but at the end of the first of its three parts and still more intently at the end of the third we looked once again to the future. Then comes the Io scene, so divided as to throw the future into still greater prominence: future, past, future; future, past, future. Hence the tremendous effect, like a goal to which the whole exposition has been straining, of the prophecy of the coming of Herakles (871-3), which, again, is abruptly broken off, and then crowned at the opening of the last movement (907-27) by the completion of that other motive, the fatal secret, which marked the culmination of the first movement and again of the second. The narrations and predictions of Prometheus have been handled with such artistic mastery of the material as to concentrate at the end of the play our whole attention on the sequel.

That sequel has been lost, but some important fragments of the second play, the *Prometheus Unbound*, have survived.

The play began with the entry of the Chorus of Titans. Many thousands of years have elapsed, giving time for many changes, on earth and in heaven. Prometheus is still chained to his rock, but he has been restored from Tartarus to the light of day. The Titans describe their voyage from the banks of Ocean, where the Sun waters his horses after their day's labour, to the borders of Europe and Asia. They are brothers of Prometheus — bound to him therefore by ties closer than those which wrung compassion from Hephaistos and brought the God of Ocean and his daughters to his solitary rock. In the war against Kronos they had sided with the old order, and for this offence Zeus cast them, with Kronos, into Tartarus. They have now been released; and Kronos, too, we may presume, in accordance with the tradition, has been removed to his new home in the Islands of the Blest. Zeus has learnt to temper his power with mercy. No doubt the Titans recount these events to their brother. They can hardly fail to make a deep impression on him; but, as at the beginning of the first play, Prometheus is silent.

His opening words have survived in a Latin translation by Cicero. He appeals to them to bear witness to his agony. Pierced by cruel bonds and tormented by the eagle whose coming Hermes had predicted, he longs for the death which is denied to him. The speech is as notable for the speaker's absorption in physical pain as his speeches in the first play are notable for his indifference to it. There is not a word of his deliverer, not a word of his secret. And he longs to die. In the first play, which represented a time when the will of Zeus had been weaker than the Moirai (515-18), he had dared Zeus to do his worst, defiantly declaring that he was fated not to die (1053). Now he laments that he is being kept alive by the will of Zeus himself. The implication is that during the interval Zeus and the Moirai have come together. The old and the new are being reconciled.

The ensuing scenes must have acquainted the audience with the changes that have taken place in the interval between the two plays; but it is likely that on this occasion the narrator is not Prometheus himself, who is hardly in a position to know what has happened, but the Titans, who, we may suppose, relate for their brother's benefit both the advances

which Zeus has made in the consolidation of his power and the mercy
he has begun to extend to his former enemies. In the first play we learnt
that, but for the intervention of Prometheus, Zeus would have destroyed
the human race; but we may be certain that any such intention has
been abandoned, because, as we shall see, the greatest of his sons is
shortly to be sent down to earth for the improvements of their lot.
Thus, if Prometheus remains obdurate, his motive can no longer be fear
for the future of mankind: it can only be resentment for past wrongs.
And if the Titans proceed to advise their brother to prepare the way for
his own release by surrendering the secret which Zeus demands of him,
appealing, like the God of Ocean, for wisdom and restraint (309-10),
their advice, unlike his, will not be ignoble: they will urge him to submit
to his old enemy, not merely because he rules the world, but because he
now rules it well. Nor can Prometheus reply, as he did to the Oceanids,
that advice comes ill from those who are not themselves in trouble
(263-5), because his brothers' sufferings have been hardly less terrible
than his own. Yet, in view of further evidence, we must, I think, assume
that Prometheus rejects their appeal. He cannot yet bring himself, by
revealing his secret before his release, to 'unsay his high language'.

In the Medicean manuscript of Aeschylus, the list of *dramatis per-
sonæ* prefixed to the *Prometheus Bound* includes the names of Ge, the
Goddess of Earth, and Herakles. As it is known that Herakles appeared
in the *Prometheus Unbound*, it is generally agreed that both names have
been inserted by mistake from another list, which gave the characters of
the second play or of the two plays together.

The Goddess of Earth was traditionally regarded as the most ancient
and in some ways the most august of the divinities of Greece – the origin
of all things into which all things return, and the fountain of all wisdom,
from whom all prophets, divine and human, drew their inspiration. And
she was the mother of Prometheus. It was to her that he appealed in his
opening soliloquy and again at the end of the first play to bear witness
to his wrongs. From her he learnt the destined course of the war in
heaven, and at her advice he took the part of Zeus. It was she who foretold to him the coming of his deliverer, and it was she who imparted to
him his secret.

It has already been noted how in the first play both Hephaistos and
the God of Ocean stressed their kinship with the prisoner, and how at
the beginning of the second he is visited by still closer kinsmen, the
sons of Earth. Their visit is followed by a visit from the Godess of Earth
herself, which will thus mark the culmination of a motive introduced at
the beginning of the trilogy. And we may infer that her purpose is similar
to theirs – to offer him her sympathy, and at the same time to urge

upon him the wisdom of submission. The voice of his mother is now added to the entreaties of the rest of his kin, beseeching him to soften his obduracy and remove the bar to his deliverance.

His secret is this. If Zeus unites with Thetis, she will bear him a son who will overthrow him. Now, in the tradition recorded by later writers, Zeus was actually in pursuit of Thetis when the revelation of the secret deterred him. Thus, the situation is highly dramatic. Prometheus has only to hold out a little longer, and the downfall of his enemy is assured. On the other hand, his mother pleads with him to submit, before it is too late, not merely in order to effect his own release, but to prevent the fall of Zeus, who, no longer the vindictive tyrant who sought the extinction of the human race, has already, in the birth of Herakles, taken them under his care. Prometheus is asked, not to quail before his adversary, but to sacrifice his pride for the sake of that very race for which he has already sacrificed far more.

With regard to the actual manner of the revelation, it should be observed that, since the Goddess of Earth is as well acquainted with the secret as Prometheus himself, all she requires is his permission to divulge it. There is no need for it to pass his lips. And, further, if she is intent on such a mission, she will take advantage of the occasion to urge Zeus to deliver Prometheus in return for his own deliverance. And what more influential mediator could be found than the goddess who is the author of the being of Zeus himself, as of all created beings, who helped him to his supremacy, who is, moreover, the personification of Right?

It is at this point, I believe, that Prometheus yields: but one further agony awaits him. After his mother's departure, he hears a rush of wings. We remember the alarm in which he awaited the coming of the Ocean Nymphs, and how they hastened to reassure him. This time his fears are well-founded. The eagle is returning to its feast. Prometheus bends his gaze in the direction from which it is approaching. From the opposite direction appears a warrior, armed with bow and spear and clad in the famous lion skin. He draws his bow and, with a prayer to Apollo, whose gift it is, he shoots the eagle down. Recognising his deliverer, Prometheus greets him as 'a hated father's son beloved,' and we may suppose that he followed up this greeting with an appeal to Herakles to release him from bondage in accordance with his destiny. Herakles, however, who has now learnt who the sufferer is, may well be reluctant to assist his father's inveterate enemy. Prometheus will then explain that he has already removed the main obstacle to their reconciliation, and will doubtless recall the services which he rendered many centuries before to his ancestress on that very spot. Moreover, he can direct him on his travels and foretell what the future holds in store for him when his labours are at an end. He is now eager to let flow the fount of prophecy, which he unsealed so reluctantly to Io, if only his own request is granted in return. Herakles 'pities the suppliant'. Prometheus is to predict his future, and in return Herakles will release him. An arrangement of this kind, parallel to the bargain struck by Prometheus with Io and the Oceanids (780-85), would enable the dramatist to reserve the climax of the actual release for the end of the scene.

The surviving fragments suffice to show that, just as the wanderings of Io covered the eastern and southern limits of the world, so those of Herakles will extend to the north and west. The two prophecies are complementary, embracing the whole surface of the earth. In particular, we know from other sources that it was Prometheus who directed Herakles to the Garden of the Hesperides and instructed him how to get the Golden Apples with the help of Atlas, to whom we were introduced in the first play. We also know that in the second the dramatist explained the origin of the constellation called the Kneeling Herakles. During his fight with the Ligurians on his way to the Hesperides, the hero's weapons gave out and he was forced to his knees. This means that Prometheus predicted that, in memory of this encounter, the image of Herakles, like that of other departed heroes, would be set after his death among the stars. That being so, the prophecy can hardly have ended with the quest of the Golden Apples, or even with the last of the hero's labours, the descent into Hades, without some allusion to his final destiny — his ascent into Heaven. It must have been carried to its proper conclusion in the deification of the hero, in harmony with the prediction to Io, which concluded with his birth.

Prometheus has now fulfilled his part of the agreement; it remains for Herakles to fulfil his. The hero mounts the rock and shatters the handiwork of Hephaistos.

We still await the result of Earth's mission to Zeus, and we also remember that at the close of the first play Zeus declared through the medium of his emissary that the sufferings of Prometheus could not end until he found another god to surrender his immortality in his stead (1026-29). It is possible, therefore, that Hermes reappears. He announces first of all that the mediation of Earth has been successful. With the revelation of the secret the cause of offence has been removed, although, for reasons which will appear immediately, it is probable that the formal reconciliation has still to be effected. Further, it is possible that Zeus transfers part of his displeasure to his son, who, as predicted of him, has delivered the prisoner without the Father's consent (771). Herakles is said to have bound himself with olive — probably in allusion to the olive planted by Athena in the Academy at Athens; and the motive for this act appears to have been his desire to avert his father's anger by binding himself vicariously on the prisoner's behalf. This point is dramatically important, because it provides a starting-point for the third play. In the regular manner of the trilogy, one difficulty is solved by the creation of another. Finally, the prisoner must find a substitute. At this point Herakles comes forward and explains that he has accidentally wounded the Centaur, Cheiron, who, suffering incurable pain, longs to die, but cannot: let him, therefore, relinquish his immortality in place of Prometheus. His offer accepted, Herakles departs, with the blessings of all present, to fulfil the remainder of his historic destiny.

If we consider the situation in which the dramatist has left us, we see that, just as in the first play the prophecy to Io raised an expectation which has only been satisfied by its fulfilment in the second — namely, the coming of Herakles — the prophecy to Herakles has now raised an expectation no less far-reaching, his deification; and our minds will not be at rest until we are assured that this, too, has been realised. It is therefore difficult to resist the conclusion that the plot of the third play was concerned, not merely with the readmission of Prometheus to Olympus, but with the future of Herakles. The destinies of the two heroes have become interlocked, and at the close of the second play our interest has been transferred in some measure to the latter.

Before leaving the *Prometheus Unbound*, let us compare its structure, so far as it can be recovered, with that of the *Prometheus Bound*. The silence of Prometheus at the opening of the first play is balanced by his silence at the opening of the second; the visit of the God of Ocean in the first by the visit of the Goddess of Earth in the second; the Daughters of Ocean, the chorus of the first play, by the Sons of Earth, the chorus of the second; the wanderings of Io in the east and south by the wanderings of her descendant in the north and west; the prophecy of the birth of the great benefactor of mankind by the prophecy of his deification. Thus, it appears that the two plays were constructed with that organic symmetry which the study of his other work has led us to expect.

The third play was entitled *Prometheus the Fire-bearer*. This epithet probably refers to the torch which Pausanias saw (mistaking it for a sceptre) in the right hand of the archaic image of Prometheus in the Academy, where, as already noted, the god was worshipped as one of the three divinities who had taught man the use of fire and were honoured with annual torch races.

We have already made some progress with the conclusion of the trilogy. In the first place, Prometheus is a suppliant, seeking readmission to Olympus. In the *Oresteia*, the suppliant was saved by the intervention of Athena, the goddess of wisdom and patroness of the city which claimed to uphold that virtue among men. The same goddess had an ancient connection with Prometheus. We are told that Prometheus assisted at her birth, when she sprang fully armed from the head of Zeus, and that the two collaborated in the creation of mankind. But above all Prometheus was granted a place in the Academy — an honour which he could not have won without the goddess's consent. Of the three fire gods, we made the acquaintance of the two elder at the opening of the trilogy, and I believe, therefore, that in the conclusion we were introduced to the youngest and greatest of the three. It is she who reconciles Prometheus with her father and invests him with the human honours that are his due.

Before his descent into Hades, Herakles visited Eleusis with the intention of becoming an initiate, but he was unable to behold the mysteries until he had been cleansed of the blood of the Centaurs: accordingly, he was purified at Agra and then initiated. We are also told that the Lesser Mysteries of Agra were founded by Demeter for the express purpose of purifying Herakles after the slaughter of the Centaurs. These traditions, preserved by Apollodoros and Diodoros, relate to Aeschylus's birthplace. They must have been known to him, and it is extremely probable that they were derived by the later writers from him. It appears, therefore, that here again the poet was working with an ulterior purpose — namely, the interception at the end of the trilogy of another and far more important feature of Athenian ritual, the Lesser Mysteries of Demeter.

The agony of Io was due in part to the jealousy of Hera, and her descendant suffered much from the same cause. Ultimately, however, when Herakles was admitted to Olympus, he was reconciled with Hera and received in marriage her own daughter, Hebe, the goddess of eternal youth. Furthermore, if the marriage of Herakles and Hebe signifies the reconciliation of Hera with the House of Io, it signifies just as clearly her reconciliation with her lord. Her hostility to Io and Herakles was prompted by conjugal jealousy, of which Zeus was the guilty cause. In the first play we saw Zeus heartlessly pursuing a mortal girl; in the second we saw him in purusit of Thetis; but in the third, when he joins with Hera in blessing the union of their son and daughter, the two stand together as guardians of the sanctity of marriage, thus marking a further step in the advancement of humanity.

In the beginning, Zeus crucified Prometheus for the salvation of mankind. In the course of time, which taught wisdom to them both, Prometheus saved Zeus from destruction and was himself saved by the son of Zeus, who, under his father's guidance, carried on the work of

Prometheus, clearing the path of human progress; and the divine feud was eventually resolved by Athena, who completed her father's purpose by her patronage of the city which stands at the summit of human civilisation. Hence, at the close of the trilogy, these three — Prometheus, Herakles, Athena — appear together as representatives of the inception, development and consummation of the idea of God, and as the founder, promoter and perfecter of the destiny of man.

If this view of the trilogy is essentially correct, it means that, for all the profound differences in their interpretation of the myth, Aeschylus was continuing the work which Hesiod had begun. The story of Prometheus has now been infused with an intellectual content far beyond the compass of the tale told by the rude peasants of Boiotia; but the advance which the new interpretation marks over Hesiod, no less than his advance on the primitive nucleus of the myth, has only been rendered possible by the underlying advancement of society itself.

It would be an interesting and profitable task to pursue the history of this myth in its successive reinterpretations through the Middle Ages down to our own day; but for the present it must suffice to conclude the subject with some remarks on what Shelley made of it.

Gilbert Murray, who believed that 'the strong tradition in the higher kind of Greek poetry, as in good poetry almost everywhere, was to avoid all the disturbing irrelevances of contemporary life', and could see 'no evidence of any political allusions' in the *Oresteia*, remarked that 'it is surprising that out of material so undramatic as a mere contest between pure evil and pure good Shelley has made such a magnificent poem' (*Aeschylus*, Oxford, 1940). It would indeed be surprising, if it were true, but, unlike Aeschylus, Shelley was in the habit of writing prefaces to his poems with the object of explaining what they were about, and in his preface to the *Prometheus Unbound* he wrote as follows:

We owe the great writers of the golden age of our literature to that fervid awakening of the public mind which shook to dust the oldest and most oppressive form of the Christian religion. We owe Milton to the progress and development of the same spirit; the sacred Milton was, let it ever be remembered, a republican, and a bold enquirer into morals and religion. The great writers of our own age are, as we have reason to suppose, the companions and forerunners of some unimagined change in our social condition or the opinions which cement it. The cloud of mind is discharging its collective lightning, and the equilibrium between institutions and opinions is now restoring, or about to be restored.

If we are curious to know what these institutions were that Shelly found in conflict with his opinions, we have only to read his *Mask of Anarchy written on the Occasion of the Massacre at Manchester*:

'Tis to work and have such pay
As just keeps life from day to day
In your limbs, as in a cell
For the tyrants' use to dwell

So that ye for them are made
Loom and plough and sword and spade
With or without your own will bent
To their defence and nourishment.

This conflict was something more substantial, as well as more disturbing, than 'a mere contest between pure good and pure evil', and it was also inherently dramatic, because it sprang straight out of contemporary strife. Only those who have studied the brutality, duplicity and hypocrisy of the ruling class of that date as revealed in their Enclosure Acts and Game Laws, their Speenhamland system and their truck system, and who stand where Shelley would have stood in relation to the sufferings no less great than are the common lot of the majority of mankind to-day, are in a position to appreciate the indignation which burns in the challenge of Prometheus:

Fiend, I defy thee! with a calm, fixed mind,
All that thou canst inflict I bid thee do;
Foul Tyrant both of Gods and Human-kind,
One only being shalt thou not subdue.

During Shelley's lifetime, the last of the English peasants had been turned out of their common fields on to the roads, and from there herded into the workhouses, prisons, cotton-mills and coal-mines, where they worked, men, women and children, in conditions still paralleled in such places as Jamaica, Johannesburg and Bombay. It was the period of the Industrial Revolution, which enriched the rich and impoverished the poor — the period in which the new manufacturing class was engaged in overthrowing the privileges of a corrupt landowning oligarchy, while the new proletariat, notwithstanding hunger and squalor and police persecution, was slowly and painfully learning how to organise for action.

Aeschylus was a moderate democrat, who had seen the long struggle between the landowners and the merchants culminate in a *concordia ordinum*, marked by the abolition of aristocratic privilege and the extension of the franchise to the whole of the citizen body. It is essential, however, to remember that this *concordia* owed its completeness to the fact that there was another class which was not free. The slaves were the proletariat of ancient democracy, and if they had not been slaves, incapable of organisation and therefore politically powerless, the overthrow of the landed aristocracy would have been followed by a struggle between them and their masters. It was only by excluding this class from his very conception of democracy that Aeschylus was able to regard the democratic revolution as a fusion of opposites symbolised in the reconciliation of Zeus and Prometheus.

Shelley was a member of the upper middle class who had transferred his allegiance to the proletariat. But this was not a slave proletariat; it was free, and already clamouring for the suffrage. Between this class and the capitalists there was no room for compromise, because their interests were contradictory, and that is what made it impossible for Shelley to accept the Aeschylean conclusion. He was bound to revolt against the idea of reconciling the champion with the oppressor of mankind. As for his alternative, even in those early days there were a few who saw more or less clearly that the only possible solution of the conflict was the expropriation of the ruling class by the class which it had expropriated; but, owing partly to the immaturity of the proletariat, which at this time was hardly conscious of its future, and partly to his own middle-class outlook, which he had not entirely outgrown, Shelley shrank from the idea of revolutionary action. Accordingly, his Jupiter is overthrown, but only by the mystical power of passive resistance.

In fairness to Shelley, it must be added that, whereas Aeschylus was celebrating a revolution which he had already seen accomplished, Shelley's revolution was at this time no more than a hope of the future; and so, for a century, it remained.

10

AESCHYLUS: THE LAST PHASE

C. J. HERINGTON

The starting-point of this essay is a fact which now seems to me almost certain: that Aeschylus' *Suppliants*-tetralogy, *Oresteia*, and *Prometheia* — in that order — form a compact group of works at the very end of the poet's career. I accept (as I think most people now do) the implication of the papyrus-hypothesis that the *Suppliants*-tetralogy must date from 466 BC or later, perhaps 463.[1] It has always been known, beyond doubt, that the *Oresteia* was produced in Spring 458. And lastly I am convinced by a number of arguments of varying type, produced over the last fifty years, that the *Prometheia* must have been written after the *Oresteia* if it was written by Aeschylus at all (which I firmly believe). The *Prometheus* must in that case belong to the last two years of Aeschylus' life: between 458 and his death in Sicily, 456/5.

These datings mean that we still have, in whole or part, a very high proportion of the tetralogies that Aeschylus actually composed in his last ten years, or perhaps even in his last seven. It could be that they represent *all* the tetralogies which he composed in this time; but even if that is not so, there is hardly space for more than one other tetralogy in the period, or two at the outside. Now my belief is that they are not merely chronologically a compact group, but that they are so artistically as well. Even more: that in these last three surviving works Aeschylus created a new art-form, something that differs *in kind* from any work that was staged under the name of tragedy, either his own or anybody else's, before or after that final decade of his life. A consequence of this will be that the three surviving examples of what I think of as a unique art-form can be used, more than is generally recognized, to explain each other; and that, in particular, the *Prometheus* begins to make more sense than it did.

That, in outline, is the position whose meaning and consequences are to be discussed in this paper. But I feel it necessary, first, to step right back and ask a question of method. There seem to be some artists whose

From *Arion* 4.3 (1965), 387–403. Reprinted with minor revisions by permission of the author and *Arion*.

works gain little or nothing in meaning through being dated at a specific point in the maker's life, and grouped with the other works of the same period. This sort of artist engineers internally consistent structures that are independent of himself: the façade is raised, is checked for symmetry and mechanical stress in all directions — and the little architect steps from behind it with a wave of the hand and wanders off anywhere, leaving behind him a thing made. With such work (I think, heretically perhaps, of the plays of Sophocles and the odes of Horace) dating and grouping seem to be largely antiquarian labor. But there exists another sort of artist, whose work, and whose relationship to the work, are altogether different. Not long ago a large exhibition of Picasso's works toured the northern parts of America, showing some of us (at least) for the first time a really representative selection of his paintings and drawings, in chronological order. The first impression of an innocent observer, after walking through the galleries from one end to the other, was: an exhibition by seven or eight different men, practising seven or eight different arts. What it actually was, of course, was an exhibition by an individual who many times, under the stress of a new technical idea or of something he had seen in the world, ruthlessly and abruptly threw overboard his previous achievement, and tried again.

Now although the point is not mathematically provable, I believe that most people who have spent any reasonable time on Aeschylus will have felt that they are having to do with this second sort of artist. As a citizen and as a poet he lives in an age of crisis. Classical society — or, if you like, modern society — is being born out of archaism. Correspondingly, tragedy is being born out of song. We cannot at any stage of Aeschylus' life say that tragedy is; we can only say that it is becoming. Aeschylus' thought, and the technique to match his thought, are dynamic and evolutionary, receptive always to what is new. Such a poet as that might begin his career with a two-dimensional imagination like a Persian carpet, close-woven with archaic centaurs, hippocamps and horsecocks; he might end it with a mind fixed on the profound space that is opened by the coming of philosophy. If that was in fact so, then the grouping of the plays by date would be an unavoidable stage towards understanding.

On these assumptions I again turn to the main position: that the *Suppliants*-tetralogy, the *Oresteia*, and the *Prometheia* (to which I shall refer from now on as 'the late group', for short) were composed in that order during Aeschylus' last ten or seven years, and that they represent most, if not all, of a phase in the tragic art which is sharply set off from anything discernible before or after.

The first step must be to survey the tragedies which lie on either side of the late group, chronologically speaking. Before 466 BC Aeschylus had already been composing for well over thirty years — a good working lifetime in itself. During that time the only two fixed dates and fixed points, so far as present knowledge goes, are the production of the *Persians* in 472, and that of the *Seven Against Thebes* in 467. Now, wildly different as these two tragedies are, thematically and musically, they yet imply the same cosmic background, and the same view of the human situation and human destiny. The cosmos here is — by comparison with what is to come in the late group — almost a comfortable one; in the sense that, however grim it is, however frightful the choices to be made within it, at least the roots of things remain the same. The archaic powers, both those in heaven and those below the earth, reign each un-questioned in their own spheres; in the *Seven*, infernal Furies and Olym-pian Apollo conspire towards the downfall of the house of Oedipus.[2] And in this universe the laws, though harsh, are not blind, nor purely deterministic. Catastrophe, when it comes, is doubly motivated: some-thing said or done in the past (an oracle, a family curse) preordains it externally, but it is only triggered off by something internal, something in the man himself. The two types of motivation are not, indeed, equally stressed in each play. In the *Persians* the disaster due to Xerxes' pride is already known when the ghost of Darius suddenly produces an oracle (otherwise unrecorded, either in history or in the actual play) which has foretold the downfall of the Persian army (*Persians*, 739–44, 801); con-versely, in the *Seven*, it is the inner rage of Eteocles — long ago destined to destruction by the Curse — that is held back from the audience until comparatively late (653 ff.). But in both plays the dual motivation of catastrophe is there for all to see. I would stress that it is not, of course, just a superficial matter of plot-mechanics; it involves, in itself, a subtle and not yet quite disproved view of human nature and destiny.

So much for the two tragedies that survive from the period before the Aeschylean late group. Paradoxically, but I believe truly, it must now be observed that their closest relatives, in some important respects, are to be found not in that late group, but in the earlier surviving plays of Sophocles: the *Ajax*, the *Antigone*, and the *Oedipus Tyrannus*, which were produced within the twenty years or so following Aeschylus' death. For those three Sophoclean plays fundamentally imply for dramatic purposes the same cosmos, and are constructed round the same double motivation, as the *Persians* and the *Seven*. In saying this, of course, I am not forgetting the great differences between the plays, and between the poets; each play has its individual soul, as it were, which at the moment I am not trying to approach. But behind all the differences I seem to see the same frame of reference, within which the drama is built. That is true, also, of yet another tragedy written down in the same period as the earlier Sophoclean plays, probably in the forties of the fifth century: the prose tragedy of Croesus, King of Lydia, which stands at the opening of Herodotus' *History*.[3] Here, in fact, the two motivations which converge towards the downfall of the hero are emphasized almost too clearly — the oracle which foredooms the end of Gyges' dynasty in the fifth generation (I. 13. 91), and the recklessness which springs from within Croesus himself.

So far as our evidence goes, then (and there seems just enough of it to exclude the possibility that we are being deluded by the accidents of preservation), tragic writing both before and in the generation after the Aeschylean late group, for all its variety in detail, moves against the background of the same universe. If there is any rift in that universe, it is between man and the unseen powers; whose laws he may challenge or misread, just as he may misread his own nature. In any of those events he, the individual, is due for destruction; but the universe itself remains as it was before, static, undivided. I repeat that the variety of movement against that cosmic background is immense, even to judge from the extant plays. And we should certainly have some shocks if the sands were to open up and yield some of the more eccentric lost tragedies of which the fragments now allow us only glimpses — Jason and the Argonauts rolling drunk on the stage in Aeschylus' *Kabeiroi*; the sword doubling back against the invulnerable flesh when the Aeschylean Ajax tries to commit suicide;[4] or the Aeschylean Priam literally weighing Hector's body in the scales against gold.[5] But there is nothing in the fragments to indicate that such plays, too, did not move within the frame of this unified, archaic universe.

It will at once be clear that the Aeschylean late group — *Suppliants*-tetralogy, *Oresteia*, *Prometheia* — will not fit into that frame at all; that from this point of view it forms a completely separate enclave in the known history of Greek tragedy before *c.* 440 BC, or rather of all Greek tragedy. But, although that is to my mind the most striking of the features that link the three works together, I do not think it is the only one, either in detail or on the grand scale. Of the many others, there are four which seem to be of special significance: the technique of trilogy-composition; the involvement of Gods in human feuds; the comic (in the technical sense of *Old Comic*) element; and the intrusion of contemporary philosophical speculation. I shall look at these in turn.

Probably the most striking feature is the first: the technique of putting together a tragic trilogy. The Aeschylean late group shows an odd, unbalanced relationship between the three plays which constitute the trilogy on the one hand, and the traditional myth which contributes its subject-matter on the other. The complete *Oresteia* is the simplest example. Its trilogic form can be symbolized as *A*, *A*, *B*: two responding plays to begin with and the third wild, non-responding. The *Agamemnon* and *Choephori* not only respond to each other in movement — murder and counter-murder — but they are also grouped together by the fact that the basic story in both, and even the characters, are in conformity with the traditional myth already known (in outline at least) a century before Aeschylus, and in part known to Homer too. (Again I should emphasize that I am not trying to touch the soul of these plays, nor forgetting that Aeschylus slants the traditional story in ways all his own. Here I am trying to view the grand overall movement, as if through the eyes of the designer as he makes his first outline, sketch-block on knee.) But the *third* member of the *Oresteia*, the *Eumenides*, has a totally different character and movement from the first two; and all the evidence which we have so far, both internal and external, suggests that its plot was freely invented by Aeschylus *ad hoc*, to resolve the issues raised, through the medium of the traditional story, in the first two plays. The only traditional legendary element visible in the *Eumenides* is, probably, the purification of Orestes at Delphi — and my own reading of the play suggests that even this element is not so much re-used by Aeschylus as perverted. Instead of a proof of Apollo's ultimate healing and reconciling power (as which it was surely intended by its inventors) it has become, in the context of this play, a proof of Apollo's inefficacy; instead of a pious and harmonious finale to Orestes' story it now serves merely as a horrific *proagon*, in which the two parties to the coming cosmic *agon* are first alternately paraded and then confronted.

The same curious principle of trilogic composition seems to have applied in the remaining two trilogies of the late group. Appallingly fragmentary as the *Suppliants*-trilogy and the *Prometheia* now are, there are still more solid reasons than one might think for this belief. To take the *Prometheia*: the basic story here, that Prometheus was bound by Zeus and later released by Herakles, is standard in Greek mythical accounts from Hesiod (*Theogony* 512 ff.) until the end of the ancient world (and beyond the end). But there is no such universal agreement as to what happened *after* the release. Hesiod says nothing on the point, and if we look to the many later ancient versions of the Prometheus-story we find the wildest diversity. Now Aeschylus' *Prometheus Bound* and *Prometheus Unbound*, for all their deliberate rehandling and censoring of Hesiod's story, were fundamentally based on that story, and presupposed a knowledge of it in their audience. In fact, we know enough of the two of them to be sure that between them they covered approximately the same legendary area as the Hesiodic version, the boundary being drawn between the two antithetic parts: the binding and the releasing (compare the murder and counter-murder in the *Agamemnon* and *Choephori*). It is a necessary inference from these facts that the third play of the trilogy — which I believe, in common with the majority of those who have considered the problem, to have once existed, and to have been entitled the *Prometheus Pyrphoros* — abandoned Hesiod entirely. And it is a likely inference, since no important pre-Aeschylean source from the Prometheus story other than Hesiod is known, that it must have contained a freely invented synthesis of the antithesis set up in the first two plays.

Finally, the evidence about the earliest of the Aeschylean late group, the *Suppliants*-trilogy, strongly suggests the same pattern. All versions of the legend of the Danaid girls, at all dates, agree on the basic story: the escape of the girls and their father from Egypt to Argos, chased by their cousins; their eventual unwilling marriage; and those 49 murders on the wedding-night. But there is no fixed tradition at all as to what happened after that night; thenceforward there are as many versions as there are tellers.[6] What is known of Aeschylus' *Suppliants*-trilogy suggests, beyond reasonable doubt, that the first two of its plays, the *Suppliants* and the *Aigyptioi*, between them contained the two responding movements that are found in the universal tradition — the enforced flight, the enforced union. The third and last play of the trilogy, the *Danaides*, evidently opened[7] with the discovery of the massacre in the wedding-chamber, on the dawn after the wedding. But the most important fragment from this play (125 Mette; one of the most famous passages of Aeschylean poetry in its own right) indicates that it, too, subsequently ran wild, like the *Eumenides* and the *Prometheus Pyrphoros*. The speaker is the goddess Aphrodite herself, who has, it must be noticed, no business in any other recorded dénouement of the Danaid legend. And she is speaking, not about the *human* sexual relationship, with which the earlier two plays of the trilogy were concerned, but about the love which unites the Earth and Sky in the spring rains:

> Now the pure Heaven yearns to pierce the Earth;
> now Earth is taken with longing for her marriage.
> The rains showering from the mating Sky
> fill her with life, and she gives birth, for man,
> to flocks of sheep and to the lifegiving wheat.
> And from that liquid exultation springs,
> perfect, the time of trees. In this I share.

It seems certain from these lines that a deity has materialized in person on the stage in the Danaids, presumably to take one side or the other in the human feud. And it further seems likely from their mutilated context (preserved on a papyrus)[8] that Aphrodite's speech dealt *at length* with the question of the relationship between male and female right across the cosmos, including vegetable and animal fertility as well as the primal marriage between Earth and Sky. This development, of course, would closely associate the ending of the *Suppliants*-trilogy with that of the *Oresteia*; where we can still observe in detail how one of the human motifs of the *Agamemnon* and *Choephori*, the relative roles of man and woman, is raised to cosmic importance in the *Eumenides*. In the latter play, as we all know, the male Olympian powers are ranged on one side, the female pre-Olympians on the other; holding the balance is the sexually ambiguous figure, Athena (daugher who has no mother, earth-deity and Olympian deity, woman in hoplite-armor); and an issue that becomes of increasing importance as the play marches to its climax is the fertility of Athenian crops, cattle, and women.

To summarize: the principle of trilogic composition that appears to obtain in the Aeschylean late group means that the first two members of a trilogy follow the outline of the traditional legend and have responding movement, while the third is largely free invention, designed to synthesize the antitheses set up in the former two. It is useless to look for such a principle of composition in anything that was written after Aeschylus' death, because of course the practice of composing connected trilogies was then almost entirely abandoned (there are only three recorded instances later than 456 BC, and no details survive of these). But we do possess one example of a connected trilogy from immediately *before* Aeschylus' late group, the Theban trilogy of 467 BC, and the comparison is startling. Here there survives only the last of the three plays, the *Seven Against Thebes*, but the titles of the two plays that stood before in the trilogy, the *Laius* and the *Oedipus*, are known, and are revealing enough for the contents. The third member of *this* trilogy — which, as already mentioned, is played out against the background of a still undivided archaic cosmos — comes to its grim end in accordance with the universal legendary tradition, with the annihilation of the princely brothers, Eteocles and Polyneices, at each other's hands. In the *Seven* there seems to be very little rehandling of the basic legend, except to make it slightly more ghastly than the versions known to Pindar earlier and Herodotus later by causing the princes to die without issue. Here the Gods do not materialize on the stage; they do not take sides in the human feud, nor are their relationships in any way affected by it; far from being divided, they join hands to bring about the disaster on the mortal plane. In fact, in the Theban trilogy Aeschylus retains both the archaic cosmos and the archaic story, dramatizing the saga right to the end.

A word should be said here about the tetralogies of Aeschylus that are represented only by fragments, and by no surviving plays. Not one can be precisely dated, but the vast majority must certainly belong to the thirty-year period before the late group; as we have seen, there is simply not room for more than a minute fraction of them in the years from 466 onwards. What little can be seen of these lost works – and it must be admitted that it *is* little – implies the trilogic technique of the Theban trilogy rather than that of the late group; dramatization, that is, of the ancient saga to the end, not free invention and synthesis in the third play. This is almost certainly true of one of the most deplorable losses from ancient poetry as a whole, Aeschylus' trilogy on Achilles;[9] the final tragedy in that, the *Phrygians or Ransoming of Hector* followed the outlines, at least, of the twenty-fourth book of the *Iliad*. And the trilogies on Ajax and on Odysseus respectively, though no one would dare to speak dogmatically about their contents, would seem to suit a straight treatment of the heroic saga, rather than the A, A, B movement of the late group.

Trilogy-technique, then, is one major feature which certainly links together the three works of the late group, and at the same time sets them sharply off from the immediately preceding Theban trilogy, if not perhaps also (though this is obviously far more speculative) from some other earlier trilogies. A second such feature has already entered this argument, and I need not add much to it here: this is the *involvement of the Gods* as partisans in the issues of the trilogy, and the concomitant split, not just on the human level, but in the cosmos itself. This happened very probably in the last play of the *Suppliants*-trilogy (we recall the speech of Aphrodite), and certainly at the end of the *Oresteia*. The *Prometheia* evidently contains this same feature, but gives an amazing twist to the pattern; for here the trilogy opens instantly with the involvement of the Gods and the cosmic split, and the humans, except the semi-human Io and (in the *Unbound*) Herakles, are kept off the stage altogether, at least in the first two plays. There is a distinct possibility, however, that the humans came back in the third play, the *Pyrphoros*; many enquirers have guessed, and with some sound reasons, that this play may have culminated in the founding of the Athenian torch-races in honour of Prometheus. If that is so, there will have been in the *Prometheia* a sort of inversion on the process seen in the *Suppliants*-trilogy and the *Oresteia* (where the problem climbed up through the human level to the divine), but the strong family resemblance is still there.

A third feature common to the late group must be stated at this time with dogmatic brevity;[10] it is the appearance in these trilogies of the forms and techniques of Old Comedy – an art which became a respectable form only in the last twenty years of Aeschylus' life. If I am right in my belief that the whole structure of the *Eumenides* is largely explainable in the light of the Old Comic convention, and that there are distinct traces of the same convention in the *Suppliants* and *Prometheus*, then this is at least further proof that Aeschylus' art was receptive, even in his comparatively advanced old age, to what was *new*: to what was new outside tragedy, as well as within it. But there is one likeness to Old Comedy (at least as we know it from Aristophanes' earlier plays thirty years later) that goes deeper than mere formal considerations. I think we are all agreed, unless we are theorists of the medieval school, that a play need not end in physical catastrophe in order to merit the name of 'tragedy'. And yet what other Athenian plays, outside the *Oresteia*, end in positive outbursts of *joy*, in a triumphal torch-procession, and with benedictions on the land for the fertility of its crops and its women? Practically the whole of the final song of the *Eumenides* consists in such benedictions, with the loud refrain 'Rejoice!'

> Rejoice, rejoice in your just shares of wealth!
> People of the city, rejoice!   (*Eum.*, 996 f.).

> Rejoice, again rejoice, our cry redoubles:
> all who in the city live!   (*Eum.*, 1014 f.).

In fact, that sort of benediction is only heard once elsewhere in Aeschylus, in the *Suppliants* of all plays (625 ff.): while for *dramatic finales* which contain such benedictions, and a torchlight procession, and the redoubled cry 'Rejoice!', we have to turn to a comedian, Aristophanes. The end of the *Peace*, for instance, combines all three (1317 ff.):

> We must carry torches . . . and pray the Gods to give wealth to the Greeks, and that we may all alike raise much barley and much wine, and eat figs, and that our women may bear us children. . . .

And then, in the final words of the *Peace* (1355 ff.):

> Rejoice, rejoice, people, and if
> you follow me you'll have cakes to eat!

The *Oresteia*, I think beyond doubt, *ended* in what the spectators could at once see was the manner of Old Comedy — though of course transposed into a nobler key. In estimating what this means we must not forget that Comedy, down till near the end of the fifth century, was much closer to its origins in actual popular religious cult than Athenian tragedy was at any stage where we have knowledge of it. Paradoxically, to the conservative religious or pious spectator, an Old Comedy was probably a more serious act than tragedy itself; in that not only by its origins, but by its costumes and the very form of many of its jokes, it concerned the most ancient and urgent of human needs — the reproduction of crops, of animals, and of the race itself. Aeschylus, it seems to me, so modelled the end of the *Oresteia* that it would appeal to that primeval religious feeling too, besides appealing to the more modern type of mentality among his audience; to the old tribal consciousness as well as to the New Learning in that hectically changing community which was the Athens of his last years.

It would be a bold man — certainly a bolder man than I am — who flatly asserted that the finales of the *Suppliants*-trilogy and of the *Prometheia* must have shared the Old Comic character of the *Eumenides*. Yet three considerations certainly point strongly in that direction. First, few who consider the extant material will doubt that those two trilogies must have ended in harmony, in a synthesis of the antitheses expounded in their first two plays. Second, the great *Danaides* fragment, quoted and discussed above, shows that the last play of the *Suppliants*-trilogy moved into the same ambit — fertility — as the *Eumenides* does; a subject which otherwise is the province of comedy, not tragedy. Third, one notes with great interest the theory already mentioned, that the *Prometheus Pyrphoros* culminated with the founding of the Promethean torch-races. Torchlight at the end of the play, with its symbolism of triumph and marriage, would again link the *Prometheia* to the *Oresteia*, and at the same time distinguish the pair of them from any other Attic drama whatsoever *except Old Comedy*; where torches appear towards the end more commonly than not, and in which three of the eleven extant finales actually consist of torchlight processions.

The last characteristic feature of the late group which I am going to speak of can be dealt with more briefly because the individual facts involved have long been recognized. There is a number of passages in the plays of Aeschylus which are so close to doctrines known to have been under discussion by contemporary pre-Socratic philosophers that mere coincidence seems ruled out. What is not so easily recognized, but is (I believe) true, is that all the reasonably certain instances of this sort of allusion are found in the plays of the late group.[11] They are not specially obtrusive in their dramatic contexts, but if one reflects on them as a whole they add up to a certainty: that in his last years Aeschylus was, at least, *aware* of the philosophical movements that were gathering in strength across the Greek world (especially in Sicily, which Aeschylus knew well in the last two decades of his life, and where, in fact, he died) — a rising hurricane which, by the end of the following generation, was to have swept away the structure of archaic thought and religion. How much does that awareness have to do with the new shape and new tendencies of the late trilogies? Are the late trilogies a sort of response by an enquiring, but still essentially religious late-archaic mind, to the coming of philosophy?

The answer to that may become clearer a little later. Meanwhile, to sum up on what has been said so far, I suggested at the beginning of this paper, first, that these three trilogies stood close together chronologically. That belief was reached in the first instance from external and technical considerations, but I hope that what has been said since may reinforce it; thematically too, and compositionally, they seem to belong together. Second, I suggested that they were in fact so different from anything called 'tragedy' before or after them that they practically constitute an art-form of their own, a very short-lived art-form that flourished, at the outside, for a decade, and was never revived. One of the trilogies concerned does not even *begin* like a conventional tragedy; the stock complaint, and a well-justified complaint, about the *Suppliants* is that it is not 'tragic'. And while the *Oresteia* may seem to begin like tragedy of the older type — the *Agamemnon* in many ways reads like a maturer draft of the *Persians*[12] — it is, taken as a whole, almost a denial of tragedy. To seek a name for the new form would be pointless; 'tragicomedy', which might have served, is already in use for something quite different. But one may look for a parallel to it, and I do not think it too fanciful to find that parallel centuries later and in a sphere far from Athens: in Dante's *Comedy*. Dante, by the way, would have called the *Oresteia* too a 'comedy' without hesitation, if we can trust the views put foward about his own work in the letter to Can Grande: *a principio horribilis et fetida quia Infernus; in fine prospera, desiderabilis, et grata, quia Paradisus . . . et sic patet quare comedia dicitur.*[13] But perhaps it is better not to quibble over names; I see more than a superficial likeness between the *things*, between Dante's Hell, Purgatory, and Paradise and Aeschylus' *Agamemnon*, *Choephori*, and *Eumenides*. In both the tripartite works there is a similar movement, a gradual climb from torment, through testing, into the light. Indeed, if Headlam's and Thomson's ideas about the Orphic symbolism of the *Oresteia* are anything like correct, there is not only a likeness but — at a vast distance — a historical connection. For there exists a certain underground current of mystical belief which flows for ever, calmly ignoring frontiers and religions.

But to come back to that troubled decade, 466–456 BC. Another of the suggestions made at the beginning of this paper was that once these three trilogies were firmly grasped as being a unique group, produced within a short period under a single impulse, they would throw considerable light on each other, and especially on the *Prometheus*. It will be worth while to end by outlining the way in which the grouping might help towards the understanding of that most problematic of all the characters in Aeschylus: Zeus.

The great argument here for the last century or more has been, of course, that the tyrant-Zeus of the *Prometheus* will not fit — that he is irreconcilable with the sublime Zeus known elsewhere in Aeschylus' work. Does he really not fit? The question is worth reconsidering.

Throughout the series *Suppliants*-trilogy, *Oresteia*, *Prometheia*, I trace two new and even more urgent preoccupations, which I believe, must explain each other. A preoccupation with the split in the cosmos; and a preoccupation with the possibility that Zeus may emerge from the chaos as the ultimate authority, *panaitios, panergetas*, all-responsible, all-worker (to quote the Chorus of the *Agamemnon*, 1486). I think we need have little hesitation about the significance of the cosmic split in these late trilogies. When archaic man runs head-on into classical free enquiry, when a tradition of static authoritarianism in politics and religion finally comes face to face with classical democracy (and it happens that the emergence of full-blown democracy, both in Athens and in Sicily, coincides very closely with the last ten years of Aeschylus' life) —when these confrontations occur all at once, the world will in fact seem to split; from the microcosm of the mind, through the state, to the divine macrocosm itself. It is almost a matter of indifference at which of those levels you think of the cleavage. Though Aeschylus (characteristically) chooses in these plays to show it primarily in its aspect of cosmic cleavage, one might think that the struggle in the *Eumenides* makes almost equal sense if you take it as the struggle between the Olympian *ego* and the infernal *id*, or, more prosaically, as that between liberal and conservative. Certainly, for our time as well as for that of Aeschylus, it seems to mean more than a momentary disturbance among fading pagan gods. It is a deadly feud from which not one of us is free.

Aeschylus, it is true, did not have so gloomy an opinion, for in these same plays, as a possible healer of the cleavage, stands Zeus. Lately an assault has been launched against the idea, so popular in the nineteenth and early twentieth centuries, that Aeschylus was the founder of a new and sublime Zeus-monotheism, and it has been held instead that all the difficulties can be swept away by assuming that his Zeus is quite primitive (that is the word used) throughout; no more developed than the Zeus of the epic poets.[14] I am coming to wonder whether this assault does not go too far and simplify too much. It has done valuable work by questioning some hardened prejudices. But even apart from the difficult question of its method (the rigidly positivist interpretation of Aeschylus' language gives me pause, because poets of all people, almost by definition, do not and cannot use words positivistically), do its results perfectly fit the phenomena?

There is, indeed, a primitive Aeschylean Zeus, no advance on the Zeus of Homer and Hesiod (or, come to that, on the woman-and-boy-chasing Zeus who appears on early fifth-century vase-paintings), but I suspect that he belongs to the dramas of the phases earlier than 466 BC. This is the Zeus who is cursorily mentioned, with no special emphasis, in the *Persians* and the *Seven*; perhaps the fully anthropomorphic Zeus who was actually brought on the stage – on the only occasion we know of in fifth-century Attic tragedy – in Aeschylus' *Psychostasia*; certainly the Zeus who mated with a cow-formed Europa in the play called *Kares ē Europe*, and who is roundly abused by Danae (whom he has seduced in the golden rain) in the satyric *Diktyoulkoi* (lines 774–84). But Aeschylus certainly knows of at least one other Zeus, who has nothing to do with Homer or Hesiod, or any writer earlier than his own day: the Zeus of that stupendous couplet from the lost *Heliades* (*The Daughters of the Sun*): 'Zeus is Aither, Zeus is earth, Zeus is heaven; Zeus is all, and whatever is beyond the all.'

The dramatic context of these words is unknown, and the play to which they belong is undated. But even as they stand, even if the play should be rediscovered and it should prove that they were qualified or denied in the next line, they surely constitute complete proof that the poet's mind was at least open to more than the epic and archaic view about Zeus. For a brief and shattering moment they let us glimpse a universe in which the orthodox polytheism and anthropomorphism simply cannot exist – in that respect strikingly similar to the universe implied in the writings of Aeschylus' senior contemporary Xenophanes (whom, so far as dates and known movements go, he could quite well have met at the court of Hieron in Sicily).

If, to Aeschylus, the concept 'Zeus' was as malleable as the *Heliades* fragment suggests, there now seems nothing to forbid the conjecture that in these last three trilogies we see a series of experiments, not only with the idea of a cosmic split, but with the idea of Zeus as the possible answer to the new and chaotic condition of heaven and earth. The experiments will be open-minded and honest, though there will underlie them a basic faith, inherited from archaism, in the simple power of the archaic supreme god. In the process of the experiments, Zeus will gradually and naturally move nearer to the centre. The same critic who has assaulted the concept of a sublime Aeschylean Zeus has also objected to the idea (likewise popular in the nineteenth and earlier twentieth centuries) of an 'evolving' Zeus, which is often brought in to solve our problems. I think he is justified, and I have learned from him not to believe in an evolving Zeus, either. But I do believe, as the whole of this paper has suggested, in an evolving Aeschylus. From that point of view I take a final look at the late group of trilogies.

The *Suppliants* was always famed for its majestic and moving Zeus-hymns.[15] And even in the days, not so long ago, when the play was commonly dated in the 490s or 480s BC, they were customarily compared with the equally splendid Zeus-hymn of *Agamemnon* 160–83, 'Zeus, whoever he may be . . . ' – without anyone's feeling much embarrassment, apparently, about the almost total absence of such august language from what would then have to be the intervening plays, the *Persians* and the *Seven*. Now that the *Suppliants* seems to be brought down within perhaps as little as five years of the *Agamemnon*, that difficulty, at least, vanishes. But what is still perhaps not enough noticed is that in both these trilogies the Zeus-hymns occur fairly early in the first play, and are placed, of course, in the mouth of the chorus. One would naturally incline to take them within rather than outside their dramatic context: as intuitive hopes by the helpless girls and the old men respectively, rather than, at that stage, as definite statements by the poet. And in fact, in the *Oresteia* we have to wait very long indeed before that intuitive hope is justified. Not only does unnatural murder have to be done, but the universe has to be parted in two, with Apollo and the Furies (and behind them, offstage, Zeus and the Fates respectively) as opposing partisans. And during the middle section of the *Eumenides* we are to have visions of a universe from which all authority has gone, leaving only that mindless and pitiless chaos across which Euripides, later on, was to move consciously all his life. (But that was after the philosophic revolution was complete.) It is only at the very end of the *Oresteia* that the gash is healed, and the original intuitions fulfilled; but it has been touch and go. We cannot know about Zeus's part in the later stages of the *Suppliants*-trilogy, for obvious reasons. The immense importance, however, that is attached to him in the extant play, suggests that he must have been heavily involved at the end also. And the *Danaides*-fragment makes it almost certain that the cosmic cleavage was there.

In almost every way, even down to minor technical and metrical details, the *Prometheia* takes a stride beyond the *Oresteia*. Here the trilogy *begins* on the cosmic level, instead of rising to it from humanity, and *begins* with a total cleavage on that level. And here Zeus, instead of being kept on the periphery of the actual struggle – instead of being the remote object of human hopes – has moved into the eye of the storm. If there was to be anything beyond the *Oresteia*, it probably had to be this. The two preoccupations, with the cosmic split and with Zeus, fuse into one, and the last question is being asked: can the archaic god survive as a viable force in the new world? We only see, now, one side of the debate, not the response. But this much seems likely. In the *Prometheus Bound* Aeschylus fearlessly and honestly shows, through the eyes of Io and Prometheus, a picture of the archaic power-god which is not really too exaggerated a caricature of the Zeus known to Homer and Hesiod, except that it has taken on political overtones. It apparently includes even Zeus the seducer, the Zeus of the *Europe* and *Diktyoulkoi*, here shown at his worst with Io. There are hints, however, both in the prophecies of the *Bound* and in the fragments of the *Unbound* itself, that in the second play a different aspect of Zeus began to be uncovered: the Zeus who freed the Titans, who at least did not prevent the coming of Prometheus' savior Herakles, who — almost unbelievably — *pitied*,[16] and who in the end came to terms with the intellectual, the *sophistēs*, Prometheus.[17]

Anything said about the final synthesis in the last play of the *Prometheia* is bound to be a guess, but here is one. Those who have claimed that the Zeus of the *Prometheia* is irreconcilable with the Zeus of Aeschylus' other works have always pointed to the great Zeus-hymns near the beginning of the *Suppliants* and the *Agamemnon*, and the absence of anything of the sort in the *Prometheia*. The guess is that when the Day of Judgment comes and all vanished Greek literature is unrolled before us, we shall find that missing Zeus-hymn — in the finale of the last play of the *Prometheia*, the *Pyrphoros*. And that it will be a hymn of joy.[18]

11

CHARACTER IN SOPHOCLES

P. E. EASTERLING

Critics are always reminding us that character-drawing in Greek tragedy was a very different thing from what we meet in the modern theatre, different and (it is implied) perhaps more limited or rudimentary. But this contrast between ancient and modern is too vague to be illuminating: we need to define exactly what kind of difference it is before we can decide whether it is important. In drama meant for live performance it can hardly be a difference of *technique*, since every playwright is limited to two basic means of character-drawing, what his figures say and do and what other people say and do to them and about them. Nor can there be much significance in differences of *convention*. Of course convention counts for something: a dramatist writing for three masked male actors, who must take all the speaking roles in his play, male or female indiscriminately, using a highly formal and declamatory style of acting in a large open-air theatre, will create characters which can be rendered in these circumstances. But there is no reason why the particular conventions of his time should limit his portrayal of character in any serious way: Lady Macbeth, after all, was written to be played by a teenage boy. Surely the differences that really demand attention are those of *attitude*.

Modern audiences, brought up on post-Romantic literature with its overwhelming emphasis on the individual, and conditioned by modern psychological terminology, expect a dramatist to be primarily concerned with the unique aspect of each man's experience, with the solitary focus of consciousness which, as John Jones puts it, is 'secret, inward, interesting'.[1] When they first read a Greek play they are naturally inclined to interpret what the characters say and do as if the ancient dramatist shared their preoccupation with idiosyncratic detail. But closer study soon makes plain that this is an anachronistic prejudice, which can all too easily lead us to irrelevant or absurd conclusions.

The prologue of *Trachiniae* will perhaps illustrate my point. The first

From *Greece & Rome* 24 (1977), 121–9, Reprinted with the excision of some words of Greek by permission of the author and the Oxford University Press.

forty-eight lines are a careful presentation of Deianira, full of significance for the rest of the play. She begins by recalling her past, how she was courted by the terrifying river god Achelous who came to her in the guise of a bull, snake, and bull-headed man. Heracles appeared and challenged him, and there was a duel; but she could not bear to watch: 'I sat apart terrified lest my beauty should bring me pain one day' (24-5). Then she describes Heracles' victory and their subsequent life together, or rather apart: Heracles always away from home performing his Labours, herself waiting in lonely anxiety. Here we have a speech of the greatest importance for our understanding of Deianira, establishing her history as the princess who was the object of violent passion and showing how her life as wife of Heracles has brought her nothing but fear, pain, and loneliness. What of the detail at line 25? In a modern writer it would certainly have to be interpreted as a glimpse of idiosyncrasy: Deianira talking about her own beauty would be revealing her self-absorption, even her narcissism . . . But the tone in Sophocles is so clear that the 'modern' interpretation does not even occur to us, and we take the line quite straightforwardly as an unselfconscious statement of the situation: it is Deianira's rank and beauty that make her a fitting battle prize for the great river god and the great hero. The phrase is picked up in a telling way later, when Deianira sees the captive princess Iole and pities her 'because her beauty has destroyed her life' (464-5). Deianira does not yet know that, like her, Iole has been fought for by Heracles; for the audience there is irony and pathos in the echo, which links the two women as victims of Love. The idea is further developed in the lyric which follows this scene (497 ff.): the Chorus recall the duel of Achelous and Heracles and the beautiful Deianira sitting apart (523-5) as an analogy to the case of Iole.

So the apparently rather incidental detail at 24-5 turns out to have an important function, which we are in no danger of failing to recognize; but later in the same prologue there is a passage which it is much easier to misinterpret, Deianira's response to the Nurse's advice. Deianira has ended her long speech with an account of her present anxieties: Heracles is still away, no one knows where, but there is reason to fear that he is in danger. The Nurse suggests sending one of his sons to find news: Hyllus, as the eldest, is the obvious choice, 'if he is concerned for his father's safety' (56-7). Hyllus opportunely rushes in; Deianira at once acts on the Nurse's advice, paraphrasing her words in a rather striking way: 'She says it is a disgrace that you are not trying to find out where your father is, as he has been away so long' (65-6). The Nurse has in fact said nothing of the kind; why does Deianira rephrase her words like this? Because Sophocles wants to give her a suitably dignified and queenly response (this is also the effect of her preamble at 61-2, 'Son, even the lowly can speak noble words . . .'), and it is dramatically important to create a sense of urgency: Hyllus must be stirred to act straight away.

Editors and critics commonly ignore these details, which give a purposeful tone to Deianira's words, and instead make much of the fact that she has failed to take action earlier and even now has to be prompted by the Nurse. Does not this mean that she is irresolute, weak-willed, helpless, timid? But it is easy to see why Sophocles leaves the decision to look for Heracles till now: the play must open at the most critical moment; and the sending of Hyllus must take place within the play, not before the action starts. Hyllus himself gives the reason why nobody has taken steps to look for Heracles before: in the past he was always successful (88-9). When the greatest of Greek heroes is away on an expedition his family expect to wait patiently at home, not to go running after him. Why make the *Nurse* suggest sending Hyllus, though? We may guess that Sophocles chose to do it like this partly because the Nurse would have had greater impact in the scene where she reports Deianira's suicide if she had already been introduced to the audience early in the play, partly because she can convey expository information about Hyllus (at 54 ff.) more appropriately than Deianira herself; and in any case it is more interesting for the audience if the action starts with someone else's response to Deianira's account of her anxieties. I suggest that, having decided to use the Nurse for these or whatever other reasons, Sophocles gave Deianira the rather dignified words at 65-6 precisely to avoid an impression of weakness.

Suppose then, that we agree to be wary of our natural preoccupation with idiosyncrasy and to distrust the modern view of what constitutes an 'interesting' character, what is there to be said positively about character portrayal in Greek tragedy, or more particularly, in Sophocles? For the ancients, at any rate, Sophocles was one of the great masters of the art, as a famous passage in the *Life* attests: 'He knows how to arrange the action with such a sense of timing that he creates an entire character out of a mere half-line or a single expression. This is the essential in poetry, to delineate character or feelings' (21). And Sophocles himself, according to Plutarch (*De prof. in virt.* 7), described his mature style as 'the best and most expressive of character'.

Perhaps it will be helpful to start by making a distinction between idiosyncrasy and individuality. For it is a striking feature of Sophocles' characters that although we are given so little circumstantial detail about them they are all clearly distinct from one another, and it does not seem to be enough to say that he is just a brilliant depictor of *types*. One might argue that in the *Tyrannus*, for example, Sophocles does indeed make us believe in Oedipus' intense experiences of fear and hope and pain, but that is as far as it goes: Oedipus could be any noble sufferer finding out the truth about himself. But I suspect that most of us when reading or watching the plays are conscious of a significant difference between Oedipus and, say, Ajax or Philoctetes, which goes beyond the basic observation made by G. H. Gellie[2] that 'these people are different because their stories are different'. Of course the stories are important; and in any case all the main and many of the minor characters had a certain pre-existing mythological identity which helped to give them individuality. It is also true that Sophocles deals in dramatic formulas, particularly that of the intransigent hero or heroine whose passionate refusal to compromise is set off by the sympathetic ordinariness of an associate.[3] But he finds ways of making the formulas work differently in different plays, so that Chrysothemis, for instance, is quite distinct from Ismene, though both have the same functional role, and Tecmessa, Deianira, and Jocasta are all sharply individualized.

This impression of individuality derives, I think, from the dramatist's ability to seize on significant detail. Much must depend on the intensity with which he explores the situations he takes from the myths; if he can recreate them in dramatic form with the fullest understanding of what happens to people and what they do and feel in real life, then he will be able to present his readers with the significant details that force them to suspend disbelief and accept his characters as individuals. This demands of us as critics that we use our imagination, as actors do when they are trying to understand a part: in other words, we have to be open to psychological insight in the dramatist's observation.

Consider the notorious scene early in *Oedipus Tyrannus*, where Tiresias tells Oedipus the whole truth about himself; but Oedipus responds only to the accusation that he is Laius' murderer (apart from giving just a fleeting hint of uncertainty at 437 and 439, when he tests the seer about his parentage). How do we explain this failure to react to the rest of Tiresias' denunciation, particularly his speech at 447 ff.? 'Fortunately', says Tycho von Wilamowitz[4] 'it cannot be explained in terms of Oedipus' psychology, because the Chorus reacts in the same way and can talk . . . only about the murder of Laius. . . . The poet's intention is a far cry from all psychological refinements, and the effect of this scene, which is still powerfully felt, does not depend on the presentation of so-called characters.' The dramatic power, he goes on, is the contrast between the knowing seer and the unsuspecting Oedipus, with Oedipus forcing the full revelation of his guilt out of Tiresias. The characters understand only what is necessary for the action and do not

hear the rest. Can one doubt that Sophocles knew he was being im-
plausible?

The essential point left out of this analysis is Sophocles' insight.
Tiresias accuses Oedipus of killing a man he *knows* he has never met, a
king what is more, whom he could hardly expect to meet and kill without realizing it in some casual skirmish.[5] Oedipus knows, therefore, that
the accusation is false; but false as it must be it comes as a shattering challenge to his sense of his identity, and there is nothing at all surprising in
the fact that he is unable to take in the rest of the seer's words, which
suggest even more outrageous and unthinkable guilt. No wonder, either,
that the Chorus are unable to grasp their significance. Thus, although
the scene may indeed have little directly to do with character-portrayal,
it does deepen our sense of the reality of Oedipus' experiences.

This impression of depth, of a solid individual consciousness behind
the words, is often conveyed by the ambiguity with which Sophocles
treats people or episodes. Take Antigone. A great many details of her
motivation are left inexplicit, but from what we are given most of us
have a full and vivid picture of that role and know how we would want
it acted. But we should not all agree — and I think this is quite an important point. It seems to be true of most great roles that they offer
scope for varying interpretation (I mean of course something more
serious than mere producer's gimmicks, like putting on Hamlet in a
space-suit). When Antigone rejects Ismene's claim to share the guilt of
burying Polynices (536 ff.), how do we interpret her motives? No doubt
it is too sentimental to say that she is using those cruel words as an
attempt to shield Ismene; some of her retorts recall the harsh way she
spoke to her sister in the prologue, when there was no third party present
(one thinks particularly of 69–70: 'I won't ask you again, I won't accept
your help if you change your mind'). On the other hand, it would be
too trivial to narrow down Antigone's reaction to simple petulance or
doctrinaire martyrhood: is it not a more whole-hearted sentiment than
that? Certainly the picture is complicated by Ismene's reiterated claim
that life without Antigone is not worth living (548, 566) and by her
remark at 570 about the love of Antigone and Haemon. Critics will go
on disagreeing; but at least Sophocles has given us something real in this
ambiguous little scene.

What I am trying to suggest is that a dramatist with a delicate sense
of the complexity of experience will often give his characters words and
actions which are susceptible of varying shades of interpretation, for in so
doing he will be imitating life. Behaviour that can be variously explained
has great dramatic potential; what bores us is either motiveless, totally
inconsequential behaviour which we cannot relate to our observation of

life, or its opposite, the over-simple, too predictable behaviour we meet in soap-opera. We welcome an imitation by the dramatist that 'character' is not a static thing detachable from people's words and actions, but a dynamic phenomenon not ultimately to be separated from what they say and do. Sophocles' extant plays abound in examples of this kind of ambiguity: the Deception Speech in *Ajax* (646 ff.); Clytemnestra's reaction to the false news of Orestes' death in *Electra* (766 ff.); Odysseus' threat to Philoctetes that he is to be left behind on Lemnos: 'We're leaving you here, we don't need you now we have the bow. There are plenty of expert archers at Troy . . . ' (1054 ff.). This can be seen as a bluff designed to force Philoctetes off the island, or as a genuine threat: readers react differently, but the important point is that Sophocles creates a situation — as in life — in which both interpretations are plausible, and he thereby gives a certain depth to his portrait of Odysseus.

One of the finest examples of Sophocles' sustained use of ambiguity comes in this same play. When Neoptolemus is carrying out the plan to trick Philoctetes, almost everything he says can be interpreted in two ways, either as direct deceit or as an indication of his growing reluctance to take part in the trickery at all. So at 431 ff., where he is talking of the Greek heroes at Troy, we know he has been instructed by Odysseus to tell whatever slanderous stories he likes about him as part of the deception (65), and this makes it hard to know how to take his denigration of Odysseus. He could just be leading Philoctetes on when he agrees with him that Odysseus is one of the wicked who survive, by contrast with the good, like Ajax and Antilochus, who die (426 ff.); but the audience knows that he was reluctant to use deceit in the first place, that he is after all the son of Achilles; and this scene shows him and Philoctetes forming a bond based on shared heroic attitudes. So at 431, for example, when he slightingly calls Odysseus a 'clever wrestler' and adds that even clever schemes are often thwarted, or at 441, when he again insults him, we cannot help wondering whether this hostility is not seriously meant. Certainly the pitiful appearance and dignified behaviour of Philoctetes affect the audience's feelings: one is bound to wonder, as one watches the scene, how far they are affecting Neoptolemus' feelings too. How long will he be able to sustain the deception?

The stage action itself is often used to contribute to the depth of the situation the dramatist is exploring. I argue elsewhere[6] that the breaking point for Neoptolemus comes when he supports Philoctetes physically, raising him to his feet after his attack of the disease (893 ff.). Sophocles puts the visual action to equally powerful use in *Electra*, when Orestes tries to make Electra set down the urn so that he can convince her that her brother is not dead after all but alive and standing beside her

(1205 ff.). In the *Coloneus* there are two great moments when the stage action greatly deepens our sense of Oedipus' consciousness. The first comes at 1130 at the end of his speech of gratitude to Theseus for rescuing Antigone and Ismene from Creon. Oedipus is overjoyed; he wants to take Theseus' hand and embrace him – but then he suddenly holds back. 'What am I saying?' His sense of his own pollution prevents him from touching Theseus or allowing Theseus to touch him; and yet one of the most insistent themes in this play has been Oedipus' passionate assertion of his innocence (e.g. 266 ff., 966 ff.). This instinctive feeling of pollution is a touch of great psychological nicety; it is worth considering the possibility that the whole sequence – Creon's kidnapping of Antigone and Ismene, and their rescue by Theseus – is designed to lead up to this dramatic moment. The second example is the famous climax at 1540 ff. when the blind Oedipus leads the way on stage, in striking contrast with his helplessness shown all through the play so far, and particularly in the prologue, where he has to be led step by step.[7]

I have said little so far about language, though this is surely one of the most important means of creating an impression of depth: if a character talks with the power of the Deception Speech in *Ajax* or Electra's opening anapaests (86 ff.) or her lament over the urn (1126 ff.) we are forced to recognize the reality of the person portrayed. I am not of course suggesting that Sophocles consistently gives each character a style of his own. There are habits of style that any character will use in certain circumstances – in an *agon*, or a narrative, or stichomythia – in response to what Miss Dale[8] called 'the rhetoric of the situation', which reminds us of the dangers of over-interpretation I mentioned at the beginning. However, one can detect some degree of characterization by style, for example in contrasts between noble and lower characters: in *Trachiniae* the differences between Deianira, the rather grand herald Lichas, and the crude old man who comes as messenger, show that it can be a fairly complex matter too. But beyond this use of style to differentiate there is a more pervasive use of language, inextricable from the poet's development of a play's themes and structure, which deepens our awareness of the particular individual at the centre of the action. This is one reason why I think we can go further than Gellie in his claim that 'the people are different because their stories are different'. What I want to suggest is that Sophocles' conception of his central character or characters influences his choice of words and images in a quite fundamental way.

Philoctetes is a clear-cut example, though each of the plays illustrates the same technique. Not only is Philoctetes given a series of magnificent speeches, full of subtle detail; he is also the focus of almost everything in the lyrics, and the play's leading images are all associated with him: the desert island with its lonely rocks and its wild beasts, the wound, the bow, the dead man. The theme of his loneliness is explored in terms both of being cut off from civilization (as in the lyric at 676 ff.: he has no neighbours, no one to heal him, no crops, no wine) and of having only the wild creatures and the rocks of Lemnos for companions — and the birds and beasts that are his prey will prey on him in turn if he is abandoned without the bow. All this, which is both literal and symbolic, creates a highly individual impression of Philoctetes, which distinguishes him sharply from other great sufferers in Sophocles. Of course he is cast in the same mould as Electra and Oedipus, but the poetry which defines him is uniquely his.

Finally, can we agree with the ancient *Life* that Sophocles captures a character in a 'half-line or single expression'? If one can allow a whole verse there is Antigone's famous 'It is my nature to join not in hating but in loving' (523); or there is Philoctetes' brief and ordinary-seeming question at 923-4: 'Stranger, what have you done to me?' This depends for its powerful impact on the cumulative effect of all Philoctetes' generous and trusting words to Neoptolemus up to this point. All through the play he has called him 'my child', 'my son', but the moment when he realizes that Neoptolemus has been deceiving him and his trust evaporates is precisely defined with 'O stranger'.

I have perhaps been implying in these notes that in the matter of characterization the differences between Sophocles and modern dramatists are ultimately unimportant, that there is nothing in modern drama that does not have its counterpart in his plays. In a qualitative sense I believe this to be true: his insight into human behaviour and his gift for expressing it in dramatic form remain unsurpassed; but it would be absurd to argue that he covers all the same ground as his modern successors. There are times, if we are honest, when we are made uneasy by the extremely public nature of his characters, as indeed by that of all characters in Greek tragedy. This is no doubt because the Greeks were interested in individuals as part of a community much more than in the individual's unique private experience, a difference of attitude which is sometimes hard for us to share or appreciate. For example, in Sophocles the loneliness and isolation of the suffering hero is a major tragic theme, but his heroes are quite unlike outsiders in the modern sense, men and women who can only define themselves meaningfully in terms that cut them off from society for good. There are many things that his characters simply do not talk about and that he and his contemporaries presumably never thought about. But that is a historical matter, something to be discussed in a quite different sort of paper.

12

AJAX

KARL REINHARDT

The *Ajax* is a drama which plunges right into the middle of the catastrophe, or its consequences; it does not begin with what had preceded that catastrophe. The subject of the tragedy is not Ajax's quarrel with Odysseus and the Atridae, or how, cheated of the arms of Achilles, Ajax resolves on vengeance, or how he is seized by madness – all of which might well have provided highly dramatic themes. On the contrary, the drama begins on an unprepared *fortissimo*: during the prologue the mad Ajax is summoned out of his tent; at this point there is a break; and what follows is virtually a new, contrasting beginning. Then comes, as the first part of the tragedy, the melancholia and death of a man fully conscious of what he is doing, and, as the second part, the dispute about his burial. We have here a kind of catastrophe-drama which shows from the very beginning how a human being has to *come to terms* with his fate, which has already been *decided*.[1] This type of structure and content is by no means common in Attic drama; of all the tragedies that survive, the *Ajax* is the only one of this kind. The *Ajax* is also unique among Sophocles' tragedies in that it opens with the entrance of a visible deity who points to the victim of its wrath. In front of the tent of Ajax, Odysseus hears the voice of his patron goddess, Athena, visible in her divine splendour only to the audience and to the demented Ajax; she summons her victim out of the tent, encourages him in his confusion, pretending to support him, but at the same time really betraying him to his enemy; and not content with this cruel behaviour, she goes on to drive home a moral (118 ff.):

Athena
    Do you see, Odysseus, how great the gods' power is?
    Who was more full of foresight than this man,
    Or abler, do you think, to act with judgment?

From *Sophocles*, translated by H. and D. Harvey, pp. 9–33 (1979). Reprinted with abridgements and revisions by permission of Barnes and Noble Books, and Basil Blackwell Publishers.

Odysseus
   None that I know of. Yet I pity
   His wretchedness, though he is my enemy,
   For the terrible yoke of blindness that is on him.
   I think of him, yet also of myself;
   For I see the true state of all of us that live —
   We are dim shapes, no more, and weightless shadow.

Athena
   Look well at this, and speak no towering word
   Yourself against the gods, nor walk too grandly
   Because your hand is weightier than another's,
   Or your great wealth deeper founded. One short day
   Inclines the balance of all human things
   To sink or rise again. Know that the gods
   Love men of steady sense and hate the proud.

The speech of the avenging deity, and the fact that the drama begins *after* the catastrophe, are both unparalleled and have therefore struck critics as odd. Those who were not content to account for this in terms of aesthetic considerations put the blame for what they considered a faulty structure on an alleged primitiveness on the part of a poet 'not yet quite sure of himself'. They tried to lessen the *fabula docet* effect, the didacticism which offends our sensibilities, by regarding it as addressed to the audience only, and by separating it from the action; as if Sophocles were making use of the goddess to mention something in passing. . . .[2] But in fact these two difficulties, the nature of the deity, and the opening of the play at the point of the catastrophe, are closely bound together. And the lesson to be drawn from the words of the goddess, however strange it may seem that she apparently stands outside the realm of mortality, gives her intervention an unmistakable meaning: this is Man before God!

But where is the origin of this to be found? The Ajax theme had already been treated in epic, in the *Little Iliad* or in the *Aethiopis*; and although it is no longer known what rôle Athena played in these works, it was certainly not the rôle she plays in Sophocles. In the *Iliad* Athena deceives Hector in his flight, in order to deliver him into Achilles' hands. But Sophocles' Athena goes much further than Homer's: she continues to play her tricks on the man after he has been betrayed. And it is this element of pointing, demonstrating, making an example of a man, which is as far removed from epic as anything can be, especially with the additional didactic element. But if it comes from neither epic nor saga, where does it come from? Is it an innovation by Sophocles? But in that case why do we have nothing else like it? And if it is Sophoclean, is it early or late? Is it developed or primitive?

These questions can now be answered, thanks to a text which has only recently been discovered. The unique elements in the *Ajax* are not to be explained by any lack of skill or any wilfulness on the part of the poet; they are due to the influence of an earlier work and reveal a style which is still bound by archaic conventions. In the light of this discovery we can now estimate for the first time how much Sophocles 'learnt from Aeschylus', as the *Vita* puts it. It is the first certain proof that the *Ajax* is an early play. It must be the earliest of all the surviving plays, certainly much earlier than the *Antigone*, which is generally considered to be the earliest.[3]

The discovery to which we are indebted for this is a piece of papyrus containing fragments of Aeschylus' *Niobe*. From the twenty-two lines — for that is all that survives, and the beginning and end of each line are lost — we may infer an unexpected amount of information concerning the history of tragedy. Like the *Ajax*, the *Niobe* was a tragedy of shattering destruction, opening — *after* the judgment of the deity, *after* the *hybris* of the heroine — with the sufferings of a character persecuted by a divine being: a drama of dumb anger, of dull pain, of the need to come to terms with the terrifying power of fate; a representation of passive pathos, with just as little 'action' as the *Ajax*. When Ajax has become conscious of what he has done, he sits absorbed in his own thoughts, brooding on his fate, without uttering a word; he reveals himself in his misery and breaks his silence in answer to the cry of his family in order to bid farewell to his little son, only to plunge immediately all the more violently into silence, without his tent. That is exactly how Niobe sat in dumb misery 'without a word during half the drama', veiled at the tomb of her children. Just as Athena points her finger at the mad hero, we learn from the new papyrus that Leto, the immortal mother, revealing herself in all her power, pointed at the mortal mother: for just as Ajax had boasted before Athena of his heroic deeds, Niobe had boasted before Leto of the number of her children. And the moral conclusion which the goddess in Aeschylus adds is astonishingly similar to the didactic passage which is put into the mouth of Athena in the *Ajax*:[4]

Leto
    Now you can see the marriage's conclusion,
    This is the third day that she has sat by this tomb,
    the living mother wailing over her dead children,
    lamenting the wretched fortune of their beauty.
    A mortal brought to ruin is nothing but a shadow.
    Mighty Tantalus will soon come here
    intent on bringing her back home again. . . .
    To you — since you are not unsympathetic — I will

explain: a god implants a fault in mortals
when he intends to ruin their house utterly.
Even so, a mortal must not speak presumptuously
but guard the fortune that the gods have sent him.
Yet in great prosperity men never think that they
may stumble and spill the full cup they're holding.
And so, exultant in their beauty, she . . . *

The same stylistic elements — the visibility of the goddess, gnomic interpretation, the victims' consciousness of their fate — are peculiar to both tragedies: even before the discovery of the papyrus a fragment [fr. 159 Nauck² = fr. 278 D Mette] was known which read:

Tantalus
My destiny, which reached up to the heavens
now plunges down to earth and says to me:
'Learn not to admire too much the things of man'.

Just as Tecmessa finally comes to Ajax pleading in vain, so Tantalus came in vain to Niobe, hoping to comfort her and to persuade her to live. . . . And even if we can never know the rest of the tragedy, enough is certain. The *Ajax* and the *Niobe* belong to the same genre.

But the similarities in external formal construction show up all the more clearly the difference between the two poets' deeper personal conceptions of tragedy. In Aeschylus the disaster falls on the whole house; husband and father share in the downfall. . . . Niobe represents the fate of her whole immoderately large family. In Aeschylus a human being even in his downfall does not stand only for himself or by himself. The ruined man is not an individual separated from the world that contains and sustains him, before Sophocles. The fact that it is necessary to make room by force for Ajax's monologue for the first time in the middle of this drama, an indication of the break-through of a new mode of speech, is at the same time the most powerful expression, and historically the most memorable symbol of a new tragic consciousness which is unknown before the time of Sophocles. The relationship between the two poets is made clear by the fact that in Aeschylus' *Women of Thrace* [fr. 83 Nauck² = fr. 252 Mette] which treated the same material, there was still the traditional messenger's report instead of a monologue, still a description of the unhappy death of Ajax instead of the speech of the isolated individual who has prepared himself for death.

But there is another innovation. We cannot understand the deeper

* [We have translated the text of H. Lloyd-Jones (Loeb Aeschylus ii), not that used by Reinhardt.]

contrast between the nature of the tragedy of Ajax and the tragedy of
Niobe if we do not realize that each is conditioned by a different type
of deity. In Sophocles the goddess has her sport with the mortal.[5] And
this sport, and everything connected with it (on the one hand the confusion of the madman trapped by his own delusions, on the other hand
the harshness and irony of the divine will) is presented in a form which
is more cruel than anything in the Ajax saga or any other work known
to us. Even more cruel than anything in Aeschylus, despite the terrible
things of which his gods are capable. That a person's intentions and impressions should clash with the reality of his nature and his surroundings,
so that everything he does and says becomes a mockery of what he
wants and believes, is a peculiarly Sophoclean motif; it appears for the
first time — admittedly in a traditional form — in the prologue of the
Ajax, and it recurs in some form or variation in every later work. And
even if in the three late works, the *Electra,* the *Philoctetes* and the
Oedipus at Colonus, the clash appears playful and secondary rather
than terrible and central, nevertheless in the end it breaks out once
more with all its old power: for finally it creates one of the most powerful scenes in the *Oedipus at Colonus.*

But what is later revealed within the bounds of a human fate appears
at the beginning in the form of the divinity in person (71 ff.):

Athena
      You there, who are binding fast your captives' arms
      With fetters, come outside! Ajax! Come out!

                              . . .

      Ajax, I call you once again!
      Is this how much you care for your old ally?
                  (*Ajax enters with a bloodstained whip from the tent, where
                        he has been lashing, not Odysseus, but a ram.*)

Ajax
      Hail, Athena! Daughter of Zeus,
      Hail and welcome! How well you have stood by me!
      I shall deck you with trophies all of gold
      From the spoils of this hunting, in thanksgiving.

Athena
      Excellent. But tell me, did you dip
      Your blade well in the Greeks' blood?

                              . . .

      Well then, if your good pleasure wills it so,
      Do execution, carry out all you have in mind.

Ajax

 I must be at my work. Goddess, I charge you to[6]
 Stand always my ally as you have today.

 If we listen to the goddess, Ajax is 'bad' and Odysseus good. But this is only the judgment of the religion of humility — admittedly, a Greek, not a Christian humility — whereas, if we disregard the voice of this religion, Ajax is great, a hero, a colossus indeed in the greatness of his heart no less than in his physical strength. Does this mean that the goddess is blind to what Odysseus sees and feels? It is obvious that the mortality of the gods has nothing to do with their power. For the function of the divine (leaving aside, that is, its function in epic poetry) seems to be to define and limit the area within which man can act, and which can be measured by the mind of man.

 The figure of Ajax the outsider is developed by Sophocles beyond the Ajax of the epic poems. Similarly, Odysseus, the figure who stands in opposition to him, develops from the crafty fox of the epic into a character of god-fearing resignation, who can recognize himself in his neighbour. What has happened to the age-old contrast between the giant and the trickster, between the archer and the warrior with his shield and spear, between the nimble, inventive, adaptable Odysseus and the stubborn, steadfast, direct Ajax? It has developed beyond Homer's representation of the spirit of two types of warrior to become a contrast between two attitudes towards fate.[7] On the one hand stands the tragically unprotected, heroically rigid and inflexible Ajax; on the other, the protected, perceptive Odysseus, well-adjusted to his fate. Sophocles sets the intransigent Ajax, the man who wanted to massacre the Achaeans out of wounded pride and ambition, and the humane Odysseus side by side, thus foreshadowing the later contrast between the inflexibility of Antigone and the mildness of Ismene. Yet a comparison between this situation and a later untragic and protected contrasting figure — for Creon too stands in the same relationship to Oedipus — shows how the *Ajax* belongs to a quite different, earlier stylistic phase: there is as yet no tension or conflict between the opposites. Each stands alone, each holds his own fate within himself, each is self-sufficient, separated from the other — not seen in relation to him. Sophocles was able to make characters stand out in contrast with each other before he could relate them to each other and involve them with each other.

 The contrast between the victim of fate and the man who knows occurs also in religious narratives, and these may well have influenced Sophocles. Odysseus' awe in the presence of the downfall of human greatness is shared by Cyrus (Herodotus i. 86.6) when he rescues his enemy Croesus — who 'was a fellow human-being' — from the pyre, 'reflecting that nothing in the affairs of mortals is secure'. But what a difference dramatic presentation makes! It concentrates the abstract opposition of fortune and misfortune into a contrast between one individual in the grip of a daimon and one untouched by any daimon.

In the *parodos* the fall of Ajax, their leader, is echoed by the fears of his followers. The one is joined by the many, the great man by small men, who are brought together by the bad news. Their urgent questions bring Tecmessa from the tent. Expressions of fear concerning the dangerous rage of the soldiers who threaten both the leader and his retinue alternate with the narrative of the behaviour of Ajax, first in his madness, then after he had recovered his senses. This gives rise to a dialogue in melic form, of a traditional type: it is no more than an extended echoing and invocation of the fate which has overtaken them all. The *parodos* of the *Trachiniae* is similar, though simpler and shorter. The form becomes more elaborate later.[8] For although there are already in the *Ajax* two voices which alternate in question and answer, the *mood* of the dialogue is still monotonous by comparison with the later, less static developed form. The outlook and attitude remain the same from beginning to end; there is no change. It is particularly noticeable that there is no final climax. On the other hand, the language, with its vividness, its lyrical description, its invocations and wealth of imagery, is as a result more continuously devoted to the central theme, the fate which they are bewailing. Sophocles' choruses reflect the stylistic development of the *epeisodia* which separate them. Just as the action is most compact, tense and well-rounded in the *Oedipus Tyrannus*, so are the choruses; and the same phenomenon occurs in the other plays. On the other hand, at the early stylistic level of the *Ajax*, there is a greater wealth of imagery, even in the dialogue, and the language is noticeably more heroic: for example, pathetic comparisons are found only in the *Ajax* and the *Trachiniae*. Indeed, an accumulation of assonance and imagery such as that at the very beginning, when the goddess reveals herself to Odysseus (7 ff.):

Athena
   . . . You've coursed him like a keen Laconian hound . . .

and Odysseus answers:
Odysseus
   Voice of Athena, dearest utterance
   Of all the gods' to me — I cannot see you,
   And yet how clearly I can catch your words.
   That speak as from a trumpet's throat of bronze! [9]

— such wealth of assonance and imagery from the heroic age never occurs again in Sophocles.

The prologue portrays the mad Ajax; the first *epeisodion* portrays him after his return to sanity. The prologue reported the madness before the madman himself appeared; in the first *epeisodion* therefore the description of the tragic hero similarly precedes his appearance on the stage — this time inside his tent, revealed to the audience by the *ekkyklema*, the wheeled platform. This lessens the emphasis on the *transition* from madness to sanity, while stressing the two points of time which affect Ajax's destiny — his state before the transition and his state after it; the latter no less serious than the former (259). For not only is there no dramatic representation of the transition on the stage; but even the account of it (though told so much more sensitively, tenderly and intimately by Tecmessa than by the goddess in her more pitiless and explicit description) is still concerned exclusively with the contrast between the *states* of madness and sanity (311 ff.) — not with the transition or the painful awakening.

Tecmessa
    He sat so, without speaking, for some time;
    Then finally spoke those fearful, threatening words —
    What should befall me if I failed to say
    What had befallen him . . .
    Now, though, quite overcome by his misfortune,
    Refusing food and drink, he sits there motionless,
    Relapsed among the beasts his iron brought down.

Compare this with the madness of Euripides' Heracles, to take a later example of the representation of insanity: we find in Euripides what is lacking in the *Ajax*, the mental change as Heracles wakes and opens his eyes, which forms the climax of the most important scene. One might imagine that it was simply because the latter is Euripidean, the former Sophoclean. But this is certainly wrong, for there are plenty of transition and transformation scenes in other plays by Sophocles: for example, the transition from error caused by deception to truth in the *Philoctetes*, the change from the last glimmer of hope to deepest despair in the *Electra*, the plunge from illusion to discovery in the *Oedipus Tyrannus*, the transformation of deepest gratitude to deepest shame in the *Oedipus at Colonus*, to mention only a few. After the *Trachiniae*, change is sought, not avoided, and takes place not off-stage but as the climax of the *epeisodia*. The *Ajax* and the *Trachiniae*, in which pathos is presented in a stationary form and in which no reversal of emotion occurs during the action, stand on one side, and all the other plays on the other. Both in language and in dramatic composition, a change has taken place between the two types of play.

Nevertheless, in this early work, once the tonality has been established, the stream of lyric poetry is more resonant, ranges more widely, and breathes more deeply and expansively than in any other play of Sophocles. The lament of Ajax, like Ajax himself, is colossal. It lacks changes and variations of mood, but the result is that its fixed contrasts resound on an unceasing note, and the horror of the circumstances can be expressed without restraint: the greatness of Ajax and his shame, the sense of his heroic being and the senselessness of his fate, the hero turning his hatred on the outside world and his misery on himself, locked in lament or shouting his heart out. . . . The first sounds issue from the closed tent, as he calls for his little son and his half-brother; then the *kommos* (lament) accompanies the revelation of the interior of the tent: the battle-field strewn with dead cattle, the hero seated in the middle amidst the laments of Tecmessa and the chorus: the *picture* turns into melic dialogue. . . . And what echoes and re-echoes in the scene, the slyness of Odysseus his arch-enemy, the falseness of the leaders of the army, the mockery of his soldiers, the landscape and the scenes of his glory . . . all these threads are woven into the harmony of the inevitable end of the *kommos* (364 ff.):

Ajax
>Here I am, the bold, the valiant,
>Unflinching in the shock of war,
>A terrible threat to unsuspecting beasts.
>Oh! what a mockery I have come to! What indignity!

Tecmessa
>Ajax, my lord and master,
>I beg you not to say such things.

Ajax
>Go away! Take yourself out of my sight!

>>>>>>>>>>>>(*He groans*)

He is no longer worthy to lift his eyes to seek help from either gods or men. Where can he flee? Where can he stay? . . . (412 ff.):

Ajax
>O
>Sounding straits of the sea
>Caves by the sea's edge, meadows on the shore,
>Long and long have you kept me here in Troyland . . .

What follows the *kommos* is very much the same in the static way in which it expresses the tragedy: it is just as much without crescendo, change, climax or descent. In the prologue Ajax and Odysseus had stood in contrast with each other without either penetrating the consciousness of the other; the same is true of Ajax and Tecmessa in the second *epeisodion*. There is no interplay of dialogue, there is not a single word which has the power to communicate and penetrate the wall between them. Each remains the prisoner of his own fate. Ajax's speech rings out as though Tecmessa were not present; and Tecmessa's plea, urgent and touching as it is, does not touch Ajax either by its vibrant tone or the power of its arguments. She does not even provoke him to contradict her. And when she pleads, she expresses herself only from her own point of view; and that is hopelessly out of touch with her husband's.

The speeches of both characters begin with the same emphasis on fate; both characters recall their fathers; both end with themselves — and again it is not a coincidence that in all the tragedies of Sophocles it is this passage that is most comparable in genre and attitude with the opening speech of the *Trachiniae*. Even if the chorus does hear Ajax's decision — let them hear it, they hear it only as the audience hears it. No advice, no directions, no words are addressed to him — Ajax's powerful survey of the hopelessness of his position, delivered to the world with such pathos, stands in isolation, unresolved (457 f.):

Ajax
And now, Ajax — what is to be done now?
I am hated by the gods, that's plain; the Greek camp hates me . . .

Tecmessa begins her speech with a solemn *gnōmē*, which is followed by the account of her fate — her plea, too, develops into a narrative imbued with pathos (485 ff.):

Tecmessa
Ajax, my master, life knows no harder thing
Than to be at the mercy of a compelling fortune.
I, for example, was born of a free father;
If any man in Phrygia was lordly and prosperous, he was.
Now I'm a slave. Such, it seems, was the gods' will,
And the will of your strong hand . . .

The rest of her plea, right down to the last detail, is based on Homer — Hector's farewell to Andromache in the sixth book of the *Iliad*.[10] But because the model is so clear, the difference that is revealed by the way in which Sophocles adapts it for the stage is particularly significant. In the epic (vi 407 ff.: the following excerpts give some idea of the content), Andromache laments:

And you have no pity on your little son, nor on me, who soon must be your widow. . . . For me it would be far better to sink into the earth when I have lost you, for there is no other consolation for me . . . since

I have no father, no mother and they who were my seven brothers all went down into Hades, for Achilles slaughtered all of them, and my father too; my mother died at home, struck down by Artemis . . . Hector, you are father to me, and my mother, you are my brother, and my husband. Take pity upon me, that you may not leave your child an orphan, your wife a widow. . . . *

Like Tecmessa, Andromache speaks of herself and her son, but mainly because these are the two things most likely to persuade her departing husband to turn back. His reply also refers to them:

All these things are in my mind also; yet I would feel deep shame before the Trojans, and the Trojan women. . . . For I know there will come a day when Ilium shall perish, and Priam, and the people of Priam. . . . But it is not so much the pain to come of the Trojans that troubles me, nor even of Hecuba nor Priam, nor the thought of my brothers in their numbers and valour, . . . as the thought of you, when some Achaean leads you off, taking away your day of liberty, in tears; and in Argos you must work at the loom of another, and carry water from the spring Messeis or Hypereia, reviled and dishonoured; and some day seeing you shedding tears a man will say of you: 'This is the wife of Hector, who was the bravest fighter of the Trojans, in the days when they fought at Ilium!' May the earth hide me under before I hear you crying and know by this that they drag you captive.*

Tecmessa's plea does not seem at first sight so very different (510 ff.):

> . . . And last, dear lord, show pity to your child.
> Robbed of his infant nurture, reft of you,
> To live his life out under the rule of guardians
> Nor kind nor kindred — what a wretchedness
> You by your death will deal to him and me!
> And I no longer have anywhere to look for help,
> If not to you. My country was destroyed
> Utterly by your spear, and another fate
> Brought down my mother and my father too . . .
>   . . . Then what fatherland
> Shall I ever have but you? Or what prosperity?
> You are my only safety . . .

And yet how *different* the two speeches are. Take, for instance the slavery awaiting the wife — Tecmessa and Andromache alike, for the future of each will be the same — when one of the Achaeans takes her away as his booty, and the remarks that will then be passed around:

---

*[This is based on the translation by Richard Lattimore (University of Chicago Press, 1951), modified to correspond with Reinhardt's phrasing.]

'See, this woman was once the wife of Hector' or 'this woman was the wife of Ajax, the greatest of all heroes.' In the epic it is the husband who thinks about this, a touch which enhances the tenderness of the situation; in the tragedy it is not the husband but the wife. That is, in the epic they speak to each other, in the tragedy they speak without communicating with each other, for each speaks his own language to which the other does not listen. The words of the wife die away without a syllable having reached her husband's ears, and vice versa. Ajax's thoughts of his father, his home, his son, respect and shame (*aidōs*) are to him reasons for committing suicide; but precisely the same ideas appear to Tecmessa as reasons for *not* committing suicide. But neither speech refers to the other, neither refutes the other; they do not touch or lead to any argument for and against; rather, they express two incompatible philosophies of life, each justified from a different, totally separate standpoint.

Instead of replying, Ajax commands that his son be brought to him.[11] Why had he been kept at a distance? When Ajax hears that it was for fear that in his madness he might attack him too, he says (534):

Yes, that would have been worthy of my evil genius.

And yet, when the child is brought to him, we forget for a moment that the hero is standing, not among dead enemies, but among dead cattle; the hero's farewell is like a farewell on a battlefield; the dissonance between the hero and his fate, his soul and his circumstances could not be more terrible (545 ff.):

Ajax
Lift him up, lift him to me. He won't be frightened,
Even by seeing this fresh-butchered gore,
Not if he really is my son.

. . .

My boy, have better luck than your father had,
Be like him in all else; and you will not be base.

He will not let the mother come near him. His solicitude for his son, the heir to his heroism, is the only thing which brings him out of the prison of his fate, the barrier erected around him by his 'daimon'.[12] But as though this were too great a sacrifice to sentiment, he has scarcely finished pouring out his heart when he calls even more impatiently for the door of his tent to be shut, so that he may retreat silently into himself again.

There can no longer be any doubt as to what will happen. The chorus which concludes this scene ends like a lament over one who has already fallen: they sing of how the mother of Ajax will cry 'woe' and beat her breast when she hears of the calamity that has befallen her child. It would be better for him to be hidden in Hades; when he left his father's house he was the best of the Achaeans, and now he has gone so far astray. . . . But when in the *epeisodion* which immediately follows Ajax steps out of his tent, he is a changed man. And now, if we are not to misinterpret what follows, we must make use of comparisons.[13] Only by comparison can we grasp the formal structure and avoid being misled by perverse modern interpretations. Has a genuine transformation taken place? Can Ajax be lying? And if he is lying, why? Or do his lies change into truth? There are as many interpretations of this passage as there are possibilities. But before we indulge in speculation, we should bear in mind that the same phenomenon recurs in the *Trachiniae* (436 ff.), the play which comes next in chronological order. So we should start by making sure that the interpretation is valid for both the *Ajax* and the *Trachiniae*.

It is true that the two speeches, both that of Ajax and that of Deianira, are speeches of deception, obviously uttered to mislead another person. Both are equally unexpected in the mouth of a person who until that point, whether standing in silence, speaking or singing, had always remained rigidly enclosed in the world to which he is bound by his own fate, apparently incapable of any difference in conduct or any change of attitude. The characters plunge into both speeches with equal abruptness; neither is preceded by any previous deliberation; neither is directed towards any goal which has been mentioned before. They are thus both very different from any form of *intrigue*, either external and caused by circumstances, or within the mind. But in that case we are entitled to speak of deception? Indeed some scholars have concluded that we cannot. Yet in both cases the deception is revealed by the reversal which follows, in which the apparent truth of the speech is confronted with the real truth. In both cases we are completely unprepared for the reversal that reveals the real truth; its effect is like the impact of a shattering blow on the chorus in both plays, an impact similar to that caused by the reversal that had revealed the apparent truth a little earlier.

But the roots of the relationship between the speeches go even deeper. They both counterfeit the truth; but, more than that, in spite of the obvious deception involved, they both unfold a tale which is rendered so convincing to the ear by the wealth of its imagery that the will to deceive does not suffice to explain its pathos. In these speeches the individual, in his loneliness and isolation, comes to realize the truth about the way in which all things fit together, in an order which is valid not only for the community of which he is no longer a part, but as the very essence of Nature, which is valid both in heaven and on earth. So the individual who has been cast out exercises his own will in spite of the circumstances by which he is bound, and frees himself not only from the ordinances of society but also from the ordinances of all existence.[14]

The eyes of Ajax are suddenly opened, he recognizes the world, but he refuses to fit into it, to submit to its ordinances, to follow the rule 'Know thyself'. Rather, he sees in the world something alien and contrary to his nature, in which he could participate only if he were no longer Ajax: 'If I were to submit to this world and its gods, who tolerate nothing that is extreme or persistent, no final Yes or No, I would hate my enemy, but, bearing in mind that he may one day become my friend, I would limit my hatred accordingly' (he alludes to the saying of Bias [Ar. *Rhet.* 1389 b, 24-5]); 'and I would do good to my friend, bearing in mind that his friendship might not endure for ever' [679-82]. He has to perish, not only because he has detached himself from his heroic environment — that was already his fate in the epic — but because the world can no longer contain him. The comparisons which he makes between himself and the world of nature are more than a rhetorical device; they are more than the dignified language of tragic diction. While they stress change as a universal law to which all realms, both the macrocosm of nature and the microcosm of man, are subject, they bear witness to a feeling concerning the world close to that of Heraclitus: 'God is summer and winter, day and night . . .' [fr. 67 Diels-Kranz[6]]. But in the words of Ajax a discord can be heard underneath the noble praise of the order of the world, an undertone of revulsion, almost of scorn of that wisdom which is the wisdom of this world (646 ff.):

Ajax
    Strangely the long and countless drift of time
    Brings all things forth from darkness into light,
    Then covers them once more. Nothing so marvellous
    That man can say it surely will not be —
    Strong oath and iron intent come crashing down.
    My mood, which just before was strong and rigid,
    No dipped sword more so, now has lost its edge —
    My speech is womanish for this woman's sake . . .

              . . .

    From now on this will be my rule: Give way
    To Heaven, and bow before the sons of Atreus.
    They are our rulers, they must be obeyed.
    I must give way, as all dread strengths give way,

In turn and deference. Winter's hard-packed snow
Cedes to the fruitful summer; stubborn night
At last removes, for day's white steeds to shine.
The dread blast of the gale slackens and gives
Peace to the sounding sea; and Sleep, strong jailer,
In time yields up his captive. Shall not I
Learn peace and wisdom? Have I not learned this,
Only so much to hate my enemy
As though he might again become my friend,
And so much good to wish to do my friend,
As knowing he may yet become my foe?

In this passage the deception grows from an irony which has deeper roots than what we generally call 'tragic irony'; here the irony arises from a dawning perception of an everlasting discord between the hero and the way in which the world is organized.[15]

It is true that the speech of deception in the *Trachiniae* does not employ the same wealth of comparisons with the world of nature as that in the *Ajax*; but Deianira disguises her intentions in the same way. She pretends to recognize and glorify a power which governs mankind, the gods and the world; but this recognition is deceptive, since she does not act in accordance with her words. Admittedly it is not the same power as that in the *Ajax*; but it is as much in conflict with the unchangeable nature of the loving Deianira as the law of change is in conflict with the inflexibility of Ajax. What Deianira pretends to recognize — that is, what she recognizes as valid for the world, but not for herself — is the law of change, confined to the only part of the world that she recognizes, her own world — Love. Just as Deianira boasts of her insight at the moment when she least possesses it, so Ajax pretends to fulfil the law 'think as a mortal should: do not presume to go further' when he is furthest from doing so [cf. *Trach.* 439, *Ajax* 677].

But in Ajax's 'speech of deception' his newly gained perception helps him to make a decision. The result of his perception was not deliberate dissimulation; similarly the result of his decision is not an intention to mislead. Rather, Ajax's own mind is the victim of self-deception to such an extent that, far from voluntarily intending to mislead, Ajax involuntarily *veils* his meaning: 'But you [Tecmessa] go in and pray to the gods that they may grant fulfilment of my heart's desire.' In this passage the words 'desire' and 'fulfilment' are both veiled; they are veiled allusions to 'the fulfilment of death' — and this is an action as far removed from a trick as it is from the usual word-play of irony; it is not even ambiguous like the 'long sleep' which Schiller's Wallenstein plans, but is the attitude of a man hiding himself in darkness (687 ff.):

Ajax

> And you, my friends, heed my instructions too,
> And when he comes, deliver this to Teucer:
> Let him take care for me and thought for you.
> Now I am going where my way must go . . .

But the veiled language is at its most veiled when it comes to the thought of the suicide weapon, the sword. It is true that Ajax needs an excuse to move away with his sword without arousing any suspicion, but it is not merely this excuse which gives his speech a secret inner meaning: his intention outstrips his words, and the 'speech of deception' becomes a monologue; his words, instead of remaining within the play, break right through its framework and address the audience. They signify: this is Ajax, this is how he veils his words, here is a man who is turning away from reality to appearances, who is renewing his allegiance to the unreal, a man who is making atonement, who is in truth unteachable, who is shutting himself off from everything – for he does not begin to shut himself off completely before the lines which give an *appearance* of participation in Society (654 ff.):

Ajax

> But now I'm going to the bathing place
> And meadows by the sea, to cleanse my stains,
> In hope the goddess' wrath may pass from me.
> And when I've found a place that's quite deserted,
> I'll dig in the ground, and hide this sword of mine,
> Hatefullest of weapons, out of sight. May Darkness
> And Hades, God of Death, hold it in their safe keeping.
> For never, since I took it as a gift
> Which Hector, my great enemy, gave to me,
> Have I known any kindness from the Greeks . . .

His thoughts circle around his death. The 'enmity' of the weapon, the 'digging' of it 'in the ground', 'Darkness' and 'Hades', the 'beyond-ness' of the 'deserted place', the 'cleansing' of the 'stain': all these are just as valid as images of his inner self, but transposed from clarity into obscuring, veiling references.[16] Deception drives Ajax into the abyss: once more he draws around himself the disguising veils of this world and its hopes which have become alien and inimical to him.

This is the key to the relationship between Ajax's 'speech of deception' and his monologue, from which it is separated by the episode in which his followers go to look for him. The relationship is one of contrast between veiling and unveiling, between illusory participation in society and the nakedness of the solitary soul in the face of death. The cleansing of the stain, the enmity of the weapon, the hostility of the

ground and the implacability of his hatred, everything that had previously
been veiled, now stands as naked as the hero himself (815 ff.):

Ajax

> He's firm in the ground, my Slayer. And his cut
> (If I have time even for this reflection)
> Should now be deadliest. For, first, the sword
> Was Hector's gift, a token of guest-friendship,
> And he of all guest-friends my bitterest foe;
> Here, too, it stands, lodged in this hostile ground
> Of Troy, its edge made new with iron-devouring stone.
> And, last, I've propped it, so, with careful handling,
> To help me soon and kindly to my death.
> This preparation I have made. And now,
> Making my invocation, as is right,
> I call first, Zeus, on you . . .

The monologue with its sevenfold invocation embraces the entire
world around him, the world in which he has his roots and from which
he is departing; friend and enemy; Hector and the Atridae; Zeus and the
Erinyes; his ancestral home and the scene of his exploits; Salamis and
Troy; light and death. This invocation is arranged in accordance with
the Greeks' view of the world as composed of pairs of contrasted antitheses. No lament, reproach, world-weariness, aversion, no hint of
melancholy, not even the melancholy of a Brutus — none of the bitterness of renunciation; right up to the very moment of his death, the
moment when he sets himself free from the ties of the world, he is
unable to lose, either in love or in hate, his preoccupation with that
same world which scorns him, and him alone, and which he, and only
he, can no longer bear. Imagine the totally different way in which
Euripides would have made Ajax put the blame on the world! Each of
the invocations is followed by a final prayer, a final greeting — except
that the invocation of death is broken off, and in its place comes a final
greeting to light (854 ff.):

Ajax

> Strong God of Death, attend me now and come.
> And yet I shall converse with you hereafter . . .
> O radiance, O my home and hallowed ground
> Of Salamis, and my father's hearth, farewell!
> And glorious Athens, and my peers and kin
> Nurtured with me, and here all springs and streams,
> My nurses, you that wet the plains of Troy,
> Farewell! This last word Ajax gives to you;
> The rest he keeps, to speak among the dead.

It is only in his speech of deception, taken in conjunction with his monologue, that Ajax is finally caught up in the incompatibility between two worlds — his private world and the everyday world. The inflexible fighter becomes the inflexible soul; the man deprived of his honour becomes the man deprived of the world, and, because he was too firmly rooted in his private world, he is punished. For the gods remain the guardians of this cosmos. The tragedy of Ajax does not take place in a world which is out of joint.

For the purpose of dramatic presentation, the contrast between what is veiled and what is revealed is set in the context of a rambling, changing inter-play of hope, awe and fear on the part of those close to Ajax; a song of jubilation at his 'unhoped-for change' (716–17) is followed by the news of the warnings of the seer, and everyone hurries to look for the hero whom they now know to be in danger. . . . The stage has to be empty to allow for the change of scene — it appears that the *ekkyklema* was used for the second time at this point:[17] now, suddenly, we are taken to a distant place, where the sword is fixed firmly into the ground, concealed by the surrounding undergrowth, and the hero stands in front of it. There also had to be provision for the actor who played the part of the living hero to be replaced by the dummy representing his dead body, which appears with the sword thrust through its chest. . . . After that, the chorus, divided into semi-choruses, re-enter from either side, with weary steps to indicate that they have come a long way in their desperate search — and then Tecmessa stops with a sudden cry at the place where the body has fallen. Now that the body has been discovered, they all stand around it, and begin the lamentation over the dead hero. His body has fallen forward, but Teucer lifts it up and displays it, covered in blood. . . .

But this is more a question of stage-management, the outer trappings of the play, an area in which the young Sophocles was fond of innovation and experiment. Furthermore, the motif 'Too late!' is not developed from the character of the fallen hero, and has no connection with his fate; he is involved in it merely for the purpose of the framework of the play. It is true that the speech of the seer, as reported by the messenger, recapitulates, interprets, and points to the future, but what a difference between this early work and the language of the Tiresias scenes in the later plays! Instead of arousing shudders of fear and unleashing threatening powers, it adds no more to the play than an anxious warning and a didactic explanation, which, in any case, after a gnomic opening, soon reverts to the epic style of reported narrative. The anecdote about the remark of Ajax which illustrates his lack of a sense of moderation is modelled on Odysseus' description of Achilles' departure

from home in the *Iliad* (ix 254);[18] and what follows is much the same.
There is no question in this scene, as opposed to those in the later plays
in which a prophet appears, of two different worlds coming into contact
with each other; the relationship between man and god, as illustrated in
this speech with examples from the past, does not go beyond the traditional framework of archaic ethics, the doctrine of moderation. Thus
the traditional type of interpretation is juxtaposed in this early work
with the power of the new style of tragedy just as sharply as the tremendous innovation of the monologue is juxtaposed with the old device
of introducing a messenger within an *epeisodion* to bring news and to
explain the situation. Scenes of this kind are no longer to be found in
the plays of Sophocles' later style.

The second part of the play — the coda or whatever you like to call
it, the dispute about the burial — is less concerned with purely theatrical
considerations than the first. For it is certainly not just tacked on for
merely external reasons, in order to make up the length of the play, as
some have thought; nor is the relationship of this part to the whole
satisfactorily explained by saying that the fate of the body was more
important to an Athenian than it is to us. Not everything which is considered important is turned into drama. The purpose of the finale is
rather to contrast the genuine greatness of the tragic hero who was
fated to die with the spuriousness and conceit of those who opposed
him, triumphed over him, and lived on — their ingratitude, pusillanimity,
envy, meanness and arrogance.

Certainly we must take the play for what it is. There is no development or forward movement; instead, one set of circumstances simply
succeeds another, and we watch a collection of contrasting figures who
are united only by their relationship to the central figure of the hero. It
is not that he has any effect on them or they on him: it is rather that
they shed light on his character, in that their characters define his by
contrast. We have already seen how Tecmessa, while embodying and
foreshadowing her own fate, provided the contrast of feminine with
masculine. Similarly Teucer defines Ajax's character by contrast: he is
the noble bastard, who is to be driven out of his own country with
curses by his father because he returns home without his greater, legitimate brother: for that incident too — which involves the same type of
pathetic deliberation as Ajax's decision to die — is presented simply in
the form of a lament of the surviving for the fallen, without being interwoven into the plot as 'action'. This preference for setting the fates of
different characters in contrast with each other, and indeed the overall
preponderance of demonstration, direct representation and didacticism
over development and forward movement, the predominance of a series

of relationships over dynamic action and gradual downfall, is the aspect
of the play which more than anything else determines the character of
the whole of the *Ajax*, not only of its last part. Thus, later, when Teucer
becomes the mouthpiece of the poet, even the relationship of both
friendship and enmity between Hector and Ajax is revealed as determined
by fate (1034): when they exchanged the sword and the belt, what a
difference between the meaning that they both attached to the action
and the meaning which in fact it was destined to have! Hector was
dragged to death, according to Sophocles, by that same belt which Ajax
had given him, and Ajax killed himself with that same sword. They had
hoped to escape the fate that hung over them, but it used their behaviour
as a means of fulfilling the divine will which operates above and beyond
the human context (1034 ff.):

Teucer
> Did not a Fury beat this weapon out?
> And was it not Aidoneus, that grim craftsman,
> Who made that other one? In my opinion,
> That was the gods' contrivance, like all other
> Destinies of men, for the gods weave them all.

Thus there would obviously be something lacking from the whole
picture if there were no opportunity for that deceitful world which opposed Ajax, and upon which he wanted to take his revenge, to express
itself; and it is the Atridae who speak for it. And the fame of the hero
whom the gods overthrew is enhanced by contrast with the lack of
moderation of the petty men who seek vengeance: the sententious
complaint of the over-commanding sub-commander Menelaus, who preserves the morality of the *polis* — and yet is unable to get the better of
Ajax to any great degree (much in his character already points to the
Creon of the *Antigone*), and the explosively quarrelsome way in which
the highest dignitary, Agamemnon, expresses his envy of Ajax's glory.
Confronted with innate worth, outward rank, as represented by Agamemnon, can only adorn itself with jangling maxims about the whole-
someness of obedience and the stability of the state: orders must inspire
fear in the army just as *nomoi* do in the *polis*, and so forth. Contrast
this petty-mindedness with the final greatness of Ajax! Contrast this
'righteousness' of the little men with the 'wrong-doing' of the great
hero!

But in order to round off the drama in this way, Sophocles made use
of the old formal device of the *agon*, or set debate — indeed, as scholars
have observed, an *agon* of a particularly antiquated type: the opponents
enter to prevent the burial, one after the other, and exit again with

threats or protests, as in the *agon*-scenes of comedy; word rebounds against word, reproach against reproach, maxim against maxim. There is so little attempt to disguise the genre that the *agon* is even described as such in the choral anapaests that introduce the second half (1163). Thus as a method of representing the opponents, the *agon* appears to our minds to be unduly restricted by the formal nature of its construction. Instead of situations which develop from the *nature* of the pervading hostility, there is a ready-made *schema*, a mere substitute for it, which has to be filled with the appropriate ingredients. Perhaps the lack of development, movement and progress is due to the traditional nature of the form. Even the grudging retraction of Agamemnon which is provoked by Odysseus makes no difference. The attitudes of the opponents at the end are just the same as they were at the beginning; the strife continues to rage in all its fury but it does not shift its ground — and in this too it is similar to the *agon*-scenes of comedy.

The tableau on the stage makes amends to us for this in one respect: all the time that the brawl is growing in intensity, Tecmessa and Eurysaces kneel in the background, guarding the body, a silent, motionless group. The child holds in his hand the hair-offerings of his family as a gift to his dead father, in the posture prescribed by Teucer (1180):

Teucer
>Take it, dear child, and guard it, and let no one
>Remove you, but cling fast, inclining over him . . .

At the end, the chorus divides, going away in groups to either side, as Teucer commands: to dig the grave, erect the tripod, fetch the armour. . . . Teucer and the boy remain by the dead man, they raise him — he is still bleeding.

Thus there is much in this play that is unique. Methods which will be discarded by Sophocles in his later work stand cheek by jowl with others which point ahead to later developments. Above all there is the conception of a single figure who is presented in only one or two situations, which is unparalleled in the later plays. To a greater extent than any of the later works, the *Ajax* seems to have been composed around this central character; the rest of the characters are seen in the light of this dominating figure, whether they interpret it, look back at it, or stand in contrast to it. But the interpretation falls short of the conception, and the form of the play seems to conform to the religious drama of the older style rather than to rise from the heart of the work. It is not until the *Oedipus Tyrannus* that both form and content grow together so as to form a perfect unity.

13

ANTIGONE: DEATH AND LOVE, HADES AND DIONYSUS

CHARLES SEGAL

Antigone's lonely journey to the cave and Hades follows an ancient heroic pattern, the dangerous quest into the unknown, which pervades ancient literature from the Gilgamesh Epic through the *Odyssey*, *Aeneid*, and beyond. Her heroic journey, however, also has a distinctly feminine character. She defies the city in the name of the house, and she takes on the role of Kore the Maiden, carried off to marry Death in the Underworld and then returned, after a period of barrenness and mourning on earth, with the joyful new vegetative life of the spring. Antigone's cave is a place of contact between worlds: between life and death, between Olympian and chthonic divinity, between gods and men. In moving into the darkness of the cave Antigone effects a passage between life and death, the familiar and the unknown, vitality and sterility. This experience is in part modeled on that of Kore-Persephone in her descent to become the bride of Hades.

Antigone, however, is a Kore who does not rise again to new life. She refers to herself repeatedly as 'bride of Hades', a term that makes the analogy with Persephone unmistakable, particularly as the association with Persephone was a regular feature of funerary practices and funerary epigrams for girls who died young.[1] Yet although the Eleusinian Demeter plays a prominent role in the fifth stasimon, there is no clear allusion to the return of her daughter. When Antigone invokes Persephone by name in the context of her imminent descent to Hades as her 'underground bridal chamber' (*nympheion*, 891, 1205), it is to Persephone as queen of the dead, 'she who has received the greatest number of my perished (kinsmen) among the dead' (893-894).

From *Tragedy and Civilization: An Interpretation of Sophocles* (Cambridge, Mass. and London: Harvard University Press, 1981) pp. 179–88. Reprinted by permission of the author. Text excerpted by the author from a lengthier chapter with certain footnotes omitted for this edition. Those referring to this essay for scholarly purposes are requested to consult the original version.

The mythic paradigm of Persephone enlarges the reversal of upper and lower realms predicted by Teiresias. Not only are rites of burial and sacrifice inverted but the Kore's cycle of descent and ascent as well. This Kore remains in the lower world and draws her living spouse down after her. We may recall again Antigone's special devotion to the cult of the dead and to 'the Justice who shares her house with the gods below' (451).

In the Kore myth the maternal figure, Demeter, remains a constant source of hope for the return to life and light. In this play that figure is Eurydice, whose name, 'the wide-ruling one', signifies the Queen of the Dead. At the end, more like Antigone's Niobe than the chorus' Demeter (cf. 1120 ff.), she mourns the hopeless death of her children and then returns to the death-filled interior recesses of the doomed house. A *mater dolorosa*, she too is drawn into the dark, Hades-like hollows of enclosure. There is no Demeter-like mother left alive to call the Kore back to life. The maternal figures of the fourth stasimon, Danae, Cleopatra, Eidothea, either suffer or inflict imprisonment and in the last example destroy rather than nurture children.

Antigone herself doubles with the grieving figure of the Great Mother. In comparing herself to the petrified Niobe, she projects an image of herself as the *mater dolorosa* as well as the maiden wedded to Hades. Logically, Antigone cannot be Kore and Demeter at the same time. Yet mythic imagery often operates with exactly this fruitfully illogical union of opposites. Here a mythic archetype is split into two contradictory and yet simultaneously coexisting aspects of the self. The Kore is also the mother at an earlier stage. So here Antigone, who takes on herself the task of burying and mourning the dead son, often the role of the mother or wife, is the Earth Mother who grieves over her children. The maiden claimed by Death, who ought to be resurrected with the new life of the year, will instead remain in the Underworld with her dead (893–894).

Sophocles' dramatic structure makes clear the discrepancy between the reality of Antigone's life and the mythic patterns to which she assimilates herself. She is a virgin girl, neither mythical *mater dolorosa* nor a maiden wedded to a god in the Underworld. Her union with death, though figuratively a marriage, is in fact a cruel, desolate end. Her future husband, a living mortal not the awesome god below, chooses the same cavernous hollow and the same doom but with no hope of any future union. The pattern of universal renewal of vitality implicit in the Kore myth contrasts also with the bleak reality facing Creon's city. It, too, has lost touch with those cosmic processes that involve passage between Olympian and chthonic realms, the interchange between life and death, renewal and destruction.

No longer a principle of continued life, this Kore-figure appropriates a *mater dolorosa*, ever-weeping Niobe, image of her own crystallized grief. No new life after a sojourn in darkness awaits her, but perpetual sadness and loss. Haemon, plunging into the cave, claims his bride-of-death as an inaccessible Kore, whom he can embrace only in a grimly funereal version of a sexual union (1236-41). In the Kore myth the grieving Demeter's withdrawal threatens to extinguish life on earth, but she relinquishes grief when Zeus 'leads holy Persephone forth from the murky darkness into the light' (Homeric *Hymn to Demeter*, 337-338; cf. 302-309). Thereupon Demeter again 'sends the grain upward from the fertile plowlands, and all the wide earth is heavy with leafage, heavy with flowers' (471-473). In this play, however, the divinely sanctioned command, 'Send up the maiden (*korē*) from the dwelling dug beneath (the earth),' is not fulfilled (1100-1101). The phrasing of these lines, literally 'send the *korē* upward,' uses the same verb of ascent (*an-hīemi*) as the Eleusinian text, where Demeter, mourning her daughter underground, refuses to 'send upward' the rising grain (*Hymn to Demeter* 307, 332, 471). Sophocles' Kore-figure, however, leaves house and kingdom plunged in darkness and sterility, both literally and metaphorically.

Each of the male characters discovers that aspect of the female appropriate to his experience and attitude. Haemon, a victim of Eros, is united with Antigone as the bride of Death. Creon will find in the female figure who dwells in the recesses of his house neither Kore nor Demeter but their complement, the grieving mother and 'wide-ruling' (Eury-Dike) Queen of the Dead, whose desolation has now spread over his entire realm. Having denied the basic ties of kinship and the sanctity of family bonds, he finds his wife a corpse, herself the 'all-mother of the corpse' (1282). As a manifestation of chthonic female power and maternal vengeance, she makes the interior spaces of his own house (*mychoi*, 1293) a dark place of corpses (1298-1300).

It is not by accident, therefore, that the tale of the disasters of his house centers on Eurydice. The full, grim account is addressed not to the chorus but to Eurydice as she emerges from the house (1181-82, 1184) to address Pallas Athena in prayer (1184). These prayers to Olympian Athena, goddess of the city in all its glory, are answered, in a sense, by Creon's belated, failed prayers to the chthonic Hecate and Pluto (1199-1200) as catastrophe inside the gates of house and city (*oikeion kakon*, 1187; *penthos oikeion*, 1249) overwhelms victories outside the gates. Creon had defended the gates and ramparts of 'seven-gated Thebes' from invaders outside, as the chorus joyfully sang in the parode (101, 122, 141). When Eurydice crosses the gate (*pylē*, 1186) of her house to the outside, it is only for a moment. Then she returns within (1255), to draw Creon with her into the dark spaces of that Hades-house, as she draws him after her into the dark, passionate grief which she 'secretly hides held down in her angered heart' (*katascheton / kryphē(i) kalyptei kardia(i) thymoumenē(i)*, 1253-54; note the powerful alliteration).

These reversals and their spatial analogues of ascent or descent find other mythical correlates in the last two odes of the play. The three myths of the fourth stasimon, Danae, Lycurgus, and the blinding of Phineus' sons, all have to do with imprisonment and deprivation of light. The first myth, that of Danae, has the closest analogies to Antigone's situation. Danae, like Antigone, 'changes the light of the sky' for a confining chamber's vault (944-946) and is 'hidden in a tomb-like chamber' (946-947; cf. 886-887). Yet this downward movement of a mortal into darkness is balanced by a happier descent on the part of Zeus, whose 'gold-flowing seed' (*gonai*, 950) accomplishes a sexual union and a reunion with life which are denied Antigone. The implicit comparison, like Antigone's own comparison of herself to Niobe, has its pathos: Antigone will be the bride of Hades, not of Olympian Zeus. Like the Niobe simile, it suggests the frustrated rhythms of fertility and renewal (cf. 827-832). For King Lycurgus, however, who corresponds much more closely to Creon, imprisonment in a cave is a punishment only, and this is appropriate to Creon's 'descent'.

In the grim third myth, the tale of the blinding of Cleopatra's two sons by their stepmother in Thrace, the motif of the cave veers between savagery and divine ancestry. Daughter of the wind god Boreas and the Athenian Oreithyia, Cleopatra 'received her nurture in distant caves, amid the winds of her father' (983-985). Yet her kinship with Boreas in the far North also connects her with the violence of nature (*thyellai*, 'winds,' usually indicates destructive storms). At the opposite extreme from the subjugated nature of Creon's city and close to Niobe in her identification with the forces of the wild, she is nevertheless deprived of the civilized city par excellence, the Athens of her mother, 'seed of the Erechtheids of ancient birth' (*sperma archaiogonōn antas' Erechtheidân*, 981-982). 'Seed' and 'birth' here take up the theme of marriage and fertility from the previous strophe.

Cleopatra's blinded sons 'have their origin from an unhappily married mother' (so Jebb for *matros echontes anympheuton gonan*, 980). *Anympheutos gona*, however, means literally 'wedless birth'. Not only does it contrast to the 'ancient birth' of her Erechtheid ancestry in the next line, but in moving from the sky god's 'birth seed' (*gonai*, 950) to the dark, cavernous spaces of dangerous stepmother it cancels out Danae's Zeus-sent, fruitful 'births' (950) and recalls the unfulfilled 'birth' of Antigone, the 'brideless bride' of Hades (*nympheusō*, 816; *an-hymenaios*,

876; *nympheion*, 891). The grim 'bride rites' (*nymphika*) of Hades in the cave will then definitively cancel 'births' (1240; cf. *nympheion Haidou*, 1205). In the same semantic field as 'birth,' 'the dragon's seed' (*spora drakontos*, 1125) is connected with the death of Creon's sons in present and in past (cf. 1302-1305). Thus Danae and Cleopatra interlock with Niobe as multivalent paradigms for the hopes of fertile marriage and their destruction in the house of Antigone and Creon. They also bring the deeper mythic pattern of Kore and Demeter closer into the foreground. The struggle between Creon and Antigone expands to include a dialectic between house and cave, city and wild nature, central Greece (Argos, Athens) and the remote periphery (Thrace) in these myths of royal women encountering divinity.

The fifth stasimon, the Ode to Dionysus, returns us again to nature's fertility (1131 ff.) and to astral imagery (1126 ff., 1146 ff.). The starlit night sky of the purifying Dionysus (1144, 1146-47) sets off by contrast Creon's figurative descent from happiness to misery (1155 ff.) and the literal details of his descent to the cave (1204 ff.).

This cave and the dark forces which it contains prove to be the final test of Creon's conception of human power and of Antigone's tragic heroism. For her it is a place of tragic isolation and tragic fulfillment, ambiguous locus of the tension between her devotion to loved ones and death-bent, stony heroism.[2] For Creon the cave symbolizes all that he has repressed. It is the subterranean reservoir of dark passions and the place of lonely encounter with love and death, Eros and Hades. The Eros which Creon denied in a crude image drawn from the arts of civilization ('There are other fields for him to plow,' 569) returns in the cave to defeat him: Eros takes his son from him and gives him to Antigone for an inverted union in the realm of the dead (1240-41).

The conflict between Creon and Antigone is not only between city and house, but also between man and woman.[3] Creon identifies his political authority and his sexual identity. 'If this victory (*kratē*) rests with her without punishment, then I am not the man, but she's the man' (484-485). The word *kratē*, 'victory', 'power', repeatedly describes his sovereign power in the state (166, 173, for example). He sees Antigone, then, as a challenge to his most important values and his self-image. 'A woman will not rule me (*arxei*) while I live', he says a little later, again linking the conflict of the sexes with political power.

In this same speech Creon confronts an opposing principle of an especially feminine kind, Antigone's 'reverence for those of the same womb', *homosplanchnous sebein* (511). On this basis Antigone defends herself against the male-oriented, civic ethic of the polis. She makes kinship a function of the female procreative power: she defines kinship in terms of the womb (*splanchna*). Thus at the end of her great speech on the unwritten laws she calls Polyneices 'the one (born) from my mother, dead' (*ton ex emēs / mētros thanonta*) whom she, for that reason, will not leave 'a corpse unburied' (*athapton . . . nekyn*, 466-467). As her defiance of Creon continues into the stichomythy, her word *homosplanchnos* some fifty lines later etymologically defines 'brother' as 'one of the same womb' (511). *Homosplanchnos* calls attention to the root meaning of the familiar word for 'brother', *adelphos*, from *a-* ('same', equivalent to *homo-*) and *delphys* ('womb', equivalent to *splanchna*).[4] In this view of kinship she reopens, on a personal level, the debate between Apollo and the Erinyes in Aeschylus' *Oresteia*;[5] however, she gives the decisive tie of blood not to the father's seed, as Olympian Apollo and Olympian Athena do (*Eumenides* 657-666, 734-741), but to the mother's womb.

Antigone's definition of kinship as *homosplanchnous sebein* reaches deep into the conflicts of values in the fifth-century polis. The establishment of Cleisthenian democracy at the beginning of the century rested, in part, on breaking down the power of the clan and blood ties; instead, allegiance to the polis was to subsume and transcend the ties of blood. Benveniste's study of kinship terminology in Greece takes this conflict back a stage further.[6] The Greek vocabulary of kinship sharply distinguishes between male and female lineage. The old Indo-European term for 'brother', *phratēr* (I.E. **bhratēr*, Latin *frater*) survives in the Greek term for the members of a phratry (*phratēr*; cf. *phratra*). The phratry consists of men united as members of the male band through the masculine, patriarchal line and 'issued mystically from the same father'.[7] Though based on kinship, it is kinship extending beyond the *oikos* into the polis, where it has political power.[8] An old term for 'brother', *kasis, kasignētos*, which may originally have denoted maternal lineage, becomes assimilated to the strictly paternal line, and the original Indo-European word for 'sister' (equivalent to Latin *soror*) is then lost. For brothers related by blood Greek then develops a new term, *adelphos*, 'of the same womb' (*a-delphys*), which denotes kinship through the mother. Symmetrical to *adelphos* is *homogastrios*, or the doublet, *ogastōr*, literally 'co-uterine', from *gastēr*, 'belly', 'womb'. Antigone's *homosplanchos* is the exact equivalent of *homogastrios*. Whether or not *homogastrios* and *homosplanchnos* are historical survivals of a pre-Indo-European matrilinear system of kinship in Greece does not concern us here. What is important for the *Antigone* is that the distinction between paternal and maternal lineage is a live issue for audiences of mid-fifth century Athens.

Antigone does not phrase her conflict with Creon strictly in terms of maternal versus paternal kinship, but that division is relevant since

Cleisthenes' reforms involved cutting across the exclusive blood ties of the clan or *genos*, where ties through the mother are more obvious.[9] As Freud long ago pointed out, paternity is only an inferential relation, whereas maternity is immediate and visual. There can be no doubt about the mother who has given birth to the child, but there is no equivalent certainty about the father who sired it.[10] It is in keeping with Creon's fierce adherence to the polis and his inferential, abstractive mentality that he leans heavily on patriarchal lineage and authority (639-647; cf. 635). His stress on patriarchy, though illogical in one sense (see 182-183), is congruent with his antifeminine, antimaternal attitude (see, e.g., 569).[11] The conflict between him and Antigone, then, is not just between family and city, but between fundamentally different concepts of life.

That conflict necessarily involves Creon's son, the extension of his power in the male line both in the city and in the house. As the victory of Orestes in the *Eumenides* reflects a successful separation of the male adolescent from his ties to the mother and an initiation into the male society of phratry and polis,[12] the death of Haemon reflects just the opposite: the failure of the political tie of the male band to pull the youth away from the mother to the city and a return to the womb as the underground cavern, the mysterious seat of life-and-death, the elemental procreative power which remains under the control of the woman, the 'All-Mother', whom Creon will soon encounter in her destructive and vengeful aspect. Haemon thereby rejects not only his father but also his adult male role of political responsibility in the city, succeeding his father to the throne of Thebes. In both literal and symbolical action he fulfills Creon's worst fear, 'alliance' with the woman (740; cf. 648-651).

The tie through blood alone, through the womb, Antigone makes the basis of her *philia*. *Philia*, which includes notions of 'love', 'loyalty', 'friendship', and 'kinship', is another fundamental point of division between Creon and Antigone. An exchange a few lines after her 'reverence for the *homosplanchnoi*' (511) sharpens the clash between the two views (522-523):

Creon: The enemy (*echthros*) is not a loved one (*philos*), not even when he is dead.

Antig.: It is my nature to share not in enmity, but in loving (*synechthein, symphilein*).

Creon here repeats his political definition of *philos* from his first speech (182-183), but now it is opposed by Antigone's fierce personal loyalties. Once more the 'sameness' of the womb cuts through that principle of differentiation that separates *philos* from *echthros*. Creon's 'politicization of burial' distinguishes between the two brothers as hostile political forces: 'The one he promotes in honor; the other he dishonors' (22).[13] To Antigone, however, those 'of the same womb' are worthy of the same degree of honor (*timē*) and love (*philia*). The *homo-splanchnoi* are to be joined in the sister's *sym-philein*.

Antigone's claim of sameness, however, overlooks a critical difference. As the first ode points out, origin from that one womb is a source of horror and pollution: the two brothers are the 'miserable wretches who, born from one father and one mother, levelled double-conquering spears against one another and so won, both of them, a common share of death' (143–146).

The contrast of 'one' and 'two', the use of the dual forms, the interplay between 'common' and 'both' in the last line all stress the pollution: 'They destroyed one another in double portion on one day, smiting and being smitten with pollution of the same hand' (*autocheir miasma*), says Creon soon after (170–172). That those so intimately linked in 'oneness' should suffer such violent 'difference' is itself the expression of an infectious division in the house. It is Antigone's tragic task to insist on the ultimate 'oneness' or 'sameness' and thereby close over this difference.

The struggle is marked in her opening words. Her striking phrase of address to Ismene, 'common self-(wombed) sister' (*koinon autadelphon*, 1), attempts to reaffirm family unity in blood against the harsh reality of Ismene's picture of the 'two' brothers who on 'one day' died with 'double hand' (13–14). Antigone's 'common' sister contrasts also with the chorus' 'common death' (146) of the two brothers. That phrasing of kinship in the first line of the play intensifies the blood tie and points back, in turn, to the deeper horrors of sameness in the house of Oedipus, the incestuous marriage and the patricide.[14] 'The woes that come from Oedipus' occur in her second line. Even her dual form when speaking of herself and Ismene in the third line has its significance, for it repeatedly denotes the polluted fratricides (recall 143–146, above) and comes to mark a shift of allegiance on Antigone's part as she leaves the living kin for her bond to the dead. Creon's path is, of course, just the opposite: he insists on 'difference' and carries it to its logical conclusion in the face of those bonds of 'sameness' which the gods finally vindicate. The list below will recapitulate:

Creon	*Antigone*
Philoi as those devoted to city	*Philoi* as kin ties
Differentiation by political loyalties	Oneness of 'same womb'
Separation from mother	Return to womb and mother (earth)
Patriarchal kinship (phratry)	Matrilinear kinship (*homosplanchnoi*)

Earth as a political territory	Earth as locus of blood kinship
Earth as plowed terrain	Earth as receiver of the dead
World above (Olympian religion)	World below (chthonic gods)
Control over nature	Fusion and sympathy with nature
Use of death	Acceptance of death
Rejection of *eros* (cf. 569)	Tragic death as 'Hades' bride'
Logos (mutually exclusive alternatives)	*Mythos* (paradox)
Future or gnomic present Calculations of time	Past (the dead, inherited curse) Timeless
Manipulative rationality	Emotionality

Parallel to the loss of the unrestored Kore in the house of Oedipus is the premature death of the unmarried son in the house of Creon. Here Creon's strength crumbles at its weakest point, that is, at the point of his own link with the cycle of generation. In the two encounters with Haemon in the middle and at the end of the play Creon has his sharpest confrontation with forces beyond his control. Haemon is Creon's link with a house through procreation. Antigone and the cave act, in a sense, as the agents of the powers of the house, earth, and death when they rob Creon of his last human ties. 'You will give one of those from your own loins' (*splanchna*), Teiresias warns, 'a corpse in exchange for corpses' (1066-67). Through Haemon Creon too feels deep physical and biological ties to the *splanchna*.[15] This word, as we have noted, generally denotes the womb and not the loins. It thus confuses Creon's rigid differentiation of male and female and thereby puts him in touch even more fundamentally with life and death.

Creon himself is deeply concerned with family solidarity, as his opening lines to Haemon make clear (639 ff.). Haemon sensitively exploits this sympathy with his father: he begins his plea, 'Father, I am yours' (635). But this concern on Creon's part only increases the pathos of his downfall through his alienation from every member of his house, living and dead (1302-1303). Exhibiting something of what Bergson called 'intellect's congenital lack of comprehension for life', he disregards until too late what his blood kin might teach him about the meaning of familial ties. Hence his house, instead of being a locus of civilized values and the place that transmits new life from generation to generation, becomes, like the house of Antigone and Oedipus, a place of death and savagery, a cavern-like 'harbor of Hades'.

Fleeing his father's house for the cave, Haemon exposes that house to the terrible savagery which in the fourth stasimon occurs in a far-off Thracian setting at the very limits of civilization. Here too the act of savagery (see *agria damar*, 'savage wife', 973) was directed against the eyes (*ommata*, 974; cf. *agria ossa*, 'savage eyes', 1231). These 'savage eyes' turned against the father by the son ironically echo the bitter father-son conflict earlier, where Haemon shouted out his bitter threat, 'Never will you see my face as you look upon me with your eyes' (764). 'Eyes' mark a progression from angry looks to deeds of bloody vengeance. Now 'the evils in the house', *ta en domois kaka* (1279–80), are the last blow to the king's tottering strength. Deeper father-son hostilities lurk in the background (cf. the Freudian equation, eyes = penis), but we cannot discuss those here.

When Creon uses the language of procreation, it is only to reinforce his authoritarian principles. Thus in his encounter with Haemon, he praises 'obedient offspring', literally 'obedient births' (*gonai*, 642). 'Begetting (*phiteusai*) useless offspring', he generalizes in his favorite mode of speech, only 'sires' (*physai*) trouble for oneself and laughter for one's enemies (645-647). Haemon's reply about the gods' 'planting' (*phyousi*) wits in men (683) takes a very different view of the process of birth as a metaphor for man's relation to nature.[16] This verb, *phyein*, involving growth, birth, procreation, not only points back to more mysterious aspects of birth (cf. 144, 866) but also includes Antigone's utterly opposite attitude toward birth, kinship, and 'inborn nature' or *physis* (see 523, 562).

Creon's demand for obedience assimilates the order of the house to the order of the city and levels out the difference between them: lack of authority, *anarchia*, 'destroys cities and overturns houses' (672-674). Scornfully dismissing ties of kinship with a slur on Antigone's reverence for 'Zeus who looks after kindred blood' (658-659), he asserts his principle that the man who is good in the realm of the house will also be just in the city (661-662). Creon's word for 'order' here, as elsewhere in this speech, is *kosmos* (660, 677, 730), the word used to describe Antigone's burial of the corpse (396, 901). The one subordinates kin ties to the 'order' of the polis; the other defies the polis to 'order' the rites owed to a dead kinsman.

14

ON MISUNDERSTANDING THE
OEDIPUS REX

E. R. DODDS

On the last occasion when I had the misfortune to examine in Honour Moderations at Oxford I set a question on the *Oedipus Rex*, which was among the books prescribed for general reading. My question was 'In what sense, if in any, does the *Oedipus Rex* attempt to justify the ways of God to man?' It was an optional question; there were plenty of alternatives. But the candidates evidently considered it a gift: nearly all of them attempted it. When I came to sort out the answers I found that they fell into three groups.

The first and biggest group held that the play justifies the gods by showing — or, as many of them said, 'proving' — that we get what we deserve. The arguments of this group turned upon the character of Oedipus. Some considered that Oedipus was a bad man: look how he treated Creon — naturally the gods punished him. Others said 'No, not altogether bad, even in some ways rather noble; but he had one of those fatal *hamartiai* that all tragic heroes have, as we know from Aristotle. And since he had a *hamartia* he could of course expect no mercy: the gods had read the *Poetics*.' Well over half the candidates held views of this general type.

A second substantial group held that the *Oedipus Rex* is 'a tragedy of destiny'. What the play 'proves', they said, is that man has no free will but is a puppet in the hands of the gods who pull the strings that make him dance. Whether Sophocles thought the gods justified in treating their puppet as they did was not always clear from their answers. Most of those who took this view evidently disliked the play; some of them were honest enough to say so.

The third group was much smaller, but included some of the more thoughtful candidates. In their opinion Sophocles was 'a pure artist' and

From *Greece & Rome* 13 (1966), 37–49. Reprinted by permission of Oxford University Press.

was therefore not interested in justifying the gods. He took the story of Oedipus as he found it, and used it to make an exciting play. The gods are simply part of the machinery of the plot.

Ninety per cent. of the answers fell into one or the other of these three groups. The remaining ten per cent. had either failed to make up their minds or failed to express themselves intelligibly.

It was a shock to me to discover that all these young persons, supposedly trained in the study of classical literature, could read this great and moving play and so completely miss the point. For all the views I have just summarized are in fact demonstrably false (though some of them, and some ways of stating them, are more crudely and vulgarly false then others). It is true that each of them has been defended by some scholars in the past, but I had hoped that all of them were by now dead and buried. Wilamowitz thought he had killed the lot in an article published in *Hermes* (34 [1899], 55 ff.) more than half a century ago; and they have repeatedly been killed since. Yet their unquiet ghosts still haunt the examination-rooms of universities — and also, I would add, the pages of popular handbooks on the history of European drama. Surely that means that we have somehow failed in our duty as teachers?

It was this sense of failure which prompted me to attempt once more to clear up some of these ancient confusions. If the reader feels — as he very well may — that in this paper I am flogging a dead horse, I can only reply that on the evidence I have quoted the animal is unaccountably still alive.

I

I shall take Aristotle as my starting point, since he is claimed as the primary witness for the first of the views I have described. From the thirteenth chapter of the *Poetics* we learn that the best sort of tragic hero is a man highly esteemed and prosperous who falls into misfortune because of some serious (*megalē*) *hamartia*: examples, Oedipus and Thyestes. In Aristotle's view, then, Oedipus' misfortune was directly occasioned by some serious *hamartia*; and since Aristotle was known to be infallible, Victorian critics proceeded at once to look for this *hamartia*. And so, it appears, do the majority of present-day undergraduates.

What do they find? It depends on what they expect to find. As we all know, the word *hamartia* is ambiguous: in ordinary usage it is sometimes applied to false moral judgements, sometimes to purely intellectual error — the average Greek did not make our sharp distinction between the two. Since *Poetics* 13 is in general concerned with the moral character of the tragic hero, many scholars have thought in the past (and many undergraduates still think) that the *hamartia* of Oedipus must in Aristotle's view be a moral fault. They have accordingly gone over the play with a microscope looking for moral faults in Oedipus, and have duly found them — for neither here nor anywhere else did Sophocles portray that insipid and unlikely character, the man of perfect virtue. Oedipus, they point out, is proud and over-confident; he harbours unjustified suspicions against Teiresias and Creon; in one place (lines 964 ff.) he goes so far as to express some uncertainty about the truth of oracles. One may doubt whether this adds up to what Aristotle would consider *megalē hamartia*. But even if it did, it would have no direct relevance to the question at issue. Years before the action of the play begins, Oedipus was already an incestuous parricide; if that was a punishment for his unkind treatment of Creon, then the punishment preceded the crime — which is surely an odd kind of justice.

'Ah,' says the traditionalist critic, 'but Oedipus' behaviour on the stage reveals the man he always was: he was punished for his basically unsound character.' In that case, however, someone on the stage ought to tell us so: Oedipus should repent, as Creon repents in the *Antigone*; or else another speaker should draw the moral. To ask about a character in fiction 'Was he a good man?' is to ask a strictly meaningless question: since Oedipus never lived we can answer neither 'Yes' or 'No'. The legitimate question is 'Did Sophocles intend us to think of Oedipus as a good man?' This *can* be answered — not by applying some ethical yardstick of our own, but by looking at what the characters in the play say about him. And by that test the answer is 'Yes'. In the eyes of the Priest in the opening scene he is the greatest and noblest of men, the saviour of Thebes who with divine aid rescued the city from the Sphinx. The Chorus has the same view of him: he has proved his wisdom, he is the darling of the city, and never will they believe ill of him (504 ff.). And when the catastrophe comes, no one turns round and remarks 'Well, but it was your own fault: it must have been; Aristotle says so.'

In my opinion, and in that of nearly all Aristotelian scholars since Bywater, Aristotle does *not* say so; it is only the perversity of moralizing critics that has misrepresented him as saying so. It is almost certain that Aristotle was using *hamartia* here as he uses *hamartēma* in the *Nicomachean Ethics* (1135^b12) and in the *Rhetoric* (1374^b6), to mean an offence committed in ignorance of some material fact and therefore free from *ponēria* or *kakia*.[1] These parallels seem decisive; and they are confirmed by Aristotle's second example — Thyestes, the man who ate the flesh of his own children in the belief that it was butcher's meat, and who subsequently begat a child on his own daughter, not knowing who she was. His story has clearly much in common with that of Oedipus, and

Plato as well as Aristotle couples the two names as examples of the gravest *hamartia* (*Laws* 838c). Thyestes and Oedipus are both of them men who violated the most sacred of Nature's laws and thus incurred the most horrible of all pollutions; but they both did so without *ponēria*, for they knew not what they did — in Aristotle's quasi-legal terminology, it was a *hamartēma*, not an *adikēma*. This is why they were in his view especially suitable subjects for tragedy. Had they acted knowingly, they would have been inhuman monsters, and we could not have felt for them that pity which tragedy ought to produce. As it is, we feel both pity, for the fragile estate of man, and terror, for a world whose laws we do not understand. The *hamartia* of Oedipus did not lie in losing his temper with Teiresias; it lay quite simply in parricide and incest — a *megalē hamartia* indeed, the greatest a man can commit.

The theory that the tragic hero must have a grave moral flaw, and its mistaken ascription to Aristotle, has had a long disastrous history. It was gratifying to Victorian critics, since it appeared to fit certain plays of Shakespeare. But it goes back much further, to the seventeenth-century French critic Dacier, who influenced the practice of the French classical dramatists, especially Corneille, and was himself influenced by the still older nonsense about 'poetic justice' — the notion that the poet has a moral duty to represent the world as a place where the good are always rewarded and the bad are always punished. I need not say that this puerile idea is completely foreign to Aristotle and to the practice of the Greek dramatists; I only mention it because on the evidence of those Honour Mods. papers it would appear that it still lingers on in some youthful minds like a cobweb in an unswept room.

To return to the *Oedipus Rex*, the moralist has still one last card to play. Could not Oedipus, he asks, have escaped his doom if he had been more careful? Knowing that he was in danger of committing parricide and incest, would not a really prudent man have avoided quarrelling, even in self-defence, with men older than himself, and also love-relations with women older than himself? Would he not, in Waldock's ironic phrase, have compiled a handlist of all the things he must not do? In real life I suppose he might. But we are not entitled to blame Oedipus either for carelessness in failing to compile a handlist or for lack of self-control in failing to obey its injunctions. For no such possibilities are mentioned in the play, or even hinted at; and it is an essential critical principle that *what is not mentioned in the play does not exist*. These considerations would be in place if we were examining the conduct of a real person. But we are not: we are examining the intentions of a dramatist, and we are not entitled to ask questions that the dramatist did not intend us to ask. There is only one branch of literature where we *are* entitled to ask such questions about *ta ektos tou dramatos*, namely the modern detective story. And despite certain similarities the *Oedipus Rex* is not a detective story but a dramatized folktale. If we insist on reading it as if it were a law report we must expect to miss the point.[2]

In any case, Sophocles has provided a conclusive answer to those who suggest that Oedipus could, and therefore should, have avoided his fate. The oracle was *unconditional* (line 790): it did not say 'If you do so-and-so you will kill your father'; it simply said 'You will kill your father, you will sleep with your mother.' And what an oracle predicts is bound to happen. Oedipus does what he can do to evade his destiny: he resolves never to see his supposed parents again. But it is quite certain from the first that his best efforts will be unavailing. Equally unconditional was the original oracle given to Laius (711 ff.): Apollo said that he *must* (*chrēnai*) die at the hands of Jocasta's child; there is no saving clause. Here there is a significant difference between Sophocles and Aeschylus. Of Aeschylus' trilogy on the House of Laius only the last play, the *Septem*, survives. Little is known of the others, but we do know, from *Septem* 742 ff., that according to Aeschylus the oracle given to Laius *was* conditional: 'Do not beget a child; for *if* you do, that child will kill you.' In Aeschylus the disaster *could* have been avoided, but Laius sinfully disobeyed and his sin brought ruin to his descendants. In Aeschylus the story was, like the *Oresteia*, a tale of crime and punishment; but Sophocles chose otherwise — that is why he altered the form of the oracle. There is no suggestion in the *Oedipus Rex* that Laius sinned or that Oedipus was the victim of an hereditary curse, and the critic must not assume what the poet has abstained from suggesting. Nor should we leap to the conclusion that Sophocles left out the hereditary curse because he thought the doctrine immoral; apparently he did not think so, since he used it both in the *Antigone* (583 ff.) and in the *Oedipus at Colonus* (964 ff.). What his motive may have been for ignoring it in the *Oedipus Rex* we shall see in a moment.

I hope I have now disposed of the moralizing interpretation, which has been rightly abandoned by the great majority of contemporary scholars. To mention only recent works in English, the books of Whitman, Waldock, Letters, Ehrenberg, Knox, and Kirkwood, however much they differ on other points, all agree about the essential moral innocence of Oedipus.

II

But what is the alternative? If Oedipus is the innocent victim of a doom which he cannot avoid, does this not reduce him to a mere puppet?

Is not the whole play a 'tragedy of destiny' which denies human freedom? This is the second of the heresies which I set out to refute. Many readers have fallen into it, Sigmund Freud among them;[3] and you can find it confidently asserted in various popular handbooks, some of which even extend the assertion to Greek tragedy in general — thus providing themselves with a convenient label for distinguishing Greek from 'Christian' tragedy. But the whole notion is in fact anachronistic. The modern reader slips into it easily because *we* think of two clear-cut alternative views — either we believe in free will or else we are determinists. But fifth-century Greeks did not think in these terms any more than Homer did: the debate about determinism is a creation of Hellenistic thought. Homeric heroes have their predetermined 'portion of life' (*moira*); they must die on their 'appointed day' (*aisimon ēmar*); but it never occurs to the poet or his audience that this prevents them from being free agents. Nor did Sophocles intend that it should occur to readers of the *Oedipus Rex*. Neither in Homer nor in Sophocles does divine foreknowledge of certain events imply that all human actions are predetermined. If explicit confirmation of this is required, we have only to turn to lines 1230 f., where the Messenger emphatically distinguishes Oedipus' self-blinding as 'voluntary' and 'self-chosen' from the 'involuntary' parricide and incest. Certain of Oedipus' past actions were fate-bound; but everything that he does on the stage from first to last he does as a free agent.

Even in calling the parricide and the incest 'fate-bound' I have perhaps implied more than the average Athenian of Sophocles' day would have recognized. As A. W. Gomme put it, 'the gods know the future, but they do not order it: they know who will win the next Scotland and England football match, but that does not alter the fact that the victory will depend on the skill, the determination, the fitness of the players, and a little on luck'.[4] That may not satisfy the analytical philosopher, but it seems to have satisfied the ordinary man at all periods. Bernard Knox aptly quotes the prophecy of Jesus to St. Peter, 'Before the cock crow, thou shalt deny me thrice.' The Evangelists clearly did not intend to imply that Peter's subsequent action was 'fate-bound' in the sense that he could not have chosen otherwise; Peter fulfilled the prediction, but he did so by an act of free choice.[5]

In any case I cannot understand Sir Maurice Bowra's[6] idea that the gods *force* on Oedipus the knowledge of what he has done. They do nothing of the kind; on the contrary, what fascinates us is the spectacle of a man freely choosing, from the highest motives, a series of actions which lead to his own ruin. Oedipus might have left the plague to take its course; but pity for the sufferings of his people compelled him to consult Delphi. When Apollo's word came back, he might still have left the murder of Laius uninvestigated; but piety and justice required him to act. He need not have forced the truth from the reluctant Theban herdsman; but because he cannot rest content with a lie, he must tear away the last veil from the illusion in which he has lived so long. Teiresias, Jocasta, the herdsman, each in turn tries to stop him, but in vain: he must read the last riddle, the riddle of his own life. The immediate cause of Oedipus' ruin is not 'Fate' or 'the gods' — no oracle said that he must discover the truth — and still less does it lie in his own weakness; what causes his ruin is his own strength and courage, his loyalty to Thebes, and his loyalty to the truth. In all this we are to see him as a free agent: hence the suppression of the hereditary curse. And his self-mutilation and self-banishment are equally free acts of choice.

Why does Oedipus blind himself? He tells us the reason (1369 ff.): he has done it in order to cut himself off from all contact with humanity; if he could choke the channels of his other senses he would do so. Suicide would not serve his purpose: in the next world he would have to meet his dead parents. Oedipus mutilates himself because he can face neither the living nor the dead. But why, if he is morally innocent? Once again, we must look at the play through Greek eyes. The doctrine that nothing matters except the agent's intention is a peculiarity of Christian and especially of post-Kantian thought. It is true that the Athenian law courts took account of intention: they distinguished as ours do between murder and accidental homicide or homicide committed in the course of self-defence. If Oedipus had been tried before an Athenian court he would have been acquitted — of murdering his father. But no human court could acquit him of pollution; for pollution inhered in the act itself, irrespective of motive. Of that burden Thebes could not acquit Oedipus, and least of all could its bearer acquit himself.

The nearest parallel to the situation of Oedipus is in the tale which Herodotus tells about Adrastus, son of Gordies. Adrastus was the involuntary slayer of his own brother, and then of Atys, the son of his benefactor Croesus; the latter act, like the killing of Laius, fulfilled an oracle. Croesus forgave Adrastus because the killing was unintended (*aëkōn*), and because the oracle showed that it was the will of 'some god'. But Adrastus did not forgive himself: he committed suicide, 'conscious' says Herodotus, 'that of all men known to him he bore the heaviest burden of disaster'.[7] It is for the same reason that Oedipus blinds himself. Morally innocent though he is and knows himself to be, the objective horror of his actions remains with him and he feels that he has no longer any place in human society. Is that simply archaic superstition? I think it is something more. Suppose a motorist runs down a man and kills him, I think he *ought* to feel that he has done a terrible thing, even if the accident is no fault of his: he has destroyed a human life, which nothing can restore. In the objective order it is acts that count, not intentions. A man who has violated that order may well feel a sense of guilt, however blameless his driving.

But my analogy is very imperfect, and even the case of Adrastus is not fully comparable. Oedipus is no ordinary homicide: he has committed the two crimes which above all others fill us with instinctive horror. Sophocles had not read Freud, but he knew how people *feel* about these things — better than some of his critics appear to do. And in the strongly patriarchal society of ancient Greece the revulsion would be even more intense than it is in our own. We have only to read Plato's prescription for the treatment to be given to parricides (*Laws* 872 c ff.). For this deed, he says, there can be no purification: the parricide shall be killed, his body shall be laid naked at a cross-roads outside the city, each officer of the State shall cast a stone upon it and curse it, and then the bloody remnant shall be flung outside the city's territory and left unburied. In all this he is probably following actual Greek practice. And if that is how Greek justice treated parricides, is it surprising that Oedipus treats himself as he does, when the great king, 'the first of men', the man whose intuitive genius had saved Thebes, is suddenly revealed to himself as a thing so unclean that 'neither the earth can receive it, nor the holy rain nor the sunshine endure its presence' (1426)?

III

At this point I am brought back to the original question I asked the undergraduates: does Sophocles in this play attempt to justify the ways of God to man? If 'to justify' means 'to explain in terms of *human* justice', the answer is surely 'No'. If human justice is the standard, then, as Waldock bluntly expressed it, 'Nothing can excuse the gods, and Sophocles knew it perfectly well.' Waldock does not, however, suggest that the poet intended any attack on the gods. He goes on to say that it is futile to look for any 'message' or 'meaning' in this play: 'there is no meaning', he tells us, 'in the *Oedipus Rex*; there is merely the terror of coincidence.'[8] Kirkwood seems to take a rather similar line: 'Sophocles', he says, 'has no theological pronouncements to make and no points of criticism to score.'[9] These opinions come rather close to, if they do not actually involve, the view adopted by my third and last group of undergraduates — the view that the gods are merely agents in a traditional story which Sophocles, a 'pure artist', exploits for dramatic purposes without raising the religious issue or drawing any moral whatever.

This account seems to me insufficient; but I have more sympathy with it than I have with either of the other heresies. It reflects a healthy reaction against the old moralizing school of critics; and the text of the play appears at first sight to support it. It is a striking fact that after the catastrophe no one on the stage says a word either in justification of the gods or in criticism of them. Oedipus says 'These things were Apollo' − and that is all. If the poet has charged him with a 'message' about divine justice or injustice, he fails to deliver it. And I fully agree that there is no reason at all why we should require a dramatist − even a Greek dramatist − to be for ever running about delivering banal 'messages'. It is true that when a Greek dramatic poet had something he passionately wanted to say to his fellow citizens he felt entitled to say it. Aeschylus in the *Oresteia*, Aristophanes in the *Frogs*, had something to say to their people and used the opportunity of saying it on the stage. But these are exceptional cases − both these works were produced at a time of grave crisis in public affairs − and even here the 'message' appears to me to be incidental to the true function of the artist, which I should be disposed to define, with Dr Johnson, as 'the enlargement of our sensibility'. It is unwise to generalize from special cases. (And, incidentally, I wish undergraduates would stop writing essays which begin with the words 'This play *proves* that . . .'. Surely no work of art can ever 'prove' anything: what value could there be in a 'proof' whose premises are manufactured by the artist?)

Nevertheless, I cannot accept the view that the *Oedipus Rex* conveys *no* intelligible meaning and that Sophocles' plays tell us nothing of his opinions concerning the gods. Certainly it is always dangerous to use dramatic works as evidence of their author's opinions, and especially of their religious convictions: we can legitimately discuss religion *in* Shakespeare, but do we know anything at all about the religion *of* Shakespeare? Still, I think I should venture to assert two things about Sophocles' opinions:

First, he did not believe (or did not always believe) that the gods are in any human sense 'just';

Secondly, he did always believe that the gods exist and that man should revere them.

The first of these propositions is supported not only by the implicit evidence of the *Oedipus Rex* but by the explicit evidence of another play which is generally thought to be close in date to it. The closing lines of the *Trachiniae* contain a denunciation in violent terms of divine injustice. No one answers it. I can only suppose that the poet had no answer to give.

For the second of my two propositions we have quite strong *external* evidence − which is important, since it is independent of our subjective impressions. We know that Sophocles held various priesthoods; that when the cult of Asclepius was introduced to Athens he acted as the god's host and wrote a hymn in his honour; and that he was himself worshipped as a 'hero' after his death, which seems to imply that he accepted the religion of the State and was accepted by it. But the external evidence does not stand alone: it is strongly supported by at least one passage in the *Oedipus Rex*. The celebrated choral ode about the decline of prophecy and the threat to religion (lines 863–910) was of course suggested by the scene with Creon which precedes it; but it contains generalizations which have little apparent relevance either to Oedipus or to Creon. Is the piety of this ode purely conventional, as Whitman maintained in a vigorous but sometimes perverse book?[10] One phrase in particular seems to forbid this interpretation. If men are to lose all respect for the gods, in that case, the Chorus asks, *ti dei me choreuein*; (895). If by this they mean merely 'Why should I, a Theban elder, dance?', the question is irrelevant and even slightly ludicrous; the meaning is surely 'Why should I, an Athenian citizen, continue to serve in a chorus?' In speaking of themselves as a chorus they step out of the play into the contemporary world, as Aristophanes' choruses do in the *parabasis*. And in effect the question they are asking seems to be this: 'If Athens loses faith in religion, if the views of the Enlightenment prevail, what significance is there in tragic drama, which exists as part of the service of the gods?' To that question the rapid decay of tragedy in the fourth century may be said to have provided an answer.

In saying this, I am not suggesting with Ehrenberg that the character of Oedipus reflects that of Pericles,[11] or with Knox that he is intended to be a symbol of Athens:[12] allegory of that sort seems to me wholly alien to Greek tragedy. I am only claiming that at one point in this play Sophocles took occasion to say to his fellow citizens something which he felt to be important. And it *was* important, particularly in the period of the Archidamian War, to which the *Oedipus Rex* probably belongs. Delphi was known to be pro-Spartan: that is why Euripides was given a free hand to criticize Apollo. But if Delphi could not be trusted, the whole fabric of traditional belief was threatened with collapse. In our society religious faith is no longer tied up with belief in prophecy; but for the ancient world, both pagan and Christian, it was. And in the years of the Archidamian War belief in prophecy was at a low ebb; Thucydides is our witness to that.

I take it, then, as reasonably certain that while Sophocles did not pretend that the gods are in any human sense just he nevertheless held that they are entitled to our worship. Are these two opinions incompatible? Here once more we cannot hope to understand Greek literature if we persist in looking at it through Christian spectacles. To the Christian it is a necessary part of piety to believe that God is just. And so it was to Plato and the Stoics. But the older world saw no such necessity. If you doubt this, take down the *Iliad* and read Achilles' opinion of what divine justice amounts to (xxiv. 525-33); or take down the Bible and read the Book of Job. Disbelief in divine justice as measured by human yardsticks can perfectly well be associated with deep religious feeling. 'Men', say Heraclitus, 'find some things unjust, other things just; but in the eyes of God all things are beautiful and good and just.'[13] I think that Sophocles would have agreed. For him, as for Heraclitus, there is an objective world-order which man must respect, but which he cannot hope fully to understand.

IV

Some readers of the *Oedipus Rex* have told me that they find its atmosphere stifling and oppressive: they miss the tragic exaltation that one gets from the *Antigone* or the *Prometheus Vinctus*. And I fear that what I have said here has done nothing to remove that feeling. Yet it is not a feeling which I share myself. Certainly the *Oedipus Rex* is a play about the blindness of man and the desperate insecurity of the human condition: in a sense every man must grope in the dark as Oedipus gropes, not knowing who he is or what he has to suffer; we all live in a world of appearance which hides from us who-knows-what dreadful reality. But surely the *Oedipus Rex* is also a play about human greatness. Oedipus is great, not in virtue of a great worldly position — for his worldly position is an illusion which will vanish like a dream — but in virtue of his inner strength: strength to pursue the truth at whatever personal cost, and strength to accept and endure it when found. 'This horror is mine,' he cries, 'and none but I is *strong* enough to bear it' (1414). Oedipus is great because he accepts the responsibility for *all* his acts, including those which are objectively most horrible, though subjectively innocent.

To me personally Oedipus is a kind of symbol of the human intelligence which cannot rest until it has solved all the riddles — even the last riddle, to which the answer is that human happiness is built on an illusion. I do not know how far Sophocles intended that. But certainly in the last lines of the play (which I firmly believe to be genuine) he does generalize the case, does appear to suggest that in some sense Oedipus is every man and every man is potentially Oedipus. Freud felt this (he was not insensitive to poetry), but as we all know he understood it in a specific psychological sense. 'Oedipus' fate', he says, 'moves us only because it might have been our own, because the oracle laid upon us before birth the very curse which rested upon him. It may be that we were all destined to direct our first sexual impulses towards our mothers, and our first impulses of hatred and violence towards our fathers; our dreams convince us that we were.'[14] Perhaps they do; but Freud did not ascribe his interpretation of the myth to Sophocles, and it is not the interpretation I have in mind. Is there not in the poet's view a much wider sense in which every man is Oedipus? If every man could tear away the last veils of illusion, if he could see human life as time and the gods see it, would he not see that against that tremendous background all the generations of men are as if they had not been, *isa kai to mēden zōsas* (1187)? That was how Odysseus saw it when he had conversed with Athena, the embodiment of divine wisdom. 'In Ajax' condition', he says, 'I recognize my own: I perceive that all men living are but appearance or unsubstantial shadow.'[15]

So far as I can judge, on this matter Sophocles' deepest feelings did not change. The same view of the human condition which is made explicit in his earliest extant play is implicit not only in the *Oedipus Rex* but in the *Oedipus Coloneus*, in the great speech where Oedipus draws the bitter conclusion from his life's experience and in the famous ode on old age.[16] Whether this vision of man's estate is true or false I do not know, but it ought to be comprehensible to a generation which relishes the plays of Samuel Beckett. I do not wish to describe it as a 'message'. But I find in it an enlargement of sensibility. And that is all I ask of any dramatist.

15

AMBIGUITY AND REVERSAL:
ON THE ENIGMATIC STRUCTURE OF *OEDIPUS REX*

JEAN-PIERRE VERNANT

In his 1939 study of ambiguity in Greek literature, W. B. Stanford notes that from the point of view of amphibology, *Oedipus Rex* occupies a special position as a model.[1] No literary genre in antiquity, in fact, uses so abundantly as tragedy expressions of double meaning, and *Oedipus Rex* includes more than twice as many ambiguous forms as the other plays of Sophocles (fifty, according to the table that Hug drew up in 1872).[2] The problem, however, is less one of a quantitative order than of nature and function. All the Greek tragedians had recourse to ambiguity as a means of expression and as a mode of thought. But double meaning assumes quite a different role according to its place in the economy of the play and the level of language where the tragic poets situate it.

It can be a matter of ambiguity in vocabulary, corresponding to what Aristotle calls *homōnumia* (lexical ambiguity); this type of ambiguity is made possible by the vacillations or contradictions of language.[3] The playwright plays with them to translate his tragic vision of a world divided against itself, torn by contradictions. In the mouths of several characters, the same words take on different or opposed meanings, because their semantic value is not the same in the religious, legal, political, and common languages.[4] Thus, for Antigone, *nomos* designates the opposite of what Creon himself, in the circumstances in which he is placed, also calls *nomos*.[5] For the young girl the word means religious rule; for Creon, an edict promulgated by the head of the state. And indeed, the semantic field of *nomos* is sufficiently extended to cover, among others, both of these meanings.[6] Ambiguity then translates the tension between certain values felt as irreconcilable in spite of their homonymy. The words exchanged in the theatrical space, instead of establishing communication

Translated by P. du Bois, from *New Literary History* 9 (1977–8), 475–501. Reprinted by permission of Johns Hopkins University Press.

and agreement between the characters, on the contrary underline the impermeability of minds, the freezing of character; they mark the barriers which separate the protagonists, and they trace the lines of conflict. Each hero, enclosed in the universe which is his own, gives a word a meaning, a single meaning. Against this unilaterality, another unilaterality clashes violently. Tragic irony may consist in showing how, in the course of the action, the hero finds himself literally 'taken at his word', a word which turns itself against him in bringing him the bitter experience of the meaning which he insisted on not recognizing.[7] It is only over the heads of the characters, between the author and the spectator, that another dialogue is woven, where language recovers its property of communication and almost its transparency. But what transmits the tragic message, when it is understood, is precisely that in the words exchanged between men there exist zones of opacity and incommunicability. In the moment when, on stage, he sees the protagonists adhering exclusively to one meaning and, thus blinded, lose themselves or tear each other apart, the spectator is led to understand that there are in reality two possible meanings or more. The tragic message becomes intelligible to him to the extent that, wrested from his former certainties and limitations, he realizes the ambiguity of words, of values, of the human condition. Recognizing the universe as full of conflict, opening himself to a problematic vision of the world, he makes himself embody the tragic consciousness through the spectacle.

The *Agamemnon* of Aeschylus may provide good examples of another type of tragic ambiguity. Implications are used in a completely conscious way by certain characters in this play to conceal in the discourse which they address to their interlocutor a second discourse, contrary to the first, a discourse whose meaning is perceptible only to those persons, actors, or audience having necessary information.[8] Welcoming Agamemnon at the threshold of his palace, Clytemnestra uses this double-keyed language: it sounds agreeably like a token of love and of conjugal fidelity in the ears of her husband; but, already equivocal for the chorus, which has a presentiment of an obscure threat, it reveals itself as completely sinister to the spectator, who easily deciphers in it the plan for death which she has contrived against her husband.[9] The ambiguity no longer marks the conflict of values but the duplicity of a character. An almost demonic duplicity: the same discourse, the same words which entice Agamemnon into the trap by concealing the danger at the same time proclaim to the world the crime about to be perpetrated. And because the queen, in the hate which she vows to her spouse, turns herself into the instrument of divine justice in the course of the play, the secret language hidden in the words of her welcome has oracular value. In speaking of the death of the king, she, like a prophet, makes it inevitable. What Agamemnon cannot understand in the words of Clytemnestra is then the very truth of what is said. Formulated aloud, this word acquires all the executive force of a curse; it inscribes into being, in advance and forever, what is enunciated by her. To the ambiguity of the discourse of the queen corresponds exactly the ambiguity of the symbolic values attached to the purple carpet spread out by her in front of the king and on which she persuades him to walk. When he enters into his palace, as Clytemnestra invites him to in terms which evoke at the same time quite another dwelling, these are indeed the doors of Hades through which, without knowing it, Agamemnon passes. When he places his bare foot on the 'sumptuous fabrics', with which the ground has been strewn, the road of purple given birth beneath his steps is in no way, as he imagines it, an almost too elevated consecration of his glory, but is instead a way to deliver him over to the infernal powers, to pledge him to death without remission, that 'red' death which comes to him in the same 'sumptuous fabric' prepared by Clytemnestra for taking him in a trap as in a net.[10]

The ambiguity which one finds in *Oedipus Rex* is quite different. It concerns neither an opposition of values nor duplicity on the part of the character who is leading the action and delights in playing with his victim. In the drama where he is the victim, Oedipus, and Oedipus alone, leads the 'play'. Nothing except his stubborn will to unmask the guilty, the lofty idea which he has of his burden, of his capacities, of his judgment (his *gnomē*), his passionate desire to know the truth at any price — nothing obliges him to push the inquiry to its end. Teiresias, Jocasta, the Shepherd try successively to stop him. In vain. He is not a man to content himself with half measures, to accommodate himself to compromise. Oedipus goes to the end. And at the end of the road which he has traced against all opposition, Oedipus discovers that in leading the play from beginning to end it is he himself, from the beginning to end, who has been played. Thus in the moment when he knows himself responsible for making his unhappiness, he will be able to accuse the gods of having prepared all, done all.[11] The equivocation in the words of Oedipus corresponds to the ambiguous status which is conferred on him in the play and upon which the whole tragedy is constructed. When Oedipus speaks, he sometimes says another thing or the opposite of what he says. The ambiguity of his words translates not the duplicity of his character, which is all of a piece, but more profoundly the duality of his being. Oedipus is double. He constitutes by himself a riddle whose meaning he will guess only by discovering himself in every respect the opposite of what he believed himself and seemed to be. Oedipus does not hear the

secret discourse which is established, without his knowing it, at the heart
of his own discourse. And no witness to the drama on the scene, apart
from Teiresias, is any more capable than he of perceiving it. It is the
gods who send back to Oedipus, as an echo to certain of his words, his
own discourse, deformed or turned around.[12] And this inverted echo,
which sounds like a sinister burst of laughter, is in reality a rectification.
What Oedipus says without wishing to, without understanding it, constitutes the only authentic truth of his words. The double dimension of
Oedipus' language reproduces, then, in an inverted form, the double
dimension of the language of the gods as it is expressed in the enigmatic
form of the oracle. The gods know and speak the truth, but they make
it known by giving it expression in words which seem to men to say
something quite different. Oedipus neither knows nor says the truth,
but the words he uses to say something other than truth make this truth
clear, without his knowledge, in a way shocking for anyone who has the
gift of double hearing, as the diviner has double vision. The language of
Oedipus thus appears as the place where two different discourses weave
themselves and confront each other in the same language: a human discourse, a divine discourse. In the beginning, the two discourses are quite
distinct, as if cut off one from the other; at the end of the play, when
all is made clear, the two discourses are rejoined; the riddle is solved.
On the tiers of the theater, the spectators occupy a privileged situation
which permits them, like the gods, to understand at the same time the
two opposed discourses and to follow their confrontation from one end
to the other, through the play.

   We understand then why, from the point of view of amphibology,
Oedipus Rex has exemplary significance: Aristotle, recalling that the
two constitutive elements of tragic plot are, besides the 'pathetic', recognition *(anagnōrisis)* and *peripeteia* — that is, the reversal of the action
to its opposite *(eis to enantion tōn prattomenōn metabolē)* — notes
that the recognition in *Oedipus Rex* is the most beautiful because it
coincides with the *peripeteia*.[13] The recognition which Oedipus brings
about in fact bears on no one but Oedipus. And this final identification
of the hero by himself constitutes a complete reversal of the action, in
the two meanings which one can give to Aristotle's formula (which is
not itself free of ambiguity): the situation of Oedipus, by the very act
of recognition, is revealed as contrary to what it was previously; Oedipus'
action ends up with the opposite result from that aimed at. At the
opening of the play, the Corinthian stranger, decipherer of riddles, savior
of Thebes, installed at the head of the city, whom the people venerate
as the equal of a god for his knowledge and his devotion to the state,
must face a new riddle, that of the death of the former king. Who killed

Laius? At the end of the investigation, the judge discovers himself identical with the assassin. Behind the progressive elucidation of the detective riddle, which forms the thread of the tragic action, what is being played out in fact is the recognition by Oedipus of his identity. When he appears for the first time, at the opening of the play, to announce to the supplicants his resolution to discover the criminal at any cost, and his certainty of success, he expresses himself in terms whose ambiguity underlines the presence, behind the question which he hopes to answer (who killed Laius?), of another problem (who is Oedipus?). In going back in his turn, the king declares proudly, 'I will bring this to light again [*egō phanō*].'[14] The scholiast does not fail to observe that there is in this *egō phanō* something concealed, something Oedipus does not mean, but which the spectator understands, 'since all will be discovered in Oedipus himself [*epei to pan en autō phanēsetai*].' *Egō phanō*: 'it is I who will bring the criminal to light,' but also 'I myself will discover myself criminal.'

What then is Oedipus? Like his own discourse, like the word of the oracle, Oedipus is double, enigmatic. From the beginning to the end of the play he remains psychologically and morally the same: a man of action and of decision, with courage nothing can beat down, with conquering intelligence, a man to whom one can impute no moral fault, no deliberate oversight of justice. But without knowing it, without having asked for or deserved it, the character of Oedipus in all his dimensions — social, religious, human — is the reverse of what he appears at the head of the city. The Corinthian stranger is in reality a native of Thebes; the decipherer of riddles, a riddle which he cannot decipher; the judge, a criminal; the clairvoyant, a blind man; the savior of the city, its damnation. Oedipus, he who for all is renowned (8), the first of men (33), noblest of men (46), the man of power, of intelligence, of honors, of wealth, finds himself the last, the most unhappy (1204-6, 1296 ff., 1396 ff.), and the worst of men (1365), a sinner (1398), a festering foulness (1396), object of horror to his equals (1306), hated by the gods (1345), reduced to beggary and exile (455, 1518).

Two features underline the significance of this 'reversal' of Oedipus' condition. In the first words he addresses to him, the priest of Zeus makes Oedipus in some way the equal of the gods: *isoumenos theoisi* (31). When the riddle is solved, the chorus recognizes in Oedipus the model of a human life which, through this paradigm, appears equal to nothingness: *isa kai to mēden* (1187-88). At the start Oedipus is the clairvoyant mind, the lucid intelligence which, without anyone's aid, without the help of a god or an omen, knew how to guess, by the resources of his *gnomē* alone, the riddle of the Sphinx. He has only scorn for the blind gaze of the diviner whose eyes are closed to the light of the sun and whose life, according to his own expression, 'is one long night' (374). But when the shadows are dispelled, so that all is made clear (1182), when light bears on Oedipus, it is then precisely that he sees day for the last time. As soon as Oedipus is 'elucidated', found out (1213), offered to the eyes of all as a spectacle of horror (1397), it is no longer possible for him to see or to be seen. The Thebans turn their eyes away from him (1303–5), incapable of looking in the face of this evil which is a 'terrible sight for men to see' (1298), this grief of which one can bear neither the telling nor the sight (1312). And if Oedipus blinds himself, it is, as he explains (1370 ff.), because it has become impossible for him to support the gaze of another human creature among the living and the dead. If he could have, he would also have stopped his ears to wall himself in a solitude cut off from the society of men. The light which the gods projected on Oedipus is too bright for mortal eye to gaze on. It casts Oedipus out from this world, made for the light of the sun, the human glance, social contact. It restores him to the solitary world of night, where Teiresias lives, who has himself paid with his eyes for the gift of double sight, the access to the other light, the blinding and terrible light of the divine.

Considered from the point of view of men, Oedipus is the clairvoyant leader, equal to the gods; considered from the point of view of the gods, he appears blind, equal to nothing. The turning around of the action, like the ambiguity of the language, marks the duplicity of a human condition which, like a riddle, invites two opposite interpretations. Human language is inverted when the gods speak through it. No matter how great, just, happy one may be, the human condition is reversed as soon as one measures it against the gods. Oedipus had 'shot his bolt beyond the others and won the prize of happiness complete' (1197 ff.). But in the eye of the Immortals, he who raises himself to the highest is also the lowest. Oedipus the blessed touches the bottom of unhappiness: 'What man', sings the chorus, 'what man on earth wins more of happiness than a seeming and after that turning away? Oedipus, you are my pattern of this, Oedipus, you and your fate! Luckless Oedipus, whom of all men I envy not at all.'[15]

If such is indeed the meaning of the tragedy, as Hellenists agree, we will recognize that *Oedipus Rex* is not only centered on the theme of the riddle, but that in its presentation, its development, its denouement, the play itself is constructed as a riddle.[16] The ambiguity, the recognition, the peripeteia, homologous with each other, are equally integrated into the enigmatic structure of the work. The keystone of the tragic architecture, the model which serves as matrix to its tragic organization and to its language, is reversal, that is, that formal scheme by which positive values are inverted to negative values when one passes from one to the other of the two planes, human and divine, which tragedy unites and opposes, just as a riddle, according to Aristotle's definition, joins together irreconcilable terms.[17]

Through this logical scheme of inversion, corresponding to the ambiguous mode of thought proper to tragedy, an instruction of a particular type is proposed to the spectators: man is not a being which we can describe or define; he is a problem, a riddle whose double meanings we have never finished deciphering. The meaning of the work depends neither on psychology nor on mortality; it is of a specifically tragic order.[18] Parricide and incest correspond neither to Oedipus' character, to his *ēthos*, nor to a moral fault, *adikia*, for which he might be responsible. If he kills his father, if he sleeps with his mother, it is not because, more or less obscurely, he hates the first or is in love with the second. For those whom he believes to be his true, his only parents, Merope and Polybus, Oedipus has feelings of filial tenderness. When he kills Laius, it is in legitimate defense against a stranger who struck him first; when he marries Jocasta, it is a marriage without affection, which the city of Thebes imposes on him with a stranger in order to permit his accession to the throne, as recompense for his exploit: 'Though I did not know, Thebes married me to evil; Fate and I were joined there. . . . I thought of her as my reward. Ah, would I had never won it! Would I had never served the State that day!'[19] As Oedipus declares, in committing parricide and incest, neither his person (*sōma*) nor his acts (*erga*) are at issue; in reality, he himself has done nothing (*ouk erexa*).[20] Or rather, during his action its meaning, unknown to him and without his having anything to do with it, reversed itself. Legitimate defense became parricide; marriage, consecrating his glory, incest. Innocent and pure from the point of view of human law, he is guilty and contaminated from the religious point of view. What he accomplished, without knowing it, without evil purpose or felonious intent, is nonetheless the most terrible wrong conceivable against the sacred order which governs human life. Like those birds which eat birds' flesh, to recall the expression of Aeschylus,[21] he is twice satiated with his own flesh, first by spilling paternal blood, then by uniting himself to maternal blood. Oedipus thus finds himself, by a divine curse as gratuitous as the election from which the other heroes of legend profit, cut off from the social bond, thrown outside humanity. He is from then on *apolis*; he incarnates the figure of the excluded. In his solitude, he appears at once not yet human, a wild beast, a savage monster, and beyond the human, bearer of a formidable religious qualification, like a *daimōn*. His stain, like his *āgos*, is only the reverse side of the supernatural power which is concentrated in him in order to destroy him: at the same time as contaminated, he is sacred and saint, *hieros* and *eusebēs*.[22] To the city which will welcome him, to the earth which will hold his corpse, he will bring the pledge of the greatest blessings.

This play of inversion is expressed, by other stylistic and dramatic procedures besides that of ambiguity, in particular by what Bernard Knox calls a 'reversal' in the use of the same terms in the course of the tragic action.[23] The reader is referred to his fine study of which we will recall only a few examples. A first form of this reversal consists in using, to characterize the status of Oedipus, a vocabulary the values of which are systematically inverted when they pass from active to passive. Oedipus is presented as a hunter on the trail, tracking down and startling the wild animal (111, 221, 475 ff.) which wanders on the mountain, hastened into flight by the hunt (467), hidden away far from humans (479-80). But in his hunt, the hunter at length finds himself the game: hunted by the terrible curse of his parents (417). Oedipus wanders and bellows like a wild animal (1260, 1265) before putting out his eyes and fleeing into the wild mountains of Cithairon (1451).

Oedipus leads an investigation, at the same time judiciary and scientific, which is underlined by the repeated use of the verb *zētein*.[24] But the investigator is also the object of the investigation, the *zēton* is also the *zētoumenon*;[25] like the examiner, the questioner[26] is also the answer to the question (1180-81). Oedipus is the discoverer[27] and the object of the discovery (1026, 1213), that very one who is discovered (*heuriskomai*, 1397). He is the doctor using a medicinal vocabulary to speak of the evil from which the city is suffering, but he is also the sick man (61, 674) and the sickness (1294, 1389, 1396-97).

Another form of reversal is the following: the terms which designate Oedipus at the height of his glory detach themselves from him one by one to come to rest on the gods; the grandeur of Oedipus vanishes in proportion as, in contrast with his, that of the gods is affirmed. At line 14 the priest of Zeus, in his first words, addresses himself to Oedipus as sovereign: *kratunōn*; at 903 the chorus implores Zeus as sovereign: *ō kratunōn*. At 47 the Thebans call Oedipus savior: *sōtēr*; at 150 it is Apollo who is invoked as savior (*paustērios*) to put a stop to the evil, as Oedipus formerly had put a 'stop' to the Sphinx (397). At line 236 Oedipus gives orders as master of the power and of the throne (*egō kratē te kai thronous nemō*); at 200 the chorus implores Zeus 'the Lord of lightning' (*astrapan kratē nemōn*). At 441 Oedipus recalls the exploit which made him great (*megas*); at 871 the chorus recalls that in the celestial laws resides a great (*megas*) god who does not age. That dominion (*archē*) which Oedipus prides himself in exercising (259, 380), the chorus recognizes as forever immortal between the hands of Zeus (905). That help (*alkē*) which the priest at 42 asks of Zeus, the chorus implores Athena, at 189, to give to them. In the first line of the tragedy, Oedipus addresses himself to the suppliants as a father speaks to his children; but at 198, to destroy the pestilence of the city, it is on Zeus that the chorus confers the title of father: *ō zeu pater*.

Even the name of Oedipus invites these effects of reversal. Ambiguous, it bears in it the same enigmatic character which marks the whole tragedy. Oedipus is the man with the swollen (*oidos*) foot, an infirmity which recalls the cursed child, rejected by his parents, exposed to die in savage nature. But as Oedipus, he is also the man who knows (*oida*) the riddle of the foot, who succeeds in deciphering, without misconstruing it,[28] the 'oracle' of the sinister prophetess, of the Sphinx with the dark song (1200, 130).[29] And this knowledge enthrones in Thebes the foreign hero, establishes him in the place of the legitimate kings. The double meaning of *Oidipous* is found again at the interior of the name itself in the opposition between the first two syllables and the third, *Oida*: 'I know', one of the master words in the mouth of Oedipus triumphant, Oedipus the tyrant.[30] *Pous*: 'the foot' — the mark imposed since birth on him whose destiny is to finish as he began, excluded, like the savage beast which his *foot* makes flee (468), whom his *foot* isolates from humans, in the vain hope of escaping the oracles (479 ff.), pursued by the curse with the terrible *foot* (417) for having transgressed the sacred laws with his lifted foot (866), and incapable from then on of extricating his foot from the evils into which he has precipitated himself by raising himself to the height of power.[31] The whole tragedy of Oedipus is thus contained in the play to which the riddle of his name lends itself. To that wise, knowing master of Thebes, whom happy omen protects, is at every point opposed the cursed infant, the Swollen Foot cast out of his fatherland. But in order for Oedipus really to know who he is, the first of the two characters which he initially assumed must be inverted until it turns into the second.

The knowledge of Oedipus, when he deciphers the riddle of the Sphinx, bears in a certain fashion on himself. What is the being, asks the sinister songstress, who is at once *dipous, tripous, tetrapous*? For *Oidipous*, the mystery is only in appearance; it is about him surely, it is about man. But this answer is knowledge only in appearance; it masks the true problem: what then is man, what is Oedipus? The pseudo-response of Oedipus opens to him the high gates of Thebes. But in installing him at the head of the state, this answer realizes, by hiding it from him, his true identity as parricide and committer of incest. To penetrate his own mystery is for Oedipus to recognize in the stranger who reigns in Thebes the formerly rejected child of the land. This identification, instead of definitively uniting Oedipus with his fatherland, instead of fixing him on the throne which he occupies from then on not as a foreign tyrant but as the legitimate son of the king, turns him into a monster whom it is necessary to expel forever from the city, to cut off from the human world.

Venerated as the equal of a god, uncontested master of justice, holding in his hands the health of the whole city — such, placed above other men, is the character of Oedipus the Wise, who at the end of the play is reversed, projected into an opposite figure: at the last rung of disgrace appears Oedipus-Swollen Foot, abominable contamination, concentrating in himself all the impurity of the world. The divine king, purifier and savior of his people, rejoins the contaminated criminal whom it is necessary to expel like a *pharmakos*, a scapegoat, so that the city, pure again, may be saved.

It is in fact by means of the axis occupied at the summit by the divine king, at its base by the *pharmakos*, that the series of reversals takes place which affects the character of Oedipus and makes of the hero the 'paradigm' of ambiguous man, of tragic man.

The quasi-divine aspect of the majestic figure who advances on the threshold of his palace, at the beginning of the tragedy, has not escaped the commentators. Already the ancient scholiast noted in his commentary at line 16 that the suppliants come to the altars of the royal house as to the altars of a god. The expression which the priest of Zeus uses, 'You see us assembled near your altars', seems so heavy with meaning that Oedipus himself asks: 'Why do you hold yourselves thus crouched in a ritual attitude of supplication towards me, with your boughs crowned with fillets?' This veneration towards a man whom one places higher than man because he saved the city 'with God's assistance' (39) because he has been revealed by supernatural favor as the *Tuchē*, the 'happy omen' (52) of the city, is maintained from one end of the play to the other. Even after the double contamination of Oedipus has been revealed, the chorus celebrates nonetheless as its savior this man whom it calls 'my king', 'standing a tower against death for my land' (1201). At the very moment when it evokes the inexpiable crimes of the unhappy one, the chorus concludes, 'To speak directly, I drew my breath from you at the first and so now I lull my mouth to sleep with your name' (1222–23).

But it is at the crucial moment of the play, when the fate of Oedipus rests on the razor's edge, that the polarity between the status of the demigod and that of scapegoat reveals itself most clearly. What is the situation at that point? We know already that Oedipus may be the murderer of Laius: the symmetry of the oracles given on the one hand to Oedipus, on the other to Laius and Jocasta, increases the anxiety that grips the heart of the protagonists and the Theban notables. The messenger from Corinth arrives in the midst of all this. He announces that Oedipus is not the son of those whom he believes to be his parents, that he is a foundling; he has himself taken him from the hands of a shepherd on Cithairon. Jocasta, to whom all is clear by now, begs Oedipus not to push the investigation further. Oedipus refuses. The queen then addresses this last warning to him: 'Unhappy one, may you never know who you are!' But once again the tyrant of Thebes is mistaken about the meaning of what Oedipus is. He thinks the queen fears that the base origin of the foundling will be disclosed and that her marriage will be revealed as a misalliance with someone less than nothing, a slave, son of a slave to the third generation (1062). It is precisely then that Oedipus draws himself up — in his battered soul, the announcement of the messenger brings forth a mad hope which the chorus shares and which it expresses joyously in its song. Oedipus proclaims himself son of *Tuchē*, of happy omen, who, reversing his situation in the course of the years from the 'little' one he was, has made himself 'great' (*mikron kai megan*: 1083), that is to say, has transformed the deformed, foundling child into the wise master of Thebes. Irony of words: Oedipus is not the son of *Tuchē*; as Teiresias predicted, he is her victim (442), and the reversal is produced in the inverse sense, bringing the great Oedipus back to what is lowest, back from the god's equal to the equal of nothing.

However, the illusion of Oedipus and the chorus is understandable. The exposed child can be a reject which one wants to get rid of, a deformed monster or lowly slave. But he can also be a hero with an exceptional destiny. Saved from death, victor of the test imposed on him by his birth, the excluded one reveals himself elect, invested with supernatural powers.[32] Having returned triumphant to the country which excluded him, he will no longer live there as an ordinary citizen, but as absolute master, reigning over his subjects in the manner of a god among men. That is why the theme of exposure figures in almost all the Greek legends of heroes. If Oedipus was rejected at birth, cut off from his human lineage, it is doubtless, as the chorus imagines, because he is the son of some god, of the nymphs of Cithairon, of Pan or of Apollo, of Hermes or of Dionysus (1086-1109).

This mythic image of the hero exposed and saved, rejected and returning as victor, continues in a transposed form, in a certain representation of the *turannos*. Like the hero, the tyrant accedes to royalty by an indirect route, outside the legitimate lineage; like him, he qualifies himself for power by his acts, his exploits. He reigns, not by virtue of

his blood, but by his own virtues: he is the son of his deeds and of
happy omen at the same time. The supreme power which he, outside of
ordinary norms, was able to conquer places him, for good and bad,
above other men, above the laws.[33] According to the just remark of
Bernard Knox, the comparison of tyranny with the power of the gods
(gods defined for the Greeks as 'the strongest', 'the most powerful') is a
commonplace of the literature of the fifth and fourth centuries. Euripides and Plato agree in speaking of *turannis isotheos*, of tyranny equal to
deity, inasmuch as it is absolute power to do all one wishes, to permit
oneself everything.[34]

The other face of Oedipus, complementary and opposed (his appearance as scapegoat), has not been so clearly defined by the commentators.
We have seen that Oedipus, at the end of the tragedy, is cast out from
Thebes as one expels the *homo piacularis* in order to 'ward off the contamination [*to agos elaunein*]'.[35] But Louis Gernet established the
relationship of the tragic theme with the Athenian ritual of the *pharmakos* in a more precise way.[36]

Thebes suffers from a *loimos* which according to the traditional
schema is manifested by a drying up of the sources of fecundity; earth,
flocks, women bear no more, while pestilence decimates the living.
Sterility, sickness, death are experienced as the same power of contamination, a *miasma* which has disrupted the normal course of life. It is a
matter then of discovering the criminal who *is* the stain of the city, its
agos, in order to get rid of the evil through him. This is what is known
to have happened in Athens, in the seventh century, when to expiate
the impious murder of Kylon, the Alcmeonids were expelled and declared impure and sacrilegious (*enageĩs kai alitērioi*).[37]

But there also exists, in Athens as in other Greek cities, an annual
rite which aims at periodically expelling the contamination accumulated
in the course of the past year. 'It is the custom in Athens', reports El-
ladios of Byzantium, 'to parade two *pharmakoi* for purification, one for
the men, the other for the women.'[38] According to the legend, the origin
of the rite lay in the impious murder committed by the Athenians on
the person of Androgeos the Cretan: to get rid of the *loimos* set off by
the crime, the custom of a recurrent purification by the *pharmakos* was
instituted. The ceremony took place on the first day of the holiday of
the Thargelia, the sixth of the month *Thargeliōn*.[39] The two *pharmakoi*,
wearing necklaces of dried figs (black or white according to the sex
they represented), were paraded through the whole city; they were
struck on the genitals with squill bulbs, figs, and other wild plants,[40]
then they were expelled; perhaps, at least at the beginning, they were
even put to death by stoning, the corpses burnt, the ashes dispersed.[41]

How were the *pharmakoi* chosen? Everything leads us to believe that they were recruited from the dregs of the population, among the *kakourgoi*, jailbirds, designated by their misdeeds, their physical ugliness, their base condition, their vile and repugnant occupation, as inferior beings, degraded, *phauloi*, the rejects of society. Aristophanes, in the *Frogs*, opposes to the well-born citizens, wise, just, honest, who are like the good money of the city, the bad pieces of copper, 'foreign, red-haired, beggars born from beggars', the latest arrivals, whom the city would not have accepted easily at random even as *pharmakoi*.[42] Tzetzes, citing the fragments of the poet Hipponax, notes that when a *loimos* struck a city, the most wretched of all (*amorphoteron*) was chosen as *katharmos* and *pharmakos* of the diseased city.[43] At Leucas, they took for purification a man condemned to death. At Marseilles, some wretch offered himself as 'cure all'. He thus gained a year of life, supported at public expense. At the end of the year he was paraded around the city with solemn curses so that the transgressions of the community would fall on him.[44] So the image of the *pharmakos* comes quite naturally to Lysias' mind when he wishes to denounce to the judges the repugnant foulness of a person like Andocides, impious, sacrilegious, informer and traitor, exiled from city to city, and seemingly marked in his miseries by the finger of god. To condemn Andocides 'is to purify the city, liberate it from contamination, expel the *pharmakos*.'[45]

The Athenian Thargelia included another panel. With the expulsion of the *pharmakos*, it associated another ritual which took place on the seventh of the month, the day dedicated to Apollo. They dedicated to the divinity the first fruits of the earth in the form of the *Thargēlos*, a cake and a pot filled with seeds of all kinds.[46] But the central element of the holiday was the carrying of the *eiresiōnē*, a branch of olive or laurel ribboned with wool, garnished with fruits, with cakes, with little flasks of oil and wine.[47] Young boys paraded these 'maypoles' across the city. They placed them at the threshold of the temple of Apollo, they hung them at the doors of private houses (*pros apotropēn limou*) to avert famine.[48] The *eiresiōnē* in Attica, at Samos, Delos, and Rhodes, the *kōpō* at Thebes, signify springtime renewal. Accompanied by songs and by an offering of gifts, their procession consecrates the end of the old season and inaugurates the young new year under the sign of the gift, of abundance, of health.[49] Society's need, by dismissing those which have faded during the year, to reinvigorate the forces of fecundity on which its life depends appears clearly in the Athenian rite. The *eiresiōnē* remains attached to the houses' doors where it fades and dries until the day of the Thargelia when the new year's green one replaces it.[50]

But the renewal symbolized by the *eiresiōnē* cannot be produced unless all contaminations of the group have been cast off, unless earth and men have been made pure. As Plutarch[51] recalls, the first fruits of all kinds which decorate the *eiresiōnē* commemorate the end of the *aphoria*, the sterility which struck the soil of Attica as punishment for the murder of Androgeos, that murder which the expulsion of the *pharmakos* ought precisely to expiate. The major role of the *eiresiōnē* in the Thargelia explains what Hesychius glosses *thargēlos: hē hiketēria*, because, in its form and function, the *eiresiōnē* is nothing but a suppliant's branch.[52]

These are precisely the *hiketeriai*, these suppliants' branches crowned with wool, which, at the beginning of Sophocles' play, the representatives of the Theban youth, grouped in classes by age, children and very young people, parade up to the gates of the royal palace and set down in front of the altar of Apollo to ward off the *loimos* oppressing the city. Another indication permits us to define more precisely the ritual scenario evoked by the first scene of the tragedy. Twice it is recalled that the city resounds with 'groans and hymns and incense' (5,186). The paean is normally a joyous song of victory and of thanksgiving. It is opposed to the threnody, a song of mourning, a plaintive melody. But we know from a scholiast of the *Iliad* that there exists another type of paean, that which is sung 'to end evils or in order that they not occur.'[53] This cathartic paean, whose memory was kept alive by the Pythagoreans in particular, also takes the form of a threnody, according to the scholiast. This is the paean mixed with sobs of which the tragedy speaks. This purifying song is used at a very precise moment of the religious calendar, at that turning of the year which spring represents, when, at the threshold of summer, the period of human undertakings begins: harvests, navigation, war.[54] Situated in May, before the beginning of the harvests, the Thargelia belong to this complex of spring holidays.

These details must have imposed on the spectators of the tragedy the comparison with the Athenian ritual so much the more easily in that Oedipus is presented implicitly as the *agos*, whose contamination it is necessary to expel.[55] From his first words he defines himself, without wishing to, in terms that evoke the character of the scapegoat: 'I know', he says to the suppliants, 'you are all sick, yet there is not one of you, sick though you are, that is as sick as I myself. Your several sorrows each have single scope and touch but one of you. My spirit [*psuchē*] groans for city and myself and you at once' (59-64). And a little further on: 'the grief I bear, I bear it more for these [others] than for my own heart' (93-94). Oedipus is wrong: this evil, to which Creon immediately gives its real name in calling it *miasma* (97), is precisely his own. But in being wrong he says, unknowingly, the truth. Because he is himself, as *miasma*, the *agos* of the city, Oedipus indeed carries the weight of all the unhappiness which overwhelms his fellow citizens.

Divine king – pharmakos: such are the two faces of Oedipus, which constitute him as a riddle by uniting two figures in him, as in an expression with double meaning, the one the inverse of the other. Sophocles attributes a general significance to this inversion in Oedipus' nature. The hero is the model of the human condition. But Sophocles did not have to invent the polarity between the king and the scapegoat (a polarity which the tragedy situates at the very heart of the character of Oedipus). It was inscribed in the religious practice and in the social thought of the Greeks. The poet simply lent it a new significance in making it the symbol of man and of his fundamental ambiguity. If Sophocles chose the couple *turannos – pharmakos* to illustrate what we have called the theme of reversal, it is because in their opposition these two persons appear symmetrical and in certain respects interchangeable. Both appear as *individuals* responsible for the *collective* health of the group. In Homer and Hesiod, the fecundity of the earth, of the flocks, of women depends on the person of the king, offspring of Zeus. If he shows himself irreproachable (*amumōn*), in his sovereign justice, everything prospers in his city;[56] if he errs, it is the *whole city* which pays for the fault of one man. The son of Cronos makes unhappiness fall back on all, *limos* and *loimos*, famine and plague all together: men die, women cease to give birth, the flocks no longer reproduce.[57] Thus the normal solution, when the divine scourge strikes a people, is to sacrifice the king. If he is the master of fecundity, and it dries up, it is because his power as sovereign is in some way reversed; his justice has become crime, his virtue contamination, the best (*aristos*) has become the worst (*kakistos*). The legends of Lycurgus, of Athamas, of Oinocles thus require, for the expulsion of *loimos*, the stoning of the king, his ritual sacrifice, or failing that, the sacrifice of his son. But sometimes the painful role of unworthy king, of sovereign in reverse, is delegated to a member of the community. The king unburdens himself on an individual who like an inverted image represents everything negative in his person. Such is the *pharmakos*: double of the king, but in reverse, like those sovereigns at carnival crowned at holiday time, when order is set upside down, social hierarchies reversed: sexual prohibitions are lifted, theft becomes legal, the slaves take their masters' place, the women trade their clothes with men; then the throne must be occupied by the basest, ugliest, most ridiculous, most criminal of men. But, the holiday once ended, the counter-king is expelled or put to death, dragging with him all the disorder which he incarnates and of which the community is purged at one blow.

In classical Athens, the rite of the Thargelia still makes clear certain traits, in the person of the *pharmakos*, which evoke the figure of the sovereign, master of fecundity.[58] The horrible person who must incarnate contamination is supported at the cost of the state, nourished on especially pure foods: fruits, cheese, consecrated cake of *maza*.[59] If in the course of the procession he is decorated, like the *eiresiōnē*, with necklaces of figs and branches, and struck on the sexual parts with squill bulbs, it is because he possesses a beneficent virtue of fecundity. His contamination is a religious designation which can be used in a beneficent sense. Like that of Oedipus, his *agos* make him a *katharmos*, a *katharsios*, a purifier. Moreover, his person's ambiguity is marked even in the etiological accounts which claim to explain the foundation of the rite. To the version of Helladios of Byzantium which we have cited is opposed that of Diogenes Laertius and of Athenaeus:[60] when Epimenides purified Athens of the *loimos* caused by the murder of Kylon, two young people, one named Cratinos, seem to have made a voluntary gift of their persons to purify the land which had nourished them. These two young people are presented, not as the refuse of society, but as the flower of Athenian youth. According to Tzetzes, as we have seen, they choose as *pharmakos* a particularly ugly being (*amorphoteros*); according to Athenaeus, Cratinus was, on the contrary, a very handsome adolescent (*meirakion eumorphon*).

The symmetry of the *pharmakos* and the legendary king, the first assuming a role below analogous to that which the second plays on high, perhaps casts light on the institution of ostracism whose character J. Carcopino has shown to be strange in many respects.[61] In the framework of the Greek city, there is no longer, as we know, a place for the person of the king, master of fecundity. When Athenian ostracism was instituted at the end of the sixth century, it is the figure of the tyrant who inherited, transposed, certain of the religious aspects belonging to the former sovereign. Ostracism aims as a rule at getting rid of that citizen who, raised too high, threatens to accede to the tyranny. But, in this completely positive form, the explanation cannot take account of the institution's archaic features. It functions every year, doubtless between the sixth and the eighth prytaneion, following rules contrary to the ordinary procedures of political and legal life. Ostracism is a judgment which aims at 'ridding the city' of a citizen by a temporary exile of ten years.[62] It is pronounced outside the tribunals, by the assembly, without there having been a public denunciation or even accusation against anyone. A first preliminary session decides by the raising of hands if the procedure of ostracism will take place or not for the year in progress. No name is pronounced, no debate takes place. If those voting have declared themselves favorable, the assembly is called back again in exceptional session some time later. It sits in the agora and not, as usual, on the Pnyx. To proceed to the real vote, each participant inscribes the name of his choice on a potsherd. This time no debate either: no name is proposed. There is neither accusation nor defense. The vote takes place without there being any appeal to reason, political or judicial. Everything is organized to give to the popular feeling which the Greeks call *phthonos*[63] (both envy and religious mistrust in regard to one who rises too high, succeeds too well) the occasion to manifest itself in the most spontaneous and unanimous form (it requires at least six thousand voters), outside all rule of law, all rational justification. For what is the ostracized reproached but for those same superiorities which raise him above the common and for his fortune, too great, which threatens to attract divine prosecution to the city. The fear of tyranny is mixed with a deeper apprehension of a religious kind, in regard to someone who puts the whole group in danger. As Solon writes: 'A city perishes by its overly great men [*andrōn d'ek megalōn polis ollutai*] .'[64]

The development which Aristotle assigns to ostracism is in this regard characteristic.[65] If a being goes beyond the common level in virtue and in political capacity, he says, he cannot be accepted on a footing of equality with the other citizens: 'Such a being in fact will naturally be like a god among men.' That is why, Aristotle adds, the democratic states instituted ostracism. In doing so, they followed the example of the myth: the Argonauts abandoned Heracles for an analogous motive. The ship Argo refused to carry him like the other passengers because of his excessive weight. And Aristotle concludes that things are in this matter as in the arts and sciences: 'A master of a chorus would not permit among his singers one whose voice would surpass in force and beauty all the rest of the chorus.'

How could the city admit into its heart one who, like Oedipus, 'has shot his bolt beyond the others' and has become *isotheos*? When it establishes ostracism, it creates an institution whose role is symmetrical to and the inverse of the ritual of the Thargelia. In the person of the ostracized, the city expels what in it is too elevated, what incarnates the evil which can come to it from above. In the evil of the *pharmakos*, it expels what is vilest in itself, what incarnates the evil that menaces it from below.[66] By this double and complementary rejection it delimits itself in relation to what is not yet known and what transcends the known: it takes the proper measure of the human in opposition on one side to the divine and heroic, on the other to the bestial and monstrous.

What the city thus realizes spontaneously in the play of its institutions Aristotle expresses in a fully conscious and deliberate way in his political theory. Man, he writes, is by nature a political animal; he then who finds himself by nature *apolis* is either *phaulos*, 'a degraded being, a subman', or *kreittōn ē anthrōpos*, 'above humanity, more powerful than man'. Such a man, Aristotle continues, is 'like an isolated pawn in a checkers game [*ate per azux ōn hōsper en pettois*].' And the philosopher comes back to the same idea a little further on, when he notes that one who cannot live in a community 'is not at all part of the city and finds himself by consequence either a brute beast, or a god [*ē thērion ē theos*].'[67]

It is the very status of Oedipus, in his double and contradictory aspect, which finds itself thus defined: above and below the human, hero more powerful than man, equal to god, and at the same moment brute beast rejected in the world solitude of the mountains.

But Aristotle's remark goes further. It permits us to understand the role of parricide and incest in the reversal which makes the equal of god and the equal of nothing coincide in the person of Oedipus. These two crimes constitute in effect an attack on the fundamental rules of a checkers game where each piece is situated, by its relation to others, in a determinate place on the checkers board of the city.[68] By making himself guilty of them, Oedipus has shuffled the cards, mixed up positions and pawns: he finds himself from then on out of the game. By his parricide, followed by incest, he installs himself in the place occupied by his father; he mingles, in Jocasta, mother and wife; he identifies himself at the same time with Laius (as Jocasta's husband) and with his own children (of whom he is at the same time father and brother), mixing together three generations of the line. Sophocles underlines this equalization, this identification of what ought to remain distinct and separate, with an insistence which has sometimes shocked moderns but which the interpreter must take fully into account. He does it with a verbal play centered on the words *homos* and *isos* (like and equal), with their compounds. Even before knowing anything of his true origin, Oedipus defines himself, in his relation to Laius, as sharing the same bed and having a *homosporon* (260) wife. In his mouth the word means that he 'sows' the same wife whom Laius 'sowed' before him; but at line 460 Teiresias takes up the term again to give it its true value: he announces to Oedipus that he will discover himself to be at once the murderer of his father and his *homosporos*, his cosower (1209–12). *Homosporos* ordinarily has another meaning: born from the same sowing, relative of the same stock. In fact, Oedipus, without knowing it, is of the same stock, just as much of Laius as of Jocasta. The equalization of Oedipus and his sons is expressed in a series of brutal images: the father has sown his sons where he was sown; Jocasta is a wife, not-wife but mother whose furrow produced in a double harvest both father and children; Oedipus has sown her who engendered him, from the place where he was himself sown, and from the same furrows, from these 'equal' furrows, he has received his children.[69] But it is Teiresias who gives all its tragic weight to this vocabulary of equality when he addresses himself to Oedipus in these terms: there will come evils 'establishing a grim equality between you and your children' (425). The identification of Oedipus with his own father and his own children, the assimilation in Jocasta of mother and wife, make Oedipus equal to himself, that is, they make him an *agos*, a being *apolis*, without common dimensions, without equality with other men, and who, believing himself equal to a god, finds himself finally equal to nothing.[70] The tyrant *isotheos* no more recognizes than could a wild beast the rules of the game which are the foundation of the human city.[71] Among the gods, who form a single family, incest is not prohibited. Cronos and Zeus attacked and dethroned their father. Like them, the tyrant can believe that everything is permitted him. Plato calls him 'parricide'[72] and compares him to a man who, by virtue of a magic ring, would have the freedom to infringe the most sacred rules with impunity: to kill whomever he wishes, unite with whoever pleases him, 'master of any action, like a god among men'.[73] Wild beasts are also not bound to respect the interdicts on which the society of men rests. They are not, like the gods, above the laws through an excess of power; they are beneath the laws, through a lack of *logos*.[74] Dio Crysostom reports the ironic remark of Diogenes on the subject of Oedipus: 'Oedipus bewails being at the same time the father and brother of his children, the husband and son of his wife; but about that cocks are not indignant, nor dogs, nor any bird.'[75] Among them there is neither brother, father, husband, son, nor wife.[76] Like the isolated pieces in the checkers game, they live without rules, without knowing difference or equality in the confusion of *anomia*.[77]

Out of the game, excluded from the city, rejected from the human by incest and parricide, Oedipus is revealed, at the end of the tragedy, incidental to the monstrous being evoked by the riddle whose solution he thought himself to have found in his pride as 'sage'. What is the creature with one voice, asked the Sphinx, who has two, three, and four feet? The question presented, confused, and mixed together the three ages through which man travels successively and which he can know only one after another: child when he walks on all fours, adult when he holds himself firmly on his two legs, old man helping himself with his staff. In identifying himself all at once with his young children and his old father, Oedipus, man with two feet, effaces the boundaries which ought to keep the father rigorously separated from the sons and from the grandfather, in order that each human generation occupy in the course of time and in the order of the city the place assigned to it. Last tragic reversal: it is his victory over the Sphinx which makes of Oedipus not the answer which he guessed, but the very question which was asked of him, not a man like the others, but a creature of confusion and chaos, the only one, we are told, of all those who go on the earth, in the air and the waters, to 'change his nature' instead of keeping it distinct.[78] Formulated by the Sphinx, the riddle of man thus admits of a solution, but one which turns itself back against the conqueror of the monster, the decipherer of riddles, to make him appear himself as a monster, a man in the form of a riddle, a riddle this time without an answer.

From our analysis of *Oedipus Rex* we can draw some conclusions. In the first place, there is a model which the tragedy puts to work on all the levels where it deploys itself: in language, with its multiple stylistic procedures; in the structure of the dramatic account where recognition and peripeteia coincide; in the theme of Oedipus' destiny; in the very person of the hero. This model is not given somewhere in the form of an image, a notion, a complex of feelings. It is a pure operative scheme of reversal, a rule of ambiguous logic. But this form has, in the tragedy, a content. To capture the countenance of Oedipus, paradigm of the double man, of man reversed, the rule is incarnated in the reversal which transforms the divine king into a scapegoat.

Second, if the complementary opposition between the *turannos* and the *pharmakos*, on which Sophocles plays, is indeed, as it seemed to us, present in the institutions and in the political theory of the Ancients, does the tragedy do anything but reflect a structure already given in the society and in common thought? We think, on the contrary, that, far from presenting a reflection of it, the tragedy calls it into question. In social practice and theory, the polar structure of superhuman and sub-human aims at delineating in its specific features the field of human life as defined by the ensemble of *nomoi* which characterize it. The sub-human and superhuman correspond only as two lines which neatly draw the boundaries within which man finds himself enclosed. On the contrary, in Sophocles, superhuman and subhuman are joined and are mixed together in the same person. And as this person is the model of man, all limits which would permit one to delineate human life, to fix unequivocally its status, are erased. When he wishes, like Oedipus, to pursue the investigation of what he is, man discovers himself enigmatic, without stability or a domain proper to him, without fixed connection, without defined essence, oscillating between the equal of a god and the equal of nothing. His real greatness consists in the very thing which expresses his enigmatic nature: the question.

Finally, the most difficult thing perhaps is not to restore, as we have tried to do, its authentic meaning to the tragedy, that meaning which it had for the Greeks of the fifth century, but to understand the counter-meanings which it has invited, or rather, how it has lent itself to so many counter-meanings. Whence comes this relative malleability of the work of art, which is also its youth and its perpetuity? If the true strength of the tragedy is in the last analysis this form of reversal which comes into play like a logical schema, we understand that the dramatic account remains open to diverse interpretations and that *Oedipus Rex* could be charged with a new meaning to precisely that extent that through the history of Western thought the problem of the ambiguity in man has been displaced, has changed terrain, and the riddle of human existence has been formulated in other terms than it was for the Greek tragedians.

16

THE *ELECTRA* OF SOPHOCLES:
PROLEGOMENA TO AN INTERPRETATION

R. P. WINNINGTON-INGRAM

The play has given rise to diverse interpretations. The greatest divergence of opinion is about the attitude of Sophocles to the matricidal vengeance. At one extreme we have a robust Homeric Sophocles, untroubled by the squeamishness of Aeschylus; at the other, an Aeschylean sensitiveness to the moral implications of the vengeance and a presumption that the Furies are only waiting for the play to end to begin their pursuit of Orestes. Adherents of the former view can point to certain epic features which Sophocles has introduced, but the constant reminiscences of the *Oresteia* are far more striking. This paper assumes (what will be in part substantiated) that Sophocles wrote with the *Oresteia* constantly in mind[1] and expected the better-educated among his audience to be reminded of it. It will be concerned particularly with the Sophoclean treatment of the Furies and will suggest that this is of fundamental importance to the interpretation of the play.

Though nothing is said about a pursuit of Orestes by the Furies of his mother, Sophocles does not, as one writer has put it,[2] omit the Furies. The word Erinys occurs four times in the play. At 112 Electra prays, among other chthonian powers, to the Erinyes; at 276 she states that Clytemnestra, when she sleeps with Aegisthus, fears no Erinys. At 491 the Chorus sing of the coming of the Erinys; at 1080 they sing that Electra is prepared to die 'having killed the double Erinys'. In addition, a reference to Erinyes is universally admitted at 1388, where the Chorus describe the avengers as 'the hounds that no one can escape'. If Sophocles had wished to write a supposedly epic version of the story, he should have scrupulously avoided a theme so closely associated by his predecessor with blood-guilt incurred by Orestes. By using this theme (as by all

From *Proceedings of the Cambridge Philological Society* 183 (1954–5), 20–27. Reprinted with revisions by permission of the author and the Cambridge Philological Society.

the innumerable reminiscences of the *Oresteia*), he insists, on the contrary, on placing himself in a relationship to Aeschylus and raises the question: did he accept or reject or modify the standpoint of the earlier dramatist? This would be true, if the above-mentioned passages stood alone. I shall endeavour to show that the theme of the Furies is in fact developed by Sophocles in close relation to the thought of Aeschylus.

Erinyes (in the singular or in the plural) are prominent throughout the *Oresteia*, not merely in the *Eumenides*.[3] In the earlier plays of the trilogy they are represented as carrying out the punitive justice of Zeus. In the *Choephori* the divine powers, Olympian and chthonian — Zeus, Apollo and the Furies — all converge to bring about the matricidal vengeance. It is not until the third play that conflict arises between the Olympians and the chthonians, between new and old gods, which is finally resolved by the persuasions of Athena. The justice which the Erinyes exercise (as Aeschylus constantly insists) on behalf of Zeus is vindictive. They administer the *lex talionis*, most clearly formulated at *Cho.* 309 ff. They are mainly (though not exclusively) concerned with bloodshed; and in that connexion they are the presiding deities of the vendetta or blood-feud. They work through human agencies: Clytemnestra, Aegisthus and Orestes are all (expressly or by implication) performing the function of Erinyes, when they carry out their acts of retaliatory justice. One act of retaliation leads to another in an apparently never-ending series. The shed blood demands its revenge on every occasion.

Orestes, for whose punishment no human agent is forthcoming, is pursued by the Erinyes themselves. The complex issues of the *Eumenides* cannot be examined here. But the play ends with the persuasion and (in some sense) transformation of the Erinyes, who nevertheless remain stern and punitive, though they cease to operate through the primitive blood-feud. The significance of this final scene resides in the manifestation of persuasion (*peithō*) as a mode of the divine power. Previously the justice of Zeus had seemed to be essentially a matter of *bia* (cf. *Agam.* 182 ff.). The Erinyes operated violently — and, moreover, blindly, automatically, rigidly, compulsively. Here there is a link with *Prom.* 516 f. This may be an important aspect of the Furies for Aeschylus. They represent the way in which the present and the future are inexorably determined by evil in the past. Only the great antithetical power of persuasion is capable of liberating mankind from this fatal and diasastrous constraint.

I have suggested elsewhere[4] that, not only Aeschylus in the *Oresteia*, but also Sophocles in the *Oedipus Coloneus* saw the nature and operation of Furies in some such light as this. I shall now suggest that a similar set of ideas is developed in the *Electra*. It will be convenient to begin with the First Stasimon (473 ff.).

The structure of the ode is very simple, the thought determined in the first instance by the ominous dream of Clytemnestra as interpreted by Electra. Strophe and antistrophe form a self-contained whole. The strophe says: Justice will come, and the antistrophe says: the Erinys will come (475 f., 489 ff.). The shift from Justice to Erinys is mediated by the reference to the dead Agamemnon, who does not forget (482f.). That the Erinys is qualified as many-footed and many-handed is a reminder that she will work through a plurality of human agents. Justice, carried out by a Fury or Furies. It is the Erinys that suggests the theme of the epode (504 ff.). It is characteristic of Fury-justice that it tends to involve a *succession* of *ponoi* (troubles) (505, 515): the descendants of Pelops were Fury-haunted since the curse of Myrtilus. One reason why Sophocles took the story back to Pelops was doubtless that it made the succession longer. 'Never yet has it stopped' (513 f.) suggests the question: will it stop now?

This chorus, about Furies and their justice, is preceded (466 f.) by Chrysothemis saying that *to dikaion* (justice) is not a subject for dispute and followed by a wrangle between Electra and Clytemnestra as to where justice lies.

The wrangle has a strong rhetorical flavour. Clytemnestra argues that she killed Agamemnon justly (528), because he had killed Iphigenia. In rebuttal, Electra sets out (554 f.) to reconcile the cases of Iphigenia and Agamemnon. We need not deny all sincerity to Clytemnestra's plea, but her tone is vulgar and forfeits sympathy. Neither is Electra's argumentation altogether satisfactory. In particular, at 558 ff. and 577 ff., she uses two arguments without perceiving their implications. (She is hoping for the return of Orestes to kill Clytemnestra: 603 ff. is quite specific.) For instance, at 577 ff., granted the worst interpretation of Agamemnon's action, was it right that he should die at Clytemnestra's hand? 'By what kind of law? Take care lest, in making this law for men, you make trouble for yourself and a change of heart. For, if we are to kill one in return for another, you (I say) would be the first to die, should you meet with justice.' What kind of law? The question is easily answered. It is the law of retaliation; the law proclaimed by the Chorus of Libation-bearers (*Cho.* 400 f.); the law which the Erinyes administer, on which Electra and Orestes intend to act, and under which, if the law is generally valid, they will themselves be liable to retaliation.

By making Electra use arguments to which she is not entitled, Sophocles keeps alive the theme of the Furies with which the preceding chorus dealt. But this is far from being the sole relevance of the Furies to this debate.

In Clytemnestra's speech 528–51 form a self-contained whole (her argument about justice). 'Justice slew him, not I alone; and you should have helped Justice, if you had been right-minded.' Clytemnestra speaks as if there were a right and a wrong conception of justice in this case. Her view is right, and Electra would see it as right, if she were not wrong-headed — if (we might say) she were open to argument. But she is not. Still, she meets Clytemnestra on Clytemnestra's terms (554 f.), and the latter welcomes the rational approach: Electra then advances arguments to which Clytemnestra's mind is equally closed. Is not all this argumentation largely beside the point? Yes, because the principle of justice to which they both appeal is the same while their applications of it are quite irreconcilable. This principle is that of retaliation, of blood for blood, the law of the Furies; and it is founded not upon reason but upon passion.[5]

Electra's reasonableness does not in fact last long. She set out to reason with Clytemnestra: she ends (from 595 onward) with an emotional outburst, to which Clytemnestra reacts appropriately. Electra has insulted her mother (613); she is shameless (615, 622, 626); Aegisthus will punish her when he returns (626 f.). We are back to the tone and circumstances of 516 ff., and it is as though the whole intervening argument had never been.

But there is a further point, brought out at the beginning and end of this debate or wrangle. 'You are always accusing me of *hybris*', says Clytemnestra (520 ff.). 'It is not insolence (*hybris*) on my part, but I speak ill of you because you are constantly speaking ill of me.' 'You cannot say that I began it this time', says Electra (552 f.). Both are concerned to fasten the responsibility on the other. But clearly an endless process is in operation, in which words and deeds both play their part. 622-5 are significant in this connexion. To the original deed of Clytemnestra Electra can (for the time being) retaliate only with words. Clytemnestra replies with deeds, but also herself with words. The process is reciprocal and potentially infinite, just as the succession of retaliatory deeds is potentially infinite. What we have in this scene, then, is the Furies at work upon the plane of words. (We may compare *Cho*. 309 f.).

Of this tragic process Electra in her calmer moments is aware. Such a moment is represented by her speech at 616 ff.,[6] which provides a general comment on the preceding wrangle. 'Though you may not think it, I am ashamed. I know that I behave unsuitably. But the fact is that your hostility and your actions compel me perforce to act as I do. It is by shameful acts that shameful acts are taught.' The choice of words is notable, if only because Electra is repeating here what she has already said in answer to the friendly criticisms of the Chorus.

We turn back to 254-309 (immediately following the Parodos). The speech begins and ends on the same note. 'I am ashamed, ladies, if you think by reason of my much lamenting that I take things too hard. But you must bear with me, since a violent force compels me to act so.' After describing the nature of this force, she ends (307 ff.): 'In such a case neither moderation or piety is possible, but in the midst of evils one is utterly bound to follow evil ways.' It is perhaps permissible to say that Sophocles lays some stress on the notion (associated with the words *bia* and *ananke*) that evil in the past sets up an inevitable compulsive process which determines evil in the future. So, in the most general light, Aeschylus conceived the action of the Furies, perpetuating evil in the process of its own punishment. It seems probable that Sophocles also associated this notion with the Furies, conceived as the presiding deities of the *lex talionis*.

This notion, which is developed in Electra's speech (254 ff.), in the First Stasimon and in the debate between Electra and Clytemnestra, is prepared in the Parodos. During the kommos, while Electra expresses her grief, courage and despair, the Chorus range more widely and are made to raise questions relevant to the themes discussed above and providing the perspective in which to view the closing words of Electra (245 ff.), when she says that, if the chthonic power of the dead is to count for nothing, if the law of blood for blood is not applied, then (in Jebb's translation) 'all regard for man (*aidos*), all fear of heaven (*eusebeia*), will vanish from the earth'. Yet the mind and actions of the bloodavenger are such as to exclude moderation and piety. This dilemma may be cardinal to the interpretation of the play.

The main intention of this paper is to call attention to the employment by Sophocles of this Aeschylean theme (or set of related themes) and to suggest that it must be taken fully into account in interpreting the play. It does not follow that, because Sophocles developed the theme, his attitude towards it was precisely the same as that of Aeschylus. Reference has already been made to a difference between the Aeschylean and Sophoclean treatments of the story. The *Electra* ends with the imminent death of Aegisthus; in the *Oresteia* Orestes is pursued by the Furies and there is a sequel. About this difference, which may or may not be fundamental, something further must now be said.

The pursuit of Orestes was already an established part of the legend. If Sophocles had wished to rule it out, he could hardly perhaps have done so specifically, but he could at least have avoided anything which positively suggested it. This he has not done. In addition to the passages already mentioned, there is one other, of debated interpretation, towards the end of the play. Aegisthus is made to speak of 'the evils of the Pelopidae, present and to come' (1498) and to throw doubt on the capacity of Orestes to foresee the future. That Aegisthus means by 'evils to come' —

and that Sophocles intended to convey — something over and beyond Aegisthus' own death would seem obvious. The only question is what weight should be attached to the remark. Now what happens after a play is strictly outside the drama and, beyond a limited point, an illegitimate field for speculation. This is only legitimate in so far as the dramatist invites it. In this play (I would suggest) Sophocles neither asserts nor denies that Orestes was pursued by Furies, but deliberately indicates it as a possibility inherent in the system of justice which he has successfully applied (1505 ff.). So much and no more.[7] For the future fate of Orestes (and Electra) is not of primary importance. What really matters is not what the Furies may do when the play is over, but what they do while the play is on.

That the play ends without a pursuit of Orestes by the Furies does not make the ending 'happier'. On the contrary. No pursuit by Furies; then no Delphi, no Athens, no Areopagus, no reconciliation of the Furies by the persuasions of Athena. The difference between the two dramatists would seem to be that Aeschylus, without minimizing the sufferings of the past and the present, has his eyes upon the future, while Sophocles is concentrated upon the present as produced by the past. This corresponds to a difference in form: the trilogy as contrasted with the single play, and to a difference in the attitudes of the poets to their leading characters. The more strongly the light is focused upon the individual caught up in the workings of the Furies, the more emphasis there is likely to be upon their unpersuaded grimness.

Herein lies the solution to an interpretative dilemma. Is this a play of ideas or a play about a person? Some critics write off the whole religious and moral issue as mere background (or framework) to a primarily psychological drama. Certainly Electra is central to the interest, as she is to the form, of the play. But there is no conflict between this fact and the working out of those general themes we have been considering, if Electra is in fact conceived and drawn as both the victim and the agent of the Furies. Hence the significance of the Parodos, in which the state of mind of Electra is conveyed with poignancy and pathos, while, concurrently, themes of general import are set in motion. Hence the importance of her speech at 254 ff. and of her scene with Clytemnestra, as revealing the tragic process in which she is involved. The conflict and contradiction are in the nature of things — in words and deeds which morality seems to demand and which yet make morality impossible.

The concentration upon Electra is another good reason why stress should not be laid on the pursuit or non-pursuit of Orestes by the Furies. The play is about Electra, and she is victimized by the Furies even before the act of matricide is committed. Nor does the punishment of Clytemnestra await the sword of Orestes. For all her bravado she has lived in fear, and she is telling the truth when she says (780 ff.): 'Neither by night nor day could sweet sleep cover my eyes, but time in its forward movement kept me living ever in the thought of death.' She was already being punished, in the course of time, by the absent Orestes and by the all-too-present Electra, about whom she makes a significant remark (784 ff.): 'For she was the greater plague that shared the house with me, ever drinking my blood – my soul's blood – unmixed.'[8] The mythological Erinyes drank the physical life-blood of their victims: Electra had been acting the Erinys to Clytemnestra, upon the psychological plane, over all the long stretch of time between the murder of Agamemnon and the action of the play; and during that same stretch of time had been suffering a degradation of which she was herself aware. The theme of 'time', with which Sophocles had a positively Shakespearian obsession, needs fuller investigation, but I would suggest that one reason why Sophocles deals so late and so rapidly with the climax of action is that he was less interested in the critical decisive moment when the Furies strike physically than in the long process of time during which, equally, they are at work.

If this line of approach is correct, the question whether Sophocles *approved* of the matricide loses much of its interest. It can still be argued that he thought it better on the whole that Aegisthus and Clytemnestra should be punished, even at such a cost. It can also be argued that, by various means, including an elaborate use of double irony, he represents the punishment as bringing disaster on its agents, and that he is primarily concerned to do this. But, in either case, he is dealing with a situation in which, thanks to the operation of the Furies, past and present, only deplorable alternatives are open. It is a grim play. Grimmer than the *Oedipus Coloneus*, because, although that too deals with the activity of Furies, there is Antigone, with her noble failures; there is Theseus, who represents a land where the Furies are, with some right, worshipped as Eumenides; there is the solemn passing of Oedipus, with its mysterious hints of reconciliation. Nevertheless, there is a common background of ideas to the two plays; and this background is Aeschylean. It may be that, in the last decade or so of his life, Sophocles, brooding upon the thought of his great predecessor, brought his own tragic thought to its most mature expression in the *Electra* and in the *Oedipus Coloneus*.

17

PHILOCTETES AND MODERN CRITICISM

P. E. EASTERLING

Philoctetes has attracted more critical attention in the last fifteen years than any other play of Sophocles, more perhaps than any other Greek tragedy. This may be partly because its themes — alienation and communication, ends and means — are familiar and important to modern readers, partly because it is a play of remarkable complexity which presents a special challenge to the interpreter. What follows is a brief attempt to take stock, to see how far there are areas of common agreement and where the important problems now seem to lie.

I begin with dramatic technique, on which much of the best recent work has been concentrated,[1] leading us to a deeper understanding of the play's extremely refined and subtle design. We can now make a number of fairly confident assumptions without having to argue from scratch about the nature of Sophocles' methods:

1. Here as in the other extant plays Sophocles releases the crucial information on which the action turns in a piecemeal and ambiguous way. If pressed too literally, as if it were historical evidence, it turns out to be inconsistent; but this is how he gives himself scope for the effects of suspense and surprise and progressive revelation. The prophecy of Helenus is expounded in a way which leaves its detail uncertain until late in the play, and (as Robinson has pointed out)[2] Sophocles makes his characters respond to it as people would in real life, interpreting the cryptic revelation of the future according to their sense of what is actually feasible in the circumstances.

Thus in the Prologue Odysseus argues, from his knowledge that Philoctetes is a man with both a bitter grievance against the Greeks and an unfailing bow, that neither persuasion nor force will have any effect (103). To him at this juncture there is only one conceivable approach to Philoctetes, stealth. This attitude is echoed in the False Merchant's

From *Illinois Classical Studies* 3 (1978), 27–39. Copyright 1978 by the Board of Trustees of the University of Illinois. Reprinted by permission of the author and the University of Illinois Press.

story (whether true or false is not important) that when Helenus said that Philoctetes must be persuaded to go to Troy Odysseus volunteered to fetch him: most likely he would do it by persuasion, he said, but if persuasion failed, by force (617 f.). Odysseus is approaching the prophecy in the pragmatic spirit that you do the best you can towards fulfilling what is foretold, crossing your fingers that whatever is beyond your control will somehow fall into place. This is what the Chorus are doing at 833 ff., when they urge Neoptolemus to make off with the bow while Philoctetes sleeps. When he refuses, saying that the god demanded Philoctetes as well as his bow, their answer is 'The god will see to that: you get the bow while you can.' This flexibility of response is not only convincing; it is also a great source of dramatic interest, which would simply be precluded if the dramatist and his characters treated the future deterministically.

2. It used often to be argued (and here Bowra's[3] interpretation was especially influential) that the point of the varying responses to the prophecy was moral and religious, that the real focus of the action was the impious neglect by Odysseus of the god's command. But detailed analysis has shown the weaknesses in this approach; and in any case modern criticism of the other plays of Sophocles has made us more and more aware that a simple moralistic formula is unlikely to work. The impiety of Odysseus as the 'real subject' of *Philoctetes* is as inadequate as the *hubris* of Ajax as the key to that play.

3. Analogous with Sophocles' ambiguous treatment of the prophecy is the ambiguity in his treatment of the characters' motivation. What, for example, does Odysseus really want, and what has he in mind at successive points in the play? Is he bluffing or not when he says that with the bow safely in Neoptolemus' possession Philoctetes can be left behind on Lemnos (1054 ff.)? How much truth is told by the False Merchant? Most important of all, how far is Neoptolemus carrying out his plan to deceive, and how far is he moved by pity and shame, *before* the moment at which he breaks? Recent criticism collectively demonstrates how little the audience actually knows — either about the prophecy or about the motivation of everyone but Philoctetes — until late in the play.

In the case of Neoptolemus, Steidle[4] in particular has drawn attention to a great many places where his words or his silence may hint that he is unhappy with the role he is playing; we must also remember that the suffering figure of Philoctetes makes a very powerful impact on our emotions, and therefore, we may suppose, on the emotions of Neoptolemus. But the important point is that almost every detail in Neoptolemus' behaviour can be variously interpreted. For example, at 461 ff., when he says he had better be going: is this simply a device for furthering the deceit, precipitating a plea for rescue on Philoctetes' part by pretending that the interview is over, just like the other interviews with casual callers in the past, or is Steidle right to see in it a hint of Neoptolemus' passivity and reluctance to take more positive action?[5] The answer is that we have no means of knowing for certain, though each critic or producer or actor will have a strong individual response and feel sure of the tone of voice in which it should be played.

4. Finally, there is the visible stage action. Recent work has taught us to recognise more readily that what we see on the stage is crucially important for the interpretation of the play. Taplin,[6] for example, has shown how the action of Neoptolemus in physically supporting Philoctetes links two highly significant scenes: 877 ff., where Philoctetes leans on Neoptolemus as he makes ready to leave Lemnos, and 1402 ff., where the same sequence follows Neoptolemus' final agreement that he will take him home. In both cases the action brings the essential solution — Philoctetes trusting Neoptolemus — as directly as possible before our eyes, and the parallelism between the two scenes deepens the meaning of 1402 ff.: *this* time Philoctetes' trust is not misplaced. Seale's[7] work on the repeated pattern of departures that turn out not to be departures points in the same direction: the play exhibits symmetries of design that ought to make us wary of the once popular view that it is all stops and starts ('Sophocles Improvises' is the title Waldock chose for his chapter on *Philoctetes*).[8]

There is another consideration which in my view needs to be recognised as fundamental, one so obvious that it is easily overlooked. This is that the technique of 'deceiving' the audience, or of withholding information in order to build up suspense or create surprise effects, must be sharply distinguished from anything that could be described as confusion. The most striking feature of *Philoctetes* as (I would argue) of all Sophocles' plays is, paradoxically enough, its lucidity. The audience are never allowed to be perplexed by the way the action is presented, though the issues may be left extraordinarily imprecise. In the Prologue, for example, the notorious ambiguity created by Sophocles as to the object of the mission — is it the bow alone, or the bow and Philoctetes? — is not perplexing because it is not even noticeable as the scene is played. Its function is to give Sophocles room for manoeuvre later, certainly not to present the audience with a puzzle to be worried over at this stage. At each point in the action the engagement of the audience's emotions is such that they have little attention to spare for questions of conflicting evidence. But audiences *can* be distracted by obscurity or implausibility and will refuse to suspend disbelief if they are; so that this impression of clarity where the situation is in fact shifting and complex depends on very considerable sleight of hand by the dramatist.

There is a good example in the scene with the False Merchant. The detail about the crucial importance of persuasion is made prominent by being set in a context where the means of winning Philoctetes are discussed at some length (610–619), and later in the play it is reaffirmed as an essential requirement by Neoptolemus (1329 ff.), but at this stage, since it is set in a speech which we know to be partly a lie, and spoken by a bogus character, we cannot be sure how valid a point it is. Thus, as Gellie[9] rightly says, 'we know, and we do not know, that Philoctetes must go willingly to Troy.' The gloss I wish to add is that we are not therefore perplexed or confused. This speech certainly confirms our feeling of distrust for Odysseus' methods, which took its cue from Neoptolemus' reactions in the Prologue, but what most occupies our thoughts here is the ordeal of Neoptolemus: is he, or is he not, going to be able to carry through the deception? His progressive insight will be a guide to our own.

It is worth considering how Sophocles creates this impression of lucidity. One important factor is his psychological sureness of touch. There is nothing an audience finds more baffling than motiveless behaviour, but if what the characters do is susceptible of explanation, even of multiple explanation, then we accept it because this is what we are used to in real life. Take the scene where Odysseus goes off saying 'We don't need you: we have the bow, and there are good archers like Teucer and myself who know how to use it' (1054 ff.). The situation is so recognisable that we do not need to look for an answer to the question whether Odysseus convinces himself as well as Philoctetes that he really is leaving Lemnos. Different actors will give different nuances to the scene — more or less calculation, more or less frustration and anger on the part of Odysseus — but the real dramatic point is of course the effect of his behaviour on Philoctetes. For the audience this must be something absolutely serious, even if at the back of their minds they feel that the play cannot end here, like this.

Another factor which is inseparable from the lucid impact of the play is its structure. Garvie[10] has convincingly shown that there is an essential three-part structure: the parts all overlap, but are still clearly to be seen as three distinct phases in the dramatic movement. First, deceit, which fails because the agent, Neoptolemus, cannot bring himself to carry it through; second, violence, which fails because the person who tries to use it, Odysseus, never succeeds in getting the bow; third, persuasion, which fails when it encounters the full force of Philoctetes' will. Garvie treats the epiphany of Heracles as extraneous to this pattern, but I prefer to see the moment when Philoctetes listens to Heracles' words as the ultimate and paradoxical success of persuasion. Even if we leave aside for the moment the question of the end of the play, it seems clear that at least up to 1407 there is what Garvie calls a 'totality of dramatic design',[11] not a mere episodic sequence of stops and starts: the Prologue states the three options (101-103) and the play enacts the trial of each in turn.

This apprehension of the play's plan very much sharpens, or so I have found, the questions of meaning to which we must now turn. If we consider what is the function of the tripartite structure certain obvious answers suggest themselves. For example, that it gives shape to the central sequence of events, the developing relationship between Neoptolemus and Philoctetes, with the result that we are made to think very hard about communication between human beings and about ends and means, facing the question *What really matters*? This is pretty clear and uncontroversial, but there is a harder question which demands an answer: if the structure also has the function of relating the human interaction of Neoptolemus and Philoctetes and Odysseus to a broader scheme of things, as it does, through the prophecy and Heracles, what weight does Sophocles give to this broader scheme, or suprahuman level? Is the prophecy a purely formal device, or does it mean something; and if so, what?

Sophocles was not after all obliged to use the prophecy. Admittedly it was there in the myth, the datum that Philoctetes and his bow were essential for the capture of Troy, and he had to find some way of motivating the expedition to fetch Philoctetes. But it would have been possible to manage without Helenus and his prediction. For example, Odysseus and Neoptolemus can have come at the instance of the Greek generals, who have decided that they must secure the aid of Philoctetes because he is the most effective archer they know, by virtue of being armed with the bow of Heracles which took Troy once before. Odysseus opts for trickery as the only possible method; when that fails because of the inability of Neoptolemus to carry it through he would like to use force, but Neoptolemus refuses to co-operate; at last Neoptolemus tries the method most congenial to him, persuasion, and offers Philoctetes the promise of glory at Troy. Even without the prophecy this could be made very convincing ('come to Troy and we will find you the best doctors, give you the greatest honours . . .'). Only in the Exodos would Sophocles really have needed a revelation of the future, when Heracles makes his dispositions. The crucial interaction of Neoptolemus and Philoctetes, the real focus of our interest and sympathy, would hardly be affected by the suppression of the prophecy.

The dramatist, however, thought the prophecy worth the price of fairly major inconsistencies. Why?

The reason can hardly be that this was his only means of conveying the sense of compelling necessity which must be part of the dilemma of Neoptolemus. The struggle within the young man's conscience would be just as real — if anything more immediately recognisable by a modern audience, at least — if that sense of necessity were equated with patriotic duty. If it was loyalty to the state that demanded the ruthless exploitation of Philoctetes then there would still be a fine moral dilemma for Neoptolemus. And clearly (following the lead of Euripides) Sophocles could have made a much more political play out of this story. As it is, he treats the theme of duty with some reserve: Schmidt[12] has pointed out, for example, that in the crucial exchange at 1222 ff. Odysseus has no moral arguments, only threats, in answer to Neoptolemus' claim that it is *dikaion* [right] to hand back the bow.

Nor does it seem that Sophocles is using the prophecy in the same way as he treats oracles in *Trachiniae* and *OT*, to make an overt contrast between divine and human knowledge which ironically illustrates the frailty and vulnerability of man. But irony is certainly there, and this perhaps is the direction in which we ought to be looking for a clue to Sophocles' interest in the prophecy.

It has, I think, to be accepted that the final exposition of the future by Heracles is authoritative, and that this validates retrospectively the account given by Neoptolemus at 1326 ff. The message is that Troy *will* fall, by the joint endeavour and freely willed co-operation of Philoctetes and Neoptolemus, and that Philoctetes will be cured. (The audience know that these things did happen.) All through the play we witness human attempts to achieve these ends, attempts which are based on reasonable, though humanly limited, assessments of the situation, such as Odysseus' claim in the Prologue that nothing but trickery will work. But these attempts successively frustrate themselves. Neoptolemus speaks more truly than he knows at 431 f.: 'Even the cunning are sometimes tripped up.' His own impassioned attempt to persuade is 'tripped up' by the trickery he has earlier employed. There is deep irony in the exchange at 1362 ff. when Philoctetes expresses surprise that he should want to go to Troy and help the Atridae who are his enemies, and Neoptolemus can only say, lamely, 'What you say is reasonable' (1373) without daring to reveal the whole truth.[13]

There is another sort of irony in the false departures that we witness on stage, particularly in the latter part of the play: Odysseus and Neoptolemus with the bow apparently abandoning Philoctetes (1068 ff.); Philoctetes and Neoptolemus leaving for Malis (1402 ff.). These departures contradict what the audience, reminded by the prophecy, must know actually happened. So in each case we feel that this cannot be the real ending and that something more ought to happen, but it is hard to see what it can be. This is particularly true of the great moment when Neoptolemus sacrifices his own interests to those of Philoctetes, which is enormously deepened by the sense that Neoptolemus is abandoning his destiny. We have to believe in his serious rejection of his future even though we remember that Troy fell. It is an insoluble contradiction, until Heracles comes and solves it.

This final stage in the action seems to me unintelligible if it is not genuinely organic, if it is only Sophocles making a gesture towards the received tradition. The logic of the play's structure and the ironical use of the prophecy surely point to the view that Philoctetes' assent to Heracles in fact fulfils the requirements of Helenus' prediction, though of course in a quite unexpected way. (Unexpected, but not unprepared; many critics have noted the trouble Sophocles has taken to make the visible presence of Heracles the culmination of a major theme.) But is Philoctetes 'persuaded' by Heracles, or is he not? This can easily turn into a rather pointless debate if we allow ourselves to be mesmerised by English terminology and make a rigid distinction between obedience to a command and compliance in response to argument: the Greeks after all used *peithomai* for both ideas. When Philoctetes says to Heracles 'I shall not disobey your words' (1447) and later speaks of the 'judgment of friends' (1467) that is one of the causes of his going to Troy, we should see the fulfilment of Helenus' words: Philoctetes is going willingly — and his whole tone in the closing anapaests is one of positive, even joyful, acceptance. It is a quibble to insist that he is not persuaded; but there is a larger and more difficult question to be answered: What is the meaning of that culminating persuasion?

If we accept the structural pattern suggested by Garvie, and further, the ultimate effectiveness of persuasion, then there is more sense in the stress that Sophocles seems to lay on Neoptolemus' growing understanding of the prophet's words. As Zwierlein[14] has pointed out, we must not treat the question of what Neoptolemus knows as an historical problem. If we press it logically we are forced to the unwelcome conclusion that despite his apparently ignorant questions in the Prologue Neoptolemus knew the details of the prophecy already. Certainly at the end of the play he can give Philoctetes a most circumstantial account of what Helenus has foretold, but the contrast between his knowledge then and his ignorance earlier emphasises not the factual inconsistency but Neoptolemus' acquisition of insight. He becomes more aware, through his contact with Philoctetes, of the meaning of the prophecy, making sense of what he had already heard but did not understand. Particularly at 839 ff., the famous 'oracular' pronouncement in hexameters, Neoptolemus seems to be expressing his 'seeing' something that he has not properly seen before. This experience is a familiar part of the process of growing up, and it has often been noticed that in Sophocles' Neoptolemus we have a study of a young man coming to maturity through experience. But it is not enough to stop there and adopt a comfortable view of *Philoctetes* as a 'character play': Neoptolemus' deepening insight must be seen as part of the play's dramatic movement and must bear on the larger question to which we are seeking an answer. Can his insight be a guide to our own? Does the prophecy have any truth to tell?

The prophecy *could* be offering some sort of illumination of the gods' purposes or some meditation on the relation between man and god, but I should be surprised if it were. The divine activity as such is far less significant in this play than in *OT* with its Apollo or *Trachiniae* with its Zeus; the lack of imaginative detail is striking by contrast. This is why I find it hard to see the real emphasis of *Philoctetes* as *either* on the ultimate rightness of the gods' purpose *or* on their cruelty in condemning Philoctetes to ten years' agony on Lemnos. Much more telling, it seems to me, is the stress given to the power of persuasion: Neoptolemus' response to Philoctetes, his willingness to be persuaded to sacrifice everything because he respects and pities Philoctetes, is matched by Philoctetes' culminating response to Heracles. And in each case it is the power of *philia* – the *philia* of *chrēstoi* [the upright], who know how to behave – that makes one man bend his will to another's. It is worth adding that Heracles seems to be more important as the *philos* and heroic mentor of Philoctetes than as representative of the gods.[15]

Steidle[16] perceptively notes the force of Heracles' words describing Neoptolemus and Philoctetes as a pair of lions each protecting the other (1436 f.): this is one sense in which the prophecy tells the truth, emphasising the importance of the relationship between Neoptolemus and Philoctetes; and their interdependence is visually demonstrated by Neoptolemus supporting Philoctetes as they go. This reading of the play, in which the words of Heracles are seen as the true climax of the dramatic movement, makes Sophocles affirm the values of *philia* – of pity and respect and human interdependence – in answer to his implied question What really matters?; but there is a final related problem which needs to be discussed, the meaning of Philoctetes' going to Troy. This after all is an important part of Heracles' revelation, and we must be able to make sense of it if we are to understand the play's morality.

Modern criticism is sharply divided: I quote a few representative views. Robinson[17] argues that the decision of Neoptolemus to take Philoctetes home is the first and 'true' conclusion; the second is lighter and slighter, avoiding historical or theological issues, but explaining how Sophocles' version can be fitted into the myth while not essentially detracting from the serious meaning of the first conclusion. Jan Kott[18] goes much further and sees the end as the ultimate absurdity. Just as in *Ajax* there is no meaning in the making of a hero out of Ajax, so in this play Philoctetes' going to Troy is the final horror: 'healing is always payment for submission.' This attitude is shared by Poe,[19] for whom 'Philoctetes' failure becomes a paradigm of the frustration and futility of mankind.'

At the other end of the spectrum there are the old-fashioned pietists, and more recently and interestingly Vidal-Naquet,[20] who sees Philoctetes' going to Troy as the re-integration of the wild man into the city, or Clare Campbell,[21] who brings out the importance of the themes of disease and cure: 'When Heracles now says both men should go to Troy, not home, Philoctetes freely agrees – he has been healed in his social nature, so he can accept physical healing, and it is in the logic of his plight that it will happen at Troy, when he rejoins the Greek body politic which had cut him off just as in despair he used to want to cut off his own foot. . . .'

Since this is a drama we need to use the design of the action and its effect on the spectator's emotions as the basis of any interpretation. Sophocles was at liberty to make the Greeks at Troy stand for whatever he chose: they have no absolute significance independent of the dramatic context. Equally there is no need to suppose that he was concerned to assert the rightness of history because it happened. The important question is What do the audience want for each of the characters as they watch the play?

Philoctetes himself is the focus of nearly all the imagery: the desert island, the wound, the bow, the dead man, are all used as means of exploring his situation and of arousing our emotional response to him. This is overwhelmingly a reaction of pity: for his brute physical suffering, lavishly described and enacted on stage, and for his mental anguish in his isolation. His suffering is the main, almost the only, theme of the lyrics, and the sense of his pitiableness is reinforced by important moments in the action, as at 248 ff., when Neoptolemus pretends never to have heard of him, and Philoctetes is desolated by the thought that even his name has vanished from the memory of the Greeks. We also admire him for his dignity and strength, his generous warmth towards Neoptolemus, his concern at the fate of the other Greek heroes, his delight at the sound of Greek being spoken, his ingenuity in managing for himself on Lemnos, most of all perhaps for his refusal to kowtow.

We badly want him to be cured and to be rescued from isolation. At the same time we understand his hostility towards the Greeks, and we do not want him to sacrifice his self-respect as the price of being healed. His wound is *both* his bitterness and wildness *and* his dignity, just as the desert island symbolises not only his alienation, loneliness and animal-like life but also his purity. Thus our feelings are mixed: we want Philoctetes to be made whole and to be honoured by society, but we do not want him to compromise with men whose methods the play makes us despise. To introduce the Christian notion of forgiveness and loving one's enemy would be to make Sophocles write a quite different play.

Or Sophocles might have written a different play again, in which going to Troy was a compelling patriotic duty: then Philoctetes' refusal would plainly be a matter of selfish pride; but he has not arranged things like this. The world of the Greeks at Troy is the ordinary world of un-heroic politics, whose methods are illustrated by the behaviour of Odysseus and sharply contrasted with the noble standards of Philoctetes and Neoptolemus and the great dead: Achilles, Ajax, Nestor. . . .[22] When Philoctetes wants nothing to do with this world we cannot blame him.

But it is also true that when Neoptolemus appeals to Philoctetes *as a friend* to go to Troy we begin to fear that he is in danger of becoming inaccessible, permanently alienated, if he will not listen; and although we endorse Neoptolemus' willingness to renounce Troy altogether for his sake we surely must feel that going to Malis is a second best,[23] not because we much care about the fall of Troy, but because it is at Troy that the cure is to be found, and it is very important to us that Philoctetes be cured, both to assuage our pity and to convince us that he is reinte-grated into society. For the healing must be a healing of mind as well as body: the language that associates the wound with death,[24] with the desert island,[25] with Philoctetes' hatred of his enemies,[26] requires us to see the cure as relating to his entire being. Being cured will mean coming back from the dead,[27] ceasing to be the solitary wild thing who is at the same time predator and prey of the island's beasts and becoming instead one of a 'pair of lions, each guarding the other's life' (1436 f.).

As Schmidt has argued,[28] Neoptolemus' action in standing by his com-mitment to Philoctetes has given Philoctetes a new heroic community to which to belong: it is no longer true that all the 'real' heroes are dead. So Troy can be used as a symbol *both* of the corrupt unheroic world of politics, which we applaud Philoctetes for rejecting, *and* of society, into which we want him to be reintegrated. This double significance is achieved in ways which illustrate the delicacy of Sophocles' technique. For ex-ample, he is careful not to raise the question of just how Philoctetes and say, Agamemnon, will greet each other at Troy. This absence of naturalism is essential to the success of the final scene, and the use of anapaests must help to create a distancing that makes credible the apparition of Heracles and the response of Philoctetes.

The double significance of Troy makes equally good sense in Sophocles' treatment of Neoptolemus. What the audience want for him is that he should be willing to be true at last to his real *physis* and sacrifice everything to his sense of what he owes to Philoctetes (94 f.); but also that the two of them should do great deeds together. Neoptolemus, we feel, will not be truly fulfilled any more than Philoctetes will if he has no opportunity for the exercise of his *aretē* in action. Sophocles is not inviting us to reject the whole idea of action in society as inevitably evil or futile, as a modern writer might. So our feelings are mixed for Neoptolemus, too: we want him to put Philoctetes first (and this is another reason why Sophocles makes comparatively little of the patriotic motive), but we also want him to be part of his society. Thus the prophecy can be seen to have more truth to tell than the value of *philia*: it also asserts the possibility of right action.

If this approach to the meaning of Troy is correct it throws some light on Sophocles' treatment of Odysseus. This ambiguous figure represents on stage the ambiguity of the world of the Greek army: he is by no means the simple embodiment of evil that he seems to Philoctetes. His goal, after all, is the restoration of Philoctetes in order that Troy shall be taken; this is the goal to which the prophecy points and which is ultimately achieved through the intervention of Heracles. But the meaning of this goal has been completely redefined by the action of the play, and at the end we are given no sense that Odysseus, to use Gellie's phrase, 'has won, yet again';[29] the inadequacy of Odysseus' arguments at 1222 ff. and his decisive defeat at 1293 ff. make it clear that Philoctetes at Troy will be doing neither his bidding nor that of the Atridae.[30]

The language of Philoctetes himself at the end of the play is not at all the abject language of the broken man who licks the boots of his exploiters: there is joy in his response to Heracles (1445) and Vidal-Naquet[31] suggests that in his address to Lemnos and its nymphs we see the wild island given a new significance: the scene is transformed and made almost pastoral, representing the re-entry of Philoctetes into the civilised world. Of course there *could* be a sinister irony in the joy of Philoctetes — the audience might be meant to think 'poor fool' as the big battalions take over — but in that case it would be hard to explain the feelings that Sophocles has generated about Philoctetes' wound and the need for cure.

The only disturbing irony at the end of the play, it seems to me, is of a kind that Sophocles uses elsewhere: the hint at 1440 ff. of the subsequent history of Neoptolemus. 'Only be careful,' says Heracles, 'to show reverence to the gods. . . .' It was Neoptolemus who killed Priam at the altar when Troy was taken, but we have not been reminded of this part of his story until this glancing hint very late in the play, and Kott is surely unjustified in treating him as a war criminal all along. Sophocles likes making these ironical references to other stories at the very end of his dramas; one might compare the end of *O.C.*, where Antigone asks to be allowed to go to Thebes in order to settle her brothers' quarrel (1769 ff.), or the reference at the end of the *Electra* to 'the present and *future* ills of the Pelopidae' (1498).

Almost all critics, I suspect, would agree that the profoundest moment in the play is Neoptolemus' decision to take Philoctetes home, which as it is enacted on stage, with Neoptolemus supporting Philoctetes, is made more significant through its recall of the earlier scene of his breakdown. At once Neoptolemus' act of listening to a friend's persuasion is echoed by Philoctetes listening to Heracles, and Clare Campbell[32] is right, I think, to suggest linking these events very closely in the stage action, so that the one shall seem to precipitate the other. Certainly they are linked in meaning: they give the answer to the question What really matters? This answer takes us away from the familiar and perhaps too schematic image of the proudly lonely Sophoclean hero to something more complex, which is echoed in the themes of *philos* and *xenos* in the *Coloneus*.[33]

18

APOCALYPSE: *OEDIPUS AT COLONUS*

CEDRIC H. WHITMAN

If the *Oedipus at Colonus* fails to exhibit the dramatic alacrity of earlier plays, it is for a good reason. The play presents the long slow reversal of the *Oedipus Rex*. Instead of the abrupt plunge down the precipice, the movement here is laboriously uphill, and endurance is the criterion. The gods who speak from the whirlwind imparted their lightning swiftness to the *Oedipus Rex*. Oedipus himself sets the tempo for the play in which, hated by the gods and abandoned, he finds his answer to them. The gods who destroyed him earlier make no further move, either for or against him, until they finally acknowledge his dignity with the affidavit of their heavenly thunder and bring to pass the moment in which he is complete. The timeless divinities are the lords of time, but Oedipus is the actor, and he looks to them for nothing save the continuation of their dread function. If time continues, endurance continues; but while time remains the same in essence, endurance grows greater, and so does knowledge. Given time, *tlemosyne* [heroic endurance] must achieve its victory.

Almost in his first words, Oedipus lists time as one of the three great elements of his moral fibre (3–8):

> Who will receive today the wanderer
> Oedipus, with some scanty charities?
> Who begs but little, and of that little still
> Gets less, but finds that it suffices him:
> For sufferings, and length of time, my comrade,
> And third, nobility, teach me content.

Previously, Oedipus had spoken of himself as the 'brother of the months' (*O.T.* 1082–83). He now has time as his constant companion. Once time had 'found him out' (*O.T.* 1213); now it stands by him as a medium

From *Sophocles: A Study in Heroic Humanism* (Cambridge, Mass.: Harvard University Press, 1951), pp. 197–214. Reprinted, with notes slightly abridged, by permission of Mrs Anne Whitman.

of greatness and even as a teacher.[1] Again, as in the *Electra*, there is a
contrast between what Oedipus is expected to learn from time and what
he actually does learn. In the scene with Creon, the latter, staggered by
Oedipus' proud replies, says that an old man in such misery ought to
have learned to be mild and acknowledge his own weakness (809 ff;
852 ff.). But time teaches every man what he really is, and in Oedipus'
case it has rather confirmed his high spirit and strength. It has, in a way,
brought the man to pass, as it brings all things to pass, especially the
most unexpected (1454 ff.). Itself a paradox, time fosters paradox, and
turns things into opposites; it is the inevitable condition of Becoming
yet in the end it reveals Being, even as Oedipus implied to Theseus in
the great speech already quoted. The gods are free of time, deathless
and ageless. Yet in the world they govern, in the events wherein they
manifest themselves, all things are inverted to their opposites, friend
becomes enemy and enemy friend, faith dies, and falsehood blossoms.
But the helpless and aged Oedipus, the prey of time, will become a timeless blessing, a member of those heroic dead whose power represented
to the Greek mind one of the most holy and inviolable forces in the
world.

This speech of Oedipus is somewhat reminiscent of Ajax' 'yielding'
speech, save that when Ajax says that in time things become their opposites, it is clear that he is resolved to be no more a part of the shoddy
flux, but to get out of time, seize Being at a blow and be himself forever.[2] The inflexible standard of the old arete compelled Ajax. But
Oedipus' virtue was one of the intellect; like the Homeric Odysseus, he
could accept time with its contradictions as the framework of man's
existence in which through devious ways he comes to fulfillment. His
inner law has made survival difficult, but necessary. For the same intellectual honesty and skill which drove him in the earlier play to find out
who he was, and to boast that he could bear the knowledge, has given
him both the will and the strength to achieve that boast.

Oedipus himself states clearly his moral independence of the gods in
the scene with his daughter. Ismene has told him that the victory in the
war depends on him, and Oedipus, half-aside, reflects on the strangeness
of the news; Ismene tries to give a pious answer (392–95):

Ismene: They say their victory lies in your hands.
Oedipus: When I am nothing, then am I a man?
Ismene: Yes, for the gods who smote now raise you up.
Oedipus: Cheap gift, to raise an old man, who fell young![3]

The rejection of Ismene's pietism is unmistakable. A little later, when

Ismene reports the prophecy that if Oedipus dies hostile to the Thebans his tomb will be an affliction to them, the old man, in deep self-consciousness of his inward power, says drily: 'A man might know that by his wits, without a god's help' (403). Indifferent to what the gods may seem to do, Oedipus trusts his intellect still; he does not really fancy the gods care about him at all (385 ff).[4] His exaltation cannot be interpreted as an act of grace, as Ismene suggests. It is a product from within, born of Oedipus' own equipment.

It has long since been recognized that Oedipus, in fundamental character, is still the same as ever. His mind, the quality which made him 'small and great', has only been deepened, not discredited by time. No less his famous wrath is vigorous as of old, and perhaps even a little more savage, as the insight and authority which motivate it grow. Innocent sufferer though he may be, he shows none of the religious transfiguration or humble self-abnegation of the Christian martyr.[5] Half of his exalted function is to bless Attica, but the other half is to have personal revenge on his enemies, and the terrible explosions which Creon and Polyneices endure show the ferocity of his hatred and anger; even Theseus gets a rather sharp answer.[6] Christian sentiment may recoil from the sheer violence of these outbursts; but the hypocrisy which they rebuke need find no sympathy. Oedipus is more right than ever in his anger, for his honesty has only grown fiercer with the years. The compromise which all expected of a condemned and polluted exile has not been forthcoming.

For all that, it is never for a moment forgotten that Oedipus is polluted, that he is the man who slew his father and married his mother. Not only his character but also his external fate remains unchanged. To emphasize this point, Sophocles has symbolized it nicely in the first part of the play by making him once more stumble into defilement. The first thing he does is to step on the consecrated ground and sit on a sacred stone. Thus throughout the prologue, first chorus, and first episode, he is technically guilty of sacrilege against the Eumenides. Eventually he makes amends, or rather sends his daughter to make them; but he is in no hurry, and in the end, it is into the most sacred and forbidden part of the grove that he turns. By this light touch the poet recalls and reasserts the same old fate of Oedipus the king – his almost innate luck of touching things which are forbidden, without knowing it. He is the man who treads blindly and innocently upon taboos. Yet even as Oedipus had formerly committed sacrilege and survived in greater wisdom and strength, so now the revelation of his error does not cause him to start up in alarm; he only asks on what land he is trespassing (39–46):

> *Stranger*: Here the dread
>   Goddesses dwell, daughters of Earth and Darkness.
>
> *Oedipus*: Let me hear by what name I should address them.
>
> *Stranger*: The people of this land call them the all-seeing
>   Eumenides; elsewhere they've other names.
>
> *Oedipus*: Graciously let them take their suppliant
>   For from this place I never shall depart.
>
> *Stranger*: What does this mean?
>
> *Oedipus*: The token of my fate.

The last line, like so many of Oedipus' remarks, is spoken as an aside and goes uncomprehended by the stranger, who at once changes the subject. But it is clear that Oedipus has passed beyond the phase where technical defilement matters. If it had been his fate alone of all men to defile what was most sacred and to suffer for it, his suffering has invested him with certain rights; for now he alone of all men may walk in the Athenian grove of the Furies and not suffer.

And what strange Furies these are, who receive their suppliant graciously — and such a suppliant — and whose grove echoes with the song of nightingales (17–18). These are purely Athenian Furies;[7] only after the first consistory of the Areopagus were the Furies given nightingale voices, when an earlier exile, 'hated of the gods', Orestes, found relief and dignity again in the equable air of Athens. Now Oedipus comes to Athens, and there is no yelping of 'insatiable, bronze-footed bloodhounds', but only the music of the birds, as if all the past evil of the Theban house were transformed by the mysterious forces of time and suffering into a present of tranquil beauty and a prospect of hope. Quite after his own fashion, Sophocles has borrowed the gentle goddesses of pain from Aeschylus and spun them magically into his many-levelled, symbolic scheme of the heroic life. Here, in the grove of these paradoxically sweet dread goddesses, Oedipus could recognize a token of his fate; and Athens too could see herself once more, as at the trial of Orestes, the defender of the weak, mediator between the suppliant and justice, the restorer of the fallen — the great role she loved to play. With characteristic finish, Sophocles brings in these nightingales again in the great ode on Athens, so that the whole episode of Oedipus' coming and acceptance is rounded off with the music of nightingales.

Error and exaltation, pollution and the song of nightingales! No union of opposites could be more Sophoclean. Nothing is denied or remitted; all the old misery, the horror of the fate of Oedipus remains unchanged and unrationalized. Nothing has been invented to show that the gods really meant well. Within and without Oedipus is the same man, save that he has added a new dimension of fortitude and knowledge. He continues to act his role with ever increasing self-consciousness.[8] He knows the 'token of his fate', and therein creates a historical self. He is the blind man who knows; he is the 'hated of God' who is innocent and noble. In this role he will win recognition.

Oedipus' battle for significance finds its core in the defense of his nobility. Those about him on the whole believe that no one could do the things which he did and yet be a good man. The lack of distinction which antiquity, until the time of Socrates, made between inner and outer values is well expressed in the famous *scolion* of Simonides:

> No man can help being bad
> Whom hopeless misfortune seizes;
> For every man who fares well is good,
> But if he fares ill, he is bad and the best on the whole
> Are those the gods love.[9]

The gods had not loved Oedipus; he had been seized with hopeless misfortune. Hence the chorus is suspicious of him from the first. When they hear who he is, their reaction shows clearly how they have formulated their feelings about him. He must be guilty, for if his murder of Laius had been the moral equivalent of mere manslaughter in self-defense, the gods would not have punished him (228 ff):

> No fated punishment comes to him
> Who avenges what he first has suffered.

The gods afflict him, he must be evil; let him get out. Antigone attempts to correct this attitude by presenting her father in the light of one undeservingly oppressed by the gods' arbitrary will (252 ff.):

> Among all men you will not find
> One who, if a god leads on,
> Has power to escape.

In these two views the fate of Oedipus is summarized respectively as a tragedy of fault and a tragedy of fate. Antigone's appeal is meant to lighten the burden of guilt, but only Oedipus himself understands fully his own innocence.

The *Oedipus Rex* can hardly have failed to stir ambiguous reactions in Athens. The passages just quoted illustrate the interpretations which his story prompts; indeed, it is even possible that between 429 and Sophocles' resumption of the myth, the much debated question of the guilt or innocence of Oedipus had already begun to divide readers into bristling camps. Sophocles may have wished to settle it once and for all by the heavy emphasis he lays in this play upon his hero's innocence.[10]

In his very opening speech, Oedipus mentions 'suffering, time, and third, nobility' as the things which have given him his strength. The emphasis upon 'nobility' is beyond question.[11] Time and suffering will do nothing for the ignoble man, except make him bitter. Even as in the *Oedipus Rex*, when he faced the imminent revelation of his parricide and incest, he knew that no external fortune could destroy his soul, so now in his old age he maintains his basic excellence. Later, when Antigone's appeal has quieted the chorus, in a speech of formal defense, he states quite explicitly that his deeds were unwilled, and that his griefs are due to no evil in his nature (263-272):

> And will you then
> Uproot me from this seat and drive me forth,
> Fearing a name alone? You cannot fear
> Either my body or my deeds; for these
> My deeds were not committed; they were suffered,
> If, as you must, you mean my history,
> My father and my mother, for which tales
> You fear me. Ah, full well I know it is!
> And yet, how am I evil in my nature,
> I who, when struck, struck back, so that had I
> Even known my victim, I'd not be condemned.

The legal claim that he killed in self-defense and ignorance is backed by the moral claim that even if he had known that his assailant was his father, he would not be morally guilty. It will be remembered that Laius had hit him over the head with an ox-goad, for no reason other than that he was in the way, a fact which perhaps lends weight to Oedipus' claim. Be that as it may, the real innocence rests, in his own eyes, upon his inward conviction of integrity. Later he says to Creon (966-968):

> For not in me, nor in myself, could you
> Discover any stain of sin, whereby
> I sinned against myself and mine.

Oedipus' rejection of the word 'hamartia' here clearly has an inward reference, while his outer misdeeds are undeniable. In a similar spirit he can use the old figure of the 'gift of the gods', always a dangerous thing to receive (539 ff.):

> *Chorus*: You have done —
> *Oedipus*: I have not done.
> *Chorus*: What then?
> *Oedipus*: I have received a gift . . .[12]

The gods and their gifts, the misery of his life; these are all externals and ineluctable. But he is himself, and the gods can do nothing to break the strong moral good he wills. Oedipus is a landmark in Greek morality, for he presents the first really clear exposition of the independence of the inner life, that doctrine which in Socrates and his followers became the cornerstone of a whole new phase of civilization.

Yet for this moral independence to be significant — to be real one might say — it had to be recognized. Herein the feelings of the fifth-century poet differed from the mysticism of Plato, the reality of whose inner world was prior and causal. For Sophocles, the hero must win in this world; whether in such a death as Antigone's or in such a life as Oedipus', the heroic victory had all its reference and significance in the purely human sphere. Hence the rising action of the *Oedipus at Colonus* shows the hero's triumph over person after person. He already has Antigone, in whom for the first time a Sophoclean protagonist has a real companion. Antigone is not a foil, she is a counterpart to Oedipus; Sophocles kept in mind the character he had given her almost forty years before and here endowed her with no little of her father's endurance (345-52). Ismene shares her position to some extent, so that in the three of them, in the scenes where the old man praises his daughters (337 ff., 1365-68), one detects the nucleus of a world in which Oedipus is accepted and honored. With them, Oedipus stands on his own terms, commanding and receiving freely their love and honor.

It is not long before the stranger of the prologue adopts a respectful tone.[13] The chorus similarly, in spite of its misgivings, is forced (76) 'to feel awe at his pronouncements' (292 ff.). But the climax of Oedipus' triumph over society appears in the scene with Theseus, who recognizes him at once as a superior being (631 ff.). It is the essentially Athenian interpretation of *aretē* which underlies this scene and makes it moving. Theseus represents Athens; without hesitation he penetrates all the disguises of fortune and circumstance and arrives at the true man. Drawn in the aristocratic colors of a legendary king, he is none the less the embodiment of the most enlightened kind of democratic individualism. Mutual recognition of virtue, as in the case of Philoctetes and Neoptolemus, can bring the great man back to the world, or, more accurately, can bring the world back to the great man, whose ethos has remained unchanged. The value of the true man, whatever his state, attains a just estimate in the liberal air of Athens. Theseus comes and listens respectfully before Oedipus, and Oedipus acknowledges his excellence (569, 1042 ff.). Hero recognizes hero as a fellow stranger in this world, knowing its uncertainty, and basing standards of behavior on its immanent sorrow (562-68). Oedipus makes for himself a world of the souls that can respect him in his tribulations, and when he departs, he is no longer isolated, but prized.

Thus, like Philoctetes, Oedipus is set free to bestow the value of himself upon the world. But those who would avail themselves of his blessing must accept the blind beggar himself and not try to use his greatness without understanding him. So too, Philoctetes' magic bow could not be separated from its lame and offensive owner. The paradox of human value must be taken whole; there is no short way. Philoctetes and disease are one; Oedipus and pollution are one. The hero's external daimon and internal daimon, that is, the inner and outer divine forces of his life, are inextricably interwoven until the great moment comes when the external yields, and the hero's inwardness may burst out and become a reality. And this is not so much a mystic process as a social one. Theseus and the Athenians could perceive that reality through the shell. They are therefore a little like Oedipus, who is blind but full of true insight: 'All he says has eyes' (74).[14] His murmured remark, 'When I am nothing, then am I a man?' conveys the whole secret. His triumph is prepared within himself, almost in defiance of the very gods themselves, and the Athenians, when they accept his paradox, are made worthy to share in his triumph.

But his triumph does not come without a struggle. The two scenes in which Oedipus sets his face against Thebes forever have occasioned much criticism. Their relevance has either been missed altogether,[15] or else explained merely in connection with the original saga, the *fabula sacra*.[16] But part of the saga is not necessarily part of the play. For the Greek dramatist, there was no *fabula sacra*; he was as free as Homer to exclude whatever detail he felt to be irrelevant. As examples of Oedipus' growing heroic powers, wherewith he settles his accounts in the world, the episodes of Creon and Polyneices clearly contribute something to the character of the protagonist;[17] but their significance is greater than that. The moral essence of these scenes is derived from the problem of the *Philoctetes*, where an individual of heroic proportions, rejected long since and cast away by his comrades, becomes once more the object of their specific personal concern.

Over and over again we are told that the Thebans, and Creon in particular, had exiled Oedipus long after the latter had ceased to feel that exile was necessary or appropriate to his misfortunes; up till that time they had kept him against his will (431-44; 765-771; 776-780). Precisely why is a question. Euripides, in the closing scene of the *Phoenissae*, makes the exile of Oedipus begin after the expedition of the Seven is over; it is therefore an act of the new king, Creon, who perhaps may be thought to have planned it in order to consolidate his power.[18] In Sophocles' play, however, Oedipus was exiled while Creon was merely regent, during the minority of the princes. The latter, apparently, had been quite passive in the matter. In the absence of conclusive evidence, it is perhaps safe to assume that the disposal of Oedipus in some way affected the various claimants' interest in the throne (418–420; 448). In any case, the very doubtfulness of the motivation suggests Sophocles' real intention: the Thebans had used the legally justifiable reason for exile, blood guilt, as a kind of political cover for more selfish motives. Oedipus himself seems to feel that he ought to be received into Thebes and buried there (406–08). Yet technically, as a parricide, Oedipus could not possibly return. The Thebans certainly had no intention of bringing him into the city, but only of keeping him near at hand (399 ff.; 600–02). One might well ask how it had been possible for him to stay in the first place, and why he thought he might return at all, if ritual pollution had really such a solemn significance.

But the fact is, such pollution was open to flexible treatment, and the sons of Oedipus and Creon had made political capital of it. And now, like Odysseus in the *Philoctetes*, Creon and Polyneices both wish to use the great man's power without accepting the man himself. The oracle told them they would conquer if they could get him back (412–416), but there is yet some question of how a hero must be received. The great contrast with the pragmatic scheme of the Thebans is the frank and generous attitude of Theseus. Not only does he feel a personal respect and kinship for Oedipus; he gives him the full rights of a citizen and even offers to take him to his own house (636–641; 643). With Theseus' example before them, even the choristers seem no longer to fear the pollution which attends the old man, and they defend him valiantly against Creon's attack (834 ff.). To be sure, the Athenians are to gain much from him, but they have not tried to achieve it by the half-and-half plan of Creon.

In the scene with Creon, the political substance of the play becomes most clear, and brings the elements of festival drama into the foreground. All that the Athenian mind felt to be politically good clashes openly with the spiritual blindness of Creon. Creon arrives in guile and departs in violence. He behaves like a tyrant — indeed, he calls himself one (851) — and he carries off women, as tyrants are supposed to do.[19] But he is also much subtler, and like most fifth-century stage tyrants, he possesses less in common with the economic dictators of history than with the clever, sophistically trained oligarchs of the war years. His obsequious carefulness before the Athenian choristers who, by a curious anachronism, are at once the subjects of Theseus and liberal exponents of democracy, includes not only respectful compliments, but even a passing intimation that he represents a majority vote (733 ff.; 758 ff.; esp.

737 ff.). With deft political skill he answers the arraignment of Theseus by trying to use Athenian institutions and the famous piety of Athens to his own advantage: he says smoothly that he is sure that Athens would never receive an unholy incestuous parricide; the Areopagus would never allow it (944-49). Creon seems to know well the principle formulated later by Aristotle, that 'we should know the moral qualities characteristic of each form of government, for the special moral character of each is found to provide us with our most effective means of persuasion in dealing with it' (*Rhet.* I, 8 [1366a]).

Aristotle further states that the end of tyranny is protection of the tyrant, while the end of aristocracy is the maintenance of education and national institutions. Clearly Creon is here a tyrant speaking in his own defense; but with great skill he uses as his principal argument the moral end of the aristocratic Theseus, namely the maintenance of Athenian piety and the court of the Areopagus. A definite political antinomy, therefore, is only thinly veiled in this scene. It appears even more clearly in Theseus' reproof, which enters almost unnecessarily into Theban manners. Creon, says Theseus, is not only unworthy of Athens, but unworthy of Thebes herself, and the Theban tradition of breeding gentlemen (913-923).

By contrast with Creon, the failed aristocrat, the mythic figure of Theseus, characterized both as the true aristocrat and the man of the polis, with its ideal of legality and true piety, points the religious question implicit in the political antinomy. Creon's well-planned references to Athenian piety miss fire. Theseus deigns no answer, but Oedipus in towering wrath bursts out in one of his terrible cannonades.[20] He defends himself from the scornful, personal taunts of Creon (960-1002), strips the veil from his pretense of justice, and then says (1003-1009):

> How fine for you to flatter Theseus' name
> And Athens, calling her well administered!
> But in your commendations you miss much;
> If any land knows how to honor gods
> With reverence, this land leads all the rest.
> Wherefrom you, plundering these girls and me,
> The aged suppliant, try to drag us off!

Creon's breach of the most holy right of the aged and the suppliant fits oddly with his otherwise scrupulous observance of religious forms in treating a parricide. He will bring Oedipus into the vicinity of Thebes as a useful object, but will not admit his technical pollution within the walls. The Thebans are thus represented as standing on the forms of piety without regarding their essence, while Athens 'knows how to honor the gods with reverence', by receiving the suppliant generously with no reservations. Far from dallying over mere religious formalities, Theseus leaves a sacrifice half-finished in order to go to battle for his guests (887-890; 897-903) — the sort of religious enlightenment which Sparta, for instance, would not risk in the crucial year of Marathon.

These details are too closely allied to the play's principal action to be regarded as merely adventitious. The paradox of seeming and being, which informs the character of the hero, is here extended to include a commentary on the spirit and the letter, in the culture and political ethics of Greece herself. In this scene, even more fully than in the great ode on Athens, Sophocles has poured out his love for the city and his faith in her as the genuine polis, where not merely the nightingales sing and the sacred olives flourish, but where also the individual man, that irreducible minimum of political or any other kind of greatness, holds his place by arete alone, and 'whatever good he may do to the city'.[21]

Scholars have long since recognized references to the Peloponnesian War in this play.[22] The shadow of bitter hatred between Athens and Thebes overhangs the whole, and with reason, for in the late years of the war, Thebes showed herself Athens' most implacable enemy, ransacking her outlying fields for anything movable,[23] and clamoring later at the peace table for demolition of her walls and enslavement of her inhabitants.[24] In the years just preceding Arginusae (406), when the *Oedipus at Colonus* was written, Athens was in desperate condition. The treasury was empty, the statues stripped of their gold; her leaders were incompetent, her population starving, every nerve was strained to the breaking point. If Thucydides, writing probably at about this same time, could call Athens 'the education of Greece', because she represented the greatest opportunity for an individual to be self-sufficient and at his best,[25] it is not so surprising that Sophocles too, with his profundity of poetic insight, should have been able to see his city historically and create a vision of her which would be as timeless as the heroism of the old Oedipus. When he speaks of Athens in the play, he never mentions her sufferings. He speaks of her as if she were inviolable, as if the sacred olive trees were not burned stumps and the land ravaged and ruined. Athens herself in those days was a pattern of heroic tlemosyne; and if Sophocles could see beyond the ruins and the stumps, it was because he saw whence Athens derived her almost incredible fortitude. The value of man was implicit in it all, and embodied in the figure of Oedipus. The man whose intellect has brought him to divine insight has come to the place where only the true counts. The ideal Athenian setting is more than a patriotic motif: in it Sophocles symbolizes the world of man's metaphysical value, the world which is the only home for Oedipus.

The picture is, of course, confessedly and purposely idealized, but it is not fiction. It is myth, which is to say, it is history distilled into meaning.

The scene with Polyneices completes the picture of society's misguided attempt to regain the great individual for its own ends. Once more, as in the *Philoctetes*, the attempt through guile and force yields to the attempt through persuasion and appeal, and once more the same refusal follows. Polyneices is no mere politician like Creon; he is very sympathetically drawn. Even though he is perhaps still too self-involved to rise above his practical need of Oedipus into a full understanding of the old man's worth, nevertheless his full admission of guilt, and especially his recognition that has come too late (1264), stamp him at once as a serious and wellnigh tragic character.[26] Therefore the appalling execrations which the old man calls down on him are the more surprising. But Polyneices really is too late, and it is only out of empty hope that he can suggest how he may make up for his sins (1269 ff.).

For Polyneices' faults are in his nature and in the nature of his will. He has put himself where he cannot turn back (1418 ff.), but he has done so not because of any moral standard, but because he wanted the throne. He is therefore in a tragic situation, perhaps, but he is not a tragic character; however genuine his penitence may be, it implies little understanding and no real morality. Fundamentally he needs Oedipus for precisely the same reason as Creon does, and he would never have come otherwise.[27] Oedipus' refusal of him rests on the same absolute standard he has always espoused. Since now Oedipus is himself all but a god, it may be said that his refusal rests on a divine standard.

The curse may seem another matter. Many scholars have argued that Oedipus was wrong to curse his son;[28] others that the curse merely illustrates Oedipus' great exaltation.[29] Still others have collected much juridical evidence to prove that Polyneices, as the very image of a bad son, by all contemporary standards deserved damnation.[30] Yet in a play about inner and outer religious standards, Sophocles would hardly allow Polyneices to be condemned on merely legalistic grounds. Polyneices is undoubtedly a bad son; yet he is drawn in touchingly human colors: in his parting from Antigone, in his rather high conception of generalship, and in the loneliness of his sorrow as he bravely accepts his fate, he carries away a good deal of our sympathy (cf. 1429 ff.; 1402-04; 1432 ff.). The simply bad son might be forgiven, one feels, if Antigone could intercede for him. If Sophocles meant us to remember only his past deeds, he should have made him appear more like them. But instead, he has deliberately given his cause some justice by making him the elder, instead of the younger brother (374 ff.).

It has been wisely noted that in the epic source the curse on the sons

of Oedipus precedes and apparently causes their strife,[31] but in Sophocles the strife came first, arising 'from some god and their own sinful
mind' (371 ff.). By the time Oedipus utters his curse, Polyneices is already on his way to the war, and is too fatally involved to turn back, as
his words to Antigone show. So the curse, which once had a supernatural
causative force, is here simply a statement of fact, though Polyneices
still refers to the Furies as the ones who will bring it to pass, as one
always speaks of a god in connection with what is true (1433).[32] Obviously it is Polyneices who will bring it to pass, for he is already doing
it, and Sophocles has made it doubly pointed by letting Antigone beg
him so movingly to desist. But Polyneices, whose name means the 'man
of the heavy curse', knows who he is. Quite aside from his past cruelty to
his father and sister, and even apart from the fact that he is still only trying
to use Oedipus, Polyneices deserves the curse because he is accursed, as
Esau was accursed long before the actual denunciation came.[33] Oedipus,
like an oracle, has simply told the truth. Once more, the supernatural
element enters in such a way that it can only be symbolic. Appropriately
enough, the last of the three gods whom Oedipus invokes to destroy
Polyneices is the War itself, the really destructive element 'which has
cast such heavy strife' between the brothers (1391).[34]

The Creon and Polyneices scenes are not loosely or poorly integrated,
from the moral point of view. From the mere standpoint of plot they
revive and restate the conflicts of the *Philoctetes*, illustrating with infi-
nitely subtle turns the world with which the great individual must deal,
in his struggle for weight, dignity, and reality. Individualism in terms of
such values means more than ordinary individualism; it is a norm of
heroic being. And the basic difference between Oedipus and Polyneices
is that Oedipus asserts his heroic right to be, while Polyneices asserts
only his right to have. Therefore the one is oracular and blessed, the
other accursed and pathetically confused in his humanity.

With the retreat of Polyneices, Oedipus' moral triumph is complete,
and the mastery which he has shown throughout the play is now symbolized in the final scene of divine mastery. The last and most impressive
of the supernatural happenings in Sophocles has this in common with all
the others: the supernatural 'cause' follows its effect. Oedipus officially
'becomes a hero', with the power of blessing and cursing. But manifestly,
the transformation which takes place in the depth of the sacred grove
adds little in itself to the power of Oedipus. The blind and aged hero
has already repulsed Creon and cursed Polyneices; before he leaves, he
pronounces the eternal blessing upon Theseus and Attica. To the Greek,
a person could become a hero only if he really was one, and Oedipus
has already exercised his full prerogatives. Viewed in their simplest and

most profound light, these prerogatives are no more than the ability to
see through the veils of circumstance into essential fact. Oedipus' words
'have eyes'. His insight attains its perfect symbol when he himself leads
the way into the grove, unguided except by what he calls 'the present
deity'; nor does he hesitate to identify himself subtly with that divine
force. The inward man has at last come true.

It is a grave mistake to overlook the moral qualities which have made
Oedipus a hero, and to regard his apotheosis as a simple act of grace on
the part of the gods, or as amends made by them for the sufferings
which he has endured.[35] The choristers, indeed, interpret it thus:

> Out of the many woes that came
> Without cause, now the god in justice
> Would lift him up. (1565 ff.)

On the other hand, they have already prayed on their own behalf, when
they heard the thunder and saw Oedipus' fate coming, to be delivered
from any share in such 'gainless grace' (akerdē charin, 1484). It is clear
that they regard the gods as the actors here, and the whole process as
fraught with danger, not only for Oedipus, but also for the passive spectators. These good Athenians, with their simple, human limitations and
their sophrosyne, know that the gods can be almost as perilous friends
as they are enemies, and they would prefer to stand apart and pray.
Oedipus himself rejects any such interpretation, however. He uses the
word 'grace', but always of the blessing he himself is to bestow on
Athens (1489).

It will be remembered with what contempt he treated the suggestion
of Ismene, in an earlier scene, when she remarked that the gods who
formerly destroyed him were now about to reinstate him (394-395).
Oedipus, with his customary brutal truthfulness, called it a cheap favor.
Indeed, the gods did little for Oedipus; he had to prove himself every
inch of the way, and it is no wonder that he omits all sanctimonious
expressions of gratitude. He speaks seriously of the gods and the world
at large only to Theseus, for the latter is the only other character of sufficiently heroic proportions to understand him in his own terms. By the
same token, Theseus alone is permitted to witness the last hour of
Oedipus. Only the large soul can fully understand how 'the gods look
well but late', how time penetrates all things, or how the noblest in man
is rooted in his essential weakness and subjection to change (1536 ff.;
607 ff.; 560 ff.). Others may grasp the words when they are spoken,
but Theseus comprehends out of his own being. And Theseus, champion
of the true Athenian religiosity, regards Oedipus himself as the grace-
bringer, not the gods. There was no Messiah in Greek theology; if man

was to come near to the divine, he must get there himself. How this can be achieved is known only to him who has in some sense already achieved it; the rest of the world will view it with limited, and doubtless frightened, eyes. As Hölderlin once wrote:

> Only those who themselves are
> Godlike ever believe in gods.[36]

Oedipus brings us to a vision of godhead, whose content and significance are Oedipus himself. Sophocles says nothing of the gods who greet him, but he has shown all he could of the man who, after long sorrow, greeted the gods.

The end, therefore, is no great change, except that it releases Oedipus from the struggle of asserting himself and the suffering which pursued the moral activity of his soul. He had exalted himself by his endurance in that activity, and the final scene shows only the universal of which the play was the particular. That universal is important, but one must not forget how it came about. It is the result of 'time, suffering, and his own nobility'. How perfectly his last words to his daughters sum up the trial of values by which he has triumphed:

> Children, it now behoves you leave this place,
> Enduring, in nobility of mind. (1640 ff.)

Endurance, nobility, mind: these are the laws of the human soul. So stated, they sound very simple, and in essence perhaps they are. But in action, which is life and the only context in which human beings can know them, they are the stuff of tragedy, the divine scheme of *ananke*, which binds the magnanimous man to himself and puzzles and outrages the philistine world, until it finally can ratify itself in a form that can no longer be denied.

19

EURIPIDES: POET OF PARADOX

ERICH SEGAL

The progress of Greek tragedy has been likened to the famous fire-relay held at the Panathenaic festival. Aeschylus, nobly bearing the torch lit with the spark of Prometheus, handed it to Sophocles who carried its splendor still further, before giving it to Euripides. But this last playwright was not only too weak to carry the torch, he could not even keep the flame alive.[1] A dramatic simile, but like so much that is said of Euripides, wholly inaccurate. We are led to believe that Euripides 'killed tragedy'. Aeschylus himself argues as much in the *Frogs*, and this gospel according to Aristophanes has been echoed through the ages, especially by vigorous apostles like Schlegel and Nietzsche. And yet there is a problem here, even for those who believe that the ancient classics never lie. Did not Aristotle consider Euripides 'the *most* tragic of the tragic poets' because most of his plays end — as the best tragedies should — sadly (*Poetics* XIII 9-10)?

No one would dispute that some of Euripidean drama presents the most unmitigated misery ever witnessed on a stage. The ruthless tyrant Alexander of Pherae was so ashamed to be crying at the sorrows of Hecuba that he had to leave the theater before the *Trojan Women* was over. But then what of the 'escape plays' like the *Helen* or the *Andromeda*, in which misery turns suddenly to mirth and — that most comic of catastrophes — marriage? Scholars can provide another convenient explanation for this Euripidean 'development' by adducing the example of Shakespeare. After the storms of *King Lear* came the smiling calm of *The Winter's Tale* or *The Tempest*. Likewise, after the tearful *Trojan Women* came the happy *Helen*. Unfortunately, Euripides will not lie still on the literary bed of Procrustes, for after the *Helen* came the *Bacchae*. And before all of them came the *Alcestis*.

To discuss Euripides is to speak in paradoxes, even Aristotelian ones. The *Poetics* insists that the dénouement of a tragedy conform with a

Originally published in *Euripides: A Collection of Critical Essays*, ed. Erich Segal (Prentice-Hall, 1968), pp. 1-12. Reprinted by permission of the author.

certain justice. Good men must not suffer ill and, most important, evil men must not prosper. This last instance, Aristotle argues, would be the most *un*tragic situation of all (*Poetics* XIII 3). In light of this, how can we evaluate Euripides' *Heracles*, whose tormented protagonist is not only totally innocent, but has been constantly hailed as the greatest benefactor of mankind? It is not a question of a hero being more sinned against than sinning. Heracles has not 'sinned' at all; in fact, even before his heroic quest he has proved himself a paragon of *pietas*. Similarly, in the *Trojan Women* the playwright goes to great pains to emphasize that Andromache has been a saintly wife (cf. lines 643 ff.), and yet Hector's widow is doomed to endure what she herself describes as a fate worse than death: a life without hope. In direct contrast, Helen, who is considered by everyone to be responsible for all the misery (and indeed *everyone* gets to indict her during the play), goes scot-free. While the Trojan widows sing sorrow in sackcloth and ashes, Helen is blithely arranging her *toilette*, so that she can appear well groomed (and, miraculously, well gowned) for her happy reunion with Menelaus. By Aristotle's own rules, this play is a paradox: 'most tragic' because of its sad ending, and most 'untragic' because the wicked Helen prospers.

It is important to realize that Euripides was an iconoclast from the beginning. We have nothing from the earliest years of his creative life, but we can see that his first extant play was a bold departure from traditional dramaturgy.[2] In the year 442 or 441, Sophocles' Antigone marched bravely to her death, lamenting that her tomb was also to be her wedding chamber (lines 891 ff.). In 438, Euripides also presented a self-sacrificing young woman who likewise dies voluntarily out of family loyalty, but who goes *to* her tomb and then *back* to her wedding chamber. And already in the *Alcestis* we see articulated the famous Euripidean life-in-death paradox which Aristophanes would so often mock.[3] Before our very eyes, a funeral has turned into a wedding, 'tragedy' has suddenly become 'comedy'. Characteristic of Euripides, the paradox is vividly visual: the bride wears black. (In the *Iphigenia at Aulis* the victim is dressed in bridal white.) Moreover, it is no accident that this change has been effected by Heracles, half-human, half-divine, a drunken Dionysiac in the service of Apollo. In the *Alcestis* we find innumerable motifs which appear again and again, with differing emphases, throughout Euripides' *oeuvre*: a sudden shift of fortune, demonstrating the potential joy-in-sorrow (and vice versa) all emphasized by verbal paradoxes in the dialogue; Salvation in the Nick of Time; *deus* (in this case, demi-god) *ex machina*; the perplexing problem of what is real and what is illusory, and perhaps most important, the evasion of limit.

A longing for escape seems to permeate all the plays of Euripides. But the question of which characters do escape and which do not defies rational analysis. Magically, a flying car arrives to rescue the 'villainess' Medea and whisk her to safety. Though her actions are the precise opposite of those of Alcestis, she enjoys the same rewards. Small wonder that Aristotle singled out Medea's *ex machina* exit for special censure (it is, of course, 'most untragic'). And yet Phaedra — who is no Alcestis, but surely no Medea either — is denied rescue from her dilemma. The famous 'escape ode' from the *Hippolytus* has significance even beyond its context, and bears quoting. Gilbert Murray's somewhat quaint translation may not be the most literal, but it is still perhaps the best known piece of Euripides in English:[4]

> Could I take me to some cavern for mine hiding,
>   In the hill-tops where the Sun scarce hath trod;
> Or a cloud make the home of mine abiding,
>   As a bird among the bird-droves of God!
>   Could I wing me to my rest amid the roar
>   Of the deep Adriatic on the shore,
> Where the waters of Eridanus are clear,
>   And Phaëthon's sad sisters by his grave
> Weep into the river, and each tear
>   Gleams, a drop of amber, in the wave.
>
> To the strand of the Daughters of the Sunset,
>   The Apple-tree, the singing and the gold;
> Where the mariner must stay him from his onset,
>   And the red wave is tranquil as of old;
>   Yea, beyond that Pillar of the End
>   That Atlas guardeth, would I wend;
> Where a voice of living waters never ceaseth
>   In God's quiet garden by the sea,
> And Earth, the ancient life-giver, increaseth
>   Joy among the meadows, like a tree.

Faced with the various miseries of life, many of Euripides' choruses yearn for the wings of a bird (e.g., *Helen* 1478 ff.), to fly from the face of disaster. But here in the *Hippolytus*, the cry for escape itself contains an ironic indication that there will be none at all. The chorus of Troezenian women wishes to travel to the edge of the earth, the Atlantic pillars. In a few moments Theseus will wish that he could banish Hippolytus to this same far-off frontier (line 1053). But the very theme of this play is no exit; hell hath no limits. In the opening lines of the prologue, Aphrodite has told us that her power (which is, among other things, the power to destroy whomever she wishes) extends even as far as the pillars of Atlas. Moreover, the paradise to which the chorus would flee has already seen one fatal chariot accident. Would Hippolytus himself find safety where young Phaëthon fell after losing control of his horses? Even at the limits of the earth, the situation strangely resembles what is about to occur on stage. Phaëthon's sisters, the 'Daughters of the Sunset' are but another — typically Euripidean — chorus of grieving women, who weep with such sorrow that their tears turn to amber. What good, then, to fly off like a bird? Grief may be transmuted, but it cannot be transcended.

The second stanza of this escape ode reminds us that the desired place of refuge was also the scene of one of Heracles' greatest triumphs, where he gathered golden apples, and shouldered Atlas' burden: the weight of the world. In a later play, Euripides' chorus can boast that the protagonist has actually journeyed to this fabled territory (*Heracles* 392 ff.):

> Thence among the singing maidens,
> western halls' Hesperides.
> Plucked among the metal leaves
> the golden fruit, and slew
> the orchard's dragon-guard
> whose tail of amber coiled the trunk
> untouchably. He passed below the sea
> and set a calmness in the lives of men
> > whose living is the oar.
> Under bellied heaven next,
> he put his hand as prop:
> there in the halls of Atlas,
> his manliness held up
> > heaven's starry halls.
> > > (trans. Arrowsmith)

What is more, just as he did in the *Alcestis*, Heracles has arrived precisely in time to rescue a household menaced with death; this time, it is his own family. But, just as the *Alcestis* turned suddenly from tragedy to triumph after the savior's arrival, here matters take the opposite course. Having successfully gone to the limits of the earth (and beneath it) Heracles is trapped. Hera sends Madness personified against him and he will not escape (line 842). This unexpected demon *ex machina* causes Heracles to murder his own wife and children. When he awakens to the full horror of his deed, he too wishes to escape as a bird:

> Oh no — what can I do? Where can I find refuge
> from these ills? Fly off with wings? Dive beneath the earth?
> > (lines 1157–58)

But no, he cannot fly. Quite the contrary, as he tells Theseus a few moments later, it is his own happiness that has taken wings and flown from him (line 1186). And why dive beneath the earth? He has, in fact, just returned from a trip to Hades, but now hell is inside his head (lines 1297 ff.). No divine epilogue relieves this new misery, not even a goddess like Artemis in the *Hippolytus*, to tell him why things must be as cruel as they are.[5] Heracles is abandoned like Sophocles' Philoctetes, although he must live forever with both wound *and* bow (cf. *Heracles* 1376 ff.), offered no promise of surcease from pain. There is, moreover, an ironic parallel between Heracles' outcry (quoted above), and *Medea* 1296 ff, where Jason, hell-bent on punishing the villainess who has just murdered the King and the Princess of Corinth, shouts that Medea would have to 'hide herself beneath the earth, or fly winged into the air' to avoid the retribution she deserves. And yet but a moment later, her hands stained with still more innocent blood, Medea will in fact soar into the sky . . . completely free. Aristotle was understandably outraged by Medea's escape; but he does not even comment upon the horrible fate of Heracles. Indeed, it is beyond the pale of rational criticism. But the question is its own answer: this is Euripides. In fact, the *Alcestis* and the *Heracles*, with the same demi-god first as savior and then as victim, present the polarities of Euripidean drama: the untragic and the hypertragic.

A similar Euripidean paradox is visible in the figure of Helen. While often vilified as the oversexed bitch who caused the Trojan War,[6] she appears in the *Helen* as 'virginal' and pure,[7] waiting to be rescued by her beloved Menelaus and, though dressed in black, to be rewedded to him during (of course) a funeral ceremony. Moreover, Helen had never even been to Troy; an image had gone in her place to cause all that slaughter.[8] In the *Alcestis*, King Admetus is a widower who is simultaneously burying his wife and marrying her again. Here Helen is a widow simultaneously burying (an image of) and marrying (the real) Menelaus. Moreover, the play concludes with the appearance, *ex machina*, of Castor and Pollux, earlier described as 'both dead and not dead' (line 138), who absolve Helen from any guilt whatever, noting with supreme irony that 'the world has few like her' (line 1687). It is small wonder that when scholars tire of calling Euripides 'the Greek Ibsen', they dub him 'the Greek Pirandello'.

Dare we ask why, according to Euripides, a 'deceitful' Iphigenia escapes from Tauris, while a 'noble' one is immolated at Aulis? We have earlier been indiscreet enough to broach this matter in the case of Alcestis and Medea. It is the same question we ask concerning the bad Helen of the *Troades* (or the *Orestes*) and the 'virgin' waiting in Egypt like patience on a monument. It is not merely a case of comparing plays, for the dramas themselves abound in contradictory characters and situations. Every play of Euripides seems to be asking a question or else boldly stating some mythical and/or visual paradox. It is easy to see why Euripides was, even in antiquity, branded 'the philosopher of the stage', and linked with men like Protagoras, whose new philosophy called all in doubt, and who composed, among other things, an *Antilogiai* (Contradictions), a kind of paean to paradox, celebrating the power of rhetoric to affirm uncertainty.

All the while Euripides was composing his plays of dubious genre and questionable morality, Sophocles was writing — there is no better term — heroic tragedy. And there are no *antilogiai* in the Sophoclean protagonist; he is a monolith, unyielding and uncompromising. If he is at odds with the world, he will leave it, but 'Ajax will 'quit himself like Ajax'. The cowardly messenger may run backward and forward while en route to bring Creon the news of Antigone's defiance, but she herself never hesitates for a moment. She never doubts that she is doing the 'right' thing. (Hegel grants Creon a case of equal 'rightness', but that does not detract from Antigone's self-assurance.) Sophocles' admiration for this sort of heroism, the divine in man, is nowhere more evident than in the well-known choral ode from the *Antigone* (lines 332 ff.) which begins:

> There are many awesome things [*deina*] in the world, but nothing more awesome [*deinoteron*] than man.

The sentiment is similar to the Hebrew psalmist's 'I will praise Thee; for I am fearfully and wonderfully made: awesome are Thy works.' The word *deinon* connotes both admiration and fear, but Sophocles is clearly focusing on what is to be admired. The world of Euripides is also full of *deina*, awesome — if rarely admirable — things, but man is definitely not one of them. In fact, what is *deinon* usually acts *upon* man. Sometimes this force has a name, like Dionysus:

> He [Pentheus] shall come to recognize
> that Dionysus son of Zeus has come into the world, undeniably a god,
> at once most awesome [*deinotatos*]
> and gentlest to mankind.
>
> (*Bacchae* 859–61)

It is the ultimate irony that Greek drama, which began, as Herodotus tells us, with the suffering of Dionysus for humanity, should culminate in a play which presents the suffering of humanity for Dionysus. This new 'god' is the supreme paradox, an irrational, self-contradicting force that is at once most benign and most horrible.[9]

But Euripides' Dionysus is not merely an external *deinon* to whom

men are as flies to wanton boys (this is Seneca's reinterpretation), it is
also a force acting from within. In contrast to the single-minded Sophoclean characters, we have Euripides' Medea, the first expression of what
Bernard Knox has called 'the unheroic temper'. Stricken with doubt,
torn by conflicting inner forces, Medea changes her mind four times in
twenty lines (1044 ff.). Finally darker Dionysiac passions conquer her
reason. The denouement of the *Bacchae* demonstrates that Pentheus is
lord of nothing, least of all his own actions. And Hippolytus, champion
charioteer, is unable to control the horses he has been training his entire
life (lines 1355 ff.). It is a striking coincidence, and all the more striking
because it is a coincidence, that Freud uses a similar image of a horse
out of control to describe the overwhelming power of the Id.[10]

Our most familiar classical tragedies have a single stage setting: the
palace of a king. From play to play the palace remains; only the monarch
changes. Today it is the House of Atreus, tomorrow the House of Oedipus – or of any royal family whom Aristotle deemed worthy of tragic
treatment. The play might depict the fall and/or rise of princes, but the
palace remained intact. Agamemnon is carried out; Orestes soon marches
in. If we seek an image to describe what Euripides 'did' to classical
tragedy, we can do no better than say he destroyed the palace. Two
particular instances come to mind. In the *Trojan Women*, Troy lies in
ruins *on the stage*. The citadel has already been sacked when the play
begins, and the heroes – princes one and all – are dead. We may argue
the topicality of this drama, reminding ourselves that the Island of Melos
had been sacked the previous year and that the *Trojan Women* was
Euripides' castigation of war. But the play is more than a reportage of
ruin; it contains as much symbolism as journalism. It is saying that in
415 BC the royal palace was a shambles and that Homer's epic heroes
no longer have a dwelling place in the Greek theater.

Still another palace was to fall. In the final play of Euripides, Dionysus
tears down the palace of Pentheus, before, in fact, he tears the king
himself into pieces. Ironically, this ultimate destruction of the dignity
of man (if not man himself), demonstrates that he is king neither over
his house nor over his mind.[11]

But the theater itself was not destroyed. The Euripidean revolution
merely changed the decor and the *dramatis personae*. In place of the
classical *reges et proelia* ('kings and battles'), Euripides brought to the
stage what Aristophanes derides as *oikeia pragmata* (*Frogs* 959), 'familiar
affairs', or still more literally, 'household things'. The living room replaces the throne room. But he did not wait until his later plays to
present these bourgeois people in their bourgeois surroundings. What is
preserved at the end of his first extant play is not so much the 'House

of Admetus' as the *home* of Alcestis.[12] We are back to where this essay —and Euripides — began.

On the authority of the Parian Marble, we can place the birth of Euripides at 484 BC. He was born early enough to know Athens in its glory and to witness the final plays of Aeschylus, notably the *Oresteia* in 458. He made his own debut in 455, a year after Aeschylus' death, with a *Peliades*, clearly some version of the Medea story, but did not win the first of his (very few) victories until 441. He is said to have written ninety-two plays, seventy-eight of which were known to the librarians in Alexandria who at the same time, possessed 123 plays by Sophocles. The fact that we still have eighteen (nineteen if we count the *Rhesus*) by Euripides and only seven by Sophocles gives some indication of the favor enjoyed by Euripides in later times.

That he was a bold theatrical innovator is indisputable. Sophocles, as Aristotle quotes him, acknowledged that Euripides presented men as they actually were — people, not paragons. Euripides therefore owns the distinction of having brought 'realism' to the stage. Visually as well as verbally, he rejected the 'epic' (or perhaps we should say 'Homeric') theater. Gone forever were the Aeschylean red carpet and purple passages. Euripides' dialogue is extremely simple, although both Aristotle and 'Longinus' recognize a sublime quality in this simplicity.[13]

It is also true that Euripides banished choral drama from the stage. His 'intrigue' plays made the chorus seem very much out of place. Fifteen Ideal Spectators may look well in a palace, but they considerably clutter up a living room. (Eric Havelock has aptly described the Euripidean revolution as 'putting on stage *rooms* never seen before'.) Time and again his choruses are cautioned to keep secrets that they have overheard; it becomes increasingly clear that they should not be there in the first place. And yet, as if to confound the scholars, Euripides finishes his career with the *Bacchae*, almost as much a choral drama as the *Oresteia*.

The vast influence of Euripides throughout the ages is ample testimony that what he gave the drama was not a *coup de grâce*, but many *coups de théâtre*. He made a deep impression on everyone, including philosophers, poets, and the apostle Paul (who quotes him in I *Corinthians*). Needless to say, the playwrights worshiped him, comedians as well as tragedians. This awe is reflected in the famous remark by Philemon, writer of Greek New Comedy, who claimed he would hang himself to meet Euripides. Euripides' influence on Seneca is well known, while the romantic comedy he inspired in Menander gave models to Plautus and Terence for their Roman entertainments. Whether Euripides 'killed' tragedy is open to debate; that he created melodrama has never been doubted. The long thread from such intrigue-plays as the *Ion* wove innumerable handkerchiefs for centuries of heroines to drop.

And in one way or another, 'Euripidean drama' is still being written. There are conscious emulations like O'Neill's *Desire Under the Elms* (from the *Hippolytus*) or T. S. Eliot's *The Cocktail Party* (from the *Alcestis*) and *The Confidential Clerk* (from the *Ion*). But other writers have more forcefully, if unconsciously, presented Euripides *redivivus*. I think especially of García Lorca and Edward Albee. The Spanish poet is justly admired for his portraits of women swept up in the tidal wave of passion. The Novia in *Blood Wedding* is caught in the very same dilemma as Phaedra, her sense of what is right (and honorable) in violent conflict with a sexual desire that is driving her insane.[14] The same author's Yerma, like Medea, is a victim of a passion which 'poisons' her, turning love into hate ('me estoy llenando de odio', she cries), and drives her to a bloody act of revenge. Edward Albee's *Who's Afraid of Virginia Woolf?* also deals with the vague boundary between love and hate and culminates, like the *Medea*, with a *Kindermord* (albeit an imaginary one) as the supreme act of vengeance. All of this proves not so much that Euripides was ahead of his time as that the issues he broached were timeless.

One final point. There is a common notion that Euripides was unpopular, unappreciated in his own day. If 'success' be measured merely by prizes won, then he surely was a failure, for he received the best-in-festival award only four times in his entire life. But this might indicate, as one scholar suggested, that the judges 'were either idiots or bribed'. It is easier to argue their aesthetic shortcomings, since this same group of arbiters also failed to give first prize to *Oedipus Rex*. But if we look carefully, we can see evidence that in the playwright's own day, the public 'adored Euripides like a god'.[15] We have Plutarch's authority that the average Athenian sailor could recite whole passages of Euripides by heart. To be singing his odes is *ipso facto* to be singing his praises.[16] And contemporary authors were not loath to alter their style in the wake of the Euripidean revolution. Sophocles himself owes a stylistic debt to his innovating contemporary, one particularly visible in the *Trachiniae* and *Philoctetes*.[17] Many scholars have even found verbal echoes. On a quiet night they can hear the voice of Alcestis in Sophocles' Deianira. And there is an interesting similarity between *Alcestis* 941 ff. and *Trachiniae* 900 ff., two passages which describe a tearful spouse wandering through the living quarters of a palace, bewailing the death of domestic happiness — with the significant distinction that in Euripides' play it is *King* Admetus who displays 'unmanly grief'.

But without any doubt the greatest contemporary admirer of Euripides was Aristophanes. His imitation was surely a form of flattery, his parody an expression of reverence. And so much of what Aristophanes had the comic license to utter, Euripides was daring to say on the 'serious' stage, not the least of which involved such frightening issues as the death of God, the New Morality, and the changing relations between the sexes. We think immediately of 'Cloud-theology' (Euripides in several passages replaces Zeus with 'Aether'), as well as the escape theme of the *Birds*. And the significance of Euripides' 'appearance' in the *Thesmophoriazusae* far transcends both parody and caricature. These two playwrights were so much alike that Cratinus, a contemporary comic author, coined the verb 'to Euripidaristophanize'. Euripides was always popular. He presented his 'familiar affairs' not so much to shock the good burghers of Athens as to please them. It is naïve to argue, like H. D. F. Kitto, that the Athenian public preferred art 'with themes of importance', and hence rejected Euripides in favor of Aeschylus and Sophocles.[18] Heroic drama, like the epic which inspired it, had run its course. The people wanted Euripides.

It is therefore fruitless to speculate on why Euripides left Athens in the last years of his life. (It is odd that scholars have not sought for 'deeper meanings' in the fact that Aeschylus died in far-off Sicily.) Whatever the reason, it was certainly not because the public — or his wife — rejected him. Euripides' 'exile' to Macedonia is far more enigmatic than Ovid's to the Black Sea. For one thing, we are at least sure that the Roman poet did not go voluntarily. To consider the various tales of Euripides' misanthropy (or misogyny) is to descend to the level of his scandal-mongering biographers, or to misconstrue Aristophanes, who, we *must* remember, was only joking. The comic poet who had mocked his friend Socrates and seen his comic gibes become tragic accusations surely knew that a Euripidean paradox like 'who knows if life is death, or death life' was no laughing matter.

20

THE VIRTUES OF ADMETUS

ANNE PIPPIN BURNETT

The *Alcestis* nowadays is commonly described as a psychological drama which has as its true subject an absurd disparity between outmoded ideals and actual human conduct. It is usually said that Euripides has portrayed the noble action of a fairy-tale heroine, then capped it with ignoble consequences. Some scholars, however, turn a skeptic's eye even upon Alcestis and her sacrifice. Those who admire the queen often assert that she dies disillusioned, while the true debunkers explain that she is dying for base reasons that show her to be as false and calculating as her mate. Critics who believe in Alcestis but find her husband unworthy of her read the play as a bourgeois-realist comedy with a plot that breaks all the rules of realism.[1] Those who find both the king and the queen to be cheap imitations of tragic nobility discover a Shavian marital fable ending with the reunion of a pair who will live unhappily ever after, each a thorn in the other's flesh.[2] Both groups believe that the secret of the play is hypocrisy, conscious or unconscious; they argue that principals and chorus often do not mean what they say, and that Euripides meant only the simpletons in his audience to take his play at face value. These critics seem to forget, in dealing with the *Alcestis*, the enormous spatial candor of the ancient theater, and the difficulty of conveying innuendo from behind a mask.

I should like to play the simpleton, and attempt a naïve reading of Euripides' *Alcestis*. The way has been prepared for many years, ever since Lesky's study of the fable's fairy-tale forms[3] showed that the story itself makes no evaluation of the husband's acceptance of his wife's sacrifice, though it plainly condemns the parents. Euripides, then, in choosing as his *mythos* the mixed tale of the bargain with death and the love sacrifice, was not choosing a story which necessarily dealt with a cad or a coward. It was doubtless within his power to give the king these

From *Classical Philology*, 60 (1965), 240–55. Copyright © 1965 by the University of Chicago. Reprinted by permission of the author and the University of Chicago Press.

qualities if he wished, but if the conventional story of a favorite of the gods was to be given a new tone of moral corruption, the change would have to be strongly made.[4] A straightforward dramatist would establish the altered ethical coloring of his king as soon as possible; a writer of more subtlety might lull his audience for a while, then suddenly force them to see the baseness of the man they had admired. In this case, however, the longer the revelation was postponed, the more shocking and incontrovertible it would have to be when made. Euripides, however, follows neither of these courses. His opening description of Admetus is of a king, hero, and favorite of Apollo. At the play's end the entire kingdom, the entire generation, has had its admiration of the man, his wife, and his friend strengthened and confirmed. The audience has nowhere been instructed to separate its judgment from that of the chorus. Nor has its attention ever been directed to what must be, in a re-evaluation of the Admetus story, the crucial moment for revision: the moment when Admetus accepted his wife's offer to trade her life for his. Euripides, in fact, has gone to considerable trouble to discourage his audience from thinking of this moment at all.

In fairy tale the bargain and its fulfilment both belonged to the king's wedding day; the family refuses, the bride insists, and at once she sinks away as her dying husband is revived. Euripides has split this single action in two, making a new chronology that stretches over an indefinite length of time. No word of his text describes the circumstances of the past bargain: how Apollo announced it, how Admetus made his canvass, how Alcestis offered herself, and how Admetus received that offer. All these matters are ignored, though three passages mysteriously suggest that Admetus was virtually dead at the time (13, 462-63, 633). The bargain is stated as fact; Apollo's first (and presumably inalterable) arrangement with the Moirai in two lines (14-15), the subsequent actions of Admetus and his family in three (15-18). The only motivation discussed is that of Apollo; he sponsored the bargain as a boon for Admetus, to show his gratitude for that man's pious hospitality. Euripides' new chronology supplies one new detail, however; in his version of the bargain, the death that was offered and accepted was not an immediate death but one set vaguely in the future, allowing a certain amount of continued common life to both the receiver and the giver. This amelioration would hardly have been added by a poet bent on condemning the king.

The play allows us to watch what happened on the day the bargain was fulfilled, but places behind a veil of time the day when Alcestis made her promise to the Fates. It was Euripides, as far as we know, who made this unmeasured chasm of years appear in the middle of the old story, and the effect of the innovation is plain. The bargain assumes the unquestioned inevitability of historical event. In the course of his play, the dramatist explores and evaluates Alcestis' decision by making her, on this later day, repeat her old reasons, but there is no similar exploration in the case of Admetus. He has no decision today, since her death cannot now be prevented, and the audience is not encouraged to think that he was allowed a decision on the long-ago bargain day. That bargain was engineered by Apollo and presented to Admetus in token of gratitude, and one thing Euripides has made his chorus say, at a crucial moment in the denouement, is that one must accept the gift offered by a god (1071, a positive version of Solon's 'inescapable are the gifts of the gods').

The visible action of the *Alcestis* represents the bargain's fulfilment, and then its remarkable dissolution. The cost is met, the article secured, then suddenly the price is returned and the purchase becomes a free gift. The audience sees Alcestis die and sees her carried out; it sees her husband take a visitor into his house and drive another away; it sees him refuse to go back into his house alone and refuse to take a strange woman in with him; then suddenly the strange woman proves to be the dead wife, and the man who bought his own life at the price of hers re-enters his house, his purchase still secure but with the price paid once more in his hands. This is the skeleton of the *Alcestis*; it acquires its flesh and form, its ugliness or beauty, from the speeches which Euripides has written for his characters. As they speak, the king and queen at least must be heard with the ordinary good faith granted to all the figures who walk the classic stage, for there is nothing in the tradition, nothing in their past, and nothing in the play's overt system of rewards and punishments to suggest that this man and woman are false. If the dramatist is playing a subtle game with the material he has chosen, if in spite of the positive evaluations of the action he himself has created he means his creatures to be doubted, he will label their lies, or show a strong contradiction between their words and their accomplished deeds.[5]

In the *Alcestis* prologue a god and a demon meet at Admetus' threshold; Apollo is just leaving the house Death is about to enter. Apollo toys for a while with the demon, pretending to dissuade him with a courteous plea, then standing aside sardonically to let him pass. He knows that Death is to lose his prey, and ignominiously, submitting to force and getting no thanks for what he will have to grant (64-71). The prologue thus shows the apparent defeat of what is bright and young and good, while promising that in the end these qualities will be victorious over the power that is black and old and evil.

As the two supernatural beings dispute, their speeches investigate the ideas of graciousness, justice and repayment. Viewed from heaven, this whole affair is merely an incident in a series of repayments, transgression for transgression, made between Zeus and Apollo (3-7). On earth there has been a series of benefactions; Apollo is here because of a positive repayment, the benefaction he returned to Admetus after his kind reception (9). Such chains of repayment must begin somewhere; the heavenly one began, according to Apollo, with Asclepius' raising of the dead — a boon to men but an evil in the eyes of Zeus. The earthly chain began with Admetus' hospitality to Apollo. In the course of the prologue Apollo asks, perhaps not quite seriously, if Death will not perform another such gratuitous initial act (60). If Thanatos had agreed, a continuing courtly exchange of favors between him and Apollo would presumably have been founded (70). Death, however, is interested in justice, in getting and giving exactly what is due on the basis of old debts and established law (30-31). An independent act of graciousness is incomprehensible to him (63).

Apollo suggests, like Athena in the *Eumenides*, that there is more to justice than Death supposes, that the quality of an act is to be considered as well as its quantity, and that repayment is to be made not only in kind but with love or hatred in addition. Admetus' hospitality was technically repaid by the tricking of the Moirai, but in addition Admetus, the man who was *hosios* ('pious'), has become dear to the god. Apollo is interested now in the death of Alcestis, not because he still has any debt to discharge, but because he shares the griefs of his mortal friend (42). In Death's way of thinking, this is contrary to justice (41). And Thanatos' refusal to become Apollo's benefactor provides an opposite case; he is to be repaid exactly, according to his own notion of justice, by receiving no thanks (70), but in addition he will become the enemy of Apollo (71). Thus the motifs of friendship and enmity are added to those of *dikē* ('justice') and repayment while the demon and the god confront each other. The ambiguous word *charis* ('graciousness') is also introduced as they converse; it is used to describe an original, gratuitous benefaction (60), or the necessary return of good for good (70).

The prologue introduces, beyond these abstractions, one concrete concept. Apollo opens the play by stepping forth from the house of Admetus and turning to address it. The house is dear to him (23), and he has acted for its aid and salvation (9, 41). He has in some sense occupied the house ever since he first entered it as a servant, and he now leaves it only because he cannot stay under the same roof with Death. Heracles will enter the house in his stead, and then Death's work will be undone. There are ten direct references to the house in seventy-six lines; a lighter but still unusual density characterizes the rest of the play, where there are at least sixty mentions of *domos* or *oikos*, and as many more to roofs, walls, gates, etc., in the total of 1163 lines.

The prologue's motifs of house and repayment, *dikê* and *charis*, are — like its symbolic action — prophetic of the play to come. As the prologue begins with an apostrophe to the house, so does the denouement (861 ff.), and at the center of the whole, marking the beginning of the reversal, is the great House of Admetus Ode (569-605). This house is the formal object of the action, and the action is moved by the mechanism of repayment. Apollo entered the house in repayment of his crime against the Cyclopes. He repaid his host by arranging for his escape from death at the price of another death, which causes Apollo to leave the house and Death to enter. Death's entrance is followed by Alcestis' exit from the house as a corpse, a departure that leaves the house temporarily emptied and diminished. Apollo, moved by his love for Admetus and his respect for the house, and also perhaps by his need to do Zeus a new disservice, brings Heracles upon the scene, and Admetus, repaying old obligations to his friend, opens his house to the agent of the god. Admetus has, in repayment to Alcestis, promised to close the house to a future wife; as part of the same repayment, he closes it also to his father and mother. Finally Heracles, repaying Admetus, keeps Alcestis from entering the House of Hades and restores the House of Admetus by sending her once more within its doors. I hope to demonstrate that this formal structure of action and motivation represents the true action of Euripides' play as a device or an emblem might.

As long as the prologue lasts, Alcestis' approaching death appears to the audience, as it does to Apollo, simply as an event in the history of the House of Admetus. The death is fixed and has been for many years; there is, as Admetus later says, a sense in which it has happened long ago (421; cf. 527). Very soon, however, it becomes immediate.

This death, although it is to be reversed, is the central fact of the drama, and it is at once created and dissected in a fashion typical of Euripides. First the causes of the death are expressed, in the barest possible form, by Apollo. Then the death is represented symbolically, as the god withdraws before its miasma and the demon enters to cut his lock of hair. Next the death is mourned by the citizens of Pherae, as they sing the *parodos*, and only at this point does the dying woman instead of the death itself become important. She is given public praise as the best of women, whose death will be the fullest expression of her *aristeia*. A third shift of focus comes with the speech of the servant woman who in effect forces the eye of the chorus to the keyhole of the women's appartments. She allows them, and the audience with them, to watch what no man could have witnessed, knowing that the purity of Alcestis' private actions will be the more blinding for having been spied upon. After this incomparable glimpse of stately preparations and heartbroken farewells, a brief ode is sung to say that there is no escape from death. The surface of the song is funereal, but the audience simultaneously anticipates both the terror of death and the joy of revival, since they know that Heracles is somehow to save the queen.

At last Admetus and his dying wife appear, and in the scene that follows, the presence, the words, and then the silence of Alcestis drive out all the consciousness of artistry or illusion. In a passage of only 150 lines Alcestis first experiences her death, in a brief and pitiful *agon* with an invisible enemy, and then explains it. She gives a crystalline statement of the reasons which led her to choose this death and of the results she wishes it to have. Then, as soon as she is assured that her death will be effective, she simply ceases to live. The child's song follows, releasing the emotion of the audience and providing testimony that the woman who spoke so clearly a moment ago is really gone. All memory of Apollo's promise is momentarily lost and death seems beyond redemption.

Euripides' prismatic technique for dramatizing this death also allows evaluations of it to come from different sources. Apollo made no judgment, he simply said the queen was young and not yet ready to die; but the chorus of citizens and the serving women have saluted the queen as the finest of women. To them her action is a just expression of her superlative virtue. Alcestis says the same of herself, and with her statement of reasons and demands the audience is allowed to test all these opinions and to judge the woman and her action for themselves.

Alcestis begins with the fact that her promise to die was freely made, not forced upon her. It was, in the prologue's terms, a gratuitous benefaction of the sort that inaugurates a repayment chain. Thanatos had objected that such actions are not required by *dikê* and are made at the expense of the benefactor. He refused to perform a minor act of graciousness, but Alcestis has decided upon a major one. What can move a human being to a freely chosen act that is in the interest of another but against his own? This is the question that Euripides explores in Alcestis' discussion of her case, a case in which the cost of her action to herself was the highest any human could pay.

The lucid economy of Alcestis' explanation has shocked some moderns,[6] but her secret is that she sees the problem as simple. She knows of course that her action will bring *kleos* and that fame is an honourable thing, but this prize she gives away to her husband and her children as consolation. For herself she wants only one thing — success. Self-sacrifice has no inherent value since life is good; it is conceivable only when careful calculation has shown that death will bring results that life could not, results that are more valuable even than life.

Alcestis chose to die rather than to live as Admetus' widow (the two existing possibilities, once Pheres and his wife had declined) because she saw that in these circumstances her death would best serve that to which her life was dedicated, her marriage. She states this with cool idealism. She would not betray her marriage bed and her husband (180–81); she honored her husband's life more than her own soul, though she loved life well (282 ff.); her children can be despots in their father's house, though she is dead, as they could not be in the house of a stepfather (280 ff.). In Alcestis' cosmos Marriage is a pure element to be named with Sun, Air and Earth (244–49). Husband and bed are one, as are husband and hearth;[7] she confides her children to Hestia (163 ff.) and to Admetus (375), for the two are inseparable in her thought. Husband, children, house, and marriage make up a single ideal concept which her death will save. It is more valuable to her than her sharp delight in life, and having seen what was best she felt that to choose any course but death would have been shameful (180; cf. Plato *Apology* 28B).

Alcestis' farewells are made to her marriage bed, the symbol of temporal union; her recommendations for the future are made to the goddess of the eternal *foyer*, from whose altar nothing can be taken away.[8] Nothing that she does has any reference to romantic love, for this concept is unknown to her. She is ruled by *philia* (279), the feeling proper among friends and members of the same family.[9] She expects to be forgotten (381,387) and assumes that another will sleep in her bed (181–82), but these things do not interest her. The success she demands is that her marriage should continue after she is gone; it must not be imitated or replaced, for her death is to make it immortal.

Alcestis dies only when the results she wants have been promised her. What she asks is specific; she says in effect: 'I refused to give our children a stepfather; I ask in return that you shall not give them a stepmother.' This finely calculated return of like for like which takes no account of the quality of the initial benefaction and which has nothing to do with gratitude or love, this repayment which cannot pretend to be worthy of Alcestis' deed, she labels 'just' (302). It is the kind of *dikê* that Death understands. Admetus agrees as a matter of course (note how his reference to Thessalian brides, line 331, echoes hers to Thessalian grooms, line 285; they make exactly paired renunciations), but he is no more satisfied than an Apollo would have been by this mean return of like for like. Hastily he adds extensions and embellishments to his covenant in the attempt to respond to her *philia*: he will not only not marry a new wife, he will grieve for this one forever, sacrificing not only the joy of future sons, but all joys. He will not only close his house to the potential enemy stepmother, he will drive away the actual enemy, the father who has behaved like a stepfather (636 ff.). A comparison of his parents' action with that of Alcestis has proved to him that they deserve not love but hatred from him (338-41; cf. her accusation of them at 290 ff.). From this day on he will be a stranger to the pleasures of music and masculine company, nor will he have any female companion to solace him.

Had he simply proposed never to install the concubine Alcestis took for granted, the effect could only have been crude. Admetus instead makes a promise that is positive, delicately stated, and filled with a powerful meaning (348-56):

> Your body's counterfeit as like as art can make
> I shall command, and place upon my bed.
> This will I embrace and this adore,
> Holding it I will call your name
> And thus in semblance will I hold the wife I have no more.
> A pleasure cold as ice I'll know
> But it may lift the weight upon my soul
> And then, perhaps, in dreams
> Your shade will come to bring my heart some cheer.
> For sweet it is in sleep to welcome friends,
> Though all too short their stay.[10]

Since he is not Orpheus (357) this will be his way of bringing his wife back from Hades. He will live in the dream he hopes to induce with the *eidolon* (image), himself a sleeping image of death, host to her phantom imitation of life. She has asked that her marriage be kept alive; Admetus determines as far as possible to keep his wife alive too, as statue and as ghost (cf. 328). At the same time he arranges to die with her; his life will be like death (288, 242-43, 278, 666, 802, 1082, 1084), its goal that moment when his corpse will lie beside death's image of her while his soul seeks her shade in the house she is to prepare below (363-68).

Admetus' promised repayment exceeds Alcestis' bid for justice and attempts to reflect something of the quality of her action. His words are approved by the chorus, which calls his promises, thus extended, *axia*, worthy of her sacrifice (370; cf. 300). Whether his actions are likewise worthy of her, whether the play as it continues is worthy of her, are the questions which next must be considered. Both dramatist and characters must meet the test of Alcestis' death: its motives, its demands, and its beauty. Alcestis has explained the results she hopes for; the audience will witness the results the playwright has arranged.

Alcestis' body is carried into the house, and Admetus accompanies it, to close the first episode. The next phase of the action is expressed in a pair of scenes in which one visitor is almost violently brought into the house and another is more violently driven away. These scenes of reception and ejection stand on either side of the axial House of Admetus Ode, the physical center of the play, a song in celebration of the welcome once given to Apollo and of the blessedness of wealth that was its reward. The two scenes occupy the space between the death and the decision to revive Alcestis and so, unless this is a very foolish play indeed, they must in some way cause or explain the happy reversal which occurs.

Pheres, as one of the refusing parents, belongs to the love-sacrifice tale, but Heracles is an intruder. An alternate and probably older version made Persephone return Alcestis to her lord,[11] and this detail is echoed in the folk-tale solution of direct divine intervention.[12] Phrynichus had made use of Heracles in his more primitive drama, but such a precedent was far from binding, and Euripides emphasizes the technical superfluity of this visiting hero in his prologue. Apollo has already cheated death once by making the Fates drunk, and on Admetus' doorstep he teases Death in the manner of a satyr-play Sisyphus about to trick Hades himself. Clearly the god could save Alcestis at once; instead he announces a story change: the bargain will be reversed, not by divine interference, but by the heroic act of a mortal. Even in this form, however, the story does not need Heracles. If someone is to wrestle with death, Admetus is on hand, and there is no dramaturgical need to bring in an outsider. Euripides emphasizes this point too, by making Admetus himself touch on the possibility of a journey to the underworld.

Heracles is plainly necessary to Euripides' particular intentions toward his story, and the dramatist as plainly wants us to realize this. The brute effect of Heracles' introduction is that something of the satyr drama invades the tragedy of Alcestis' death and salvation, echoing the drunken Moirai in the story of Admetus' escape. A more subtle result is the restored prominence given to the king. Admetus had figured in a god-come-to-visit story in which he was rewarded for his piety with wealth, a beast chariot with which to win a wife, and escape when he was threatened with death.[13] He had also figured in a love-sacrifice tale. The two stories had no essential connection, but had been given a point of contact through Apollo when the final reward for hospitality that ended the first became the bargain with death that began the second tale. Euripides succeeds in conflating the two, by refusing Persephone and choosing Heracles, an envoy of Apollo's, to act as Alcestis' savior. By means of this semi-divine friend he is able to stage a version of the god-come-to-visit story concurrently with his drama of the love-sacrifice. He can thus consider, in a single play, the characteristic virtues of both Alcestis and Admetus.

As soon as Admetus has sent his friend indoors the audience is reminded of that other, gratuitous act which stands with Alcestis' decision as one of the two mortal causes of everything seen on the stage. The reception of Heracles is the double of Admetus' original reception of Apollo and will have the same sort of consequence; this much is made explicit in the ode which follows (605; cf. Apollo at 68–69). Thus Admetus, making the first move of his new life, is shown to re-enact the past. He faces a second test of hospitality, more difficult than the first, since Heracles' arrival is apparently so untimely. However, his new duty to Alcestis (his promise to mourn and yet to live as if his wife were still alive) coincides with his continuing duty as a nobleman. His simple impulse to deny Alcestis' death shows him the way, and he has soon fulfilled Apollo's requirement by offering the hospitality of his house to Heracles. When the traveler's fateful entrance into the guest quarters has been accomplished, Admetus explains his reasons (553–60). He could not have turned his friend away, for to do so would have threatened the reputation of his house and the future reception of its members elsewhere. Whereas Alcestis saw the house from within, an enclosed space with the marriage bed at its center, Admetus honors its outward aspect. For him the house includes the city (553), a city which has obligations toward other cities. The house where Alcestis' children are to rule is also the *polis*, and he values its good name more than his own sharp need to grieve alone for his wife. Even the servant, whose views are much more limited than his master's, recognizes that Admetus was governed by *aidos*, the sense of proper reverence felt toward one's family and the gods (823).

Once, before the play began, Admetus had taken in a guest without realizing the full meaning of his action, and he will do so again, before the play has ended. The three actions are given such heavy echoes that they stand each as a type of the other two. Apollo was presumably unrecognized; Heracles is recognized only as a friend, not as a savior; Alcestis will be veiled. In every case Admetus acts out of respect for his house: the desire to give it its due and to preserve in this way its ideal existence in men's opinion. The first reception resulted in *philia* (42), the second has friendship as its partial cause (1037); in the final case, the desire that a friend shall not become an enemy causes the reception (1106) which has the return of Alcestis' *philia* as its effect.

In the scene that follows, this act of friendship and welcome is matched by an act of enmity, as Pheres is abused and driven away. The primary fairy-tale identification of Pheres is not as father but as one who refused to do what Alcestis did, and Euripides has done his best to preserve this single character for the old man. When he arrives on the scene one fact and only one is known about him, but it has been stated four times over: Pheres, though ripe for death, refused to exchange his life for his son's (Apollo, 16; Alcestis, 290-92; Admetus, 338-39; Chorus, 468-70). His presence now makes possible the completion of the central inquiry of the play; through him the dramatist can consider again what it is that could induce a human being to give up his life for another. The woman who chose to die has given her reasons; now, in the presence of her corpse, the audience hears the explanation of the man who refused.

Pheres begins with a fair speech in praise of Alcestis. If there was a convention for portraying the hypocrite, the actor probably followed it here, for Euripides has made Pheres' own words prove him disingenuous. He begins by saying that he would sympathize and share in his son's misfortunes (614), but soon he admits that whether Admetus be wretched or joyful is no concern of his (685-86). Alcestis he calls wise (615) when he thinks he has benefited from her action (625), an idiot (728) when it is suggested that he might have done as she did. The noble deed (623) becomes a stupid error when he imagines himself performing it (710). He congratulates Alcestis on her most glorious life in his first speech (623), but reveals in his next that he does not believe in glory (726). He wishes her well in Hades (627), then states his own conviction that the time below is long but never sweet (692-93). With each self-contradiction he proves what Admetus had earlier said (339) — he is a friend only in words.

When his trumpery offering of praise has been rejected, Pheres states his reasons for refusing to save his son, beginning at the same point that Alcestis had chosen. No debt bound him to die for Admetus, and he loved life. *Dikê* was enough for him, and *dikê* meant holding on to the same tangible things that Alcestis had decided to relinquish. The house, for him, was a complex of lands and flocks (687) to be counted and consumed, not a complex of ideals to be preserved. He values only the sweets of this earth (693) and thus the best life is the longest one. Pheres does not care for reputation and he admits that he knows nothing of sympathy; it is his own fate a man cares about, not that of anyone else (712). And in so denying *philia* he isolates himself from every other being in the play save Death alone; all the rest, from god to slave, experience what it is to live with two souls instead of one (Admetus, 883-84; cf. Apollo, 42; the household, 192-93 and 825; the chorus, 210-12; Alcestis, 313-19; Heracles, 1010). Thus the problem posed by Apollo was even simpler for Pheres than it had been for Alcestis, since self-sacrifice is inconceivable to a man who stands outside society, recognizing nothing but material goods. Such a man could easily allow his own kin to be protected by one who was not of their blood, though he thus betrayed his house as well as his son.

Pheres freely admits that his present good fortune is owed to Alcestis

(620-21; 625), and he comes with a token repayment. She, however, had not intended to be his benefactor, and so his gift is refused. Admetus then proceeds to withdraw the advantages which had come to the old people through Alcestis' sacrifice, and as he explains himself he repeats words that she had spoken (651-52; cf. 295-96). He charges Pheres with responsibility for Alcestis' death, and honoring the symmachy of marriage makes her enemy his and that of his house. Pheres is forbidden access to the hearth where her spirit resides, and is driven away from the halls that belong now to her children. The old parents will have, however, exactly what they bargained for (662-66, 735-36). Pheres had chosen, not honorable death for himself and survival for his son, but continued life for himself and death for his son. Burial at the hands of his son had not then seemed important to him. Now Admetus says in effect: 'You have the continuing life that you wanted; you will also have the rest of your choice, the dead son and a burial by strangers.' He renders his father the sort of justice the old man had proclaimed, the calculated *dikê* of Thanatos, and could say now in his father's words, 'How do I wrong you? What do I deprive you of?' (689) Admetus casts off his father, not by doing any violence to the man, but by announcing his own symbolic death (666).[14] At the same time he declares that he will substitute Alcestis, although she is dead and an outsider, for his living father and mother; she will receive the honor and care due by tradition to Pheres and his wife (646-47). And so Admetus states again the two fictions of the paradoxical dream in which he will live if live he must: Alcestis remains alive and he is dead. When Pheres is gone, Admetus moves away at his wife's side to the grave where he would join her (897-99).

In receiving Heracles, Admetus repeated his original reception of Apollo; in refusing Pheres he seems to repeat Apollo's confrontation with Death. As in the earlier scene, a young and powerful figure comes out of the house, meets an old man[15] who has entered from the *parodos*, and a dispute about Alcestis ensues. Admetus, like Apollo, argues that the old are meetest for death, while Pheres, like Thanatos, denies it. Pheres accuses Admetus of having too little respect for established custom, as Death had reproached Apollo. Apollo asked a favor; Thanatos refused; Apollo answered, 'It will happen anyway, by another agency, and you will get no thanks but become my enemy.' Admetus had long ago asked a favor and Pheres had refused; now Admetus says, 'It has happened anyway, by another agency, and you will get no thanks but be my enemy.' The visual and verbal parallelism suggests that the Pheres scene has been constructed with a special intention. This scene is the play's *agon* in the technical sense, and it is made to seem almost a life and death struggle. One of the curiosities of the *Alcestis* is that it has four separate *agons*, all reflections of the heroine's central match with death. She gives in after the briefest resistance (259-63), but Apollo teases Thanatos, Heracles wrestles with the greedy demon, and Admetus drives off her human enemy, the immediate cause of her demise. In so doing he duplicates one of Heracles' other exploits, the defeat of the demon Old Age (a figure scarcely distinguishable from a Ker or from Death himself).[16] The spectator is left with the subrational sense that the ugly figure whom Apollo allowed to enter the house has now been driven off by Admetus.

In the paired scenes upon which the plot of the *Alcestis* turns the spectator watches Admetus begin to act. He repays a friend of the house with a benefaction and its enemy with enmity; the one who has threatened his house is driven away and the one who will save it is taken in. Since Heracles is young and jolly, a banqueter and a bringer of life, while Pheres is old and mean and associated with death, the king has shown himself truly king by driving out old Hunger and bringing in Wealth and Health.[17] Like a celebrant at the Anthesteria he has said to Pheres, 'Get out, Death';[18] to Heracles like the citizens of Thasos, 'Come dwell with us,' 1151.[19] These actions strengthen his house, and likewise strengthen his alliance with Alcestis, as he makes her friends his friends, her enemies his.[20]

As Admetus has an *agon* in Alcestis' name, so he also has a *pathos*. *Philia* means sharing both the good fortune and the suffering of another being (1054, 1103, etc.), living with two souls (see 900, where Admetus would have given Hades two souls instead of one, and its contradiction to 54),[21] and the full experience of what this can mean reaches Admetus on his return from the tomb. In spite of his fictions,[22] he is to suffer life, not death, and he realizes that here, at last, he has outstripped his wife in unhappiness (935-36). The scene (861-961) in which he greets the humiliating actuality of an unwanted life is the mirror image of her farewell to a richly desirable world. She, before, with face unstained by any tear, had moved serenely through a much-loved house where linen lay folded in orderly chests. Admetus now loathes the very walls of the building and cannot enter where she is not; he cries out and longs for death, as he imagines the sordid minutiae of the life that awaits him in this ill-kept house filled only with emptiness. Her tears fell only once, in farewell to the bed she would not betray; in the service of that same bed, now deserted (925), he must waste his spirit in a struggle with each day's petty lusts (950-53). She willed the joy of her good fame to those she left behind, but Admetus looks forward to the agony of knowing himself slandered by enemy tongues (954-60).

At this point the natural results of Alcestis' death have had their full description. The sacrifice is a success, as far as mortal endeavour can make it so, for Admetus has maintained the external life of the house she died to preserve. Her action has found its *dikê*, its narrow due, but the real has not become the ideal. The immortal marriage will be a grievous phantom thing at best and the continuing house will be shadowed by slurs on its master's reputation. But the world is not fully defined by the natural, and Euripides will not allow the story to end this way. Apollo has sent Heracles and he by a miracle brings to husband and wife a true *charis* (1101; cf. 1074), something far beyond the limits of mere justice.

Heracles re-enters, the first words in his mouth a description of the reciprocal duties of friendship (1008-11); as Pheres is the false kinsman so Heracles is the true friend. His protestations, unlike those of the old man, are borne out by his actions. He claims that Admetus' deceit has caused him to fail in his own friendly duty of sympathy; it has also laid him under a new obligation to his host, since Admetus had meant with his deception to serve their friendship (855-60).[23] By returning Alcestis he can erase the evil fortune he had failed to share, and he can repay the host who so honored his arrival. And by keeping what he is doing a secret, he can even return in kind Admetus' well-meaning deceit. Here the direction of Apollo is more than ever evident, for Heracles' heavy sprightliness serves many more purposes than he can suppose. The disguise of Alcestis allows Admetus a symbolic repetition of the act that first earned him Apollo's patronage as, for the third time, he receives a god-sent guest. The veil causes Alcestis, whose death had deprived the house of its spirit, to return in the guise of Hestia herself; it also allows her to witness a test of her husband's promised faithfulness. Only her corpse was present when Admetus, for her sake, quarreled with his father; now she hears him make public his plan to love and honor her, though she is dead, until he dies himself (1085-96).

The trick being played on Admetus creates the peculiar, happy tension of this scene. It makes this third test of friendship, hospitality, and faith by far the most difficult of all. Admetus must close his door to betrayal of his wife and yet open it to the gift of his friend and the gods (1071). He must reject what he takes to be a False Alcestis without depriving himself and his house of the true presence of his wife. The audience watches Admetus' nobility guide him once again in a situation he does not wholly understand. The entertainment of this woman will, he believes, bring him a grief more bitter than any he has left (1069), but rather than damage his friendship with Heracles (1106) he will accept this further suffering. Heracles' ironical offer of a joyful reward does not tempt him (1101); his resistance breaks only when his friend urgently begs the favor (1107). His plain statements that he can have nothing to do with the girl (1056, 1090) have served to separate the threat to Alcestis from the threat to himself, and thus he agrees to receive the property of Heracles (at the cost of pain to himself), while he refuses to accept a substitute for his wife. In so acting he completes the salvation of Alcestis (1020, 1119) and bears out the chorus' prediction that his aristocratic piety, incomprehensible to themselves, will find a reward at last (600–605, the close of the House of Admetus Ode). And in fact Admetus crosses his threshold not with his friend's property but with his own wife restored, for Heracles sees to it that he shall receive the recognition token, the touch of Alcestis, before the eyes of the audience. Husband and wife step back into their restored house each in his own character and each aware of his new felicity.[24] Their alliance has been strengthened, the false friendship of Pheres is at an end, the true friendship of Heracles is firmer than before (he will return, 1152), and the reputations of king, queen, and house have been fixed forever by the miracle. Admetus and Alcestis are harbored now in a better life than any they had known before (1157), and at last the ideal is become real. The Homeric description of the best of marriages has found its perfect illustration (*Odyssey* VI 182–85):

. . . for a better and higher gift than this there cannot be, when with accordant aims man and wife have a home. Great grief it is to foes and joy to friends; but they themselves best know its meaning.

(trans. Palmer)

When Admetus and Alcestis close the play by walking back into their castle, they do not merely exit through a conventional palace-front set. They enter a place altogether different from those dim and planless tragic palaces which seem to contain no more than a noose or a blood-filled bath. They have idealized the House of Admetus, but Euripides has made it real, no longer a façade but an interior. The House of Admetus has storerooms and chests, household altars, throne room, guests' quarters, men's hall, and a *thalamos* with its marriage bed. In it one may bathe or feast or play the lyre, scold a servant or listen for a woman's call of greeting. It is a house where dust can gather and children cry. It was not the poet's vulgarity that dictated these details, though Aristophanes would have it so. The subject of the play is the salvation of this house, and by a miracle it, like Alcestis, has been saved whole, an ideal clothed again in full reality.

The play has shown a pair of human beings faced with a number of choices. Each was able to discriminate between real and apparent qualities and each valued certain timeless things above the joy or pain of the moment. Both follow the path of virtue and it brings them grief and separation, but a god is interested in their case and he, by reversing nature, reunites the pair, restores their happiness, and gives their ideal transcendent reality. This is not the sort of tale we have been taught to expect from Euripides, but he has told it. The pleasure he took in dramatizing it is evident, for the pathetic emotion of the death scene, the hard accuracy of the quarrel, the bitterness of Admetus' return from the burial, and the complicated sport of the final moments all display the characteristic Euripidean talents at their height. In addition, the pervasive recurrence of a bit of wordplay suggests that Euripides saw in the Admetus–Alcestis *mythos* other opportunities not strictly dramaturgical.

'Who can say if what we call life is not death, and death life? ' (Frag. 638 Nauck) sounds fully as foolish out of context as Aristophanes intended it should. In the *Alcestis*, however, Euripides shows the kind of profit he could make from such a paradox. He uses it as if for decorative effect, but in fact it lies at the heart of his subject, with Alcestis herself its embodiment. When Admetus begins his ambiguities about the state of his wife with 'of her I have a double tale to tell,' 519 (cf. 521 and 525), he is only repeating the play's initial description of Alcestis: 'You could say that she was living and you could say that she was dead' (141). The two conditions are always mixed in her. She has in a sense been dead for many years (527); when she first enters the chorus has already described her funeral, and when she returns to the house in the end she still has the touch of Death upon her. While she is in her tomb, the living declare that they too are dead (825, 1082); she on the other hand is to be treated as if she were yet on earth (329, 992-99, 1096). They lead a life that is not life (242-43), she lies in a tomb that is no tomb (995). The only ease Admetus hopes to find in life is death (1086), though by his own definition he and all mortals with him are dead already (527). Everywhere this 'double tale' is told. When Heracles, like the impatient comic poet, objects that there is generally thought to be considerable difference between the two states, Admetus answers, 'You indeed may think so, but I see the matter otherwise' (528-29).

Euripides constructed his drama so that there would be at its core a time when life and death, Heracles and Thanatos, were housed under a single roof. This is the situation within, while the House of Admetus Ode is sung, and this is the situation which provides the technical causation of the plot's reversal. The simultaneous celebration of banquet and funeral serves to provoke the outraged slave, producing the revelation that moves Heracles to save Alcestis. The sounds of mourning and rejoicing have been kept from sacrilegious mingling by the ritual foresight of Admetus, bent on carrying out to the letter his promise to Alcestis (548). Nevertheless they have risen from the house in the same moment (760) in a double strain that finds a fanciful echo later just before the miracle of Alcestis' return, when Admetus mixes the remembered music of his wedding with the present music of his grief (915 ff.).

A house in which a corpse is laid out while a feast goes forward is a plain but profoundly suggestive image in a drama of death and its reversal. Heracles, the satyrlike glutton, creates this symbolic situation,[25] and Euripides makes him also its exegete. Fallen upon an elegiac mood, he decides to share the secret of life with the man who serves him; his speech is remarkably close to another, put into Apollo's mouth by Bacchylides as the moral of Admetus' escape from death (782-91; cf. Bacchylides III 76 ff.):

> Every man must die;
> There's not a living soul who knows
> If he'll be here tomorrow.
> Fate creeps on unseen
> And neither book nor spell can teach you
> When the end will come.
> Since what I say is true,
> Be of good cheer and drink!
> Make today your own
> And leave the rest to fate.
> Honor Kypris, that sweet god,
> For she is fond of men.

Anyone who will not live this way, he concludes, ends with a life that is no life at all. He thus repeats the old lesson in Dionysiac terms, his own example (added to that of the drunken Moirai) enforcing the notion that this is the way, not just to happiness but to salvation. He has hardly finished when he learns of Alcestis' death. Off he goes to surprise Thanatos, hardly sober, still wreathed, his tuneless song echoing yet. He makes the day his own by sharing his victory with a friend, honoring the Aphrodite of Admetus' marriage.[26]

Even Heracles at his most buffoonish slips into the paradoxical way of talking which assumes that life may not be life; even for him there is an ideal life to be sought. He states the commonplace, positive side of the proposition, in contrast to Alcestis' heroic negative statement. The ordinary man is to take what best pleasure the day may offer and not count the number or the rewards of the days to come, since he may die tomorrow. This is the exact opposite of Pheres' rule of life; the old man, who ends with a life that is no life at all, thinks always of tomorrows — how sweet, how few, they are. Heracles on the contrary says, 'Today is sweet: live as if there were no tomorrow.' The noble man is to follow the same lesson, according to Heracles' example, in a bolder and more elevated form. Heracles' victory and Alcestis' sacrifice teach him that the day's best pleasure may be an exercise of virtue, even though choosing it should mean counting the days to come at precisely naught, risking death today or fixing it for tomorrow. The difference between life and death is nominal, that between a virtuous act and a shameful one absolute.

Euripides has made of his *Alcestis* an elegant mystery play for the uninitiate, the revelation of a world in which friendship may resurrect and virtue is the key to miraculous blessedness. This saving virtue is bred in a mind that makes life and death its simultaneous guests; the virtuous man hears always the mixed strains of dirge and revelry, for the knowledge that he may die tomorrow is also the knowledge that he may be snatched from death. A man who understands what Heracles taught will not argue always from *dikê*, but will be free to perform the uncalculated act of graciousness, and such a man may attract the favor of the gods, who know how to be gracious in return. Gods do sometimes befriend mortals, for there is an aspect of divinity that interests itself in man, cutting simples for Asclepius or urging the Moirai to tipple, opposing the will of Death and the justice of a jealous Zeus. His own play becomes a final figure for what Euripides says about life under the dominion of such a company of gods, for in it tragedy, comedy, and satyr drama touch and intermingle. Death and Old Age are real, and are only temporarily defeated, but this time, at least, Heracles the satyr-savior did appear, as if in answer to the hymn addressed to him by Orphic votaries (*Orphic Hymn* 12):

> Come blessed one, purveyor of all healing means,
> Evil demons exorcise with waving wand;
> Loose your feathered arrows and harsh death remove from us.[27]

21

THE *MEDEA* OF EURIPIDES

BERNARD M. W. KNOX

In 431 BC Euripides competed against Sophocles and Euphorion with three tragedies, *Medea*, *Philoctetes*, and *Dictys*, followed by a satyr play, *Theristae*; he was awarded the third prize.[1]

But his *Medea* left a deep and lasting impression in the minds of his Athenian audience; comic parodies,[2] literary imitations,[3] and representations in the visual arts[4] reflect its immediate impact and show that the play lost none of its power to fascinate and repel as the centuries went by. It struck the age as new, but like all innovative masterpieces, it had its deep roots in tradition; it looks back to the past while it gropes for the future. In it we can see what Euripides took over from his predecessors and contemporaries, how he transformed what he learned from them, and what he invented and was to refine and develop as his own unique tragic vision in the last twenty years of his long dramatic career.

He has been fascinated by this story from the very beginning. His first offering in the Dionysiac contest (in 455 BC, only three years after the staging of Aeschylus' *Oresteia*) included the *Peliades*, the story of Medea at Iolcos, her deceitful promise to rejuvenate old Pelias, its king, and the king's death at her hands. Some time later (we do not know the date — it may have been before the *Medea* or after it),[5] Euripides produced the *Aegeus*, the story of Medea at Athens, married to old Aegeus, its king, and her unsuccessful attempt to engineer the death of his son Theseus. In 431 BC, twenty-four years after his first production, he staged the play we have, the story of Medea and Jason at Corinth.

We know that the version of the myth which he used in this play was not imposed on him. The many variants of the legend which can still be found in ancient mythographers and commentators as well as in the fragments of lost epics show that he had a wide freedom of choice.[6] One account had Medea kill her children unintentionally (she was trying to

From *Yale Classical Studies* 25 (1977), 193–225. Reprinted by permission of the author and *Yale Classical Studies*. The author has kindly allowed certain footnotes to be shortened and others to be omitted. Those referring to this essay for scholarly purposes are requested to consult the original version.

make⁻ them immortal and something went wrong with the formula);
in another the children were killed by the Corinthians in a revolt against
Medea, whom they had appointed queen of Corinth; in yet another
Medea killed Creon, left her children in the temple of Hera, and fled to
Athens — whereupon Creon's kinsmen killed the children and spread
the rumor that Medea had done it. At least two of these versions (and
probably more besides) were available to Euripides, but he made his
own by combination, addition, selection. In it, Medea, far from being
queen of Corinth, is a refugee there. Deserted by her husband, Jason,
she is to be deported, but she kills Jason's bride, the bride's father
(Creon, king of Corinth), and her own children, whose bodies she leaves
in the temple of Hera Akraia before she departs for Athens. And it seems
to be suggested by the evidence that the murder of the children by
Medea herself is Euripidean invention.[7]

Out of the old stories available to him, Euripides created a new one
— a version more shocking, more physically and psychologically violent
than anything he found in the tradition. What is even more remarkable
is the way he handles it. How was he to present such a shocking series
of actions to an Athenian audience in the theater of Dionysus?

There were several possibilities open to him. He might have made
Medea a Clytemnestra figure — a magnificent criminal whose violence
represents the primitive past of the race, posed against the civilized,
rational values of male democracy, represented in this case by Jason. He
might have created a version of the story in which Medea was punished
for her crimes and so have shown the working of the justice of the polis,[8]
represented by Creon, or of Zeus, announced by a god from the machine
— Hera, perhaps would have been appropriate, or that old standby,
Apollo. He might have presented us with a Medea who murdered her
children while insane, like Ino (who is actually referred to in the play),
or one who murdered in cold blood but was then consumed by everlasting
remorse, like Procne. But he did none of these things: what he did was,
like the endings of so many of his plays, unexpected.

The prologue introduces the situation swiftly — a wife abandoned
with her children for a royal bride in a foreign city. Medea will take no
food, listen to no comfort, no advice: she will only weep and rage. But
it soon becomes clear that she is no passive sufferer. 'I am afraid,' says
the Nurse; 'she is planning something dreadful.' As the action develops,
we begin to feel the brooding menace of the unseen figure behind the
stage door; she is planning suicide or revenge and the Nurse fears for the
children's lives. Soon we hear Medea's desperate cries from inside the
stage door, her curses, her wishes for death and general destruction.

This is no ordinary woman wronged: in fact, the stage situation may have reminded the audience of a play they had (probably) seen some years before[9] – the *Ajax* of Sophocles. There too we hear the hero's desperate and terrifying cries from inside the stage building,[10] where, like Medea, he lies, refusing food;[11] there too a woman fears for the protagonist's child (and has had it taken away to safety).[12] And there are many other resemblances. Both Ajax and Medea fear more than anything else in this world the mockery of their enemies;[13] for both of them a time limit of one day is set;[14] both in a set speech explore the possible courses of action open to them and, rejecting alternatives, decide – the one for suicide, the other for revenge.[15] And these similarities are enforced by some striking verbal parallels between the two plays.[16]

These resemblances are not coincidence. Medea, in fact, is presented to us, from the start, in heroic terms. Her language and action, as well as the familiar frame in which they operate, mark her as a heroic character,[17] one of those great individuals whose intractable firmness of purpose, whose defiance of threats and advice, whose refusal to betray their ideal vision of their own nature, were the central preoccupation of Sophoclean tragedy. The structure and language of the *Medea* is that of the Sophoclean heroic play. This is the only extant Euripidean tragedy constructed according to the model which Sophocles was to perfect in the *Oedipus Tyrannos* and which, through the influence of that supreme dramatic achievement and its exploitation by Aristotle as a paradigm, became the model for Renaissance and modern classical tragedy: the play dominated by a central figure who holds the stage throughout, who initiates and completes – against obstacles, advice and threats – the action, whether it be discovery or revenge.[18] Other Euripidean tragedies are different. *Hippolytus* is a drama with four principal characters.[19] Hecuba, who is on stage throughout *The Trojan Women*, is no dominating figure but a passive victim, as she is also in the play named after her, until she turns into a revengeful Medea figure at the end. Pentheus, Heracles, and Andromache are victims rather than actors. Electra in her own play comes nearest to Medea in stage importance, but she cannot act without Orestes, and in the *Orestes* he shares the stage with her. *Phoenissae* has no central character at all and the *Ion*, *Iphigenia in Tauris*, and *Helen* are plays of a different type, in which the 'incurable' tragic act is avoided. The *Medea* is the only Euripidean tragedy (in the modern sense of that word) which is tightly constructed around a 'hero': a central figure whose inflexible purpose, once formed, nothing can shake – a purpose which is the mainspring of the action.

Medea is presented to the audience in the unmistakable style and language of the Sophoclean hero.[20] These have been isolated and discussed elsewhere;[21] all that is necessary here is to demonstrate their presence and function in the *Medea*. She has the main characteristic of the hero, the determined resolve, expressed in uncompromising terms: the verbal adjectives *ergasteon* (791), 'the deed must be done', and *tolmeteon* (1051) 'I must dare'; the decisive futures — especially *kteno*, 'I shall kill' — this word again and again. The firmness of her resolve is phrased in the customary Sophoclean terms *dedoktai* (1236), *dedogmenon* (822) — 'my mind is made up'. She is deaf to persuasion; she will not hear, *akouei* (29). She is moved by the typical heroic passions, anger, *orge* (176 etc.), wrath, *cholos* (94 etc.). She exhibits the characteristic heroic temper daring, *tolma* (394 etc.), and rashness, *thrasos* (856 etc.). She is fearful, terrible, *deine* (44 etc.) and wild, like a beast, *agrios* (193 etc.). She is much concerned, like the heroes, for her glory (810); she will not put up with injustice (38), and with what she regards as intolerable (797). Above all, she is full of passionate intensity, that *thumos* which in her case is so marked a feature of her make-up that in her famous monologue she argues with it, pleads with it for mercy, as if it were something outside herself. Like the heroes, she feels that she has been treated with disrespect, *etimasmene* (20), *atimasas* (1354 etc.); wronged, *edikemene* (26 etc.); and insulted, *hubriz*' (603 etc.). Her greatest torment is the thought that her enemies will laugh at her, *gelos* (383 etc.). Like the Sophoclean heroes, she curses her enemies (607 etc.) while she plans her revenge. She is alone, *mone* (513) and abandoned, *eremos* (255 etc.), and in her isolation and despair she wishes for death.

Like the Sophoclean tragic hero, she resists alike appeals for moderation and harsh summonses to reason. She is admonished, *nouthetoumene* (29) by her friends but pays no more attention than a rock or the sea waves. She is begged to 'consider', *skepsai* (851), but to no avail: she cannot be persuaded, *peithesthai* (184) or ruled, *archesthai* (120). The chorus beg her as suppliants, *hiketeuomen* (854) to change her mind, but to no effect. To others her resolution seems to be stupidity, folly, *moria* (457 etc.), and self-willed stubbornness, *authadia* (621);[22] she is like a wild animal, a bull (92 etc.), a lioness (187 etc.).

As in Sophoclean heroic tragedy, there is also a secondary figure whose pliability under pressure throws the hero's unbending will into high relief. It is not, in this play, a weak sister, like Ismene or Chrysothemis, but a man, like Creon in the *Antigone*; in fact, he has the same name, Creon; he is king of Corinth. He comes on stage, his mind made up: he has proclaimed sentence of immediate exile for Medea. She must leave at once: he is afraid of her. Her eloquent appeal falls on deaf ears: his resolve, he says, is fixed, *arare* (322). She will never persuade him (325). But she does. He yields, though he knows that he is making a mistake, and gives her one more day.

However, the structure of the *Medea* does differ from that of the Sophoclean hero play in one important respect: the hero (like Clytemnestra in the *Agamemnon*) must conceal her purpose from everyone else in the play, except, of course, the chorus, whom (unlike Clytemnestra) she must win over to her side. Consequently, a characteristically Sophoclean scene is missing: the two-actor dialogue in which the heroic resolve is assailed by persuasion, threat, or both — Ismene to Antigone, Creon to Antigone, Chrysothemis to Electra, Tecmessa to Ajax. But there *is* a speech in the *Medea* which rolls out all the clichés of the appeal to reason, the summons to surrender which, in Sophocles, all the heroes have to face. It is typical of Euripides' originality, of the way he makes things new, that this speech is delivered by Medea herself.

It is her false declaration of submission to Jason, her fulsome confession that she was only a foolish emotional woman, the speech that lures him to his doom. 'I talked things over with myself,' she tells him, 'and reproached myself bitterly.' As she reports her self-rebuke, she pulls out all the stops of the Sophoclean summons to reason. 'Why do I act like a mad woman [*mainomai* 873] and show hostility to good advice [874]? Shall I not rid myself of passion [*thumou* 879]? I realize that my judgment was bad [*aboulian* 882] . . . . I raged in pointless anger [883] . . . I was mindless [*aphron* 885] . . . . I confess I was full of bad thoughts then . . . but have come to better counsel now [892–93]. My anger has subsided [898].' And later, when Jason accepts her apologies, she says, 'I shall not disobey you [*apisteso* 927]. What you did was best for me [*lōista* 935].'

Jason is understanding and sympathetic. 'I congratulate you on your present frame of mind — and I don't blame you for things past. Anger is something you have to expect from a woman. . . . But your mind has changed for the better [911].' As he turns from Medea to his sons, Euripides puts in his mouth a subtle variation on a Sophoclean theme: the threat to the hero that he or she will realize the need for surrender in time. 'You have realized what the best decision is,' he says to her, 'though it took time [912].' He has swallowed the bait — hook, line, and sinker: the way is now prepared for the murders that will wreck his life.[23]

This speech is part of Medea's grand design; these formulas of dissuasion masquerading as terms of submission are the instruments of her revenge. As if this were not a sufficiently daring adaptation of the patterns of the heroic play, Euripides presents us with another. There *is* one person who can and does pose a real obstacle to Medea's plans, who can effectively confront her with argument — Medea herself.[24] In the monologue she delivers after she hears that her fatal gifts have been delivered into the princess's hands by her children, she pleads with herself, changes her mind, and changes again and then again to return finally and firmly to her intention to kill them. When the children look at her and smile, she loses her courage. 'Farewell, my plans!' (1048). But then she recovers. 'Shall I earn the world's laughter by leaving my enemies unpunished? No, I must dare to do this!' (1049-51). Then a sudden surge of love and pity overcomes her again and she addresses herself to her own *thumos*, her passionate heroic anger, as if it were something outside herself. 'Do not do it. Let them go, hard-hearted — spare the children!' (1056-57). But her *thumos* will not relent: the children must die. In this great scene the grim heroic resolve[25] triumphs not over an outside adversary or adviser but over the deepest maternal feelings of the hero herself.

This presentation in heroic terms of a rejected foreign wife, who was to kill her husband's new wife, the bride's father, and finally her own children, must have made the audience which saw it for the first time in 431 BC a trifle uneasy. Heroes, it was well known, were violent beings and since they lived and died by the simple code 'help your friends and hurt your enemies' it was only to be expected that their revenges, when they felt themselves unjustly treated, dishonored, scorned, would be huge and deadly. The epic poems do not really question Achilles' right to bring destruction on the Greek army to avenge Agamemnon's insults, nor Odysseus' slaughter of the entire younger generation of the Ithacan aristocracy. Sophocles' Ajax sees nothing wrong in his attempt to kill the commanders of the army for denying him the armor of Achilles; his shame springs simply from his failure to achieve his bloody objective. But Medea is a woman, a wife and mother, and also a foreigner. Yet she acts as if she were a combination of the naked violence of Achilles and the cold craft of Odysseus, and, what is more, it is in these terms that the words of Euripides' play present her. 'Let no one', she says, 'think me contemptible and weak, nor inactive either, but quite the opposite — dangerous to my enemies, helpful to my friends. Such are the qualities that bring a life glory' (807 ff.). It is the creed by which Homeric and Sophoclean heroes live — and die.

She is a hero, then, but since she is also a woman, she cannot prevail by brute strength; she must use deceit.[26] She is, as she admits herself, a 'clever woman', *sophe*, and this cleverness she uses to deceive everyone in the play, bending them to her frightful purpose. Creon is tricked into giving her one day's grace; she knows that his initial bluster hides a soft heart[27] and fawns on him (her own term, *thopeusai* 368) to gain time. Aegeus is tricked into promising her asylum in Athens: tricked is the word, for if he had realized that she intended to destroy the royal house of Corinth and her own children, he would never have promised her protection. She knows this, and that is why she binds him by a solemn oath. And Jason she takes in completely by her assumption of the role of repentant wife: she showers him with such abject self-abasement, such fawning reiteration of all the male Greek clichés about women (she even says: 'A woman is female – it's her nature to weep,' 289), that one wonders how Jason can believe it. But she knows her man. 'That's the way a sensible woman *should* act,' he says (913).

And so the poisoned gifts are taken to the new bride; Medea, when she hears that they have been delivered and accepted, successfully resists the temptation to spare the children, and then, after savoring at length (1133-34) the messenger's frightful description of the poison's effects, she kills her sons. Her revenge is complete when Jason comes to save them; she holds their bodies in the chariot sent by her grandfather Helios, and, safe from Jason, taunts him with the wreck of all his hopes, his childlessness. The end of the play sees her leave to deposit the children's bodies in Hera's temple and then go off to Athens.

She triumphs.[28] She will always suffer from the memory of what she did to the children, as she grudgingly admits to Jason (1361-62),[29] but she has her full and exquisite revenge. 'These children are dead,' she says to him, 'that is what will torment you' (1370). And she escapes the consequences of her action, goes safely to Athens.

This is very unlike what happens to most Sophoclean heroes. Ajax triumphs in a way, but he is dead; Oedipus wins a kind of victory, but he is blind; Antigone's victory comes after she has hanged herself. This complete success of Medea is connected with another feature of the way she is presented which is also in sharp contrast with the Sophoclean hero. She is quite sure, from start to finish, that the gods are on her side.

All the Sophoclean heroes feel themselves, sooner or later, abandoned by gods as well as men: their loneliness is absolute, they can appeal only to the silent presence of mountains, sea, and air.[30] But Medea from her first appearance has no doubts that the gods support her cause. She appeals to Themis (ancestral law) and Artemis (woman's help in child-birth!) to witness Jason's unjust action (160); she calls on Zeus, who, she says, knows who is responsible for her sorrows (332), swears to avenge herself in the name of Hecate,[31] 'the mistress I revere above all others, my chosen helpmate' (395 ff.). She asks Jason if he thinks the same gods by whom he swore fidelity no longer reign in power (493), appeals again to Zeus (516), and calls exultantly on 'Zeus, the justice of Zeus and the light of the Sun' (764), as she sees her plans for revenge ensured by Aegeus' promise of shelter in Athens. After the murder of the children she is still confident, in her confrontation scene with Jason, that Zeus is on her side (1352), and she makes plans to deposit the bodies of her sons in the temple of Hera Akraia (1379). When Jason appeals to the avenging Erinyes and blood retribution (*Erinys . . . Dike* 1389 f.), she dismisses his claim to divine protection with scorn: 'What god or spirit listens to *your* prayers?' (1391). She never wavers from her faith that what she does has divine approval.[32] She can even say, to the messenger who brings the news from the palace which seals the fate of the children: 'These things the gods and I, with my evil thoughts, have contrived [1013–14].'

'The gods and I' — she sees herself as their instrument and associate.[33] And the play gives us no reason to think that she is wrong. On the contrary, it confirms her claim in spectacular fashion. All through the play, appeals are made to two divine beings, Earth and Sun. It is by these divinities that Aegeus is made to swear the oath that he will protect Medea from her enemies once she reaches Athens; it is to Earth and Sun that the chorus appeals at the last moment, begging them to prevent the murder of the children, and Jason, in the last scene, asks Medea how, with her children's blood on her hands, she can look at Earth and Sun. 'What Earth will do we shall not be told,'[34] but Helios, the Sun, is clearly on Medea's side. Not only are the poisoned gifts sent to the princess an inheritance from Helios (and the poison acts like a concentration of the sun's fire), but, more important, it is Helios who sends Medea the chariot on which she escapes to Athens. 'In the gods' name,' says Jason, 'let me touch the soft skin of my sons' (1402–3). But *his* appeal to the gods has no effect; 'Your words are wasted' (1404), Medea tells him, and draws away in her chariot as Jason appeals again to Zeus. The chorus ends the play with lines which appear in our manuscripts at the end of several other Euripidean plays; some critics have thought them inappropriate here,[35] but they are obviously and squarely in their right place:

> Zeus on Olympus has many things in his store-room:
> the gods bring to pass many surprising things.
> What was expected is not fulfilled.
> For the unexpected the gods find a way.
> So this story turned out.

Medea's appearance as a heroic figure, as the murderer of her children who escapes the consequences of her actions, apparently with the blessing of the gods, must have seemed to the audience surprising beyond description. Euripides himself, like the gods, has many things in his store room; he has defied expectation and found a way for the unimagined.

II

But he has another surprising thing in his store room: Medea's final

appearance. She has been on stage since near the beginning of the play;
she leaves only toward the end, when she goes through the palace door
to murder her sons. When she enters again, to face Jason, she is on the
chariot sent by Helios, her grandfather, high up in the air. This last detail
is not clearly stated in the text, but no other stage arrangement would
explain why Jason cannot reach her and must beg her to let him touch
the bodies of his sons. She must be either on the roof of the stage building
(but that would present mechanical difficulties) or in the *mechane* —
her chariot swung out over the stage area on a crane. In either case, she
is high up and out of reach. But this is the place reserved in Attic tragedy
for gods; this is not, as the chorus of the *Electra* says, the pathway of
mortals (1235-36). And as the scene progresses, this hint that she has
become something more than mortal is confirmed. Her situation, action,
and language are precisely those of the divine beings who in so many
Euripidean plays appear at the end in power to wind up the action, give
judgment, prophesy the future, and announce the foundation of a
religious ritual.[36]

From her unapproachable position on high, she interrupts and puts a
stop to the violent action of the human beings on the lower level (Jason
is trying to break down the palace door). In this she is like Apollo in
the *Orestes*, Athena in the *Ion* and *Iphigeneia in Tauris*, the Dioscuri in
Helen, and Hermes in the *Antiope*.[37] She justifies her savage revenge on
the grounds that she has been treated with disrespect and mockery
(1354-55), like Dionysus in the *Bacchae*; in this she is like Aphrodite in
the *Hippolytus* prologue, Athena in the prologue to the *Troades*. She
takes measures and gives orders for the burial of the dead (her own sons
1378 ff. and the princess 1394) like Thetis in the *Andromache*, Athena
in the *Suppliants* and *Erechtheus*, Hermes in the *Antiope*, and the Dioscuri in the *Electra*. She prophesies the future (the ignominious death
of Jason) like Thetis in the *Andromache*, Athena in the *Suppliants* and
Ion, the Dioscuri in *Electra* and *Helen*, Apollo in *Orestes*, and Dionysus
in the *Bacchae*. She announces the foundation of a cult (for her own
children in Corinth 1328 ff.) like Artemis in the *Hippolytus* and Athena
in the *Iphigenia in Tauris* and *Erechtheus*. She announces her departure
and destination (1384 ff.) like the Dioscuri in *Electra* and Apollo in
Orestes.

And Medea speaks in phrases which recur in the pronouncements of
the gods from the machine. 'Why are you trying to break down the
doors with crowbars?' she asks Jason. 'Stop!' *pausai* (1319). 'Why are
you directing a pursuit?' Athena asks Thoas at the end of the *Iphigenia
in Tauris*. 'Stop!' *pausai* (1437). So Apollo speaks to Menelaus in the
Orestes: *pausai* (1625). This is not the only command Medea issues from

the *mechane*: like the gods she is prone to imperatives. She dismisses Jason. 'Go!' she says to him, 'and bury your wife,' *steiche* (1394). So Athena in the *Ion* dismisses Ion and Creusa: 'Go!' *steicheth'* (1616), and the Dioscuri in *Electra* send Orestes on his way to Athens with the same word: 'Go!' *steich'* (1343).

Medea shows the same merciless, even vindictive, attitude toward Jason that characterizes the Euripidean gods. 'The children are dead. This is what will give you pain,' she says to him, using the same word, *dēxetai* (1370), that Artemis uses in the *Hippolytus* when she rebukes Theseus: 'Do my words pain you?' *daknei* (1313). Like Artemis, she holds out the prospect of more suffering to come. 'Listen to what comes next — you will cry out in even greater agony,' says Artemis (1314), and Medea tells Jason: 'You are not sorrowing yet. Wait until you are old' (1396). A statement of Artemis about the ways of gods with men sums up what Medea might have claimed: 'Those who are evil we destroy, children and home and all' (1340-41) — except that Medea's more exquisite revenge is to leave Jason alive and alone amid the ruin of his hopes for his sons and his marriage.

Medea is presented to us not only as a hero, but also, at the end of the play, by her language, action, and situation, as a *theos* or at least something more than human. She does not start that way, but that is how it ends. Ends, that is to say, in *this* play: she is going to Athens, as she tells us, and what form she will assume there we are not told. It is not likely that Euripides' audience was worried about that point: they must have been sufficiently taken aback by the appearance of Medea, the murderer of her sons, in the 'habiliments of the goddess', assuming the attitude and using the language of the stage *theos*.

It is very hard to imagine what it meant to them (and what it should mean to us), for there is no parallel to it in Attic drama. Peleus in the *Andromache* is told that he will become a *theos* (1256) and is given a rendezvous for his apotheosis (1265 ff.), but it does not take place on stage. Helen, at the end of the play which bears her name (1667), is given a similar assurance (not fulfilled on stage) and in the *Orestes* she actually appears on the right hand of Apollo, on her way to rejoin Castor and Polydeuces in the heavens (1631 ff.), but she does not say anything. There *are* two cases in which a human being at the end of the play performs one of the functions of the *deus ex machina*. In the *Heraclidae*, Eurystheus, on the point of death, gives instructions for his burial (1036) and reveals a Delphic oracle which gives his buried corpse protective powers for Athens in future wars (1032 ff.). (However, he expressly forbids a cult of his grave 1040-41.) In the *Hecuba*, the blinded Polymestor prophesies the transformation of Hecuba and the deaths of Agamemnon and Cassandra (1259 ff.). These are faint and partial approximations, but there is nothing remotely comparable to Medea's full exercise of all the functions of the *theos* and her triumphant godlike departure through the air.

The effect of this investment of Medea with all the properties and functions of stage divinity must have been to bring home to the audience the conviction that Medea is not merely an individual woman wronged and revengeful; she is, at the end, a figure which personifies something permanent and powerful in the human situation, as Aphrodite clearly does, and Dionysus also. These two were Olympian deities, worshipped in state cult and portrayed in temple sculpture, but the Greek imagination created many other *theoi*, was apt, in fact, to see a *theos* in every corner. 'All things are full of gods,' said Thales, and from Hesiod on through the fifth and fourth centuries, Greek literature presents us with *theoi* who represent almost every phase of human activity and circumstance — poverty, plague, reputation, force, helplessness, ambition, time, and sorrow, to name just a few. A sentence of Menander gives a clue to what lies behind the proliferating theogony: adding a new *theos* to the unofficial pantheon — shamelessness (*Anaideia*) — he says: 'Whatever has power is now worshipped as a god.'[38]

Medea, in her last appearance, certainly has power but it is not easy to define exactly what she represents. There is a *theos* in Aeschylus which bears some resemblance to her: the house-destroying *theos* of the *Seven Against Thebes*, (720-21). But this *theos* is almost immediately (723) identified as an *Erinys*, and that will not do for Medea; in fact, as a spiller of kindred blood, she should be their allotted victim, as Jason vainly hopes she will be (1389). Revenge — *dike* in the simplest sense — certainly has something to do with it, but she is more than Lesky's 'Dämon der Rache';[39] there would have been no need to give her the style and appurtenances of a *theos* for that — as seems clear from the figure of Hecuba in the last scenes of the play which bears her name. Perhaps the appearance of this ferocious incarnation of vengeance in the place of an Olympian god is meant to reinforce in the audience's mind that disconcerting sense of the disintegration of all normal values which the play as a whole produces, to emphasize visually that moral chaos which the chorus sang of earlier:

The spell cast by sworn oaths has faded; respect for others no longer remains anywhere in Greece, it has taken wing up to the sky. (439 ff.).

But Medea as *theos* must also represent some kind of irresistible power, something deeply rooted in the human situation, as dangerous as it is universal. It has something to do with revenge for betrayal, but its peculiar ferocity must stem from the fact that before she was a hero and through her action became a (stage) *theos*, she was a woman.

It is clear from Medea's very first speech that this strange drama, which uses Sophoclean heroic formulas to produce a most un-Sophoclean result, is grounded in the social reality and problems of its own time. There can be no doubt, to anyone who reads it without prejudice, that the *Medea* is very much concerned with the problem of women's place in human society. I do not of course mean to revive the idea, fashionable in the early years of this century, that Euripides is a feminist.[40] Even though tradition has it that speeches from the *Medea* (in the translation of Gilbert Murray) were read aloud at suffragette meetings (a careful selection, no doubt), it is not likely that Sylvia Pankhurst would have admitted Medea to membership in her league. Euripides is concerned in this play not with progress or reform[41] but (just as in the *Hippolytus* and the *Bacchae*) with the eruption in tragic violence of forces in human nature which have been repressed and scorned, which in their long-delayed breakout exact a monstrous revenge. The *Medea* is not about woman's rights; it is about woman's wrongs, those done to her and by her.

III

This aspect of the play is usually ignored or dismissed — on the grounds that Medea is atypical: she cannot be considered a figure relevant to the problems of Athenian society because she is an oriental barbarian and also a witch.[42] 'Because she was a foreigner', says Page, 'she could kill her children: because she was a witch she could escape in a magic chariot.'[43] The second half of this magisterial pronouncement kills two birds with one stone; in addition to denying the play any relevance to Athenian society, it also disposes of the awkward questions raised by Medea's appearance as the *theos* on the machine — she is just a witch on a glorified Hellenic broomstick. Since Page gives no other evidence that Medea is a witch, what he seems to mean is rather: 'since she can escape in a magic chariot, Medea is a witch.' But supernatural winged chariots are hardly an identifying mark of witches: they are properties, in Greek mythology, of gods, of Apollo, of the Attic divinity Triptolemos, above all of Helios, the sun (who is, of course, Medea's grandfather). And yet Medea as a witch or sorceress appears as a regular feature of most discussions of the play.[44] There are of course passages in ancient literature which present us with lurid pictures of Medea as a figure resembling our conception of a witch. In the following lines, for example, she addresses her prayer to Hecate:

For thee, my hair flowing free as is the custom of my race, I have paced
the sacred groves barefoot. I have called down rain from dry clouds,
driven the waves to the sea-bottom . . . changed the order of the seasons
. . . brought wheat to harvest in the winter time.

Another poet gives us a detailed descripton of the witches' brew she
cooks for old Aeson:

And all the while the brew in the bronze cauldron boiled and frothed
white: in it were herb-roots gathered from Thessaly's lonely vales . . . and
hoar-frost taken at the full of the moon, a hoot-owl's wings and flesh, a
werewolf's entrails also, and the fillet of fenny snake, the liver of the
stag.

The first of these passages is from the *Medea* of the Roman dramatist
Seneca[45] and the second from the *Metamorphoses* of Ovid.[46] It is, in
fact, in the Roman poets of the first centuries BC and AD (Horace, Virgil,
and Lucan) that something resembling our conception of a witch first
appears, to give literary shape to the medieval witch of Christian times
who serves the devil instead of Hecate but claims the same powers to
raise the dead, curse, blight, transform, and prophesy. From the contents
of Ovid's cauldron to that of Shakespeare,

> Finger of birth-strangled babe
> ditch-delivered by a drab
> make the gruel thick and slab,[47]

there runs an unbroken line. But it does not go back as far as the fifth
century BC. The term 'witch', with its medieval overtones of black magic,
ugliness, and malevolence, has no place in a description of Euripides'
Medea.

There is, however, one incident in Medea's career, well-known to the
fifth-century audience, which, though it does not justify the anachronistic use of the term 'witchcraft', does associate her with the use of magic
— her deliberately unsuccessful attempt to rejuvenate old Pelias by
cutting him into pieces and boiling him in a pot. Interestingly enough,
this is not magical practice, but a deliberate murder which uses other
people's belief in magic to mask its real nature. Still, it is at any rate a
magical context for Medea and it was a popular story; Sophocles dramatized it in his *Rhizotomoi*,[48] and it was the subject of the *Peliades* at the
very beginning of Euripides' career as a dramatist. It would therefore
have been very easy for him to emphasize this aspect of Medea's action:
the material was familiar, needing only an emphasis on the dramatist's
part to bring it to the surface of the audience's memory and cast a baleful spotlight on Medea the sorceress. But he hardly mentions it, and

when he does, it is in the blandest of terms. It is described simply as a murder — 'I killed Pelias, the most painful way to die, at the hands of his own daughters' (486 ff.) — without any of the sensational details. In fact, when one thinks how naturally a scathing reference to this episode would have fitted into Jason's desperate invective at the end of the play,[49] it seems as if Euripides was doing his best to avoid the subject altogether.

And in any case, in the play Euripides wrote, Medea has no magical powers at all. Until she is rescued by the god Helios, and is herself transformed into some kind of superhuman being, she is merely a helpless betrayed wife and mother with no protection of any kind. She has only two resources, cunning and poison.

Perhaps it is the use of poison which has led so many critics to use the word 'witch'. For the only fifth-century Greek word for witch that the dictionaries can suggest is *pharmakis*, which means of course a woman who deals with love charms, drugs, and poisons. This certainly applies to Euripides' Medea, but it has nothing to do with witchcraft. Love charms, drugs, and poisons are the age-old last recourse of the unloved or vengeful wife in fifth-century Athens, modern Egypt, nineteenth-century India, or for that matter Victorian England — everywhere in fact before the scientific detection of poisons made these things too dangerous (for the poisoner) to use. And Medea is not the only *pharmakis* in Athenian literature. Deianira in Sophocles' *Trachiniae* tries to win back her husband's love with a love charm which, like Medea's gift to the princess, is a poisoned robe (and has the same effect on its victim).[50] The stepmother, in Antiphon's speech, gives her husband a love charm (drinkable this time) which kills him; the prosecution claims that was exactly what she intended.[51] The Athenian princess Creusa (no barbarian witch this one) uses in Euripides' *Ion* a poison just as magical as Medea's[52] to try to kill the boy she thinks is her husband's bastard son. All three of these ladies use poison, intentionally or not, to redress the balance of their unequal struggle with their husbands, but no one dreams of calling them witches.

Of course, Greek men did not approve of such feminine initiatives, but they did not invest them with the supernatural and diabolical associations of the modern word 'witch'. In any case, the particular function of the medieval witch — cursing, producing barrenness in women, a murrain on the cattle, disease and death for whole families — was in the ancient world not the province of specialists but the normal recourse of ordinary individuals. This is all too clear to anyone who studies the hate-filled inscriptions known as *defixiones*, which show, from the fifth century on, ordinary persons in Greece and elsewhere, solemnly recording on tablets of lead or pieces of broken pottery their spells for the painful destruction of their neighbors and business rivals. 'I call down on An-drotion a fever to recur every fourth day until he dies,' runs one of the milder specimens —scratched on a fifth-century Athenian potsherd.[53]

Medea then, in the body of the play, has no supernatural powers or equipment. All she has is a very powerful poison, but this merely puts her in the same class as Deianira and Creusa. These are of course not the parallels cited by the proponents of Medea the witch. They cite Circe and Hecate. But Hecate is a great goddess and of course Circe is a god-dess too, as Homer plainly tells us.[54] The Medea of the body of the play is not comparable in any way with these powerful figures.

But if to call Medea a witch falsifies the situation, she is also, according to many modern critics, a barbarian, an Oriental, and therefore equally irrelevant to the problems of Greek society. This case is most eloquently argued by Page.

She is just such a woman as his audience would expect a foreign princess to be. She has nearly all the features of the type — unrestrained excess in lamentation, a readiness to fawn on authority, the powers of magic, childlike surprise at falsehoods and broken promises. . . . It was natural then that Medea should be unrestrained in the expression of her sorrow, like a Phrygian or a Mysian . . . she was like a wild beast in her grief and anger. And then in a moment she changes her mood and cringes before the King . . . a second time . . . before Aegeus, a third time before Jason. Respect for authority was the primary cause. The Oriental was accustomed to despots whose word was law. . . . Broken promises Medea finds it . . . difficult to forgive. . . . The contrast of truthful barbarian and lying Greek had long been a commonplace.[55]

The case could not be more eloquently stated, but it is flawed. Medea is indeed unrestrained in the expression of sorrow, but the comparison should be 'like Ajax, Odysseus, Achilles, Heracles'.[56] She is compared to a wild beast, but so, sooner or later, are all the Sophoclean heroes.[57] The way she fawns on Creon, Aegeus, and Jason has nothing at all to do with respect for authority; she is deceiving them all, and two of them she is luring to their ruin.[58] As for her 'childish surprise at falsehoods and broken promises', this is a trait she shares (apart from the prejudicial adjective) with Creusa, Philoctetes, and of course the Greek chorus of the *Medea*.

Page finds that 'above all the inhuman quality of the child-murderess was a typically foreign quality. The chorus could think of only one other example in the legends of Greece — Ino' (though, as he points out in a note, 'they might have added at least Agave and Procne'). But Page does not produce any eastern stories which will serve as cogent parallels.

In fact, as an example of the 'appalling cruelty' of 'foreign countries', he cites Astyages, who 'set a Thyestean feast before Harpagos'. But the adjective 'Thyestean' gives the game away – that's a *Greek* story! – and the list of Persian atrocities which follows contains nothing which cannot be paralleled, or for that matter bettered, from Greek myth and history.[59]

'No *Greek* woman would have had the heart to do what she has done'; Page quotes Jason to sum up his case. But dramatic characters do not necessarily speak for their creator. And this speech is neatly cancelled out by one of Thoas', the barbarian king in the same dramatist's *Iphigenia in Tauris*. Informed that the captured Orestes has murdered his mother, he exclaims (using exactly the same verb as Jason, *etlē*) 'Apollo! Not even among the barbarians would anyone have the heart to do what he has done' (1174).

In any case, there is no suggestion in the play that anyone regards Medea as a barbarian, except of course, in the end, Jason. The chorus of Corinthian women fully approve of her first announcement that she plans revenge on her husband (267-68). When she makes clear that this means death not only for Jason but also for the king of Corinth and his daughter, they raise no objections. In fact, in the choral ode which follows they sing exultantly of honor coming for the female sex. When she tells them that her plans have changed – she will now kill the princess, 'whoever touches her', and also Jason's sons – they cry out in protest. But it is only the murder of the children which appalls them. Their protest brushed aside, they say only that she will be the unhappiest among women. Where they could have intervened decisively – the scene in which Medea entraps Jason by feigned humility – they remain silent. Finally, after listening to the messenger's ghastly account of the deaths of the king and his daughter, their only comment is 'It seems as if heaven today were bringing much evil on Jason – as he deserves!' (1231-32).

The chorus obviously feel that Medea's situation might well be their own: as far as they are concerned, she speaks like and for them, and when after the offstage murder of the children they sing their antistrophe, far from suggesting that she is a witch and oriental barbarian (and surely this was the place to make Page's point), they find a parallel in their own Greek tradition. 'Only one woman, only one, have I heard of who in time past raised her hand against her children. It was Ino, driven mad by the gods' (1282 ff.). The foreignness of Medea was fixed in the legend and it suited Euripides' purpose, since it made possible the liquid fire and the chariot of the sun, but Euripides' Medea, in her thought, speech, and action is as Greek as Jason, or rather, as Ajax and Achilles.

IV

But she is a woman and her first speech, that of a woman speaking to women, exploits and appeals to their feelings of sympathy. It is of course one of the most famous speeches in Greek tragedy. No more howls of despair, or threats of suicide — she comes out of the house to win the support of the chorus for her still nebulous plan for revenge. She is apologetic, conciliatory, a foreigner who must carefully observe the proprieties. But her life, she says, has been destroyed; her husband, who was everything to her, has turned out to be the vilest of men.

'Of all the creatures that have breath and intelligence, we women are the most afflicted.' We buy our husbands with our dowry — her argument proceeds — not knowing if they will be good or bad, go into a new home unprepared for the new life. If we work hard and make a success of it, we're lucky; if not, death would be better. The man, when he tires of our company, can go out for distraction; we are forced to keep our eyes steadily on one single human being. They say we live at home in safety, while *they* fight the wars — what fools! I'd rather stand in the battle line three times than go through child-bearing once.

It is magnificent rhetoric, and it wins their heart. But it is not, as has so often been claimed, *just* rhetoric. It has its vital function in the construction of the drama, but it must also reflect some contemporary reality, for dramatists, especially the greatest dramatists, are not philosophers, not original thinkers; they reflect and use, dramatize and intensify, the thought and feeling of their time. And in fact there are many signs that in the intellectual ferment of late fifth-century Athens, the problem of women's role in society and the family was, like everything else, a subject for discussion and reappraisal. In Euripides' *Melanippe Desmotis*, for example, someone (presumably the heroine) makes a long polemical speech demonstrating woman's moral and religious superiority to man (Page, *GLP* 112). The *Lysistrata* of Aristophanes is of course a hilarious comedy, but it has a deeply serious undercurrent of feeling, and the heroine of the play, the woman who organizes her sex on both sides to stop the war, is wholly sympathetic — it is quite clear that her creator admired her. J. H. Finley long ago drew attention to the resemblances (some of them verbal) between Medea's speech and the arguments against marriage set forth (from the man's point of view) by Antiphon the sophist.[60] And one cannot help suspecting that much later, Plato, when he says in the *Republic* that to divide mankind into male and female for the purposes of public life or education or anything, except the begetting and bearing of children, is just as absurd as to divide it into the long-haired and the bald,[61] may well be adapting to his own purpose, as he so often does, ideas that were first put into circulation by the sophistic radicals of the fifth century.

Even if it is conceded that the role of women in family and society was a problem under discussion in fifth-century Athens, it may be objected that it was a theme a tragic poet might well avoid, and that even if he did choose to handle it, he would never take as his protagonist a woman who butchered her own sons. Yet this same strange combination of infanticide and programmatic speech about the lot of women appears in another tragedy produced before 414 (how many years before, we do not know).[62] Its author is none other than Sophocles. His *Tereus* told the story of the Athenian princess Procne, married to Tereus, king of Thrace. She persuaded him to bring her sister Philomela from Athens to join her. Tereus, on the way home, raped Philomela, and then cut out her tongue so that she could not denounce him. But Philomela wove the story of the outrage on a piece of embroidery and so Procne learned the truth. She killed her son by Tereus (his name was Itys), cut up the flesh, cooked it, and served it up to Tereus who ate it. The gods, in pity and disgust, changed all three of them into birds: Tereus to a hoopoe, Philomela to a swallow, and Procne into a nightingale, whose song is a perpetual mourning for Itys.

This metamorphosis almost certainly did not take place on stage (though Tereus in *The Birds* of Aristophanes complains that Sophocles gave him a beak), and in fact we have very little idea of how Sophocles treated this horrendous tale. But among the few fragments that survive there is one speech of Procne, the wronged wife, which runs as follows:[63]

Now separated (from my family), I am nothing. Many a time I have observed that in this case our sex, the female sex, is nothing. When we are children, in our father's home, our life is the most pleasant in the world; young girls grow up in thoughtless delight. But when we reach maturity and intelligence, we are expelled, bought and sold, far away from the gods of our fathers and from our parents, some to barbarians, some to houses where everything is alien, others to houses where they meet with hostility. But all this, when one night has joined us to our husband, we must acquiesce in, and pretend that all is well.

We do not know the context of this speech but its content is astonishingly close to Medea's opening address to the chorus, and it is made by a woman who, like Medea — but in even more gruesome circumstances — kills her child to punish her husband. The attribution of such sentiments to two such similar characters by two different playwrights suggests that the lot of women was, in late fifth-century Athens, very much a question of the day, and also a subject that fascinated the tragic poets.

Even those who recognize that Medea's speech is not merely the rhetoric of an oriental witch but a reflection of Athenian social conditions, usually tamp down its explosive potential by explaining that since women in fifth-century Athens (unlike women today) were confined to the home, children, and servants, excluded from active, social, economic, and political life, some such protest was only natural in the work of an intellectual dramatist. Though this view of woman's lowly position in fifth-century Athens has been doubted by influential scholars in recent years,[64] it seems to me, on the whole, to be fairly close to the truth. But what is no longer true is the implied comparison which makes our own society look extremely advanced in this matter and permits smug and carefully qualified understanding of Medea's protest as a historical curiosity. For our own complacency about the freedom of women in modern industrial democracy has been exploded by the literature of the militant women's movement of the last decade. In fact, almost everything the play says about women's position in society is still relevant (except perhaps for the dowry, but that is still an important matter in France, Italy, and, above all, in Greece), and the startling universality of Euripides' play is clear from the fact that it says some things that do not seem to have occurred to anyone again[65] until Simone de Beauvoir wrote *Le Deuxième Sexe*.

Medea's speech wins over the chorus, but now she has to deal with Creon and his sentence of immediate expulsion. He is afraid of her, and one thing which contributes to his fear is the fact that, as he says himself, she is a clever woman (285).[66] 'Clever' is not an adequate translation of *sophe* — but then, there isn't one. It is a word used in the fifth century to describe not only the skill of the artisan and the poet, not only the wisdom won by experience and reflection, but also the new intellectual, enlightened outlook of the great sophistic teachers and the generation they had taught. This is why Creon fears her; it is on this point that she must reassure him, and she does. She admits that she is *sophe* — an intellectual, a person of great capacity — but points out that it has not done her any good. She speaks in generalities, but it is clear enough what she is talking about. Men distrust superior intelligence in general, but they really fear and hate it in a woman. *Sophos*, a clever man, is bad enough, but *sophe* — a clever woman!

This is not the first time, Creon — it's one of many — that my reputation thwarts and harms me. No one who has his wits about him should have his children taught to be unusually clever (*sophous*). They will be called lazy, indolent, and, worse than that, they'll win the jealous hatred of their fellow-citizens. If you offer new and clever ideas to fools, they'll think you are good for nothing, not clever. And then again, if the city

at large ranks you above the recognized intellectuals, *they*'ll be your
bitter enemies. This is what has happened to me, exactly this. I am
clever; some hate and envy me; others find me withdrawn, others just
the opposite, and still others offensive. I am not so clever.

These lines have sometimes been seen as Euripides' bitter reflections on
his own isolation as an advanced and intellectual poet. There is much
truth in this view, but the lines are also Medea's, the complaint of a
woman of great intellectual capacity who finds herself excluded from
the spheres of power and action.

  She wins her one day's delay from Creon and tells the chorus her
plans; so far, they do not include the murder of the children. The chorus
evidently approve, for they plunge straight into the great ode which
celebrates the new day coming for the female sex.

> The waters of the sacred rivers run upstream;
> the right order of all things is reversed.
> Now it is *men* who deal in treachery:
> now covenants sealed in heaven's name are worthless.

So much for Jason's betrayal. But they go on.

> Legends now shall change direction,
> Woman's life have glory.
> Honor comes to the female sex.
> Woman shall be a theme for slanderous tales no more.

> The songs of poets from bygone times shall cease
> to harp on our faithlessness.
> It was not to our minds that Phoebus, lord of melody,
> granted the power to draw heavenly song from the lyre:
> for if so, we would have chanted
> our own hymns of praise
> to answer the race of man.

> Time in its long passage has much to tell
> of our destiny as of theirs.

  This is an extraordinary passage. All the songs, the stories, the whole
literary and artistic tradition of Greece, which had created the lurid
figures of the great sinners, Clytemnestra, Helen, and also the desirable
figures (from the male point of view) of faithful Penelope and Andromache — all of it, Hesiod's catalogues of scandalous women, Semonides'
rogues' gallery of women compared to animals, is dismissed; it was all
written by men. The chorus has suddenly realized the truth contained
in the Aesopian story of the man and the lion who argued about which
species was superior.[67] Shown as proof of man's dominance a gravestone

on which was carved a picture of a man downing a lion, the lion replied: 'If lions could carve sculptures, you would see the lion downing the man.'

Xenophanes had remarked that if cows, horses, and lions had hands and could paint pictures and carve statues, they would have made gods looking like themselves. It took Euripides to apply the revolutionary implications of that statement to the relation between men and women. 'Legends now shall change direction; woman's life have glory,' sings the chorus, but the future tense is unnecessary. Euripides' play itself is the change of direction.[68]

For though he has spared us no detail of the hideous revenge Medea exacts from her enemies, he has presented that revenge in heroic terms, as if she were not a woman but an Achilles or Ajax. She has no doubts about the rightness of her course – her one moment of hesitation she dismisses as cowardice. Like Achilles in his rage against Hector, she surpasses the bounds of normal human conduct: Achilles wishes that his spirit (*thumos*) would drive him to strip Hector's flesh from his body and eat it raw, and he does treat his enemy's body shamefully. Medea kills her sons to make Jason a lonely, childless man. The one is as heroic, and tragic, as the other.

But Achilles relents. Medea does not. Her final words to Jason are full of contempt, hatred, and vindictive triumph: her rage is fiercer than the rage of Achilles, even of Ajax: it has in the end made her something more, and less, than human, something inhuman, a *theos*.

But this was only to be expected. For Ajax and Achilles have run their full course as men in the world of men, earned their share of glory, used to the full the power and skill that was theirs, before their time came to die. But Medea is a woman: no matter how great her gifts, her destiny is to marry, bear and raise children, go where her husband goes, subordinate her life to his. Husband, children, this is all she has; and when Jason betrays her, the full force of that intellect and energy, which has nowhere else to go, is turned against him.

One passage in their last confrontation is revealing. 'Did you really think it right to kill them,' he asks her, 'just because of what goes on in bed?' (*lechous*, 1367). And she answers: 'Do you think that is a small suffering for a woman?' It is a great suffering – for she has nothing else. It was to this marriage that she devoted all the courage, skill, and intellect she possessed – to save Jason in Colchis, to murder Pelias, for his sake, in Iolcos; to this marriage she has devoted all her energy, all her power. She could have been a queen, and who knows what besides, in her own country; she gave it up for her marriage. And when that was taken away from her, the energy she had wasted on Jason was tempered to a deadly instrument to destroy him. It became a *theos*, relentless, merciless force, the unspeakable violence of the oppressed and betrayed, which, because it has been so long pent up, carries everything before it to destruction, even if it destroys also what it loves most.

22

ON EURIPIDES' *MEDEA*

EILHARD SCHLESINGER

I

In the past twenty years critics have fastened their attention upon the great monologue of Medea (1021-80) and found therein the essence of the tragedy. This speech is undoubtedly the drama's poetic culmination, but at the same time we should realize that this is not the whole play but only one of several speeches of the protagonist. We are dealing with the words in the fifth *episode* which Medea directs first to her children and the chorus, but then more and more to herself. The structure and style of this speech has been brilliantly studied by Schadewaldt.[1] The children return from Creusa to whom they have given the deadly gifts in accordance with their mother's plan. Medea sees that her revenge has begun to materialize, that now it will inevitably take the course which she herself had determined, and that the fate of her children has thereby been irrevocably decided. Yet at the same time the sight of her children makes her also feel the whole monstrosity of her design.

Because actors wore masks and performed at a great distance from the audience, an ancient dramatist could not convey his meaning through the sort of facial expression, which would be effective in the cinema today. Euripides, however, in a masterly fashion is able to achieve the same effect through the words of the heroine: 'Why, children, do you look upon me with your eyes?' cries Medea (1040 f.), 'why do you smile so sweetly that last smile of all?' They have carried out their task and now must inevitably die. At this point her maternal instincts rebel once more, and in the ensuing verses of the monologue we find two Medeas opposing one another, or rather the two forces that are fighting for control over her: the *bouleumata* 'reason' and the *thymos* 'passion.' The opposition is so strong that at the climax of the soliloquy Medea

Originally published in *Hermes* xciv (Jan. 1966), pp. 26-53. Translated and slightly abridged by Walter Moskalew in *Euripides: A Collection of Critical Essays* (Prentice-Hall 1968), pp. 70-89. By permission.

plainly identifies herself with the *bouleumata*, while the *thymos* becomes a second person whom she resists and addresses in the vocative: 'You must not do these things! Poor heart, let them go, have pity upon the children' (1056 ff.).

The word *thymos* here certainly means passion or a passionate temperament — a usage also found among Pre-Socratic philosophers like Heraclitus and Democritus.[2] Yet we should not overlook the fact that this passage, despite its strongly rhetorical coloration, is nevertheless a transformation of an old poetic device.[3] Even in the *Iliad* a hero addresses his 'proud spirit.'[4] But here *thymos* is not unbridled emotion, what Plato calls *thymoeidês*, nor do the *bouleumata* stand in direct opposition to it as a rational principle, in the manner of the charioteer in the *Phaedrus* who keeps a tight rein on the two horses, *thymos* and *epithymia*.[5] For Medea at one point refers to her revenge plan as *bouleumata* (1044) and then later uses the same term for her thoughts opposing the revenge and especially the murder of her children (1079). This word therefore can not refer to a specific part of the soul or a specific psychic force.[6] *Bouleumata* are rather thoughts, considerations, or plans that serve various and even opposing aspects of the soul. Nor should one regard *thymos* as a narrowly psychological term, for the old meaning it has in epic poetry — vitality, vital energy — is still strongly felt.

Medea is determined to act; she has not merely thought of it, nor has she struggled to the decision. In a sense the revenge is imposed upon her by her own nature. She must will it of necessity, and this she knows very well. Even before the great monologue begins, the revenge is already a closed matter, and so is the murder of her children, for *this* is the essence of her revenge. But it is very important that she herself come to grips with this fact. The force within Medea that reacts to this necessity is not an opposing will, but rather a simple longing for happiness struggling against a destiny that has forced her to perform deeds of superhuman proportion, 'heroic' deeds in the Greek sense of the word. What is said here in the language of the latter half of the fifth century differs very little from the sentiments expressed in Hector's monologue in *Iliad* XXII and in the great speech of Achilles in *Iliad* IX. It has therefore been incorrectly maintained that in this monologue Medea struggles with the decision to murder her children, that the tragic conflict of the whole drama lies essentially in the assault of passion on her maternal feelings, which here in the monologue finally impels her to decide to kill her children. Such is generally the view of those who adhere to the theory that this is 'psychological drama.' Yet the interpretation of their opponents is equally unsatisfactory, even though we cannot deny that they have helped interpret the tragedy by vigorously pointing out certain inconsistencies.

Zürcher sees in Medea's monologue a proof of his theory that the Euripidean characters are not psychologically consistent creations.[6a] He feels that Medea's motivation to kill her children is complex; that it is not *exclusively* her innate passions which drive her to this, for she herself speaks of her children's death as a *necessity*. Euripides presumably had joined two motifs: infanticide as both *revenge* and *inevitability*. In the second part of the monologue, as the heroine gradually comes to her senses, she says (1062 f.): 'Force in every way must have it they must die, and since this must be so, then I, their mother, shall kill them.' That these verses create a problem of interpretation is of course no new discovery. In addition to this they are also repeated in 1240 f. Most editors, among them Page in the latest edition of his commentary, simply bracket them. The question belongs first of all to the realm of verse repetitions in our text of Euripides, and it has in fact been already examined in that context.[7] We also pass over the textual problem, which we can do more readily, because bracketing only lessens the difficulty pointed out by Zürcher, but does not remove it altogether. These verses certainly remain in the speech which Medea delivers at the end of this *episode*, when she prepares to go inside and actually carry out her plan (1240 f.). Admittedly this is somewhat less awkward than having the motifs of *revenge* and *inevitability* placed side by side, but the problem can in no way be eliminated through brackets. *At least once* in this scene Medea maintains that in every way it is inevitable that her children die, in which case it is better that *she* rather than her enemies kill them. She herself expresses this thought for the first time here, but it is essentially what the chorus had already said at the beginning of the fourth *stasimon* (976 f.): 'Now there is no hope left for the children's lives. Now there is none. They are walking already to murder.' If Zürcher's assertion were correct, that hereby a new motif for the death of the children is introduced, then Medea's words could only have the following meaning: Although at one time I have toyed with the thought of killing my children, it was no absolute decision. But now, when I see them before me, I understand that I cannot do such a thing. I shall let them live — take them with me to Athens, where they will further cheer me. But no, it is too late for that. They have already brought the deadly gifts to the king's daughter and have thereby become murderers in the eyes of the Corinthians. By letting them live I shall only deliver them to the vengeance of my enemies. The deed has inevitably sealed their doom.

Yet such an interpretation of the monologue is certainly false. It is difficult to see why an invocation to the avenging spirits of Hades (1059) should introduce the idea of inevitability, if inevitability does not motivate the vengeance, but is rather an unforeseen accident. More important and decisive is another consideration. We should ask ourselves why the children must necessarily fall into the hands of the Corinthians. Medea had never doubted that she would be able to save herself after carrying out the deed. Her only question, before the appearance of Aegeus, was where she would flee and what would become of her. Here in the monologue she does in fact contemplate taking her children with her to Athens. It is indeed possible to save them, in which case we can speak neither of the 'inevitability' of their death, nor of a juxtaposition of two opposing motifs, unless we wish to maintain that Euripides had fused two different accounts of the myth. Indeed there did exist a version where Medea's children were killed by the Corinthians.[8] This variant must have been the origin of the festival that is mentioned in the *exodos* of the tragedy (1381 ff.). Yet it is highly unlikely that Euripides should have arbitrarily chosen discordant motifs from different traditions.

Actually we are not at all dealing with two separate elements: infanticide as *revenge* and *inevitability*. The death of Medea's children is inevitable because it is a necessary part of her vengeance on Jason, which is also inevitable because Medea *must* revenge herself, although here it is better not to speak of a psychological need for vengeance. We cannot resolve this question by an interpretation of the monologue alone, for the monologue itself can be fully understood only when viewed in the larger perspective of the play. Then the objections raised against the last twenty verses will also disappear.[9]

II

To be able to picture the tragedy in its totality, let us follow Goethe's advice and start by examining *how* the play is constructed. This question will be simplified if we consider more closely two things which had already been noticed and criticized by Aristotle, who twice in the *Poetics* finds fault with the dramatic technique of the *Medea*. In the first instance (1454 b 1) he deals in general terms with the *lusis*, the unravelling of the plot, and demands that it should follow naturally from the action of the play. For this reason he considers it improper to resolve the complications of a drama through unexpected external interventions for which the audience has not been prepared in the course of the action. This kind of ending he calls *lusis apo mēchanēs*, or *deus ex machina* as we usually term it.[10] As an example of this faulty *lusis apo mēchanēs* he cites the *Medea*. This criticism can refer only to the sun-god's dragon-chariot, in which the heroine escapes the fury and vengeance of Jason. It is indeed strange that Aristotle should have chosen this particular play as an example, for there are many more obvious instances of *deus ex machina* in Attic tragedy. The intervention of Helios to send his granddaughter the chariot must have appeared especially arbitrary and artificial to him. He must also have had the impression that this kind of departure was incompatible with the character of Medea as she had been presented in the course of the dramatic action.[11] But it seems to me even more conspicuous that neither Seneca nor Corneille dispensed with the dragon-chariot, even though in other respects the French dramatist very clearly improves certain weaknesses of the Euripidean play, especially the appearance of Aegeus, the second scene to which Aristotle also voiced an objection.

This unexpected ending must first of all seem completely superfluous. We have already said that Medea could very well have escaped in a purely human manner, as indeed the messenger who reports the deaths of Creon and Creusa, advises her to do (1122 f.). She could have killed her children immediately after the monologue and fled. Her safety in itself is therefore no sufficient justification for the *lusis apo mēchanēs*. That is certainly correct in itself, but had Medea left in this manner, it would have been a fearful escape. The messenger does in fact say (1122 f.): 'Medea, run for your life, take what you can, a ship to bear you hence or chariot on land!' Yet from the point of view of theatrical effectiveness the flight of Medea was an inappropriate ending. The revenge had to be complete. Who the victor was had to be physically manifest. The lone figure of Jason grieving over the bodies of his sons would not have created this unequivocal impression. True theater demands not a stealthy, but a mighty exit.[12] There had to be a final confrontation in which the contrast between the triumphant Medea, full of derision and scorn, exhibits the bodies of her children to completely annihilate Jason, thus creating a lasting impression for the audience. This can only be achieved if the heroine has unusual means at her disposal, for without them she is helplessly exposed to the fury of her husband. Seneca emphasizes this by having Jason appear on stage not alone but in the company of a military escort. Anouilh in his version also supports this point, even though he forgoes the *ex machina* solution. His play also contains a final confrontation, but instead of a triumphal exit he has Medea plunge into the flames of her children's funeral pyre, made from the chariot in which she and Jason had originally fled to Corinth. Anouilh is the great adaptor of Greek tragedy to the contemporary stage, and it is interesting to observe how skilfully he interprets the original before transposing it into a modern idiom. Although a cursory glance at his works may leave the impression that they have little more than the name in common with their ancient models, in reality he is recreating the true essence of the

Attic art form in a twentieth century mold. The suicide of Medea may therefore be a correct interpretation of the Euripidean tragedy, but it represents a mode of expression that is modern rather than Attic. No doubt Euripides could not have his Medea die in this way, precisely because she was the granddaughter of Helios. She *had* to depart avenged and victorious, and by having her go off in the chariot of the sun, Euripides falls back upon the mythical nature of his protagonist, which was so well known to his audience.[13] In the course of the play he had presented Medea as completely human. She is well aware of her divine origin, but this merely intensifies her pride and makes her feel even more keenly the humiliation she has endured. She never speaks of superhuman faculties, nor does she count on miraculous powers to bring her plans to fruition. The reference to her knowledge of drugs, *pharmaka* (394 f.), surely has no such connotation. In the whole play she is merely a woman, an extraordinary woman to be sure, but still entirely human. If the poet emphasizes her divine origin only once and near the end of the play, it must be to achieve a specific theatrical effect. Yet in fact what he does here differs very little from the common practice of all Greek writers from Homer onward, who employ a motif when it is called for, and abandon it whenever it conflicts with a particular poetic intent.[14]

If, however, we wish to justify fully this transgression against Aristotelian canons, we should not be content with seeing it as a mere striving for theatrical effect. We must realize that the whole structure of the tragedy not only requires, but is throughout directed to this ending. But first we must understand the poet's intent. Strohm has pointed out[15] that the *exodos* of the play corresponds in detail to the second *episode*, but drew no further conclusions from his discovery. This *episode* presents their confrontation after Jason had left Medea to marry the daughter of the king. The actual breach of faith lies outside the beginning of the play, while the prologue and the first *episode* show the effect of Jason's infidelity upon Medea. In this confrontation, Jason is master of the situation and speaks first; in the *exodos* the roles are reversed. The difference between the characters clearly emerges from the similarity of the two scenes. Jason is not portrayed as a temperamental man; he does not come to provoke Medea or to gloat over her misfortune. He is calm, objective, and completely convinced of the correctness of his action. This gives him a feeling of confidence and superiority, which unintentionally exacerbates Medea's already aroused temper and wounds her still more deeply with its tone of pitying condescension. In both scenes the dialogue is begun by the character who controls — or thinks he controls — the fate of the other (Jason 446-64, and Medea, 1317-22), and after his exit it is concluded by a passionate outburst on the part of the weaker antagonist (Medea, 623-26, and Jason, 1405-14). In between lies the actual altercation. First the weaker answers the address of his opponent (Medea, 465, and Jason, 1323-50), who in turn tries to refute his arguments (Jason, 522-87, and Medea, 1351-60). Then follows an excited debate in the usual manner of the *agon*, which in the *exodos* consists almost exclusively of short exchanges of dialogue. The correspondence in the structure of the scenes is further stressed by verbal reminiscences: there are the same insults, accusations, and declarations that the opponent's actions have made him an abomination in the eyes of gods and men. They both regret having met each other. All the instances which Medea cites in the second episode to prove her past kindness to Jason and his present ingratitudes are again picked up by Jason in the *exodos*, who sees them as stages in the progress of his misfortune. Euripides certainly wanted us to perceive the relation between these two scenes, and he could only have achieved this effect by using the dragon-chariot, for without it, a final confrontation between Jason and Medea would have been impossible.

This correlation makes the two scenes cardinal points of the whole tragedy. Not only do they form the beginning and end of the dramatic action, but they also contrast as image and its reflection. For the *exodos* represents an exact reversal of the situation in the second *episode*. Between these points we see the gradual transformation of the initial situation into its opposite. This development is decisively influenced by the machinations of Medea, which are further determined by other factors. The second *episode* and the *exodos* provide the framework for this intrigue but are not part of it. In these scenes the protagonists meet in open and unrestrained hostility, and as Strohm has correctly observed,[16] Medea does not make the slightest attempt to deceive her husband in their encounter. The first objection of Aristotle, which directed our attention to the *exodos*, has thus enabled us to establish two stable points of reference and thereby grasp the structure of the entire tragedy. The main action begins at verse 446. All that precedes — the prologue, the *parodos*, the first *episode*, and the first *stasimon* — is a kind of prelude.

Generally, in Greek tragedy the plot consists of a change from one state to its opposite, or *metabasis* as Aristotle calls it (1452 a 16). This change can be from good fortune to bad or vice versa (1451 a 13 f; 1453 a 12 ff.). Thus in the *Medea* the helpless victim of the decree emerges victorious on all fronts, while the master of the situation, who fancied that he was able to determine the fate of Medea and fulfil all his desires, becomes in the *exodos* a man completely annihilated. On the surface it seems that we actually have a double plot, for two characters whose lives are inextricably bound together experience a change: Jason from prosperity to misery and Medea the reverse. We might even get the impression that Jason is the tragic hero, while Medea, whose *metabasis* is a turn for the good, is lacking in true tragic stature. But such a view is undoubtedly false, for Medea is surely the tragic heroine. A double plot there is, but the concepts of *eutuchia* and *dystuchia* [good and bad fortune], which Aristotle must have formulated while thinking of the *Odyssey*, have as little application here as they have to the fortunes of Sophocles' Creon and Antigone.

Nevertheless, an interpretation of the play cannot be content with this rather tentative conclusion, but must try to define more clearly the essence of the tragedy. But the final triumph, for which Euripides introduces the notorious magic chariot, and especially certain expressions in the last speech of the protagonist, present an enormous problem. Jason says to her at the beginning of their heated exchange (1361): 'You yourself are grieved and share the pain,' to which Medea answers: 'That's true, but much less grieved, since you can mock no more.' Details like these, as well as the final picture in general, at least tend to diminish the sense of tragedy, and this is surely why objections to the chariot of the sun have been raised time and again.

III

What we have considered up to now has at least provided us with a few points of reference, from which we can follow the plot with greater confidence. Again another aspect criticised by Aristotle is of crucial importance: the appearance of Aegeus in the third *episode*. But to appreciate the significance of the scene, we should first briefly discuss what has preceded.

What we have called the prelude is subdivided into two parts by the entrance of Creon (271): the first part embracing the prologue, the *parodos*, and the first long speech of Medea; the second including the Creon scene and her second speech after his departure. The first *stasimon* is almost a final reflection on this prelude, which it further rounds out by having the second two *strophes* echo themes from the prologue of the nurse.[17] Essentially, the prologue and *parodos* present the condition into which Jason's decision has put Medea and her attendant women. Purely material consequences are also mentioned — for example, the fate of exile which now awaits Medea — but the emphasis is above all on her emotional state. Thus the words of the nurse introduce the essential facts in a rather different manner from the simple, almost dry style of the later Euripidean prologues. She begins with a wish for the

impossible that provides the whole initial scene with an emotional undertone, and immediately exposes a motif which will dominate the whole
play: the wish to undo the past, the cursing of all ties with Jason, and the
remorse for having become completely estranged from her family
through crimes she committed on his behalf. From this motif Anouilh
fashioned the main theme of his play. There follows in twenty-five
verses the equally vivid account of Medea's state of mind. First her
despair and deep regret for having left her homeland, then her hatred,
which is aimed not directly at Jason but at the children (36): ['she
hates the children']. This first mention of Medea's offspring is somewhat
unexpected after: 'From her own misfortune the poor woman has
learned how sweet it is not to be cut off from one's country.' The nurse
then immediately goes on to speak of something else. In Medea's hatred
she sees a potential for horrible deeds, but these are unrelated to the
children. She can imagine the murder of Creusa or even Creon and Jason,
but not the killing of the children. The agitated mode of expression and
disconnected train of thought is meant to mirror the nurse's emotional
state and thereby increase the tension. To her mind Medea's hatred of
the children is associated with the preceding curse on her ties with
Jason, of which the children are a constant reminder. The nurse fears
that her mistress will be driven to a deed which could only make her
situation worse: 'She is frightening and anyone who arouses her enmity
cannot emerge victorious' (44 f.). But there is no prophecy of infanticide
here. It would also be wrong to conclude from this that the cause of
their death is an unnatural hatred their mother bears them. The hate
Medea speaks of is directed against her whole life with Jason and against
all that reminds her of it. In the lyric passage shortly thereafter Medea
curses not only the children and the father, but she even calls herself
odious, summing up her feelings with the words: 'Let the whole family
perish' (114). The unexpected mention of her children reveals that they
are vital to the main theme of the tragedy. And at this very moment
they appear themselves, ingenuous and naïve, as they return from their
games accompanied by their tutor (46). Here we perceive that the whole
plot revolves around Medea's children and, furthermore, the child in
general as well as the relationship of man and wife to child is a motif
which recurs again and again, especially in the choral odes.[18]

   To understand any poetic treatment of a traditional myth, it is important to know the extent of the author's changes and transformations.[19]
A knowledge of the details that have been added, omitted, or especially
stressed can greatly advance our appreciation of a work of art. Unfortunately here we find ourselves in a rather disadvantageous situation. The
information that has primarily come down to us in the scholia is too

scanty for an adequate reconstruction of the Medea story before Euripides.[20] Nor do we know whether the tragedy's crucial motif — Medea's infanticide — was invented by the poet or was part of the existing traditional material. Lesky comes to the resigned conclusion that we will probably never be able to resolve this question.[21] Kerényi, however, maintains that the infanticide was an old traditional ingredient of the myth.[22] His explanations seem convincing, but rest exclusively on internal evidence. Yet, there is no doubt that in his tragedy Euripides wished to establish firmly the motif of infanticide, whether he invented it himself or culled it from tradition.

With Medea's anapests, which are uttered offstage (96 ff.), a lyric passage begins in which the emotional stress reaches a climax and then again gradually subsides with the *antistrophe* of the chorus (173 ff.), until we return to the realm of *logos* in the speech of Medea at the beginning of the first *episode*. What is here presented in lyric form (augmented by music and dance) is essentially no more than what the nurse had already told us, and this correspondence may be seen both in the arrangement of motifs and from verbal reminiscences. For example, the image of Medea dissolving all her days in a flood of tears (25) is later picked up in the anapests of the nurse (141) and the choral *strophe* (159). Four times we hear Medea's voice offstage, and in each case the nurse comments upon it, first alone and then with the chorus. Something new is introduced with the choral *antistrophe*. The heroine's first utterance is purely an expression of her despair and a wish to die, her second the realization of her enormous suffering leading to the curse, which we have quoted above. After the pause during which the chorus moves into the *orchestra*, Medea's third outburst reiterates in more violent form the curse which she calls down upon herself as well as the wish to find a release from her hateful life in death. Her last words are somewhat more specific, for here she unleashes even more violently her rage over Jason's infidelity and in her hatred wishes death for him and Creon's daughter. Yet her last outcry returns to the remorse for having left her country and broken all ties through the murder of her brother.

By repeating in lyric what had already been said in the prologue, Euripides emphasizes the dominant motifs of the drama: Medea's children, her rootlessness and homelessness, as well as the plight of woman in general. One could compare the whole scene to an operatic overture, in which through repetition and variation the themes of the whole composition are entwined. There is no action in our sense of the word. Despair, impotent rage, and remorse would have been the reactions of any woman under such circumstances, yet among these a very individual note is struck in the end: 'Medea is frightening.' She cannot be treated like this with impunity. She will react. The chorus' wish to speak to Medea is perfectly natural at this point. The nurse undertakes the mediation (184 ff.), and at the beginning of the first *episode* the heroine appears already somewhat composed, determined to take her own fate into her hands. The whole situation from the prologue to the *parodos* can be best summarized by an image which the nurse employs in the anapests (106 ff.). She would like to remove the children and she warns them of their mother's wild temper and feelings of hatred. Then she speaks of a 'cloud of wailing' still forming, but which their mother as her passion increases will soon inflame with lightning. This part of the prelude reminds one of the great *parodoi* of the *Persians* or the *Agamemnon*, creating a mood as well as displaying the underlying tensions which are bound to lead to a storm.

The first speech of Medea adds little that is new. The motifs of the homelessness of an exile and the plight of woman in the existing social order occupy most of the space,[23] and only at the end does it become clear that she is firmly bent on revenge, although its form is still uncertain. Only in very general terms does she say that her husband, Creon, and Creusa will have to pay the penalty (260). She does not say how this is going to happen, and the time of her revenge remains likewise indefinite. It is important to realize that the action can only be set in motion as the result of an external impetus.[24] It is clearly indicated where the impulse will come from and what it consists of. In speaking to the nurse the tutor mentions a rumor (70 ff.) that Creon is thinking of banishing Medea and her children. This exile is the new development which swells the heroine's vindictiveness and forces her to carry out her designs at once, if she will realize them at all.

Such is the content of the Creon scene and the second speech of Medea which follows it. Furthermore, this scene is of very special significance, because it contains a small but independent subplot which completes the picture of Medea's character and also sets the stage for the climax of the tragedy. Creon wants to remove Medea from Corinth, because, as he openly admits, he is afraid of her. He justifies his fear from everything he knows of her. She is *sophē* [shrewd] and *kakōn pollōn idris* [versed in many evil arts] (285), she has every reason to be angry, as Creon well understands, and they all know of her threats to destroy the three perpetrators of her misfortune — Jason, Creon, and his daughter. A kind of tragic irony characteristic of this play lies in the fact that the measures he takes to assure his own and his family's safety actually increase the danger and hasten his downfall. Because of this new outrage, Medea is driven to decisive and swift implementation of her scheme, which is exactly what Creon wished to avoid. Now he becomes the victim of her first machination. The king wishes Medea to go at once. He himself will make sure that she crosses the borders as soon as possible, and he will not return home until he has expelled her (275 f.). Under such circumstances Medea does not have the slightest chance of carrying out her vengeance, and must first of all entreat a postponement. The king himself unconsciously provides her with the means of luring him into the trap. When Medea again bewails her lost homeland (328), Creon replies that *next to his children* he too loves his country most of all. The children motif reappears, but here its significance goes beyond mere effect on the audience. Medea uses Creon's revelation in two ways. She comes to realize how much children mean to a man, and immediately exploits this, pointing out the distress of her own children in appealing to Creon's paternal feelings. Thus he grants her a day's grace, even though he knows all too well that in doing so he is committing a grave error (350). Yet Creon's statement also shows her that she can wound Jason most deeply by killing his children. It is *here* that the thought of infanticide first occurs to her.

Medea's belief that such a revenge is effective and therefore necessary is strengthened in the second *episode*, when Jason declares that the main reason for his action was precisely his concern for the children (562 ff.). Of course, Jason's children are also hers, and herein lies her own tragedy.

In the speech (364 ff.) with which the first *episode* ends, she gives free rein to her indignation. She decides to carry out her revenge this very day. It is still the same as in the first speech — a wish to murder the king, his daughter, and her husband, but now she wonders how to do it. Should she openly kill her enemies with a weapon? That would not be a satisfactory revenge, for in so doing she herself might perish and become the laughing-stock of her enemies. She therefore decides to use poison, a method in which she is especially well versed. But she now suddenly interrupts herself. What is going to happen to her when her enemies are dead? She is, after all, without home or shelter. If she cannot find these, she cannot be truly victorious. In that case she might as well die, and it would indeed be better to seize a sword, kill her enemies, and face the consequences of her action. She sets herself a time limit, during which she will try to find some place of refuge. The only consequence of Medea's appearance is that she is now firmly resolved to take vengeance this very day. But what, and above all, how she will do this still remains uncertain. Yet, when she now confronts Jason in the second *episode*, we are fully aware of her predicament.

Her long enumeration of all she has done for Jason rounds out the exposition and completes the account of past events. We actually do not learn anything new about Medea, but her position is now placed in the context of Jason and his world. The *agon* at once brings both situations and the corresponding human attitudes into clearer light, and throws them into relief by means of antithesis. Kurt von Fritz[25] rightly stresses the contrast of the characters and especially the depreciation of one who was formerly a Greek national hero. But here we are not so much interested in the legendary past, as in the role that this character plays within the dramatic framework. It is of course completely erroneous to dismiss Jason's attitude here and in the fourth *episode* as mere cynicism; we may call him a weakling and Lothario who has pulled himself up by the hem of Medea's skirt to become a hero in the Argonautic expedition. Nevertheless, it is worthwhile to examine the Euripidean Jason more closely. To understand his relationship with Medea, we must first ignore the stereotyped marital conflicts presented in the contemporary cinema. Things are more complicated here. Jason is not the husband who, tired of his wife, has fallen in love with another woman and now loses his head. We may take him at his word when he repeatedly denies his love for Creusa.

To understand Euripides' Jason we may best begin with a motif already mentioned, that of an exile's rootlessness. It is important to note that the fate of homelessness has completely different meanings for Jason and for Medea. Medea's own situation becomes painful only when Jason leaves her. With an expression that reminds us of Andromache's words to Hector, she states that her husband was everything to her (228). Leaving her country, her mother and father, in fact even murdering her brother and severing all ties with her family, epitomize the plight of the woman who relinquishes her entire previous existence to follow her husband. Medea, however, does not exchange one mode of life for a similar one. In order to lead a purely human existence with Jason she separates herself from a family descended from the sun-god and therefore related to both the divine and heroic worlds. The failure of her relationship will be all the more painful because she has sacrificed so much for it.

Jason describes the same situation rather differently (551 ff.): 'When I came here as a fugitive from Iolkos, overcome with countless, inescapable difficulties, could I possibly have found a better remedy than marrying the daughter of the king?' He had to flee his own country, and now that he is in a foreign land, his main concern is to build a new life. But for him, the son of a king, merely existing is not enough. Even in Corinth he wants to be what he was, to live 'worthy of my ancestry' (562), and this means that he, his family, and his descendants must become firmly rooted in that community. Now he is offered the opportunity to ally himself with the king's family, to make the children of his first marriage the stepsons of the princess, and one day to ascend the throne of Corinth. This would be extremely advantageous not only for him but for his children, and in the end could even benefit Medea, if she would only be sensible. He, therefore, seizes the opportunity; he cannot comprehend how someone might reproach him for this and be concerned with such a trifle as the *lechos* [life in bed]. But it is in this very point, the *lechos* of which Jason speaks repeatedly, that the main difference lies. For him marriage and children, indeed, all human ties, are only a means to an end. The value of life depends on social status and its perpetuation in generations to come. That is why children are important for him. It would be most convenient if one could have children without women, for then there would be no annoying complications like his present conflict with Medea. Jason on many occasions speaks of women and the female point of view, which he compares to the male. This antithesis of the male and female world is also a motif which passes through the whole play, above all in the choral odes. Medea herself continually appeals to the feeling of solidarity among the members of her sex. Such an antithesis is nothing new in Greek literature. We think at once of *Iliad* VI, but there we do not find a gulf separating the two realms; Andromache's world differs from Hector's, but does not oppose it. What divides Hector from his family is not a completely different scale of values, but the painful necessity of being brave. In Euripides, however, the male world is completely dehumanized. Jason is the child of a noble family, whose every effort is directed exclusively toward gaining status, and whose idea is to live well and to feel no want (559 f.). Opposed to him stands Medea as a woman and as a champion of human values and personal relationships.

IV

We now come to the second dramatic incident to which Aristotle objects: the entrance of Aegeus. The king of Athens chances to pass through Corinth on his journey from Delphi to Troezen. Medea asks and obtains the desired asylum. She now has a harbor for her plans, where she can fasten the cable (769 f.). The appearance of Aegeus is without a doubt the turning-point of the drama (1452 a 21 f.). This fact has only been questioned by modern interpretations that have tried to see the climax in the great monologue, of which we have spoken at the outset. Aristotle thinks that this turning-point is poorly constructed, because the appearance of Aegeus is *alogon* (1461 b 20 f.). The appropriate translation here is probably not 'irrational' or 'silly', but rather 'absurd' or 'dragged in by the hair.'

Aegeus is already married when he meets Medea (673). The very reason for his journey to Troezen, the consultation with Pittheus regarding the Delphic oracle, is eliminated, when as gratitude for his help Medea holds out to him the prospect of being blessed with the offspring he so desires (717 f.). We can assume that Aegeus abandons the journey, for when he leaves, the chorus utters a conventional blessing in which it speaks of his return home (760).

Aristotle surely had none of these things in mind when he called the scene *alogon*, nor can he be referring to the fact that Aegeus comes unexpectedly and by chance, because he himself says that a good *peripeteia* occurs contrary to expectation (1452a4). Perhaps we might better understand Aristotle's objection if we compare the arrival of Aegeus to the reversal in Sophocles' *Oedipus Rex*, which the philosopher cites as an exemplary *peripeteia*. In this play, when the search for the murderer of Laius has come to a dead end, a messenger comes from Corinth and announces the death of Polybus, whom Oedipus believes to be his father. With this revelation the discovery of the truth is at once made possible. Yet even here it is a chance happening and in no way follows from the sequence of events that Polybus will die at this particular time. It is even less inevitable that the messenger must be precisely the man who many years ago had received the child Oedipus with the pierced feet from a herdsman of Laius, and who could therefore say with every certainty that Oedipus is not a Corinthian. Nevertheless, there is significant difference from the reversal of the *Medea*. Oedipus' ties with the royal house of Corinth are well known; he himself had just given Jocasta a detailed account of his youth. The death of Polybus at the appropriate moment is of course not inevitable, but it is nevertheless in the realm of what is possible and imaginable. It is also not improbable that the very man who has played such a special role in the life of Oedipus, and who rejoices that the child of those days will become king of his city, should be the one to bring the message. All this then, to turn again to Aristotle, lies not in the realm of the *anangkaion* [inevitable], but it is surely within the *eikos* [probable].

In contrast, the arrival of Aegeus in Corinth seems forced, for from the content of the play we cannot infer the slightest connection between Medea and Aegeus or Athens. But there is a real relation between the journey of Aegeus and the Medea plot, though it lies below the surface and is not as easily perceived as in Sophocles' play. Its nature is purely poetic, for what ties together these seemingly disparate actions is again the children motif. Childless Aegeus has gone to Delphi to inquire what he must do to get offspring; from there he journeys to Troezen, because he does not understand the oracle and needs someone to interpret it for him. The child, however, as we have already observed several times, is the central theme of the tragedy. Again a man appears who desires progeny, and most likely for the same reasons as Creon and Jason. For the third time Medea sees how important children are to a man. Just as she had exploited this knowledge with Creon, she now achieves her goal by promising Aegeus that with her magic arts, she will help him have children. The meeting with the Athenian king is the last link in a chain of evidence that proves Jason would be most vulnerable where his children are concerned. Aegeus' arrival not only marks the reversal which brings about the beginning of the revenge action and the *metabasis*, but it also determines once and for all the specific form of the revenge — infanticide.

After Aegeus' departure, Medea can begin to act, and she does, first of all explaining to the women of the chorus the details of her revenge plan which have now been crystalized. Corneille was very puzzled by this announcement. He thought, quite correctly from his standpoint, that it was highly improbable that none of these many witnesses should have informed the king of Medea's intentions. In Attic tragedy, however, the poet had to accept the presence of the chorus as a convention. Moreover, Corneille has even failed to recognize how very skilfully Euripides employed the constant presence of the chorus, making it a kind of confidant to the protagonist, thereby affecting many variations on the theme of women's solidarity against men. By appealing in the prelude to their common womanly interests which are thwarted in the existing social order, Medea has already asked the chorus at least to help her revenge by keeping silent, and she repeats time and again that it is their duty as women to stand by her.

From the beginning the children play a decisive role in Medea's plan (774 ff.). Through them she gains access to the royal house, which she must have to achieve her ends. The children are sent on the pretense of asking permission to stay in Corinth. Since this also accords with Jason's wishes, she can count on his support and has him summoned (820), so that in the fourth *episode* she can make him the unsuspecting instrument of her plot. The children will convey wedding gifts to his young bride Creusa, but these will be poisoned and bring death. Here, in contrast to her previous revenge speeches, she mentions neither Creon nor Jason. She says only in very general terms that the girl and anyone who touches her will die a miserable death (788). All attention is focused exclusively on Creusa, who is the prime object of Medea's revenge. Medea kills her not out of jealousy but to prevent her from bearing children to Jason (804 f.). She then states what she *must* do next: 'I shall kill my children' (790 ff.). It is the first clear revelation of the main theme, and it shocks the chorus immensely. But her *thymos* will not allow her to be made a laughing-stock. And infanticide is the form the revenge must inevitably take, for that alone can cause the supreme agony (793 ff.).

Medea herself realizes that this revenge will result in her own annihilation as a human being, and yet she admits in 1013 ff: 'The gods and I, in a kind of madness, have planned it so.'[26] In a sense Euripides' heroine perishes with the children, much the way Anouilh presents it in the final scene of his brilliant version. The granddaughter of Helios may stand in triumph on her dragon-chariot, but Medea the woman is dead.

23

THE *HIPPOLYTUS* OF EURIPIDES

BERNARD M. W. KNOX

The usual critical treatment of the *Hippolytus* of Euripides is an analysis in terms of character, an analysis which, whatever its particular emphasis, is based on the Aristotelian conception of tragic character and the relation between character and reversal of fortune. In the case of the *Hippolytus*, this analysis, far from arriving at a generally accepted line of interpretation, has produced nothing but disagreement. Is Hippolytus the tragic hero,[1] destroyed by an excess of chastity, a fanatical devotion to the goddess Artemis? Or is Phaedra the tragic heroine,[2] and the conflict in her soul the tragic conflict of the play? The claims of Theseus should not be neglected; his part is as long as Phaedra's, and the Aristotelian word *hamartia* is used to describe his conduct by the goddess Artemis (1334).

Such divergence of views is natural in a play which develops so many characters so fully; though literary statistics are distasteful, the size of the parts in this play (an important statistic for the actors, at any rate) shows how difficult the problem of emphasis is. Hippolytus speaks 271 lines,[3] Phaedra and Theseus 187 apiece, and, surprisingly enough, the Nurse has more lines than either Phaedra or Theseus: 216.[4] The attempt to make Phaedra the central figure of the play seems perverse — why not the Nurse? She too has her conduct described as *hamartia*[5] — and even Hippolytus is not a central figure on the scale of Medea, who speaks 562 lines in a play of similar length, or Oedipus, who has 698 in the *Oedipus Tyrannus*, a play which is a little longer. The search for a central tragic figure in this play is a blind alley. When the action is so equably divided among four characters, the unity of the work cannot depend on any one, but must lie in the nature of the relationship of all four. In the *Hippolytus*, the significant relationship between the characters is the situation in which they are placed. It is exactly the same situation for

From *Yale Classical Studies* 13 (1952), 3–31. Reprinted by permission of the author and *Yale Classical Studies*. The author has kindly allowed certain footnotes to be shortened and others omitted. Those referring to this essay for scholarly purposes are requested to consult the original version.

each of them, one which imposes a choice between the same alternatives — silence and speech.

And we are shown that their choice is not free. Aristotle's comments on the tragic character assume, to some extent, that the human will is free to choose. But the freedom of the human will and the importance of the human choice are both, in the prologue of the *Hippolytus*, expressly denied. In no other Greek tragedy is the predetermination of human action by an external power made so emphatically clear. In the *Oresteia*, where each word and action is the fulfillment of the will of Zeus, the relation between human action and divine will is presented always in mysterious terms; the will of Zeus is an inscrutable factor in the background which is clearly revealed only at the close of the trilogy. And while Clytemnestra is on stage in the *Agamemnon*, we are not distracted by any feeling that her purpose as a human being is not decisive; in fact, it is the most important thing in the play. Sophocles' Oedipus has fulfilled and is still fulfilling the oracles of Apollo, but it is Oedipus, a human being making human decisions, who commands our undivided attention. And significantly, the prophecy of Apollo is presented as exactly that, a prophecy and not a determining factor; Apollo predicts, but does no more — it is Oedipus who acts.

Both the *Oedipus* and the *Agamemnon* may be ultimately, in logical (though not necessarily religious) terms, determinist, but dramatically they emphasize the freedom of the human will. But the *Hippolytus* begins with a powerful presentation of an external force which not only predicts but also determines; Aphrodite tells us not only what will happen but announces her responsibility and explains her motives. It is a complete explanation and one which (even if it were not confirmed in every particular by another goddess at the end of the play) we are bound to accept. Aphrodite is one of the powers which rule the universe; and though what she says may shock us, we must accept it as true.

The play, from this point on, should be simple, the unrolling of an inevitable pattern. But Euripides has a surprise in store. As we watch the human beings of the drama, unconscious of the goddess's purpose, work out her will, we are struck by their apparent freedom. In no other Greek tragedy do so many people change their minds about so many important matters. Here again Euripides is departing sharply from the procedure of his fellow dramatists. Clytemnestra's purpose in the *Agamemnon*, concealed from the chorus and her victim by the resolution of that male-thinking brain, dangerously close to the ironic surface of her speech of welcome, triumphantly achieved when she stands over Agamemnon's body — this inflexible purpose is the straight line along which the whole play moves. Oedipus' determination to know the truth, carried relentlessly to the brink of the abyss and beyond, is the line of development of the greatest plot in western tragedy. But in the *Hippolytus* the line of development of the characters' purposes is a zigzag. Phaedra resolves to die without revealing her love, and then makes a long speech about it to the chorus. The Nurse urges her to reveal it, regrets her action when she hears her mistress speak, and then returns to urge Phaedra on to further lengths of speech. And Hippolytus, when he learns of Phaedra's passion, first announces his intention to tell Theseus the truth and then changes his mind and keeps silent.

'In this world, second thoughts are best,' says the Nurse (436). Three of the principal characters have second thoughts (the Nurse, in fact, has not only second but third and fourth thoughts); the play makes an ironic juxtaposition of the maximum dramatic complication of individual choice with a predetermined and announced result. The choice of one alternative then the other, the human mind wavering between moral decisions, accepting and rejecting in a complicated pattern which emphasizes the apparent freedom and unpredictability of the human will — all this is the fulfillment of Aphrodite's purpose.

The choice between speech and silence is the situation which places the four principal characters in significant relationship and makes an artistic unity of the play. But it does much more. The poet has made the alternations and combinations of choice complicated. Phaedra chooses first silence then speech; the Nurse speech then silence, then speech, then silence; Hippolytus speech then silence; the chorus silence; and Theseus speech. The resultant pattern seems to represent the exhaustion of the possibilities of the human will. The choice between silence and speech is more than a unifying factor in the play; it is a situation with universal implications, a metaphor for the operation of human free will in all its complicated aspects. And the context in which it is set demonstrates the nonexistence of the human free will, the futility of the moral choice.

The goddess Aphrodite presents the issue and announces the outcome. Her preliminary work is done (23); the moment has arrived for the consummation of her design, the punishment of Hippolytus (21). But there is still one recalcitrant detail, Phaedra's determination to remain silent. 'She, poor woman, is dying in silence. No one in the house shares the secret of her disease' (39-40). But this last obstacle will be removed; things will not fall out this way (41). The truth will come out (42). And Theseus will kill his son.

In the scene between Phaedra and the Nurse, we are shown the first stage of the accomplishment of Aphrodite's purpose — Phaedra's change from silence to speech. Her words are the involuntary speech of delirium,

the breakout of her suppressed subconscious desires. But this delirium
is also the working of the external force, Aphrodite, who predicted this
development and now brings it about before our eyes. Phaedra's wild
fantasies make no sense to the Nurse and the chorus, but their meaning
is clear to the audience. Her yearning for the poplar and the grassy
meadow, for the chase and the taming of colts on the sand, is a hysterical
expression of her desire for Hippolytus (210-11).

The Nurse calls her outburst madness (214), that is, meaningless
speech, and Phaedra, when she comes to her senses, calls it madness too
(241), but in a different sense, passion. She has revealed nothing, but
she has for the first time put her desire into words, and broken her long
silence. Her passion has overcome her judgment (240); in her case the
choice between silence and speech is also a choice between judgment
and passion. In the next few lines she defines her dilemma, poses the
alternatives, and sees a third course open to her (247-49). To be right
in judgment, that is, in her case, to remain silent, is agony; passion, in
her case, speech, is evil. Better to make no choice and perish — to perish
unconscious of the alternatives, to abandon judgment and choice, to
surrender free will.[6] This is what she comes to in the end, but she has
not yet reached such desperate straits. She is still in the no man's land
between the alternatives of speech and silence, for her delirious outburst
has not revealed her secret to the Nurse. But it has brought her a
momentary relief and thus weakened her determination. She is now less
able to withstand the final assault on her silence which the Nurse, at the
request of the chorus, proceeds to make.

The Nurse has little hope of success; she has tried before and failed —
'Phaedra keeps silent about it all' (273), she tells the chorus. But she
makes a last attempt. The essence of her practical viewpoint can be seen
in her reproach to Phaedra when she gets no answer; for her there is no
problem which cannot be resolved by speech. 'Well, why are you silent?
You should not be silent, child. Either you should refute me, if I say
something wrong, or, if I say what is right, you should agree with my
words' (297-99). She gets no answer still, and in an angry reminder to
Phaedra that she is ruining her children's future, she mentions, without
realizing its significance, the name of Hippolytus. This fortuitous thrust
provokes a cry of agony and a plea for silence. 'I beseech you, in future,
be silent about this man,' (312).

The Nurse does not realize the reason for Phaedra's agitation, but
she senses the moment of weakness and presses her advantage. She now
makes a frontal attack on Phaedra's silence; throwing herself at her
mistress' feet, she seizes her hand and knees. It is the position of the
suppliant, the extreme expression of emotional and physical pressure

combined, and it is enough to break Phaedra's weakened resolution. 'I will grant your request,' (335). 'My part is silence now,' replies the Nurse, 'and yours is speech,' (336).

Phaedra finds speech difficult. She invokes the names of her mother and sister, examples of unhappy love, and associates herself with them. But she finds it hard to speak plainly. 'If only you could say to me what I must say myself' (345). This is her wish, to break silence and yet not speak, and she actually manages to make it come true. In a dialectic maneuver worthy of Socrates himself, she assumes the role of questioner and makes the Nurse supply the answers and repeat the name Hippolytus, this time in a context which leaves no doubt about its significance. 'You have said it,' she says to the Nurse, 'you did not hear it from me' (352).

This revelation is more than the Nurse had bargained for. She who saw only two attitudes toward speech for Phaedra — rebuttal or agreement — can adopt neither herself; she has no advice to give, no solution to propose. She is reduced to despair and silence; she who reproached Phaedra for wishing to die now resolves on death herself. 'I shall find release from life in death. Farewell. I am no longer living' (356-57). The full meaning of her words to Phaedra is now clear to us and to her. 'My part is silence now. Speech from this point on is yours.'

Speech is Phaedra's part now, and she pours out her heart to the chorus. The relief of speech, which first forced itself on her in a delirious outburst, is now the product of conscious choice. She tells the chorus the path her judgment followed (391): first of all, to hide her sickness in silence (394). But this proved insufficient; more was needed, to subdue her passion by self-control (398-99). And when this failed, she resolved on a third course, to die. She is still resolved to die; her change from silence to speech has made no difference to the situation, for she can depend on the silence of the chorus and the Nurse. But she has had the comfort of speech, told her love and despair to a sympathetic audience, and what is more, an admiring one. 'Honour? Who hath it? He that died o' Wednesday,' says Falstaff, and this is the essence of Phaedra's dilemma too. She has resolved to die in silence to save her honor. But this very silence means that she cannot enjoy her honor while living, and it will not even be appreciated after her death. No one will ever know the force she overcame and the heroic nature of her decision. Death in silence involved an isolation hard for any human being to bear, and she makes it clear that her desire to be appreciated was one of the forces driving her to speech. 'May it be my lot', she says, 'not to pass unnoticed when I act nobly, and not to have many witnesses when my acts are disgraceful' (403-04).

Now she can act nobly, die rather than yield to passion, and yet not pass unnoticed. The chorus, the representatives of the women of Tro-ezen,[7] recognize and praise her nobility (431-32). Phaedra can have her cake and eat it too. But it is not destined to end this way, as Aphrodite said in the prologue.

For the Nurse now intervenes again. Her passion and despair silenced her and drove her from the scene when she realized the nature of Phaedra's sickness. But she has changed her mind. She has now rejected silence, which abandoned Phaedra to her death, and chosen speech, which is designed to save her life. 'In human life', she says, 'second thoughts are somehow best' (435-36).

Phaedra's silence was judgment; her speech was at first passion. But in the Nurse's case these relationships are reversed. Her passion, despair, drove her to silence, and her speech now is the product of judgment. It is speech (*logos*) in both senses of the Greek word, speech and reason; the nurse here represents the application of human reason to a human problem.

The 'reason' behind the Nurse's lines is one stripped bare of any restraint of morality or religion, though it uses the terms of both. The speech is a masterpiece of sophistic rhetoric, in which each argument points toward the physical consummation of Phaedra's love. But this is a conclusion which the nurse is clever enough not to put into words. She leaves the implied conclusion to work on Phaedra's weakened reso-lution and contents herself, to conclude her speech, with specific advice in which every phrase is an ambiguity: 'bear your love (as you have so far)' or 'dare to love' (476), 'subdue your love (as you have so far)' or 'make it subject to you, turn it to your own good' (477), 'incantations and charmed words' (478) to cure her of her passion[8] or to make Hip-polytus love her. The Nurse is probing to see what effect her speech will have on Phaedra; she does not dare commit herself fully yet.

She gets a violent reaction. These are too fair-seeming words (487); Phaedra asks for advice that will save her honor, not please her ears. But she has made an important admission; the Nurse's words did please her ears (488). The Nurse sees the weakness in Phaedra's defense and pushes hard. She speaks bluntly and clearly now. 'You need not graceful words [so much for honor] but the man' (490-91). This is plain speaking, and Phaedra replies with an angry and agonized plea for silence (498). But the Nurse presses her advantage and pushes the verbalization of Phaedra's suppressed wishes to a further stage; she has already mentioned 'the man', and now she invokes 'the deed' (501) — the act of adultery itself.[9] This word brings out into the open the consummation which Phaedra rejected with such horror in her speech to the chorus (413-18), but now it is attractive as well as repulsive – like love itself (348) – and Phaedra now reveals that if the Nurse continues to put evil in a fair light (505), she will come to it and be consumed in what she now flees from (506).

The Nurse is clever enough to return to ambiguities, the love charms (509), which will relieve her sickness without disgrace or damage to the mind. The Nurse thus returns to her original proposal; this is the same circular movement of her earlier interview with Phaedra, in which the name 'Hippolytus' was the point of departure and return. And here, as there, the closing of the circle with the repetition makes clear the meaning of the words. Phaedra must know now, after all that has been said, what the Nurse means by 'love charms'. But the ambiguous phrasing is a triumph of psychology on the Nurse's part. She remembers how Phaedra tried to evade responsibility by a verbal fiction before – 'If only you could say to me what I must say myself' and 'You have said it. You did not hear it from me' – and she gives her mistress the same opportunity again. And Phaedra takes it. Her question is not 'What will be the effect of this love charm?' but 'Is it an ointment or something to drink?' (516). She has abandoned her critical intelligence and surrendered control over her own choice; she is now following the third and most desperate of the three courses she saw before her. 'To be right in judgment is agony, passion is evil, best of all is to perish without judgment or choice.'

That she surrenders control of her actions here is made clear and also plausible by the relationship between Phaedra and the Nurse which the words and tone of the next few lines suggest. She is now a child again, and the Nurse does for the grown woman what she had always done for the child – evades her questions, makes light of her fears, relieves her of responsibility, and decides for her. 'I don't know', she says, in answer to Phaedra's question about the nature of the love charms. 'Don't ask questions, child. Just let it do you good' (517). To Phaedra's expression of fear that her secret will be revealed to Hippolytus, the nurse replies, 'Leave that to me, daughter. I'll take care of that' (521). With a prayer to Aphrodite (523), 'co-operate with me', and a statement that she will tell her thoughts to 'friends within the house', the Nurse goes into the palace. And Phaedra lets her go. She has gone through the cycle of conscious choice, first silence, then speech, and come at last to abandon choice all together and entrust her destiny to another. And the result will be, as she said herself, destruction.

For that result she does not have long to wait. 'Silence' (565), is the word with which she follows the closing line of the choral stasimon to open the next scene. She is listening to what is happening inside the house, where Hippolytus is shouting at the Nurse. What Phaedra both feared and longed for has come true; Hippolytus knows of her love.

The opening lines of the ensuing dialogue show Hippolytus in his turn confronted with the same choice, between silence and speech. He must choose between telling Theseus what he has heard, and remaining silent, as he has sworn to do. His first reaction is a passionate announcement that he will speak, an appeal to earth and sun to witness what he has just heard (601-2). To the Nurse's plea for silence (603), he replies, 'Impossible. What I have heard is dreadful. I cannot keep silence' (604). This impulse to speak is, as in Phaedra's case, passion overriding judgment, but the passion which inspires him is not the same. Behind Phaedra's delirious words and subsequent conscious surrender to the Nurse's questioning, we can see the power of Aphrodite working in her. But Hippolytus' outburst is the shocked and incredulous reaction of the virgin mind, the working of Artemis in him. And in his case, as in Phaedra's, the passionate impulse endangers the chief objective of the conscious mind; Phaedra's speech endangers her honor, that *eukleia* which is her life's aim,[10] and Hippolytus' speech endangers his highest ambition, reverence, *eusebeia*,[11] for it involves breaking the oath he swore to the Nurse. Though they make their choices in different order (Phaedra choosing first silence, then speech; Hippolytus first speech, then silence), the parallel is striking. And the agent who brings about the change of mind is in each case the same, the Nurse.

The connection between the two situations is emphasized not only verbally and thematically but also visually. For the Nurse now throws herself at the feet of Hippolytus, as she did at Phaedra's, and clasps his hand and knees, as she did hers. The supreme gesture of supplication is repeated, to meet with the same initial resistance and final compliance. But this time she begs not for speech but for silence.

Hippolytus rejects her request with the same argument she herself had used against Phaedra's silence. 'If the matter is good', he says, 'it will be better still when published' (610) – a line which recalls what the Nurse had said to Phaedra, 'Then you will be even more honored if you tell' (332). Hippolytus launches on his passionate denunciation of women. The violence of his speech relieves the passion which made him ignore his oath, and he ends his speech with a promise to keep silence (660). He will respect the oath. 'Don't forget this, woman,' he says to the Nurse, 'it is my reverence which saves you' (666). Hippolytus too changes his mind: 'in this world second thoughts are somehow wiser.'

But Phaedra's situation is desperate. She does not believe that the disgust and hatred revealed in Hippolytus' speech will remain under control – 'He will speak against us to his father,' she says (690) – and even if she could be certain of Hippolytus' silence, she is not the woman to face Theseus with dissimulation. She wondered, in her long speech to the chorus, how the adulteress could look her husband in the face (415-16), and even if she had the necessary hardness, the situation would be made difficult, to say the least, by Hippolytus' announced intention to watch her at it (661-62). Now she must die, as she intended from the first, but she can no longer die in silence. That would no longer be death with honor (687-88). Speech has brought her to this pass, and in order to die and protect her reputation she now needs more speech. 'Now I need new words,' she says (688).

'May I not pass unnoticed when I act nobly,' she said in the beginning, 'nor have many witnesses when I act disgracefully' (403-4). She got the first half of her wish — the chorus was witness to her noble resolution to die in silence — but the second half was not granted. Hippolytus is a witness to her weakness, and he must be silenced. To this motive for action against him is added the hatred of the rejected woman who has heard every word of his ugly speech.[12] The 'new words' which she finds, the letter to Theseus accusing Hippolytus of an attempt on her virtue, will save her reputation and satisfy her hatred. They will guarantee the ineffectiveness of Hippolytus' speech, if speak he does, and they will also destroy him.

But there are other witnesses to be silenced too, the chorus. She asks them to hide in silence what they have heard (712), and they agree. They bind themselves to silence by an oath. Thus the chorus, like the three principal characters so far seen, chooses between the same two alternatives, and seals its choice, silence, with speech of the most powerful and binding kind, an oath. The chorus will not change its mind.

The preliminaries are now over, and the stage is set for Hippolytus' destruction. Phaedra commits suicide, and Theseus finds her letter. What happens now, whether Aphrodite's purpose will be fulfilled or fail, whether Hippolytus will live or die, depends on whether Theseus chooses silence or speech. He does not keep us waiting long. 'I cannot hold it inside the gates of my mouth,' he says (882-83). But it is not ordinary speech. By the gift conferred on him by his father, Poseidon, he can speak, in certain circumstances, with a power that is reserved for gods alone — his wish, expressed in speech, becomes fact. In his mouth, at the moment, speech has the power of life and death. And he uses it to kill his son. 'Father Poseidon, you gave me once three curses. With one of these, wipe out my son' (887-89).

Here the last piece of the jigsaw puzzle of free will is fitted into place to complete the picture of Aphrodite's purpose fulfilled. And Theseus' curse is at the same time a demonstration of the futility of the alternative which the second thoughts of Phaedra, Hippolytus, and the Nurse have suggested. 'Second thoughts are somehow wiser' — they were not for these three. Perhaps first thoughts are best. But Theseus is the one person in the play for whom second thoughts would have been wiser, and he gives himself no time to have them. He acts immediately, without stopping to examine the case or consider alternatives; to abandon judgment and perish — Phaedra's last desperate course — is Theseus' first impulsive action.

The alternatives before these human beings — first and second thoughts, passion and judgment, silence and speech[13] — are chosen and rejected in a complicated pattern which shows the independent operation of five separate human wills producing a result desired by none of them, the consummation of Aphrodite's purpose. The fact that the moral alternatives are represented by silence and speech is not merely a brilliant device which connects and contrasts the situations of the different characters; it is also an emphatic statement of the universality of the action. It makes the play an ironical comment on a fundamental idea, the idea that man's power of speech, which distinguishes him from the other animals, is the faculty which gives him the conception and power of moral choice in the first place.

The Greek commonplace is most clearly set forth in a famous passage of Aristotle's *Politics* (1.1.10). 'Man alone of the animals possesses speech. Mere voice can, it is true, indicate pain and pleasure, and therefore it is possessed by the other animals as well . . . but speech is designed to indicate the advantageous and the harmful and therefore also the right and the wrong: for it is the special property of man, in distinction from the other animals, that he alone has perception of good and bad and right and wrong and other moral qualities.[14]

It is clear that Euripides was familiar with the idea, for he makes at least one ironical reference to the contrast between man, who has speech, and the animals, which do not. Hippolytus, in his furious invective, wishes that women could be provided with dumb animals instead of servants like the Nurse. 'Animals with bite instead of voice should be housed with them, so that women could neither speak to anyone nor get speech back in return' (646–48). Here he wishes that speaking beings could be made dumb, but in his own moment of trial and agony before Theseus he reverses his wish, and begs an inanimate object, the house, to speak in his defense. 'House, if only you could somehow send forth a voice and bear witness . . . ' (1074–75).

Speech is what distinguishes man from the other animals. But in the *Hippolytus* its role is not simply to point out the distinction between right and wrong. It is presented not as the instrument which makes possible the conception of moral choice and expresses moral alternatives, but as an explosive force which, once released, cannot be restrained and creates universal destruction. 'To what length will speech go?' (342) asks the Nurse, when she has finally succeeded in opening Phaedra's lips. It goes far enough to ruin all of them. It assumes many forms: Phaedra's delirium, the Nurse's cynical argument, Hippolytus' invective, Phaedra's letter, Theseus' curse — and in all these forms it is the instrument of Aphrodite's will.

The *Hippolytus* is a terrible demonstration of the meaninglessness of the moral choice and its medium, speech. But it is not a mechanical demonstration; the unifying and meaningful situation is the key to the play, but that does not mean that character is unimportant. The demonstration is in fact powerful precisely because the choices and alternations of choice made by the human beings are in each case the natural expression of the individual character. As has often been re-marked, if the prologue were removed, the action would still be plausible. The external directing force works not against but through the charac-teristic thoughts and impulses of the characters involved. But the brilliant delineation of character in the *Hippolytus* does more than motivate the action plausibly. The characters, like the situation, have a larger dimen-sion of meaning than the purely dramatic; they are individual examples which illustrate the fundamental proposition implied in the situation — the futility of human choice and action.

The four characters involved are very different: different in purpose, action, and suffering. But they all go through the same process. Action in each case, far from fulfilling conscious purpose, brings about the opposite of that purpose. The individual purpose is the expression of a view of human life and a way of living it; in each case this view is ex-posed, by the individual disaster, as inadequate. And the view of human life implies, in turn, an attitude toward the gods; these attitudes are in each case proved unsound. The human beings of the world of the *Hippolytus* live out their lives in the darkness of total ignorance of the nature of the universe and of the powers which govern it.

Phaedra's purpose and way of life can be summed up in one word, the word which is so often on her lips: *euklees*, 'honorable'.[15] She has a code of honor proper for a princess, an aristocratic and unintellectual ideal. From first to last this is Phaedra's dominant motive, except for the fatal moment when she surrenders her initiative to the Nurse. It is to preserve this honor that she takes her original decision to die in silence; to enjoy appreciation of her honor she indulges in the luxury of speech to the chorus; and to rescue her honorable reputation from the consequences she ruins Hippolytus and brings guilt and sorrow on Theseus. But it is all to no purpose. In the end her conspiracy of silence is a failure and her honor lost. Hippolytus and the chorus keep the oaths that they have sworn and remain silent; the house cannot speak; but the goddess Artemis coldly reveals the truth to Theseus, who learns not only that his wife had a guilty passion for Hippolytus but also that she has tricked him into killing his innocent son. Phaedra's attempt to save her honor has proved an expensive failure.

Not only is her purpose baffled and her code of conduct shown to be inadequate; her concern for her honor is dismissed by the gods as irrelevant. Both Aphrodite and Artemis treat Phaedra's honor with complete indifference. 'She is honorable – but still, she dies' (47), says Aphrodite, and when Artemis reveals the truth to Theseus she makes it clear that she is concerned with the reputation not of Phaedra, but of Hippolytus. 'I have come', she says to Theseus, 'to show that his mind was just, so that he may die in honor' (1299) – to save his reputation. Phaedra's passion, far from being buried in silence so that she can be honored after death, will be the subject of song in the ritual cult of Hippolytus. 'It shall not fall nameless and be silenced, Phaedra's passion for you' (1429-30).

Phaedra's purpose, to save her honor, is one consistent with her ideal of conduct and her life as she has lived it so far. It is characteristic of the Nurse that her purpose has nothing to do with ideals; it is specific and practical – she wishes to save not Phaedra's honor but her life, and to that end she will use any means which promise success. Her love for Phaedra is the motive for her actions from first to last. But in the end she succeeds only in destroying Phaedra's honor and her life as well; she hears herself rejected utterly and cursed by the person to whom she has devoted her entire life and whose well-being is her only objective.

The Nurse has no aristocratic code of conduct. Her word is not honorable, *euklees*, but *logos*,[16] speech, reason, argument. She believes in, and tries to effect, the settlement of human problems by human reason, *logos*, expressed in speech, *logos*, which influences others as argument, *logos*. This is in fact not an aristocratic attitude but a democratic one, and the Nurse has another quality characteristic of Athenian democracy, flexibility.[17] She can adapt herself quickly to new situations, seize a new ground of argument – a capacity illustrated by the fact that she shifts her ground in the play not once, like Phaedra and Hippolytus, but three times. She is in fact so flexible that her attitude is not a consistent moral code at all, but merely a series of practical approaches to different problems. It is natural therefore that the Nurse should be made to speak in terms that clearly associate her with the contemporary sophists, who, like her, had a secular and confident approach to human problems, the rhetorical skill to present their solution convincingly, and a relativism which, expressed as the doctrine of expediency, enabled them to shift their ground, as the Nurse does, from one position to another.

For the Nurse, when she first talks to Phaedra, the choice between speech and silence is meaningless. She behaves only in the choice between speech and speech. 'You should not be silent, child. But either refute me if I speak badly, or agree if I speak well' (297-99). This implies her basic confidence that no problem is beyond the power of human reason, but when she hears the first hints of what is wrong with Phaedra (337-42), her confidence begins to falter. 'To what lengths will speech go?' she asks. And when she understands the truth, she tries to stop Phaedra's speech, 'Oh. What will you say?' (353). She abandons hope of saving Phaedra's life, and consequently has no further use for her own. She goes off to die.

She comes back with her confidence renewed. She is now ashamed of her emotional reaction, her inadequacy (435). Second thoughts are best. What has happened to Phaedra is not 'irrational' (437), not something beyond the powers of reason and speech.

The powerful speech into which she now launches is easily recognizable as contemporary sophistic rhetoric at its cleverest and worst; it is a fine example of 'making the worse appear the better cause'. It is the devil quoting scripture; she cynically accuses Phaedra of *hybris* (474), insolence and pride toward the gods. She uses the stock sophistic argument to justify immoral conduct, the misdemeanors of the gods in the myths. And she reveals, in her description of the way of the world — the husbands who conceal their wives' infidelities, the fathers who connive at their sons' adulteries — a cynicism which is the well-known result of sophistic teaching, the cynicism of a Cleon, a Thrasymachus. Only a hardened cynic, in fact, could fancy that Hippolytus could be corrupted. And the Nurse's argument takes this for granted. Speech is all that is needed, winning words and in a double sense — the love charms and also her pleading the cause of love which will charm Hippolytus into compliance.

When we next see her, she is begging for silence. Speech has unloosed forces beyond her control, and she now persuades Hippolytus to remain silent. But Phaedra has overheard their interview and now resumes control of the situation. She pours out on the Nurse all the fury and hatred which Hippolytus' terrible denunciation has roused in her. She uses the verbal loophole the Nurse so cleverly left her; 'Did I not tell you to be silent?' (685-86) and curses her terribly, calling on Zeus to blast her with fire and destroy her root and branch (683-84). But the nurse is still not silenced. 'I can make a reply to this, if you will listen' (697), she says, and she maintains her practical, unprincipled viewpoint — 'If I had succeeded, I would be one of the clever ones' (700). And desperate though the situation is, she still has a way out. 'There is a way to save you, even from this situation, my child' (705). But the Nurse, her way out, and the whole concept of *logos*, reason and speech, for which she stands, are rejected by Phaedra in one biting phrase, 'Stop talking' (706). And we hear no more of the Nurse.

The worldly, practical approach to the problem has proved no more successful than Phaedra's simple code of honor. The Nurse's one purpose, to save Phaedra's life, has, when translated into action, ensured her death. And the Nurse's outlook implies a view of the gods, a skeptical view, which is ironically developed in a play which has begun with the appearance of the goddess Aphrodite in person. The Nurse reveals her basic skepticism in her opening speech (176-97), in which she dismisses speculation about future life as unprofitable. Life as we know it is painful, she says (189-90), but as for some other thing, dearer than life, darkness enfolds it and hides it in clouds (192-93). There is no revelation of what lies beneath the earth (196). Later, when she recognizes the power of Aphrodite, she still expresses her belief in 'scientific' agnostic terms. 'Cypris was no god, then, but something greater, whatever it may be, than a god' (359-60). This rationalism of hers is the most unsound of all the views of the order of the universe expressed or implied by human beings in the play, and by a supreme irony this representative of skeptical thought is chosen to be the most important link in the chain of events which Aphrodite has forged. The Nurse's 'reason' is the driving force in the process which brings Phaedra and Hippolytus to their deaths.

Hippolytus' purpose and his ideal is put before us early in the play; it is to live a life of piety and devotion to the virgin goddess Artemis. 'I am in your company, and exchange speech with you,' he says to the statue of Artemis. 'I hear your voice though I may not see your face. May I round the final mark of the course of my life even as I have begun' (85-87). He hopes to round the final mark, to run the full course of a life of reverence and piety, but his prayer is to be ironically fulfilled this very day. At the end of the play, he hears Artemis' voice though he cannot see her face, and exchanges speech with her as he lies dying, but he has been cut off in full career, his chariot wrecked. And before that he will have suffered the spiritual agony of seeing his father condemn and curse him as a hypocritical adulterer, a man whom it would be a mockery to associate with Artemis.

Like Phaedra, he is an aristocratic figure; in fact, most of the commonplaces of the aristocratic attitude are put into his mouth in the course of the play.[18] But he is also an intellectual and a religious mystic.[19] His principles, unlike Phaedra's, are clearly and consistently formulated; for him the most important thing in life is *eusebeia*, reverence toward the gods.[20] 'I know first of all how to treat the gods with reverence' (996), he says when defending himself against his father's attack. Except for the moment of passion when he threatens to break his oath and speak, he is guided in every thought and action by his *eusebeia*. And when he finally decides for silence and his oath, he emphasizes this motive: 'Know this, woman, it is my reverence which saves you' (656), he says to the Nurse. He might have said 'It is my reverence which destroys me,' for all through his father's bitter onslaught he stands by his principles, respects his oath, and keeps silent about Phaedra's part in the affair. As was the case with Phaedra and the Nurse, it is the central concept of his whole life and character which destroys him.

And, like them, he represents an attitude toward the gods. It is a religious position which is intellectual as well as mystic. His reverence for the gods manifests itself mainly in the worship of one goddess, Artemis; he completely rejects another, Aphrodite. The position is logical; on the intellectual plane, the worship of Artemis is clearly incompatible with the worship of Aphrodite, and acceptance of the one does constitute rejection of the other. The mass of humanity can ignore the contradiction, as the old servant does in the opening scene and just as most Christians manage to serve Mammon as well as God. But for the man who has dedicated his life to God, or to a goddess, there can be no compromise. Hippolytus must choose one or the other, 'Man must choose among the gods as the gods choose among men,' (104), he says to the servant.[21] And Hippolytus has chosen Artemis. It does not save him. He dies in agony in the prime of youth, and before he dies he has to go through the mental agony of hearing himself, the virgin soul (1006), treated by his father as a lustful hypocrite. And he sees himself in the end as a man who has spent his life in vain: 'In vain have I toiled at labors of reverence before mankind' (1367-69). He even goes so far as to wish that human beings could curse the gods, and though he is reproached by Artemis for this sentiment, he shows his disillusion in his farewell to her. 'This great companionship of ours, you find it easy to leave' (1441).[22] His reverence is inadequate, not merely as a way of life but also as a religious belief; it cannot stand unmoved in the face of reality — the knowledge that his privileged association with Artemis made him not a man to be envied but a pitiful victim, and that all the goddess can do for him is promise to kill another human being to avenge him.

Theseus is an early Attic king, but with the customary anachronism of Athenian tragedy, he is presented as a fifth-century statesman. His characteristic expression of thought and feeling is that of the man in the public eye, the man who is always conscious of his audience. When he states the charge against his son and invokes Poseidon's curse, he calls on the city to hear (884), making it an official act. Even in his mourning for Phaedra he is conscious of his public stature (817), and in his tirade against Hippolytus he speaks to the audience as often as he does to his son (943, 956). And he supports his action by an appeal to his reputation; if he is worsted by Hippolytus, the monsters he conquered in his heroic youth will no longer serve as proof that he is harsh to evildoers (976-80). His life is devoted to the maintenance of a reputation; even in his private sorrow he never forgets that the eyes of Athens are upon him.

He is a statesman, but not, like his son, an intellectual. He is the man of action; this point is emphasized by his impulsive act, his appeal to his heroic past, and his contempt for speech (*logos*). This appears clearly in his attack on his son; he describes Hippolytus as one who pursues evil with 'pious words' (957). 'What words', he says, 'can argue more effectively than this woman's corpse?' (960-61) 'Why do I try to compete with you in words on this matter?' (971). He follows this last remark with action, the proclamation of banishment; he is a man not of words but of deeds. When he called Poseidon's curse on his son he did not wait, as Artemis reminds him later, for proof or prophecy or cross-examination, but followed his impulse. He is like another Athenian statesman, Themistocles, who, says Thucydides, was best at intuitive action in an emergency, and the best man to decide immediate issues with the least deliberation (1.138); Theseus acts with the swift decision of a Themistocles, an Oedipus. But he is wrong. And his mistake destroys the thing to which he has devoted his life. It is a mistake he can never live down, his public reputation is gone, as Artemis coldly tells him: 'Hide yourself in shame below the depths of the earth, or take wing into the sky . . . among good men there is now no portion you can call your own' (1290-95).

Theseus, too, has a distinct religious attitude. His is the religion of the politician, vocal, formal, and skin-deep, verbal acceptance but limited belief. He first appears on stage wearing the wreath of the state visitor to an oracle, and he can roundly recite the names of the gods in public proclamation or prayer — 'Hippolytus . . . has dishonored the awful eye of Zeus' (886), but he only half believes in all this. He prays to Poseidon to kill his son, and before the day is out, but when the chorus begs him to recall his prayer he replies: 'No. And in addition, I shall exile him from this land' (893). That revealing phrase 'in addition' is expanded in the succeeding lines. 'Of these two destinies he will be struck by one or the other' (894). Either Poseidon will strike him down or he will live out a miserable life in exile. The hint of skepticism is broadened when the messenger arrives to announce the disaster. He claims that his news is of serious import (1157) to Theseus and all the citizens of Athens, but Theseus' first thought is of political news: 'Has some disaster overtaken the neighboring cities?' (1160-61). Informed that Hippolytus is near death he asks, 'Who did it? Did he get into trouble with someone else whose wife he raped, as he did his father's?' (1164-65). And only when the messenger reminds him of his curse does he realize the truth. 'O gods, Poseidon, then you really were my father, you listened to my curses' (1169-70). It is a revelation which proves the unsoundness of his skepticism, and he accepts it with joy. But he will live to regret it and wish his prayer unspoken. 'Would that it had never come into my mouth' (1412).

Theseus has gone through the same cycle as the other characters of the play. All four of the characters live, and two of them die, in a world in which purpose frustrates itself, choice is meaningless, moral codes and political attitudes ineffective, and human conceptions of the nature of the gods erroneous. But two of them learn, at the end of the play, the truth which we have known from the beginning, the nature of the world in which they live. They learn it from the lips of Artemis, as we have already heard it from the lips of Aphrodite. Artemis comes, like Aphrodite, to reveal (1298); she confirms, expands, and explains the process of divine government, of which the prologue was our first glimpse.

These two goddesses are powers locked in an eternal war, a war in which the human tragedy we have just witnessed is merely one engagement. In this particular operation, Aphrodite was the active agent and Artemis the passive; Artemis now informs us that these roles will be reversed — there will be a return made for this in which Artemis will assume the active role and Aphrodite the passive. The terms in which she explains her passivity in this case to Theseus make clear that this is permanent war, an eternal struggle in which the only losses are human lives.

'This is law and custom for the gods,' she says (1328). 'No one wishes to stand hostile against the energy of a god who has a desire — we stand aside always' (1329-30). The authority for this law and custom, as Artemis makes clear, is Zeus himself; but for her fear of Zeus, she says, she would not have allowed Hippolytus to die. What has happened, then, is no anomaly, but the working of the system of divine government of the universe, an eternal pattern of alternate aggression and retreat. And we can see from what Artemis says that when she has the active instead of the passive role, she will be as ruthless as Aphrodite was in this case.

The words which describe Aphrodite's direction of human affairs are thus equally applicable to Artemis; they constitute a description of the function of divine government as a whole. And there are two words, repeated throughout the play at crucial moments and in significant contexts, which characterize the nature of the government of the universe. One of these words, *sphallein*, describes the action characteristic of the gods, and the other, *allōs*, describes the human condition which results from that action.

Sphallein, to trip, throw, cast down. It is Aphrodite's own word for her action in the play. 'I throw down those who despise me' (6). The literal accomplishment of this metaphorical threat comes when the bull from the sea 'throws' the horses of Hippolytus' chariot (1232). But this action is not confined to Hippolytus. The word recurs in connection with all the principal characters of the play. 'You are quickly thrown,' (183), says the Nurse to Phaedra in her opening speech. She is referring to Phaedra's sudden changes of mind, the capriciousness of the sick woman who vacillates between staying indoors or out, but the words have a terrible significance in the light of what happens later when Phaedra changes her mind about something more important. Speaking of her own love for Phaedra and wishing, for her own peace of mind, that she did not love her so much, the Nurse laments the fact that 'consistent conduct in life' (261), 'brings, so they say, not pleasure but overthrow' (262). It is true enough; the one consistent attitude in her, her love for Phaedra, brings her to ruin, and the words describe more exactly still the attitude and practice of Hippolytus, who is as consistent as the Nurse is flexible, as single-minded as the Nurse is versatile.

Phaedra, after she has heard Hippolytus denounce her and all her sex, sees herself as 'thrown' (671). As Theseus reads the fatal letter, the chorus prays to an unnamed god not to throw the house (871). And when Theseus explains to Hippolytus how he could curse and condemn him, he uses the same word; 'I was tripped and thrown in my opinion by the gods' (1414). It is this remark of his which provokes Hippolytus' wish that the human race could curse the gods.

The goddess trips, throws, leads astray, frustrates – all these are meanings of *sphallein*, and the word which describes the operation of the human will in these circumstances in *allōs*: otherwise, differently, wrongly, in vain. This adverb is used to describe the operation of human will throughout the tragedy; the character's actions produce results opposite to their purpose, things turn out 'otherwise'. 'Our labor is all in vain' (301), says the Nurse of her efforts to make Phaedra speak; the word has a double sense here, for the Nurse succeeds in her final attempt, but the results are not what she intended. 'Vainly', says Phaedra to the chorus, 'have I pondered in the long watches of the night, seeking to understand how human life is ruined' (375–76). This understanding she never attains, but it is given in all its fullness to Theseus and Hippolytus at the end of the play. 'In vain, in vain,' chants the chorus, 'does the land of Greece increase sacrifice of oxen to Zeus and Apollo . . .' (535-37). 'In vain', says Hippolytus in his agony, 'have I performed labors of reverence before mankind' (1367-69).[23] And the Nurse, speaking specifically of humanity's ignorance of anything beyond this life, characterizes the whole human situation with the same word (197). 'We are carried off our course, led astray, supported vainly, by myths.' In the context, it is of course a rationalist criticism of popular beliefs, but the verbal pattern of the whole poem invests it with a deeper meaning. We are borne astray, carried to a destination we did not intend, by myths, myths in which the Nurse does not believe, but which the appearance and actions of the two goddesses in the play prove to be not myths in the Nurse's sense, but the stuff of reality. The underlying meaning of the Nurse's words is brought out by the emphatic manner in which both goddesses are made to emphasize their connection with myth; myth, *mythos*, is the word they use of their own speech. 'I will quickly reveal the truth of these words [myths]' (9), says Aphrodite; Artemis, after telling Theseus the truth, asks him cruelly, 'Does my word [story, myth] pain you?' (1313). Human beings are indeed borne astray by myths, the goddesses who trip their heels and thwart their purpose. Humanity is merely the 'baser nature' which 'comes between the pass and fell-incensed points of mighty opposites.'

Of the nature and meaning of Aphrodite and Artemis in this play much has been written, and there is little to add. They have many aspects; they are anthropomorphic goddesses, myths, dramatic personalities with motives and hostile purposes and they are also impersonal, incompatible forces of nature. They are indeed 'mighty opposites', and that opposition may be expressed in many terms — positive and negative, giving and denying, increase and decrease, indulgence and abstinence — but what Euripides has been at some pains to emphasize is not their opposition, but their likeness. The play is full of emphatic suggestions that there is a close correspondence between them.

When Hippolytus describes the meadow sacred to Artemis from which he has made the wreath he offers to her statue, he mentions the bee (77), which goes through the uncut grass in spring. It is an appropriate detail, for the name *melissa*, bee, was given to priestesses of Artemis,[24] and the bee is in many contexts associated with virginity.[25] But some five hundred lines later the chorus compares Aphrodite to a bee, 'She hovers like a bee' (562-63). This transference of symbol from the appropriate goddess to the inappropriate one is strange, and it is reinforced by another striking correspondence. The chorus, early in the play, describes Artemis, under one of her many titles, Dictynna. 'She ranges through the marsh waters, over the land and over the sea, in the eddies of the salt water' (148-150). And later, the Nurse, describing the power of Aphrodite to Phaedra, uses similar language; 'She ranges through the air, and she is in the wave of the sea' (447-48). The function of these surprising echoes[26] is to prepare us for an extraordinary feature of Artemis' concluding speeches: she repeats word after word and phrase of Aphrodite's prologue. These two polar opposites express themselves in the same terms. 'I gained a start on the road long ago' (23), says Aphrodite, and Artemis uses the same unusual metaphor — 'And yet I shall gain nothing, and only give you pain' (1297), she says to Theseus. 'I shall reveal' (6), says Aphrodite; and Artemis says that she comes 'to reveal' (1298). 'I am not unnamed' (1), says Aphrodite, and Artemis takes up the phrase; 'not unnamed shall Phaedra's love for you fall and be silenced.' Both of them claim, in similar words and with opposite meanings, that they reward the reverent and punish the wrongdoer (5-6 and 1339-41), and each of them, with the same characteristic word, *timōrēsomai* (21 and 1422), announces her decision to kill the other's human protégé.[27]

They are opposites, but considered as divinities directing human affairs, they are exactly alike. The repetitions emphasize the fact that the activity of Aphrodite and the passivity of Artemis are roles which will be easily reversed. And the mechanical repetition of Aphrodite's phrases by Artemis depersonalizes both of them; we become aware of them as impersonal forces which act in a repetitive pattern, an eternal ordered dance of action and reaction, equal and opposite. From the law which governs their advance and retreat there can be no deviation; Artemis cannot break the pattern of movement to save Hippolytus, nor can she forgive Aphrodite. Forgiveness is in fact unthinkable in such a context; it is possible only for human beings. These gods are, in both the literal and metaphorical senses of the word, inhuman.

Artemis does indeed tell Hippolytus not to hate his father (1435). But this merely emphasizes the gulf between god and man. She does not, on her plane, forgive Aphrodite; rather, she announces a repetition of the terrible events we have just witnessed: a new human victim is to die to pay for the loss of her favorite. 'The anger of Cypris shall not swoop down on your body unavenged. For I shall punish another man, with my own hand, whoever chances to be most loved by her of mortals, with these inescapable arrows' (1420-22). This, together with the promise that his memory will be the myth of a virgin cult, is the consolation she offers Hippolytus for the fact that she stood aside and allowed him to be destroyed. She cannot weep for him — that is the law which governs the nature of gods (1396) — nor can she stay by him as he dies. 'It is not lawful for me to see the dead and defile my eye with their dying breath' (1437–38). And she withdraws, leaving father and son alone.

It has often been remarked that this disturbing play ends on a note of serenity. Méridier's comment is typical: 'le dénouement s'achève, grâce à la présence d'Artémis, dans un rayonnement de transfiguration. Et cette scène finale, où la tristesse déchirante s'épure peu à peu et s'apaise dans une sérénité céleste . . . '[28] The ending is serene, but the serenity has nothing to do with Artemis, who throughout her scene with Hippolytus coldly and insistently disassociates herself from him,[29] so that he bids her farewell with a reproach. The serenity comes not from the goddess but from the two broken men who are left on stage after she withdraws.

Hippolytus forgives his father. To err is human, as Artemis says to Theseus (1434); but to forgive is not divine. It is an action possible only for man, an act by which man can distinguish himself from and rise above the inexorable laws of the universe in which he is placed. And though Hippolytus recognizes that he is following Artemis' advice,[30] he shows too that he is fully conscious of the fact that in forgiving he is doing what she cannot do. As he forgives his father, he calls to witness his sincerity 'Artemis of the conquering arrow' (1451). The epithet is not ornamental; it recalls vividly Artemis' announcement of her intention to repay, twenty-five lines before — 'with these inescapable arrows I shall punish another.' Hippolytus calls to witness his act of forgiveness the goddess who canot herself forgive.

It is significant that Artemis leaves the stage before the end of the play; her exit closes the circle which began with Aphrodite's entrance. Within its circumference, the human beings of the play fulfilled through all the multiple complications of choice an external purpose of which they were ignorant. But Aphrodite's purpose is now fulfilled; she has no further use for these creatures, and Artemis has gone. The play ends with a human act which is at last a free and meaningful choice, a choice made for the first time in full knowledge of the nature of human life and divine government, an act which does not frustrate its purpose. It is an act of forgiveness, something possible only for human beings, not for gods but for their tragic victims. It is man's noblest declaration of independence, and it is made possible by man's tragic position in the world. Hippolytus' forgiveness of his father is an affirmation of purely human values in an inhuman universe.

24

THE *TROJAN WOMEN*

D. J. CONACHER

It has commonly been argued that the *Troades* is a play signally lacking in dramatic structure.[1] Some critics have condemned, or at least severely censured the work on these grounds, others have found it intensely moving, even as drama, despite this alleged defect, but however judgments have varied, the general impression of the play conveyed by the critics is that it presents a succession of unrelieved and ever deepening woe. Few will question the varied and striking successes of individual passages: the brilliant Cassandra episode, with its effective contrasts of frenzied lyric and strong dramatic exposition; the vivid choral description of the Trojan Horse *débâcle*; the final *kommos*, as the Queen and her women beat upon the soil in their last farewell to the Trojan dead. More contrived, but intensely interesting for its own sake, is the set debate between Hecuba and Helen on the question of the latter's guilt. However we may regard the incident in relation to the rest of the play, the rhetorical verve of this confrontation, in a life-and-death struggle, of the mythical and the rationalistic interpretations of Helen's story provides one of Euripides' most arresting scenes.

With all these riches, is the *Troades* still a play which fails to combine its effects within an organic dramatic structure? This seems improbable when we notice that those who like the play praise it for its final and total impact. The power of this play increases steadily until it is finished; its closing lines leave us with a sense of completeness which no mere series of episodes, however striking in themselves, could possibly evoke.

In considering the dramatic structure of the *Troades*, we should remember that it completed a trilogy which was at least loosely connected in theme: thus the whole of the present play may be regarded as in some sense a conclusion. This does not mean that it need not have a structure of its own, with its own beginning, middle and end, but it is

From *Euripidean Drama: Myth, Theme and Structure*, pp. 137–45. Copyright © University of Toronto Press 1967. Reprinted by permission of University of Toronto Press.

quite reasonable to suppose that this fact may have a certain limiting effect on the play as a whole. Consider the *Eumenides* in relation to the *Agamemnon*: no elaborate analysis of either play is needed to observe that the structure of the last play of the trilogy is far less complex, just as its tensions are far less tightly drawn. There are certain obvious reasons why this should be the case generally in connected trilogies. Psychological considerations aside (a series of three plays of the power and complex tensions of an *Agamemnon* would surely reach a point of diminishing returns), the sheer density of material, both actual and potential, must be far greater in the early part of the trilogy. Every critic knows that even within any single play, the structural complexities will be greater in the earlier half or two thirds of it, as the poet seeks to make his revelations gradually in the particular dramatic form required. In the proportions of a closely connected trilogy we may expect to find not the same but an analogous situation. Each play has its own end to reach, its particular material to realize. But in the first play, *all* of the material must be present either actually or potentially, and elaborate structural devices may be needed to effect the anticipatory ironies so essential to Greek drama. (In the case of the *Agamemnon* anticipatory irony often gives place to veiled prophecy; consider how much the role of Cassandra is influenced by the subsequent development of the trilogy.) The total amount of unrevealed material gradually decreases as the trilogy proceeds, so that progressively less elaborate structures are required. In the case of the *Troades* something of the same process is at work, though to a lesser degree.

In most tragedies which we know, cause and effect, with sometimes an ironic perversion of purposive action, determine structure. (This is as true of *Macbeth* and *King Lear* as it is of *Oedipus Tyrannus* and *Hippolytus*.) In the *Troades*, on the other hand, the time for action has passed; Troy and her leaders have fallen and all that remains to be shown is the long passion of the Queen and her women who have survived the cataclysm. A mere sequence of disaster, however, does not make a drama, and in default of real action on the part of Hecuba there appears a faint outline of policy and even of a curious intermittent hope which punctuates the sufferings. Again and again, this hope is stamped out and gives away to desolation, only to flicker forth in some new place until its final quenching at the end of the play. Thus a certain rhythm is introduced into what would otherwise be a mere chain of woeful experiences, and it is this rhythm which informs the structure of the play.

In all this, the anticipatory 'preparations' of the prologue do not come amiss. Fluctuations in the Trojans' attitudes toward the gods reflect, to some degree, the alternations just described. Viewed in this light, the play's progression might be regarded as the gradual recognition, on the part of Hecuba and her women, of the truth about the gods which the prologue has already expressed, by satiric implication, to the audience.

We may best appreciate this rhythm of hope and desolation if we read through the play rapidly, pausing only to note the dominant tone of each part, the major effect of each incident. The Chorus too, as one would expect in a play so dominated by pathos, will be seen to play an important part in reflecting the changing moods of the dramatic passages.

Both the *Hecuba* and the *Troades* begin, when the prologue is over, with a lyric passage from the Queen, but two passages show very different reactions on her part to the sufferings which surround her. In the former play, Hecuba begs her fellow-slaves (as they now are) to lift her, a tottering old woman, into the open air (59–63). In the opening lyric of the *Troades*, Hecuba shows a full awareness of her woes, but here her first words give *herself* the command to raise her head (98), and soon she is expressing a kind of 'policy in desolation' which she is to follow, and bid others to follow, throughout the play. 'Sail with the flood; steer with your destiny; sail with the winds of chance; set not your prow against the flux of life' (102–4).

The repetition of the word *daimon*, which occurs four times in the opening lyric, is interesting and effective. It is one of Euripides' favourite words for that indefinite divine power, a shade more definite than *tychē*, which affects the destinies of men. Here the poet's insistence on the term, and his emphasis on the changing winds of fate (101) keeps fresh and immediate the impression already made on us by the fickle gods of the prologue. Hecuba is well aware that the gods have, at least for the present, turned away from her, but she does not as yet rail against them or explicitly despair of their return. Yet there is already a hint of bitterness in the nostalgic reference at the end of her monologue to the triumphal strains with which she used to lead the chorus in praise of the gods of Troy:

. . . how strange my clamour now, like to a mother-bird's over her nestlings, not like the song I used to sing in Trojan choruses, leaning on Priam's sceptre, honouring the gods.   (146–52)

Here the Chorus of Trojan women enters. Their fluttering terror, their anxious cries ('What is the news? What will happen to us all? Already the ships are moving. . . . What chieftain will take me as his slave?') Hecuba answers with the same resolute acceptance of their desperate plight which she has already shown: 'I know not, but I guess the worst' (163).

In the *stasimon* which follows, the captive women develop their speculations about their future home. Vignettes of many states and colonies of Greece are included in these lyric wanderings; in the fears and preferences which the Chorus shows, the poet allows (in addition, no doubt, to some contemporary references)[2] a few gleams of hope to lighten the gloom. Thus, while one singer shudders at drudgery in Corinth, another prays that she may reach that 'illustrious happy land of Theseus.' Sparta, home of Helen and Menelaus, is of course the most dreaded of all, but good reports are heard of Thessaly which, for its wealth and beauty, is chosen next to Athens itself as the favourite place for slavery!

The entry of Talthybius announcing the bitter facts of the Greek choices seems timed to quench these optimistic flashes. Agamemnon is to wed Cassandra, the sacred virgin of Apollo; Andromache is to go to the son of her husband's slayer and Queen Hecuba to Odysseus, the Greek whom she most despises; Polyxena, the youngest and fairest, the Greeks will sacrifice upon Achilles' tomb. These dooms could hardly be worse; a new access of woe finds expression in Hecuba's passionate outburst against 'that hateful tricky monster' (282 ff.) who is to be her master.

Suddenly the gloom is rent asunder by the triumphant entry of Cassandra, shrieking ecstatically of her coming nuptials:

Raise high the marriage torch. . . . Hymen, Lord Hymen! Blessed is the bride-groom and blessed too the bride — I who am to serve the royal bed of Agamemnon at Argos! Hail, Lord Hymen, hail!   (308–14)

As Cassandra links her mother's bereavements with her celebrations, and the name of Hecate with that of Hymen, we soon catch the baleful irony, the sardonic exaltation, beneath this girlish carolling, and soon the inevitable cry to Phoebus Apollo confirms our guess that Cassandra's mockery is buoyed up by some real secret joy. (This is the twist which gives a special brilliance to the Cassandra scene: the joy with which she greets her coming marriage, and which so shocks her mother and the Chorus, is a real joy, though its reasons are the reverse of those which might be inferred from a literal reading of her lyric.) All these hints are soon fulfilled in the 'sane' speech with which Cassandra (like her Aeschylean counterpart) explains her lyric. Her 'marriage' will bring death on Agamemnon and the hated house of Atreus in turn will perish in matricidal murder (354–64).

To these sardonic satisfactions, Cassandra adds further consolations to the Trojans. The war has profited them more than their conquerors: for the sake of one woman, Greeks have died far from home, without family, without burial, while the Trojans have gained the greatest glory in dying for their native land. Even Paris has gained a kind of fame in marrying Zeus's daughter! (365–99).

It is Cassandra's fate never to be heeded by her people. Her speeches here, which should provide the one great relief to Trojan gloom, have no effect. We know and Cassandra knows that the Greeks in turn will suffer, but by Apollo's trick the knowledge must still be hidden from those who need this satisfaction most. The Queen who has earlier raised her head in the midst of her miseries (98 ff.) now bids the woman let her lie, and a new cynicism breaks into her habitual prayers.

'Let me lie where I have fallen. . . .' This indeed seems the final despair of Hecuba. Yet when Andromache mutters her envy of the dead Polyxena, the Queen rounds on her: 'Life can never be as bad as death! Death is a nothingness, but in life is hope' (632-33).

In the rhythm of the play, the main significance of this debate between Hecuba and Andromache is the resurrection of hope which Hecuba again provides. Andromache's speech is disappointing: a set rhetorical exercise on two unrelated themes: 'Death *versus* unhappy living' and 'The proper deportment of wives and widows.' The speech abounds in the bitter ironies and classic dilemmas of pathetic rhetoric; only the peroration addressed to Hector's shade saves it from banality. Yet once again, Hecuba finds solace. The sight of the young mother Andromache reminds her of the one remaining hope; Andromache must live to raise her son and Hector's son: '. . . Troy's mainstay now, for children sired by him may build again; our city may exist again' (703-5). Hardly has this hope been uttered when Talthybius enters with the dread announcement that Astyanax is to be cast from the battlements.

Now for the first time even the Chorus turns against the gods. Hecuba has already blamed them, though briefly (696). Andromache has blamed everyone: the Greeks, of course (764-65), Helen in the most savage terms (766-69), even Priam and Hecuba, by implication, for letting Paris grow up (597 ff.); but most emphatically she blames the gods (597, 599, 775-76). And now the Chorus, remembering Ganymede and Tithonus, Troy's fairest offerings, murmur 'Vain indeed for Troy were these love-charms of the gods!' (858-59).

With unconscious irony, the Chorus' words provide the cue for Menelaus, another cast-off of love, who summons Helen, the love-charm which has caused the Trojans' woe. Structurally too the entry of Helen is excellently placed, for only such a challenge could revive the flagging powers of Hecuba. At the sound of Menelaus' threats on Helen's life, Hecuba utters a new prayer of hope in the justice of the gods:

You who contain the Earth, yet dwell upon it, Whoever you are, Zeus, hard-guessing for the wise, whether the necessary laws of nature or the mind of man, I pray to you: for walking silent ways you guide in accord with justice the affairs of man.   (884-88)

This 'new prayer', as Menelaus calls it in surprise (889), has occasioned much learned comment from the critics. Wilamowitz,[3] for example, observes (with certain qualifications) that Hecuba is actually invoking a power like the divine air of Diogenes or the world mind of Anaxagoras, which according to the philosophers controlled the world and all its motions and thought. More significant, perhaps, is this critic's observation that at this point Hecuba dares believe, now that Helen is apparently to be brought to justice, that this law of nature works, in some incomprehensible way, in accordance with justice. In any case, we may agree that this prayer recalls to the audience daring contemporary views on the gods; it serves too as prologue to Hecuba's coming refutation of Helen's 'traditional' defence of her sin ('It was the gods. . . .'). For, in the debate for her life which now ensues (919 ff.), Helen follows and even improves upon the orthodox interpretation: first Hecuba and then Priam are guilty, the one for bearing, the other for not destroying, the fatal fire-brand Paris; next Aphrodite was the cause, for when Paris came to abduct her the god was with him and not even Zeus himself can resist Aphrodite. How insistent, in contrast to Hecuba's prayer, is the anthropomorphism now! The passage is, moreover, enriched by several Euripidean 'improvements'. To the traditional 'Homeric' defence of Helen that the fault was Aphrodite's, Helen adds the boast that thanks to the lure of her beauty Greece was saved, for had Paris accepted either Hera's or Pallas' bribes, instead of Aphrodite's, Greece would have been enslaved. Again, in having Helen ask herself the crucial question: 'What indeed was I thinking of, to abandon home and country for that foreigner?' (946-47), the poet makes this alleged pawn of the gods undergo a moment of uncertainty before letting her accept 'the divine excuse' again.

Hecuba's attack on Helen's arguments begins with a defence of Pallas Athena and Hera against the charges of folly implied in Helen's story. This questioning of myths disparaging the gods is, of course, common in Euripidean drama; usually however, such passages abandon the anthropomorphic level of mythology on which such discreditable stories of the gods are based. Consider, for example, Heracles' argument at *Heracles* 1341-46 which ends, '. . . the god, if he be really god, needs nothing,' and comparable passages in the *Hippolytus* (120), the *I.T.* (389-91) and the *Bacchae* (1348), where we find the same implication that by nature the gods should be above human passions. In the present passage, Euripides with more attention to dramatic relevance keeps Hecuba's argument on the anthropomorphic level: why should *these* goddesses, Hera who has already got Zeus, and Athena, who has chosen a virgin's life, barter their favourite states to win a prize for beauty? (976-81). Not till she deals with Aphrodite does the more typical Euripidean rationalism begin to intrude into Hecuba's argument:

My son was peerless in his beauty; on seeing him your mind *became* the god of love. For folly is men's 'Aphrodite'; hence is the name derived from foolishness (*aphrosynēs*)   (987-90)

Hecuba wins the debate; she persuades Menelaus that Helen has willingly abandoned him. But it is Helen, or rather Helen's beauty, which finally carries the day. Before Helen's entry, Hecuba has begged Menelaus not to look upon her, lest desire sap his resolution (891). Now despite more blustering from Menelaus, she hears him postponing Helen's death till they reach Argos. She persuades him not to allow Helen on the same ship as himself, but one feels that she is now fighting a losing battle. The gloomy ode which follows substantiates this sense of defeat. It begins (1060-80) with more direct reproaches to Zeus than the Chorus has yet permitted itself ('So, Zeus, you have betrayed your Trojan temple, your Trojan altar . . .' [1060 ff.] and 'In vain our sacrifices, in vain the reverent music of our choirs' [1071 ff.]); it ends with a prayer for Helen's death at sea (even as she holds her 'golden mirrors, delight of virgins' – a nice touch) in terms which clearly indicate fear of Helen's re-establishment in Sparta.

After the scene with Helen, there are no further resurrections, however slight, of Trojan hope. Two brusque entries of Talthybius, once with the body of Astyanax, once to announce the final burning of Troy and the order for departure, evoke two moving laments from Hecuba. (Talthybius is a harsh, sinister figure in the *Troades*, very different from the sympathetic Talthybius of the *Hecuba*; here he is used to represent the impersonal cruelty of the Achaeans; though personally guiltless of the deeds and instructions he relates, we cannot but sympathize with Cassandra's scornful comment on the type he represents [424-426].) Hecuba's lament for Astyanax opens with a castigation of Achaean cowardice and closes with a pathetic reminiscence of Hector, suggested by the imprints left on Hector's shield on which the body of the child is to be buried. But it is Hecuba's account of the tender relations between herself and her little grandson which leads to the heart of this ultimate desolation:

It is not you who bury me, but I you, the younger one; an old woman, without city, without child, buries this pitiful corpse. Vain were my nursings, my many kisses, and vain too my dreams for you, of old.
                                                                              (1185-88)

In these final passages, both Queen and Chorus seem to turn completely from the gods: 'From the gods, naught but trouble . . . in vain our sacrifices!' (1240, 1242). 'Why call upon the gods? They heard us not, when called upon before' (1280-81). When Hecuba does call upon them, it is more in indignation than in prayer: 'Son of Cronos, Lord of Troy, begetting father, have you seen what things unworthy of the Trojan race we suffer?' and the Chorus, which has earned its own share of tragic knowledge, replies, 'He *has* seen — and the great city has become nothing. Troy is no longer' (1288-93). In this last *kommos* between the Queen and her woman, as the smoke from the burning city rises in the background, we have reached the end of that rhythm which false and intermittent hope has lent to this theme of suffering. Yet even here there is something more than the mere desolation. It appears first in Hecuba's echo of that consolation suggested earlier by Cassandra: the recognition that, in a sense, Trojan greatness and future fame depend on this utter ruin which the gods have sent. The stature which the ruined Hecuba acquires in these final scenes reminds us of the special kind of nobility which the ruined Oedipus (in Sophocles' *O.C.*) possesses. This feeling for the nobility of an Oedipus, or a Hecuba, derives in part from the aura of almost superstitious awe with which the Greeks surround those necessarily great personages who had suffered the ultimate in woe and yet endured. It derives in part, also, from the awareness which such strangely privileged beings have finally acquired of their real position in relation to the gods, or (in non-mythological terms) to the outside forces, merciless, because impersonal, which frame their destiny, and which can no longer hurt them more.

In the final lament, Hecuba has abandoned hope and vain cries to the gods, but she is still not passive. Still she leads her women in the one invocation which has any meaning left: the Trojan soil, the earth, and beneath it, the vast familial crowding of the dead.

25

ORESTES

CHRISTIAN WOLFF

The plot of *Orestes* is Euripides' invention. It comes like a parenthesis between two well-known stories, one of Orestes' return to avenge his father and reclaim his house and rule (the subject of Aeschylus' *Choephoroi* and the *Electra* of Sophocles and Euripides), the other, its sequel, of Orestes' purgation, trial, and acquittal in Athens (the subject of Aeschylus' *Eumenides*). But though its action is new and without mythical precedent, the play is filled with echoes of these familiar stories. Thus Euripides partly repeats his own *Electra*. As in that play there had been a plot to kill Clytemnestra, so in *Orestes* a plot is hatched to kill Tyndareus' other daughter, Helen (cf. 1421 ff., 1588, *Electra* 976). The famous call to the dead Agamemnon to assist his children in their vengeance (*Electra* 677 ff., already an adaptation of *Choephoroi* 479 ff.) re-echoes when Orestes, Electra, and Pylades ask for help in their plot against Helen (1225 ff.). Then, as Clytemnestra had been lured off to her death by Electra (*Electra* 1128 ff.), so Electra now draws Helen's daughter Hermione into the palace to be held hostage and possibly killed (1123 ff.). Finally, drawing on Sophocles, the scene in which Helen cries out offstage as though she were being killed while Electra onstage shouts her rejoicing (*Orestes* 1301 ff.) recalls the latter's exultation when Clytemnestra is killed in the older poet's *Electra* (1409 ff.).

Each of these echoes, however, creates effects of dislocation. Not an aging, corrupt queen, killer of her husband, but the young and innocent Hermione is now victim. Invoking Agamemnon's help is far less relevant in a plot on Helen than it had been in enacting vengeance on the wife who murdered him. Here, in fact, this traditional motif directly contradicts an earlier moment in the play where Orestes imagines that, had he asked his father whether or not to kill Clytemnestra, Agamemnon would have supplicated him on his knees not to do it (288 ff.). What appears at first to be a formal repetition, somewhat misplaced, sets off a characteristically Euripidean dissonance, and then marks the contradictions of

Originally published in *Euripides: A Collection of Critical Essays*, ed. Erich Segal (Prentice-Hall 1968), pp. 132–49. Reprinted by permission of the author.

his protagonist's motives. Orestes' remorse for one killing is wiped out by the project of another. More generally, the new sense of the plot of *Orestes*, set into relief by echoes of *Electra*, has been well outlined by one commentator as follows: 'the former crime [that is, killing Clytemnestra], at divine behest [Apollo's command; cf. *Orestes* 1665], is accomplished by human agency; the latter crime [killing Helen], at human behest [it is Pylades' idea, 1105], is blocked by divine agency [the final reappearance of Apollo].'[1] In *Electra* Orestes had committed a crime under divine compulsion; now he sets out spontaneously to commit another whose necessity is doubtful. Clytemnestra had been a guilty victim. Helen has her guilt, but nothing makes it clear that Orestes should be her punisher; and Hermione, another prospective victim, is an innocent bystander. Set against *Electra*, the action of *Orestes* appears to be motivated by a kind of gratuitous self-indulgence.

But the play not only recalls a past story, it also anticipates its traditional sequel, and again there are shifts of meaning. Orestes' trial for murder, forecast at the end of *Electra* and represented in Aeschylus' *Eumenides*, becomes in this play a trial before the public assembly of the citizens of Argos. Yet where Orestes had been acquitted at his traditional trial, he is now condemned; not on grounds of justice, but for patently political reasons. Euripides has, in fact, represented the trial at Argos with transparently contemporary features — notably two speakers typifying, respectively, an Athenian demagogue (903 ff.), such as Cleophon (as the scholiast suggests), and the politician of adaptability (888 ff.) perhaps a caricature of Theramenes (cf. Aristophanes, *Frogs* 538 ff.). Apollo, appearing at the end of the play, will finally forecast the old trial at Athens, assuring justice and Orestes' acquital; the jury will be made up of gods (1650), not men as in the tradition represented by Aeschylus. But where, a spectator in the Athens of 408 might have asked himself, are the gods or such an administration of justice as would give a man fair trial in his city at such a time? Juxtaposing his new plot with the old myth, Euripides now lays bare the gap between everyday reality and the ancient story. It is a familiar way with him, but never does he take it quite so far. This new plot moves as far from its traditional conclusions as possible. Orestes, condemned to death, unregenerate, abandoned by whatever gods had led him on, reaches the point of killing Hermione, setting his ancestral house on fire, and destroying himself, Electra, and Pylades. Then Apollo appears and turns the action about to force its traditional conclusion. The torches are stayed (they might recall the torches carried in celebration at the end of the *Eumenides*). Orestes will be purified and given new trial, and he will marry Hermione at whose neck he holds his sword.

One might suppose Euripides, as he is so often accused of doing, means to negate the myth completely. Yet not only does *Orestes*, for all the novelty of its plot, parallel parts of a traditional story, but it is also filled with reminiscences of other tragedies and the sound of legendary names — Glaucos the sea-god, Ganymede, Oiax the brother of Palamedes, Odysseus, Telemachus, the Achaian herald Talthybius, the hero Diomedes, Hector, Leda, and the Dioscuri. And, most notably, we never cease hearing about the mythical backgound of Orestes' race, the names and stories of Tantalus, Pelops, Atreus, Thyestes, Aerope, Agamemnon, and Iphigenia; and of Troy and Helen. The old stories weigh heavily on this new one, conjuring up an endlessly oppressive past, a weight accompanying Orestes' own crime (cf. 28 ff., 164 ff., 192 ff., 289 ff., 374 f., 392 ff., 505 ff., 526 ff., 546 ff., 819 ff., 1587 ff., 1648 ff.).

The plot of *Orestes*, then, stands in a twofold relation to the myth. As it is new and seems to depart from the familiar mythical tradition, it represents a break with the past. But, as it is dense with references to that past, this break effects no release. The past has no more viable connection to the present, but is still a burden on it. This burden is so great that the present — the plot of the play — appears to lose its substance, to lead nowhere, to achieve nothing. The new story, in terms of the traditional continuity of the myth to which the play returns in the end, might just as well not have taken place. Euripides dramatizes a sense of emptiness and superfluousness, something, one suspects, of the contemporary mood in Athens, and perhaps something of a more general sadness.

The action itself, to consider it more closely, falls into two parts. In the first Orestes, Electra, and then Pylades are together in a situation that is desperate but begins by holding some hope, in Menelaus' help and possibly a reasonable decision from the Argive assembly. That hope is shown, in a series of encounters, to be vain. Orestes and his sister are condemned to death and prepare to take their own lives. Then, suddenly, they decide instead to plot revenge on Menelaus for his treachery, a project that takes up the latter half of the play. The procedure from one part to the other, like that of the play throughout, is by abrupt, unexpected (but carefully devised) shifts. These are reflected in the central figure of Orestes, in his unpredictable oscillations between sanity and madness, and in the contradictions of his mood and purposes.

As the play opens his situation is critical twice over. Outwardly he faces a trial for murder before a hostile city which holds him completely captive. Inwardly he appears overcome by guilt, the effects of which erupt in a physical illness resembling epilepsy. His inner disturbance in turn is given two definitions. In accordance with the tradition, it is represented as the work of the furies (37, 317 ff.; cf. 408, 410, 423). But then, when Menelaus asks, 'what disease destroys you?' (395 f.), Orestes answers, *hē synesis, hoti synoida dein' eirgasmenos* ('the intelligence — that I am conscious of my terrible deeds'). A psychological abstraction articulates an inner condition which before had been called, in the language of myth, the work of the furies. In the same spirit Orestes recognizes that 'it is not my appearance' — his haggard and unkempt looks — 'but my deeds [*erga*, which can have the sense of 'reality', as in *Trojan Women* 1232] that torment me' (388); and that 'my body is gone, but the name has not left me' (390; cf. 398 f.). The characteristic Greek habit of antithesis here serves to give rational formulation to an internal state, and so breaks through the surface of the myth.

But, in the characteristically Euripidean way, rational articulation is not commensurate with larger circumstances or human character. Orestes, having expressed this kind of insight into his own condition, straightway forgets it. He needs to be saved from both his madness and the outward circumstances of Argos' hostility. To Menelaus he can appeal for help only in the latter case; there is no human help for madness. But he does not consider what help would save him if the madness continues. Orestes forgets the question of his guilt. Although we have seen him haunted to distraction by the memory of his deeds, he can be equally ready to shift the blame for them to Apollo (276, 285 f., 591 ff.; cf. 416). This contradiction is then accompanied by another. Exhausted by his conscience, Orestes is indifferent to whether he lives or dies, and yet again he is anxious only to live and argues passionately for it (644 ff., 677 ff., cf. 382 f.). Menelaus turns out to be no help. The Argives convict Orestes, and again he is resigned simply to die (1023 f.).

Here, having gone through a cycle of suffering, reaction, and final defeat, the first part of the play's action ends. That the protagonists have exhausted all their hopes and resources will underline the sense of irrational and gratuitous action that follows, the second half of the play. Just as they are ready to die the thought of revenge sparks a new plot. Menelaus' betrayal will be avenged by killing Helen. And as that plot is elaborated, hope for survival is once more raised (1172 ff.; cf. 1152); Electra suggests holding Hermione hostage to force Menelaus to help.

Orestes is passive, originating neither of these proposals, though he then pursues both with enthusiasm. He exemplifies how susceptible for any action whatever a man may be who has nothing to lose. Thus, in turn, neither he nor Electra nor Pylades notices either the practical or the moral contradictions in their plans. They do not consider how Menelaus could in fact help them, locked in as they are on all sides (430),

surrounded by armed guards (444, 761 ff.), and objects of all Argos'
hostility (cf. 1530). Menelaus seems to be as powerless as he claims
(688 ff.). He has had to bring in Helen secretly by night for lack of
means to protect her against the anger of the citizens (57 ff.). He might
have helped by speaking for Orestes at his trial, as he promised (704 ff.),
and did not. But that time is past; now Menelaus is no use. In moral
terms, the condemned trio do not reconcile their claim to go down
fighting in a noble death (cf. 781, 1093, 1152) and the ignoble object
of that fight — killing a woman and using an innocent girl as hostage.
(The question of what is noble, *kalon*, was raised aready with Clytemnestra's death [194; cf. 417] and reduced to a paradoxical formulation,
to kalon ou kalon, 'the noble [beautiful, proper] [which is] not noble'
[819], by which the word, and value, lose their simple sense [cf. 610,
891, 1106, 1131, 1213, 1316, 1614].)

As these contrary motives are revealed, the original uncertainty about
whether or not to accept death persists. The ideals of facing death nobly
and of suicidal recklessness alternate with an intense desire to survive.
Having said he would 'freely' give up his life to be avenged on Menelaus
(1170 ff.), Orestes indulges immediately the hope of survival: 'would
that an unhoped-for salvation befall those that kill and die not — that is
my prayer; what I wish is sweet — even by speech to delight the mind
cheaply with winged fables' (1173–76). When the conspirators pray to
Agamemnon, it is first that they be saved (1234, 1238), and then that
they meet with success, without specifying survival or vengeance (cf.
1243 and 1172), and closing with the vague epigram, 'we are bound, all
of us, either to live or die' (1245), which catches one of the play's
refrains, the protagonists' always wavering purpose: 'to live or die' (758,
848, 1152; cf. 1174).

Electra deceives Hermione by asking her to plead with Helen for
their lives (1334 ff.). But Orestes tells the girl when he has captured her
that she will be 'a salvation to us, not yourself' (1348). Electra next
looks forward only to revenge (1350 ff.). The action that follows and
the report of it by a Phrygian slave concerns itself only with that, the
attempted killing of Helen. Then, as the Phrygian is cornered by Orestes
and grovels at his feet begging to be left alive, the pursuit of life re-
emerges in a grotesquely comic light. 'To live', the Phrygian pleads, 'is
everywhere more sweet than to die for those who are sensible' (1509).
'Sweet' echoes Orestes' earlier sudden hope of survival (1175 ff.), though
he had also called 'sweetest' a death in common with Electra (1054).
('Those who are sensible [sane, shrewd]' *tois sôphrosin*, recalls, if it
were necessary, that Orestes is probably mad [cf. 254, 502].) When he
asks shortly after, 'as a slave do you fear Hades which will free you

from ills?' (1522), he echoes his own words of appeal to Menelaus for 'escape from ills' (448). The Phrygian answers that every man, even a slave, looks on the light 'with pleasure' (1523). Orestes approves: 'well spoken; your intelligence saves you' (1524); and he calls the fawning of the slave frantic for his life by the same name, *synesis*, he had earlier given his consciousness of guilt, on whose account he was ready to die (395 ff.). Now he appears willing to spare the wretch's life (1524 f.), yet he shifts once more: 'but I shall change my mind' (1526). Finally the slave runs off, and Orestes, before going after him, announces that he had no intention of killing him in the first place, for he – this killer of women – does not consider a eunuch slave, neither man nor woman, worth killing (1527 f.).

This brief scene recapitulates the play. Orestes plays viciously at an indecision with which he is himself really afflicted. The slave in turn is a distorted reflection of the Orestes who had cried out for his life (644 ff., 677 ff.), and whatever pathos those cries had expressed is not grotesque ridicule. And the cause of that ridicule is Orestes himself. He taunts the slave, dangling the lure of life before him, as he himself has been taunted, bedeviled, and harassed – by circumstances, gods, men, and the impulses of his own mind. Orestes in his dejection had said to Menelaus that 'we are enslaved to the gods, whatever the gods are' (418). He now acts out divine arbitrariness upon another slave, his own image.

There follows the second confrontation of Menelaus and Orestes, which should represent the consummation of the plot for survival. But Orestes first threatens to destroy Menelaus – whom he had planned to make his means of safety – Hermione, and the palace, 'house of his fathers', by fire (1594 ff.), which would kill himself, Electra, and Pylades as well. The matter of rescue comes up just at the end of the scene. First Orestes bypasses it, asserting his right, not simply to live, but to rule in Argos (1600 ff.). Then Menelaus, no longer able to endure the threats to his daughter's life, cries out, 'what shall I do?' (1610; cf. 596) 'Persuade the Argives not to kill us,' says Orestes. But that is evidently impossible; it is much too late for any persuasion. Menelaus simply admits his helplessness: 'you have me' (1617). That had been the object of the plot for survival, and now it is Orestes' cue to call for the palace to be set on fire (1618 ff.). Irrationally grounded, the pursuit of life turns into a suicidal holocaust.

The *Orestes* begins by suggesting a moral conflict made internal, turning on its protagonist's sense of guilt, but that issue, mostly under the pressure of outward circumstances, is dissipated. (There is one brief reminder of it in the last scene, when Menelaus claims he is at least pure 'in hands', that is, free of ritual pollution, to which Orestes rejoins, 'but not in mind' [1604].) The plot turns outward to revenge and survival. But as the presuppositions of these are at cross purposes, the actions that result negate themselves. The play opens with Orestes' desperate situation; the first part of it ends with the exhausting of all hope; and the latter part reaches once more its point of departure, Orestes' imminent death. Apollo's final appearance, then, breaks the cycle and restores the myth's traditional conclusion, that Orestes is saved. But returning to the myth is a further negation of human actions. Orestes' plan of revenge, for which he had, finally, been willing to lay down his life, is canceled. Insofar as that plan was criminal, Apollo's appearance and the return to the myth are providential – but that point we shall consider later. Thus far we have noticed a disjunction between the mythical elements and the immediate action of the play, which suggests a sense of the super-fluous or gratuitous. This sense now appears as well in the bafflement of human purpose which that action demonstrates.

'Change in all things is sweet,' Electra says to Orestes, restless in his sickness (234). 'Yes', he answers, 'for it gives the illusion [*doxa*] of health, and seeming [*to dokein*] is better, even if there is no truth' (235-36). Illusion and seeming in every form dominate the play. The project for survival, we saw, was born out of wishful thinking (1173 ff.). Euripides represents a world whose real substance has become elusive and men who shy from realities too hard to bear, preferring hope in illusion. But delusion and madness can follow. 'Even though you may not be sick,' Electra tells her brother, 'but only imagine you are, it is an affliction and perplexity for mortals' (314-15). 'You see nothing of what you imagine you know clearly,' she assures him (259). Orestes responds by recoiling from his sister's embrace, thinking her a fury (264 f.). At the end of the play, finally, Orestes tells Apollo, recalling the god's com-mand to kill Clytemnestra, 'the fear came upon me that I was imagining the voice of some demon [*alastōr*] and not yours' (1668-69; cf. *Electra* 979). We are made to look back on the possibility that the basis of the whole action, Orestes' matricide, was inspired by a delusion.

This inner doubt of Orestes, in turn, is dramatized by action that is often baffling. The play deludes its audience about what is happening. Euripides' noted flair for the theatrical here creates effects not only spectacular and surprising, but deceptive and illusory as well. They are climaxed in the representation of the plot against Helen. Orestes and Pylades have gone into the palace, while Electra stands watch outside with the chorus. The chorus leader imagines that someone – a country-man – has come up and is lurking about the house (1269), only to decide that it was no one, 'contrary to what you [Electra] imagined' (1274). Shortly after, a cry is heard from inside, '. . . I am wretchedly perishing' (1296), and the chorus tentatively identifies Helen's voice, 'so one might conjecture' (1298). She cries out again, 'Menelaus, I am dying' (1301). Such cries of victims from offstage are frequent in tragedy (e.g. Aeschylus' *Agamemnon* 1343 ff., *Choephoroi* 870 ff., Sophocles' *Electra* 1404 ff., Euripides' *Hecuba* 1035 ff., *Electra* 1165 f.). Nor is there any doubt that those who utter them are in fact being killed. Here Euripides first diverts our attention with the appearance of Hermione, whom Electra lures into the palace — which has become strangely silent (1301-52). Then the chorus shouts to cover, they say, the groaning inside, so that no help might come 'before I really see the bloody corpse of Helen . . . or hear an account from one of the servants, for I know some of the things that happened, but about others I know not clearly' (1357-60).

We are led explicitly to expect one of two regular features of a Greek tragedy, either the opening of house doors to reveal those who have been killed inside or a messenger speech telling what has happened off-stage. The doors remain shut. We probably (our text is uncertain; cf. 1631-32) will not see Helen again. And the messenger speech seems to be put off by another interruption, the entrance of a Phrygian slave in panic flight from Orestes and Pylades (1369 ff.). He wails out his fear almost incoherently in a kind of virtuoso aria, a monody in free se-quences of lyric meters. The chorus breaks in with single, spoken lines, trying to elicit from him what has happened. He must be our messenger, in the place of the usual dispassionate and orderly narrator. Euripides' theater cannot be more surprising.

The Phrygian's account works its effect by both the events he reports and the manner in which he reports them. He describes a piece of duplicity and its attendant confusion and disorder. There is an illusory quality in things, and men set out to delude one another as well. So far we have seen Menelaus' duplicity toward Orestes and Electra's deceiving of Hermione. The play also shows another kind of deception in hypocrisy, especially Helen's (126 ff.; cf. 1122 f.), and in flattery, as in Orestes' appeal to Menelaus (670 ff.) and his suspicion of the Phrygian: 'you please with a coward's tongue, but these are not your thoughts within' (1514). Now Orestes and Pylades are described deceiving Helen by claiming they are her suppliants for their life (1414 ff.). But in part they really are suppliants for their life, though they sometimes forget it. They are as much deceived as deceiving.

The manner of the slave's report is partly accountable because, unlike the usual messenger, he is directly affected by the play's action. Thus when he calls out 'where can I escape, flying to the bright air or sea . . .?' (1376 f.) he echoes numerous Euripidean heroes in distress (cf. *Hippolytus*

732 ff., 1290 ff., *Heracles* 1157 f., *Ion* 796 f., 1238 ff., *Andromache* 861 ff.). There is probably an element of self-parody here (anticipating Aristophanes' *Frogs* 1352 f.), but Euripides also gets an effect of dislocation similar to the ones described earlier with the repetitions of the *Electra* and other tragedies in the *Orestes*. An incidental figure, a foreign slave, expresses feelings usually reserved for aristocratic Greek heroes. The world has become so disordered that anyone may occupy the stage's center. Further, that not only an affected party but also a foreigner should be our informant indicates how an event may be obscured as it is communicated and suggests an effect of relativity. As the Phrygian appears outlandish to a Greek, so he tells what he has seen with the amazement of an outsider.

After his cry for escape, the Phrygian invokes Ilium and recalls its downfall on Helen's account (1381 ff.), and again different spheres of reference clash. As cowering slave he is a familiar type, the degenerate oriental, proverbial for cowardice (cf. Arisotophanes' *Birds* 1244). Yet now we hear he saw Ajax at Troy (1480) and remembers Odysseus (1404), and he reminds us that the valiant Hector was also a Phrygian (1480). When he describes Helen, whom the play has shown with unsparing realism as vain, unfeeling, self-interested, and insignificant, he uses language reminiscent of the sinister and beautiful figure in Aeschylus' *Agamemnon* (cf. 1386 ff. and *Agamemnon* 681 ff., 742). His actual narrative begins with a Homeric image, 'Hellenes, two twin lions . . .' (1401; cf. *Iliad* V, 548, X, 297), also used by Aeschylus (*Choephoroi* 937), and Sophocles (*Philoctetes* 1436). And he echoes Homeric similes when he compares Orestes and Pylades to mountain boars (1459; cf. *Iliad* XI, 324, XII, 42, XVII, 282). But their actions do not match these epic descriptions. The 'twin lions' fall in simulated tears at Helen's feet (1410), the 'mountain boars' only stand 'facing the woman' (1460). Furthermore, these epic figures are out of harmony with the references to animals, preying and hunting, found elsewhere in the play. To the Phrygian, Pylades is also a 'murderous serpent' (1406; cf. *Iliad* XXII, 93 ff.) and Orestes 'a serpent, slayer of his mother' (1424), a phrase already used by Tyndareus (479). Menelaus will exclaim over the horrors committed by 'twin lions — I shall not call them men' (1555). The Phrygian's poetic periphrase now describes irrational savagery, what Tyndareus, referring to lawless revenge, had called 'bestiality', *to thēriōdes* (524).

Doubt and disorder attend these disparities. The Phrygian next describes Helen's confused attendants, his fellow slaves, scattered and routed. A stock joke about cowardly Phrygians (cf. 1448) is played out, and the various fates of the anonymous slaves are ticked off in comic catalogues (1448 ff., 1475 ff., 1486 ff.). The confusion of the scene is represented by continuous and abrupt shifts of style. Aside from the pathetic Euripidean manner, as in the cry for escape, the epic features, and the echoes of other tragedies already noticed, there are extravagant exaggerations of Euripides' own lyric style, such as the constant use of repeated words, sound patterns, anaphoric sequences, invocations, and a variety of metrical effects. Frantic outbursts, narrative, commentary, and genre scenes, such as Helen at her weaving (1473 ff.), flash by for our distraction. The whole monody is 147 lines long. At the end of it we hear that Helen has 'vanished' (1495), and 'what followed', the slave says, 'I know not' (1498). The messenger cannot report what should have been a foregone conclusion, Helen's death and the manner of it. He ends by remarking on futility — Menelaus' untold trouble and suffering to regain Helen from Troy has gone for nothing (1500 f.).

Like the short scene noticed earlier between the Phrygian and Orestes, the monody is a mirror — a distorting mirror — of the play's moods and themes. Its opening cry for escape voices a longing shared by all the actors (cf. 598 and 1376). The slave's abject fear recalls Tantalus' terror in punishment (6), Orestes' fear of the furies (38, 270, 312), Clytemnestra's terror before death (825), Helen's fears before the Argives (102, 104, 118) and before death (1296, 1301, 1465), Electra's and Pylades' fears for Orestes (757, 859; cf. 1255), and it looks forward to the chorus' fear, finally, of Orestes' actions (1537 f.; cf. 1324) and Menelaus' for his daughter's life (1598, 1609). When the Phrygian laments the fall of his city, Ilium, whereby he was made a slave (1381 ff.), his recollection of a doomed city — of which we are reminded throughout the play — is like the reiterated laments for the fall of a great house (332 ff., 807 ff., 960 ff., 1537 ff.), backdrop for the downfall of Orestes, its last scion (cf. 664, 673). More generally, the monody reflects the contradictory movements within the play as a whole and the doubtful and suspended action that results; the punishment of Tantalus (5 ff., 982 ff.) is everyone's inheritance. And the frustration of the actors is dramatized by the expectations which are denied their audience. We still do not know what has happened — the success of Orestes' plot and the fate of Helen. (The latter will not be resolved until Apollo's final appearance; Menelaus is certain she is dead and will not believe a rumour that she has escaped [1556 ff.], though Orestes repeatedly insists she is alive [1580, 1586, 1614], having, however, also spoken as though she were dead [1512, 1534].)

This lack of knowledge of course heightens the play's sense of excitement — a sense which Euripides effects by inventing a plot previously unknown to his audience. But thus he must lose some of the advantages that the use of a familiar story allows, notably occasions for tragic irony and a sense of inevitability. In their place there is some room for comedy, as in the figure of the Phrygian, and decorative elaborations and archaisms of form and style, as well as stylistic experiments such as the Phrygian's monody and its earlier counterpart, Electra's finely wrought lyric solo (982–1012) – both probably vehicles for the same virtuoso performer. And since its characters are more corrupt than virtuous, and sometimes simply mad, *Orestes* lacks some of the commonly accepted qualifications for a tragedy. Commentators often call it a melodrama. But that should not distract us from its underlying seriousness. It is too systematic in its elaborations of disorder to be taken lightly. Its action has too much of the nightmare about it, a nightmare dreamed by an uncertain world, oppressed by fear and guilt and a memory which longs for release of terrible things that have been done (cf. 213–16, 325–27). It is possible that *Orestes*, like the *Trojan Women* (both plays about the aftermath of a famous catastrophe), is a kind of indictment of public conscience.

The moving force of the whole story is revenge. Orestes' initial misfortunes are the result of it. His way out is to pursue it yet again. Revenge is what both the myth and Euripides' invented plot have in common. As it is related to justice, and so more than a private matter – the 'wild kind of justice', Francis Bacon called it – it raises questions about political order. The theme of revenge makes us see Orestes' world as it claims to administer justice; and, more remotely, it might make us think of the gods as they are said to show men justice.

In Euripides' *Electra* Agamemnon was avenged, but under circumstances of doubt (*Electra* 966 ff.), and remorse followed (1190 ff.). Yet the vengeance was ordered by Apollo, though other divinities, the Dioscuri, say that he acted unjustly and unwisely (1254 ff., 1302). But 'where Apollo is a fool,' Electra remarks, 'who is wise?' (972). Justice has its claims and Clytemnestra deserved punishment, as her brothers (the Dioscuri) and her father Tyndareus agree (1244, *Orestes* 499, 505, 538). But the conditions under which that claim has to be made are obscure, an obscurity indicated by calling Apollo unwise. The Dioscuri, in turn, say that because of 'necessity', they could do nothing themselves (*Electra* 1301; cf. 1247 f.). The problem of justice involved in avenging Agamemnon, as far as gods are concerned, has reached an impasse, which is where *Orestes* begins.

Before he comes to trial Orestes faces the private indictment of his grandfather Tyndareus, who most clearly defines his injustice: he should not himself have exacted vengeance but should have prosecuted Clytemnestra by the procedures of civil law (500 ff.); though the deed, killing Clytemnestra, was just, the doer of it was not (538 f.). (The same argument of course, applies to Orestes' attempted killing of Helen.) Orestes cannot answer this. And yet, as many have observed, Euripides makes the indictment possible by a violent anachronism. The old story takes place before civil justice existed. Aeschylus used the myth to show how that form of justice must emerge from and supersede an older familial system of vengeance. Sophocles in his *Electra* confines the plot completely within the myth, where no public justice exists. But Euripides confronts the myth with contemporary circumstances: Tyndareus refers to homicide laws [512 ff.] which were reinscribed within the year before the production of the *Orestes*. And so Orestes' injustice can be defined in rational terms, but somehow not adequately, because the displacement of an action out of the old story into a contemporary context is irrational. One might think Euripides means again to discredit the myth, revealing the barbarity of the old story when it is set in a civilized context. But the myth is not so much discredited as simply given. In fact, it recoils on that civilized context which might first have appeared to discredit it.

Tyndareus' accusation actually rests on a specious argument. 'His championing of legal process is not so much anachronistic as futile. The law could not be invoked against the reigning queen, and the old man conveniently forgets that Orestes was a child at his father's death. The legal customs he extolls had not in fact been invoked by anyone.'[2] Furthermore, he first praises laws that call for exile, rather than death, as a punishment (515), and then goes on to urge that Orestes, and Electra as well, be executed (536, 613 ff., 915 f.). For the rest, his character is distinguished by an attempt to blackmail Menelaus into supporting the conviction of Orestes (536 f., 623 ff.) and by a concern only for outward forms. He assumes that 'fair and unfair are evident to all' (492) and that Orestes, therefore, by his wretched appearance alone, must be guilty (533). He is the only person in the play to take seriously Orestes' pollution and the interdict against speaking to him (481), and yet, carried away by his accusations, he addresses him anyway (526 ff.). Tyndareus begins by expressing an ideal of justice and leaves in a fury of vindictiveness (609 ff.).

After the private accusation comes the public trial before the assembly of Argos. Like the other main event in the play, the plot against Helen, we are allowed to see it only through the eyes of a messenger, at one remove. The Phrygian's account is colored by his fear and overelaborate to the point of distraction. The messenger who reports Orestes' trial is partial, a retainer of Agamemnon's family (868 ff.), and his account is as schematic and truncated as the Phrygian's is overlong. The issues of the trial, at least as we hear them, are oversimplified and thus obscured.

The words 'just' or 'justice' occur nowhere in the account (contrast *Eumenides* 511 ff., 675, 699 f.). Orestes does not plead the command of Apollo in his defense. The countryman who alone supports him passes over the fact that it was not just 'a woman' Orestes killed (925), but his mother. The demagogue who carries the assembly with his recommendation of the death penalty offers, in the report, no argued prosecution at all. The only reasonable proposal, exile (512 ff.), is passed over. Violence of speech (903 ff.) alone persuades the crowd, which allows itself to be moved by the private interests of a few — the friends of the usurper Aegisthus (894) and Tyndareus, who is not even an Argive (915). There is no rational functioning of justice in the public sphere. The myth of revenge might have seemed barbarous in the civilized world, but in fact it reveals the barbarity of civil justice debased. Orestes is part of a world as flawed as he is.

His injustice in the killing of Clytemnestra, to which he explicitly admits (646 f.), is, like the myth, given, a kind of legacy. The question of blame and responsibility comes from the past. Thus one might say that the more pressing question which the play sets is, given injustice, what is there to be done? Orestes indicates that dilemma when he says to Tyndareus, 'do not say this deed [taking vengeance on Clytemnestra] was wrong [*ouk eu*], but that we the doers of it acted to our misfortune [*ouk eudaimonōs*]' (600 f.; cf. the sophistic defense of Helen that claims she 'did no wrong' [*ēdikēsen*] but 'suffered misfortune' [*ētuchēsen*], Gorgias, *Helen* 15). He tries to shift attention from past injustice to present release, and at the same time he implies a shift from a criterion of virtue to one of happiness, from a judgment of wrong action to a freedom for well-being. But, as the myth is reasserted at the play's end and cancels its action, so there is no escape from this past.

In the present, justice can only be distorted. Orestes pleads with Menelaus: 'I am unjust; in exchange for this evil I ought to receive from you an injustice; for unjustly did my father Agamemnon assemble Greece and come to Ilium . . . to heal the unjust wrong of your wife' (646-50). By this grotesque and obsessive logic the principle of reciprocity substitutes for that of justice. Agamemnon, argues Orestes, gave ten years to get Helen back: Menelaus should give him one day; Agamemnon sacrificed his daughter Iphigenia: Orestes will not require Menelaus to kill Hermione (656 ff.). He asks, then, for what he thinks his due, a return for what Menelaus has received (643; cf. 244, 452 f.). The play refers to a number of debts or favors owed. Hermione owes Clytemnestra her upbringing in Helen's absence (64, 109); Orestes owes his to Tyndareus (460 ff.), and he uses for a part of his defence a claim that he owed his existence more to his father than his mother (555 ff.; cf.

Eumenides 658 ff.). But rendering what is due, *apodidonai* (cf. 643, 652, 1075, 1585), is countered by violation of favor, betrayal, *prodidonai* (cf. 575, 722, 1057, 1087, 1165, 1236, 1463, 1588). The intense loyalties of Electra, Pylades, and Orestes, the countryman at the trial, and the messenger are offset by the betrayals of Clytemnestra and Menelaus. And where betrayal may result from calculating self-interest, loyalty as the play describes it is passionate beyond reason. Its intensity is easily shifted to the pursuit of vengeance.

And that is everywhere. The avenging spirits, first of his father (581 ff.), then of his mother, hounded Orestes. Oiax wants to avenge his brother Palamedes (433 f.); Tyndareus his daughter; Aegisthus' friends seek revenge for him (cf. 894). And then Orestes would have vengeance on Menelaus, while Pylades justifies killing Helen as vengeance for Greece (1133 ff.). Finally, Menelaus will want revenge of Orestes (cf. 1534). Orestes' pursuit of vengeance appears as only an extreme instance of a universal impulse, originating, like his first killing, in pressures from the past, and then, like his second attempt, continuing spontaneously, or rather because of a corrupting habit ingrained by causes that have become irrelevant. The old story of revenge, with its continual reversals, reflects its contemporary context — the constant shifts and revisions of power, climaxed in the years just before this play by the oligarchic revolution of June, 411, followed by the government of the Five Thousand in September of that year, and a return to the democracy by June, 410; and in their wake cycle upon cycle of vengeance and reprisals, probably the greatest evil of Athenian political life. Earlier in the century Cleon, according to Thucydides, had argued for swift reprisals against Mytilene as 'the injured party proceeds against the offender with the edge of his anger too blunted, but the requital that follows most closely upon the injury best matches its vengeance' (III, 38, 1). Anger, *orgē*, and passion, *thumos*, feelings that pervade the *Orestes*, are taken for guides in the place of rational calculation. In a famous passage Thucydides notes 'the enormity of revenges' under the pressure of civil disorders; that 'to get revenge on someone' was thought more of than not to have suffered injury in the first place; and that 'the leading men dared the most terrible deeds and executed revenges even more awful . . . limiting them only by their momentary pleasure' (III, 82, 3-8). And two years after the production of *Orestes*, Aristophanes' chorus still appeals for mildness after changes of party and government, calling on the Athenians to rid themselves of 'terror' and give up 'anger', *orgē* (*Frogs* 688, 700); to end reprisals and temper the urge to vengeance. As in *Orestes*, the political life of the city depends, in some measure, on a solution of the problem of revenge.

'Passion [*thumos*],' says Aristotle, 'has in it a certain pleasure, for it is combined with hope for revenge' (*Eud. Ethics* 1229 b 32 f.). There is, finally, a hedonistic, self-indulgent quality in the impulse to vengeance, proverbially sweet (cf. Thucydides VII, 68, 1-2). The characters in *Orestes* are all carried only by the tides of their feelings — whether Orestes at one extreme, or the nervous Menelaus at the other — which, in a kind of vacuum, cut off from traditional and public supports, acquire an extreme intensity that must somehow be satisfied. The loyalty and devotion between Electra, Orestes, and Pylades is one such satisfaction. But as Orestes' situation becomes utterly hopeless, and nothing more can be done for him, devotion is frustrated and the feelings thus released turn outward and look for gratification in vengeance. Both the particular spur of that vengeance and its general context is betrayal. We have noticed the disjointedness of the play. In every way it presents divisions and discontinuities — between the traditional myth and the immediate action, between the past and present, between impulses to life and to death, between intention and achievement, between nobility and madness, between justice and politics, between fact and delusion, and — in style — between an almost naturalistic realism and lyric extravagance. Orestes' sense of betrayal at the hands of Menelaus is the specific cause for his plot of vengeance, but Menelaus' seems only a particular instance of a more general betrayal, which is represented by this disjointed nature of the world. Revenge, then, becomes an irrational response to the world's failure to render what one imagines is his due. It could be an attempt to force repayment on the loss between what seems and what is. And it is an exasperated explosion of feeling after all human intentions are denied. Until his last-minute appearance, Apollo is the mythical representation of this betrayal in things. When Electra assures Orestes, 'I shall not let you go,' *outoi methēsō* (262), she is made to echo Apollo's promise to him in Aeschylus' *Eumenides*, 'I shall not give you up,' *outoi prodōsō* (64). Human loyalty would take the place of divine. But it is far from sufficient. Apollo finally appears.

He comes to restore a mythical conclusion to a situation that has moved as far as seems possible from its mythical basis. His appearance is abrupt, but only the last in a series of surprising entrances: Tyndareus', Pylades', and the Phrygian's. When Orestes reappears to corner the slave, the chorus acknowledges the pattern: 'Look, here is a novelty succeeding novelties' (1503). The god has been mentioned only twice since Orestes last blamed him for his misfortune (597 f.), once, after the trial, as author of Orestes' ruin (995 f.) and once, in passing, as the builder of Troy's walls now fallen (1388). As the plot moves away from the myth, the god is forgotten. And yet there are a few indications he might return.

'He delays,' says Orestes, in answer to a question about the god's help, 'such is the nature of the divine' (419 f.). Orestes' last words about Apollo indicate his helplessness without the god: 'where might one still escape if he who gave the command [to kill Clytemnestra] will not keep me from death?' (598 f.). And all the ensuing action bears him out. There is no human solution. The chorus, then, prepare for the possibility of Apollo's coming by turning back to the myth and a traditional statement of the gods' overruling power: 'A deity holds the end [*telos*] for mortals, the end, wherever he wishes. It is a great power. By an avenging demon this house has fallen, fallen, by blood, by Myrtilus' fall from the chariot' (1545 ff.; cf. *Ion* 1615, Aeschylus *Agamemnon* 1487). But they only look backward to a former crime, and see ruin before them now.

Apollo's appearance, surprising and yet somehow expected, appropriately concludes the play. It marks the most violent break in the continuity of the action thus far, yet it alters nothing of what the play had shown about human helplessness. *Orestes* includes an indictment of human character and the political world. Apollo bypasses both. He will 'set things right' in Argos (1664), ignoring the city's hostility to Orestes and the decision of its assembly. He announces the deification of Helen, who will become a 'salvation' for those at sea (1637), the same Helen whose character we had seen so harshly exposed, and who, the god himself recalls, had been a cause of so many deaths (1641). We noticed earlier the reconciliation he brings about between Menelaus, Orestes, and Hermione. The play had raised a question about human survival. The god solves it by ignoring the terms in which it was set, the substance of the play's action.

It was remarked that insofar as the plot of *Orestes* diverged from the myth it lost a sense of inevitability. The most fantastic possibility might then be realized, one, for instance, which Orestes puts forward as unthinkable — namely, that Hermione should be killed as Iphigenia was killed (658 ff.). But before the play is over Hermione is almost killed. She is saved only by a still more fantastic possibility, the last-instant interference of a god. Apollo's appearance is thus a sign of the extreme range of life's possible reversals. His coming suggests how fantastic it is that we survive at all.[3] And yet this god had originally ordered Orestes' crime, as he himself reminds us (1665), and so represents also the obscurity and pressure of the past. He shows that these are still present and, by his prophecies (e.g., 1654 ff.), that they continue into the future as well. The arbitrariness of his interference is the most disturbing demonstration yet of the simply irrational course of things. It recalls Orestes' arbitrariness with the Phrygian slave, differing only as the god has more power and uses it now to restore a traditional order. The plot which Euripides invented for the action of this play moves in cycles which show how futile human action is, coming always back to its starting point, a desperate and helpless strait, and how thus, without achievement, it was insubstantial and empty of all but passionate feelings. For this condition Apollo has no cure. Euripides shows us human beings who cannot save themselves. But the way the god saves them denies their humanity, or rather, finally, isolates it. The break between the new plot — 'human beings as they are' — and the myth — the received, poetic vision of order — is beyond healing. What is remarkable is the unflinching steadiness with which Euripides can look at this segment of humanity he has chosen to represent, in all its degenerate and criminal nature. And, rather than overwhelm us with the bitter and scornful judgment he must make, he mourns, behind a façade of theatrical virtuosity. *Orestes* has no substantial resolution or catharsis. Apollo sees to that. Thus it is not in the usual sense a tragedy. In fact, it curiously anticipates the themes of Aristophanes' *Frogs*, that serious comedy — the downfall of a city and political life because of a deficiency and degeneration of human virtue; the vindictiveness of human feeling; and the death of tragedy. The *Orestes* is filled with innovations which may surprise, but also disappoint, the expectations which traditional tragedy fulfilled. Part of its peculiar 'tragedy' is that true tragedy is no longer possible, as Euripides suggests by turning to one of tragedy's most used myths for his most experimental play.

26

EURIPIDES' FINAL PHASE: THE *BACCHAE*

HANS DILLER

At the beginning of this century, Gilbert Norwood's *Riddle of the Bacchae* influenced scholarly opinion to begin viewing the play as enigmatic because of its attitude towards religion.[1] Euripides was regarded as a critic of the Olympian gods. Divinities like Apollo in the *Elektra* and *Ion* or Hera in the *Herakles* were seen as frivolous, even malicious agents of human misfortune. Still worse, they seemed indifferent to the suffering of their own children (e.g. Zeus in *Herakles*). Many gods completely ignored those who piously worshipped them — as in the *Trojan Women*.

By contrast, the *Bacchae* presents the story of a Theban king, Pentheus, who denies and persecutes the new god Dionysos, and of the god's complete triumph over his adversary. The atmosphere leaves no doubt that the Bacchic experience and its effects on the human soul are real. At the end of the history of classical tragedy, in his very last years, in a play produced only after his death in Macedonia[2] Euripides retells the story of the god whose celebration had been at the origin of Attic tragedy. The myth had already been treated by Aeschylus[3] who preserved many typical features of the old mythic miracle-working in its plot.[4]

Using a very ancient pattern it showed Dionysos on the one side as leader of the chorus of his devotees and on the other his adversary. Even in its external structure it was in many ways more primitive than other contemporary tragedies.[5] Did it also preserve the spirit of the ancient myth? Did Euripides intend here, perhaps under the influence of the earthy Macedonian Dionysos-cult,[6] to describe a kind of religious 'conversion?' This was the nineteenth-century interpretation.[7]

Yet in this Euripidean tragedy the god's triumph was gained at the expense of a cruelty which could hardly have had the poet's approval,

Originally published in German as 'Die Bakchen und ihre Stellung im Spätwerk des Euripides', *Akad. Mainz* 1955, Nr. 5, pp. 453-71. Translated with minor revisions for this collection by the editor and Dr G. Mander.

even as an admonitory example. The tearing-apart of the persecutor by his own mother — who, admittedly, was also guilty of denial of the god — was an action with which even a religious fanatic would not have wanted to identify himself. In a time which saw Euripides primarily as an enlightened and rationalist writer, the matter was turned upside down and Pentheus was taken to be the representative of reason and order seduced by an imposter and brutally killed by a lot of misguided fanatical women. As Lucretius put it, 'Such are the evils religion can cause.'[8]

Fortunately, the discussion did not remain on this level. The idea that Euripidean tragedy does not set out to discuss or even preach philosophy has increasingly gained ground. Rather, Euripides presents the tension between human beings or between man and his environment, as it were, the contradiction of the rational and the irrational. This is particularly true of the *Bacchae*.[9]

Once this antinomy is recognised, there still remain various possibilities of how sympathy and antipathy may be distributed between protagonist and antagonist. Opinions of the *Bacchae* range from the assumption that the play was 'a fullhearted glorification of Dionysos'[10] (of course, of a Dionysos, as Euripides saw him) to the view that Euripides considered sympathy and antipathy futile to explain an elemental force like Dionysos.[11] Another view was that Euripides 'recognised but hated Dionysos'.[12]

With such a wide spectrum of interpretations it might be useful to investigate how Euripides dealt with and presented, in dramatic terms, the tension created in the world by the eruption of the Dionysiac. The answer might tell us something about the anthropological insight and artistic power of Euripides in his old age and locate the *Bacchae* more firmly in his late work.

The world of Dionysos as presented in the play is a unified entity. Yet its spiritual dimensions are so immense that its unity has been doubted, and it was assumed that Euripides fused genuine Dionysiac features more or less successfully with technical instructions on how to lead an innocuous life.[13] But the colourful intermingling of wild ecstasy with calm tranquility, of everyday life with unaccustomed events, is characteristic of the Dionysiac. This constitutes its attraction and its danger. Its almost irresistible fascination lies in the liberation from ego-boundaries, the escape from the limitations and miseries of human existence. The Maenad who rushes into the mountains from the narrow confines of city life leaves behind the ordinary life of her quotidian existence (140). Spatial removal becomes the symbol of Dionysiac bliss in other ways (402-15). Even the elderly forget their age and go into the mountains (188, 194). The physical limitations of man are abolished. He acquires immense speed (167 f., 446, 727 ff., 1090 f.), immense strength (734 ff., 945 ff., 1109 ff., 1125 ff., 1206 ff.), as well as the joyous awareness of these powers. The wine as 'breaker of sorrows' is only one symbol among others for this victory over the narrowness of human existence (280 ff., 382 ff., 769 ff.). What Nietzsche presented as characteristic of the Dionysiac in fact happens: the *principium individuationis* is overcome, the limitations of nature are transcended. Man and beast, man and nature unite. The Bacchae suckle young animals (699 ff.), the soil tapped lightly gives people whatever they desire to drink (142, 704 ff.). Mental barriers are overcome; in Bacchic hallucinations man sees the future (298 ff.). The god vanquishes his enemies by mere terror (302 ff.) or by a supernatural, powerful physical effort (734 ff., 1109 ff., 1125 ff., 1206). Here is the nature of the Dionysiac: it imperils not only the enemies but also the followers of the god, who lose control of their imagination. Agaue takes Pentheus for a wild beast, and the enormous strength she derives from her Dionysiac intoxication makes her kill her son while in the grip of delusion.

It is true that in the *Bacchae* only the god's adversary and the Theban women who first denied him are punished by falling into a Dionysiac ecstasy; only they become victims of this danger. The chorus of Lydian women who accompany the god and give the play its name sing only of the bliss of Bacchic life. Unless threatened by external forces, it is a life of mystic purity (72 ff.) which bestows the clear conscience of piety in observance of the gods' rituals (cf. 370 ff. the prayer to *Hosia* and 114, *hosiousth'*). The same women who, in the opening song, praise the intoxicating mood of a Bacchic night, how it passes in shrill music, orgiastic dancing, and the tearing up of the bleeding sacrificial animal – are a premonition of what is to come. In the first stasimon the same women claim (in contrast to Pentheus) calmness, moderation, and abstemiousness as the principles of life (387 ff.), and they are happy to share these principles with the common people (416 ff.). The cult of Dionysos, which Pentheus opposes as a new religion, appears in the choral songs and in the words of the seer Teiresias as consonant with religious tradition. To fight against it is thus equally as damnable as fighting against traditional religion (890 ff., 200 ff.). And at the end these same women who had praised the peace found in the god sing the praise of revenge (876 ff.),[14] revelling in the thought of how a mother's revenging hand dripped with the blood of her own child (1153 ff.).

Here is a whole complex of ideas which needs to be resolved before we understand the tragedy. The anti-Dionysiac opposition must also be presented, even more so because most of what the chorus sings is in reaction to the behaviour of the opposition. To look at the opposition means, in particular, to interpret the character of Pentheus. It has rightly been noted that the tragedy's title is not *Pentheus*, but *The Bacchae*; that it deals with the epiphany, fight, and victory of the god, and that the human characters are merely permutations of the way the god can be encountered.[15] But in order to grasp the Dionysiac, the central phenomenon of the tragedy, we must understand the motives for resistance to it and the way that resistance is overcome. This can only be done through the character of Pentheus, since Teiresias and Kadmos surrender at once to the new god, and though Agaue and her sister are initially Dionysos' enemies and treated by him as such, we learn nothing of their kind of resistance nor how they are overcome by the god. We only see Agaue's awakening from the delusion. On the other hand, we accompany Pentheus on his way, first as persecutor, then as victim of the god. The latter we are told in a messenger's report, and the very last thing we see is the head of the dismembered man carried onto the stage by his own mother.

What are Pentheus' motives for his battle against the god? The views about his behaviour and his character correspond to those taken towards Dionysos. Pentheus has been seen as a rationalist and a martyr to 'enlightenment', but we have demonstrated how, from the beginning, his behaviour is anything but rational.[16] It has, therefore, been put forward that, on the contrary, he is a man of *thymos* [temper].[17] This is factually more correct and very Greek, but it merely explains *how* Pentheus reacts to Dionysos, not *why*. The views about his relationship with the city of Thebes which he rules are equally contradictory. His action has been explained as that of the responsible ruler who tried to keep law and order in the city, in the face of Bacchic misbehaviour.[18] The way a responsible ruler speaks can be seen in Eteocles' opening speech in Aeschylus' *Seven Against Thebes* or from *Oedipus Rex* (58 ff., 443). Pentheus behaves quite differently. Characteristics of the typical tyrant in tragedy have been found in him, and that is decidedly more correct.[19] When one of his subjects says that he fears the quickness of his mind, his irascible and 'too kingly' manner, we recognise a detailed description of tyrannical traits. Yet this certainly does not fully describe Pentheus, not even in his relationship to his city. We shall have to return to this relationship later. One thing, however, can already be said in this context to be characteristic of his nature: he feels he has to take action in his capacity as ruler (225 ff.),[20] and he is proud of his action. 'Alone of all the others, I dare it, I alone am a man', he says before the fatal reconnaissance expedition against the Bacchae. And Dionysos confirms scornfully: 'You are sacrificing yourself for this city, you alone' (962 f.).

For Pentheus to take action means above all to punish. In the relationship with his grandfather Kadmos (which is certainly not without its touching moments) he shows his love by looking for the enemies of his grandfather — on his own initiative and without having been asked by the old man — in order to 'discipline them' (1320-2).

Can this acting at any cost be expanded into a more complete picture of Pentheus' behaviour throughout the entire tragedy? Some have tried to dispense with individualistic characterisation and to see in Pentheus — fitting the characterisation by Dionysos, 45, and by Agaue, 1255 — the *theomachos*, the godfighter *par excellence* who had been a vivid figure in Greek mythology since the time of the epic.[21] This is correct in terms of the history of types, but in factual terms too vague. Moreover, we have to consider that the verb *theomachein*, which we first encounter in late Euripides, has already moved decisively towards abstraction. In the *Bacchae* (325, 1255) and in the *Iphigenia at Aulis* (1408) the verb means a hopeless fight against the inevitable.[22] It is important for the understanding of this tragedy that, from the very outset, Pentheus' fight will inevitably be in vain. But this makes it even more urgent to discuss why he began it.

Recently, there have been attempts to explain Pentheus' behaviour in very intricate psychological terms, based on the notion that 'the god who is his undoing is in reality inside himself, his conceit, his arrogance, his vanity, his insecurity, even his lustfulness.'[23] This hint was expanded into a full analysis of the *Bacchae* and a characterisation of Pentheus in which violence, power, lust, desire for fame, and repressed sensuality are seen as manifestations of Dionysiac forces. Pentheus is poisoned by a desire for power and fame, the source of Dionysiac madness — and the tragedy is said to prove this.[24] Why he does not use these traits to serve rather than oppose the god is explained by arguing that Pentheus has to suppress his inclinations for the sake of the citizenry.[25] His fight with the god is in reality a fight against himself, and the repression leads to a tragic explosion. Pentheus is an isolated Bacchant — a contradiction in terms — and thus fated to perish.[26]

I have nothing against depth psychology and I also do not endorse the view that Euripides was not able or willing to create 'unified' characters.[27] But I am sceptical about a psychology which tries to find motivation from outside the drama to explain the reversal which turns the enemy of the god into his wayward follower. Nevertheless, we have to consider this psychological approach because its premise, that the god finally overcomes Pentheus from within, is correct. Yet this does not mean that Pentheus' decision against the god is also of Dionysiac origin. And there is the further question of whether the case of Pentheus is as abnormal as the psychological interpreters make him, or whether his decision and his downfall are not about something much more universal.

From the beginning Pentheus has a wrong impression about the reasons for the Dionysos cult among the Theban women. The movement started in Thebes while he was out of the country. When he came back he heard that the women had swarmed into the mountains to worship the god, but that this was only a pretext for sexual and drunken excesses (215 ff.). He adheres to this view until the end (233 ff., 259 ff., 454, 487). The wish to observe the Bacchae in their excesses ultimately leads to his death (814, 1060). Since he is repeatedly informed of the true facts (314 ff., 683 ff.) he cannot be regarded as the victim of misinformation.[28] Yet it could be said that his misconception results largely from his own conclusions. Dionysos, in his human disguise as the leader of the Bacchic movement, has 'the gracefulness of Aphrodite in his eyes' (236). And this is merely the external shape of something very essential in the Bacchic cult. We have seen that the Dionysiac lifts man above his limitations as an individual and as the member of a species, and that his followers regard this as a particular blessing. Yet man cannot activate this state by his own effort but is, rather, carried away by a force stronger than himself. The maenadic condition is of being possessed by god, and like Euripides, Plato will later say that in this state man performs feats not merely physically but also mentally beyond his normal power. Like Teiresias in the *Bacchae*, Plato considers the mantic to belong to this realm.[29] The songs of the chorus often express the readiness to surrender to this power, convinced that it will bring peace and happiness to all men.[30] In the Helen scene of the *Iliad* Homer already calls this surrender to irresistible attraction 'Aphrodite',[31] and it is characteristic of the way Pentheus' mind works that he ascribes the new movement which has enthralled the women to the most obvious and trivial context which his experience suggests to him (216).

Pentheus opposes this surrender. To him it leads to the triumph of the absurd (242 ff.) whose followers fill him with almost physical revulsion (342 ff.). Whatever is unusual, i.e. beyond his own experience, rouses his resistance and scorn (216, 467). The fact that the movement comes from a foreign land goes against his national pride (483, 1034). These are individual traits. But they are the expression of a universal human reaction. For Pentheus does not face some arbitrary new fact, but rather the epitome of all that is new and unexpected. And as we have found when characterising the Dionysiac, this demands that man admit it to his innermost being, and by so doing, surrender the right to examine it. We have seen that for Plato as well as for Euripides, the Bacchic experience was a model for 'enthusiastic' action and creation.

And we now should add that Plato also regarded as a problem the fact that this kind of action was beyond human control.[32] To be sure, Pentheus is not asked to become a Bacchant himself, even though the renegades Kadmos and Teiresias give him an example. But he would have to accept the Bacchic activities which started without his permission. It is evident when applying the simplest psychological notions of tyranny that it must have been unbearable for him to allow into his city a foreign power which apparently had a stronger influence over people than he had himself.[33] As a man of action and initiative he had to defend himself, particularly since the foreign and new element was besieging him with outrageous demands.

He finds the women of his town have disappeared to perform suspicious actions. He sees two old men, his own grandfather, the former king together with the seer, in Bacchic clothes and postures which look grotesque for men their age. He has to listen to speeches which intensify the provocations — from Teiresias' definition of the Dionysiac[34] which, in spite of its rationalistic theology, makes it appear no less irrational and sinister, to an etymological interpretation of the myth of the god's birth which makes the absurd seem even more absurd. Finally hints of the god's future power and of his demands to be worshipped rouse the ruler's jealousy. His grandfather advises him to recognise the birth story, which he himself had hitherto considered a pious lie (26 ff.), for the sake of family prestige. This reflection of the god's appearance among men is certainly anything but attractive.

It thus becomes understandable that Pentheus resists surrender or even calculated compliance to divine 'enthusiasm'. Yet that neither qualifies him as a pioneer of enlightenment nor a hero. What drives him on is the need simply to assert himself intellectually, to preserve his most basic existence. Even under a flood of new and strange impressions we have to try to orient ourselves, and the attempt at methodical orientation is, as such, usually based on a minimum of concepts or ideas. The greater the influx of unintelligible impressions, the less able he is to withstand them. Pentheus, too, lacks sufficient means to face the new movement, having merely the will to assert himself. He orients himself mentally by applying the most obviously banal concepts, his knowledge of the effect of sex and alcohol, family gossip and national prejudices. It has been rightly said that he applies the vulgar standard of average experience to everything.[35] Thus it does not seem accidental that Pentheus' opponents repeatedly bring up his descent from Theban Sparta and therefore from the earth (213, 264, 995 f., 1025-28, 1155, 1274, 1315, in particular 537-44).[36] The earthborn 'Giants' are the mythological example for the fight against the gods. Just as the *theomachos* became the supreme symbol for the hopeless battle against the inevitable, the Giant is the symbol for the rebellion of the Lower forces against the Higher. Ultimately, the Higher triumphs over the earth-bound Giants by virtue of the superior mobility, the capacity to survey wide expanses and transcend frontiers. Pentheus, too, remains earthbound in his thoughts. The area he rules is small, and his thinking slow in spite of the swiftness of his actions. He is no match for his winged enemies.[37]

He will lose the fight about *sophia* [wisdom].[38] The chorus predicts this in its first stasimon: Pentheus' *sophon* is not *sophia* (395); the Bacchae do not envy him for it (1005). Wisdom and insight are with those who surrender to the god (390, 1151), because they know that he is the true wise one who can take vengeance on his enemies (877 ff., 882 ff.). Old Teiresias is readily accepted in the circle of those clever enough to throw their lot in with the right side (179, 186) because they can distinguish true *sophia* from false (200 ff., 266 ff., 311 ff.). The chorus accepts Teiresias' equation of the belief in the new god with the worship of ancient tradition (200 ff., 890 ff.). This is surprising at first (see above p. 359). But if this was not regarded as a cheap trick of Dionysos' followers, it was to be assumed that Euripides deliberately spoke anachronistically from a fifth-century perspective.[39] It is preferable, however, to use the explanation which remains within the confines of the tragedy. The general readiness to fulfil the demands of religion without examination, knowing that this amounts to an alliance with the stronger power, has always been a prerequisite for the pursuit of any religious cult.[40] In this respect the new Dionysiac cult also fulfils the demands of tradition.[41]

The word *sophia* which we first encounter in a technical context (*Il.* XV 412, Hes. *Op.* 648) denotes the grasping of a situation or a task and the ability to master it. Pentheus tries to comprehend the new situation which arises with the appearance of Dionysos, and he believes that he will be able to master it with the help of his own meagre experience. The god really understands the situation and is sure of how he can destroy his enemy.

This shows itself as soon as the two meet. The scene in which the captured Dionysos stands in front of the king, uncannily calm, even gentle (436 ff.) is full of ambiguity in the god's declarations to Pentheus (466, 470, 478, 494, 498, 500, 502). But it is not the ambiguity which Teiresias uses towards the king in Sophocles' *Oedipus Rex*. In Teiresias' words there is the truth about Oedipus, though half-veiled, but later in retrospect, Oedipus will have to accept it as valid. Yet the scene from the *Bacchae* (apart from a pun about his name (508), which is only word-play) is not concerned with the truth about Pentheus, but with the truth about the god, i.e. his identity vis-à-vis the captured man. For Dionysos has assumed human shape. He does not reveal himself during the play even to his followers. Even to them he manifests himself not in appearance, but simply by invocation as a god (576 ff., 1074 ff.) and continues the game of hide-and-seek towards them in a positively fastidious manner (cf. especially 629). He is not recognized by his followers until he has used them as tools for his plans (Agaue, 1297 ff., Pentheus, 1113-21).[42] He plays the same game of hide-and-seek as Pentheus' prisoner. It has rightly been said that it is a game of cat and mouse and that Dionysos in his behaviour towards his adversary aims not to convert, but to confuse and entangle him more deeply.[43] This is the intended and achieved effect of the miracles which the captured god produces. A fire and the collapse of buildings in the palace precinct and phantom apparitions confuse Pentheus while the prisoner easily escapes. Pentheus is frightened by the fire, deceived by the apparitions, torn between his anxiety about the fire and about the prisoner, fighting in vain until he is exhausted, while the god looks calmly on and goes away — and then, when Pentheus believes him fled, suddenly reappears. This is the image of a confused, disoriented man, confronted by the playful caprice of an unintelligible, superior force.

Thus the confused and disoriented man cannot stop trying to find out what his opponent is up to. Even though he seems to have formed an opinion about the deception that has been concocted, he feels a victim of his own curiosity. The latter is already evident during the prisoner's interrogation, and when the miracle of the god's liberation and the shepherd's report about the maenads' dangerous miracles in the mountains have called him to renewed activity, the god traps him by exploiting this very curiosity (811 ff.). The attempt to watch the Bacchae in action is 'rationalized'[44] as a military reconnaissance operation (838, 916, 956, 981) — which, by the way, is factually not as striking for Euripides as it may seem to us.[45] Pentheus' ideas about the depravities of the Bacchae and his wish to watch them in action (among them, his own mother) have repeatedly and confidently been interpreted as the expression of a depraved imagination and of repressed and frustrated lust. And, as we have seen, this has led some scholars to extreme conclusions about Pentheus' psyche.[46] Yet we have also seen that such psychologizing leads away from the tragedy. We must stick to the material at hand. Pentheus really wants to discover something by this operation, but it is something to confirm his prejudices (814, 1060). He wants to convict the Bacchae of debauchery, which he says he would deplore but which (as Dionysos knows) would actually please him (814 ff.). It would expose the hated enemy and annihilate him morally.

For, from the beginning, Pentheus' behaviour towards the Dionysiac contains an element of emotion as well as the insecurity of not understanding the enemy. He has decided, out of human self-defense and on the basis of everyday experience, to fight the unusual force which is confusing and erupting, overwhelming and tearing people from their accustomed environment. Taking sides already implies emotion, and thus his first appearance is already emotionally charged. The passion increases with every new incomprehensible demand he has to accept and comprehend. It reaches a peak when his disorientation is at its most intense and the external danger has apparently become threatening. The emotion brings him close to madness and thus to exactly what he considers the characteristic danger of the opposition (326, 359, cf. 399, 887, 999). In the grip of emotion the earthborn loses the ground under his feet. He starts to 'fly' (332)[47] and to show that form of excitement which is typical of the Bacchae (214, cf. 1268; 'ecstasy' 359).

Yet the similarity with Bacchic frenzy is only external; he is not yet gripped by actual Bacchic ecstasy. He lacks its most important characteristic, dream-like certainty and unswerving purpose. He feels extremely insecure and only in this state of disorientation when he has lost control over himself, does the Dionysiac overwhelm him in order to destroy him. The stranger who in reality is Dionysos says so himself (850): 'Dionysos, now bring it to an end. You are not far. Take revenge on this man. Cause him to lose himself. Let giddy madness strike him'.

And for the first time, in this specifically Dionysiac delusion, which makes everything appear easy to him, Pentheus stops being himself until he re-awakens in the face of death. The *Bacchae* is the tragedy of the power which forces a man to divest himself of his identity and most brutally compels those who try most forcefully to hold on to themselves.

In the efforts to link the *Bacchae* to other works by Euripides there have been few attempts to probe its connections with the other late tragedies. On the other hand there have often been comparisons made with *Hippolytos*.[48] Both works are interpreted as dramas about the revenge of a neglected, elemental force. But though there are certain broad similarities, the two tragedies are very different in structure.[49] The unacknowledged force of the Dionysiac confronts Pentheus initially from outside, and then creeps into his mind, destroying him from within. Agaue can only kill Pentheus because his own madness brings him into her circle. The neglected Aphrodite, however, works to destroy Hippolytus through another human being: his stepmother Phaidra. And even if we are to see the *semnotēs* [pomposity] of Hippolytus at the beginning of the play as his fatal flaw, this still bears no proportion to the terrible destruction he suffers. Our sympathies are much less ambiguously engaged than in the *Bacchae*, where the relation between the offense and the destruction of Pentheus — terrible as it is — is more fatefully balanced. Most important, Hippolytos is not prey to the human disorientation which is at the centre of the *Bacchae*. Phaidra is in the grip of a hopeless passion; Hippolytos is deeply frightened and indignant; but both are quite aware of the situation in which they find themselves. Theseus falls victim to a very simple deception. The *Bacchae* is quite different, in that the ambiguity and incomprehensibility of events stirred up by the god awakens and intensifies the passion.

A play whose structure is far more similar to the *Bacchae* is another of Euripides' late works, *Ion*.[50] Here too the god (Apollo) has led a human being (Kreusa) into such a complicated dilemma that she misunderstands the real situation, can no longer tell a friend from foe, and is led to a passionate action which might cause a mother to kill her own son. Yet *Ion* is the untragic opposite of the *Bacchae*. The god who acted out of his own embarrassment did not intend as much harm, and thus takes care that the real relationship is revealed in time. Before this happens, however, a situation has evolved which astonishingly resembles the catastrophe in the *Bacchae*: like Pentheus, Kreusa turns from being the persecutor to being the persecuted, and to her horror finds herself suddenly face to face with an indignant crowd at whose head she sees her own flesh and blood. Except here, when compared to the catastrophe in the *Bacchae*, mother and son have changed roles (*Ion* 1250 ff.). After all the strain of disorientation under which the god brought Kreusa to the brink of desperate action (and thus of her own death), there is a final difficult moment solved by a *pia fraus* [innocent deception] of Kreusa's husband Xuthos, the precondition for a final happy end: Xuthos is to accept Ion as his son instead of the son of the god (1540 ff.). Athena confirms that this *pia fraus* is really the divine will which will benefit men (1561 f., 1601 ff.). Like the deception recommended by Kadmos to Pentheus (333 ff.), it too involves a birth story. And it is instructive, moreover, to compare Kadmos' words about the suppression of secret doubts with what Ion (1520 ff.) says to his mother when he suspects that he might not be the god's son, but the offspring of a mortal indiscretion (cf. *Bacch*. 26 ff.).

Life is full of uncertainty and ambiguity. If one wants to survive, it is best not to look too closely, to leave things unexamined and undecided. Euripides makes Orestes in the *Elektra* say those words about how to judge human values,[51] but they are also valid in a wider context of life and its meaning. Diogenes Laertius (2.33) reports than when Socrates heard these Euripidean verses, he left the theatre muttering disapproval. For the moralist, such resignation was not acceptable. But this was not

Euripides' last word, or at any rate not his only word on the matter. For him, however, this statement describes one possibility of human behaviour, if the play is not to end in tragedy. Pentheus does not leave the facts which offer themselves to him unexamined and undecided and because, instead of acceptance he chooses another, worse approach, he perishes miserably.

There is a third possibility apart from the non-tragic and the horrific-tragic — the tragic-heroic. This is the approach in *Iphigenia at Aulis*. Iphigenia translates the apparently senseless caprice of fate which chose her of all people, the uninvolved person, to be sacrificed to guarantee the success of the expedition to Troy, into a challenge which claims her of all people to fulfil a great idea: the salvation of Greece from the barbarian threat. This translation is Iphigenia's very own doing. The others admire her, but they do not understand her and the chorus says expressly, 'O maiden, your resolve is noble, but what *Tyche* and the Goddess bring is sick.' (1402 ff.).

What *tyche*, blind random chance, has in store for Iphigenia is 'sick.' At the end of *Ion* the same force raises Ion and Kreusa to utmost happiness. Here too the reversal, 'one day in the bright light of the sun' (1516) is incredible and overwhelming, particularly for the happy couple. How it can be endured, whether it can be borne at all, is the external question which admits to many different answers in Euripides' late tragedies. And it is now instructive to see how in all the richness of Euripides' inexhaustible imagination and creativity there are certain structural forms which, symbolically, present the reversal of fortune. Like Pentheus in the *Bacchae*, like Kreusa in *Ion*, Iphigenia, too, stands face to face with an enraged crowd just before the impending catastrophe. Not, however, confronted with her next of kin come to kill her unwittingly, but with her still-unknown apparent bridegroom Achilleus, who is her protector first and then becomes her admirer.

For fortune always changes the roles in this way. It makes the most familiar person appear strange and hostile, and the stranger appear familiar. Late Euripides found an expressive way to present this changing *tyche*. It always was one of the most important elements of tragedy, to be sure, and Sophocles' *Oedipus* is already an unforgettable presentation of this fall from the pinnacle of power and popularity into the abyss of misery and shame. But this contrast evolves out of the linear course of the tragedy. To present a sudden reversal rising from an incomprehensible situation, Euripides found structures which are immediately striking in their external shape.

Kreusa persecuted Ion because he, the 'stranger', tried to insinuate himself into her ancient Athenian family. When her attempt to murder him fails, the persecutor not only changes into the persecuted person, she also becomes the 'strange woman' in the environment because she broke the Delphic peace (1221). In the *Bacchae*, the reversal from persecutor to persecuted in the fate of Pentheus manifests itself in the image of the hunt: Pentheus who chased Dionysos and the Bacchae (228, 352, 434 ff., 451, 866 ff.) literally becomes the chased deer which Agaue and her sisters in their delusion take to be a beast of prey and tear to pieces (848, 977 ff., 1107 f., 1169 ff., 1202 ff., 1237 ff., 1255, 1278). The tragedy contains further reversals: the man who wanted to see the Maenads (811 ff., 912 ff.) is being seen by them (1075); the man who was indignant about the Bacchic apparel of Teiresias and Kadmos (248 ff.) and undressed the captured god with glee (493 ff.) dresses himself in Bacchic clothes and perishes in them (821 ff., 912 ff., 1115).

When the course of fortune is accepted, the reversal presents itself in another form: Iphigenia who was enticed to Aulis, following her mother as dependent child (607 ff.; 613 ff.), now takes the directing on herself and proceeds to her own sacrifice (1458 ff.; 1467 ff.). Euripides presented a similar reversal in another late play a few years earlier: in the beginning of the *Phoinissai*, Antigone climbs the palace roof to see the enemy army which is besieging Thebes. She mounts the stairs, hesitantly, a shy girl who ventures forth anxiously from the security of the house. An old man, the pedagogue, has to lead her by the hand (88 ff., 103 ff.). At the end of the tragedy, the same Antigone leaves home with Oedipus, her father, and goes into exile. Now she is leading the old blind man and gives him her hand (1710 ff.). The words with which she makes her entrance and the words with which she introduces her exit are without doubt deliberately related (cf. 103–5, 106~1700–1, 1714–15).

In this deliberate consonance of contrasting situations, Euripides in his final plays found an effective way of expressing his understanding of the reversal of human fortune:

> Many are the forms of what is unknown.
> Much that the gods achieve is surprise.
> What we look for does not come to pass;
> God finds a way for what none foresaw.
> Such was the end of this story.

(Bacchae 1388–92)

27

TRAGEDY AND RELIGION: THE *BACCHAE*

THOMAS G. ROSENMEYER

I

The *Bacchae* is not intrinsically a religious drama. This flies in the face of certain criticical assumptions which have recently gained currency. It has been suggested that Euripides' chief object in writing the drama was to give a clinical portrayal of what Dionysiac religion, hence Dionysus, does to men. According to this view, the *Bacchae* is a more or less realistic document, perhaps an anthropological account of an outburst of manic behavior, of a psychosis analogous to certain phenomena reported from the Middle Ages and not unknown in our own troubled times. The play has even been compared with a modern imaginative treatment of mass psychosis, Van Tilburg Clark's *Oxbow Incident*. I feel that this is mistaken, and for a very simple and obvious reason. Whatever one may say about the ancient tragedians, about the extravagant character of many of the plots, about the implausibility of much that is said and done, the fact remains that the writers are interested in what is typical, in the generic, or, as Aristotle has it, in the universal. To attribute to Euripides a study in abnormality is to indulge in an anachronism. Euripides is not the kind of dramatist, like Sartre, whose poetic urge is stimulated by small grievances rather than catholic insight. Nor is Euripides a scientific observer of sickness; he does not record, he creates. His material is ritual and mythical, and some of it is clinical; but the product is something entirely different.

Pindar once uses the tale of Perseus cutting off the head of the Medusa as an image symbolizing the act of poetic creation: living ugliness is violently refashioned into sculptured beauty. The ferocity of the *Bacchae* is to be seen in the same light. By an act of literary exorcism the cruelty and the ugliness of a living experience are transmuted into the beauty

Originally published in *The Masks of Tragedy* by T. G. Rosenmeyer, pp. 125–49. Copyright © 1963 by T. G. Rosenmeyer. Reprinted by permission of the author and the University of Texas Press.

of a large vision, a vision which is not without its own horror, but a horror entirely unlike that felt at the approach of the god. It is the kind of horror which Plato touches on in the *Symposium* and the *Theaetetus*, the sudden weakness and awe which get hold of the philosophic soul at the moment when she comes face to face with a like-minded soul and jointly ventures to explore the ultimate. Dionysus is only a means to an end; Euripides exploits the Dionysiac revels to produce a dramatic action which helps the spectators to consider the mystery and the precariousness of their own existence.

Aeschylus, notably in his *Agamemnon* but also in some of his other extant plays, appeals to the audience with an interplay of sounds and sights. With Aeschylus, language is not an instrument but an entity, a vibrant self-sufficient thing, working in close harmony with the brilliant objects filling the stage of the *Oresteia*. The word textures pronounced by the chorus, like the sentence patterns of the actors' speeches, stir the audience as violently as the sight of a crimson tapestry or the vision of evil Furies on the roof. Behind this sumptuous drapery of color and sound, personality takes second place. The characters are largely the carriers of images and speech. Sophocles introduces the personal life, the *bios*, into drama. Now a man is no longer largely the pronouncer of words, the proposer of ideas and emotions, but an independent structure involving a past and a future, a point of intersection for ominous antecedents and awful prospects. This emergence of the organic character, of the heroic life as the nucleus of drama, was a fateful step in the history of literature. Aeschylus also, in some of his later plays, adopted the new structuring for his own purposes.

Euripides goes further. He rejects the autonomy of speech as he rejects the autonomy of the personal life; instead he attempts to combine the two in an organic mixture of his own. In the *Ion* he gives us a parody of the pure *bios* form; mythology is squeezed into a biographical mold, with unexpectedly humiliating consequences for the great hero. In the *Bacchae*, on the other hand, it is in the end not the persons who count, nor the words or sound patterns though the play may well be the most lyrical of all Euripidean works, but the ideas. The *Bacchae*, in spite of its contrived brutality and its lyricism, is a forerunner of the Platonic dialogues. The smiling god is another Socrates, bullying his listeners into a painful reconsideration of their thinking and their values. That is not to say that we have here an intellectual argument, an academic inquiry into logical relations. Rather, the *Bacchae* constitutes a poet's attempt to give shape to a question, to a complex of uncertainties and puzzles which do not lend themselves to discursive treatment. There is no clear separation of thesis and antithesis, of initial delusion and liberating doubt, nor is there anything like a final statement or a solution. Nevertheless the poem is cast in the philosophical mode. Sophocles, in the *Oedipus Rex* or the *Ajax*, takes a heroic life and fashions its tragic nexus to the world around it or to itself. Euripides, in the *Bacchae*, takes an abstract issue and constructs a system of personal relations and responses to activate the issue. He builds his lives into the issue, instead of letting the life speak for itself as Sophocles does.

The issue derives from a question which is simple and raw: What is man? As Dionysus remarks to Pentheus (506),

> Your life, your deeds, your Being are unknown
> to you.

For Plato, the human soul is a compound of the divine and the perishable, a meeting place of the eternal beyond and the passionate here. In the *Phaedrus* he puts the question more concretely. Socrates suggests that it is idle to criticize or allegorize mythology if one has not yet, as he himself has not, come to a satisfactory conclusion about his own nature and being (230 A):

I try to analyze myself, wondering whether I am some kind of beast more heterogeneous and protean and furious than Typhon, or whether I am a gentler and simpler sort of creature, blessed with a heavenly unfurious nature.

The word that I have translated as 'creature' is the same that appears in Aristotle's famous definition of man as a 'political creature,' or rather, as 'a creature that lives in a polis.' 'Political animal,' the usual translation, is unfortunate, for in his definition Aristotle clearly throws the weight of his authority behind the second alternative of Plato's question. Man is not a ravaging beast, but a gentler being. But perhaps Aristotle is not as fully sensitive as Plato to the difficulty posed by the alternative. Is man closer to the gods or to the beasts?

Another question which is linked to the uncertainty about the status of the human soul is: What is knowledge? Or, to put it differently: How much in this world is subject to man's insight and control? Greek philosophical realism, beginning with the Eleatics and reaching its greatest height with Plato, taught that reality is unchanging, static, difficult of access, and that in general men come to experience it only through the veil of ever-changing patterns of sensory impulses. There is an inexorable friction between total Being and partial Appearance. Man is constrained to deal with the appearances, but at his best he comes to sense — or, according to Plato, to know — the reality behind the phenomena. The breakthrough to the reality is a painful process; it can be achieved only at the cost of injuring and mutilating the ordinary cognitive faculties. The perfectionists, including Plato in the *Phaedo*, submit that the breakthrough becomes complete only with the complete surrender of the senses whose activity stands in the way of the vision of reality. That is to say, the perceptual blindness and the phenomenal friction cannot be resolved except by disembodiment and death.

Now if this, or something like it, is the philosophical issue which Euripides is trying to dramatize, he is at once faced with a grave artistic difficulty. How is he, as a dramatist, to convey the universal scope of Reality and the beguiling contradictoriness of Appearance, without rendering the formulation banal or bloodless or both? The statement 'Dionysus is all' would be worse than meaningless. It should be emphasized again that Euripides is not trying to say poetically what could also, and better, be said discursively. What does a poet-metaphysician do to clothe the range of abstract issues in the living and self-authenticating flesh of poetry? Is it possible for a dramatist to convey ideas without having his characters preach them ex cathedra, which is by and large the situation we find in the *Prometheus Bound*? Can a philosophical idea which is refracted by a process of poetic mutation continue to score as a factor in a metaphysical argument?

To begin with, the Greek writer has an advantage over his modern colleagues. The ancient conventions of tragedy stipulate that the dramatic nucleus be essayed from a spectrum of approaches. From prologue to chorus to characters to epilogue, each constitutive part of the drama contributes its specific orientation. In the end the various perspectives coalesce into one and invite a unified though never simple audience response. This is the desired effect; sometimes the merging of the lines of coordination is not complete, and the spectators are left without a certain key to gauge their participation. Goethe's *Faust* is, perhaps, once again a fair example of such a case on the modern stage. The author is saying something profound about man and reality, but for various reasons the play leaves us with the impression of partial statements instead of a total imagining, because of the vast scope of the action, because Goethe has inserted certain curious elements of diffusion and fragmentation, and because he tries to play off one culture against another in an attempt to universalize the compass of the theme. Any Greek play is likely to be more successful on this score. The traditional spectrum of perspectives is offset by an extreme succinctness of speech and thought, by a narrow conformity to Greek ways, by an economy of character, and, last but not least, by the condensatory effect of hereditary myth. Myth is itself a condensation of many experiences of different degrees of concreteness. Greek drama simply carries forward the business begun by myth.

Dionysus, who is Euripides' embodiment of universal vitality, is described variously by chorus, herdsmen, commoners, and princes. The descriptions do not tally, for the god cannot be defined. He can perhaps be totaled but the sum is never definitive; further inspection adds new features to the old. If a definition is at all possible it is a definition by negation or cancellation. For one thing, Dionysus appears to be neither woman nor man; or better, he presents himself as woman-in-man, or man-in-woman, the unlimited personality (235):

> With perfumes wafted from his flaxen locks
> and Aphrodite's wine-flushed graces in
> his eyes . . .

No wonder Pentheus calls him (353) 'the woman-shaped stranger,' and scoffs at the unmanly whiteness of his complexion (457). In the person of the god strength mingles with softness, majestic terror with coquettish glances. To follow him or to comprehend him we must ourselves give up our precariously controlled, socially desirable sexual limitations. The being of the god transcends the protective fixtures of decency and sexual pride.

Again, Dionysus is both a citizen, born of Semele, and a Greek from another state, for he was raised in Crete, like the Zeus of the mysteries — surely this is the implication of lines 120 ff. — *and* a barbarian from Phrygia or Lydia or Syria or India, at any rate from beyond the pale of Greek society. It is not as if the conflicting pieces of information had to be gathered laboriously from various widely separated passages in the play. All of them are to be found in the entrance song of the chorus. After the introductory epiphany of the god himself, the women of the chorus begin to assemble their picture of Dionysus, and it is indicative of what Euripides means him to be that even these first few pointers should cancel out one another. It happens to be true historically that Dionysus is both Greek and non-Greek; recently discovered Mycenean texts have shown that the god's name was known to the Greeks of the Mycenean period. It now appears that the foreign extraction of Dionysus may have been a pious fiction of Apollonian partisans. Dionysus the popular god, the god of mysteries, the emblem of surging life in its crudest form, of regeneration and animal passion and sex, was endangering the vested interests of Apollo, grown refined and squeamish in the hands of the gentry and the intellectual elite. One of the defense measures, and there were many, was to declare Dionysus a foreigner, a divinity whose ways, so the propaganda went, offended the true instincts of the Greek. There was some apparent justification for this. The genuinely foreign deities who were being imported into Greece often were kindred in spirit to Dionysus. At any rate the propaganda took hold. At the end of the fifth century all Greeks tended to believe that Dionysus came from abroad; and yet they considered him one of their own, a powerful member of the Olympian pantheon. Euripides exploits the discrepancy to the advantage of his purpose; he uses it to emphasize the unbounded, the unfragmented nature of the ultimate substance. But the arrival from foreign lands signifies a special truth; it highlights the violently intrusive character of the Dionysiac life, of the unlimited thrusting itself into the limited and exploding its stale equilibrium, which is a favorite theme of Pythagorean and Greek popular thought.

But all this would be bloodless metaphysics, dry-as-dust allegory, were it not for Euripides' grasp of the essential irony enunciated in the passage of the *Phaedrus* and skirted in Aristotle's aphorism. Man is both beast and god, both savage and civilized, and ultimate knowledge may come to him on either plane, depending on the manner in which the totality communicates itself. It is as an animal, as a beast close to the soil and free of the restrictions of culture and city life, that man must know Dionysus. But that means that in embracing Dionysus man surrenders that other half of himself, the spark of the gentle and celestial nature which, the philosophers hope, constitutes the salvageable part of man's equipment. The incongruity of the two planes, the political and the animal, becomes the engrossing puzzle and the energizing thesis of the play. The double nature of man is what the play is really about; the ambivalence of Dionysus is pressed into service largely in order to illumine the ambivalence of human cognition reaching out for its object, for the elusive pageant of truth.

II

In the *Bacchae* men are identified with animals, not as in Aesop where the beasts aspire to be men and become moral agents, but as in a Gothic tale where intelligence and social grace and responsibility are renounced and the irrational, the instinct of blood and steaming compulsion, take their place. Characteristically this way of looking at life paralyzes value judgment. The gulf between men and animals is erased, but whether this is a good thing or not is by no means clear. When the women of the chorus, for example, call Pentheus a beast they do not mean to flatter him. He is the son of Echion, who was sprung from dragon's teeth, and there is dragon blood in his veins (1155). He is said to be a fierce monster (542) whose acts make one suspect that he was born of a lioness or a Libyan Gorgon. His mother also in her moment of visionary bliss sees him as a lion rather than as a man. For her, however, this is not a matter of disparagement; if anything, embracing a lion seems to her to offer a glimpse of perfection. Not so the chorus; in the passages cited they show an incongruous pride in human shape and human achievement. But in the fourth choral ode, as they reach their highest pitch of passion and frenzied insight, they issue their call (1017):

> Appear, in the shape of a bull or a many-headed
> serpent, or a lion breathing fire!

In their first ode also they refer to Dionysus as the bull-horned god wreathed in snakes (100 f.). The god Dionysus, the stranger-citizen, the hermaphrodite, at once superman and subman, is a beast, for which the chorus praises him. This is the sacred dogma. Even Pentheus, once he has fallen under the spell of the god, acknowledges him as a bull (920):

> And now, leading me on, I see you as
> a bull, with horns impacted in your head.
> Were you a beast before? I should not wonder.

And Dionysus answers:

> Yes, now you see what is for you to see.

But what of Pentheus' own beast-likeness? Are the women suggesting that human beastliness is a mere parody of divine beastliness, and therefore to be condemned? Or have the ladies of the chorus not yet traveled the full length of the Dionysiac conversion, and retain a vestige of civilized values? Their abuse of Pentheus is couched in terms which expose them as imperfect Maenads. Contrast that other chorus, the band of Bacchantes hidden from our sight, whose mysterious acts of strength are reported to us in the messenger speeches. From them rather than from their more civilized sisters on the stage we expect the pure lesson of the new faith. And in fact they preserve no trace of a false pride in human separateness. They carry the tokens of animal life on their backs and entertain the beasts as equal partners (695):

> And first they shook their hair free to their shoulders
> and tucked up their fawnskins . . .
> . . . their spotted pelts
> they girt with serpents licking at their cheeks.
> And some clasped in their arms a doe or wild
> wolf cubs and gave them milk . . .

Under the aegis of Dionysus, men and animals are as one, with no questions asked. The philosophical message is tolerably clear. But the vestigial bias of the pseudo-Maenads onstage is more than a temporary deviation from the orthodox Bacchic faith. In the interest of the message it would have been wiser to abuse Pentheus as a man, incapable of going beyond the limitations of his anthropomorphism. The beast imagery in the choral condemnation of Pentheus is cumulative and emphatic. The praise of Dionysus does not blot it from our memory. It is, in fact, intended to serve as a counterpoint. The animal shape rules supreme; but when all parties have been heard it is not at all clear whether one ought to approve or not. The judgment is suspended and values are held in abeyance.

It is a mistake to consider the Dionysiac ecstasy a perversion of social life, an impasse, a negative situation. The *Bacchae* does not tell a story of maladjustment or aberration. It is a portrayal of life exploding beyond its narrow everyday confines, of reality bursting into the artificiality of social conventions and genteel restrictions. Waking and sleeping are deprived of their ordinary cognitive connotations; who is to say that sleeping, the drunken stupor which succeeds the rite, does not expand one's vision beyond its commonplace scope? In the *Ion* the premium is on wakefulness; in the *Bacchae* we are invited to rest in a gray no man's land which is halfway between waking and sleep, where man shelves the tools of reason and social compact and abandons himself to instinct and natural law (862 ff., trans. Philip Vellacott):

> O for the long nights of worship, gay
> With the pale gleam of dancing feet,
> With head tossed high to the dewy air —
> Pleasure mysterious and sweet!
> O for the joy of a fawn at play
> In the fragrant meadow's green delight,
> Who has leapt out free from the woven snare,
> Away from the terror of chase and flight,
> And the huntsman's shout, and the straining pack,
> And skims the sand by the river's brim
> With the speed of wind in each aching limb,
> To the blessed lonely forest where
> The soil's unmarked by a human track,
> And leaves hang thick and the shades are dim.

This is the *strophe* of a choral ode; in the *antistrophe* the chorus invokes the divine order of things — *physis*, nature — which will assert itself eventually in spite of men (884)

> who honor ignorance and refuse
> to enthrone divinity . . .

The verses cited picture the pleasure and awe of identification with non-human nature, with the life of the fawn bounding free of the snare but never quite eluding the hunter, a life of liberty which is yet not free. The

animal senses the sway of natural law even more strongly than the man.
Strophe and *antistrophe*, the vision of animal escape and the address
to natural compulsion, are part of the same complex. But in the text
they do not follow one upon the other; they are separated by that rare
thing in Greek poetry, a refrain which is repeated once more identically,
at the end of the *antistrophe*. Refrains in Greek tragedy always have a
solemn ring; they are felt to be echoes of ritual hymns. The fixed severity
of the repetition is something foreign within the headlong flow of the
dramatic current. The mind accustomed to pressing on after the determined advance of ideas and plot is abruptly stopped in its tracks; time
ceases for a while and the cold chill of monotony reveals a glimpse of
Being beyond the Becoming of the human scene.

Here is an attempt to translate the refrain as literally as the sense
allows (877, 897):

> What is wisdom? Or what is more beautiful,
> a finer gift from the gods among men,
> than to extend a hand victorious
> over the enemy's crown? But beauty
> is every man's personal claim.

Wisdom equals tyranny, beauty equals vengeance. The hunted and the
hunter have their own jealous notions of wisdom and beauty, but their
pretensions are drowned in the vast offering of the gods, the dispensation
of natural law, and the survival of the strongest. This is what the refrain
seems to say; the message agrees well with the propositions of *strophe*
and *antistrophe*. But note the didactic quality of the speech, the question
and answer, and particularly the academic formulation of the last line,
which in the Greek consists of only four words: 'Whatever beautiful,
always personal.' It is a line which might have come straight from the
pages of Aristotle; better yet, it reminds us of a similarly scholastic
passage in a poem by Sappho in which she contemplates various standards
of beauty and preference and concludes: 'I [think that the most beautiful
thing is] that with which a person is in love.' The poetess speaks of a
'thing,' using the neuter gender, and of 'a person,' any person desiring
the thing. Like a good teacher she starts her discussion with a universal
premise. Then, as the poem draws to its conclusion, she discards the
generality and focuses on the living girl and on the I, the specific poles
of her love whose reality constitutes the authority for the writing of the
poem. But the philosophic mode of the earlier formulation remains important; it reminds us that the specific poles of her present love are at
the same time representatives of a universal rhythm. In Euripides' ode,
also, it is this universal rhythm which comes into view through the

hieratic stillness of the refrain and particularly through its last line. The words are almost the same as those of Sappho; the difference is that between a vision intent upon the small joys and sufferings of love, and a vision which comprehends man in the sum total of his powers and feebleness. The refrain may well be the closest approach to poetry shedding its disguise and showing itself as metaphysics pure and simple.

But the glimpse is short-lived, and the clarity immediately obscured. Again it is the chorus itself which is the chief agent of confounding the analysis. It does so by combining in the Dionysiac prospects of its songs the two sides, the real and the ideal, which are inevitably connected in the experience. Both ritual and hope, slaughter and bliss, dance and dream, the cruelty of the present and the calm of the release, are joined together as one. The paradise of milk and honey and the orgy of bloody dismemberment merge in a poetic synthesis which defies rational classification. Of this creative insight into the contradictoriness of things I have already spoken. To complicate the picture even further, Bacchic sentiments are superimposed on traditional choric maxims. In an earlier ode which begins with a condemnation of Pentheus' words and an appeal to the goddess Piety, the women sing (386, 397):

> Of unbridled mouths
> and of lawless extravagance
> the end is disaster . . .
>
> . . . .
>
> Life is brief; if a man,
> not heeding this, pursues vast things
> his gain slips from his hands.
> These are the ways, I believe,
> of madmen, or of
> injudicious fools.

We recognize the familiar adage of 'nothing in excess,' the motto of bourgeois timidity and sane moderation, at opposite poles from the Dionysiac moral of vengeance and expansiveness and the bestialization of man. The injunctions of moderation and knowing one's limits run counter to the hopes of those who worship Dionysus. The two people who live up to the injunctions, Tiresias and Cadmus, come very close to being comic characters, as we shall see directly. Why, then, does Euripides put the pious precept into the mouth of a chorus whose primary artistic function is to communicate precisely what it is condemning, the spirit of unbridled mouths and lawless extravagance? It may be noted that such injunctions in Greek tragedy are often illusory. Setting off as they do a heroic imbalance or a cosmic disturbance, they underscore the poignancy of the action. But in this particular instance the use of the Delphic motto is even more startling than usual. The direction of the metaphysical impact is rudely deflected and the opacity of the poem enhanced by this conventional reminder of irrelevant quietist values.

While the Theban women are away celebrating, the foreign votaries are in Thebes. This is a mechanical displacement necessitated by what Greek tragedy permits; for the Dionysiac revels must be reported rather than seen, and so the true Maenads are offstage. But that puts the chorus in an anomalous position. They are worshipers of Dionysus, but they must not behave like worshipers. Few Euripidean choruses are less intimately engaged in the action and in fact less necessary to the action. It is the chorus offstage that counts. Hence the curious mixture of half-hearted participation and distant moralizing, as if the poet were not entirely comfortable with the choral requirements. This may account for the perplexing admixture of Apollonian preaching which I have just mentioned. It may account also for the remarkable poetic color of many of the choral utterances. The poet, making a virtue of the necessity, calls attention to the detachment of the chorus from the heart of the plot — though not from the heart of the philosophical issue — by giving it some of the finest lyrics ever sounded in the Attic theater. This is not the place for a close appreciation of the poetry; that can be done only in the original. The analysis of ancient poetry is a difficult thing; there are few men who combine the necessary scholarly equipment with an understanding of what poetry is about. Further, some of the clues to such an understanding which in modern poetry are furnished by the experience of living speech are missing for the Greek. Nevertheless few readers can expose themselves to the choral odes of the *Bacchae* without realizing that this is poetry of the highest order. Imagery has little to do with it; in this as in most Euripidean plays the choral poetry is even less dependent on metaphor and simile than the dialogue. There is some pondering of myth to be sure. But perhaps the most important thing about the odes is the wonderful mixture of simplicity and excitement. The women do not beat around the bush; their interest in life is single-minded, and they declare themselves with all the fervor of a unitary vision. This does not, of course, say anything about the poetry as poetry, but it may explain why the lyrics of the *Bacchae* touch us so powerfully.

There is one image, however, or rather a class of images, which ought to be mentioned: the container filled to the bursting point. In their first ode the chorus uses the trope three times. They sing of Dionysus stuffed into the thigh of Zeus, golden clasps blocking the exit until such time as the young man may be born (94 ff.). They call on Thebes, nurse of Semele, to (107)

> teem, teem with verdant
> bryony, bright-berried;

the city is to be filled to the rooftops with vegetation, as a sign of the
presence of the god. For illustration we should compare the famous
vase painting of Exekias in which Dionysus reveals himself in his ship to
the accompaniment of a burst of vegetation. Finally the women caution
each other to be careful in their handling of the thyrsus, the staff of the
god (113):

> Handle the staffs respectfully;
> there is *hybris* in them.

In all three instances it is the fullness of the container which is stressed,
not the spilling over. But as the play advances, containment proves inadequate. At the precise moment when the stranger is apprehended by
Pentheus' men, the Maenads who had been imprisoned earlier are set
free (447):

> All by themselves the bonds dropped off their feet;
> keys unlocked doors, without a man's hand to turn them.

Their liberation is as real as the binding of the stranger is false.

The most striking *mise en scène* of the inadequacy of the container
is the so-called palace miracle. Like that of the other passages, its function
is symbolic rather than dramaturgical; after it has happened it is never
mentioned again. It is not necessary to the progress of the plot, only to
the effect and the meaning of the poem. We need not worry much whether
the stage director engineered the collapse of a column or a pediment, or
whether the spectators were challenged to use their own imaginations,
though I am inclined to assume the latter. At any rate, the vision of the
palace shaking and tumbling is the most explicit and the most extended
of a series of images pointing to the explosion of a force idly and wrong-
fully compressed. Eventually this concept converges on what I have
called the friction between total Being and fragmentary Appearance,
the friction which is worked out also through a series of antinomies: the
brute wildness of the thyrsus versus the spindles abandoned in the hall,
the fawnskins versus the royal armor, the civic proclamation versus the
bleating shout, the beating of tambourines versus the steady clicking of
the loom. Dionysus disrupts the settled life, he cracks the shell of civic
contentment and isolation. Probably the most important word in the
play, as a recent critic has well pointed out, is '*hybris*.' It occurs throughout, and always in a key position. But it is not the *hybris* of which the
tragic poets usually speak, the *hybris* which figures also in the legal
documents, the thoughtless insolence which comes from too much social

or political power. In the *Bacchae*, *hybris* is quite literally the 'going beyond,' the explosion of the unlimited across the barricades which a blind civilization has erected in the vain hope of keeping shut out what it does not wish to understand. That is not to say that the word is not used also in its more conventional sense, especially with reference to the campaign of Pentheus. As a result, the efforts of Pentheus take on the aspect of a parody of Dionysiac impulsiveness.

Similarly the hunt is a principal symbol because it catches the futility of organized, circumscribed life. From the vantage point of the larger reality, all worldly activity appears both hunt and escape. Hunting and being hunted are the physical and psychological manifestations of Appearance, the monotonous jolts of the process of generation and decay. Agave cries when approached by the herdsman (731):

> Run to it, my hounds!
> Behold the men who hunt us! Follow me,
> brandish your thyrsus and pursue them!

The Maenads are resting; they are communing with the god and sloughing off the sense of separateness when they are violently pulled back into the world of Appearance and resume their game of hunting and being hunted. In this case it is Appearance which causes the disruption; Being and Appearance are so related that one as well as the other may be the cause of disturbance and dislocation. There is a perpetual pull between them which never allows either to win a lasting victory. Without the constant friction there would be no tragedy; without the violent disruption of one by the other there would be no dismemberment. *Sparagmos*, the sacred dismemberment of the Dionysiac rites, is both a means to an end and an autonomous fact. As a means to an end it supplies the frenzied exercise which terminates in the drugged sleep. The explosion of energy, the tearing and mutilation of a once living body, leaves the worshiper exhausted and readies the soul, through a numb tranquility, for the mystic union with the god. But the dismemberment operates also as a self-validating event. Through it, symbolically, the world of Appearance with its contradictions and insufficiencies is made to show itself as it really is. The destruction of Pentheus, then, is not simply a sardonic twist of an unspeakable bloody rite, but a fitting summation of the lesson of the play. The limited vessel is made to burst asunder, refuting the pretentions of those who oppose Dionysus, of the partisans of unreality.

III

Who is Pentheus, and why is it he who dies rather than one of the other Thebans? When the stranger raises the question whether the king knows who he really is, he answers (507):

Pentheus, the son of Agave and of Echion.

Thus Pentheus identifies himself as a member of the ruling house, as an officer of the State. He bears a name which establishes his position within the hereditary political structure of his city. Even at the moment of death he throws off the leveling disguise of the ministrant and cries (1118):

Mother, it is I, your son
Pentheus, the child you bore in Echion's house.

In the judgment of Dionysus this pride in the house, the emphasis on the limited life, is ignorance. But is it commensurate with the punishment which Pentheus receives? Is there not something about him as a person which is more likely to justify the violence of his undoing? To ask the obvious question: Does Pentheus not exhibit an arrogance which cries out for retribution?

Here we must step gingerly. It is to be remembered that the action of the *Bacchae* is not primarily borne or promoted by the characters. Euripides does not in this play operate with idiosyncrasies but with lives. Suffering is constructed as the measurable content of a life, not as the unique unquantifiable experience of a specific irrational soul. And the lives, also, are largely catalysts for the release of social complications.

These complications have nothing to do with the arbitrary contours of individual dispositions, but answer directly to the needs of the author's metaphysical purpose. The personal relations brought into play are devised chiefly as one of the means for the author to invoke his philosophical riddle. In the *Alcestis* character is all; in the *Bacchae* it counts for very little. It is sometimes said that the tragedy of Pentheus is not that he tried to do what was wrong but that he was the wrong man to do it — that he was, in fact, not a political strongman but precisely the unbalanced, excitable type of person who most easily falls a victim to the allurements of the Dionysiac indulgence. In other words, the character of Pentheus is too Dionysiac to allow him to oppose Dionysus successfully. But this argument will not stand up. Pentheus is no more and no less excitable or unstable than most of the heroes of Greek tragedy. An Odysseus, or a Socrates, is no more fit to stand at the center of a high tragedy than a Pecksniff or a Tanner. Odysseus is not a whole man, as Helen is not a whole woman; they are exponents of a partial aspect of the human range: intelligence in the case of Odysseus, love in the case of Helen. But Pentheus is a whole man, precisely as Oedipus is, or as Antigone is a whole woman. And because he is whole he is vulnerable, more vulnerable than the men and women who are weighted in one direction or another.

Of course he is not a moderate. His order to smash the workshop of Tiresias (346 ff.) is not well considered. He happens to be right; Tiresias appears to have turned disloyal to Apollo, and so will no longer need his oracle seat. Under the democratic spell of Dionysus, everybody will do his own prophesying. But even if Pentheus were unjustified in his harshness toward Tiresias, his lack of moderation, or, to put it more fairly, his capacity for anger, does not necessarily discredit him. Stability, self-control, discretion smack too much of asceticism and puritan artifice to provide a solid basis for tragic action. Pentheus is a whole man, with none of his vitality curtailed or held in check. But he is also a king, a perfect representative of the humanistic Greek ideal of the ordered life, a political being rather than a lawless beast. Being Aristotle's 'creature living in a polis,' he is destined to ask the wrong sort of question, a political question, when faced with the reality of religion. His query (473),

> What profit do the celebrants draw from it?

shows the political or educational frame of his thinking. The twentieth century, unlike the eighteenth, is once more inclined to the view that the question of usefulness when applied to religion misses the point, that religion cannot be adjusted to a system of utilitarian relations. But where did Euripides and his contemporaries stand on this issue? In all probability Pentheus' question did not strike the audience as irrelevant; it may, in fact, have impressed them as noble and responsible. At the end of the fifth century, as we can see in the *History* of Thucydides, the preservation of social and political institutions and traditions had become the overriding topic of discussion to which all other values tended to be subordinated. The *Bacchae* demonstrates that this sort of nobility, the exaltation of the political and educational thesis, is as nothing before the primary currents of life. But a nobility which goes under is not the less noble for its defeat. Pentheus dies, and the nature of his death, particularly of the preparations which lead to his death, is deplorable. But the fact remains that his stand, and only his, can be measured in positive moral terms. Clearly the force which kills him eludes ethical analysis.

Because Pentheus is a king he offers a larger area to be affected by the deity. His responses differ from those of other men less in their specific quality than in their intensity. As a king he suffers for the group; his name, as Dionysus reminds him (508), means 'man of sorrow.' But there is nothing Christlike about him. He proposes to live as a rational man, to leave everything nonrational, everything that might remind us of man's original condition, behind him. Love and faith, the Christian antidotes of the dispassionate intellect, have not yet been formulated. In Plato, characteristically, it is love and reason together, or love-in-reason, which refines man and weakens the animal in him. Nonreason, in the fifth century BC., is neither love nor hatred but religious ecstasy. This Pentheus means to fight, for he knows it is wrong. Pentheus is not a romantic hero, he does not search for a hidden truth. The same thing is true of the others; both the characters and the chorus are, each of them, convinced that they know best and that their way of life is best. For Pentheus the best is Form, the tested and stable limits of responsibility, law, and control. Against the chorus, which espouses the cause of excitement, of formlessness and instability, Pentheus is the champion of permanence and stability. Neither his anger nor his defeat are valid arguments against the merits of this championship. Like Ajax, Pentheus is identified with armor (781, 809); like Ajax, the armed Pentheus, confined in the panoply of embattled civil life, turns against the forces which are wrecking his fragile cause. As a functionary he represents order and limit; as a man he is whole and robust and fully alive.

This cannot be said about Cadmus and Tiresias. For one thing, they are old men, their life force is diminished and stunted. This means that they cannot suffer as Pentheus can. It also means that they have come to terms with the world; there are no issues left for them to battle out, no difficulties over which to fret. Cadmus is a fine specimen of the *arriviste*, proud of the achievements of his grandson, but even prouder of the inclusion of a genuine god in the family. The god must at all costs be kept in the family, even if it becomes necessary to mince the truth a little. Here is Cadmus' humble plea to Pentheus (333):

> And if, as you say, the god does not exist,
> keep this to yourself, and share in the fine fiction
> that he does; so we may say that Semele bore
> a god, for the greater glory of our clan.

The distinction between truth and falsity, between order and disorder, is of no importance to him. At his time of life, a good reputation is a finer prize than a noble life, no matter whether the reputation is deserved or not. Tiresias likewise is not concerned with essentials. This Tiresias is not the Sophoclean man of truth, the terrible mouthpiece of mystery and damnation, but, of all things, a clever sophist, a pseudo-philosopher who strips away the mystery and the strangeness of the superhuman world and is content to worship a denatured, an ungodded god. A squeamish deist, he does not hold with the miracles and the barbarisms of popular faith. In his lecture to Pentheus he pares down the stature of Dionysus to render him manageable and unoffending (272 ff.). Point one: he is the god of wine (280)

> which liberates suffering mortals from
> their pain.

That is to say, he *is* wine (284), precisely as Demeter *is* grain. By allegorizing the old stories and identifying the gods with palpable substances, we can dispense with whatever is not concrete and intelligible in the traditions about Dionysus. Point two: he is a perfectly natural god. The distasteful tale about Zeus sewing him up in his thigh produces a quite satisfactory meaning once it is understood that the grating feature is due to a pun. Like Max Müller in a subsequent era of facile enlightenment, Tiresias believes that the mystery of myth is caused by a linguistic aberration; with the discovery of the cause, the mystery disappears.

Finally, in the third part of the lecture, Tiresias does pay some attention to the irrational virtues of the god, to his mantic powers and his ability to inspire panic in strong men. But this part of the assessment is underplayed; it is briefer than the other two, and one feels that Tiresias adds it only in order to have a weapon with which to frighten Pentheus. The reference to soldiers strangely routed and to Dionysiac torches at home in the sanctuary of Delphi is not a confession but a threat, calculated to appeal to Pentheus in the only language he understands: the language of military and political authority. Tiresias' heart is not in the threat; what interests him is the theological and philological sterilization of the god. Neither he nor Cadmus really understands or even wants to understand what the god has to offer. But they know that his triumph is inevitable, and so they try to accept him within their lights. They are fellow travelers, with a good nose for changes of fashion and faith. To take them seriously would be absurd; a Tartuffe has no claim on our sympathy.

They do not understand; hence nothing happens to them.[1] Pentheus, on the other hand, is fully engaged, and he is a big enough man to perceive the truth beyond his own self-interest. He is capable of appreciating the real meaning of Dionysus; though he does not approve, he understands. But understanding, in a man of his power of commitment, is tantamount to weakening, and in the end, to destruction. This is what Euripides dramatizes with the sudden break-up of Pentheus' royal substance. Abruptly the officer of the State turns into a Peeping Tom. One shout of the god (810) and the manly general becomes a slavish, prurient, reptilian thing, intent on watching from a safe distance what he hopes will be a spectacle to titillate his voyeur's itch. The civilized man of reason is gone, and in his place we find an animal, living only for the satisfaction of his instinctual drives.

Is the rapid change psychologically plausible? Once more, the question is not pertinent. There is no character in the first place, only a comprehensive life-image to symbolize one side of a conflict which transcends the terms of a uniquely experienced situation. Whether it is possible for such a man as Pentheus is shown to be in the first half of the play, to turn into the creature he becomes after his conversion by Dionysus, is a question on which psychoanalysts may have an opinion but which does not arise in considering Euripides' purpose. The truth is that the change is not a transition from one phase of life to another, much less a lapse into sickness or perversion, but quite simply death. When a tragic hero in the great tradition is made to reverse his former confident choice, especially if this happens at the instigation of the archenemy, the role of the hero has come to an end. We remember Agamemnon stepping on the crimson carpet, after Clytemnestra has broken down his reluctance. The blood-colored tapestry is a visual anticipation of the murder. Instead of the corporeal death which will be set offstage, the audience watch the death of the soul. With Agamemnon slowly moving through the sea of red the contours are blurred and the king of all the Greeks is annihilated before our eyes. Aeschylus uses a splash; Euripides, less concretely but no less effectively, uses a change of personality.

That the hero has died in his scene with Dionysus becomes even clearer when the god, with a Thucydidean terseness, announces the physical death (857):

> Now I shall go and dress him in the robes
> he'll wear to Hades once his mother's hands
> have slaughtered him . . .

His death, then, is an agreed fact both while the chorus sings their ode to Natural Necessity and also during the terrible scene which follows in which Pentheus arranges his woman's clothes about him. The King joins the Maenads, but he goes further than they, for he adopts the bisexuality of the god. All this is meaningful as a picture of the complete and devastating victory of reality over unreality, of the natural over the institutional life. But it is not without its psychological aspect, and here, curiously, we may see an ironic parallel to one of Plato's most troublesome concerns. In his discussions of dramatic poetry, Plato takes it for granted that the spectacle affects the soul of the spectator, even to the extent of transforming it in its own likeness. This is what drama demands; the audience must allow what they see to shape their souls, without struggling against the impact. Plato recognizes the legitimacy of the demand, and decides that therefore drama is too dangerous to have around in a healthy body politic, except the kind of drama whose effect is beneficial. Pentheus also is about to see a spectacle, a Dionysiac drama of the type which as a responsible man of the city he had condemned. Euripides knows that Plato's act of censorship is in a hopeless cause. A life which does not reach out to embrace the sight of a greater reality which tragedy affords is incomplete. Watching a play may mean a partial sacrifice of the soul, a surrender to the unlimited and the irrational, but we cannot do without it. Pentheus holds out against it for some time, but in the end he throws down his arms, with such finality that his soul comes to be transformed and enriched even before he goes off to spy on the mysteries.

Pentheus is drunk, without the physical satisfaction of strong drink (918):

> Ho, what is this? I think I see two suns,
> two cities of Thebes each with its seven gates!

This is one way of formulating his conquest at the hand of Dionysus. Drunk he sees more keenly, or at any rate more completely:

> And now, leading me on, I see you as
> a bull . . .

And Dionysus replies:

> Yes, now you see what is for you to see.

For the first time Pentheus' eyes are sufficiently opened to see the god in his animal shape. His vision is broadened; but his role as Pentheus is finished. The disintegration of the king is made particularly painful by the emphasis on the feminine clothing. Which Dionysus assisting as his valet (928) the one-time upholder of the *vita activa* becomes fussy and vain about the details of his toilette. Does the cloak hang properly? Is he to carry the thyrsus in his right or in his left hand? The energies which had once been directed toward the mustering of armies and the implementation of public decisions are now bestowed on the arrangement of his Bacchic vestments. Along with this attention to the correct fashion — behold, another Tiresias — to the external signs of his newfound anonymity, there goes an internal change which is equally preposterous. The blocked doer turns into an uninhibited dreamer (945):

> I wonder if my shoulders would support
> Cithaeron and its glens, complete with Maenads?

His speech, formerly royal and violent and ringing, has become pretty and lyrical; he pictures the women (957)

> like birds in the thickets,
> contained in the fond coils of love's embrace.

Compare this with his earlier comment (222) that the women

> slink off by devious ways into
> the wild and cater to the lusts of males.

His imagination has been fired, his surly prejudices are gone. The vision which neither Cadmus nor Tiresias was able to entertain has come to Pentheus and is inspiring him. The Bacchianized Pentheus is a visionary and poet. But it is a poetry which lacks the saving grace of choice. He contemplates the prospect of his mother carrying him home from the mountains, and the prospect pleases him. The political man has become woman *and* child. Having rid himself of the social restrictions and classifications, he savors infancy, a sentient creature for whom the mother's cradled arms offer escape and bliss. He is woman and child and beast, an amorphous organism susceptible to all influences and realizing itself in a life of instinct and unthinking sense. The victory of Dionysus is complete; the king is dead, and the man has been found out, in the god's image.

28

FEAR AND SUFFERING IN AESCHYLUS AND EURIPIDES

JACQUELINE DE ROMILLY

It would be a long but not difficult task to demonstrate the importance of these two emotions in the entire works of these tragic authors.[1] But the results would only be conclusive, however, if they were drawn from direct comparisons. After all, it is undeniable that there is as much 'suffering' in Aeschylus as there is 'fear' in Euripides. Our concern is rather to establish which of these two emotions each author emphasizes. We should therefore compare specific descriptions of these sentiments. But what instances should we choose? Indeed, there is scarcely anything in common between the terror which seizes Orestes at the end of the *Choephoroi* and Electra's pained anxiety at the prospect of someone unforeseen possibily arriving. Both these instances can be subsumed under the term 'fear', and yet one would hardly want to use them to demonstrate a difference of psychology, inasmuch as they are particular reactions to different stimuli. For this reason it seemed more valuable and significant to deal only with cases that are truly parallel. And since both Aeschylus and Euripides have many themes, dramatic techniques and even actual scenes in common, it would seem wisest to examine the relative emphasis each author places on fear and suffering in moments that are truly similar.

Under these circumstances we would inevitably see how on each occasion there is a kind of emotional symmetry between the two authors, one using fear as a mode of expression, the other employing suffering for the same purpose, one author using 'anxiety' before the event, the other 'suffering' after the event.

Perhaps the paramount tragic theme common to both authors is the effects of war. Both men knew it first hand, and both evoked its cruelty. Each of them described the anguish and confusion of cities taken by

Originally published in *L'Evolution du pathétique d'Eschyle à Euripide*, pp. 69–76 (Société d'Edition 'Les Belles Lettres', Paris 1961). Translated for this collection and slightly abridged by the editor.

assault and sacked. Yet how different are the natures of their descriptions. On the one hand we have Aeschylus' *Seven Against Thebes*, a play completely pervaded with descriptions of war. Granted, the city is not captured and will not be. And yet from their first entrance until the great scene of the shields, the women of the chorus never cease for an instant to imagine and discuss the imminent disaster. And they persist despite Eteocles' remonstrances. Their capture is anticipated in their imagination, the images unfold in a kind of great chaotic disorder. These are the women who are dragged along as 'widows of the defenders, alas, young and old together — dragged by their hair like horses, their clothes in tatters.' Thus there is chaos everywhere. 'When a city falls, alas, numberless are its sufferings. One conqueror may take prisoners, the other may kill them, still another may set the city on fire. Smoke will stain the entire city. The furious breath of Ares beats down the men and desecrates all they revere.'[2] But all these evocations by the Theban women have their impetus in anxiety: 'What will become of me?' they cry (297).[3]

Euripides, on the other hand, prefers to dwell on disasters which have already occurred. He loves to have them evoked after the fact by the women who have had to suffer them. Through the medium of their suffering he has them gasp out their memories. In this case we should examine the *Hecuba* or the *Trojan Women*, for — by a rather remarkable coincidence — both plays take place among captive women after the fall of Troy. It would be difficult to say with certainty which of these plays should be considered the earlier, because the facts in both plays are not consistent. And if the *Trojan Women seems* to be the earlier, it is perhaps only because its action takes place before the very walls of Troy.[4] And yet in each play the capture of the city has already occurred, an event one would logically expect to inspire mourning, but not anxiety. We find here the same themes repeated by Aeschylus now presented in a completely different tone.

The chorus in *The Septem* merely evokes an imagined scene of women being dragged along against their will with wild and brutal violence. But in the *Trojan Women* they actually appear before us. Here in a series of successive episodes we see one weeping woman after another each bemoaning all that they are leaving behind. Cassandra is but one example. After Talthybius says (419): 'Follow me to the ships,' she leaves the stage, enraged but still proud, on her way to captivity. The next episode shows us Andromache, entering on a Greek chariot (617: *agometha*). She has already prepared for departure and laments her destiny in the long scene at the end of which they begin to take her son away from her (774: *agete*). Finally in the *Hecuba* it is merely a memory, as the chorus of captive Trojan women sing 'I was dragged away, having seen my husband dead, dragged across the vast expanse of waves' (937: *agomai*). The violence has diminished somewhat; and fear gives way to sadness.

It is the same with the smoke of burning cities. Although the *Trojan Women* does conclude with the flames that will be the ultimate destruction of the city,[5] nonetheless in both Euripidean plays what is evoked is rather the morrow of a conflagration, with its somber traces of smoke. The Trojan women speak of it in the present (586–588): 'The sad end of my city where the ashes are still smoking.' The chorus of the *Hecuba* also says it,[6] but in the perfect (911–912): 'Everywhere smoke has blackened you with its sorrowful stain.'

It would now follow that the descriptions of that infamous night have also changed in tone. What causes sadness now is the contrast between the joys of a normal life and the mourning which replaces it. In the *Hecuba*, the women remember how they were seated before the mirror arranging their hair when they first heard the shouts of the Greeks. In the *Trojan Women*, they recall the songs and festivity with which they welcomed the notorious wooden horse. Neither of these scenes is at all violent,[7] but rather sad, immediate and natural. And their laments are mixed with an evocation: 'I have been ruined, sad captive that I am'; 'I am damned! Never more will I walk upon your soil'; 'But stricken by sadness I have succumbed to grief'.[8] A favourite Euripidean word, *talaina* [wretched, long-suffering] has a bitter echo which permeates the play from beginning to end.

If we add to this the fact that in the *Andromache*, the characters also hark back to the misfortunes following the capture of Troy, and its chorus devotes yet another stasimon to this recollection,[9] we will understand that this is a theme and an attitude dear to Euripides' heart. One might say that in his tragedies he loved to echo and re-echo the sobs of women in mourning, as wretched in one camp as in the other,[10] and a bitterness for a happiness forever lost.

The comparison between these different texts would be extremely characteristic if it did not give rise to a possible objection, which at first glance would seem quite serious. After all, Aeschylus also evokes those same tears of women in mourning. Indeed, he devoted an entire play to comment on defeat and massacre: *The Persians*. Here Aeschylus has also chosen to situate the action after the events, using the pain of those who were present to evoke memories of the battle, and to take as his protagonist the King's mother with all her sorrow. Aeschylus even makes the entire second part of the tragedy (with the exception of the scene with Darius), into a huge fresco of despair. And this play lacks the austerity and anonymous piety with which the *Septem* concludes. Here the dead are named in a long terribly real series, and the individuals play a role along with the conquered King and his mother. Aeschylus' decision to commemorate the Athenian victory in this particular form would seem to deviate sharply from the difference of dramatic emphases we have just established.[11] And yet all one has to do is re-examine the *Trojan Women* after reading the *Persians* to see how very different the tone is. Now and then in the *Troades* we do find an expression of grief or a lament for a dead person which might recall Aeschylus.[12] Yet the atmosphere of the two plays is quite different. For one might say that Aeschylus has done everything possible to inform his tragedy with a great sweeping forward motion which, every time it comes to a halt, brings back moments of anxious waiting, and with this waiting, fear.[13] The first 248 verses of the play — before the arrival of the messenger — is but one long cry of anguish. Then suddenly the messenger appears and announces the disaster. The chorus responds to his words with cries and sobs. For the moment at least, is not the period of anxiety completed? Not at all. For now the queen expresses her dread at the possibility of learning of Xerxes' death. Moreover, even after giving his first bit of news, the messenger has not said all. The long speech, deftly divided into successive phases (keeping the end to be the object of Darius' predictions), causes a certain amount of anxiety to remain, an anxiety which gradually emerges, with each successive revelation. Indeed, how could it be otherwise? The unending anxiety in the *Persians* is no accident, and it cannot be explained simply as a product of a playwright's clever technique. There are reasons far more profound: in the world of Aeschylus every misfortune becomes a sign of divine anger — with the fear of more to come. Consequently, even after the messenger has said everything he knows, a mood of fear still pervades the scene. And while the chorus agonises over what will henceforth become of the Persian imperial power (584 ff.), the queen, on the other hand, seeks to appease these gods, for their wrath still terrifies her about what yet may come:[14] 'Friends, whoever has known misfortune knows that from the very day a wave of evil has fallen upon them, men incessantly fear everything, whereas those who have a happy life believe that fate will bring them only joy. For me today everything is ridden with fear; all that appears before my eyes is the hostility of the gods, and all that touches my ears is the sound of catastrophe, saying that my pain will never cease — so great is the terror that grips my heart!' (598 ff.). Both she and the chorus want to know, to know when all this evil will at last come to an end (632).[15]

Thus the final threnody is really the only part of the tragedy devoted to grief pure and simple. Again we should note that even then, five out of the eight pairs of strophes are matched questions and responses, and contain a new bolt of pain which gives rise to yet another anxiety.

Therefore the apparent exception to the rule which the *Persians* supposedly represents, is in fact a confirmation: even when dealing with a real historic event, when Aeschylus wanted to describe a people stricken by a disaster, he still endowed his description with a force that made it a regular succession of grief followed by dread. In this sense, Aeschylus' tragedy stands in stark contrast to the futile laments which punctuate the entire *Trojan Women* turning it into a long series of misfortunes which come without having been feared. There is no remedy for these ills, and the only emotions they can evoke are suffering and resignation.

We can also compare the *Trojan Women* to another Aeschylean play. Both playwrights share a penchant for great scenic effects which are intended to create a moving and forceful impression. The *Trojan Women* concludes with just such a grandiose effect: Talthybius comes to announce that the time has come to depart; the captive women must go to the ships while what is left of Troy will be put to the torch, so that only ruins will remain. At first Hecuba wants to hurl herself into the fire of her burning city; but then she watches the fire, 'Ilium is but a flame; it scorches the roofs of Pergamum' (1295-1296). She and the chorus now throw themselves to the ground, beating the earth with their hands as a sort of farewell to the dead, just as the city itself is collapsing:

Hecuba Did you see, did you hear?
Chorus   The crash of the citadel.
Hecuba The earth shook, riven
Chorus   to engulf the city
                                      (1325-1326 Lattimore).

This spectacular ending inevitably evokes another: that of Aeschylus' *Prometheus Bound*. There the scenic effects, whatever they might have been, were destined to suggest the catastrophe which the Titan himself describes just as he is about to disappear, swallowed with his rock by the earth: 'But now there is action and no more words. The very earth shakes while, in its depths, the voice of thunder is roaring. Brilliant lightning bursts and burns; a cyclone stirs the dust, the winds blow wildly at war against each other; the sky and the sea commingle' (1080 ff.). But if the action is similar, we must nonetheless bear in mind this end of *Prometheus* is not the end of the entire trilogy. Even during his downfall there remain threats and calls for revenge. Indeed the last words of the hero are not complaints at his misfortune but mighty proclamations against the iniquity of his suffering: 'O my majestic mother, and you, O sky, who makes the sun circle the world with its light, you see the injustices I must endure?' (1091 ff.). The crash which hurls Prometheus down with his apocalyptic roars, marks only one phase in a greater struggle, whereas when Pergamum falls at the end of the *Trojan Women*, the play (and the trilogy) ends on a note of irremediable misery.

Thus the facts are consistent. Unless a god makes a surprise visit to interrupt the course of events, human beings in Euripides must surrender. And thus in Euripidean drama the only ending is suffering.[16]

The difference in orientation which characterises the scenes we have studied may also be found in the plays as a whole. In a study written long ago, F. M. Cornford made the following observation: whereas in Aeschylus half of the so-called *kommoi* are lamentations, two-thirds of the *kommoi* in Sophocles are in this category, and eighteen of the twenty-one Euripidean *kommoi* are lamentations.[17] A nice proportion, but hardly surprising. For in the world of Euripides no one waits, no one stays on guard, men simply bend before a catastrophe which is already inevitable.

29

FROM TRAGEDY TO PHILOSOPHY:
IPHIGENIA IN AULIS

BRUNO SNELL

If the growth of Aeschylean tragedy does in fact closely parallel the intellectual development of Attica (and hence of Greece, which is to say the intellectual development of Europe in general), then the ultimate proof of this must lie with a demonstration that the path of evolution continues in the direction taken by Aeschylus. This study does not aim to chart the whole course in every detail, but merely to approach the next decisive turn — the transition from drama to philosophy, and this is clearly heralded in the last plays of Euripides. It is the *Iphigenia in Aulis* that brings us right up to the point where art is on the verge of becoming contemplation. The characteristically Euripidean conception of human conduct in this particular tragedy has been misunderstood, and was so even in antiquity.[1] Only by recognizing the nature of this conception can we discern how the gradual awakening of the human consciousness (a process that can be traced throughout the tragedies of Aeschylus) inevitably continues beyond tragedy, thus eventually determining the end of tragedy, as it had its beginning. The tragic arose from the awareness of the necessity of making decisions and reached its full development as the decisions engendered a growing sense of urgency and perplexity. As man's consciousness passed through these various stages, the result was that the characters of Euripides' later plays came to differ from Aeschylean characters in that they possessed a considerable and necessarily more developed 'self-awareness.' The *Iphigenia in Aulis* can reveal this with remarkable clarity.

The play begins with a moving, almost chilling image of a man wavering and irresolute. It is the dead of night (9-11):

Original title 'Euripides' aulische Iphigenie'. From 'Aischylos und das Handeln im Drama', *Philologus Supplementband* 20 Heft 1 (1928), 148-60. Translated by Walter Moskalew for this collection in a slightly abridged form, by permission of *Philologus*.

> No voice is there of birds even,
> or of the seas' waves.
> The silence of the winds
> holds hushed the river.

But Agamemnon restlessly paces about and in despair looks up at the Dog Star Sirius blazing on high. He calls his old servant (16-18):

> I envy you, old man,
> I am jealous of men who without peril
> pass through their lives, obscure,
> unknown.

Agamemnon's state of mind is decidedly unheroic. In his hand he holds a letter he has written, erased, and written again. Now at last, after sealing and then unsealing it, after casting it down in tears and then picking it up, he has decided to send it off and he hands it to the old man. The letter is meant to cancel another one written shortly before. The seer Calchas had promised that the Greek fleet would be detained in the harbor until Agamemnon sacrificed his daughter. At first the king Agamemnon ordered that the army be disbanded and sent home, but his brother Menelaus induced him to fetch his daughter. An oath sworn long ago binds Agamemnon to recover his brother's abducted wife. That is why he had written the first letter summoning Iphigenia, although he did not dare to tell his wife the truth; instead, he sought to lure his daughter by pretending she would be married to Achilles. Now he regrets his decision. After much painful vacillation he dispatches a second letter to countermand the first one and send Iphigenia back. That night he furtively reveals his agony to his aged servant. Agamemnon, who is supposed to be commanding the Greeks, cuts a very unbecoming figure here as he confesses his shame and remorse, and declares how much he envies the old man for the life he leads — unencumbered by choice and ambition.

The servant steals away with the letter, but Menelaus intercepts both him and his message. Agamemnon now must face his brother and be reproached for the spinelessness and impotence of which Agamemnon himself is quite plainly and painfully conscious. Initially, when the expedition against Troy was being readied, he had fawned on all the Greeks, because he was driven by ambition to command, but no sooner assured of authority, he became arrogant and unapproachable. We begin to feel that this lust for power, with which he is charged, derives from a desire to hide his own insecurity behind a façade of outward prestige, and that even the gruffness with which he treats his underlings merely masks his inner weakness.

Agamemnon's reactions to his brother's charges reveal with what psychological subtlety Euripides has depicted him. At once he bristles and retorts that he will not sacrifice his daughter to another's selfishness. And then he proceeds to the attack, for he, too, knows his brother well: Menelaus is setting out to recover Helen, who though unfaithful still bewitches him and rules his passions. The motives guiding his actions are purely self-seeking, for it is to gratify an utterly shameful love that he asks his brother to surrender his daughter. Yet Menelaus is no more stable and self-assured than Agamemnon. As soon as a messenger announces that Iphigenia is close by and will soon arrive, and as Agamemnon gives way to more lamentation, Menelaus' resolution and obdurate strength evaporate. Overcome by pity at the sight of his brother's tears, he abandons his earlier severity and renounces his claim.

The brothers' sudden exchange of roles reveals Euripides' deft and ingenious grasp of what was dramatically effective. Menelaus stops demanding Iphigenia's sacrifice, because he realizes that he was wrong in asking for her death merely to regain his unfaithful Helen. Now he proposes that the troops be disbanded and sent home, which is exactly what Agamemnon had originally wanted to do. But the moment that allows Menelaus to transcend his selfishness also breaks him, for when he realizes that the world extends beyond the horizon of his immediate concerns, his apparent strength dissolves into sentimentality and pity. Just as his love for Helen, which had determined his actions, derived not from strength but weakness (his inability to resist her spell), so now his compassion and understanding for his brother is merely another manifestation of the same frailty. By shifting his ground Menelaus reveals himself as an equally hollow man, one who has no solid core, no fixed center that governs his inner being.

At first glance Agamemnon appears to develop in exactly the opposite direction. Iphigenia's arrival convinces him that he must sacrifice her, for now the other chieftains and the army would be unlikely to give up the expedition. The seer's utterance had assured a propitious voyage if she should die at the altar of Artemis. If Agamemnon tried to prevent the sacrifice, he would face a hopeless fight with all the Greek chieftains. He therefore decides to give up his daughter for reasons of self-preservation and political expediency.

Agamemnon is the exact counterpart of his brother. For the latter, the perception of higher goals is little else than wallowing in sentimentality, for the former, action is little else than the perception of one's advantage. The tragic balance between objective and subjective forces which we find in Aeschylus is thereby upset. Instead we have a fluctuation between capriciousness and anxiety, between inordinate personal demands and a profound fear of reality confronted.

In the first part of the play Agamemnon's movement from initial vacillation to firm resolve thus constitutes the main plot; the juxtaposition of Menelaus' contrary development functions primarily as a foil. With Agamemnon's decision, which to him seems ineluctable, the drama reaches its first point of equilibrium.

Only now does Iphigenia make her entrance, and from this moment on she dominates the play, as she moves from her initial fear to a ready acceptance of death. She picks up the plot the very instant Agamemnon takes a firm stand. But his strength is only artificial and external, imposed by necessity, for he lacks the inner freedom to make a decision on his own. The freedom within Iphigenia's grasp is of a very different sort. She is a young girl, who has lived at home, protected and untouched by outside forces, who now for the first time catches a glimpse of the world, and with anxiety and hope seeks to discern what life has in store for her. Indecision does not characterize her nature the way it does the king's. Hers is the uncertainty of inexperience, of one who on her first outing gropes along the way, and for that reason feels herself constrained by her world. When Iphigenia enters the play, lack of freedom characterize both her and Agamemnon. Yet the freedom she attains by accepting her death is radically different from Agamemnon's arbitrariness at the beginning of the play. He is solely concerned with furthering his own personal ambitions, and when he actually is forced to decide and act, collapses. Iphigenia, on the other hand, demonstrates the nature of her mettle the first time she faces a choice. She has the ability to infuse the events with a deeper significance, to see that the matter transcends her future as well as that of Helen and Menelaus. She can recognize that something higher is at stake, and in so doing leaves her father's pathetic perplexity far behind. This development of her character dovetails nicely with the movement of the plot — and it also makes good psychological sense.

And yet there is something peculiar here. To be sure, the course of events is intelligible within the context of the play itself, but from an external perspective much of it must seem rather odd. What has induced Euripides to represent the great epic heroes as such weaklings that a mere child can triumph over them? The world in which we find ourselves is fundamentally different from the heroic. The great vital forces which have guided the actions of Homeric man have disintegrated and dissolved. Menelaus' love for Helen has become a pathetic weakness — the pining of a cuckolded husband for his runaway wife. The regal dignity of Agamemnon is debased to vanity and ambition. Every grand and lofty impulse which had ennobled Homeric man is in Euripides reduced to mere pettiness and whim. His characters are no longer obsessed

by the intrinsic value and significance of their goals. They have neither
the force of will nor the conviction to struggle for something higher
than personal advantage; Euripides has become interested in the psychology of action.[2] And even when someone does take a heroic stand, it
tends to raise suspicions, for one cannot deny that there is something
intoxicating and frenzied about Iphigenia's self-sacrifice. Drama has
taken a rather disconcerting turn.

The criticism which has been leveled against Euripides from Aristophanes to Nietzsche is essentially justified: Euripidean art is discordant
and problematic. Our joy at its many beauties is frustrated by some
troubling questions. What kinds of beings are these characters? What
kind of man is their creator?

The best of what has been said about Euripides was uttered with
malice. For those who understood him best did so precisely because
they themselves were also conflicted and torn. They had to struggle
with the same inner misery and despair which Euripides depicted on
stage, and for which he himself could find only a questionable resolution
in the *Iphigenia*.

It is thus difficult to remain dispassionate.

In Homer the instances that arouse pity are rather insignificant. There
is Thersites, who can be dismissed with blows and laughter, and even
then he has had almost more than his share of attention. One could
define him as a purely negative character, for baseness is not an entity in
itself, but merely the absence of heroic virtue. What is unusual about
Thersites is merely the fact that though he does not measure up to the
demands of heroism, he nevertheless lays claim to speaking as an equal.
He exists in a society whose nature is fixed and where each individual
has but a single value and a single goal.

But what are the norms that apply to the actions of Agamemnon in
Euripides? Aeschylus was still controlled and protected by the superhuman powers, by his belief in the justice of the gods, and by his respect
for the *polis* for which he lived. The Euripidean man, however, stands
alone in a precarious and confusing world, as Orestes exclaims in the
Electra (367-79):

Alas,
we look for good on earth and cannot recognize it when met, since all
our human heritage runs mongrel. At times I have seen descendants of
the noblest family grow worthless though the cowards had courageous
sons; inside the souls of wealthy men bleak famine lives while minds of
stature struggle trapped in starving bodies. How then can a man distinguish man, what test can he use? the test of wealth? that measure means
poverty of mind; of poverty? the pauper owns one thing, the sickness

of his condition, a compelling teacher of evil; by nerve of war? yet who, when a spear is cast across his face, will stand to witness his companion's courage? We can only toss our judgments random on the wind.

Euripidean man cannot discriminate because he has no fixed standards. He has severed the ties that bound him to state, society, and religion.[3] But Euripides was not the sort of man who would 'toss judgments random on the wind'. Iphigenia's heroism and subsequent rescue by the goddess make it quite clear that the poet still hoped somehow to apprehend that which is fixed and permanent, even though he fully understood that knowledge was exactly what had led to the present disintegration. It was the intellect which had been undermining the old values throughout the fifth century. Wars and disasters had certainly also done their share. But insofar as the wars grew more desperate and barbaric, as the individual states progressively lost sight of loftier objectives and instead came to be guided by whim, to that degree they too are not causes but merely symptoms of the general chaos. This is a development that reflects a universal easing of constraints — a freedom gained through the intellect. The sophists, taking pride in a name derived from wisdom, had brought on this enlightenment, and Euripides in turn had learned from them. Nevertheless, it is quite wrong to brand him as a rationalist or to call him simply the poet of the enlightenment. For the rationalistic optimism of the sophists, who thought that through their learning they could control life, is completely alien to him.

Euripides has been both praised and blamed for priding himself on his learning. But such a view is too narrow and one-sided. Obviously we must not overlook verses such as the following praise of the reclusive life of contemplation: 'blessed is he who has acquired knowledge' (*fr.* 910). Yet it is unlikely that keen intellect ever caused any other Greek as much agony as it did Euripides. His plays are replete with instances where characters speak of knowledge as a dangerous burden — and in this he is a true follower of Aeschylus. We are here not even discussing such common sentiments as the notion that knowledge does not necessarily coincide with an honorable disposition, or that knowledge makes a bad man even worse. Such ideas might seem trivial to us. But for the time of Euripides they embodied an insight of considerable import, since even before Socrates the Greeks were much more inclined than we to regard virtue as a form of knowledge. Considering that in the earlier period ethical standards had strict and specific applicability, knowledge of them inevitably implied a desire to reach such standards.

The sophists claimed that they taught how to obtain a good result, whatever that was. For any notion of good and evil was easily revealed as questionable and elusive. Thus during this period there arises the

monstrous possibility that perhaps knowledge does not necessarily coincide with striving after the good. The cunning calculation of possible
consequences in order to protect oneself from harm is a form of *hybris*,
an evil which Aeschylus had not yet come to know.

When Agamemnon says: 'I hate a smooth tongue in a rogue' (333),
he utters a sentiment that derives from experience with sophistic rhetoric.
But the distrust of knowledge runs even deeper among the characters of
the later plays. Nor is it directed solely at the craftiness of jurists. Thus
the following occurs in the *Iphigenia* (924-25):

> Thought not too clear is sweet at times,
> but knowledge also is a boon.

And elsewhere we read (*Electra* 294-96, cited by Stobaeus 3.27 as a
passage from the *Antiope*):

> Untutored men are pitiless,
> Only the wise can pity. And they pay
> a price for their too-subtle knowledge.

Clear thought and subtle knowledge are a curse, and the curse is the
oiktos [compassion] – the grief and pity for the world. It is a familiar
chord which reverberates here, one first struck in the *Prometheus* of
Aeschylus.

Only in the light of these passages do characters such as Agamemnon
in the *Iphigenia* become completely intelligible. His grief and misery
derive from 'knowing too much'. Because he is constantly plagued by
the question of what comes next, he keeps anticipating the future. This
is what guides his actions and also distinguishes him from the Homeric
Agamemnon.

In Euripides Agamemnon envies the old man for his obscurity (19):

> Least of all do I envy
> those vested with honors.

The old man answers (20):

> Oh, but these have a glory in their lives!

He still believes in the old values, which Agamemnon no longer accepts
(21-23):

> Ah – a glory that is perilous, and
> will trip them as they walk.
> High honors are sweet
> to a man's heart, but ever
> they stand close to the brink of grief.[4]

The man who has begun to examine and ponder his actions will find glory, honor, and all that used to guide human action dissolving into nothing. One could also say that this despair comes not from knowing too much, but too little. The disintegration of fixed values and standards has made man dependent entirely on himself — and the *Iphigenia in Aulis* begins with Agamemnon alone in the solitary, silent countryside. Man is helpless before this all-powerful world, and before his own self he is perplexed. Knowledge no longer suffices to penetrate the wasteland he has created himself.

Within Euripidean tragedy this perplexity is not even resolved through some more deeply apprehended form of knowledge. It was rather Socrates who provided the solution by posing the liberating question: What is the good? The old dilemma about what man should do became a timeless philosophical problem removed from the here and now, from particular circumstances, and from individual human agents. The answer was to be found not in action, but in contemplation. Such profound knowledge does not yet reveal itself to Euripidean man, for whom the old world has crumbled but no new wisdom has yet arisen from the ruins.

The goddess abducts Iphigenia. It is this unspoiled and unreflecting being who triumphs. Euripides, as the reflecting man, perceives the natural state of woman (who somehow stands in a direct relationship with life) in a manner that is not naive, but thoroughly sentimental. Iphigenia is the only one in the whole tragedy who finds a way out of herself to the universal. She is not driven to this by some feminine instinct affirming primordial ties, since she dies for an idea, an idea in fact that had little appeal in the time of Euripides. She sacrifices herself for Greece to bring about a victory over the barbarians. This Iphigenia is not a very realistic creation, for she is designed to serve a certain poetic, even moral, purpose. The figure of Agamemnon is less pleasing, less 'poetic,' but much more true to life.

It is possible to illustrate from other late plays of Euripides how his characters fall into two categories. Some are drawn with realism and keen psychological insight, reflecting all that Euripides knows about the human soul; others are almost fairty-tale characters, beings removed from life, striving after some lofty ideal. Compared with Iphigenia, Sophocles' Antigone (who might more appropriately be called an ideal character) is life-like, for she is more deeply rooted in the troubles of this world. She derives her idealism from the fact that she sees life as simple and grand. Iphigenia, on the other hand, rises above an existence that is chaotic and dies for an ideal. Just as the sense of life's misery originates in the keen intellect that has grasped the futility of human action, so too is the transcendence of this life a product of contemplation. The quiet exuberance, the pathetic gesture, betray Iphigenia's underlying uncertainty, and suggest that her actions are not natural or primary responses. Even her self-sacrifice is grounded in a feeling of powerlessness. Her own life matters little (how different she is from the Aeschylean Eteocles!), but she does have faith in a higher purpose. This disparity between insignificance and the loftiness of her ideal is what makes Iphigenia's death so pathetic. The heroic has here assumed the form of the pathetic, because the break between the weakness of man and the triumph of a spirit aspiring to something higher is complete. Even the heroic figure lacks a center, just as the piteous minor characters do. For the vital core is shattered — except that here it is replaced by an ideal.

Both aspects of Iphigenia, her weakness and her heroism, are intellectually determined. And that is why in both cases this raises misgivings from an artistic perspective. Later contemplation led from here to a division of the world into the world of thought and the world of the senses, a division influenced by the distinction between Being and Seeming (introduced by the Ionian and the western Greeks). But the legacy of tragedy assured that the Platonic idea became the 'idea of the good'. It is a progressive awakening of consciousness that passes beyond drama into the realm of philosophy, and thus from poetry into prose.

With Euripides the relationship between knowing and doing enters a new phase, because for him the significant act is the conquest of weakness and doubt. Thus the typical course of events in his late plays is precisely the one we find in the *Iphigenia in Aulis*: the play begins with uncertainty and vacillation and gradually leads up to heroism. Sophoclean drama moves in exactly the opposite direction. Sophocles begins with action that is confident and consistent, but which in the course of the tragedy becomes unraveled, to reveal itself as impotent and empty. The *Oedipus Rex* is, of course, the classic example, but the same progress is also evident elsewhere. It is characteristic of Sophocles' intermediate position that he should present the clearest juxtaposition of action and knowledge, because in his plays the tragic reversal coincides with the translation from *prattein* (doing) to *theōrein* (contemplating). The opposing forces are thus most balanced, and their conflict less disruptive than in the other two tragedians.

The typical course of an Aeschylean tragedy revealed an even earlier stage in the relationship of contemplation to action. For Aeschylus doubt was merely a passing phase, hence the original action retained its validity even beyond death. Thus for Aeschylus the tragic act means pursuing one's path to the end; for Sophocles, submitting when the path ends; for Euripides, entering upon the path. The crucial issue for

Aeschylus is not to falter, even in the face of knowledge; for Sophocles, to adapt oneself to knowledge; for Euripides, to rouse oneself into action from whatever knowledge there is.

The artistic possibilities of grappling with the problem of action were thus exhausted as far as the ancient world was concerned. And there was no way back. The necessary step beyond tragedy led to the point where contemplation sought to control action and to examine its norms and laws. Socrates' question concerning 'the good' had removed the possibility of doubt from dramatic action.

A notion long-rooted in the old social order of the *polis* and of the aristocracy, namely that *aretē* rested on knowledge, had thus emerged in a new form. A *single* decision was called for now – a turning to the ideal. There was no longer room for the making up of one's mind piecemeal in particular tragic situations. The old values, once so vital, had fallen prey to the same contemplation which now determined the new norms and values. And just as ancient tragedy historically appears between these two manifestations of the human spirit, so too the problem of the tragic character in Greek drama resides between the polarities of primitive *acting* and the contemplative knowledge about such action, between the old constraint and the new freedom of the man who makes his own decisions – and is morally autonomous.

NOTES

O. Taplin: Emotion and Meaning in Greek Tragedy (pp. 1-12).

1. One of my purposes in *The Stagecraft of Aeschylus* (1977) is to elucidate this 'grammar' of dramatic technique. W. Jens' *Die Bauformen der griechischen Tragödie* (1971) is an attempt, far from successful but none the less enterprising, to compile the whole of this 'grammar'. Disciples of Walter Jens at Tübingen contribute sections (of greatly varying quality) on the structure of opening and closing scenes, on the acts and choral songs, speech, stychomythia, lyric dialogue, and monody; there are also three parerga on supplication, props, and the significance of on- and off-stage.

2. This point is hammered home by Brian Vickers, *Towards Greek Tragedy* (33 ff., esp. 41-2). Vickers' confutation in his section 'Metaphysics and Mystiques' (3-51) of various 'transcendant schemes' which have been vainly imposed on Greek tragedy is one of the best parts of a stimulating, if uneven, book. The most influential account of the Greek theatre as ritual has probably been Ch. i of Francis Fergusson's *The Idea of a Theatre* (Princeton, 1949).

3. I relegate a couple more hobby-horsical reflections to a footnote. Another motive for the search of ritual may be the desire of some to find religious or quasi-religious motives for all valuable human activities so that they are all done to the greater glory of god (even if it is the wrong god). Another more modern motive is the desire of the 'counter-culture' to stress all that is anti-rational, impulsive, and 'primitive' in our life. The driving forces of this movement are too complex and too close for analysis, but they include the decline of traditional religion, disillusion with scientific 'progress', Freudian psychology, expression of solidarity with non-Western cultures, and simple revolt against whatever system is nearest at hand. Greek tragedy, they gather, was a 'primitive ritual', so it is annexed as a venerable support for these cultural trends. But the ancient Greeks are treacherous allies. The undeniable powers of the irrational, the cruel, and the impulsive are clearly recognized by Greek tragedy, but they are not admired; they are rather forces of destruction and inhumanity.

4. The authoritative account is Pickard-Cambridge's *The Dramatic Festivals of Athens* (1968, ch. ii, 57-125).

5. This should be put in its place a fragment of the fourth-century comedian Antiphanes which has been taken much too seriously. His character is trying to show that comedy is much harder to compose than tragedy because you have to make up the story:

> I have only to mention Oedipus, and they know the rest
> that his father was Laius, his mother Jocasta,
> who his daughters are and his sons,
> what he is going to suffer, what he has done . . .

The crudity of this proves, in a sense, the opposite of what it purports to prove.

6. There is an interesting exercise in comparison to be found in the fifty-second (so-called) *Oration* of Dio Chrysostom (Loeb Classical Library, vol. iv, ed. A. L. Crosby, 338 ff.), in which he discusses the three *Philoctetes* plays of Aeschylus,

Euripides, and Sophocles (only the last survives). The fixed elements are that Odysseus and others have to fetch Philoctetes from Lemnos to Troy: the differences between the three plays move them worlds apart.

7. This dialogue occurs at the most harrowing moment of *Jude the Obscure* when Jude and Sue have discovered the violent death of their children:

'Nothing can be done' he replied.
'Things are as they are, and will be brought to their destined issue.'
She paused, 'Yes! Who said that?' she asked heavily.
'It comes in the Chorus of Agamemnon. It has been in my mind continually since this happened.'

To move from the sublime to the less than sublime see the very title of Cocteau's version of *Oedipus, La Machine Infernale* (1934). The prologue voice says, 'Spectator, this machine, you see here wound up to the full in such a way that the spring will slowly unwind the whole length of a human life . . .' The radio comedy show *I'm Sorry I'll Read That Again* ended its version of *Oedipus* 'My fate, my fate are killing me!'

8. Aeschylus' *Persians* is the exception which proves the rule. Not only is the play not a tragedy about Athens, but the Persian rulers are given the status and distance of tragic heroes indistinguishable, dramatically speaking, from the usual figues of the heroic age. Even those who generally agree with my case would until recently have made an exception of *Eumenides* and granted that it contains political propaganda. But it seems to me that Colin Macleod in his article on the unity of the *Oresteia* (1973) is completely convincing in his denial of specific topical allusions and in his claim that the play is political in a much more ideal and time-free sense. On the 'dramatic illusion' of Greek tragedy see the first and last chapters of David Bain, *Actors and Audience* (Oxford, 1977).

9. See, for instance, Anne Righter, *Shakespeare and the Idea of the Play* (London, 1962, repr. Penguin, 1967).

10. Excellent translations of the more important fragments are collected in the first section of *Ancient Literary Criticism*, ed. D. A. Russell and M. Winterbottom (Oxford, 1972).

11. Some fragments of Gorgias are in Russell and Winterbottom (op. cit.), but for a translation of all the little that survives see that by George Kennedy in *The Older Sophists*, ed R. K. Sprague (South Carolina, 1972, 30 ff.). The standard text is in Diels, *Die Fragmente der Vorsokratiker* (vol. ii, 7th ed., rev. Kranz, Berlin, 1951–4).

12. A Phonetic rather than literal transcript brings out Gorgias' use of the letters r, then l, then t to vary the predominant emotional p: *prikē peripobos kai eleos poludakrus kai potos pilopentēs*.

Albin Lesky: Decision and Responsibility in the Tragedy of Aeschylus (pp. 13–23)

1. B. Snell, *Aischylos und das Handeln im Drama, Philologus SB* 20, Heft 1 (1928).

2. *Proc. of the Cambr. Philol. Soc.* 186 (1960), 27.

3. *Form and Meaning in Drama* (London, 1956), 4.

4. Aeschylus, *Agamemnon* xxvii.

5. *Etudes de Lettres* 6 (1963), 73–112 (*Bull. de la Fac. des Lettres Lausanne*). On all these questions, cf. also H. Lloyd-Jones, 'The Guilt of Agamemnon', (printed

below); his interpretation corresponds in many cases with that developed here and in *Hermes* 66 (1931), 190.

6. *Sitzb. Akad. Wien. Phil. hist. Kl.* 221.3 (1943).

7. Op. cit. 101.

8. This paper was delivered to the Joint Meeting of Greek and Roman Societies at Cambridge in August 1965. The author wishes to thank Prof. R. P. Winnington-Ingram and Mr F. H. Sandbach most warmly for their help with the English of the text.

Helen H. Bacon: The Shield of Eteocles (pp. 24-33)

1. The following authors, not referred to elsewhere in the text or notes, have greatly helped me, in some cases to conclusions quite different from theirs – E. Fraenkel, 'Die sieben Redepaare im Thebanerdrama des Aeschylus', *Sitz. Bay. Akad. phil.-hist. Klasse* (1957, 3). B. Snell, 'Aischylos und das Handeln im Drama', *Philologus*, suppl. 20 (1928), 1-64. F. Solmsen, 'The Erinys in Aischylos' *Septem*' *Trans. Amer. Philol. Ass.* 68 (1937), 197-211, and *Hesiod and Aeschylus* (Cornell University Press, Ithaca, 1949). E. Wolf, 'Die Entscheidung des Eteokles in den *Sieben gegen Theben*', *Harv. Stud. Class. Philol.* 63 (1958), 89-95.

The translations are mine. I regret the necessity of making them so ruthlessly literal.

Since lines 1004 to the end do not enter into my discussion the question of their authenticity is of no direct importance for this paper. I am strongly swayed by the arguments of H. Lloyd-Jones ('The End of the *Seven Against Thebes*', *Class. Quart.* n.s. 9 (1959), 80-115) to regard them as authentic. Their discontinuity in tone and imagery with the rest of the play is perhaps to be explained by the fact that they are the conclusion not of this play alone, but of the whole trilogy.

2. H. Patzer, 'Die Dramatische Handlung der *Sieben gegen Theben*', *Harv. Stud. Class. Philol.* 63 (1958), 97-119.

3. A. Lesky, 'Eteokles in dem Sieben gegen Theben', *Wiener Studien*, 73 (1960), 5-17. B. Otis, 'The Unity of *Seven Against Thebes*' (*Gk. Rom. Byz. Stud.* 3 (1960), 153-74) came to my attention when this essay had already gone to the printer. My analysis parallels his in making Eteocles' achievement of insight into his relation to the Erinyes the unifying fact of the play. I reach very different conclusions about what it is that Eteocles comes to understand.

4. Eteocles and Polyneices are referred to as *philoi* (i.e. related by blood) to each other, just as Laius, whom Oedipus met only as he murdered him, is included among those who are *philtatoi* in *O.T.* (line 366).

5. H. Lloyd-Jones (op. cit. p. 85 n.3) makes a strong case against the view of Wilamowitz and others that Aeschylus presents the Argives as barbarians who do not even speak Greek. See also H. Bacon, *Barbarians in Greek Tragedy* (Yale University Press, New Haven, 1961), 17.

6. This is one of the commonest ways of warding off an evil spell (see Kuhnert in Pauly-Wissowa s.v. *fascinum*). For each Argive (except Amphiaraus, who casts no spell) Eteocles has a word or a symbol, or both, whose purpose is just this (see below for the magic and counter-magic employed by the brothers against each other). From this we must conclude that Eteocles relies on magic no less than the attackers do. T. Rosenmeyer in his chapter on *Seven* (*The Masks of Tragedy* (University of Texas Press, Austin, 1963), 5-48) is the first critic to discuss the pervasive importance of the shields and the fear magic associated with them. He argues,

however, that there is no appeal to magic in the shield device of Polyneices or the speeches in which Eteocles calls up the Theban champions. His interpretation of the play depends to a large extent on the implications of the contrast he finds here.

7. R. Lattimore (*The Poetry of Greek Tragedy* (The Johns Hopkins Press, Baltimore, 1958), 39–45) argues that the fact that Thebes has seven gates is a crucial element in the fate of Eteocles. If so, it is likely that the symmetries suggested verbally were also indicated in the staging. As the seven gates have seven attackers with seven shield devices we can expect to *see* on stage the seven defenders with their seven shields, each one claiming the protection of one of the seven gods whose statues stand on the stage.

8. See G. H. Chase, 'The Shield Devices of the Greeks', *Harv. Stud. Class. Philol.* 13 (1902), 61–127.

9. Though this, and related phrases, sometimes refer to the night rather than the moon (Aesch. *Pers.* 428 and Eur. *I.T.* 110, *Phoen.* 543), in context in this passage it can only refer to the moon. So also Pindar *Ol.* 3.20. For eyes as shield devices see Chase, ibid. 105.

10. In *Aeneid* 4.6 *Phoebea lampade* is definitely the sun.

11. W. Schadewaldt, 'Die Wappnung des Eteokles', *Eranion, Festschrift für H. Hommel (Tübingen*, 1961), 105–116.

12. Op. cit. 13.

S. M. Adams: Salamis Symphony: The Persae of Aeschylus (pp. 34-41)

1. This point Aeschylus, because his design so requires, leaves vague until the time for explanation comes; Herodotus naturally makes it perfectly clear, with his account of chains and proclamation.

2. The discarding of Atossa when her functions have been performed has often been noted; later drama would have required the projected meeting with her son.

3. Incidentally, if the question arises in their minds, this passage serves to inform the audience that the Persians know about *Apate* and *Ate* and so will be able to understand the lesson when it comes; the word *hybris* is withheld until Darius's final explanation.

4. The stasimon may thus, I think, be read with 93–100 in their manuscript position. With O. Müller's transposition of these verses to follow 114 (accepted by Smyth and Murray) the effect of the metaphor (87–90) is not lost. Foreboding emerges in the metaphor; the old men seek to overcome it by dwelling on Persia's might and valour and divine mission to wage wars; this leads to the thought of the Sea, and the foreboding reappears in the *double entendre* (112–14); then comes the *Apate* passage, which leads directly to foreboding unrestrained.

5. With 252 cf. 59–60.

6. The extraordinary expression 'they are mangled by the voiceless children of the deep' (577–8) is not arbitrary grotesquery: the Sea is undefilable; its own 'children' devour its offenders and prevent its pollution.

7. To the standard Hellenic milk, water, honey, and wine are added, for foreign flavour, olives and garlands of flowers. The stilted language in which all these are described appears to be the language of ritual, based on the principle that you make a thing more potent if you describe it in magnifying terms.

8. It seems to have been very well known. In the *Agamemnon*, when Aeschylus is setting forth the *hybris* shown by the Greeks in captured Troy, he drives home the point by repeating, almost exactly, a verse from it: *Ag.* 527 = *Pers.* 811.

9. Cf. *Ag*. 385–98.

10. Cf. 198–9, 468, 537–8, 834–6, 846–8, 1017, 1030, 1060.

11. Not even 'all at one stroke, they pitifully gasped upon the shore.' (976–7): the picture is in harmony with the general design; these men are victims cast up the Sea.

The translation of *The Persians* by A. J. Podlecki (Prentice-Hall, 1970) has been used for the following lines: 249–52; 345–6; 352–4; 412–13; 433–4; 472–3; 515–16; 577–8; 807–8, 976–7. Used by permission of Professor Podlecki.

H. Lloyd-Jones: The Suppliants of Aeschylus (pp. 42–56)

1. *P. Oxy*. 2256, fr. 3 (Part XX, p. 30).

2. *Eumenides* (Göttingen, 1833), 123; cf. *Griechische Literaturgeschichte*, 2^3, 88; cf. Boeckh, *Tragoediae Graecae principum rel.* (1808), 54.

3. See G. Mueller, *De Aeschyli Supplicum tempore atque indole* (Diss. Halle, 1908), 67 f.

4. Notably G. Mueller in the dissertation just quoted. Although Mueller reached a wrong conclusion, his work has great merits; his refutation of the historical arguments for a late date is particularly good.

5. By W. G. Forrest, *Class. Quart.* n.s. 10 (1960), 240, l. 3. My disagreement with Mr Forrest over the *Suppliants* does not mean that I fail to appreciate his ingenious and learned article.

6. A. Andrewes, *Probouleusis* (Oxford, 1954), 7.

7. *Il*. 22. 99 f.

8. 6. 83.

9. Aristotle, *Pol*. 1303 a 6; Plutarch, *De Mul. Virt.* 245 F. See the discussion by Forrest, loc. cit. 221 f.

10. See Forrest, loc. cit. 239, who quotes E. Cavaignac, *Rev. Phil*. 45 (1921), 102–6.

11. Authority is no substitute for argument, nor will the isolated treatment of details suffice. It is not enough to show that a particular expression is unusual; it is necessary to show that the expression in question could not have been used by Aeschylus.

12. F. R. Earp, *The Style of Aeschylus* (Cambridge, 1948). Studied in his way, according to this author, the tragedians become three old friends whose little ways we know (p. 5).

13. *Class. Quart*. 30 (1936), 116 f.

14. *Tragodoumenon Libri Tres* (Cracow, 1925), 133 f.; cf. E. B. Ceadel, *Class. Quart*. 35 (1941), 66 f.

15. See G. Mueller, loc. cit. 52 f.

16. See G. Mueller, loc. cit. 46 f.

17. At 490; the speech must be given to Danaus (cf. 500, 504).

18. *Dithyramb, Tragedy and Comedy*, 87 f.; *Theatre of Dionysus in Athens*, 31 f.; *Dramatic Festivals of Athens*, 241 f.

19. *Aischylos: Interpretationen* (1914), 4.

20. See Maas, *Griechische Metrik*, ch. 76 (on pp. 53–4 of my English translation); cf. *Hermes* 64 (1929), 461 f. = *Kl. Schr*. iv. 479.

21. Maas, loc. cit.; Kranz, *Stasimon* (1933), 272.

22. In his introduction to Denniston and Page, *Aeschylus, Agamemnon* (Oxford, 1957), xxx.

23. *Hermes* 64, loc. cit.
24. See *Greek Metre*, ch. 76.
25. *Griechische Tragoedien*, 1^4, 221.
26. W. B. Stanford, *Aeschylus in his Style* (Dublin, 1942), 112.
27. I have developed these reflections somewhat further in a review of John Jones's remarkable book *Aristotle and Greek Tragedy* (London, 1962) in *The Review of English Studies* 15, no. 58 (1964), 221 f. Cf. also *Gnomon* 34 (1962), 740; *Class. Quart.* n.s. 12 (1962), 187.
28. *Die Struktur des Eingangs in der Attischen Tragödie* (*Tübinger Beiträge* 10, 1930), 1; *Gnomon* 10 (1934), 413; also in the preface to the reprint of Droysen's translation of Aeschylus in Kröners Taschenausgabe (152).

H. Lloyd-Jones: The Guilt of Agamemnon (pp. 57-72)

1. This paper formed the first of my J. H. Gray Lectures given at Cambridge in 1961; it has also been given at other places. I am grateful to those who have helped to improve it, and particularly to Professor E. R. Dodds and Mr G. E. M. de Ste Croix.
2. See D. L. Page's preface to *Aeschylus, Agamemnon*,' ed. J. D. Denniston and D. L. Page (Oxford, 1957); and my article 'Zeus in Aeschylus', *Journ. Hell. Stud.* lxxvi (1956), 55 f.
3. Eduard Fraenkel, *Aeschylus, Agamemnon* (Oxford, 1950), iii, 625.
4. *Rheinisches Museum* ciii (1960), 76 f.
5. B. Daube, *Zu den Rechtsproblemen in Aischylos' Agamemnon* (Zürich, 1939), 147 f.
6. 'Morals and Politics in the Oresteia', *Proc. Cambr. Phil. Soc.* 186, n.s. 6 (1960), 19 f.; on this point see pp. 27-8.
7. *Proc. Brit. Acad.* xxviii, 22.
8. *Aeschylus, Agamemnon*, ii, 441.
9. *Der Agamemnon des Aeschylus* (Zürich and Stuttgart, 1957), 23.
10. *Aeschylus, Agamemnon*, ii. 371 f.; cf. *Proc. Brit. Acad.*, loc. cit. 22-3.
11. See Denniston and Page, op. cit. 120.
12. In *Theōria* (*Festschrift für W. H. Schuchhardt*) (Baden-Baden, 1960), 69 f.
13. *Trans. Amer. Philol. Ass.* lxviii (1937), 197 f.
14. *Agam.* 1485-6; Sophocles, *Trach.* 1278.

Ann Lebeck: Imagery and Action in the Oresteia (pp. 73-83)

1. Lines 532-3, 1286-8, 1318-19, 1429-30, 1527, 1562-4 (first formulation as a proverb), 1658.
Throughout her essay, Professor Lebeck refers to Eduard Fraenkel's 3-volume edition of the *Agamemnon* (Oxford 1950), abbreviated as 'Faenkel'.
2. Lines 122-3, 309-14, 400-4, 556-8, 803-5, 888, 930, 1007-17.
3. On the relation of feast and sacrifice which increases the similarity between the two, see ch. 2, n. 15.
4. However, at the close of *Eumenides*, motifs of ritual and sacrifice regain their customary propitious significance. See Froma I. Zeitlin, 'The Motif of the Corrupted Sacrifice in Aeschylus' *Oresteia*', *Trans. Amer. Philol. Ass.* 96 (1965): 498-508.

5. This term refers specifically to the ritual cry which women raise when the sacrificial victim is struck. See Wegner, 'Ololyge', *RE*, XVII[2] (1937), 2493–94; cf. J. A. Haldane, 'Musical Themes and Imagery in Aeschylus', *Journ. Hell. Stud.*, 85 (1965): 37–38.

6. The sacrifice metaphor has already been developed at some length in the lion parable where, however, it is not yet brought into alignment with Agamemnon's murder.

7. Zeitlin in *Trans. Amer. Philol. Ass*. 96: 467–8, points out the ominous implication in the recurrence of *histēmi* (to stand), first referring to Cassandra (1038), then to the victims (1057).

8. Almost all commentators take *thuousan* in 1235 as 'raging' without comment on the possible sense 'sacrificing' which, in the vicinity of *epōloluxato*, it must surely suggest. A. W. Verrall, *The Agamemnon of Aeschylus* (London, 1889), 141, notes that it is probably intended to convey both meanings.

9. In the juxtaposition of *bomou* and *epixēnon*, one finds again the union of sacrifice and cruel feast which characterizes the banquet of Thyestes. Regarding the latter word Fraenkel observes that Cassandra is to be 'not sacrificed, but slaughtered and hacked to pieces like a beast, the flesh of which is cut up small for the kitchen on the chopping-block' (593).

10. Cf. *Cho*. 577–8. On Zeus *sōtēr* (the savior), also called Zeus *teleios* (the accomplisher), see Ulrich Fischer, *Der Telosgedanke in den Dramen des Aischylos, Spudasmata*, VI (Hildesheim, 1965), 128–30.

11. L. Zichen, 'Opfer', *RE*, XVIII[1] (1939), 601.

12. A similar fusion of blood and lustral water occurs in 1092, if one accepts Fraenkel's explanation of the MS reading *pedorrantērion*. He suggests, iii, 495–6, that this neologism is based on the word *perirrantērion*, a vessel used for lustral water.

13. For example, i. 137.

14. On the difficulties of interpretation presented by these lines, see Fraenkel, iii, 663–665.

15. See Gustave Glotz, *Etudes sur l'antiquité grecque* (Paris, 1906), 110.

16. Otto Hiltbrunner, *Wiederholungs – und Motivtechnik bei Aischylos* (Bern, 1950), 61.

17. Jean Dumortier, *Les Images dans la poésie d'Eschyle* (Paris, 1935), 76, comments 'Aeschylus begins by using mere allusions, barely sketched similies, mere outlines. The entire picture does not appear in its full clarity until the very end of the drama.'

18. Lesky in *Hermes*, 66: 194–5. Fraenkel, iii, 808–9, points out that in *Agamemnon* the actual murder weapon, Aegisthus' sword, receives little emphasis compared with the robe, weapon of Clytemnestra.

19. The image of Troy's capture as a hunt is introduced by the omen which portends its fall. The sight of eagles preying on a hare leads Calchas to prophesy, 'in time does this expedition capture Priam's city' (126). *Agreō*, an Aeolic form of *haireō* occurring in tragedy only here (LSJ s.v.), does not literally mean 'to hunt down'; its resemblance to *agreuō*, however, might suggest this meaning to the hearer. The prototype of the omen created by Aeschylus is that in *Iliad* 2.303 f. There as well the capture of Troy is revealed by an animal seized as prey.

20. See *Eum*. 322, 416, 745, 791–2, 821–2, 844–5, 879, 1033.

21. *Pace* Friedrich Solmsen, *Hesiod and Aeschylus* (Ithaca, New York, 1949), 179 n. 4: 'No relation should be constructed between the joint invocation of *Zeus basileus* (Zeus the king) and *Nux philia* at *Ag*. 355 and the situation of the *Eumenides*.' It is impossible not to do so since Night and the Erinyes are both prominent in this lyric.

22. *Les Images*, 71.

23. It appears prior to this in 867–868, 1048, and 1115–16. Following Clytemnestra's speech it becomes the spun fabric of a spider (1492), the woven robes of the Erinyes (1580), and the toils of Dike (1611).

24. Compare *pedais* in 493 and *pedas* in 982.

25. This subject is treated in detail by Richard Broxton Onians, *Origins of European Thought* (2nd ed.; Cambridge, Eng., 1954). See particularly ch. 28 of part 3. Here the following examples will suffice. In Homer: *pedaō* used of death or constraint, for example, *Il.* 4.517 or 22.5. Cf. *Od.* 3.269; 4.380, 18.155; 23.353. And among other peoples there are the Norns of Norse Saga, Fate goddesses who spin and bind (Onians, 353–6). In Hindu mythology there is the death god Yama whose name means, among other things, rein, curb, or bridle, the act of checking or curbing, suppression, restraint. See Sir Monier Monier-Williams, *Sanskrit-English Dictionary* (Oxford, 1956), s.v. In the *Mahābhārata* Yama is described 'holding a noose, with which he binds the spirit after drawing it from the body' (ibid., and Onians, 358–62).

26. On this 'rhythm' of the trilogy see Lesky in *Hermes* 66, 196–7, and Karl Reinhardt, *Aischylos als Regisseur und Theologe* (Bern, 1949), 79–80.

27. Fraenkel, ii, 41. Similar inauspicious use of a word connected with the marriage ritual occurs in the Cassandra scene. The nightingale mourns a life *amphithalē kakois* (flourishing on both sides with sorrow 1114). As Fraenkel, iii 522, notes, 'this word, which clearly belongs to cult-language, points regularly to blessing and prosperity.' During the bridal feast, a child who must be *amphithalēs* (with both parents living) went round with bread in a winnowing basket crying *ephugon kakon heuron ameinon* ('I have fled evil, gained prosperity'). This formula also played a part in the rite of initiation into the mysteries (Demosthenes, *De Cor.* 259 [313]). The two ceremonies, that of marriage and that of mystical initiation, are similar in other respects as well. Another reference to a specific rite appears in 1178–79: Cassandra likens her prophecy of ruin as yet obscure to a bride not yet unveiled in the ceremony of *anakalypteria*. On the marriage ceremony, see Heckenbach, 'Hochzeit', *RE*, VIII² (1913), 2132.

28. Nilsson, *Geschichte der griechischen Religion*, i, 493–4. It is precisely because she is sacrificed to Artemis that Iphigenia can be called *proteleia naōn* with a play on *proteleia gamōn*. One need not have recourse to the version of the story found in Euripides' *I.A.* where Iphigenia is enticed to come under pretext of marriage with Achilles.

29. Despite the testimony of ancient scholia and lexicographers, Fischer, *Telosgedanke*, 60–3, holds that the three occurrences of *proteleia* in *Agamemnon* have no connection with the marriage ceremony. As proof of this he cites a fifth-century Attic inscription where the word is used of initiation rather than marriage. Having begun with this *argumentum ex silentio*, he then proceeds in circular fashion, adducing the passages in *Agamemnon* as proof of what he wants to prove about them. 'Originally the concept of *proteleia* means an introductory rite, in other words, some kind of introductory activity. The later dominant meaning of 'pre-wedding sacrifice' . . . is not found in Aeschylus at all', (p. 63). Yet in *Iphigenia at Aulis*, some fifty years after the trilogy, the word unequivocally refers to wedding sacrifices (*I.A.* 718). Moreover, when the three passages of *Agamemnon* are considered as part of a larger pattern of imagery, one is almost forced to conclude that *proteleia* has the same connotation here as it does in later antiquity: preliminary sacrifice, specifically that which precedes the marriage ceremony.

30. Onians, *Origins of European Thought*, 426.

31. *telos* recurs in the *Oresteia* almost as frequently as *dike* and its cognates. See William B. Stanford, *Ambiguity in Greek Literature* (Oxford, 1939), 157: 'The whole play is full of references to differently conceived *telē*, all of which are eventually reconciled in Aeschylus' final solution of the tragic situation.' The significance of this repetition is also discussed by Philip Wheelwright, *The Burning Fountain* (Bloomington, Indiana, 1954), 259-60.

32. Fischer, *Telosgedanke*, 9, distinguishes three specific levels of meaning. First, the simplest sense: any human action which implies a fixed goal. Next a *telos* fixed by fate, imposed on man; in this connection the word is often associated with the Erinyes and the hereditary curse which they embody. Third is the *telos* of divine power and perfection which finds fulfillment in the will of Zeus.

33. The association of this word with the mysteries and the implications of this fact for the *Oresteia* should not be overlooked despite the disfavor incurred by the views of George Thomson — see 'Mystical Allusions in the *Oresteia*', *Journ. Hell. Stud.*, 55 (1935), 20-34; see also his commentary. One may not agree with all of Thomson's conclusions, but it is difficult, if not impossible, to overlook the elements in the trilogy which led him to form those conclusions. What Thomson overemphatically calls 'allusions to the mysteries' might be better termed imagery and themes drawn from the sphere of mystery religion; for example, imagery of light and darkness, the theme of salvation and *apallagē ponōn* (deliverance from strife), and significant repetition of the type discussed here, especially that in the second stasimon and the carpet scene. (Compare Plato's *Phaedrus* where similar imagery and repetition is employed, its connection with the mysteries unequivocal.)

Such a suggestion as the foregoing is sometimes dismissed with, 'But we know from Aristotle that Aeschylus was not an initiate.' That is to mistake the issue. Initiate or not, Aeschylus seems to have been on the same wavelength as the initiated, to have been absorbed in the poetic celebration of a mystery not unlike their own. Or so, at least, it appeared to his contemporaries, as *The Frogs* of Aristophanes and that selfsame passage in the *Nichomachean Ethics* show.

34. *pelomai* and *tellō*, to turn, to come into being, to become, and *telson*, the turning point in ploughing, are related words. See Hofmann, *Etymologisches Wörterbuch des Griechischen*, s.v.

35. In addition to the meanings already mentioned the word has another connotation of importance to the *Oresteia*. There is the *telos*, or fulfillment, of Dike which comes *teleōs*, at last. Compare Hesiod, *Erga*, 217-18, and Solon's elegy to the Muses (Diehl fr. 1; Bergk fr. 13), 17-32. Daube, *Zu den Rechtsproblemen*, 116-18, observes, 'the distinguishing characteristic of the gods, their ability in the end to bring their will to fulfillment, is repeated through *telos* and formulated through related expressions.'

36. Clytemnestra prays to Zeus *teleios* the god who gives decision in battle as well as the fulfiller of prayers. In persuading Agamemnon to walk upon the carpet she has already waged one battle, attained one victory, achieved one *telos*. She now prays for favorable outcome in the second battle and fulfillment of the second *telos*, Agamemnon's murder. See Fischer, *Telosgedanke*, 127-8.

37. Several associative connections link this passage to 1385-92. One prior to, one after, Agamemnon's death, both allude to that death in a similar manner, the second openly, the first in veiled terms. Lines 966-74 refer to Zeus *teleios*; 1385-92 play upon the third libation offered Zeus *sōtēr*. Zeus *teleios* is identical with Zeus *sōtēr*: both epithets designate the god who receives the third libation (see Fischer, 127-9). In the first passage Zeus makes the grape yield wine, a

dramatic irony which suggests bloodshed. In the second Clytemnestra sheds Agamemnon's blood like a libation of wine to Zeus *sōtēr*. The first uses motifs of root
and foliage along with seasonal change from heat to cold. The second describes
blood as a shower of rain which refreshes the plant as it gives birth to seed. Thus
the same complex of ideas and imagery appears in both passages. As Fischer, 131,
puts it, the second is the 'Enthüllung' (revelation) of the first.

R. P. Winnington-Ingram: Clytemnestra and the Vote of Athena (pp. 84–103)

1. Cf. W. B. Stanford, in *Class. Quart.* 31 (1937), 92 f. *Agam.* 11.
2. E.g. Jaeger, *Paideia* i, 327. 'In Aeschylean drama man is not yet a problem
in himself, he is merely the instrument of Fate. It is Fate itself that is the problem.'
Broadly true, this may need some qualification in the case of Clytemnestra. The
more austere, however, is the view taken of Aeschylean characterisation, the more
is it incumbent on the critic to give proper weight to this characteristic of Clytemnestra (largely irrelevant to the traditional story) in considering the general themes
of the trilogy.
3. Thomson's arguments (*Oresteia* II, ad 59) for her presence at 83 are convincing.
4. *kratei* is a natural word for a house-slave to use, but obtains a broader significance as the play develops (see Daube, *Zu den Rechtsproblemen in Aischylos'
Agamemnon*, 39 ff.); it is closely associated with *nikan*, etc.
5. Headlam, *Cambridge Praelections, 1906*, 110. This does not mean that
the ode is intended to express a sequence of emotions in the Chorus. But their
train of thought is such that they end in a greatly changed mood. (I say this to
avoid a possible misunderstanding.)
6. Thus it is the male Chorus, not Clytemnestra, whose beliefs and disbeliefs
are conditioned by their hopes and fears. (This characteristic of the Chorus is put
to brilliant use at 1346 ff. in order to ease the difficulties of the dramatic situation:
note esp. 1366 f., which gives them their excuse for not entering the palace.)
7. 600, 602, 603, 604, 606 ff., 612
8. The intervening *stasimon* bears on Clytemnestra through the theme of
Helen, though their relationship is not yet fully brought out, and on Iphigeneia
through the theme of heredity.
9. See Thomson on 877 (his 868).
10. See Thomson on 889–94 (his 880–5).
11. 258–60.
12. Cornford (*Thucydides Mythistoricus*, 160) speaks of 'the proud and
masterful princess, at the death-grip now with the principle of Agamemnon's lord-
ship', and presents the issue in terms of a historical transition from matriarchy to
patriarchy. Snell (*Philologus*, Suppl. xx. i. 122 f.): 'The murder of Agamemnon is
also an act for liberation on the part of Clytemnestra.'
13. See p. 91.
14. 'An open act of pride which will symbolise the sin he is about to expiate'
(Thomson, *Oresteia* i, 25).
15. E.g. Daube, 127 n. 11. But if the behaviour of Agamemnon is not psychologically interpreted here, the critic is liable to misinterpret the scene at Aulis also,
since the two scenes are parallel and in both the same Agamemnon acts out of the
same weakness (see Méautis, *Eschyle et la trilogie*, 178 f.).
16. The tone of Agamemnon's speech (914 ff.)? He is at once worried and

gratified by her fulsome praises; at once cautious and unsuspecting. One can hardly agree with Méautis (op. cit. 180) that 914 f. is 'une bonne plaisanterie' spoken with a broad smile.

17. Compare the tone of 832 ff.

18. Cf. Headlam, *Praelections*, 129.

19. Thomson, *Oresteia*, i, 26.

20. Hence the irony of 1084.

21. Cf. Pohlenz, *Die griechische Tragödie* i, 100, E. Fraenkel, *Die Kassandra-szene der Orestie*, 9.

22. Daube points out (op. cit. 182) that, unlike Aegisthus, Agamemnon is not culpable in Attic law. But the Chorus do not attempt to defend him on this score, any more than in his treatment of Iphigeneia. For Aeschylus he was guilty on both counts of an offence against marriage (see below).

23. The two spheres over which her imagination had ranged commandingly in her first great speeches to the Chorus (see p. 85). It is of the second of these speeches that Wilamowitz could say: 'that Clytemnestra, the woman who sat at home could describe the conquered city . . . is truly improper. Nowhere else do we find such naïve dramaturgy . . .'. (*Aischylos Interpretationen*, 167 f.). When Wilamowitz erred, his errors were upon the same lordly scale as his successes!

24. When the fountains of her tears had dried up (887 f., cf. 1525).

25. And are, therefore, relevant to the argument about parentage in the *Eumenides* (see p. 98).

26. Since Apollo stands forth as the champion of marriage (*Eum.* 211 ff.), it is interesting to note a parallel between his argument there and Clytemnestra's here (1412 ff.). Where Apollo says to the Furies, in effect: 'You pursue an offence by a child, but not an offence by a wife against her husband', Clytemnestra says to the Chorus: 'You pursue an offence by a wife against her husband, but not an offence against a child.'

27. If the *daimon* represents, as in a sense it does, an evil heredity, Clytemnestra does not share in this heredity. It is hardly to the point to suggest (Daube, op. cit. 192) that she had acquired the family curse by marriage. Helen and Clytemnestra are both extraneous circumstances used by the *daimon* to effect its purposes.

28. Note the specious lucidity of 1583-6, which omit the one point damaging to his case (yet already known to the audience from 1193).

29. Note esp. 1623. This characteristic reappears in the *Choephori*.

30. 1625-7 are, without doubt, addressed to Aegisthus (see Fraenkel, *Aeschylus: New Texts and Old Problems*, 21 f.) The sexual theme is further emphasised at 1639, at 1643 f., and at 1671 (the conventional view).

31. The circumstances of his death were mentioned as recently as 491 ff.

32. On the ascription of 691-9 to Electra see *Class. Rev.* 60 (1946), 58 ff.

33. Cf. 749 f. See Méautis op. cit. 233 f.

34. It matters little whether, or in what version of the story, she killed her husband with an axe. The stress is on the epithet and on the first half of it.

35. *bia* is significant and the periphrasis should not be emended away as by Thomson, *Class. Rev.* 56, 71.

36. Thus 924 f. return to 912; 927 to 910 f.; 928 to 908 — leaving the discussion of motive and the man-woman theme in the centre of the design.

37. And by expressing those conditions in economic terms offers a fundamental generalisation about men and women.

38. Entering on *dikē* (573), he interrupts Athena, whose account of her

thesmoi (laws) is postponed till 681 ff. When it comes, it picks up many of the ideas thrown out in the preceding chorus and shows how her new order preserves such merits as the Furies could claim. Meantime, we have a scene which displays the inadequacies of Apollo's compromise.

39. Which is *philtaton*, 'nearest and dearest.' Compare and contrast, therefore, Apollo's commentary on marriage (216). But has either of these bonds the priority over the other? If 605 f. insist on the horror of matricide, perhaps they also imply the question: is the bond between mother and son any closer than that between husband and wife?

40. Cf. *Cho*. 559, but perhaps the days of his infallibility are over.

41. Thomson, *Oresteia* i, 62.

42. Moreover, as Thomson points out (*Aeschylus and Athens*, 278), the more advanced democrats, at least, would not willingly admit the infallibility in political matters of an oracle which had such close connexions with the Dorian aristocracies.

43. Which his own agents employed in the *Choephori* (557, 726, 888).

44. See Thomson ad loc.

45. *Agam*. 918.

46. He loses his temper because the charge of inconsistency which they make, and to which the attention of the jury is specially called (642 f.), is true. His abusive language (644) recalls 68 ff. and 185 ff., and it is this abuse of the beings with whom he is really so closely involved that gives the clue to his inconsistency.

47. A constant theme: *Cho*. 71 ff., 520 f., *Eum*. 261 ff. Note particularly *Agam*. 1019 ff.

48. Thomson ad loc.: Aly, *Philologus*, Suppl. xxi, 40 (who argues that Aeschylus introduced the doctrine from Sicily).

49. We are made to feel that the matricide is not just another crime, but the very climax of horror, which is particularly associated with the word *teknon* (child) (e.g. 829, 896, 922).

50. *Agam*. 1525.

51. As unnecessary, and therefore as significant, as the reference to the 'unfortunate incidents' at 632.

52. 'The young hare in the womb on which they feast is the child of Clytemnestra' (J. T. Sheppard, *Class. Rev*. 36, 8).

53. 676. On the ascription of 676 f. to Apollo see *Class. Rev*. 49, 7 f. Apollo adds a piece of testimony in favour of his contention (662–6: see below), and an appeal to the self-interest of the jurors (667–73).

54. Thomson, *Aeschylus and Athens*, 289.

55. It is unnecessary, for the purposes of this article, to go into the question whether Athena casts a vote in addition to laying down the principle of 'acquittal if the votes are equally divided'.

56. Not in terms of the psychology of Orestes, which is of comparatively little importance in the *Choephori*, and of less in the *Eumenides*. At the most we can say that he is given some personal motives, over and above the duty of vengeance, i.e., the desire to recover his father's throne and wealth, and to terminate his own exile. What is more relevant, perhaps, is the absence of personal relationship between him and Clytemnestra. The bond between mother and son is here as tenuous and abstract as it could very well be. This, of course, has the effect of emphasising the general sociological issue, but it also helps to make the acquittal of Orestes morally tolerable.

57. Orestes, in his speech of thanks, joins 'the third Saviour' (758 ff.) with Pallas and Loxias. The motives which he ascribes to Zeus are those which he has

found in his patron Apollo, including a violent detestation of the Furies. But this is not the spirit of the succeeding scene.

58. Cf. esp. 573, 580 f., 609–15.

59. The reference to Phlegra at 295 prepares this hint of force.

60. Cf. 850. The relationship between Zeus and the Furies, which is the basic metaphysical problem of the trilogy, cannot be discussed here.

61. Such advance as the Delphic code may have made upon the justice of the Furies need not be discussed here.

62. Op. cit., 288: cf. 289 ('the principle of male precedence, now formally ratified as the basis of democracy . . .'); 291 ('the matricide is acquitted by an appeal to historical expediency'). Professor Thomson's treatment of the whole subject raises many questions upon which anthropologists are far from agreed. For the purposes of the present argument, it can be granted that Aeschylus was consciously envisaging the change from a tribal to a democratic society, in the former of which women enjoyed a greater freedom than in the latter. The actual setting of the story is, of course, the aristocratic half-way stage in which the institution of marriage is firmly established and male supremacy strongly marked, and in which the blood-feud is seen operating within the family and not the clan. Nor is it necessary to examine the hypothesis that the Erinyes were – and were thought by Aeschylus to be – originally associated with matrilineal descent. In the trilogy they have, in theory, an equal interest in both parents (cf. *Eum.* 512). The dramatic situation forces them, however, to be bitter partisans of the mother (cf. *Eum.* 210), though they do not – and could not logically – disparage the man–father in the way that Apollo disparages the woman–mother.

63. Op. cit., 306 (in discussing the *Supplices*, on which see below).

64. And the Watchman, the Herald, and the Elders – all dominated by the queen's superior personality. The Elders, in particular, play the feminine role to her.

65. See Gomme, *Essays in Greek History and Literature*, 89 ff.

66. Zimmern, *Greek Commonwealth*, 329 ff. gives a well-balanced account.

67. Cf. D. S. Robertson in *Class. Rev.* 38, 51 ff. and Thomson, op. cit. 308. It is clearly impossible to discuss the problems of this trilogy adequately in a footnote. Perhaps the evidence does not permit a final verdict on the crucial question whether the objection of the Danaids was to marriage with their kin or to marriage as such. In either case, however, the sons of Aegyptus, in attempting to force themselves upon the Danaids, were committing an act of *hybris* (see H. G. Robertson in *Class. Rev.* 50, 104 ff., with references in his p. 107 n. 2), for which they – all but one – suffered an appropriate punishment. The clearest evidence for this (and it is also impartial) is in *P.V.*, 856 ff. 'If that was the crime of the sons of Aigyptos, it was a crime enjoined in democratic Athens by an express provision of the law and committed regularly by the dramatist's contemporaries in the happy belief that by so doing they were serving simultaneously the gods, the state and their own interests' (Thomson, op. cit. 306). But perhaps this happy belief was not fully shared by the dramatist.

68. For the sensibility of the artist is bound to detect and likely to reveal the flaws that inevitably mar the harmony of any social or political system. It is this, in part, which gives him his social importance. Thomson assumes, on rather inadequate evidence, that Aeschylus regarded the wealth of the community as now equitably distributed (op. cit. 289). I see no reason why he should not have praised the just achievements of Athenian democracy without being blind to its actual or potential defects.

69. 970 (*peithous*). It is Zeus only who, for Aeschylus, represents absolute

wisdom and justice, and he is inscrutable. All other deities — Artemis, Apollo, Hermes, the Furies, even Athena — represent aspects, approximations, partial and imperfect harmonies.

C. J. Herington: Aeschylus: The Last Phase (pp. 123–137)

1. A convenient publication, translation, and discussion of this papyrus is that by H. Lloyd-Jones in his Appendix to H. W. Smyth's *Aeschylus*, Volume ii (second edition, 1957), 595 f.

2. This point is well made by F. Solmsen in *Trans. Amer. Philol. Ass.* 68 (1937), 204.

3. Herodotus I, chapters 6–91, *passim*. If Professor D. Page is right, this Herodotean story will have been based itself on an early fifth-century tragedy or group of tragedies by an older contemporary of Aeschylus; see *A New Chapter in the History of Greek Tragedy* (Cambridge, 1951), with some startling evidence in support (*Trans. Cambr. Philol. Soc.*, 186 n.s. 8, 1962). In that case we should have the record of *three* tragic works, earlier than the Aeschylean late group, which presupposed the undivided cosmos discussed here. But it is right to add that Page's theory, excellently argued as it is, still faces certain difficulties, and does not yet seem to be generally accepted.

4. Aeschylus, *Threissai*, fr. 292 in Mette's collection of the fragments.

5. Aeschylus, *Phryges e Hektoros Lytra*, fr. 254 Mette.

6. The ancient versions of the Danaid story are surveyed, for example, by J. Vürtheim, in *Aeschylos' Schutzflehende* (Amsterdam, 1928), 10 ff.

7. Evidence: fr. 124 Mette (43 Nauck, Murray). Although the exact reading of this fragment is in dispute, its general drift and reference seem fairly certain.

8. *Oxyrhynchus Papyri*, Volume 20 (1952), 21 f.; reprinted by Mette as fr. 125. The tiny fragments of the nineteen lines which preceded those translated in my text here contain one, possibly two, references to *cattle* (lines 2, 6); and perhaps references to *the mating of cattle* (line 2, as restored by Mette) and to *parturition* (line 7).

9. It probably consisted of the tragedies *Myrmidones, Nereides*, and *Phryges e Hektoros Lytra*; see Mette's collection of the fragments, pp. 70–92.

10. For the detailed arguments (as I see them) I refer to my article on Aeschylus and Old Comedy in *Trans. Amer. Philol. Ass.* 94 (1963), 113 ff. Some new considerations are added here.

11. Summarily: (1) *Suppliants* 556 ff. implies a theory of the risings of the Nile otherwise attributed to Aeschylus' younger contemporary Anaxagoras (fr. A42; cf. J. Vürtheim, *Aeschylos' Schutzflehende*, 79 ff.). (2) *Danaides*, fr. 125 Mette, seems closely related to passages in Empedocles (frs. B71–73; cf. *Phoenix* 17 (1963), 195 n.). (3) Apollo's 'biology' in *Eumenides* 658 ff. abruptly introduces almost the sole Athenian reference to a problem known to have been under discussion by six non-Athenian philosophers and medical men in the middle years of the fifth century (evidence collected by A. Perretti in *Parola del Passato* ii (1956), 241 ff.). (4) *Prometheus* 88 ff. (allusion to the Four Elements, and perhaps to Empedoclean thinking? Compare, e.g. *Phoenix* 17 (1963), 180 ff.). (5) *Prometheus* 459 ff., on the excellence of arithmetic (evidently a Pythagorean notion; cf. G. Thomson, note on lines 475 f. in his edition of the play).

12. Noticed at least as early as 1663 by Stanley (quoted by E. Fraenkel in his edition of the *Agamemnon*, i, 43), and often since.

13. Paragraph 10, ed. Arnaldo Monte, *Le Lettere di Dante* (Milan, 1921).

14. H. Lloyd-Jones, 'Zeus in Aeschylus', *Journ. Hell. Stud*. 76 (1956), 55 ff.; compare D. Page in his and J. D. Denniston's edition of the *Agamemnon* (Oxford, 1957), xix ff.

15. *Suppliants*, 86–103, 524–99.

16. *Prometheus Unbound*, fr. 326 Mette (199 Nauck, Murray).

17. *Prometheus Bound*, 186–92.

18. See also *Phoenix* 17 (1963), 236–43, where some reasons are put forward for suspecting, not only that such a hymn once existed, but that echoes of it may still be heard in the solemn finale of Aristophanes' *Birds*.

P. E. Easterling: Character in Sophocles (pp. 138–145)

1. *On Aristotle and Greek Tragedy* (London, 1962), 33.

2. *Sophocles: A Reading* (Melbourne, 1972), 209.

3. See in particular B. M. W. Knox, *The Heroic Temper* (Berkeley and Los Angeles 1964), chs. 1 and 2.

4. *Die dramatische Technik des Sophokles* (Berlin, 1917 repr. 1969), 78.

5. Sophocles later explains Oedipus' failure to recognize Laius as a king by emphasizing that Laius was on a visit to the oracle, with only a modest retinue (750 ff.).

6. *Illinois Classical Studies* 3 (1978), 27–39.

7. Jebb has a sensitive note on this passage.

8. Euripides, *Alcestis* (London, 1954), xxvii.

Karl Reinhardt: Ajax (pp. 146–166)

1. 'No one can find what we call dramatic action in this play unless he knows before he starts that he has to find it' (Tycho von Wilamowitz-Moellendorff, 51).

2. E.g. Pohlenz, *Die griechische Tragödie* (1930), 186, and *Erläuterungen*, note to p. 174.

3. On the question of the date: *Ajax* 1295, where Teucer taunts Menelaus with his mother's adultery, cannot be used for dating purposes. It is a very Peloponnesian story: a disgraceful love-affair between Aërope and a slave, before she becomes the mother of Agamemnon and Menelaus. It is retold *in extenso* in Euripides' *Cretan Women*, produced in the year 438. The discrepancy between the genealogies in Euripides and Sophocles – one mentions Pleisthenes, the other omits him – has been pointed out by Pohlenz, *Erläuterungen*, 51. It is true that Wilamowitz (in *Lyrische und dramatische Fragmente* ed. W. Schubart and U. von Wilamowitz-Moellendorff), Berliner Klassikertexte, v, 2 (1907), 71, believed that Sophocles was alluding to Euripides' play at this point. But if we are looking for an allusion to a tragedy, we should not forget that Sophocles himself wrote an *Atreus* and no less than two plays called *Thyestes*, into which these events may well have been introduced in passing.

4. There has been lively discussion concerning the identity of the speaker, especially since this affects the emendations to some extent. The extant lines were regarded as a speech of Niobe by the first editor, Vitelli, and most recently by A. Lesky, *Wiener Studien*, lii (1934), 1 ff.; as a dialogue between a confidante of Niobe and the leader of the chorus by, among others, W. Schadewaldt, 'Die Niobe des Aischylos', *Sitzungsberichte der Heidelberger Akademie* (1934), Abh. 3 (with

detailed commentary). The reasons for my own view that Leto is speaking are given in the first edition and, in more detail, in *Hermes*, lxix (1934), 233 ff. A. Körte, who in *Hermes*, lxviii (1933), 252 ff., suggested Niobe as the speaker, supported my view in *Archiv für Papyrusforschung*, ix (1935), 249. The most recent discussions are: Karl-Ernst Fritsch, Diss. Hamburg (1936), and A. von Blumenthal's report on Sophocles in Bursian's *Jahresbericht* (1938), 134.

(The early date of the *Ajax* is now generally accepted; but few scholars think the *Niobe* fragment so important for dating as Reinhardt believed. For a text and discussion of the *Niobe* fragment, see my appendix to the Loeb edition of Aeschylus, ii, 556 ff. A vase published by A. D. Trendall, *Revue Archéologique*, ii, 1972, 309 ff. favours the suggestion that the speaker of the passage from the *Niobe* is not Leto, but a nurse; cf. O. P. Taplin, *Harv. Stud. Class. Philol.* lxxvi (1972), 60 ff. (Reinhardt's attempt to gain further support for his dating from the supposed relevance to the contemporary situation of *Ajax*, 1185 ff. seems to me misjudged.) – Hugh Lloyd-Jones)

5.   Sophocles seems to have been the first to deviate from the epic tradition by turning the madness into a ruse of Ajax's patron goddess. In the epic, Athena was able to direct Ajax's madness, which had already broken out, against the cattle. But in Sophocles the madness only begins with that veiling of the senses by which the goddess protects the Greeks (51). Ajax's actual plan of revenge is not madness, and he feels no repentance for it. This innovation too is clearly intended to cast more blame on the hero.

6.   'Charge you:' this is not the normal verb used in a prayer. This shows the same attitude as 774.

7.   On the prehistory of the representation of Ajax as the giant, son of the 'giant' Telamon, see Von der Mühll, 'Der grosse Aias', *Basler Rektoratsprogramm* (1932).

8.   The late Sophoclean *parodoi* of the *Philoctetes* and the *Oedipus at Colonus* are quite different: there are two voices, each with its individual rhythmic movement. Thus in the *Philoctetes*, where the relationship between Neoptolemus and his followers might appear to be similar to that in the *Ajax*, we find an alternation between a desire for knowledge and explanation, between lament and enlightenment, and between astonishment and prophecy. At the end, at the finale of the *parodos*, there is a great increase in pace, and the alternating pattern of the stanzas is interrupted when the approaching footsteps of Philoctetes are heard, while at the same time there is a reversal of roles: for now Neoptolemus asks the questions and the chorus gives the answers. There is nothing like this in the early *Ajax*.

9.   This, too, is Homeric; cf. the cry of Athena when Achilles hastens to the ditch. (It is in fact Achilles whose voice is compared to the trumpet, not Athena (*Iliad* 18, 219 ff.)) That the *Ajax* is also linguistically closer to epic than any other of Sophocles' plays is demonstrated by Jebb's commentary, lii; on this see Pohlenz, *Erläuterungen*, 50. The comparison of the trusty old *paidagogos* with an old race-horse in *El.* 25 is not to be confused with *pathetic* similes: this is reminiscent of the aristocratic type of expression, familiar to us from Plato's *Symposium*, Aristophanes, etc.

10.   Ever since antiquity the commentators have noted the similarity and sometimes even something of the difference between the two passages, and attribute the latter to the fact that Tecmessa is the slave and Andromache is the legal wife. But how can that possibly be a sufficient explanation? As if it were impossible for Ajax to have a sympathetic understanding with a slave whom he loves!

11. He has already called for him from his closed tent; this is therefore not a result of Tecmessa's plea.

12. Here too it is characteristic of Ajax that he speaks of his son's future *fate* as a hero; the comparison between youth and age, 554 ff., is similar to *Trachiniae*, 144 ff. in its gnomic style.

13. On the 'speech of deception' see Wolfgang Schadewaldt, *Neue Wege zur Antike*, viii (1929), 70 ff.; Wilamowitz, *Hermes*, lix (1924), 249 ff. (= *Kleine Schriften*, iv. 343 ff.); Welcker, *Kleine Schriften*, ii. 264; and the commentaries.

14. The ends of these two speeches are also similar, *Ajax*, 684 ff. and *Trach.* 467 ff. *Ajax*: 'But these things will be taken care of.' (This refers to his future friendships and enmities.) 'But you go in and pray to the gods that they may grant fulfilment of my heart's desire.' Similarly *Trach.* 467 ff.: 'But let all that drift away on a favourable wind. To you I say: tell lies to others if you like, but tell the truth to me.' In both passages the similarity does not lie only on the surface; the wish which appears to be benevolent really carries a sinister meaning: my friendships and enmities will be well taken care of when I am dead. Similarly in the other case: 'But let all that drift away on a favourable wind'; Deianira seems to accept the new liaison so calmly, but in fact she herself invites the danger which it implies. (I translate: 'with a favourable wind'; Radermacher's interpretation seems to me untenable. The accompanying wind is also 'favourable' in Aeschylus' *Septem*, 690: favourable, that is, for the downfall, since that is the direction in which Apollo is forcing the house of Laius.)

15. The comments of Wilamowitz, *Hermes* (lix), 1924, 249 ff (= *Kleine Schriften*, iv, 343 ff.), on this passage are very odd. Ajax's comparisons with the world of nature mean nothing to him; he ignores the tragic element in the tone of the speech; and he analyses it as follows: first, Ajax intended to apply 'a universal law', but suddenly, after a 'new reason had occurred' to him in the form of the *gnomē* of Bias on friendship, 'he could no longer pronounce the lie that he was giving in, but had to take refuge in an ambiguous expression . . .' 'He loathes having to deceive', so that he 'soon gives up deception' and so forth. A complete reversal, then, according to Wilamowitz. Just imagine the actor, suddenly called on to express loathing of deception, and then inability to continue the deception! How is he to express this loathing? There is nothing about it in the text, so presumably he has to stop to insert a mimed interlude and no doubt other nuances so as to show his disgust. . . .

Moreover, imagine someone on the brink of suicide who is 'disgusted' by having to tell the 'lie' that he is going for a walk!

On the comparisons see also W. Schadewaldt, *Monolog und Selbstgespräch* (1926), 87.

16. Wilamowitz, *Hermes* lix, (1924), 250 (= *Kleine Schriften*, iv, 344), in order to explain Ajax's behaviour, refers to Pollux, viii, 120. So too Radermacher's commentary. But we would be failing to respond to the tragic tone of the passage if we were to take it as no more than a description of an effective magic ritual, as a plausible reason for Ajax to leave the stage. Ritual magic is accommodated to the tragic framework only in the sense that it draws attention to Ajax, in that it no longer appears as magic but as an action, that is, an act of dissimulation. Similarly, washing off the stain is the 'proof' which is 'to be found' so that he may demonstrate that he is a worthy son of his father, 472.

17. It is usually assumed that the stage remains empty for a while, and that Ajax then enters from the side through the *parodos* or behind a hitherto unnoticed bush, buries his sword in the earth in silence, and when he has done this stands in

front of it and speaks. Not to mention the impossibility of conveying the effect of great distance in this way, or the problems raised by the miming, this arrangement would also entail that the main scene, where Sophocles says 'Behold, the man', is thrust to one side of the stage instead of occupying the centre. This would have an extremely strange effect on the end of the play. No lamenting retinue, no funeral procession leaves the stage. The chorus exits in groups to either side; Teucer and the boy remain alone by the body and lift it up. This is the end. But how is the stage to be cleared? How will the group around the dead man leave the scene? Are the bushes to suffice for that too? He would have to be carried out eventually. But he could only be dragged along – by Teucer and the boy! And no curtain falls to hide them. The *ekkyklema* resolves all the difficulties. The width of this apparatus would allow its wings, its scenery, and the necessary properties to be pushed out together from the rear wall. Ajax's speech to his sword could begin at the same moment as the new scene was being pushed forward. Since its function was to reveal what cannot be seen on the stage, the *ekkyklema* could probably represent not only an interior but also a distant scene if necessary.

E. Bethe, *Rheinisches Museum*, lxxxiii (1934), 21 ff., tries to prove that the *ekkyklema* was never used. But there are too many arguments for its existence, not only from the comic poets, but also from indications in the texts themselves. The subject requires investigation in a monograph.

18. Cf. Radermacher's commentary, where the evidence is given.

Charles Segal: Antigone: Death and Love, Hades and Dionysus (pp. 167–176)

1. See J.-P. Guépin, *The Tragic Paradox* (Amsterdam, 1968), 141 and n. 35. For Antigone as the bride of Hades and the connections with Persephone see R. C. Jebb, *Sophocles, The Plays and Fragments*, Part III *Antigone* (Cambridge, 1891) on 1204; J. C. Kamerbeek, *The Plays of Sophocles* Part III *Antigone* (Leiden, 1978) on 801–5; H. J. Rose, 'Antigone and the Bride of Corinth', *Class. Quart.* 19 (1925), 147–50; P. Roussel, 'Les fiançailles d'Haimon et d'Antigone', *Rev. Et. Grec.* 25 (1922), 71, who points out also the inversion of the nuptial to the funeral procession.

2. For the care and the 'in-between' state of Antigone see Karl Reinhardt, *Sophokles*[3] (Frankfurt a.M., 1947), 90. This heavy emphasis on the cave may be Sophocles' invention. According to Ion of Chios (740 Page) she was burnt with Ismene by a son of Eteocles in a temple of Hera.

3. For the male–female conflict see 525, 678–80, 741, 756, and also Ismene in 61–2 and Creon in 290. See in general C. Segal, 'Sophocles' Praise of Man and the Conflicts of the *Antigone*' (1964), in Thomas Woodward, ed., *Sophocles: A Collection of Essays* (Englewood Cliffs, N.J., 1966), 69–70; Kamerbeek on 484–5; R. F. Goheen, *The Imagery of Sophocles' Antigone* (Princeton, 1951), 88; J. H. Kells, 'Problems of Interpretation in the *Antigone*', *Bull. Inst. Class. Stud.* 10 (1963), 51–2.

4. In Aesch. *Sept.* 1031–2 Antigone laments the doom of her house connected with the burial of Polyneices with the cry 'Terrible the common womb – *koinon splanchnon* – from which we were born from our wretched mother and ill-fated father.' *Homosplanchnos* is used at *Sept.* 889–90 also in connection with the curse of the incestuous house, but in a somewhat different sense, as referring to the double fratricide. For *splanchna* of the womb and birth, see also Pindar, *Ol.* 6.43 and *Nem.* 1.45.

5. See Froma I. Zeitlin, 'The Dynamics of Misogyny: Myth and Mythmaking in the *Oresteia*', *Arethusa* 11, (1978), 149–84.

6. See in general Émile Benvéniste, *Le Vocabulaire des institutions indo-européennes* (Paris, 1969), i, 212–15, 217–22.

7. Ibid., i, 222.

8. The relation of the phratry to the significant political unit of the deme under Cleisthenes is not entirely clear. There seems to have been some overlap, and the phratries had some political significance: see W. K. Lacey, *The Family in Classical Greece* (Ithaca, N.Y., 1968), 92, 95–7.

9. See Lacey, 90–9.

10. For Greek views of filiation in the mid-fifth century and their relation to these issues see Zeitlin, *passim*, esp. 168–74 with the references in the notes on pp. 180–1.

11. For these contradictions in Creon's use of the family as a model of civic order (cf. 659 ff.) see Seth Benardete, 'A Reading of Sophocles' *Antigone*, II', *Interpretation* 5.1 (1975), 32–5.

12. See Zeitlin, 160 ff.

13. See Seth Benardete, 'A Reading of Sophocles' *Antigone*, I', *Interpretation* 4.3 (1975), 152, 176, 183.

14. See e.g. 51–2, 56–7, 146, 172 of the two brothers; 864–5 of Oedipus' incest. Compounds in *auto-* also mark Antigone's defiant burial of her brother: 503, 696, and also 821, 875, 900. Note Creon's use of *autocheir* in 306 to brand the criminal nature of the burial. Cf. also 700, 1175, 1315, and Benardete (above, n.13), 149; Kamerbeek on 49–52 and 172; B. M. W. Knox, *The Heroic Temper*, Sather Classical Lectures 35 (Berkeley and Los Angeles, 1964), 79; W. H. Will, '*Autadelphos* in the *Antigone* and the *Eumenides*', *Studies presented to D. M. Robinson* (St. Louis, 1951), 553–8. For *koinos* of the family curse cf. 146. The word also describes Antigone's exclusive allegiance to kin ties in 539 and 546. Contrast Creon's political usage ('common decree', 162) and the larger sense of the word beyond the perspectives of both protagonists in 1024, 1049, 1120.

15. The two passages contain the only occurrences of *splanchna* in this sense in the extant Sophocles. The word occurs one other time, in a different sense, at *Ajax* 995.

16. Note also Creon's use of *physis* as a criterion of authority in 727; contrast Haemon in 721. Goheen, 89 remarks Antigone's 'instinctive identification of *physis* and *nomos* as part of her identification of herself with a final order of things that is partly natural and partly divine.'

E. R. Dodds: On Misunderstanding the Oedipus Rex (pp. 177–188)

1. For the full evidence see O. Hey's exhaustive examination of the usage of these words, *Philol.* 83 (1927), 1–17; 137–63. Cf. also K. von Fritz, *Antike und moderne Tragödie* (Berlin, 1962), 1 ff.

2. The danger is exemplified by Mr P. H. Vellacott's article, 'The Guilt of Oedipus', which appeared in *Greece and Rome* 11 (1964), 137–48, shortly after my talk was delivered. By treating Oedipus as a historical personage and examining his career from the 'common-sense' standpoint of a prosecuting counsel Mr Vellacott has no difficulty in showing that Oedipus must have guessed the true story of his birth long before the point at which the play opens – and guiltily done nothing about it. Sophocles, according to Mr Vellacott, realized this, but unfortunately

could not present the situation in these terms because 'such a conception was impossible to express in the conventional forms of tragedy'; so for most of the time he reluctantly fell back on 'the popular concept of an innocent Oedipus lured by Fate into a disastrous trap'. We are left to conclude either that the play is a botched compromise or else that the common sense of the law-courts is not after all the best yardstick by which to measure myth.

3. Sigmund Freud, *The Interpretation of Dreams* (London, Modern Library, 1938), 108.

4. A. W. Gomme, *More Essays in Greek History and Literature* (Oxford, 1962), 211.

5. B. M. W. Knox, *Oedipus at Thebes* (Yale, 1957), 39.

6. C. M. Bowra, *Sophoclean Tragedy* (Oxford, 1944), ch. v.

7. Herodotus I. 45. Cf. H. Funke, *Die sogenannte tragische Schuld* (Diss. Köln, 1963), 105 ff.

8. A. J. A. Waldock, *Sophocles the Dramatist* (Cambridge, 1951), 158, 168.

9. G. M. Kirkwood, *A Study of Sophoclean Drama* (Ithaca, 1958), 271.

10. C. H. Whitman, *Sophocles* (Cambridge, Mass., 1951), 133-5.

11. V. Ehrenberg, *Sophocles and Pericles* (Oxford, 1954), 141 ff.

12. B. M. W. Knox, op. cit. ch. ii.

13. Heraclitus, fr. 102.

14. Sigmund Freud, op. cit. 109.

15. *Ajax* 124-6.

16. *O.C.* 607-15; 1211-49.

Jean-Pierre Vernant: Ambiguity and Reversal: On the Enigmatic Structure of Oedipus Rex (pp. 189-209)

1. *Ambiguity in Greek Literature* (Oxford, 1939), 163-73.

2. A. Hug, 'Der Doppelsinn in Sophokles Oedipus Koenig', *Philologus*, 31 (1872), 66-84.

3. 'Nouns are finite in number, while things are infinite. So it is inevitable that a single noun has several meanings.' Aristotle, *De Sophisticis Elenchis*, 1, 165a 11.

4. See Euripides, *Phoen.* 499-502: 'If all men saw the fair and wise the same men would not have debaters' double strife. But nothing is like or even among men except the name they give – which is not the fact' (tr. Elizabeth Wyckoff, in *Euripides V*, ed. David Grene and Richard Lattimore [New York, 1968]).

5. The same ambiguity appears in the other terms which hold a major place in the texture of the work: *dikē, philos* and *philia, kerdos, timē, orgē, deinos*. Cf. R. F. Goheen, *The Imagery of Sophocles' Antigone* (Princeton, 1951), and C. P. Segal, 'Sophocles' Praise of Man and the Conflicts of the Antigone', *Arion*, 3, 2 (1964), 46-66.

6. Benvéniste, in his *Noms d'agent et noms d'action en indo-européen* (Paris, 1948), 79-80, has shown that *nemein* retains the idea of a regular attribution, of an apportionment ruled by the authority of customary law. This meaning takes account of the two great series in the semantic history of the root **nem. Nomos,* regular attribution, rule of usage, custom, religious rite, divine or civic law, convention; *nomos,* territorial attribution fixed by custom, pastureland, province. The expression *ta nomizomena* designates the whole of what is owed to the gods;

ta nomima, the rules with religious or political value; *ta nomismata*, the customs or coinage having circulation in a city.

7. In the *Antigone*, at line 1481, Creon condemns the young girl who has transgressed 'the established *nomoi*'. Toward the end of the play, at 1113, disturbed by the threats of Teiresias, he swears to respect from then on 'the established *nomoi*'. But from the one expression to the other, *nomos* has changed meaning. At line 481 Creon uses it as a synonym of *Kerugma*, a public edict proclaimed by the head of the city; at 1113, the word has found again, in the mouth of Creon, the meaning which Antigone gave it at the start: religious law, funeral ritual.

8. As the Watchman says: 'For those who know, I speak, for those who do not know, on purpose, I hide myself [or, I forget: *lēthomai*]' (38-9). We find a good example of amphibologic dexterity at line 137: almost every word is susceptible to a double interpretation. We can understand 'massacring a trembling hare with her brood before she has given birth' and also 'sacrificing a poor trembling creature, his own daughter, at the front of the army'.

9. Cf. Stanford, 137-62. Some examples: in her first words, Clytemnestra, recalling the sufferings she has known in the absence of her husband, declares that if Agamemnon had received as many wounds as rumour had it, 'his body would have more holes than a net of mesh' (868). The expression has a sinister irony: it is exactly in this way that the king is going to die, caught in the net of death (1115), the web with no exit, the fishnet (1382) that she, with Aegisthus, stretches around him (1110) – the gates, *pulai* (604), the dwellings, *domata* (911), to which she alludes several times are not those of the palace, as those who hear believe, but, according to the established expression, those of Hades (1211). When she affirms that the King regains in her *gunaika pistēn, domatōn kuna*, she says in reality the opposite of what she seems to: *gunaik' apistēn*, a faithless woman, who has behaved like a bitch (606-7). As the scholiast remarks, *kuōn* (bitch) means a woman who has more than one man. When she evokes Zeus as *Teleios*, the Zeus by whom all is achieved, in order that he accomplish (*telei*) her wishes (973-74), it is not of the Zeus of the happy return that she thinks, as one might imagine, but of the funerary Zeus, master of death 'who ends all'.

10. We may compare lines 910, 921, 936, 946, 949 on the one hand, and 960-1, 1383, 1390 on the other, and we will note the sinister play on words *eimatōn baphas* (960), dyeing of cloths, which evokes *haimatōn baphas*, dyeing of blood. (Cf. *Choephoroi*, 1010-1213.) We know that in Homer blood and death are called *porphureoi*. According to Artemidorus Onirocriticus, 1.77 (p. 84, 2-4, Pack): 'The color purple has a certain affinity with death.' Cf. Louis Gernet, *Problèmes de la couleur* (Paris, 1957), 321-4.

11. Cf. R. P. Winnington-Ingram, 'Tragedy and Greek Archaic Thought', in *Classical Drama and its Influence: Essays Presented to H. D. F. Kitto*, ed. M. J. Anderson (London, 1965), 31-50.

12. Here again we will send the reader back to the work of Stanford and to the commentaries of R. Jebb, *Oedipus Tyrannus* (1887), and of J. C. Kamerbeek, *The Plays of Sophocles; Commentaries*, Pt. 4, *The Oedipus Tyrannus* (Leiden, 1967). We will mention only a few examples. Creon has just spoken of the brigands, in the plural, who killed Laius. Oedipus responds: how would the murderer (*ho lēstēs*) have been able to commit this act without complicity? (124). The scholiast notes: 'Oedipus thinks of his brother-in-law.' But by this singular, Oedipus, without knowing it, condemns himself. As he will recognize a little further on (842-7), if there were murderers, he is not guilty, but if there was one single man, the crime is evidently chargeable to him. At lines 137-41, there are three

ambiguities: (1) In dispelling the contamination, he does it not for faraway friends, but himself, for himself – he does not understand how well he speaks. (2) The murderer of the king could be tempted to lift his hand against him; in fact, Oedipus strikes out his own eyes. (3) In coming to help Laius, he serves his own cause – no, he will destroy himself. The whole passage 258–65, with its conclusion, 'For these reasons, as if Laius were my father, I will fight for him' is ambiguous. The phrase 'If his lineage had not aborted' also means 'If his lineage had not been sworn to a destiny of unhappiness'. At 501, the threat of Oedipus to Creon, 'If you believe that you will attack a relative without paying for it, you deceive yourself', turns against Oedipus himself: he will pay for the murder of his father. At 512–73, a double meaning: 'He would not have claimed that I killed Laius', but also 'He would not have revealed that I killed Laius.' At 928, the position of *hēde*, between *mētēr* and *tōn teknōn*, brings together *gunē* and *mētēr*: his wife, who is also his mother. At 955–6: 'He announces to you that your father Polybus is dead'; but also, 'He announces to you that your father is not Polybus, but a dead man.' At 1183, Oedipus wishes for death and cries out, 'O light, would that I have seen you for the last time!' But *phōs* has two meanings in Greek: light of life, light of day. It is the meaning which Oedipus does not mean to say which will come true.

13. *Poetics*, 1452a, 32–33.

14. 132. All subsequent references to the play, with line numbers included parenthetically in the body of the essay, are taken from the translations by David Grene, in *Sophocles I*, ed. David Grene and Richmond Lattimore (Chicago, 1954).

15. Ibid., 1190–6. In this sense tragedy, since before Plato, runs counter to the point of view of Protagoras and of the 'philosophy of enlightnment' developed by the Sophists in the fifth century. Far from man's being the measure of all things, it is god who is the measure of man, as of the rest. Cf. Bernard Knox, *Oedipus at Thebes: Sophocles' Tragic Hero and His Time* (New Haven, 1957), 150 ff., 184.

16. Cf. again, E. R. Dodds, 'On Misunderstanding the *Oedipus Rex*', *Greece and Rome*, 2nd Series, 13 (1966), 37–49.

17. *Poetics*, 1458a, 26. We may compare this scheme of reversal with that which one finds in the thoughts of Heraclitus, especially fr. 88, expressed by the verb *metapiptein*. Cf. Clémence Ramnoux, *Héraclite ou L'homme entre les choses et les mots* (Paris, 1959), 33 ff., 329.

18. Concerning this specificity of the tragic message, see 'Tensions et ambiguités dans la tragédie', in *Mythe et Tragédie en Grèce ancienne* (Paris, 1973), 23.

19. *O.C.* tr. Robert Fitzgerald, in *Sophocles I*, ed. David Grene and Richmond Lattimore (Chicago, 1954), 525, 539–40.

20. Ibid., 265 ff., 521 ff., 539.

21. *Suppliants*, 226.

22. *O.C.* 287.

23. Knox, *Oedipus at Thebes*, 138.

24. *O.T.* 278, 362, 450, 658–59, 1112.

25. Cf. Plutarch, *De Curiositate*, 522c, and *O.T.* 362, 450, 658–59, 1112.

26. *O.T. skopein*: 68, 291, 407, 564; *historein*: 1150.

27. Ibid., *heurein, heuretēs*: 68, 108, 120, 440, 1050.

28. Euripides, *Phoen.* 45.

29. Ibid., 1505–6.

30. *O.T.* 58–9, 84, 105, 397; cf. also 43.

31. Ibid., 876. See Knox. *Oedipus at Thebes*, pp. 182–4. Upon arrival, the messenger from Corinth asks: 'Do you know where Oedipus is?' As Knox observes,

the three lines 924-6 end on the name of Oedipus and on the interrogative adverb *hopou*, which gives: *mathoim' hopou-Oidipou-hōpou*. 'These violent puns', writes Knox, 'suggesting a fantastic conjugation of a verb "to know where" formed from the name of the hero who, as Teiresias told him, does not know where he is (413-14) − this is the ironic laughter of the gods whom Oedipus "excludes" in his search for the truth.'

32. Cf. Marie Delcourt, *Oedipe ou la légende du conquérant* (1944), where this theme is amply developed and where its place in the Oedipus myth is well shown.

33. Including the matrimonial laws recognized as the norm by the city. In 'Mariage de tyrans', in *Hommage à Lucien LeFevre* (1954), 41-53, Louis Gernet, recalling that the prestige of the tyrant originates in the past in many of its aspects and that his excess has models in legend, observes that 'for Periander the mythical theme of incest with the mother was raked up again. This mother is called *Krateia*, which means sovereignty.'

34. *The Trojan Women*, 1169; *Republic*, 568, 360 bd.

35. On Oedipus *agos*, see 1427; and also 656, 921, with comments of Kamerbeek, *Plays of Sophocles*, on these passages.

36. In a course taught at the Ecole des Hautes Etudes but which has not been published; see now J. P. Guépin, *The Tragic Paradox* (Amsterdam, 1968), 89 ff. Delcourt, *Oedipe*, 30-7, underlined the relations between the rite of exposure and that of the scapegoat.

37. Herodotus V. 70.71; Thucydides I. 126-7.

38. Photius, *Biblioteca*, 534 (Behber), cf. Hesychius, s.v.

39. The sixth of Thargelion, birthday of Socrates, is, Diogenes Laertius tells us (2. 44), the day on which the Athenians 'purify the city'.

40. Photius, *Biblioteca*; Hesychius, s.v. *kradiēs nomous*: Tzetzes. *Chiliades* V. 729; Hipponax, frs. 4 and 5, Bergk.

41. Scholia to Aristophanes. *Frogs*, 730, *Knights*, 1133. Suda, s.v. *pharmakos*, Harpocration, citing Istros, s.v. *pharmakos*, Tzetzes, *Chiliades*, V. 736.

42. Aristophanes, *Frogs*, 730-4.

43. Tzetzes, *Chiliades*. The scholiast at Aristophanes, *Knights*, 1133, writes that the Athenians supported, to serve them as *pharmaloi*, people extremely *ageneis kai achrestous*, of low origin, wrongdoers; the scholiast at *Frogs*, 703, that they sacrificed, to drive away the famine, *tous phaulous kai para tēs phuseōs epibouleuomenous*, beings degraded and deformed (literally: those who have been mistreated by nature); cf. Delcourt, *Oedipe*, 31 n. 2.

44. Leucas: Strabo. 10.9, p. 452; Photius, s.v. *Leukatēs*. Massilia: Petronius in Servius, *ad En.*, 3. 57; Lactantius Placidus, *Comment. Stat. Theb.*, 10, 793.

45. *Against Andocides*, 108. 4: *Tēn polin kathairein kai apodiopompeisthai kai pharmakon apopempein*. Lysias uses a religious vocabulary. On *diopompein*, *apodiopompeisthai*, *apopempein* and the rites of expulsion, the *pompaia*, cf. Eustathius, *ad Odys.*, 22, 481. In *O.T.* at 696, the choryphaeos, after the quarrel which has opposed Creon and Oedipus, wishes the latter to remain the 'happy guide' of the city, *eupompos*. On this point also, the reversal will be complete: the leader will be led back, the *eupompos* will be the object of the *pompaia*, of the *apopempsis*.

46. Plutarch, *Quaest. Conv.*, 717 d; Hesychius, s.v. *Thargēlia* Schol. to Aristophanes, *Plutus*, 1055, and *Knights*, 729, Athenaeus, 114 a, Eustathius, *ad Il.*, 9. 530.

47. On the *eiresiōnē*, cf. Eustathius, *ad Il.* 1283, 7, *Schol. to Aristophanes*,

Plutus, 1055; *Et. Magnum*, s.v. *eiresiōnē*; Hesychius, s.v. *Koruthalia*; Suda, s.v. *Diakonion*; Plutarch, *Life of Theseus*, 22.

48. *Sch. Aristophanes, Plutus*, 1055, *Sch. Aristophanes, Knights*, 728: *hoi men gar phasin hoti limou, hoi de hoti loimou*. Eustathius, *ad. Il.*, 1283, *apostrophē limou*. In the religious calendar, the *eiresiōnē* occurs again in the month *Puanepsiōn*, at the time of the holiday of the Oschophoria. The month of *Puanepsiōn* marks the end of the summer season as the month Thargeliōn (or the month immediately preceding *Mounichiōn*) marks its beginning. The ritual offering of the *puanion* (Athenaeus, 648 b) on the seventh of the month of autumn corresponds to the offering of the *Thargelos* on the seventh of the month of spring: in both cases, it involves a *panspermia*, a porridge of all the seeds of the earth's fruit. In the same way, the springtime procession of the *eiresiōnē* corresponds in the myth to the departure of Theseus (Plutarch, *Life of Theseus*, 18, 1 and 2), its autumnal procession to the return of the same hero (ibid., 22, 5-7). Cf. L. Deubner, *Attische Feste* (Berlin, 1932), 198-201, 224-6; H. Jeanmaire, *Couroi et Couretes*, (Paris, 1939), 312-13, 347 ff.; J. and L. Robert. *Rev. Et. Grec.*, 62 (1949), 106.

49. Talisman of fertility, the *eiresiōnē* is sometimes called, like the *Thargelos, euetēria, hygieia*, prosperity and health. The scholiast at Aristophanes, *Knights*, 728, notes that the seasons, *hai hōrai*, are 'attached to the branches'. Plato, *Symposium*, 188 a, writes that when the seasons allow just measure in their ordering (relationships of dry and humid, of hot and cold), they bring to man, animals, plants *euetēria* and *hugieia*; when on the contrary there is *hubris* in their mutual relations, *loimoi* appear, numerous sicknesses, which come over animals and plants also. The *loimos* manifests a disorder of the seasons close enough to the disorder of human conduct that the second may aso draw in the first; the rite of the *pharmakos* realizes the expulsion of human disorder; the *eiresiōnē* symbolizes the return to the good order of the seasons. In both cases, it is *anomia* which is averted.

50. Aristophanes, *Knights*, 728, and the *Scholion, Plutus*, 1054. 'The least spark would set it aflame like an old *eiresiōnē*' (*Wasps*, 399). We can compare the drying out of the spring bough with the drying out of the earth and men, in the case of *limos* (*limos*, famine, is often associated with *auchmos*, dryness). Hipponax, cursing his enemy Boupalos, this *agos* whose expulsion he desires, would like to see him *xēros limō*, dried out from hunger, paraded like a *pharmakos* and like him whipped seven times on his genitals.

51. Plutarch, *Life of Theseus*, 22, 6-7. Cf. 18, 1: after the murder of Androgeos 'the divinity ruined the land, striking it with sterility and sicknesses, drying up the rivers.'

52. Hesychius, s.v. *Thargēlia*: *kai tēn hiketērian ekaloun Thargēlon*, cf. also Plutarch, *Life of Theseus*, 22, 6 and 18, 1; Eusathius, *ad Il.* 1283, 6.

53. *Schol. Victor. ad Iliad.*, 10, 391: 'Paean: that which one sings to end evils and in order that none occur. Primitive music was related not only to banquets and dancing but also to the threnodies. It was still honored during the time of the Pythagoreans, who called it purification (*katharsis*).' Cf. also Aeschylus, *Agam.*, 645; *Choephori*, 150-1; *Sept.*, 868, 915 ff. Cf. L. Delatte, 'Note sur un fragment de Stesichore', *L'Antiquité classique*, 7, No. 1 (1938), 23-9. Albert Severyns, *Recherches sur la Chrestomathie de Proclos*, ii (Liège, 1938), 125 ff.

54. L. Delatte, 'Note sur un fragment'; Stesichorus, Fv. 37, Bergk = 14 Diehl, Iamblichus, *V.P.*, 110, Deubner; Aristoxenos of Tarentum, fr. 117 Wehrli: 'To the inhabitants of Locris and Rhegium who consulted the oracle to learn how to cure the madness of their women, the god answered that it was necessary to sing paeans

in the spring for sixty days.' On the importance of spring, which is less a season like the others than a break in time, marking at the same time the renewal of the products of the earth and the depletion of human reserves in this critical moment of 'welding' of one agricultural year to the other, cf. Alcman, fr. 56 D = 137 Ed.: 'The Seasons (Zeus) made them three, summer, winter, autumn as the third, and a fourth, spring, when everything flowers and grows but one cannot eat his fill.'

55. *O.T.* 1427; see n. 35 above.

56. Homer, *Od.*, 19, 109 ff.; Hesiod, *Works*, 225 ff.

57. Hesiod, *Works*, 238 ff.

58. On this double aspect of the *pharmakos*, cf. Lewis Richard Farnell, *Cults of the Greek States*, iv (Oxford, 1907), 280–1.

59. Suda, s.v. *Pharmakous*, Hipponax, Fr. 7 (Bergk); Servius, *ad Aen.*, 3, 57, Lactantius Placidus, *Comment. Stat. Theb.*, 10, 793: *publicis sumptibus alebatur purioribus cibis.*

60. Diogenes Laertius, 1, 110; Athenaeus, 602 cd.

61. J. Carcopino, *L'Ostracisme athenien* (1935). The principal texts are conveniently assembled in the work of A. Calderini, *L'Ostracismo* (Como, 1945). We owe to Gernet the idea of the comparison between the institution of ostracism and the rite of the *pharmakos*.

62. *Methistasthai tēs poleōs*, cf. *Et. Magnum*, s.v. *ex ostrakismos*, Photius, s.v. *ostrakismos*.

63. We note, in *O.T.* the presence of the theme of *phthonos*, in regard to the one who is at the head of the city; see 380 ff.

64. 'It is from the storm-cloud that snow and hail strike. Thunder issues from the resplendent lightning. It is from men too great that the ruin of the city comes.' Solon, Fr. 9–10 (Edmonds).

65. *Politics*, III, 1284 a 3 ff.

66. In a lecture which he gave in February, 1958, at the *Centre d'études sociologiques*, but which has not been published, Louis Gernet noted that between the two opposed poles of the *pharmakos* and the ostracized there is occasionally produced, in the play of the institutions, something like a short circuit. Such was the case in the last application Athens knew of ostracism. In 417 there were two persons of the first rank whom one might expect to see designated by the vote. The two confederates acting in concert succeeded in having the ostracism fall on a third thief, Hyperbolos, a demagogue of low rank, generally hated and despised. Hyperbolos was thus ostracized but, as Gernet observed, ostracism was not taken up again; horror-stricken by this 'shunting error', which underlined at the same time the polarity and the symmetry of the *pharmakos* and the ostracized, the Athenians were forever disgusted with the institution.

67. *Politics*, 1, 1253 a 2–7. To define the degraded being, the subman, Aristotle uses the same *phaulos* which the scholiast uses to characterize the *pharmakos*. On the opposition brute beast – hero or god, cf. *Nic. Ethics*, 7. 1145 a 15 ff: 'As to the status opposed to bestiality, one could doubtless not do better than to speak of super-virtue, heroic and divine, in short. If it is rare to find a divine man . . . bestiality is no less rare among men.'

68. In the expression of Aristotle which we quoted conforming to the usual translation, 'like an isolated pawn in a checkers game', there is not only opposition between *azux*, an odd counter, and *pettoi* or *pessoi*, the normal pawns which the players use. Cf. J. Treheux, 'Sur le sens des adjectifs *peridzux* et *peridzugos*', *Revue de Philologie*, 32 (1958), 89. In fact, in the category of games which the Greeks

designated by the verb *pesseuein*, there is one to which they gave the name *polis*. According to Suetonius, '*polis* is also a type of dice in which the adversaries took pawns, placed as in checkers (*petteutikōs*) on squares marked off by crossed lines. Not without wit, they called cities (*poleis*) the squares thus marked off and dogs (*kunes*) the pawns which were opposed to each other.' According to Pollux 'the game where one moves many pawns is a checkers board, provided with squares, marked off by lines. They call the board *polis*, the pawns *kunes*.' Cf. J. Taillardat, *Suetone: Des termes injurieux. Des Jeux grecs* (Paris, 1957), 154-5. If Aristotle, in order to define the *apolis* individual, refers to chess, it is because, in the Greek game, the checkers board which marks off the positions and the respective moves of the pawns is susceptible, as its name indicates, of representing the order of the *polis*.

69.   Cf. 1256-7, 1485, 1496-8: *k'ak tōn isōn ektēsasth'humas, hōnper autos exephu*.

70.   On this 'nonequality' of Oedipus in relation to the other Thebans, among whom some, like Teiresias and Creon, claim the right to equal status opposite him, cf. 61, 408-9, 544, 579 and 581, 630. The last wish the fallen Oedipus expresses concerning his children is that Creon 'not make them equal with myself in wretchedness' (1507).

71.   'One cannot speak of virtue apropos God any more than of vice apropos a beast: the perfection of God has more honor than virtue and the wickedness of the beast is of another kind than vice.' Aristotle, *Nic. Ethics*, 7, 1145 a 25.

72.   *Republic*, 569 b.

73.   Ibid., 360 c. It is in this context that it is necessary, we believe, to understand the second *stasimon* (863-911) about which very diverse interpretations have been proposed. It is the only moment when the chorus adopts a negative attitude with regard to Oedipus — tyrant; but the criticisms which they associate with the *hubris* of the tyrant appear entirely displaced in the case of Oedipus, who would really be the last, for instance, to profit from his situation to reap 'gains without justice' (889). In fact, the chorus' words concern not the person of Oedipus, but his status 'apart' within the city. The feelings of quasi-religious veneration with regard to this man who is more than a man are transformed into horror as soon as Oedipus reveals himself as the one who could formerly have committed a crime, and who seems today no longer to lend credence to the divine oracles. In this case, the *isotheos* no longer appears as the guide to whom one can abandon himself, but as a creature unbridled and lawless, a master who can venture all, permit himself all.

74.   *Logos*, word and reason, is what makes man the only 'political animal'. The beasts have only a voice, while 'discourse serves to express the useful and harmful, and, as a result, the just and the not-just: because it is the proper character of man in relation with the other animals to be the only one to have the consciousness of the just and the non-just, and other moral notions, and it is the community of these feelings which engenders family and city.' Aristotle, *Politics*, I, 1253 10-18.

75.   Dio Chrysost., 10, 29; cf. Knox, *Oedipus at Thebes*, 206; cf. also Ovid, *Metamorphoses*, 7, 386-7: 'Menephron had to couple with his mother, as wild animals do!' Cf. also 10, 324-31.

76.   At the beginning of the tragedy, Oedipus strives to integrate himself into the line of the Labdacids, from which, as a foreigner, he feels himself distanced (cf. 137-41, 258-68); as Knox writes, 'The resounding, half-envious recital of Laius'

royal genealogy emphasizes Oedipus' deep-seated feeling of inadequacy in the matter of birth . . . and he tries, in his speech, to insert himself into the honorable line of Theban kings' (56). But his unhappiness resides not in the too great difference which separates him from the legitimate line, but in his belonging to this very line. Oedipus worries also about a base origin which would make him unworthy of Jocasta. But there again his unhappiness springs not from too much distance but from too close proximity, from the complete absence of difference between the lines of the spouses. Worse than a misalliance, this marriage is incest.

77. Bestiality implies not only a lack of *logos* and of *nomos*, it is also defined as a state of 'confusion' where all is jumbled and mixed by change: Aeschylus, *Prometheus Bound*, 450; Euripides, *Suppliant Women*, 201.

78. Cf. the argument of Euripides' *Phoenicians: allasei de phuēn monon.*

R. P. Winnington-Ingram: The Electra of Sophocles: Prolegomena to an Interpretation (pp. 210-216)

1. Cf. Headlam in G. Thomson, *The Oresteia of Aeschylus*, ii, 217; J. T. Sheppard in *Class. Rev.* 41, 2-9.

2. C. H. Whitman, *Sophocles*, 161.

3. Detailed references and argument will be found in *Journ. Hell. Stud.* 74, 16 ff. and *Gnomon* 23, 414 ff.

4. *Journ. Hell. Stud.* 74, 16 ff.

5. Words of intellectual or quasi-intellectual content are also prominent in the debates between Electra and Chrysothemis, particularly between 1013 and 1057, where we find no less than seventeen terms which imply (more or less) rational consideration. But what determines the different attitudes of the two sisters in the same circumstances is certainly not the validity of their intellectual processes so much as a difference of *physis* (nature). But this important theme cannot be pursued here. The 'intellectual' words of the dialogue are picked up at the beginning of the stasimon; and we should note that the filial piety of the birds, which wins them the description of 'wisest' (1058), is a matter of instinct and not of reason.

6. Having made Clytemnestra angry, she becomes calmer herself.

7. Sophocles here opens a window upon sinister possibilities, just as, in the *O.C.*, he ends with Antigone preparing to play her part in the *Antigone*. The similarity is only not precise in so far as the approaching fate of Antigone has the greater certainty.

8. Cf. *Cho.* 577 f.

P. E. Easterling: Philoctetes and Modern Criticism (pp. 217-228)

1. Following the trail blazed by Tycho von Wilamowitz in 1917 (*Die dramatische Technik des Sophokles*).

2. D. B. Robinson, 'Topics in Sophocles' *Philoctetes*', *Class. Quart.* 19 (1969), 47.

3. C. M. Bowra, *Sophoclean Tragedy* (1944), 261 ff.

4. W. Steidle, *Studien zum antiken Drama* (1968), 169 ff.

5. Op. cit. 178.

6. O. Taplin, 'Significant actions in Sophocles' *Philoctetes*', *Gk. Rom. Byz. Stud.* 12 (1971), 27 ff.

7. D. Seale, 'The element of surprise in Sophocles' *Philoctetes*', *Bull. Inst. Class. Stud.* 19 (1972), 94 ff.

8. A. J. A. Waldock, *Sophocles the Dramatist* (1951), ch. X.

9. G. H. Gellie, *Sophocles: a Reading* (1972), 144.

10. A. F. Garvie, 'Deceit, violence, and persuasion in the *Philoctetes*', *Studi Classici in Onore de Quintino Cataudella*, vol. i (1972), 213 ff. J.-U. Schmidt, *Sophokles Philoktet, eine Strukturanalyse* (1973), 249 ff. also analyses the play into three phases although his interpretation differs in detail.

11. Art. cit. 214.

12. Schmidt, op. cit. (n. 10 above), 221 ff.

13. Cf. Schmidt, 234 ff.

14. O. Zwierlein, review of Steidle, in *Göttingische Gelehrte Anzeigen* 222 (1970), 208 ff.

15. Cf. Taplin, art. cit. (n. 6 above), 39.

16. Op. cit. (n. 4 above), 187; cf. Schmidt, op. cit. (n. 10 above), 247.

17. Art. cit. (n. 2 above), 55.

18. J. Kott, *The Eating of the Gods* (1974), 162 ff. The quotation is from p. 169.

19. J. P. Poe, *Heroism and Divine Justice in Sophocles' Philoctetes* (1974) = *Mnemosyne* Suppl. 34. The quotation is from p. 51.

20. P. Vidal-Naquet, 'Le Philoctète de Sophocle' in J.-P. Vernant and P. Vidal-Naquet, *Mythe et tragédie en Grèce ancienne* (1973), 161 ff.

21. C. Campbell, 'A Theophany,' *Theoria to Theory* 6 (1972), 82 f.

22. Schmidt, op. cit. (n. 10 above), 94, brings out the importance of 410–52 for making these standards clear; Philoctetes' hostility is confined to the *kakoi* of the Greek army.

23. Cf. B. M. W. Knox, *The Heroic Temper* (1964), 139.

24. 796 f.; 861; 945 ff. (cf. 1018; 1030).

25. 182 ff.; 265 ff.; 279 ff.; 311 ff.; 691 ff.

26. 631 ff.; 791 ff.; 1043 f.; 1113 ff.

27. Cf. 624 f., 1198 f. and the passages cited in n. 24 above. Knox, op. cit. (n. 23 above), 141.

28. Op. cit. (n. 10 above), 246.

29. Op. cit. (n. 9 above), 157.

30. Cf. Taplin, art. cit. (n. 6 above), 37; Schmidt, op. cit. (n. 10 above), 231; 246.

31. Art. cit. (n. 20 above), 179.

32. Art. cit. (n. 21 above), 81 ff.

33. An earlier version of this paper was delivered at the triennial conference of the Greek and Roman Societies on 31 July 1975. I am grateful for the criticisms and suggestions which were put forward in the discussion following the paper.

Cedric H. Whitman: Apocalypse: Oedipus at Colonus (pp. 229–243)

1. Cf. *O.C.* 7, 22, 437 f.; 580; in Creon's case, it has failed to teach wisdom, 930 f. See also on the *Electra*, and notes 25–6.

2. *Ajax* 678-682. Cf. *O.C.* 614 f. In the *Ajax* passage, such caution and reserve about friendships is an utter reversal of the Homeric standard. For Oedipus, however, the man of *gnomē*, these changes are in the order of things, and consistent with wisdom. So also the concept of *to mathein* appears (lines 117 f.) in a constructive and good light, impossible to the hero of the strictly aristocratic tradition of *phua*.

3. Cf. *Philoctetes* 1030. Is it conceivable that Sophocles counted the lines of this play as we do in our editions, and purposely placed this essential paradox at line 393? The technique was not unknown to Dante. See n. 11.

4. See U. v. Wilamowitz in T. v. Wilamowitz, *Die dramatische Technik des Sophokles* (Berlin, 1917), 334, and Max Pohlenz, *Erläuterungen* (= vol. ii of *Die griechische Tragödie*, Leipzig, 1930), 364, for interpretation of *sōthēnai* as 'homecoming'. The idea is well answered by Karl Reinhardt, *Sophokles* (Frankfurt, 1933), 214 n. 1.

5. Cf. E. Rohde, *Psyche* (Freiburg and Leipzig, 1894), 535 ff. G. Perrotta, who agrees that Oedipus is unchanged, apparently for this reason makes light of the apotheosis and claims that a hero is not a demigod (*Sofocle*, Messina and Florence, 1935), 560 f.). Once more, the interpretation of the play had suffered from an unhistorical intrusion of basically Christian values in the case of Perrotta, and perhaps of basically Orphic ones in the case of Rohde, who feels that Oedipus lacks purification.

6. See, for instance, *O.C.* 760 ff., 960 ff. (against Creon); 1383 ff. (against Polyneices), 593 (to Theseus).

7. Pausanias, i, 28. 6, notes the specific absence of horrendous attributes in the Athenian cult of the Eumenides, in contrast with the picture given by Aeschylus. This whole austere but terrorless conception of the Erinyes appears to have been a typically Athenian one.

8. For this aspect of ancient psychology, see Thomas Mann, 'Freud and the Future', *Essays of Three Decades* (New York, 1947), esp. 420-6. See also the Joseph series in general.

9. Simonides, 4, 7-12 (Diehl).

10. Besides the passages already quoted, see *O.C.* 142, 266 ff., 258-91, 521-48, and 960 ff.

11. The importance of the triad in Sophocles, and especially of the third member of the triad, has been studied with illuminating results in an essay by St. John Thackeray, 'Sophocles and the Perfect Number', *Proc. Brit. Acad.* 16 (1930), 15-44.

12. Solon I, 63-64 (Diehl); cf. *Il*. 3, 64-6; cf. Soph. 964 (Pearson) and Hesiod *Erga* 82-8. These are the clearest examples of the idea in Sophocles, but 'gift' frequently has sinister overtones, especially in the *Trach*. 494 ff., 555 f., 758, and *Ajax* 662, 665, 817, and most of all 1029-37, where the gift of an enemy is described in the light of a device of the gods. This comes close to being the 'gift of the gods', which is inescapable, and has nothing to do with moral deserts, as Oedipus' distinction, lines 539 f., shows.

13. *Daimonos* is perhaps correctly 'luck', but it is luck with a divine element, in contrast to *tychē*.

14. The blind man's insight recalls, of course, Teiresias, and the whole knowledge problem of the former play.

15. Cf. W. Dopheide, *De Sophoclis arte dramatica*, 77, who says the Polyneices episode is no part of the plot, but a little tragedy in itself. The suggestion of C. Robert, *Oidipus* I (Berlin 1915) 474 ff., only seems more historical than this. Robert

thinks that Polyneices represents Sophocles' own son Iophon, who is thought to have tried to seize his heritage before his father's death by having him pronounced *non compos mentis*. Even if Iophon's suit actually took place, which is doubtful, it is very unlike Sophocles to dramatize a humiliating family dispute in a tragedy, and thrust himself to the fore. In any case it explains nothing about the play.

16. Cf. U. v. Wilamowitz in Tycho v. Wilamowitz, 371 (answer to Robert), and 317 f., and 367, where it is skillfully shown that the Polyneices scene is firmly connected with the original saga. Wilamowitz exhibits his customary acumen in unearthing sources, but he too has failed to integrate Polyneices artistically with the play.

17. Cf. F. Allègre, *Sophocle* (Lyons, Paris 1905) pp. 299–305; C. M. Bowra, *Sophoclean Tragedy* (Oxford 1944) pp. 329 ff.; Pohlenz (above, n. 4) vol. i 364 ff.; and Reinhardt (above n. 4) 227 for such views.

18. The writer of the ancient *Argumentum*, however, feels it is inadequately motivated.

19. Herod, iii. 80. Creon's attack on Antigone suggests his character in the *Antigone*.

20. This passage, the fullest defense which Oedipus gives, should long ago have silenced the argument that he was responsible for his misfortunes through his bad temper. The simple truth of Oedipus' remarks at 991–6 seems inescapable.

21. Thuc. ii,37. Reinhardt, 223, goes so far as to suggest that Pericles himself is behind the figure of Theseus. But Pericles had been dead now for twenty years, and the shape of Sophocles' mind was more ideal and generally historical than specific.

22. For instance, *O.C.* 703 ff., 1533 f.

23. See the Oxyrhynchus Historian, Grenfell and Hunt, *Ox. Pap.*, no. 842, col. xiii, 28 ff.

24. Xen. *Hell.* ii, 2, 19.

25. Thuc. ii, 41. 1.

26. Perrotta, 606, feels he is quite as much a hero as Eteocles in the *Septem*, and is modeled on him.

27. Cf. *O.C.* 1280 with 1344 f.

28. Cf. Perrotta, 610, who thinks Sophocles disapproved of the curse and that the thunder which follows it is a correction of his attitude. Actually, Oedipus himself tells us the sign is a summons from Zeus. Perrotta feels that Oedipus is exalted in spite of his character, and with as little reason as he was destroyed in the former play. Cf. Reinhardt, 230.

29. Cf. Allègre, 299 ff., and Bowra, 329 ff. Also, apparently, Turolla, *La poesia di Sofocle*, 197 (I have this reference second-hand). Patin, *Sophocle*, 243, thinks Sophocles did not know what to think of it!

30. Pohlenz, *Gr. Trag.*, 365, and *Erläut.*, 102, urges the laws governing *trophē* and *threptēria*. He suggests comparison of *O.C.* 352, 446, 1265, 1362–5. Cf. Bowra, 327 ff. for a similar view and more evidence, and Weinstock, 197.

31. *Thebaid, fgs.* 2 and 3; cf. Bowra, 325.

32. Note the characteristic 'double motivation'.

33. See Thomas Mann, *Joseph and His Brothers*, trans. by H. T. Lowe-Porter (New York, 1945), 141 f.

34. *O.C.* 1391. Oedipus does mention having cursed both his sons before, lines 1375 f., but the context indicates no more than that he had stated before what he states now, and that both times it was true. Curses take the form of a wish, as oracles of a command, but both essentially only indicate what must be

true, when it is viewed without the element of time. Oedipus is so near the state of a god that he can speak as from outside of time.

35. Cf. Pohlenz, 363, and Bowra, 314 ff.

36. 'An das Göttliche glauben / Die allein, die es selber sind', F. Hölderlin, 'Menschen beifall' (trans. F. Prokosch).

Erich Segal: Euripides: Poet of Paradox (pp. 244–253)

1. This image was surely inspired by Aristophanes' *Frogs* 1085 ff. The 'he to Hecuba' incident is recounted by Plutarch, *Pelopidas* 29.

2. It is not enough to dismiss the 'innovations' of the *Alcestis* by noting that it was presented in place of the usual satyr-play. Besides, on this same occasion Euripides presented the *Telephus* which, according to Aristophanes, was even more 'scandalous'.

3. e.g. *Alcestis* 242–3: Admetus will 'live and not live' for the rest of his days. Also lines 518–21: Admetus tells Heracles that his wife 'has died and not died'.

4. *Hippolytus* 732 ff. Although T. S. Eliot would later complain that Gilbert Murray 'interposed between ourselves and Euripides a barrier more impenetrable than the Greek language', the lines printed have caught the fancy of many English writers (e.g. Galsworthy), who quoted them time and again.

5. And yet Artemis does not even allow Theseus to express his own longings for escape. When she appears at the end of the *Hippolytus*, she says (lines 1290 ff.) that she knows *he* would like to dive beneath the earth or fly away like a bird, as if, sadistically, to remind him that all routes leading away from torment are sealed off.

6. And in matters of sex, Euripides never minces words. Helen's lust is referred to as (among other things): *aplēstia lechous*, 'insatiable bed-hunger' (*Andromache* 218).

7. In the very first line of the play, Helen describes herself as waiting faithfully by the 'beautiful-virginal', *kalliparthenoi*, waters of the Nile.

8. Despite its ostensibly comic aspect, the *Helen* is a far more vehement anti-war statement than *The Trojan Women*. Helen may have gone to Troy in name only, but the soldiers who went as men and are *returning* only as names on the casualty list (cf. lines 399 ff.) would not be comforted by this.

9. This point was first – and best – articulated by E. R. Dodds, in his landmark essay, 'Euripides the Irrationalist', *Class. Rev.* 43 (1929), 97–104.

10. Sigmund Freud, 'The Ego and the Id', *Complete Psychological Works* xix, ed. James Strachey (London: The Hogarth Press, 1961), 25.

11. See Norman O. Brown, *Life Against Death* (New York, 1959), 16: 'True humility, he [Freud] says, requires that we learn from Copernicus that the human world is not the purpose or the center of the universe; that we learn from Darwin that man is a member of the animal kingdom; and that we learn from Freud that the human ego is not even master in its own house.'

12. And what makes a home is, of course, *philia*. This bond of humanity is all that remains for a grieving Theseus or Heracles, and even at the conclusion of the *Bacchae* for Agavê and Cadmus.

13. Aristotle *Rhetoric* iii. 2; 'Longinus', *On the Sublime* xv.

14. In his famous eulogy of Euripides (*On the Sublime* xv), 'Longinus' states that the Greek playwright 'works hardest and best' at portraying *love* and *madness*.

15. *Paideia* i. 380.

16. In *Nicias* 29, where Plutarch tells the pretty story of how Greek sailors, captured in Sicily, gained their freedom by being able to quote Euripides, he goes on to describe how, after these men returned to Athens, whenever they encountered the playwright, they would warmly thank him 'with *love* in their hearts'. Such incidents are usually ignored by those who would build a case for 'unloved Euripides', the social outcast brooding alone in his cave by the sea.

17. Sophocles presents a unique literary example of an author dealing not merely with what Harold Bloom calls 'the anxiety of influence', i.e. the great tradition of Aeschylus weighing heavy upon him, but the innovations of a younger playwright as well. On the former, see R. P. Winnington-Ingram, *Sophocles: An Interpretation* (Cambridge, 1980), 3 *et passim*.

18. H. D. F. Kitto, *The Greeks* (Baltimore, 1951), 129.

Anne Pippin Burnett: The Virtues of Admetus (pp. 254–271)

1. Most recently Bruno Snell, *Poetry and Society* (Bloomington, Ind., 1961), 83 ff. Snell sees Alcestis as embodying the archaic virtue of the wife, in the company of an Admetus who is husband only in name, a Pheres who is likewise a false parent, and a Heracles so perversely idealized as to prove that the 'true friend' does not exist in the real world. U. Albini, 'L'*Alcesti* di E.,' *Maia*, xiii (1961), 1–29, offers a nonironical reading in which, however, Admetus is shown as consistently weak.

2. K. von Fritz, *Antike und moderne Tragödie* (Berlin, 1962), 301–21, inspired by Browning, finds an Alcestis disillusioned on the day of her death, and T. Rosenmeyer, *The Masks of Tragedy* (Austin, Texas, 1963), 224, 227, 229, discovers her to be hard, cruel, and vindictive. Rosenmeyer (with Browning) believes that Admetus learns as the play proceeds, but von Fritz finds no improvement in him. C. R. Beye, 'Alcestis and Her Critics', *Gk. Rom. Byz. Stud*, ii (1959), 124, speaks of the 'lifeless and selfish grounds on which Alcestis chose to die', and concludes, p. 127, 'neither Admetus nor Alcestis are very attractive people' (*sic*).

3. A. Lesky, 'Alkestis, der Mythus u. das Drama', *SB Akad Wien* (*Ph.-hist. Kl.*), cciii: 2 (1925), 1–86; cf. his summary of recent German *Alcestis* criticism in *Die tragische Dichtung der Hellenen* (Göttingen, 1956), 157–61.

4. Remnants of what the Athenian audience knew as the story exist in a fragment of a drinking song (schol. of Praxilla, Frag. 21 Bergk), eight lines of Bacchylides (3. 76–84), six lines of the *Eumenides* (723–28), and one scrap of the play by Phrynichus (Frag. 2 Nauck²). In none of these passages is there any suggestion that Admetus was anything but the type of the man so loved by a god that he was granted an extraordinary fortune. L. Weber has attempted a 'reconstruction' of the Phrynichus play in *Rheinisches Museum* lxxix (1930), 35 ff., but his results are at best hypothetical; the only things securely known of this piece, which may have been tragic, satyric, or burlesque, are that Thanatos appeared and that at some point a wrestling match was reported.

It might be noted that Plato, when he mentions the Alcestis story (*Symp.* 179 B–C) shows no consciousness that the old evaluations have been questioned. Nor did late antiquity, which must have known the story chiefly through Euripides, find anything in it unsuitable to the exaltation of family grief and the promise of salvation: see refs. to plastic representations of the myth in *RE*, I (1903), 1513–14, *s.v.* 'Alkestis' (Escher), and the exx. collected by L. Bloch, *Alkestisstudien* (Leipzig,

1901), Figs. 1-4 at end of text; add G. Q. Giglioli, 'Sarcofago di Genova col mito di Alcesti', *Arch. class.*, v (1953), 222-31.

5. It has been cited as evidence of Admetus' hypocrisy that his expressions of grief are excessive (scholars of another turn of mind have found his 'tragic flaw' in the honest excess of his grief), but his phrases are conventional: they can be paralleled in tragedy (e.g., Soph. *Ajax* 588; *O.T.* 1217-20; Eurip. *Hipp.* 817 ff., 1410, 1456) and were imitated in grave inscriptions.

If Admetus were shamming grief in the farewell scene, covering his actual relief at having found a substitute, his falsity would be comparable to that of Clytemnestra on hearing of Orestes' death; and the Aeschylean example shows how careful a tragedian must be, even with a lady of Clytemnestra's reputation, to provide his audience with external evidences and corroborating witnesses of hypocrisy.

6. But in its defense, note A. Lesky, *Tr. Dicht.*, 159.

7. Cf. Eurip. Frag. 318 Nauck[2].

8. M. P. Nilsson, *Gr. Rel.*, i, 314.

9. See Snell, loc cit., on *philia* in marriage. Some moderns, recognizing that Alcestis is not acting 'for love', conclude that she is either calculating or disenchanted; others, confusing her salute to her bed with a romantic gesture, believe that she is acting 'for love', and that Admetus is a brute for not returning her feeling. She tells the audience and Admetus that reason, not passion, moved her; had her motive been passion, her choice would have been less to her credit (cf. *Medea* 526-31). Phaedrus, in the *Symposium*, tried to make Alcestis a figure for the power of *eros* (179 C), but he is corrected at 208 D.

10. A great deal of nonsense has been written about this passage, proving only that scholars take their Krafft-Ebing too seriously. The ideas of death, simulacra, resurrection, and marriage had a strong association, since every year at the Anthesteria the dead Dionysus was imaged by a mask fixed to a post, then brought to life to enjoy the ritual of his marriage (see Nilsson, op. cit., i, 551, 555; G. van Hoorn, *Choes and Anthesteria* (Leyden, 1957), 24-5; and for use of a Dionysus herm in the *hieros gamos*, see Hetty Goldman, 'The Origin of the Greek Herm', *Amer. Journ. Arch.* xlvi (1942), 58-68, esp. p. 66 and fig. 9). The statue motif occurs also in the story of Laodameia (Hyg. *Fab.* 103, 104), about whom Euripides wrote a tragedy (see U. von Wilamowitz-Moellendorff 'Sepulcri Portuensis imagines' (1929), *Kl. Schr.*, v: 1 (1937), 524-7, where it is argued that Admetus' speech proves that Laodameia's love was impious and perverse!). Here the wife who would not betray her husband though he was dead (Frag. 655 Nauck[2]), and who kept him alive as best she could with a statue in her bed, was rewarded with his miraculous brief return to life. Admetus, grieving and rejoicing over the image of his wife, becomes the masculine counterpart of Venus with Adonis, and prefigures the initiates described by Firmicus Maternus *De err. prof. rel.* 22. This complex of ideas finds expression in the later practice of heroizing the dead by means of statues in the guise of Dionysus or Aphrodite, as Charite did Tlepolemus (Apul. *Met.* 8. 7; cf. [Plut.] *Amat.* 753 F; and note in illustration M. Gütschow, *Atti d. Pont. Acad. Rom. di Arch.*, Ser. iii, Mem. iv: 2 (1938). Pl. xvii). One of the effects of Euripides' use of the statue motif in the *Alcestis* is that her resurrection is understood poetically as the breathing of life into a statue, a process which may have been dramatized in Sophocles' satyr play *Pandora* (see F. Brommer, *Satyrspiele*[2] (Berlin, 1959), 52).

11. Wilamowitz, *Isyllos von Epidauros* (Berlin, 1886), 57 ff.; note, however, Preller-Robert, *Gr. Myth.*[4], ii: 1, 32, where it is argued that the earliest version of all left Alcestis in the underworld.

12. Lesky, *SB Akad. Wien*, cciii: 2, 27, 30.

13. Paus. 3. 18. 6; Apollod. 1. 9. 15; Hyg. *Fab*. 50, 51; the details may have originated with Hesiod, see Wilamowitz, *Isyllos*, 68 ff. Cf. J. T. Kakrides, *Hermes* lxvi (1931), 235 ff.

14. His father in a sense casts him off in return by charging him with murder; the term *phoneus* (730) is precisely as accurate as the *haima* of 733 is real, but Pheres can thus revenge himself. The mention of Acastus creates a dim echo of the story of Aegisthus' daughter who charged Orestes with the murder of her father.

15. For death as an old man, bald, ugly, and almost naked, see C. Smith, 'A Vase with a Representation of Heracles and Geras', *Journ. Hell. Stud*. iv (1883), 100 ff.

16. P. Hartwig, 'Heracles und Geras', *Philol*., l, (1891), 185 ff.

17. See O. Kern, *Arch. f. Religionswiss*., xv (1912), 642, for an argument that a public ritual of this sort existed at Athens in the early 4th cent. F. Cornford, *The Origin of Attic Comedy* (London, 1914), 78, compares the Pheres scene with the final agon of the *Clouds* and its preceding whipping scene, viewing it as an example of the conflict of the Young King and the Old King. The Imposter scenes of Old Comedy would seem to offer a closer parallel (esp. the gift-bearing imposters of the *Birds*); these figures are often stripped of their clothing or attributes, as Pheres is stripped of his fatherhood and his share in Admetus' house.

18. Van Hoorn, op. cit. 20; Nilsson, op cit., i, 564.

19. For apotropaic door inscriptions naming Heracles, see *Bull. corr. hell*. lxxxvi: 2 (1962), 608–9; for a general description of Heracles as protector of door and hearth, see Ch. Picard, 'Hercule, héros malheureux et bénéfique', *Hommages à Jean Bayet* (Brussels, 1964), 561 ff.

20. He thus makes his city like the prosperous god-loved city described at *Eumen*. 984-6.

21. This play's figure of an experience, in one body, of the suffering of two souls, because of *philia*, is expressed in the opposite form in the proverb '*philia* is one soul living in two bodies' (G. H. Opsimathes, *Gnōmai* (Leipzig, 1884), 19).

22. These fictions are reinforced now by the chorus: Alcestis' tomb is to be no tomb but a shrine (999; note *sebas* and its echoes from Admetus at 279 and 1060).

23. Heracles' speech, 1017 ff., has often been misunderstood. He says, 'I blame you for having caused me to behave unsuitably, though certainly I have no wish to add pain to your suffering.' The condition which arouses his blame is *pathōn tade*, which is explained by *estepsa krata* and *theois eleipsamēn spondas* (1015: cf. 859-60). He does *not* blame the general tenor of Admetus' actions; he sees them as a form of *euergesia* at 860, and says explicitly *ainō men, ainō* at 1093, as if to correct any misunderstanding of his *memphomai*.

24. Alcestis' silence is sometimes treated as if it were a sullen silence, evidence that she means to begin a lifelong tongue-lashing as soon as she gets her husband into the house. The silence has a complex of serious causes, both dramaturgical and poetic. However many actors Euripides had to work with, he needed a silent Alcestis here, because he had to demonstrate somehow verbally and visually, the fact that the woman truly had been dead. If she spoke now, the audience could hardly be blamed for becoming a congress of Verrallians who refused to believe that she ever had been buried. The extent and wonder of the miracle can only be proved by showing it to be not quite complete yet. In addition, Admetus is to be given a part in Alcestis' salvation: it is not secured until the recognition touch. For

the ritual three days, see the inscription from Iulis cited by H. J. Stukey, 'Purity', *Trans. Amer. Philol. Ass.* 67 (1936) 295.

25. For parallels to the mixed strains, see Aesch. *P.V.* 555; *Agam.* 700 ff.; *Choeph.* 342 ff.; (Bion) *Lament for Adonis* 87 ff.; for association of death and marriage, Artem. *Onirocrit.* 2.65. Heracles' gluttony, a fixed motif of satyr drama, is a reminder of his cornucopia, his role as bringer of plenty, his companionship with Dionysus, and his mystical connections; see R. Stiglitz, 'Herakles auf dem Amphorenfluss', *Jahreshefte Oest. Arch. Inst. Wien* 44 (1959), 113-41. It is time for modern critics to abandon the 18th-cent. view of this scene, superbly expressed by Voltaire: 'Il ne faut pas disputer les goûts; mais il est sûr que de telles scènes ne seraient pas souffertes chez nous à la foire.' (*Dict. philos.* I, s.v. 'Anciens et Modernes'.)

26. For Aphrodite *zygia* as goddess of marriage, see V. Magnien, 'Vocabulaire grec reflétant les rites du mariage', *Mélanges Desrousseaux* (Paris, 1937), 295; the evidence (*IG*, II-III², 4533) is not strong enough to justify Magnien in calling this one of Aphrodite's cult titles, since Ariphron's paean appears in a variant version, without the word *zygia*, at Ath. 15.702A.

27. *Hymn.* 12; G. Quandt, *Orph. Hymni* (Berlin, 1955), 13-14.

B. M. W. Knox: The Medea of Euripides (pp. 272-293)

1. Cf. the *hypothesis* attributed to Aristophanes of Byzantium. Sophocles came in second.

2. Cf. Ar. *Th.* 1130, *Ran.* 1382; Eupolis, *Demoi* K90; Strattis, *Medea* K33-35 (apparently a full-length travesty); Plato K30; Eubulus K26; Alexis K176; Philemon K79. Cantharus K, 1, p. 764 *Medea*.

3. W. H. Friedrich's 'Medeas Rache', in *Vorbild und Neugestaltung, Sechs Kapitel zur Geschichte der Tragödie* (Göttingen, 1967), 7-56, now reprinted in Wege der Forschung lxxxix, *Euripides*, ed. E.-R. Schwinge (Darmstadt, 1968), 177-237, is a brilliant comparative study of later versions of the *Medea* which works backwards ('Von Grillparzer zu Euripides') to an illuminating discussion of all features of the Euripidean original.

4. L. Séchan, *Etudes sur la tragédie grecque dans ses rapports avec la céramique* (Paris, 1925, repr. 1967), 396-422; D. L. Page, *Euripides, Medea* (Oxford, 1938), lvii-lxviii; A. D. Trendall and T. B. L. Webster, *Illustrations of Greek Drama* (London, 1971), 96-7.

5. There seems to be a consensus that the *Aegeus* was produced before the *Medea*: see, for references, A. Lesky, *Die Tragische Dichtung der Hellenen* (Göttingen, 1972), 305, n. 27. There is, however, no external evidence for the date except vase paintings (on which see T. B. L. Webster, *The Tragedies of Euripides* (London, 1967), 79-80, 297-8). But the argument from vase paintings assumes too much; how do we know that the representations, frequent after 430, of Medea at Athens were not inspired by the *Aegeus* of Sophocles? Or of some other dramatist? Or by no dramatist at all? The fragments themselves are insignificant, and dates based on metrical statistics are in this case quite worthless.

6. See the discussion in Page, *Euripides, Medea*, xxi ff.

7. I am convinced by Page's demonstration (xxx ff.) that Neophron's *Medea* is later than that of Euripides. (For a survey of the controversy see Lesky, *Tragische Dichtung*³, 301; Lesky agrees with Page.) K. v. Fritz, *Antike und moderne Tragödie* (Berlin, 1962), 386 (reprint of an article published in 1959), believes that Neophron's

careful motivation of Aegeus' appearance was known to Euripides but deliberately avoided by him ('mit einer gewissen absichtlichen eigenwilligen Nichtachtung') for a purpose.

8. In the *Medea* of Carcinus there seems to have been a trial: Medea used the argument from 'probability' (Arist., *Rh.* 1400ᵇ9).

9. On the date of the *Ajax* see now Lesky, *Tragische Dichtung*³, 180 n. 2.

10. S., *Aj.* 333, 339, 342–3.

11. E., *Med.* 24; S., *Aj.* 323, 324.

12. S., *Aj.*, 531, 533, 535.

13. E. *Med.* 383, 404, 797, 1049, 1355, 1362; S., *Aj.*, 367, 382, 454, 961, 969, etc. The four resemblances between the two plays discussed above are noted by A. Maddalena, 'La *Medea* di Euripide', *Rivista di Filologia Classica* (1963), 137–8.

14. E., *Med.* 355; S., *Aj.* 756.

15. E., *Med.* 364–409; S., *Aj.* 430–80.

16. E., *Med.* 974 (vengeance); S., *Aj.* 685, 967 (suicide). E., *Med.* 93; S., *Aj.* 585, 326. Compare also E., *Med.* 47–48 and S., *Aj.* 552 ff. (children unconscious of the sorrows of their elders). E., *Med.* 173 ff., and S., *Aj.* 344 ff. (the chorus feels that the protagonist's passion will be calmed by their presence).

17. Maddalena, 'La *Medea*,' 133–4, draws attention to Medea's concern for honour.

18. W. Steidle, *Studien zum antiken Drama* (Munich, 1968), 152 n. 1.

19. Cf. pp. 311 ff. below.

20. In 431 B.C., of course, the only Sophoclean hero plays we can be certain Euripides knew are the *Ajax* and the *Antigone*. The characteristic mood, language, and situation of this type of drama were however, already present in the Aeschylean *Prometheus Bound* and in any case stem from Homer's *Iliad*. (Cf. B. M. W. Knox, *The Heroic Temper* (Berkeley and Los Angeles, 1964), 45–52.) The case for Sophoclean influence on the *Medea* is strengthened by the fact that no other extant Euripidean play deploys the full armory of Sophoclean heroic situation and formula.

21. Knox, *Heroic Temper*, 10–44.

22. On this word cf. Friedrich, *Vorbild und Neugestaltung*, 51–2 (Wege der Forschung lxxxix, *Euripides*, 233–4).

23. On Jason's 'Blindheit' with regard to Medea see von Fritz, *Tragödie*, 349 ff.

24. Cf. D. J. Conacher, *Euripidean Drama* (Toronto, 1967), 195: 'Medea herself is really the only one capable of resisting Medea.'

25. Cf. Schlesinger, 'Euripides' Medea', below.

26. Cf. von Fritz's brilliant analysis (*Tragödie*, 361 ff.) of lines 407–9.

27. Cf. von Fritz, *Tragödie*, 395 ff. (with a defense of the last two lines of Creon's speech, athetized by some critics).

28. Cf. W. Steidle, *Studien*, 166–7; H. Diller, *Entretiens sur l'antiquité classique* vi (Geneva, 1960), 32.

29. Cf. Steidle, *Studien*, 167 n. 90.

30. Knox, *Heroic Temper*, 33–4.

31. This invocation of Hecate is often cited as part of the evidence that Medea is presented throughout as a sorceress, a witch. Cf. Page on line 364; on line 367 he cites *Ion* 650 (which must be a misprint for 1050), but that passage is an invocation of Kore in her aspect of *Einodia*, not Hecate, and asks her aid for Creusa's plan to poison Ion. (For 'witchcraft' and poison, see below, section III.) But there

was an aspect of Hecate which had nothing to do with sorcery or poison but rather with the home and woman's functions in it. An effigy of Hecate stood in front of every house door (A., *Fr.* 742 Mette, Ar., *V.* 804, *Ra.* 366), women asked Hecate's advice as they left the house (Ar., *Lys.* 64), and played games with their daughters in her honor (ibid. 700 − 'hausliche Kult der Hekate' says Wilamowitz ad loc.); women called on her in childbirth (A., *Supp.* 676 ff.). Hecate is obviously an ambiguous figure, and Medea's devotion to her cannot be interpreted as an attitude typical of a sorceress unless reinforced by the context (which it is not).

32. Cf. also 22, 169, 209, 1372.

33. It is typical of Jason's blind misunderstanding of his situation (and Medea's) that he can call her, in the teeth of the evidence, 'woman most hateful to the gods' (1323-4).

34. H. D. F. Kitto, *Greek Tragedy* (3d. ed., London, 1961), 199.

35. 'Here they seem a little inapposite', Page, *Euripides, Medea*; 'The final verses of the Chorus . . . certainly have no place here', Lesky, *Tragische Dichtung*[3], 309.

36. The argument which follows in the text assumes that the appearance of a *theos* on the *mechane* was a spectacle familiar to the audience of 431 B.C., though it is of course true that all the extant examples of this phenomenon are dated (some certainly, the others probably) later than the *Medea*. (The first version of the *Hippolytus*, however, probably had a *deus ex machina* − cf. Webster, *Tragedies of Euripides*, 65, 70 − and may have preceded the *Medea*.) It seems unlikely, in view of the exact correspondence of all the features of Medea's final appearance with the functions of the *deus* in the later plays, that this can have been the first use of this device. The *mechane* itself was used in the Aeschylean *Psychostasia* and possibly in his *Carians or Europa* (cf. T. B. L. Webster, *Greek Theatre Production* (London, 1956), 12), and the appearance of a god at the end of the play to bring a conclusion occurs in the Aeschylean *Prometheus Bound* and (probably) in the lost *Danaides*.

37. Cf. D. L. Page, *Greek Literary Papyri* (Cambridge, Mass., and London, 1941), 68. One may compare also the end of the *Erechtheus* of Euripides (C. Austin, *Nova Fragmenta Euripidea* (Berlin, 1968), 36), where Athena intervenes to prevent Poseidon from destroying Athens by earthquake.

38. A. Koerte, *Menandri quae supersunt.* II (Leipzig, 1959), fr. 223.

39. Lesky, *Tragische Dichtung*[3], 309.

40. L. Bloch, 'Alkestisstudien', *Neue Jahrbücher*, band 7 (1901), 30.

41. Cf. K. J. Reckford, 'Medea's First Exit', *Trans. Amer. Philol. Ass.* 99 (1968), 239.

42. W. Schmid, *Geschichte der griechischen Literatur*, band III (Munich, 1940; repr. 1961), 360.

43. In view of the total disagreement with Page's overall conception of the *Medea* expressed in this article, it seems only fair to acknowledge at this point my deep indebtedness to his masterly commentary on the text.

44. This is especially true of critics writing in English and French. See, for example, G. M. A. Grube, *The Drama of Euripides* (New York, 1941; repr. 1961), 152-4; A. Elliot, *Euripides' Medea* (Oxford, 1969), on lines 395, 1317; D. W. Lucas, *The Greek Tragic Poets*[2] (London, 1959), 199: 'a genuine witch'; Conacher, *Euripidean Drama*, 188-9; Cunningham, 'Medea', *Class. Phil.* 49 (1954) 153; Reckford, 'Medea's First Exit', 333, 374; L. Méridier, *Euripide*, t. I (Paris 1926; repr. 1965), 119: 'une magicienne redoutable' etc. The evidence is surveyed in C. Headlam's editon of the play, (Cambridge, 1904) as an appendix, 'Medea as a sorceress'

(105-7). Headlam's conclusion is that 'Euripides . . . in his play wisely keeps this occult power somewhat in the background and it greatly conduces to the dramatic effect that his heroine impresses us as a woman, not as a witch.'

In recent German (and more rarely Italian) literature, the normal, human aspects of Euripides' Medea have been emphasized (see H. Rohdich, *Euripideische Tragödie*, (Heidelberg, 1968) 44-6, for citations and discussion). Rohdich himself speaks of 'the poet's effort to divest Medea of the monstrous nature inevitably ascribed to her and to make her identifiable to the audience as a normal woman' (41). This goes too far in the opposite direction; Medea is not a 'normale Frau' but an extraordinary one, as her presentation in heroic terms makes clear.

45. Lines 752 ff. (excerpted).

46. 7. 262 ff. Translated by Rolfe Humphries, *Ovid's Metamorphoses* (Bloomington, Ind., 1957).

47. *Macbeth* 4.i.30 ff.

48. The three surviving fragments (A. C. Pearson, *The Fragments of Sophocles* (Cambridge, 1917), 534-6) contain in their 14 lines more of the atmosphere of sorcery than can be found in the 1,420 lines of Euripides' play.

49. Jason mentions her betrayal of her father and murder of her brother (1332-4) but then proceeds directly to the murder of his own sons.

50. The messenger speeches describing the effects of the poison in both plays have often been compared: see, e.g., Page, *Euripides, Medea*, xxvi n. 4.

51. Antiphon, 1.14 ff.

52. E., *Ion* 1003 ff.

53. M. P. Nilsson, *Geschichte der griechischen Religion*[3], vol. i (Munich, 1967), 801 (with illustration).

54. *Od*. 10.136, 220, 297, etc.

55. Page, *Euripides, Medea*, xix.

56. V. di Benedetto (*Euripide*, 33) takes issue with Page on this point: 'At least in this respect the character of Medea is no less 'Greek' than Alcestis and Phaedra'.

57. Cf. Knox, *Heroic Temper*, 42-43.

58. Cf. di Benedetto, *Euripide*, 37-38, on Medea's icy calculation and cold cunning.

59. There is a passage in the *Andromache* which charges the barbarian races with incest (father and daughter, mother and son, brother and sister) as well as murder of kin: but the speaker is Hermione who, with her father Menelaus, kidnaps Andromache's child, forces her to leave sanctuary by threatening to kill it, breaks the promise made to spare its life, and would have murdered mother and child if not prevented.

60. J. H. Finley, *Harv. Stud. Class. Philol.* 50 (1939), 65 ff. = *Three Essays on Thucydides* (Cambridge, Mass., 1967), 92-4. Cf. also Reckford, 'Medea's First Exit', 336 ff.

61. Pl., *R.* 5.454 c-e.

62. The date of production of Aristophanes' *Birds* (414) is the *terminus ante quem*. T. B. L. Webster, *An Introduction to Sophocles*[2] (London, 1969), 4, dates it before 431 on 'external evidence' which (176-7) turns out to be its resemblance in theme and (reconstructed) 'diptych form' to the *Trachiniae*, which he also dates before 431. W. Buchwald, *Studien zur Chronologie der attischen Tragödie* (Königsberg, 1939), 35 ff., also puts it before *Medea*: it was the model for Medea's murder of her sons. Others, basing their proposals on 'contemporary allusions', have dated it nearer to 414. There is no certainty, or even probability, here.

63. Pearson, *Fragments of Sophocles*, 583. I follow Jebb's interpretation of the difficult opening lines.

64. A. W. Gomme, 'The Position of Women in Athens', *Class. Rev.* 20 (1925), 1–25 (reprinted in *Essays in Greek History and Literature* (Oxford, 1937)); H. D. F. Kitto, *The Greeks*[2] (Harmondsworth, 1957), 219–36.

65. With the startling exception of Geoffrey Chaucer; cf. n. 67.

66. This phrase is taken by many proponents of Medea the witch as evidence for their case. But, though 'wise woman' meant 'witch' in seventeenth-century English, the Greek word *sophe* has no such connotation. The *sophia* Creon fears is the craft that rescued Jason from his pursuers at Colchis and brought death to Pelias: these are *kaka* (evils) in the sense defined by von Fritz (cf. n. 26). Medea of course deliberately misunderstands his drift, but the charge she is evading is not 'witchcraft'. And her argument, after all, is soundly based. Her *sophia* has brought her to her present state, a woman abandoned in a hostile country.

67. Hausrath Hunger 264: cf. Babrius 194 (Crusius) and Chaucer, *Wife of Bath's Prologue* 692 ff.

> Who peyntede the lioun, tel me who?
> By god, if wommen hadde written stories
> As clerkes han withinne hire oratories
> They wolde han written of men more wikkidnesse
> Than all the mark of Adam may redresse.

68. Cf. I. Caimo, *Dioniso* 6 (1937–8), 4.

Eilhard Schlesinger: On Euripides' Medea (pp. 294–310)

1. Wolfgang Schadewaldt, *Monolog und Selbstgespräch* (Berlin: Weidmann, 1926), 193 ff.

2. Heraclitus *Diels-Kranz* 22 B 85, Democritus *Diels-Kranz* 68 B 236. See also the other occurrences listed in Kranz's index.

3. See Page's commentary on this passage.

4. e.g. *Iliad* 10. 98.

5. According to Lesky in 'Zur Problematik des Psychologischen in der Tragödie des Euripides,' *Gymnasium* lxvii (1960), 10 ff., the tragedy of Medea lies in the conflict of *thymos* = *hedonai* and *bouleumata* = *gnome*.

6. This question is examined in detail by Hans-Dieter Voigtländer, 'Spätere Überarbeitungen im grossen Medeamonolog,' *Philologus* ci (1957), 217 ff. See also Lesky's reply to A. Rivier, *Entretiens sur l'antiquité classique*, tome vi (Vandoeuvres-Genève, 1960), 83.

6a. [W. Zürcher, *Die Darstellung des Menschen im Drama des Euripides*, Basel, 1947.]

7. Philip W. Harsh, 'Repetitions of Lines in Euripides,' *Hermes* lxxii (1937), 446 f. Cf. also Page's commentary.

8. Parmeniscus in the gloss on 264.

9. Cf. Bruno Snell, 'Das früheste Zeugnis über Sokrates,' *Philologus* xcvii (1948), 125 ff.; Gerhard Müller, *Studi Italiani di Filologia Classica* xxv (1951), 65 ff.; and Hans-Dieter Voigtländer, loc. cit.

10. Cf. Andreas Spira, *Untersuchungen zum Deus ex machina bei Sophocles und Euripides* (Kallmünz/Opf, 1960).

11. It is interesting that almost all the participants in the conference of the Fondation Hardt share Aristotle's dissatisfaction with the ending of the tragedy. See

the discussion on the lecture by Kamerbeek, *Entretiens*, 30 ff. Cf. N. E. Collinge, 'Medea ex machina,' *Classical Philology* lvii (1962), 170 ff.

12. Cf. Hans Diller, *Entretiens*, 32.

13. Collinge stresses particularly this significance of the dragon-chariot.

14. W. Schmidt, *Geschichte der griechischen Literatur* (Munich, 1929), i. 149.

15. Hans Strohm, *Euripides: Interpretationen zur dramatischen Form, Zetemata*, 15 (1957), 3.

16. Loc. cit.

17. Lines 431 f.; cf. 1 f.; 433 ff.; cf. 34 f.

18. See 329, 340 ff., 562 ff., 669 ff., and especially the anapests in 1081 ff.

19. Cf. Günther Zuntz, *Entretiens*, 36.

20. Most of the material is contained primarily in the glosses of Parmeniscus on 9 and 264. Cf. Carl Robert, *Die griechische Heldensage*, III. i, 870 ff.; Karl Kerényi, *Die Heroen der Griechen* (Zürich, 1958), 266 ff.; K. von Fritz, 'Die Entwicklung der Jason-Medeasage und die Medea des Euripides,' *Antike und moderne Tragödie* (Berlin, 1962), esp. p. 333.

21. *Entretiens*, 31.

22. Preface by Karl Kerényi in *Medea: Euripides, Seneca, Corneille, Cherubini, Grillparzer, Jahnn, Anouilh, Jeffers, Braun*, ed. by Joachim Schondorff (Munich and Vienna: Theater der Jahrhunderte, 1963).

23. Cf. Hans Diller, 'Umwelt und Masse als dramatische Faktoren bei Euripides', *Entretiens*, 89 ff.

24. Cf. Jacqueline de Romilly, *Évolution du pathétique d'Eschyle à Euripide* (Paris, 1961), 119.

25. Op. cit., above, n. 20.

26. See Rex Warner's translation of the *Medea* (first published in 1944; reprinted in 1946 by John Lane, The Bodley Head, Ltd., London; also published in 1955 by the University of Chicago Press in the *Complete Greek Drama*, edited by David Grene and Richmond Lattimore) for the following lines: 1040 f., 1056 f., 1062 f., 976 f., 1122 f., 1013 f.

B. M. W. Knox: The Hippolytus of Euripides (pp. 311-331)

1. 'The chief character is Hippolytus, and it is around him that the drama is built.' G. M. A. Grube, *The Drama of Euripides* (New York, 1941), 177. See also L. Méridier, *Euripide* (Paris, 1927), Tome 2.19.

2. See David Grene, 'The Interpretation of the *Hippolytus* of Euripides', *Class. Phil.* 34 (1939), 45-58.

3. This and the following figures are based on Murray's Oxford text.

4. This figure does not include vss. 780-1 and 786-7, which Murray, with several manuscripts and the support of the scholia, assigns to the Nurse. It is dramatically more effective that the Nurse should disappear from the play after Phaedra's dismissal (708-9). In any case, the phrasing of the verses which Murray assigns to the Nurse indicates a speaker who did not know that Phaedra was going to commit suicide; the Nurse knew this only too well (cf. 686-7).

5. By Phaedra in vs. 690.

6. For a different interpretation see E. R. Dodds, 'The *Aidōs* of Phaedra and the Meaning of the *Hippolytus*', *Class. Rev.* 39 (1925), 102-10.

7. This is emphasized by the formal opening of Phaedra's address to them (373-4). Cf. also 710, when she makes her final request to them for silence.

8. For *philtra* with deterrent effect, see, for example, Tibullus 1.2.59–69; Nemes., *Buc.* 4.62 ff.

9. For this sense of *ergon*, see *LSJ* s.v. 1.3.c.

10. See below, n. 15.

11. See below, n. 19.

12. See Méridier's excellent comments in *Euripide*, 19.

13. Though the choice between silence and speech has no further significance for the action – which has been determined beyond recall by Theseus' curse – it still recurs as a reminiscent theme in the second half of the play. Thus, Hippolytus urges his silent father to speak (911), in words clearly designed to recall the Nurse's plea to Phaedra (297). And the bull which comes from the sea to fulfil Theseus' curse does its deadly work in silence (1231).

14. Cf. Isoc., *De Antidosi* 253–57, *Nicocles* 5–9; X., *Mem.* 1.4.12.

15. Cf. 423, 489, 688, 717; also 405 (*dyskleā*). In 47 Phaedra is called *eukleēs* by Aphrodite.

16. Cf. 288 to 514, *passim*.

17. Cf. Thucydides 2.41.

18. For example, 79–81, 986–9, 1016–18.

19. But not an 'Orphic'; that ghost is laid by D. W. Lucas in *Class. Quart.* 40 (1946), 65–9.

20. Cf. 84, 656, 996, 1309, 1339, 1368, 1419, 1454.

21. This is one, at least, of the meanings of this compressed statement.

22. The words recall Aphrodite's comment on the relationship between them (19).

23. The verbal context of this last appearance of *allos* is almost identical with that of its first (301).

24. Cf. scholia ad Pi., *P.*4. 106; Ar., *Ra.* 1274 (= A., *Fr.* 87).

25. Cf. Verg., *G.* 4.197 ff..

26. They are pointed out by Grube, *The Drama of Euripides*. He remarks on the 'ominous similarity' of 148 and 448 and the 'interesting echo' (*melissa*).

27. Cf. also *mythos* (9 and 1313) and *bouleumasi* (28 and 1406).

28. Méridier, *Euripide*, 24. For a similar view, more fully and more soberly developed, see S. M. Adams, 'Two Plays of Euripides', *Class. Rev.* 49 (1935), 118–19.

29. Cf. 1396, 1404, 1436, 1437–9.

30. Cf. 1442–3.

D. J. Conacher: The Trojan Women (pp. 332–339)

1. See, for example, H. Steiger, 'Warum schrieb Euripides seine *Troerinnen*?' *Philologus* lix (1900), 362–3, and the comments there cited. Cf. also Wilamowitz, *Troerinnen, Einleitung*, 263, 'The *Trojan Women* does not present any progressive action, but is rather a series of scenes which converge at the same final point . . .' and Gilbert Murray, 'The Trojan Trilogy of Euripides', in *Mélanges Glotz* ii (Paris, 1932), 645, '. . . the only movement . . . the gradual extinguishing of all the familiar lights of human life . . .'

2. See H. D. Westlake, *Mnem.* (1953), 181–91.

3. Wilamowitz, *Troerinnen, Einleitung*, 283 and n. 1.

Christian Wolff: Orestes (pp. 340–356)

1. N. A. Greenberg, 'Euripides' *Orestes*: An Interpretation', *Harvard Studies in Classical Philology*, lxvi (1962), 162.
2. G. M. A. Grube, *The Drama of Euripides* (London, 1941), 384.
3. Greenberg, op. cit. 189 f.

Hans Diller: Euripides' Final Phase: The Bacchae (pp. 357–369)

1. G. Norwood, *The Riddle of the Bacchae*, London 1948.
2. Schol. Ar. *Ran.* 67.
3. See the survey in Dodds, *Euripides Bacchae*, ed. with Introd. and Comm.[2] (Oxford, 1953), xxxvi ff. K. Deichgräber 'Die Lykurgie des Aischylos', *Nachrichten der Gesellschaft der Wissenschaften in Göttingen* 1939, 231 ff.
4. G. Murray is particularly impressive on this in *Euripides and his Age*[2] 1947, 117 ff.
5. Cf. Dodds, Comm. xxxiii ff.
6. This impression (in the sense of influence rather than conversion) is stressed in particular by Wilamowitz, *Griech. Trag.* iv, 1923, 123 f.; M. Pohlenz, *Griech. Trag.*[2] 1954, 450. On the other hand the impression created by the introduction of orgiastic cults (Sabazios, Bendis) in Athens during the Peloponnesian War should not be underestimated (Dodds, Comm. xx ff.).
7. Since this view is no longer held, it may be enough to mention the survey in Dodds, Comm. xxxviii. The doxographic survey by R. Nihard, *Mus. Belge* 16 (1912), 91 ff. may still be useful.
8. In particular G. Norwood, (above, n.1). Very limited in the sense of a 'symbolic' interpretation, Norwood's *Greek Tragedy*[4] 1948, 277 ff.; *Essays on Euripidean Drama*, 1954, 52 ff. A. W. Verrall, *The Bacchants of Euripides and other Essays*, 1910, 1 ff. Related to this tendency yet without Norwood's and Verrall's extreme conclusions are W. Nestle, *Euripides als Dichter der griechischen Aufklärung*, 1901, 74 ff. and P. Masqueray, *Euripide et ses ideés*, 1908, 145 ff. This view was taken up again, though in modified form, by L. H. G. Greenwood, *Aspects of Euripidean Tragedy*, 1953 (interpretation of the *Bacchae*, p. 48 ff. in particular). (Cf. also *Gnomon 26* (1954), 126 ff.).
9. A pioneering work, which did away with the unproductive philosophical alternative question in Euripides, was the paper by E. R. Dodds, 'Euripides the Irrationalist', *Class. Rev.* 43 (1929), 97 ff. G. Murray saw the antinomy, particularly in the *Bacchae*, as 'a bewildering shift of sympathy' in the course of the play (*Euripides and his Age*[2], 121): compare also A. Lesky, *Griech Trag.* 1938, 220 f.; M. Pohlenz, *Griech. Trag.*[2], 458. Of fundamental importance for the discussion of the *Bacchae* apart from Dodds's Commentary are the individual analyses by F. Wassermann, *Neue Jahrbücher für Philologie und Pädagogik* 5 (1929), 272 ff. (and now supplementing them, *Festschrift Robinson*, 1953, 559 ff.) and R. P. Winnington-Ingram, *Euripides and Dionysus* (Cambridge, 1948).
10. Murray[2], 122.
11. Dodds, *Class. Rev.* 102 ff.; Comm. xli ff.
12. Winnington-Ingram, 179.
13. W. Schmid, *Geschichte der griechischen Literatur* (Munich, 1940), i.3 (1940), 666 f. sees a 'certain contradiction' between the 'anakreontic-sympotic philosophy' of part of the choral songs and the wild Dionysiac orgiastic which

determines the dramatic structure of the whole work. The conclusions drawn from this are of a merely biographical nature and do not need to be discussed here as we are dealing with the unity of the *Bacchae* as a work of art.

14. Statement of Dionysos' self-characterisation 860 f.: *theos, deinotatos, anthropoisi d'ēpiōtatos* (compare Dodds, Comm., 1953).

15. Wasserman, 272 ff.: Winnington-Ingram, 161.

16. Dodds, Comm. xl.

17. K. Deichgräber, *Hermes*, 70 (1935), 331.

18. Pohlenz², 458; Deichgräber, 330.

19. Dodds, Comm xl, a highly readable amusing characterisation.

20. 'Man of action', Winnington-Ingram, 20.

21. Wasserman, 275.

22. On the development of the concept from epic via tragedy to Hellenistic philosophy, compare J. C. Kamerbeek, *Mnemos*. iv. i, (1948), 271 ff.

23. Wilamowitz, *Griech. Trag.* iv. 143.

24. Winnington-Ingram, 54.

25. Ibid. 160.

26. Ibid. 55, 58.

27. W. Zürcher, *Die Darstellung des Menschen im Drama des Euripides*, Basel, 1947. Also the review by G. Miller, *Gnomon* 21 (1949), 167.

28. Thus Deichgräber, 330.

29. Plat. *Ion* 533e6, 534a5, d1, *Phaedr*. 244c, where, as is well known, the pun *manikē-mantikē* is connected to the tracing of the matter from *enthusiasmos*, as in *Ba*. 289–301. It is of fundamental importance that in *Ion* the spiritual works from *enthusiasmos* are compared to the *Bacchae*'s miraculous deeds, as in Aischines of Sphettos, fr. 11c Dittmar (compare Pohlenz, *Aus Platons Werdezeit*, 188) and that in *Ion* 534d1 the mantic also appears. For originally, it was, of course, the madness of Apollonian obsession which caused the mantic, yet Kassandra in Euripides' *Hecuba* and *The Trojan Women* is already called a Maenad or Bacchant. *Hec*. 121, 676 expressly relates to her visionary gifts (material in Pohlenz, n.2, 150). Plutarch, *de Pyth. or.* 6, p. 397a relates the words of Heraklitos that the Sybil is talking *mainomenō stomati . . . dia ton theon. (Vers.*⁶ 22B 92). The pun that is more than a pun might go back as far as Heraklitos.

30. See in particular the words of blessing at 72 ff., 135 ff., 902 ff. and *hetera megala phanera t'* (other great and clear things) at the textually difficult passage 1006 f. (Murray², 127, Winnington-Ingram, 179; on the text Dodds (193).

31. *Il*. 3. 395. In Euripides see *Phoen*. 399, also (with a rationalistic twist) *Troad*. 988 f.

32. See *Apol*. 22b, c, *Menon* 99b ff., *Ion* 533b ff.; also my paper 'Probleme des platonischen *Ion*', *Hermes*, 83 (1955), 171 ff.

33. This view is confirmed by line 803 where Pentheus rejects an agreement with the Bacchae as *douleuein douleiais emais*.

34. Concerning the speech by Teiresias see G.M.A. Grube, *Trans. Amer. Philol. Ass*. 66 (1935), 41; Winnington-Ingram, 48 ff.

35. Dodds, Comm. xli.

36. Cf. Kamerbeek, *Mnemos*. iv. i (1948), 280 ff.

37. The provoked Bacchae are 'winged' in the rapid speed of their movement (748, 1090); winged also is the poet who creates in the trance of *enthusiasmos* (Plat. *Ion* 533b 4). Yet the genuine madman also 'flies' (*Theogn*. 1053), and in this sense the word is used by Pentheus when, in effect, he has lost control over himself (322; cf. Dodds ad loc.).

38. For the central meaning of the quarrel about *sophia* in the *Bacchae* see Winnington-Ingram 88, 167–70. As to the doubts about the value of knowledge expressed by the old Euripides, see B. Snell, *Philol. Supp.* 20 (1928), 1, 156; Dodds, *Class. Rev.* 43, 100 f.

39. Dodds, Comm. 90 ff.

40. Cf. G. M. A. Grube, *Trans. Amer. Philol. Ass.* 66 (1935), 40, n. 2.

41. The Choral song 862–911 starts from an actual situation, like all such songs in the *Bacchae*. Yet, in the Epodos, the chorus finally finds a traditional form for its affirmation of traditionalism, too. It starts from the fact that the enemy is falling into the trap and the danger is over. The Bacchae are as free as deer in the forest who have escaped the hunters' traps. (For a reversal of the situation see below). They will be able to celebrate the nocturnal Bacchic feast again (862–76). The enemy's cunning has collapsed, the chorus has shown real *sophia*. The god has protected his followers and rewarded them with the highest honor of letting the victorious head fall on to the enemy's hand (877–81, 897–901). The god's revenge falls on those who do not honour him in their rage. One should adhere to religious tradition which is as firmly based as nature (882–96; 895 f.). After this affirmation of tradition the chorus speaks in two general beatitudes 902–5 again about the actual situation, the happy overcoming of danger; it is the 'day's fortune' which alone is praised as secure. In everything else human fortune is fluctuating and uncertain because of an infinite number of possibilities and equally infinite number of hopes. The uncertainty of fortune, the treacherousness of hope because of which only the favorable moment can be treasured, is a motif of archaic poetry. What Euripides says in 905–11 is expressed in similarly conventional thought and words in the early poem by Pindar *Pyth*. 10, 59–62, unconventionally in *Pyth*. 8, 88–97.

42. The omission of 1113 (Nauck; cf. Markelbach, *Rheinisches Museum* 97 (1954), 374 n. 3) seems impossible to me, since the important stage of Pentheus' awakening from Bacchic madness has to be prepared for.

43. Wasserman, 277.

44. Dodds, Comm. 167, Winnington-Ingram, 104.

45. Cf. *Heraclid*. 390–2.

46. Cf. above, p. 361 with nn. 24–6.

47. Cf. p. 448 n. 37.

48. Emphasised particularly by Dodds, *Class. Rev.* 102 f., Comm. xli.

49. But see the legitimate qualifications of Winnington-Ingram, 174.

50. The structural similarities with the *Bacchae* demonstrated in the following confirm the late dating of *Ion* which scholars increasingly accept. See Wilamowitz, Euripides *Ion* 406 ff.; Pohlenz, 165 n. 2; W. H. Friedrich, *Euripides und Diphilos*, 1953, 13 f.: G. Zuntz, *The Political Plays of Euripides*, 1955, 64 n. 1.

51. *El*. 379. Cf. B. Snell, *Philol*. 20, 1928, 1, 153 f.; Dodds, *Class. Rev.* 43 (1929), 100. Cf. also the words of Iocasta to Oedipus. Soph. *O.T*. 979.

Thomas G. Rosenmeyer: Tragedy and Religion: The Bacchae (pp. 370–389)

1. The metamorphosis which Dionysus inflicts upon Cadmus in the epilogue is a datum from mythology. Because of the bad state of preservation of the final portion of the play we do not know how Euripides motivated the metamorphosis, and what the punishment – for such it is said to be (1340 ff.) – is for.

Jacqueline de Romilly: Fear and Suffering in Aeschylus and Euripides (pp. 390-395)

1. I have pointed out the significance of 'fear' in Aeschylus in *La Crainte et l'angoisse dans le théâtre d'Eschyle* (Paris, 1958). B. Snell underscores the importance of this emotion in *Aischylos und das Handeln im Drama, Philologus* Suppl. (1928), 164 n. 8.

2. *Seven Against Thebes* 325-9; 338-44. I cite only a small passage from a much longer description.

3. In Aeschylus there is but a single description of the sacking of a city which does not take place *before* the event – and not inspired by fear. At least it is imagined before it is actually announced: Clytemnestra's evocation of what the sack of Troy may have been like (*Agamemnon* 320 ff.). Moreover, she concludes by expressing the fear that the conquerors will be in danger if their actions are excessively brutal. There is more of this same sentiment expressed in the two succeeding *stasima*.

4. In principle, *Hecuba* is regarded as the earlier: Cassandra is still present (88), and Polyxena – who is dead in the *Trojan Women* (621) – is still alive. But on the other hand the army is no longer at Troy (8).

5. See below p. 394.

6. We have the present at 477.

7. The most general – and chaotic – description is at *Trojan Women* 557-65, where it concentrates – yet again in Euripides – on the image of 'tender infants', clutching with frightened fingers at their mothers' clothing.

8. *Trojan Women* 518 (translation slightly altered); *Hecuba* 913; 942.

9. 1010 ff. (cf. 293 ff.). Here it is Troy itself that is *talainan talainan* (miserable). Moreover, the laments do not come from the victims. The instance is somewhat akin to that in *Agamemnon*. (See above, n. 3.)

10. *Androm.* 1037 ff.; cf. also, *inter alia, Helen* 1107 ff., *Hec.* 1107 ff., *Tro.* 1084 ff.

11. On the other hand, we will not dwell here on the notion that the *Agamemnon* deplores the misfortunes of the Trojan war. Aeschylus emphasizes this theme, but in the commentary of the chorus. He never makes an explicit statement of the sorrows and suffering caused by the war (the weariness is mentioned at 551 ff.). His descriptions of mourning are very strong, but always from a distant viewpoint, and as part of a great chain of crime and retribution.

12. The mournful perfect *bebasi* ('they are gone') repeated at *Persians* 1002 and 1003 is also repeated at a significant moment in *Andromache* (1023 and 1027) as well as twice in line 582 of the *Trojan Women*. We find it again in the *Suppliant Women* (1139) and *Orestes* (971).

13. Cf. Snell, (above n. 1), p. 67.

14. Yet even when she speaks of sacrificing to the gods, she must, in some way, excuse her behaviour and constant anxiety about what may come (525-6): 'I know it is for what has already happened, but perhaps we may henceforth have a happier future.'

15. This is the meaning of the scene with the ghost of Darius. This has a curious aspect, for though he comes from the dead he expresses disquiet about the future of his family – as if he did not know it.

16. One might even say that in other scenic effects we find the same disparity: the winged chariot that flies Medea off at the end of the play which bears her name recalls the winged chariot – or chariots – of the Oceanids in *Prometheus Bound*. But the latter is merely an aspect of the Oceanids' divinity, and merely

calls attention to a concern with which their fear was not all bound up. On the other hand, Medea's chariot seems to have but one purpose: to situate husband and wife for a moment both out of reach yet within earshot, so their enmity can be welded into final and indissoluble suffering. The *Triptolemus* of Sophocles is too little known for us to make any judgments about the wingèd chariot used therein.

17. *Class. Rev.* 27 (1913), 41 ff. This was called to my attention by Professor J. C. Kamerbeek, who was kind enough to read an earlier draft in which most of the ideas were first put forth.

Bruno Snell: From Tragedy to Philosophy: Iphigeneia in Aulis (pp. 396–405)

1. See Arist. *Poet*. xv. 1454a: 'The fourth point is consistency: for though the subject of the imitation, who suggested the type, be inconsistent, still he must be consistently inconsistent. As an example . . . of inconsistency, the Iphigenia at Aulis, – for Iphigenia the suppliant in no way resembles her later self' (trans. S. H. Butcher).

2. Pasquali in his 'Studi sul drama attico, II. Menandro e Euripide' (*Atene e Roma* 21 (1918), 9 ff.) has shown how the increasing instability of the characters in the late Euripidean plays prepares the way for Menander. Particularly good are Pasquali's observations about the characters of the *Iphigenia in Aulis*.

3. H. Drexler (*Gnomon* 3 (1927), 448 ff.) points out very nicely how already Alcestis is the embodiment of an 'ideal', of an *aretē*, rather than a representation of what can be observed in life.

4. See Charles R. Walker's translation of the *Iphigenia in Aulis* (© 1958, by The University of Chicago) for lines 9–11 and 16–23; Emily Townsend Vermeule's translation of the *Electra* (© 1959, by The University of Chicago) for lines 367–79.

The translator wishes to thank Professor James H. Day of Vassar College for many valuable suggestions.

GLOSSARY

agōn: an argument between two characters, in which each vehemently attempts to convince the other. (The same word is also used for an athletic event, or a duel on the battlefield.)

aidōs: shame.

alastōr: avenging deity.

anagnōrisis: recognition on the part of a tragic character of his or her true state.

anankē: necessity.

anapaests: one of the typical meters of tragic verse, based on the anapaestic measure (∪∪−).

antistrophe: the second major section of a lyric ode, metrically identical to the first (the strophe).

aretē: excellence or prowess.

aristeia: heroic deed, heroism.

atē: blindness of the heart, infatuation.

Atē: a goddess, the above personified.

choreutae: members of the chorus.

chorikon: short choral song.

coryphaeus: leader of the chorus.

daimon: a superhuman spirit or force.

deus ex machina: 'god from the machine', i.e. a divinity who suddenly appears at the end of a tragedy (suspended from the crane, or *mēchanē*), to solve an otherwise insoluble situation. By extension, a literary metaphor for an unmotivated ending.

deuteragonist: the second actor, or the second-ranking set of roles in tragedy, assumed by that actor.

didaskalia: production record.

dikē: justice.

ekkyklema: a platform which rolls out to reveal the interior of a stage palace.

epirrhematic scene: a portion of a tragedy involving a dialogue between a character and the chorus.

episode (*epeisodion*, pl. *epeisodia*): the dramatic action in tragedy which occurs between choral odes (corresponding to 'acts' in a modern play).

epode: the final major section of a choral song.

erinys: fury (pl. *erinyes*).

exodos: the final scene of a tragedy, often concluding with the chorus singing as they march off.

gnome: a proverbial saying.

hamartia: mistake, tragic error (often called, anachronistically, a tragic 'flaw').

hapax legomenon: a word or phrase that is known to have been used but once.

hybris: excessive pride, outrage.

hypothesis: ancient plot summary of a play (cf. Latin, *argumentum*).

kleos: fame for heroic achievements.

kommos: lyric dialogue between a principal character and the chorus (often a lament).

kōmos: revel.

koros: surfeit.

LSJ: Liddell and Scott, *Greek–English Lexicon* (rev. by H. Stuart Jones)

logos: speech, rational account, or statement.

mēchanē: see above, *deus ex machina*.

moira: fate, portion.

mythos: story, or plot of a play.

orchestra: circular 'dancing floor' in the Greek theater.

parodos: the chorus' entrance song (or first choral ode).

pathos: suffering.

peithō: persuasion.

peripeteia: the Aristotelian 'reversal' in tragic plots.

philia: the love of friendship or family relationship.

phthonos: envy.

physis: nature, essential quality.

polis: city-state.

prologue: all that section of a tragedy before the parodos.

RE (sometimes P-W): *Paulys Realencyclopädie der classischen Altertums-wissenschaft.*

rhēsis: formal set-speech.

skolion: drinking-song (not to be confused with scholion, a scholar's marginal note in a classical manuscript).

sophia: wisdom (or occasionally, cleverness).

sōphrosyne: moderation, self-control.

stasimon (plural: stasima): any of the choral odes after the parodos (q.v.).

stichomythia: swift dialogue, with brief and curt exchanges.

strophe: the first major section of a lyric ode, metrically identical to the second (the antistrophe).

tetrameter: a line of four measures (generally equivalent to eight major stresses in English).

themis: divinely ordered, or primordial, right.

Themis: goddess, incarnation of the above.

theos: divinity.

thymos: the seat of the passions, temper, rage.

tlēmosynē: heroic endurance.

trimeter: a line of three measures (equivalent to six major stresses in English).

tychē: random change, capricious fortune, bringing either good or evil.